ECONOMICS:
INSTITUTIONS AND ANALYSIS

Fourth Edition

Gerson Antell / Walter Harris

AMSCO SCHOOL PUBLICATIONS, INC.
315 Hudson Street   New York, N.Y. 10013

AUTHORS:

Gerson Antell, Curriculum Consultant, Junior Achievement, and former Assistant Principal for Social Studies, Hillcrest High School, New York City, is coauthor of *Economics for Everybody* and *Current Issues in American Democracy* (both Amsco).

Walter Harris, Former Principal at Sheepshead Bay High School, New York City, and Former Director of Education, The Kolburne School, New Marlboro, MA, is coauthor of *Economics for Everybody* and *Current Issues in American Democracy.*

Consultants:

Dominick J. Camastro, Lead Teacher, Social Studies, Erasmus Campus, High School for Business and Technology, Brooklyn, New York.

Arthur D. Grazzo, Jr., Former Social Studies Teacher, Williamsville East High School, East Amherst, New York.

Edward R. Waite, Social Studies Chair, Port Chester High School, Port Chester, New York.

Text and Cover Design: Merrill Haber

Cover Art: Veer Incorporated

Compositor: Stratford Publishing Services

Text Illustrations: Burmar Technical Corporation

Please visit our Web site at:
www.amscopub.com

When ordering this book, please specify:
R 795 P or ECONOMICS: I & A, FOURTH EDITION, PAPERBACK
or
R 795 H or ECONOMICS: I & A, FOURTH EDITION, HARDBOUND

ISBN 1-56765-663-3/NYC Item 56765-663-2 (Paperback edition)
ISBN 1-56765-667-6/NYC Item 56765-667-5 (Hardbound edition)

PREFACE

Economics: Institutions and Analysis, Fourth Edition, provides an introduction to the study of the U.S. economic system. The function of an economic system is to produce the things that people need and want. None has been so successful in this effort than ours. How our economic system "does its thing," some of the controversies generated by the system, and its role in the global economy is the subject matter of economics, and of this book.

Some of you may be thinking that a course in economics sounds like a journey to the far side of the moon. Unlike history, English, mathematics, and other subjects with which you are well acquainted, a course in economics may be a first-time experience. But as you read and learn more about the subject, you will find that economics is concerned with many things with which you are already familiar. For example, from the time you were born, you have been a user of goods and services. You also know something about where those goods and services come from. You have visited shops, ridden buses, gone to the movies, and in ever so many other ways seen people and places in the workaday world. You know, too, that in exchange for the work they do, the services they perform, or the goods they sell, people earn the money they need to purchase the goods and services they want. You also know from the services you have seen it perform and the taxes you have paid to it that government is a major player in our economy. The costs of government are shared by us all. Goods and services, banks, jobs, money, taxes, government policies, and business operations are all part and parcel of the study of economics.

Economic activities extend well beyond the community or region in which you live. While the goods that you and others consume may have had their origins in the town, state, or region of the country in which you live, most have been made in other sections of the United States, or in a foreign land. More than ever before, economic activities are global in their scope.

Economic topics and issues are discussed again and again on television, radio, and the Internet, as well as in books, magazines, and newspapers. As the complexity of the economy increases, what you need to know in order to cope with problems of everyday living increases as well. Whether you are a teenager, young adult, or senior citizen, the quality of the life you lead may well depend on how well you manage your income and spending.

You will also find that much of what economics is about has to do with the world of work. Whether you own a business or work for someone else, a knowledge of economics will help you in your future career.

Finally, as a citizen you will have the opportunity to vote on a variety issues affecting the economy. The more you know about economics, the better able you will be to understand those issues and vote intelligently.

The textbook is divided into eight units of two to four chapters each. The first unit serves as an introduction to the fundamental economic questions societies must answer and the forces affecting their decisions. The next four units focus on the principal players in the U.S. economy: businesses, labor, consumers, and government. The chapter on consumers is called "Personal Economics" to reflect this chapter's emphasis on economic skills you need to learn to participate in the economy. The sixth unit discusses the role of money and banks. The seventh unit serves an important function: showing how the government helps manage the economy and how it meets certain economic challenges. The eighth unit of the text focuses on the global economy and how the United States fits into that framework.

The book contains a number of features designed to make it easier to understand. Difficult words and phrases, many unique to the vocabulary of economics, are italicized and defined as they are introduced. They appear again in the Glossary, which may be found after the last chapter of the book. More than 200 illustrations in the form of photos, cartoons, graphs, diagrams, and tables have been strategically placed throughout the text as means of helping you to understand its contents. Many of the illustrations have captions that provide further information. Some captions have questions to challenge your understanding of the content of the illustrations.

All chapters have a matching exercise related to important vocabulary words found in the chapter. And all chapters have a multiple-choice exam on important concepts introduced in the chapter. This exam is followed by a set of critical thinking questions. Most chapters end with a major skills exercise and a list of suggested Internet sites on the subject of the chapter.

Economics: Institutions and Analysis, Fourth Edition, is a thoroughgoing revision of a well-proven economics text. We carefully scrutinized all aspects of our earlier editions—organization, content, illustrations and exercises—to determine whether they are still appropriate for today's students. As a result of this review, some topics were dropped, while others were either lengthened, shortened, or added. Throughout this new edition, we have personalized the material with references to everyday experiences.

The authors invite your criticisms, questions, and comments. We hope that your study of this book will enrich your understanding of your own life, and of your role in the nation's economy and the global economy. Finally, we hope that the book will help you to become a more intelligent participant in our democratic society.

GERSON ANTELL

WALTER HARRIS

CONTENTS

FEATURES

Makers of Economic Thought

Economic Issues

Mini-Readings

Case Studies

Personal Economics

CHAPTER 1
Economics: The Basic Questions

OVERVIEW

An ancient tale relates the story of Aladdin, who bought a lamp with magical qualities. Simply by rubbing the lamp, Aladdin could conjure up a genie who would grant him any wish. Food, clothing, jewels, castles, and trips to anywhere were his for the asking. No need for a job, or money, in Aladdin's world—not as long as he had that lamp and its wonderful genie.

Alas, the story of Aladdin is a myth. No one in real life, not even the world's wealthiest people, can be in more than one place at a time, or afford to buy everything they want. If they could, there would be no need for the study of economics, and this book would not have been written.

Instead of Aladdin's world, we live in a world where there is simply not enough of everything to go around. Unable to "have it all," people need to economize, that is, to pick and choose in such a way as to get the most for their money. This involves them in the process of economics. Every day we engage in economic activities. We have to make economic decisions as buyers and sellers and as workers and business owners.

After reading this book, you will have a better understanding of why people make one economic decision rather than another. Furthermore, you will have the knowledge you will need to make sound decisions as you evaluate your own daily economic choices.

In this chapter, you will learn the answers to the following questions:

- What is economics?

- What are the four factors of production?

- What fundamental questions must all societies answer?

- How do economic systems answer the WHAT, HOW, and WHO questions?

- What do economists do?

- What part does money play in the economy?

ECONOMICS: THE STUDY OF SCARCITY AND CHOICE

Have you ever gone shopping for clothes with $90 in your wallet only to find that the things you wanted to buy added up to something around $190? Did you go home empty-handed? Probably you did not. Like most people, you likely spent your $90 on those items that you needed or wanted the most, and did without the others.

Business firms and governments face the same kinds of decisions: None can afford everything at the same time. Instead, they try to satisfy as many of their wants with the resources available. For example, a manufacturer unable to afford both might have to choose between an advertising campaign and a factory modernization program. In a similar manner, a town might have to choose between modernizing its high school and building a parking garage.

Economists refer to the things that individuals and institutions want as either goods or services. *Goods* are tangible items of value, things that we can see or touch. We can classify scissors, medicines, and textbooks as goods because they are tangible. *Services* are intangible things that have value. Intangibles can neither be seen nor touched. Haircuts, medical care, and education are examples of services.

As we use goods and services to satisfy our wants, we consume them. For that reason, people who buy goods and services for personal use are called *consumers*. The act of buying final goods and services is called *consumption*.

The ingredients that go into the production of goods and services are the factors of production. Whereas human wants are virtually unlimited, the factors of production needed to satisfy those wants are relatively scarce. Thus, scarcity is a fact of life, one with which every individual and institution must deal by choosing among available resources.

Economics Defined

We can define *economics* as the study of how people and societies use limited resources to satisfy their unlimited wants. To put it more simply, economics is the study of *scarcity* and *choice*.

THE FACTORS OF PRODUCTION

As we just learned, the ingredients that go into the production of goods and services are *factors of production*. This section discusses these four factors—human resources, natural resources, capital resources, and entrepreneurship—and shows how they are related to human wants and needs.

Human Resources

Economists use the terms *human resources, labor,* and the *workforce* to describe the people whose efforts and skills go into the production of goods and services. Without human resources, goods and services could not be produced.

Human resources influence the production of goods and services in two ways. First, the size of the workforce affects the amount of goods and services produced. If a country has too few workers, it will be unable to make full use of its other resources. It may then encourage its citizens to have larger families or it may promote immigration. It may also encourage the importation of goods produced abroad.

Numbers of workers alone, however, do not determine how much a society can produce. More important is *labor productivity,* which is the amount each worker produces in a specified time. Productivity, in turn, is affected by (1) the skill of the labor force, (2) the quality and quantity of machinery and tools available per worker, and (3) *technology* (society's knowledge of production or production methods). The United States has twice the population of Bangladesh, yet the United States produces well over 20 times the amount of goods and services that Bangladesh does. U.S. productivity is so much higher than Bangladesh's because the United States has more advanced technology. Compared to Bangladesh, the United States has more advanced equipment and its workers are better educated in the use of this technology.

Natural Resources

Natural resources are materials obtained from the land, sea, and air. They include soil, minerals, fish, wildlife, water, and timber. (Economists sometimes use the word "land" to mean natural resources of all kinds.) In order to benefit from their natural resources, people must have uses for them and the means of obtaining them.

Some regions of the world have low standards of living because they have few natural resources. In economic terms, *standard of living* refers to the quantity and quality of goods and services that are available to an individual or a society.

Scarcity of natural resources forces all societies to make economic choices. What choices have been made on uses for this land?

The only way to improve the living standards of these regions is to strengthen the regions' other productive factors—labor, capital, and management. Switzerland, Denmark, and Japan each has limited natural resources, but each also has a high living standard because its other resources are highly developed.

For centuries, the Native American Shoshone of present-day Utah had what we now consider an inadequate standard of living. They ate seeds, roots, and an occasional rabbit or other animal. They created only the simplest shelters and clothing. Today, the same land produces abundant quantities of vegetables, beef, and dairy products, and supports a much larger population at a much higher standard of living.

How is it possible that today's inhabitants get so much more out of the land than did the ancient Shoshone? The answer is that the present-day inhabitants apply modern technology to the land, such as drought-resistant crops and labor-saving machinery.

Although all natural resources are limited, some can be replaced or renewed while others cannot. We can replant forests after trees have been cut down. We can restock streams and lakes with fish and restock woodlands with animals. Plants and animals are examples of *renewable resources.* Mineral ores and fuels, however, cannot be replaced. They are *nonrenewable resources,* since once they are consumed they are gone forever.

Shortages of some natural resources have prompted governments to enact laws that would: (1) limit the consumption of nonrenewable resources (such as certain minerals), and (2) require the restocking of renewable resources (such as forests).

🏵 Capital Resources

The machines, tools, and buildings that we use to produce goods and services are called *capital, capital goods,* or *capital resources.* A factory that manufactures shirts is a form of capital because it produces those goods. Schools are capital because they house a service industry—education. The term "capital" as it is used here should not be confused with money, which in other contexts is also called "capital."

Capital is eventually used up or worn out in much the same way that an automobile or washing machine wears out from use. This process of using up or wearing out machines is a form of deterioration. The accounting term we use to measure the decline in the value of capital goods is called *depreciation.* If new capital is not produced to replace capital that has been used up (that is, depreciated), fewer goods can be produced. In order to increase production, a nation must produce more or better capital goods than are needed merely to make up for goods that are worn out, used up, or just no longer useful.

Suppose that Country X has $100 billion in capital goods. Let us also assume that the goods have a usable life of 20 years. At the end of one year, one-twentieth, or $5 billion worth of the capital goods, will have been consumed. We can see, therefore, that unless Country X adds $5 billion worth of capital goods to its stock, it will have less capital at the end of the year than there was at the beginning. It also follows that if Country X wants to increase its supply of capital goods, it will have to invest more than $5 billion on them each year.

The production of capital goods is called *capital formation.* Because capital goods are so vital to the production of goods and services, capital formation is an essential economic process in all societies.

HOW CAPITAL FORMATION TAKES PLACE.   Unlike consumer goods (such as food, clothing, and shelter), capital goods do not immediately satisfy human wants. Instead, they are used to produce other goods or services—either consumer goods or services or other capital goods. It is important to keep in mind that capital produced in the present will satisfy human wants at a future time.

The amount of consumer goods and services and capital goods that a nation can produce at any one time is limited. Therefore, capital formation requires a decision to do without some consumer goods now in order to have more later. After World War II (1941–1945), for example, Japan had little capital formation and few consumer goods. Its industries had been destroyed in the bombing. For a number of years, the Japanese invested heavily in capital goods and produced very few consumer goods. They made the decision to do without consumer goods then in order to have more goods later. Today, of course, Japan is able to produce large quantities of consumer goods for its population and for export.

Capital formation takes place when individuals and businesses set aside a portion of their income as savings. Savings enable the banks that receive the deposits to make loans to those wanting to buy capital goods. In this way, a business in need of a new machine can call upon a bank for a loan to finance the purchase.

Entrepreneurship

While land, labor, and capital are necessary ingredients in the production of goods and services, someone has to assemble them in such a way as to get the job done. This process, known as *entrepreneurship,* is the fourth factor of production. Entrepreneurship describes the process by which individuals called *entrepreneurs* create new enterprises or improve existing ones. Entrepreneurs are the "idea people" who spend the money and time to assemble the factors of production and assume the risks necessary in starting a business. If things work out as planned, entrepreneurs are likely to profit. If not, they will lose money. That it is a risky business is evidenced by the fact that in the United States two out of every three new businesses fail within the first two years of operation.

THE FUNDAMENTAL QUESTIONS OF ECONOMICS

As we learned earlier, the study of economics comes down to this simple fact: there is not enough of everything to go around. Unable to have everything we want, we need to pick and choose from among the alternatives so as to get the most out of our resources. What is true for individuals is also true for society as

Entrepreneurs such as this woman risk their money in starting a business in hopes of making steady profits.

a whole. Society must try to *allocate* (distribute) its resources in such a way as to get the most for its money. Along the way, society needs to answer some fundamental economic questions.

- WHAT goods and services should be produced?
- HOW should they be produced?
- WHO will receive the goods and services that are produced?

✴ WHAT Goods and Services Should Be Produced?

When a society's resources are fully employed, production in one area can be increased only by decreasing production in another. It follows that what is true for a society also applies to businesses. If a shopping center is built on what was once farmland, that land can no longer be used to grow food. Workers building a sports arena cannot be employed at the same time building a hospital. Machines needed to produce 100 four-door sedans and 100 convertibles can produce more sedans only by taking some of the machines away from the production of convertibles. The result would be more sedans built but fewer convertibles. Unable to have everything, individuals and institutions need to choose between those goods and services they will buy or produce and those they will forgo.

In analyzing how people make their choices, economists generally speak of trade-offs, opportunity costs, and marginalism.

TRADE-OFFS AND OPPORTUNITY COSTS.   Economic decisions (such as decisions to buy, produce, and invest) involve trade-offs. A *trade-off* takes place when one thing is given up in order to obtain something else. The answer to each of the following questions involves a trade-off:

- Should I buy an apple pie or a cheesecake?
- Should the town convert this land into a parking lot or a playground?
- Should we apply these funds to newspaper and magazine advertising or use them for ads on television?

Economists refer to the trade-off of the value of one good or service for the value of another as the *opportunity cost* of the choice. If you choose to play basketball on a summer afternoon instead of going swimming, it could be said that the opportunity cost of your basketball game is the afternoon's swim. Similarly, the opportunity cost of building the shopping center is that many acres of farmland are lost.

MARGINALISM.   Another explanation for economic choices involves *marginalism*. As used in economics, the term marginalism refers to the usefulness of adding one more item to the production of a product or service. For example, a fast-food restaurant with five employees hires an additional, sixth worker. The business owner in this example is applying marginalism by weighing the additional benefits resulting from the decision to hire that sixth worker against the additional costs of an added worker.

✺ HOW Should Goods and Services Be Produced?

There is more than one way to make an automobile, build a school, or extract minerals from the ground. In producing something, management can combine factors of production in many ways. In manufacturing automobiles, for example, management decides whether to employ 100 workers using existing machinery or introduce labor-saving machinery that requires only 40 workers. In this example, management estimates how much the new equipment would reduce costs and improve output.

In considering building a new school, city planners determine whether they want a sprawling, one-story school that requires three acres of land or a multi-story building that requires less than one acre of land but will increase construction costs for the school.

Before extracting ores from the ground, mining companies decide which mining technique yields the least waste and smallest cost of operation for a given output.

In each of these examples, management decides how to combine the factors of production most efficiently. In the first example, management considers a mix of labor and capital. In the second example, it considers land as well as labor and capital. The third example involves consideration of various methods of combining land and capital.

HOW goods are produced often affects an entire society. In parts of our country, the destruction of forests, the overgrazing of grasslands, and poor planting methods have resulted in soil erosion and floods. Smoke from our factories, industrial wastes emptied into our streams, and agricultural pesticides seeping into our groundwater have led to the pollution of lakes, streams, and air. The increased use of machines in factory production has changed the entire character of our labor force and has made it harder for unskilled workers to find jobs.

✺ WHO Should Receive the Goods and Services Produced?

Since it is not possible to produce enough of everything to satisfy everyone, we might ask, "WHO shall receive the goods and services produced?"

Should everyone have an equal share? Or should some people be allowed to have more than others? Should goods and services be awarded according to people's contributions to society? Or should we divide goods and services according to need? If people are to be paid in accordance with their contributions or needs, how are these factors to be measured? Who will do the measuring?

In the United States, a neurosurgeon's income may be ten times that of a schoolteacher. In Great Britain, a neurosurgeon may earn only four times as much as a schoolteacher. In China, the difference may be less than two times.

Among the wealthiest individuals in the United States are the most successful professional athletes. In many other countries, however, professional athletes can hardly earn a living. The United States answers the question "WHO shall receive the goods and services produced by the economy?" in one way; Britain answers it in another; and China, in still another. We will learn more about the "WHO" question in the next chapter, pages 24–47. For a full discussion of how wages are determined in the United States, see Chapter 8, pages 162–183.

ECONOMIC SYSTEMS: SOCIETY'S ANSWER TO WHAT, HOW, AND WHO

So far, we have learned that:

- Scarcity is an economic fact of life. Human wants are greater than the resources needed to satisfy them.
- In making their choices, societies have to answer three questions: WHAT goods and services should be produced? HOW should they be produced? WHO should receive the goods and services that are produced?

The way a society answers the WHAT, HOW, and WHO questions defines its economic system. Economic systems are often classified as traditional, command, or market economies.

Traditional Economy

Many of the world's people live and work in what is called a *traditional economic system*. Traditional economies are located mostly in rural areas of South America, Asia, and Africa. There are certain features common to all traditional economies. Economic life is characterized by a self-contained community. Usually the chief occupation is farming, but it might be fishing or herding. The family is the main organizational unit of economic life. Production is carried on using the same kinds of tools and techniques that were used for many generations past. People produce only enough goods to meet the needs of their family, and sometimes a little more for sale to others. WHAT is produced and HOW it is produced are not the result of conscious planning but, rather, a matter of custom and tradition.

A person's career in a traditional economic system is largely determined at birth. Men learn the trades of their fathers, while women tend the home and care for the children. Men and women alike work the land or care for their herds in accordance with time-honored traditions. Inventions and innovation are less common in traditional societies than in other groups.

WHO receives the goods and services produced in a traditional society today is largely based on the size of the family's holdings. Usually the family with the largest holding of land or livestock (such as sheep, cattle, and camels) has more than a family with a smaller holding of land or livestock. Ownership of such property is handed down in the family from generation to generation. So, once again, it is tradition that determines the WHO answer in a traditional economic system.

💢 Command Economy

In a *command economy,* the fundamental questions of WHAT, HOW, and WHO are pretty much decided by a central authority, usually the government. During the years of the cold war (1948–1991), the Communist nations of Eastern Europe and the Soviet Union had command economies. Although the degree of

Workers on this Soviet collective farm were bringing in the harvest in 1930. Who determined what was to be planted and who would do the work?

power exercised by the central authority varied from one country to another, the principal means of production in these places were in government hands.

Since government owns most of the industry in command economies, central-planning agencies determine WHAT is to be produced and HOW it will be produced. In the Soviet Union, for example, Communist party leaders wanted powerful armies and increased military might. Therefore, central planning agencies allocated funds, workers, and other resources to build up the military power of the nation. As a result of central planners' decisions to emphasize military production, fewer resources were available for the production of consumer goods and services.

In a command economy, the central authority also decides WHO will receive the goods and services produced. Government agencies set wage scales and determine the living standards that people in different walks of life will enjoy. Since insufficient resources in the former Soviet Union were allocated to producing consumer goods, these goods were in short supply. Few Soviet workers could afford automobiles, air conditioners, or comfortable housing. Moreover, those who could have afforded to pay the price of, say, an air conditioner often found that the stores had none available for sale. Those in positions favored by the Soviet government (such as scientists, astronauts, athletes, and government officials) did not have these problems. These people lived in comfortable housing. They shopped in stores especially set aside for them where they could buy things unavailable to others.

Market Economy

The opposite of the centrally directed command economy is the decentralized *market economy*. In a market system (such as we have in the United States), the major decisions as to WHAT, HOW, and WHO are made by individuals and businesses (buyers and sellers) who voluntarily exchange goods and services at a particular price. Compared to a command system, government in a market economy plays a much less important role.

Buyers and sellers in a market system make their wishes known in a marketplace, or market. A market can be located anyplace where goods are bought and sold. Markets are often compared to polling booths. Buyers "vote" for the goods and services they want by buying them. Sellers who best satisfy the wants of buyers are "elected" to stay in business through the profits they earn from their sales. Sellers who fail to satisfy buyers' wants are, in effect, voted "out of office." In the 1990s, most nations that had command economies (like those in Eastern Europe) adopted some form of market economy. To prepare themselves for the introduction of the market system, many Eastern European countries sent economists and other scholars to the United States to study the economic system there firsthand.

While entrepreneurs are sometimes needed to organize production in command and traditional economies, the rewards for what they do in those economic systems are more or less fixed (by tradition or the government). By contrast, the potential to earn profits in a market economy is in some instances almost unlimited. This provides a huge incentive to entrepreneurs in a market economy to innovate, create, and assume risk.

 # WHAT DO ECONOMISTS DO?

Economists are the professionals who study the ways society allocates its resources to satisfy its wants. Economists spend much of their time gathering and analyzing data. These activities enable them to identify problems and suggest solutions.

 ## Microeconomics vs. Macroeconomics

The kinds of problems economists study can be classified as either microeconomic or macroeconomic. *Microeconomics* is the study of the effects of economic forces on individual parts of the economy, such as business firms, households, and workers. When executives of a firm think about what would happen to sales if the company increased its prices, they are wrestling with a microeconomic problem.

Macroeconomics is the study of the impact of changes on the economy as a whole. Economists in this field try to answer questions like "What will be the effect of a tax increase on consumer spending?" and "How will a decrease in the defense budget affect the nation's businesses?"

 ## What Is vs. What Ought to Be

Economists deal with two worlds: (1) the world that is (and was) and (2) the world that ought to be. The study of what *is* focuses on the causes and effects of specific events. For example, federal minimum wage laws set the lowest wage that most workers can be paid. If members of Congress were thinking of increasing the minimum wage, they might ask economists to find the answers to questions like "How would a 10 percent increase in the minimum wage affect business profits?" and "What effect would such an increase have on the unemployment rate?" Both questions deal with the world that is.

Like everybody else, though, economists have sets of values that often influence how they view economic problems. For example, some economists support minimum wage laws because they believe that these laws promote greater economic equality. Other economists, by contrast, oppose such laws, believing that they harm the whole economy. Similarly, economists often disagree about whether government should enact programs to help special groups, such as the homeless, small business owners, farmworkers, and savers.

🗲 Using Economic Models

An *economic model* is a simplified way of looking at an economic problem. It may be expressed in the form of a statement, graph, or mathematical formula. For example, an economist might say that there is an *inverse* (reverse) relationship between the price of steak and the sales of steak. The economist's statement model could also be expressed graphically, as in Figure 1.1.

It could also be expressed mathematically as:

Sales of steak is a function of the price of steak

	(Ss)	=	*f*	×	*(Ps)*
or	*(Ss)*	=	*f(Ps)*		

Economists create models to make predictions about how a change in one variable will affect others. Suppose, for example, that an economist was asked to report on the advisability of replacing existing factory equipment with new machinery. After gathering the facts, she would prepare a model (graphic, mathematical, or statement) on which a prediction could be based.

Similarly, government economists might be asked to predict the effect of a tax cut on employment. The economists would prepare a model based on the available information. They would use the model to make their predictions.

A good model helps economists understand the consequences of economic activity and to predict changes. However, even a good economic model is not perfect; it cannot predict with 100 percent accuracy. In most instances, however, economic predictions are more accurately made with models than without them. For that reason, economists will continue to use models as tools of economics.

Figure 1.1 **Economic Model of Steak Sales**

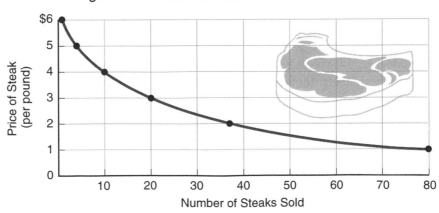

Ceteris Paribus: Other Things Being Equal

Working in laboratories, physical scientists (such as physicists and chemists) can test their theories in a controlled environment. Economists and other social scientists, however, deal with human behavior, which is often unpredictable. Such behavior can rarely be observed under laboratory conditions.

To help bring order into their studies, economists rely on an assumption known in Latin as *ceteris paribus* (other things being equal). Economists know, for example, that there is a relationship between the price of a good and the quantity of the good that people will buy. As prices increase, consumers buy less; as prices decrease, consumers buy more. But there can be any number of exceptions to these rules.

- Athletic shoes selling for $120 a pair may outsell identical footwear peddled for $30 a pair.
- For special occasions, some people shop in the most expensive stores in town.

By relying on *ceteris paribus,* however, economists can ignore these and other exceptions by simply saying that people will buy more of an item at a lower price than at a higher one, all other things being equal.

Ceteris paribus enables observers to focus on one or two variables while, at the same time, recognizing that other variables exist.

THE ROLE OF MONEY

Before there was such a thing as money, people swapped something of value for whatever it was that they wanted. Such an exchange is called *barter.* The barter system worked well on a simple level. When someone with a hunger for fish and a rabbit to swap found a person with a fish and a yearning for rabbit stew, an exchange could take place. Barter, though, has serious shortcomings because it is based on the idea of "double coincidence of wants."

Consider, for example, the case of someone with a hog to swap and a desire for a dozen eggs. Even though an egg farmer might be happy to have a hog, a dozen eggs are worth much less than a hog. How could the egg seller make change? He or she could not. Then again, what would happen if the egg farmer did not want a hog? In both cases, the likelihood is that the exchange would not take place. Problems like those were eliminated with the invention of money. Like an automobile engine that relies on oil to keep it running smoothly, the economy looks to money to smooth its way.

But what is money?

Money can be anything (yes, *anything*) that is generally accepted in payment for goods and services. Many things have served as money in the past. The ancient Romans used salt. The Aztecs in Mexico used cacao beans. Fishhooks, arrowheads, and shells were money to some Native Americans. When used as money, fishhooks, shells, and many other commodities served as *mediums of exchange.* That is, they enabled people to exchange one good or service for another. In colonial times in North America, ferry operators accepted fur pelts in payment for moving people and goods across rivers. They did so knowing that they could pay for the things they needed with those same pelts. In this example, fur served as a kind of money.

Whatever people use for money, it is a lot simpler system than barter. Thus the person with a rabbit to sell and an appetite for fish need only find a buyer for rabbit. With the money received from the sale of the rabbit, the shopper can buy a fish from any seller.

Because money was generally more acceptable if it was durable and easy to carry, metallic money became popular early in the history of civilization. Around the year 2500 B.C., ancient Egyptians produced one of the earliest kinds of metallic money in the form of rings. About 400 years later, the Chinese began using gold cubes as money. The first metal coins were struck in the 8th century B.C. by the Lydians, a people who lived in Asia Minor (present-day Turkey).

The first people to develop paper money were the Chinese. Italian traveler Marco Polo reported on its use in China in the late 1200s. During the late

People of the Pacific islands of Yap once considered huge stone discs such as these to be money.

Middle Ages in Europe, merchants and other travelers sought to protect themselves from highway robbers by exchanging their gold coins (which the robbers wanted) for goldsmiths' receipts (which the robbers found useless). The receipts could be exchanged back to coins by designated goldsmiths in other cities. In time, the receipts became so popular that people used them to pay debts without bothering to exchange them for coins.

What Does Money Do?

Money provides a *medium of exchange,* a *standard of value,* and a *store of value.*

MEDIUM OF EXCHANGE.   With money, a woodcutter who wants shoes does not have to find a shoemaker who wants wood. Or, to use a more modern example, a plumber who wants shoes does not have to find a shoe-store owner whose pipes leak. The plumber can sell his services to anyone, because the money he receives in payment will also be accepted by the shoe store. For her part, the storekeeper can use her receipts from the sale of shoes to purchase the things she wants. In this way, money serves as a medium of exchange.

STANDARD OF VALUE.   Money provides a convenient standard with which we can express the value of different items. Thus, a paperback book selling for $12 is equal in value to 20 candy bars selling for 60 cents a piece.

STORE OF VALUE.   Because money can be saved for future use, it provides a means of storing value. Thus, our egg merchant can save the money earned from the sale of eggs and use the savings at a later date to buy an expensive item.

What Kinds of Money Do We Use?

Like people everywhere, the money used by Americans on a daily basis is most likely to be in the form of currency and checks.

CURRENCY.   *Currency* is money issued by the federal government. All U.S currencies are *legal tender.* This means that they must be accepted in payment for debts. Thus, if you owe a store $1,000, it does not have to accept your jewelry or even your check in payment. It must, however, accept the currency you offer it.

All forms of U.S. currency are known as *fiat money.* Fiat money has value because the government says it does, not because of its natural value. Thus, a dime consists of copper and nickel that would be worth far less than ten cents if the dime were melted down for its metallic content. Similarly, the paper upon which a $5 bill is printed is worth hardly anything at all. Although there once was a time when the "melt value" of coins was close to their face value and there existed a certain quantity of gold- and silver-backed paper currency, this is no longer the case.

There are two kinds of currency in circulation in the United States: *coins* and *paper currency.*

Coins.   The government produces pennies, nickels, dimes, quarters, and half-dollars primarily for the convenience of making change for a dollar. For that reason, coins are also known as "fractional currency." In addition, it produces a small number of coins worth $1. U.S. coins are *token money.* That is, their metallic value is far less than their face value. In all, coins make up about 4 percent of the nation's money supply.

Paper Currency.   Paper currency is printed by the Treasury Department's Bureau of Engraving and Printing. Paper currency makes up about 46 percent of the money supply. In all, then, currency accounts for 50 percent of the nation's money supply—the remaining 50 percent consists of checks.

CHECKBOOK MONEY.   Although we tend to think of only paper currency and coins as money, they represent a fraction of the total money in circulation. Most transactions are paid for by check. *Checks* are orders written by individuals or firms directing a financial institution, in which they have accounts, to pay specified sums to the person named on the check. People who have money on deposit in accounts that offer check-writing privileges can order banks to make payments.

In a later chapter, you will learn more about where money comes from and why its value is constantly changing.

S U M M A R Y

Economics is the study of how people and societies use scarce resources to satisfy unlimited wants. In making choices, societies have to answer three basic questions: WHAT goods and services should be produced? HOW should they be produced? WHO should receive the goods and services that are produced? The way a society answers these three questions depends on whether the economic system is a traditional, command, or market economy.

Economists study the way an economy allocates its resources. Microeconomics is concerned with the effects of decisions by individuals, firms, and government on various parts of the economy. Macroeconomics is the study of changes on the economy as a whole. Economists focus on the world that is, but they may also be concerned with the world as they think it ought to be. Economists use models, or theories, to simplify the way they look at economic problems. A model may be expressed in the form of statements, graphs, or mathematical formulas. Economists rely on *ceteris paribus* (other things being equal) so they can focus on one or two variables while recognizing that other variables exist.

Money can be anything that most people are willing to accept in payment for goods or services. Long ago, money replaced the barter system and is now used in all societies. Money provides a medium of exchange, a way of calculating value, and a store of value.

The principal kinds of money used in the United States are currency, in the form of paper money and coins, and checkbook money. Currency is issued by the federal government. Checks constitute about half of the nation's money supply.

REVIEWING THE CHAPTER

BUILDING VOCABULARY

Match each term in Column A with its definition in Column B.

Column A

1. standard of living
2. good
3. factor of production
4. economics
5. capital formation
6. entrepreneurship
7. trade-off
8. marginalism
9. economic system
10. macroeconomics

Column B

a. the evaluation of the usefulness of adding one more item in the production of a product or service

b. the study of the forces affecting the economy as a whole

c. the way a society answers the WHAT, HOW, and WHO questions

d. an ingredient that goes into the production of a good or service

e. the study of how society uses limited resources to satisfy unlimited wants

f. the production of capital goods

g. a tangible item of value

h. the quantity and quality of goods and services available to an individual or society

i. the giving up of one thing to obtain something else

j. the bringing together of the factors of production

UNDERSTANDING WHAT YOU HAVE READ

1. "All societies must economize because human wants are unlimited, but resources needed to satisfy these wants are limited." This statement means that society must (*a*) use its resources in such a way that it gets the most out of them (*b*) save as much money as possible (*c*) keep its budgets balanced (*d*) prohibit the use of its resources.

2. Economists differentiate between goods and services. Which *one* of the following best illustrates a payment for a service? (*a*) $1.95 for a hamburger (*b*) $18.95 for a textbook (*c*) $15,000 for a new automobile (*d*) $10 for a haircut.

3. The opportunity cost of an increase in the local police force is (*a*) the government goods or services that people will give up in order for the government to hire additional police (*b*) the cost of the additional police (*c*) the cost of training new recruits (*d*) the amount by which taxes may be increased to pay for the additional police.

4. "An individual's role in the economy is most likely determined at birth, and goods and services are produced according to time-honored methods." Which economic system fits this description? (*a*) traditional (*b*) command (*c*) market (*d*) highly specialized.

5. In which type of economic system are consumers most likely to determine what goods will be produced? (*a*) market economy (*b*) traditional economy (*c*) command economy (*d*) wartime economy.

6. Microeconomists study questions such as (*a*) What will be the effect of taxes on consumer spending? (*b*) How will a decrease in the defense budget affect a nation's businesses? (*c*) How will an increase or decrease in interest rates affect business spending? (*d*) How will the decisions made by firm X affect consumer demand for the products produced by that firm?

7. An economic model (*a*) enables economists to predict economic activity with 100 percent accuracy (*b*) is a complex way of looking at an economic problem (*c*) can be expressed only with graphs or mathematical formulas (*d*) helps economists understand economic activity and predict changes.

8. Each of the following is an example of currency, *except* a (*a*) dime (*b*) $1 bill (*c*) check for $5 (*d*) penny.

9. Under what circumstances might peacock feathers be called "money"? (*a*) if they were very rare (*b*) if they were all identical in size and shape (*c*) if everyone accepted them in payment for goods and services (*d*) if they could be easily divided into equal parts so as to "make change."

10. Money provides a "store of value" because it (*a*) can be used to buy valuable goods in stores (*b*) is easily carried (*c*) may be saved for future use (*d*) packs a great deal of value into a small volume.

THINKING CRITICALLY

1. Why is economics called a study of scarcity and choice?

2. "HOW goods are produced often affects an entire society. Natural resources, we have learned, are limited. While some natural resources can be replaced or renewed, others cannot." Discuss the implications of these statements for people who make decisions concerning the use of mineral resources, fossil fuels (oil, coal, and natural gas), forest resources, and water resources.

3. Economic decisions are likely to be influenced by the opportunity costs involved. Explain in terms of opportunity costs your answer to each of the following questions. (*a*) Should the United States undertake a program to land astronauts on Mars? (*b*) Should your community build a new hospital? (*c*) Should your family buy a new automobile? (*d*) Should the federal government give financial support to a U.S. Olympic team?

4. "People cannot eat machinery or factory buildings. That is why poor countries should concentrate on agriculture and leave manufacturing to the industrialized nations." Explain why you agree or disagree with this statement.

5. In the United States, a neurosurgeon's income may be ten times that of a schoolteacher. In a country with a command economy, the difference might be less than two times. How can you explain the fact that individuals doing the same work in different countries do not earn comparable salaries?

6. During the early Roman era, the merchants of Rome frequently traveled beyond the empire's borders to trade with other peoples. Summarize the trading difficulties that probably arose in the barter economies they encountered.

SKILLS: | Analyzing the Production Possibilities Curve

The *production possibilities curve* illustrates in graphic form the economic concepts of scarcity and opportunity cost. "Scarcity" may be the most significant word in economics. It forces individuals and societies to choose from among the things they want. If they choose one combination of goods and services, they must give up another. To illustrate the concept of scarcity, consider an imaginary country called "Ravinia." A tiny nation, Ravinia produces two categories of goods: necessities and luxuries. (*Necessities* are those goods and services needed to sustain daily life. *Luxuries* are goods and services that add pleasure to life but can be done without.)

In a recent survey, Ravinian economists determined the following:

• With the labor force fully employed and producing nothing but necessities (food, clothing, and shelter), 600 million tons can be turned out in one year.

• With the labor force fully employed and producing nothing but luxuries (jewelry, yachts, and candy), 110 million tons can be created in one year.

• If Ravinia chooses to turn out both luxuries and necessities, various combinations of each can be produced.

Table 1.1 shows that if Ravinia chooses to produce 300 million tons of necessities in a given year, it can also generate up to 90 million tons of luxuries. Suppose, however, that the Ravinians want more than 90 million tons of luxuries—say, 100 million tons. Would they be able to produce the additional 10 million tons of luxuries? Yes, but in so doing they would have to take some of the resources that had been engaged in the production of necessities and shift them to luxury production. The table tells us that producing 10 million more tons of luxuries will result in a 50 percent reduction in the production of necessities. In economic terms, the opportunity cost of producing an additional 10 million tons of luxuries is 150 million tons of necessities.

▷ TABLE 1.1   PRODUCTION POSSIBILITIES IN RAVINIA

If necessities produced are:	The maximum production of luxuries can be:
600 million tons	0 million tons
550 million tons	40 million tons
500 million tons	55 million tons
400 million tons	80 million tons
300 million tons	90 million tons
150 million tons	100 million tons
0 million tons	110 million tons

By transferring the information in the table to a line graph and connecting the plotted points, we can create a production possibilities curve, as shown in Figure 1.2. A production possibilities curve shows the possibilities for production when all resources (land, labor, capital, and level of technology) are fully and effectively employed. In actuality, a nation is likely to produce less than it is capable of producing.

Suppose, for example, that Ravinia's present production is at point U. At U, the nation is producing 300 million tons of necessities and 45 million tons of luxuries. These amounts are well below Ravinia's capacity, and the Ravinians have fewer goods and services available to them than the economy is capable of producing. Therefore, Ravinia is under-employed.

Suppose, however, that the Ravinians want to produce 550 million tons of necessities and 80 million tons of luxuries, as depicted by point H. Is this possible? Figure 1.2 shows that it is not possible under present conditions to expand production to point H. The production possibilities curve indicates a limit beyond which production cannot expand using current resources. Expanding the economy beyond the production possibilities curve would require additional resources. Increasing the size of the labor force or acquiring more and better tools and equipment could lead to increased production. So too could improved management techniques. For the nation's economic planners, the production possibilities curve represents a limit they must constantly strive to exceed.

1. Explain the statement "scarcity may be the single most significant word in the field of economics."

2. Define a production possibilities curve.

3. According to the table on page 21, how many tons of luxuries could the Ravinians produce in a year in which they turn out 400 million tons of necessities?

4. What are *opportunity costs*?

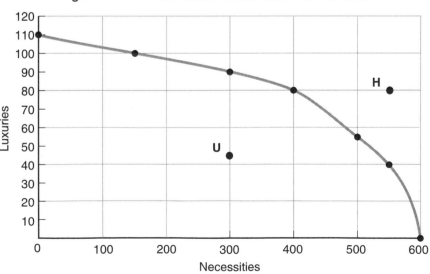

Figure 1.2 **Production Possibilities in Ravinia**

5. What would be the opportunity cost to Ravinia if it chooses to increase its production of necessities from 500 to 550 million tons at a time when its resources are fully employed?

6. You have been asked by the Ravinian government for your opinion as to the state of its economy. Current production levels stand at 200 million tons of necessities and 80 million tons of luxuries a year. What would you tell the Ravinians? Explain your answer.

7. Ravinia is now producing 500 million tons of necessities and 50 million tons of luxuries. It would like to hold its production of necessities at current levels and increase production of luxuries to 80 million tons. What are Ravinia's chances of success? Explain your answer.

CHAPTER 2

The United States Economic System

OVERVIEW

As you walk down the aisles of a supermarket, do you ever wonder how all the packaged foods, household products, and fresh produce got there? Many items may have traveled hundreds or thousands of miles in their journey to the grocery shelves. The store may have received its grapes from Chile, oranges from Florida, and tomatoes from California. Then, as one lot of produce is sold, a fresh supply appears, as if by magic.

What is true of grocery stores applies equally to most other enterprises: The goods and services they sell seem to be available whenever you need them. In all, some $10 trillion worth of goods and services are produced annually by the U.S. economic system. Incredibly, this outpouring functions without government design or direction. Somehow, the more than 146 million people involved in running the economy are able to do so without central direction. As a result of those efforts, the U.S. standard of living is one of the highest in the world.

How does our economic system produce and distribute goods and services without centralized management and direction? How does the U.S. economy answer the fundamental economic WHAT, HOW, and WHO questions? *(WHAT goods and services should be produced? HOW should they be produced? WHO should receive the goods and services produced?)* As you read this chapter, you will learn the answers to these and the following questions:

- What are the principles of the free enterprise system?

- What is specialization?

- How are the economic activities of consumers, business, and government related?

- How does a market system function?

- What are the economic goals of the United States?

PRINCIPLES OF THE U.S. ECONOMIC SYSTEM

The economic system of the United States is known as *capitalism.* In this system, the means of production are privately owned, and the fundamental questions of WHAT, HOW, and WHO are answered by the market rather than by tradition or an economic plan. Capitalism is founded on certain principles, the most important being free enterprise, private property, the profit motive, consumer sovereignty, and competition.

Freedom of Enterprise

The free enterprise system takes its name from the freedom people in the system enjoy to enter any legal business and conduct it as they see fit. Those who venture into the business world hope that they might be quite successful at it. They know, however, that they also risk the possibility of loss.

Freedom of enterprise has its limitations. Because *public utilities* (industries that serve the public interest, such as gas and electric companies) are often the only source of a certain product in a community, government often regulates what they provide and how much they can charge. To protect consumers, government requires certain professions to be licensed. Most other businesses are subject to various other types of government supervision and regulation. Despite all these limitations, individuals have considerable freedom to organize and operate their businesses as they choose.

Private Property

Having the *right to private property* means allowing individuals to own property and use it in any lawful manner they choose. The right of individuals to own the means of production (such as factories, farms, and stores) is one of the basic principles of capitalism. (In some command economies, by contrast, the means of production are owned by the government.) Like most other rights, property rights in the United States are subject to limitations. Government may, for example, tax those who own or inherit property. Similarly, the principal of *eminent domain* gives government the power to seize property it intends to use for some public purpose (such as to make room for building a road or school). Eminent domain requires, however, that government pay a fair price for the property it seizes.

⚡ Profit Motive

The principal reason why entrepreneurs go into business is to earn profits. *Profits* are what remain after the expense of doing business is subtracted from a firm's income. Unlike wages and salaries, which are more or less fixed, profits are uncertain. If business is poor, the firm might not earn any profits. If the business is successful, there is no telling how much it might earn.

To improve profits, firms try to keep costs down while, at the same time, increasing income. Thus, profits provide entrepreneurs with an impartial measure of their firm's success and failure. When profits are increasing, entrepreneurs know that they must be doing something right; when profits fall, they know that something is wrong. Either way, entrepreneurs rely on the signals profits provide to keep their operation on track. Economists describe the willingness of entrepreneurs to risk financial loss by organizing and launching a business enterprise as the *profit motive.*

⚡ Consumer Sovereignty

Just as people in business can produce and sell their goods and services as they wish, consumers are free to choose which goods and services they will buy (and which they will reject). However, even though sellers they can produce whatever they want, they know that unless they please their customers (consumers), their business will fail. Consequently, if consumers are unwilling to purchase purple ballpoint pens, manufacturers will stop producing them. On the other hand, if consumers want yellow ballpoints, manufacturers will do what they can to produce them. Economists describe the need to give consumers what they want as *consumer sovereignty.*

Consumers' likes and dislikes are expressed in a kind of marketplace election. Consumers "vote" for a product by buying it and "vote" against it by choosing not to buy it. The most successful businesses are those that either can "anticipate the market" by correctly predicting what consumers will want or can successfully create a demand for their products through advertising. Four decades ago, few parents would have thought of buying disposable paper diapers for their infants. In those days, diapers were made of cloth. The development of the disposable diaper was followed, however, by huge advertising campaigns that created a demand for the product. Today, more babies are diapered with disposables than with cloth diapers.

Consumer sovereignty can be limited by government policy. If government requires much titanium for making aircraft, then less of this scarce metal will be available for consumer products, such as paint. Consumer sovereignty is also limited when there are but two or three producers of a product. Most lightbulbs, for example, are manufactured by three producers. These manufacturers can pretty much determine the size, shape, wattage, and price of their products.

In what was one of the most costly business mistakes of the decade, executives of the Ford Motor Company in 1958 assumed that the public wanted another midsize automobile. This assumption led them to produce and promote an entirely new line, which they called the "Edsel." The public, however, did not want another midsize family car. After swallowing millions of dollars of losses in only three years, Ford shut down its Edsel division. Consumer demand for a decades-old car is another matter. A restored and operable Edsel is worth more today than when it sat on showroom floors.

Competition

The rivalry among sellers in the same field for consumer dollars is called *competition*. As we just learned, the profit motive is the driving force that pushes business firms to produce particular products or services. We also learned that consumers are free to choose what goods and services they want and from whom they wish to purchase those goods and services. The Ford Motor Company, for example, learned the hard way in the 1950s that consumers preferred other models of automobiles (many produced by General Motors and the Chrysler Corporation) to their Edsel.

For a while, Apple Computer and IBM pretty much dominated the personal computer market. Then as others saw how profitable this market was, more companies entered it. To win a share of the personal computer business, these other firms had to offer products or services that were either better or at lower prices than those of either Apple or IBM. Competition pressures business firms to constantly try to provide the best services and to create the best products at the lowest possible prices. This is the way that companies appeal to consumer sovereignty and, thus, earn greater profits.

SPECIALIZATION AND THE ECONOMY

Jack and Mildred Green live in an apartment in a large city with their two teenage children, Ted and Laura. Jack works as a mechanic for a bus company, and Mildred is a manager in a law firm. Ted and Laura go to school. On a typical day, the Greens consume many of the same goods and services as do other families in their income bracket. They spend money for food, clothing, utilities (such as telephone service, gas, and electricity), recreation, a car, a television set, and all the many other items that go along with modern living. They also use such government-provided facilities as schools and highways.

It is likely that the Greens produce none of the goods and services that they consume. They live in a society where work is so specialized that few people are able to provide for more than a tiny fraction of their own needs. Mr. Green repairs buses, while Mrs. Green helps run a law office. In addition, both parents work at raising their children and caring for their home. How are the Greens able to obtain the hundreds of goods and services that they need and want in order to live comfortably?

The Greens, like millions of other residents of the United States, must count on the efforts of other people to provide them with most of their needs. This dependence on the labor of others was not always the rule in the United States and elsewhere. In the past, people relied mostly on their own efforts and nature's abundance to provide what they needed. Frontier families in this country had to grow their own food, build their own homes, and make their own clothing. Even today in traditional agricultural societies, each family provides most of the goods and services that its members consume.

The economic independence seen in traditional agricultural societies is not possible in the United States. Instead, the U.S. economy features *specialization*. In an industrial society, jobs are highly specialized. Workers perform one specialized task and depend on other workers to provide them with the things they need. There are many advantages to specialization. By concentrating on one activity, for example, workers produce more because they become highly skillful at what they do.

Just as individual workers become more efficient at their specialized tasks, so do companies. Many small companies produce only one type of good (such as dresses) or provide just one type of service (such as dry cleaning). Specialization encourages the efficient use of capital. If a business needs to use a delivery truck only twice a week, it is wasteful for the business to purchase and maintain its own truck. The business can use its capital more efficiently by hiring the services of another company, one that specializes in making deliveries. Specialization also promotes *innovation* (new ways of doing things). Companies that produce only a few products are able to concentrate on developing new machines and production techniques that will increase production, improve quality, and lower costs for these products.

Specialization is possible only where markets are large enough to support them. In New York City, for example, there are dozens of shops that sell only handbags. Others sell only pianos. By contrast, most small towns do not have a single shop selling only pianos. The number of potential customers is too small in a small town to support such highly specialized shops. In large cities, though, there are thousands of potential buyers for pianos. Such a market can support perhaps a dozen piano shops. Stated as an economic principle, the degree of specialization is limited by the extent of the market.

How are 146 million people, working at thousands of different tasks, able to produce the hundreds of thousands of goods and services that people want, in the quantities that can be sold, and at the price that people are willing to pay? And how are these goods and services distributed to where they are needed? We will answer these questions in the pages that follow.

THE CIRCULAR FLOW OF ECONOMIC ACTIVITY

People receive income from a number of sources and spend it in a variety of ways. Workers receive wages and buy consumer goods. Business owners receive profits and pay their employees and suppliers. Landlords receive rent and purchase maintenance services and fuel for their buildings. Lenders earn interest and spend part of it on new loans or other investments. No matter how money is earned, it returns to the economy when buyers purchase the things they need or want.

Economists describe the stream of funds that is constantly passing back and forth between the public and the businesses of the country as a *circular flow.* Figure 2.1 represents this circular flow of funds. Businesses send out funds to the public in the form of wages to employees, rent to landlords, interest to banks

Figure 2.1 **Circular Flow of Money**

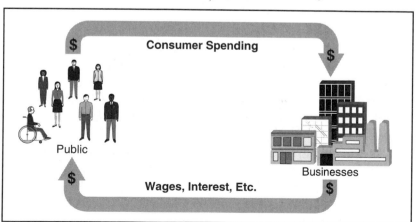

Figure 2.2 **Circular Flow of Goods and Services**

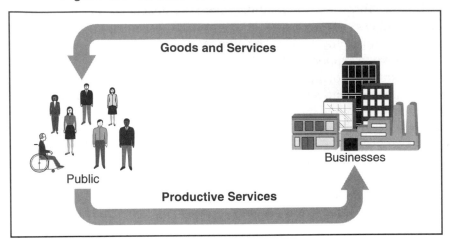

and bondholders, dividends to stockholders, and other payments. The public, as consumers and investors, sends money back to the business community.

In addition to the circular flow of funds between businesses and the public, there is also a circular flow of goods and services. The goods and services produced by businesses are purchased by the Greens and other consumers. Consumers in turn sell their productive services to businesses—in the Greens' case, to a bus company and a law firm. The flow of goods and services is illustrated in Figure 2.2. Businesses provide goods and services to the public (consumers), and the public provides productive services (land, labor, capital, and management) to businesses.

Now we have two circular streams moving in opposite directions. One carries money from the public to businesses and back again; the other carries goods and services between the same parties. These two flows are combined in Figure 2.3.

Adding Government to Our Model

So far we have limited the discussion of economic activity to the public and business sectors of the economy. To complete the picture, we must add government. The public's relations with government are similar to its relations with businesses. The bus company that Jack Green works for is owned by the city. The city uses his productive services to provide a service to the public—in this case, transportation. The money that the public pays to the bus company in the form of fares is used by the city for wages, office expenses, equipment and supplies, and the like to individuals and business firms. Other city income, such as tolls and sales taxes, returns to the public in a similar way.

In Figure 2.4, the inner loop represents the money flow between the public and government. The upper portion of the inner loop represents the taxes that the public pays to provide government with the major part of its income. The

Figure 2.3 **Circular Flow of Money, Goods, and Services**

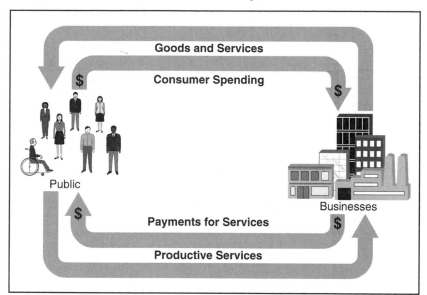

Figure 2.4 **Circular Flow of Money, Goods, and Services Between the Government and the Public**

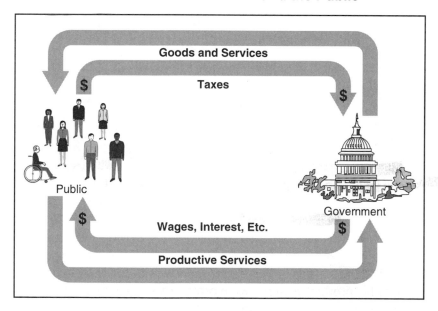

lower portion of the inner loop indicates the payments that government makes to the public in the form of wages, rent, welfare, interest, and so on.

The outer loop in Figure 2.4 shows (at the top) the flow of government goods and services to the public, and (at the bottom) the flow of productive services of individuals who provide labor or other services to the government.

A similar flowchart would represent the economic exchange between business and government. Productive services flow from businesses to government—as, for example, if Mrs. Green's law firm were to do some legal work for a government agency. Business firms also provide government with goods, such as office furniture, paper, and military hardware. Productive services flow from government to businesses, as when businesses use the Postal Service to send and receive mail. The size of the streams of money, goods, and services that flow between consumers, businesses, and the public is constantly changing.

Money flows from government to businesses in the form of fees (such as those charged by Mrs. Green's law firm) and other payments. Money flows from businesses to government as taxes, tolls, postage, fees, and so on.

Using the preceding information, one could construct a chart showing the circular flow of goods and services, and of money, between businesses and government. If we combine this information with the relationships described in Figures 2.1 through 2.4, we get a picture of the general flow of economic activity among the three major sectors of our economy: government, businesses, and consumers (the public). This economic activity is shown in Figure 2.5.

Circular flowcharts give a bird's-eye view of the economy and help us to see how changes in one part of the economy may affect the other parts. For example, when we read in the newspaper that the government plans to increase spending, we will understand that this could lead to an increase in the size of the total economic flow. Similarly, a reduction in the amount of goods and services purchased by the public will reduce the amount of income received by businesses and will thus reduce the size of the total flow of spending.

Gross Domestic Product

The magnitude of the streams of goods, services, and payments that flow among consumers, businesses, and government is constantly changing. Economists call the total value of the goods and services produced in a single year the *gross domestic product* (*GDP*). Since goods and services produced by the economy are purchased by either consumers, businesses, or government, the GDP can be expressed as $C + I + G = GDP$.

Where

C = consumer spending

I = investment (business spending)

G = government spending

(*Note*: Components of GDP are discussed in more detail in Chapter 18.)

Economists classify circular flows and the factors affecting them as macroeconomic events. Remember that macroeconomics deals with the economy as a whole, while microeconomics studies its parts.

Figure 2.5 **Circular Flow of Economic Activity Among the Public, Businesses, and the Government**

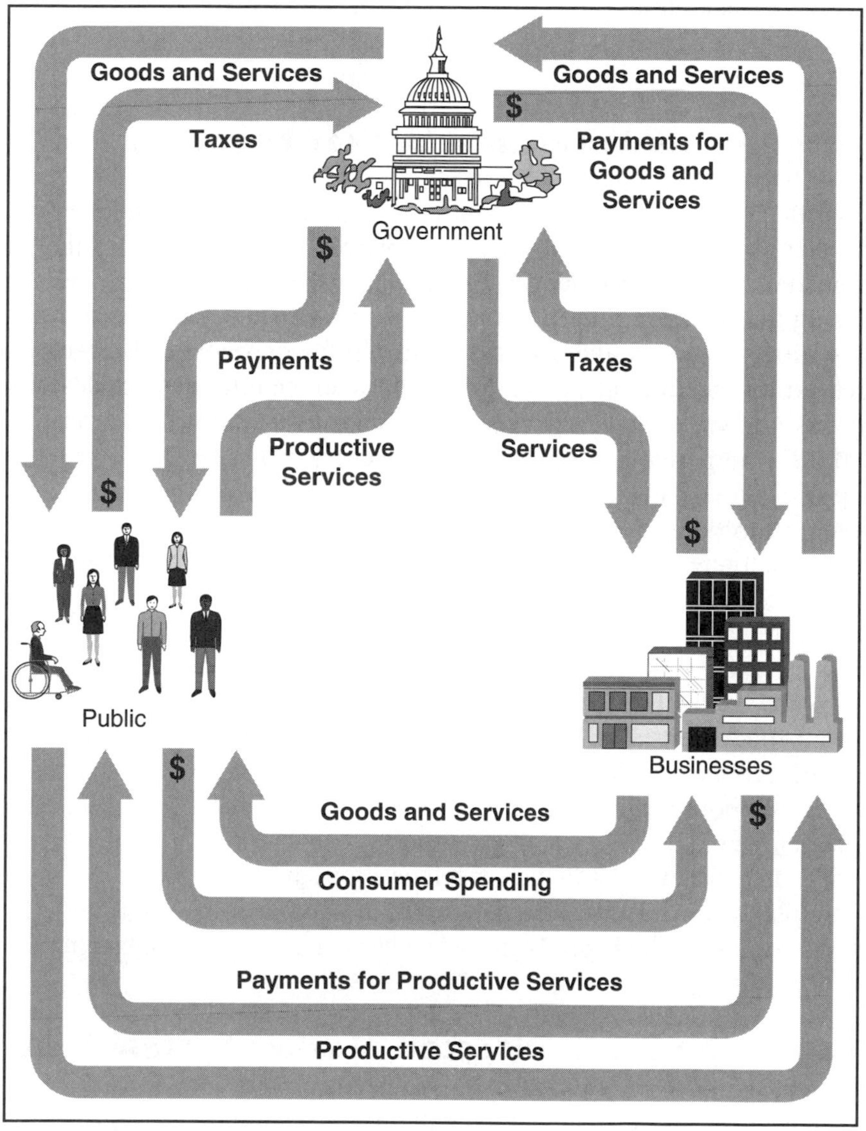

THE UNITED STATES ECONOMY IS A MARKET SYSTEM

A market is any place or circumstance in which goods or services are bought and sold. If you rent a videotape, you become part of the video rental market. Similarly, if you take an after-school job in your local grocery store, you become part of the food industry's labor market.

Since the buyers and sellers who make up a market do not have to meet face to face, markets can exist without a meeting place. In the NASDAQ stock exchange, for example, millions of shares of securities are bought and sold daily by buyers and sellers who never meet.

Dollars as Votes in a Market Economy

Circular flowcharts can illustrate the role of markets in the economy. Figure 2.6 shows the flow of goods and services between businesses and the public (households). In addition, the diagram shows the markets that are involved in the money transactions.

Figure 2.6 likens markets to an election. In the upper half of the flowchart, households "vote" for the things they want by casting their "ballots" (money) for goods and services at a certain price. Businesses put up their "candidates for office" (the goods and services they produce) so as to attract the greatest number of "votes" (dollars). The votes represent demand and the candidates represent supply. As sales are made, businesses receive the "votes" of the electorate (consumers' dollars), and their "candidates" (their goods and services) are either elected (purchased) or defeated (not purchased).

In the lower half of the flowchart, the roles are reversed: Households are the sellers and businesses, the buyers. Here the "candidates" running for election are the factors of production supplied by households: labor, buildings, and machinery. The "votes" are the dollars paid by businesses for the factors of production. Money flows from firms as part of their cost of doing business, and households receive payments in the form of wages, rent, interest, and profits.

What does the circular flowchart tell us about markets? Markets provide the "polling place" for buyers and sellers. Out of the never-ending round of elections, the prices at which goods and services will be sold are determined.

How the Price-Directed Market System Works

Like many other teenagers, Ted Green and his sister Laura are concerned with keeping up with their friends. Ted stopped going to his father's barber so he can use a stylist who cuts hair in the latest fashion. Laura recently talked her parents into buying her a stereo system so that she could start collecting her own CDs. Then the other day, Laura and her mother visited FoundSound, their local stereo store. Mrs. Green was amazed to see how many CDs the store carried that catered to her daughter's taste. Although Mrs. Green did not recognize most of the titles, the salesclerk assured her that business had never been better.

How was it that Ted Green was able to find a hairstylist who offered the latest look? Why did Laura Green have no difficulty locating the CD titles for which she was looking? Did a government agency direct that hairstylists be assigned

Figure 2.6 **The Role of Markets in Our Economy**

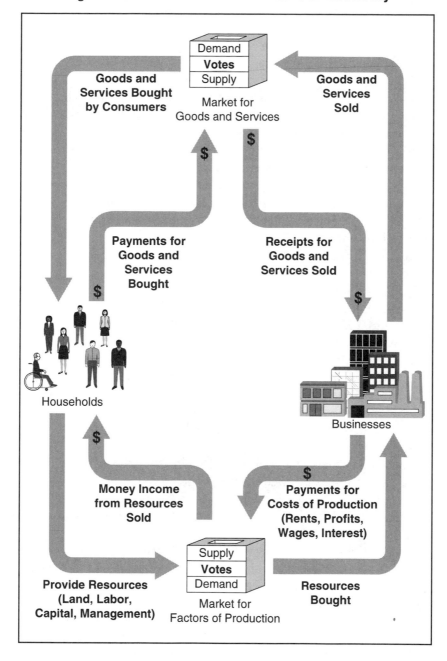

to neighborhoods in which their skills were in demand? Did a government supply board issue a list of CDs that music shops had to carry? Of course not.

The decisions to supply the goods and services that consumers like Ted and Laura were willing to pay for were made by thousands of individuals and business firms acting in their own interest. Taken together, the economic decisions made by the nation's business enterprises and those who buy from them have come to be known as the "market system" or "market economy."

🌀 The Role of Prices

Some economists compare the market system to a factory fueled by prices.

Ted Green's hairstylist became very popular. Recently, she raised her price to $35 per cut. "That's too much money," Ted said to himself. "I'm going back to the barber Dad uses. He'll do the job for half the price. Then I can use the money I save on haircuts to buy some new clothes."

Meanwhile, Laura was excited about an ad she saw in the morning newspaper. FoundSound was running a "One-Day-Only, Half-Off-Everything Sale!!"

"Half off everything," she exclaimed. "I can hardly wait till school's out. I'm going to buy a hundred CDs!"

"With what?" her friend Rebecca asked. "Half off doesn't mean it's free, you know."

"OK," Laura agreed, "so I'll buy one CD. And if I have enough left over, I'll buy another one, too."

Laura's and Ted's decisions to buy and not to buy were affected by the prices of the goods and services in which they were interested. As a matter of fact, almost every decision made by buyers and sellers is influenced in some way by the price of the product in which they are interested. Consumers compare the prices of goods they want to buy. Workers try to get the highest price, or wage, for their labor. Producers consider the prices, or cost, of the items needed for production and the prices they will be able to charge for the goods and services that they produce.

Indeed, price is such an important factor in the U.S. economy that economists often describe it as a "price-directed market system."

PRICES AFFECT WHAT GOODS AND SERVICES WILL BE PRODUCED.   How did it happen that FoundSound had the CDs that Laura Green wanted? With so many people willing to pay the price for its products, the store saw an opportunity to add to its profits by ordering more CDs from its suppliers. Moreover, FoundSound knew that if it did not have the recordings its customers wanted, they would simply buy them from its competitors.

What is true for FoundSound applies to all business firms. They must offer the products that customers want. They must do so at a price (1) that customers are willing to pay and (2) at which the firm can afford to sell.

In other words, while you and all your friends might love to buy a new mountain bike for $25, your local bike shop is not likely to offer any at that price. Why? Rather than profiting from the sale, it would lose money on the sale. If you and your friends, however, were willing to pay $500 for such a bike, the store would make sure that there were plenty from which to choose.

We can see, therefore, that the fundamental economic question of WHAT goods and services are produced in a market economy is ultimately decided by the prices that consumers are willing and able to pay for the things they want. If customers will pay the price, they can have just about anything they want. If they are not willing to pay the price, they will have to do without.

PRICES AFFECT HOW GOODS AND SERVICES ARE PRODUCED. Business firms are constantly seeking ways in which to increase their profits. Since profits represent the difference between income and costs, a surefire way to increase profits is to reduce costs while maintaining or increasing income.

In their never-ending search for lower costs, business firms constantly seek to improve the way in which they combine the factors of production (natural resources, human resources, capital, and management). In the recording industry, for example, manufacturers have to decide how many workers are needed to package and ship compact discs. The extent to which the manufacturers can, in part, rely on machinery for those operations affects both selling prices and profits. Although machines can be expensive to buy, in the long run using machines is often less costly than hiring additional workers. Similarly, retail shops have to decide how much of their operations they can turn over to computers. Does it make more sense, for example, to hire five employees and also use computers or have six employees doing the necessary operations without computers? Usually the use of computers reduces the number of workers needed. Buying and maintaining computers, though, is costly. The final determination as to how to combine the factors of production depends on estimates as to which combination will result in the lowest cost. Since individual business firms in a competitive market have little or no control over prices, their efforts to reduce costs can make the difference between profit and loss.

PRICES AFFECT WHO WILL RECEIVE GOODS AND SERVICES. Chapter 1 described how economic systems everywhere must wrestle with the problem of scarcity. Since there is not enough of everything to go around, societies have to find ways to ration the things they produce. The U.S. economic system, like all market economies, relies on prices to ration its output. Those willing and able to pay the price asked for a good or service can obtain it. Those unable or unwilling to pay the price will simply do without.

Since we have to pay for the goods and services we want, the amount of things that we can have depends on our income. For the most part, the income that people earn comes from the jobs they hold, their savings and investments, and (in some cases) business profits.

In most instances, the size of an individual's income determines the amount of goods and services that person can buy. Here again, price comes into play because the amount that people earn is largely a result of the price employers are willing to pay for their services and the availability of workers willing to accept that wage. There are millions of people willing to pay to see the best tennis, football, and baseball players in action. In contrast, there are only a handful of people who can perform at championship levels. Consequently, some of the highest paid people in the country are athletes.

Adam Smith

The year 1776 was a landmark in the history of the West for at least two reasons. First, a new vision of political freedom was proclaimed in the American Declaration of Independence. Second, a new vision of economic freedom was heralded when Scottish economist **Adam Smith** published *An Inquiry Into the Nature and Causes of the Wealth of Nations.* So great was Smith's impact upon Western thinking that he came to be known as the "father of modern economics."

Born in Scotland in 1723 and educated at Oxford University in England, Smith returned to his native land to teach for a time at the Univer-

sity of Glasgow. In 1763, he began a three-year tour of Europe, during which he met with a number of prominent thinkers. Returning to London in 1766, Smith spent the next ten years writing *The Wealth of Nations.* In 1778, Smith was placed in charge of the customhouse in Glasgow, and he held that post until his death in 1790.

In Adam Smith's time, most European nations followed the doctrine of *mercantilism.* The mercantilists believed that gold and silver were sources of wealth. Governments, therefore, ought to do everything they could to build up their nations' supply of these precious metals. Since most governments followed the mercantilists' doctrine, they enacted laws whose purpose was to enlarge their nations' supplies of silver and gold. The laws limited the economic activities of their colonies in such a way that the net effect of trade was to build up the home country's supply of silver and gold. Britain's imposition of mercantilism on its colonies was one of the principal causes of the American Revolution.

Smith strongly disagreed with the mercantilists. Wealth, he said, sprang from the production of goods and services, not from the accumulation of gold and silver. People cannot eat precious metals, nor can they be sheltered by them in storms, or warmed by them in winter. Those who want to measure the true wealth of a nation, Smith said, should look to the amount of goods and services available for each of its citizens, not the size of its treasury.

How, then, can a government encourage the production of the greatest quantity of goods and services? Here is where Smith's break with mercantilism is most clearly seen. Government, he wrote, could serve the economy best by keeping its hands off business. To the French (who had first proposed such a policy), the idea was described as *laissez-faire* (literally, "let them do"). *Laissez-faire* achieved enormous popularity in Britain as a result of *The Wealth of Nations.*

Why should government allow businesses to conduct their affairs without interference? Left to their own devices, Smith said, businesspeople would seek to make the greatest profits by turning out the greatest quantity of goods and services at the lowest possible prices. These low-cost goods and services would have to benefit society as a whole. Smith put it this way:

> Every individual . . . intends only his own gain; and he is in this . . . led by an *invisible hand* to promote an end which was no part of his intention. . . . By pursuing his own interest he frequently promotes that of the society more effectually than when he really intends to promote it.

The "invisible hand" that Smith saw guiding business along a path of public good was, in reality, the pursuit of profits. This took place in a market subject to the laws of supply and demand, which we will discuss in the next chapter. To allow the laws of the marketplace to function, Smith supposed the philosophy of *laissez-faire.* But Smith was also a realist. He recognized that government would have to intervene in the economy to preserve competition and to protect the general welfare.

The Wealth of Nations deals with many other subjects besides *laissez-faire,* among them labor, production, income distribution, rent, and taxation. Later economists would look to Smith's ideas as the springboard for the development of their own theories in each of these fields.

Smith's influence was dramatized in 1983 when the Nobel Prize in Economics was awarded to **Gerard Debreu** of the University of California at Berkeley. (See Chapter 9 for a discussion of the Nobel Prize Winners in Economics.) Debreu's prize was awarded in recognition of his work on a fundamental question of economics: How do prices operate to balance what producers offer for sale with what buyers want? Debreu developed a mathematical foundation that could be used to demonstrate the laws of supply and demand in action in a modern economy. In this way, the invisible hand of the 18th century became a mathematical reality in the 20th.

Similarly, rents (the price of housing) in poorer sections of town are lower than rents in more prosperous areas. This difference exists because (1) people who can afford higher rents are often unwilling to live in poorer areas and (2) landlords in poorer areas have to offer lower rents in order to find tenants.

We see, therefore, that prices provide the answer to the question "WHO will receive the goods and services produced in a market economy?"

💢 Evaluation of the Market System

We can gain a better understanding of the market system if we look at its advantages and disadvantages.

ADVANTAGES.   Among the most frequently cited advantages of the market system are the following:

1. The market system is the most efficient of all economic systems. In their quest for profits, producers compete with one another for the consumers' dollars. Since consumers prefer to buy the best products at the lowest prices, producers must constantly strive to increase their efficiency. They can do this by improving their products and services and reducing their costs. Those producers who succeed are rewarded with increased sales and profits. Those who fail stand to lose money and their businesses.

2. The market system is more sensitive to consumer demand than other economic systems. Since entrepreneurs are in business to earn profits, they do everything they can to produce or offer the things consumers "elect" to buy. They do this to increase their sales and their profits. For similar reasons, entrepreneurs stop producing or offering certain things as soon as they realize that these goods and services are no longer wanted.

3. The market system provides the most freedom for individuals and business firms, and least direction and control by government. Business firms are free to produce and sell their goods and services in whatever *lawful* way they choose. Similarly, consumers are free to choose from among competing goods and services—the products that best satisfy their wants.

4. The market system rewards those in accordance with the value the economy places on their contribution. How well individuals and families live is determined by their income. The income that individuals and families earn in a market system is largely based on how society, rather than government, values what they put into it. In later chapters, we will discuss the factors that account for differences in incomes.

DISADVANTAGES.   The market system is not without its shortcomings. Some of the more serious of these are discussed below.

1. The market system does not provide all of the goods and services needed by society. Although it is true that there are private roads, private schools, and private hospitals, it is highly unlikely that private individuals and groups would be willing or able to pay for the construction of the thousands of needed public schools and hospitals and the hundreds of thousands of miles of needed public roads. Little in the price system ensures that natural resources will be preserved or life and property protected. This is not to say that private businesses do not take measures to protect life or to attempt to restore natural resources (for example, by replanting trees). These actions, however, are by no means certain. Why does the market system fail to provide some essential public goods and services? The reason is that people are often willing to buy products only if they acquire the right to exclusive use of those products. They do not want to pay for goods and services that the public can also use. Food and clothing are examples of *private goods and services.* They are customarily enjoyed only by those who pay for them. Streets, police protection, national defense, foreign relations, and public health services are *public goods and services.* They benefit us all whether we pay for them or not. But since those who use public goods and services cannot always be made to pay for the cost of providing them, private sellers will not produce them. Therefore, where public rather than private goods and services are concerned, society must find ways other than the price system to determine WHAT things to produce, HOW to produce them, and WHO will receive them.

2. The market system does not adequately provide for the needs of all the people. Critics often point to the large number of people living in poverty in the United States. In a recent year, the figure was some 36 million persons. While the market economy generally does a good job of rewarding the most efficient and productive citizens, it does not provide adequately for all. Examples of groups often not sufficiently provided for are single-parent households headed by a woman, children, members of many minorities, and the mentally ill. Critics of the market system maintain that all people are entitled to a decent standard of living whether or not they are capable of earning it.

3. The market system is likely to experience periods of expansion and contraction of business activity. Widespread unemployment and personal hardship often accompany the contraction of business. Unlike other economic systems in which workers are guaranteed jobs regardless of business conditions, the U.S. market economy has witnessed periods of high unemployment. In recent decades, the federal government and state governments have taken an active role in economic affairs to lessen the impact of those periods. As a result, there has been no repetition of the Great Depression of the 1930s when U.S. President **Franklin D. Roosevelt** said ". . . one-third of a nation . . ." was ". . . ill-housed, ill-clad, ill-nourished." Although government action has helped to compensate for swings in the business cycle, critics maintain that the need for such government intervention reveals weaknesses in the market system.

4. The market system cannot account for many harmful costs of doing business. Consider, for example, a coal-powered manufacturing facility that spews harmful pollutants into the atmosphere. To economists, both the coal that powers the machinery and the air currents that carry off the smoke are resources. But they are significantly different kinds of resources. Coal, on the one hand, is privately owned. It must be paid for by those who use it. Coal, therefore, is one of the costs of doing business. Air, on the other hand, belongs to all of us. Traditionally, the cost of cleaning it up does not have to be paid entirely by those who pollute it. To economists, coal represents an *internal cost*—a cost that is part of the expense of doing business. By contrast, air is an externality, or *external cost. Externalities* are business costs paid for by society as a whole. Since the market system does not impose a penalty for polluting the air, the coal-powered manufacturing facility has no economic reason for changing its policies. (Manufacturers do, however, have legal reasons for not polluting. Local, state, and the federal government impose hefty fines on polluters.)

OUR NATION'S ECONOMIC GOALS

How we deal with economic issues depends on our economic goals. Although some disagreements exist over what our country's economic goals should be, most people in the United States include the following in their list.

Economic Freedom

Americans have guarded their traditional economic freedoms as carefully as their political freedoms. Workers in the United States take for granted their right to accept or reject a job. In some nations, workers do not have this right. U.S. workers can form labor unions that are free to strive for better working conditions—another economic freedom not enjoyed in all nations.

Economic freedom includes the right to spend or save money as one wishes and to own the goods one has purchased. It also includes the right of business-people to own property and make a profit. Of course, our economic freedoms (like our political freedoms) are limited by rules of law. The right of business-people to run their own firms does not permit them to produce or sell merchandise that endangers the health or safety of others.

Economic Justice

Most Americans agree that everyone should have equal economic opportunity regardless of nationality, age, sex, race, or income level. Not everyone agrees on what constitutes equal economic opportunity or what steps should be taken to ensure it.

In a market economy, those with special skills or wealthy families generally earn higher incomes than others. At its extremes, the unequal distribution of income results in some people becoming billionaires while others live in poverty and/or homelessness. In these circumstances, government is often called on to do something to make income distribution fairer. Government efforts to redistribute income may focus on solutions extending over the long and/or the short run. Long-term strategies focus on improving education and training as a way of improving workers' skills. This, in turn, qualifies them for higher-paying jobs. In the short term, taxes can be designed to take more from high-income groups than those with lower incomes. Similarly, government programs such as welfare and other benefits may be enacted to aid those in need.

Economic Stability

A period of economic stability is one in which changes in the level of prices, employment, and business activity are modest. In stable times, prices of most goods and services remain at levels that people can afford, and jobs are plentiful. An important economic goal, therefore, is to maintain stable prices and employment.

Unfortunately, there have been times when the United States has experienced economic decline or inflation. During an economic decline, business activity falls off, workers lose their jobs, and many resources lie idle. When the decline is severe, as it was during the 1930s, it is called a *depression*. A milder decline is known as a *recession*.

Inflation is a general rise in prices. During inflation, people find that unless their incomes are increasing as fast as prices, they cannot buy as much as before. Inflation is particularly cruel for people with fixed incomes, such as pensions.

The hardships resulting from depression and inflation led Congress to take action to maintain national economic stability. The **Employment Act of 1946** declared that it is the responsibility of the federal government "to promote maximum employment, production, and purchasing power." In later chapters in this book, we will discuss how our government tries to maintain the nation's economic stability.

Economic Efficiency

A nation must make the best use of its resources to provide the greatest quantity of the goods and services that its citizens want. How well it achieves that goal is a measure of the nation's economic efficiency.

Economic Security

People like to know that in times of illness or unemployment and in old age, they and their families will be provided for. They may set aside a portion of their earnings in the form of savings, insurance, and other investments for that purpose. Many business firms and labor unions provide their employees and members with insurance and retirement plans.

Because *economic security* is so important and many people could not otherwise obtain it, all levels of government have established programs to offset the risks resulting from loss of income. Examples of such programs are Social Security, unemployment insurance, welfare, and savings deposit insurance.

Economic Growth

Most people want more of the goods and services that make for a rising standard of living. But the society as a whole can obtain more only if it is producing more. An increasing output of goods and services is called *economic growth*. Some question whether unlimited economic growth is desirable. For example, as production increases, pollution and the loss of natural resources also increase.

S U M M A R Y

The U.S. economic system of capitalism rests on the principles of free enterprise, private property, the profit motive, consumer sovereignty, and competition. In modern economies, people and businesses specialize. Individuals and businesses must rely on the labors of others to supply them with most of their needs. The circular flow model describes the stream of funds, goods, and services constantly passing back and forth among consumers, businesses, and government. In our market economy, prices determine WHAT goods and services will be produced, HOW they are produced, and WHO will receive these goods and services.

The market system has many advantages, including efficiency and sensitivity to consumer demands. It does not, however, provide all of the goods and services needed by society. Moreover, it does not ensure stability of production and employment.

REVIEWING THE CHAPTER

BUILDING VOCABULARY

Match each item in Column A with its definition in Column B.

Column A

1. capitalism
2. public utility
3. circular flow
4. profits
5. consumer sovereignty
6. competition
7. eminent domain
8. internal cost
9. external cost
10. gross domestic product

Column B

a. the rivalry among buyers and among sellers in the same field

b. the power of government to seize property it intends to use for some public purpose

c. the dollar value of all goods and services produced by an economy in a single year

~~d.~~ an economic system in which the means of production are privately owned

e. a cost of a business that is paid for by society as a whole

~~f.~~ an industry that serves the public interest

g. a cost of business paid for by the business firm

~~h.~~ the amount of money left over after subtracting business expenses from business income

i. the freedom to choose which goods one can buy

~~j.~~ the stream of funds, goods, and services passing back and forth among households, businesses, and government

UNDERSTANDING WHAT YOU HAVE READ

1. The greatest degree of economic specialization is most likely to be found in (*a*) a traditional agricultural society (*b*) a frontier farming community (*c*) a poor rural area in India or Latin America today (*d*) an industrial society such as that of the United States.

2. Which *one* of the following forces will be most influential in determining the number of pairs of brown as compared to black shoes a manufacturer will produce in a market economy? (*a*) government directives (*b*) views of production supervisors' spouses (*c*) consumer demand (*d*) factory workers' preferences.

3. In an economic system operating under capitalism, the fundamental questions of WHAT, HOW, and WHO are answered by (*a*) tradition (*b*) the market (*c*) a government agency (*d*) congressional legislation.

4. In the circular flow of economic activity, we see that businesses (*a*) receive money but no productive services from households (*b*) receive money from both government and households (*c*) sell more goods to government than to households (*d*) receive no money from government.

5. All other things being equal, if consumers are willing to pay more for an item, it is likely that (*a*) more of that item will be produced (*b*) less of that item will be produced (*c*) producers will continue to produce regardless of production costs (*d*) the price of that item will be reduced.

6. Which *one* of the following is most influential in causing firms to produce the goods and services that the public wants? (*a*) the profit motive (*b*) competition (*c*) consumer sovereignty (*d*) the needs of the public.

7. Competition and the desire for profits pressure business firms to (*a*) provide inferior services to consumers (*b*) provide consumers with the goods and services they want (*c*) produce products of poor quality (*d*) charge high prices for products and services.

8. In a market economy, consumers can have just about anything they want if they (*a*) are willing and able to pay the price (*b*) belong to the ruling party (*c*) are famous persons (*d*) have enough friends.

9. Which *one* of the following statements is a major criticism of the market system? (*a*) It rewards inefficiency and waste. (*b*) It is insensitive to changes in consumer demand. (*c*) It fails to deal with certain harmful side effects of production. (*d*) It encourages the overproduction of goods and services that no one really wants.

10. Which *one* of the following statements is said to be a major advantage of the market system? (*a*) It is the most efficient of all economic systems. (*b*) It ensures that natural resources will be preserved. (*c*) It always provides for essential public goods and services. (*d*) It provides adequately for the needs of all U.S. citizens.

THINKING CRITICALLY

1. Some people claim that a command economy is more efficient than a market economy. In support of this position, they remind us that in time of war the U.S. government has found it necessary to assume wide economic powers. These powers have included controlling prices, wages, and hours of work, along with rationing certain goods that are in short supply. Opposing this position are those who point to the events in Europe following the breakup of the Soviet Union in 1991. The nations formed out of the USSR, as well as the nations of Eastern Europe, have all abandoned command economies in favor of market economies.

Answer *each* of the following questions by giving *two* reasons, with explanations for each.

a. Why do you agree or disagree that a command economy is more efficient than our market economy?

b. Why do you think the United States abandoned central planning after World War II?

c. Why do you think countries that were formerly part of the Soviet Union are trying to develop market economies today?

2. Assume that three members of the nation's leading rock group were recently seen at a popular club wearing buttoned shoes. Consequently, many fashion-conscious young men and women have sought to do the same. (*a*) How would the public inform shoe manufacturers that it wanted shoes with buttons? (*b*) What economic factors would shoe manufacturers consider before deciding to produce the buttoned models? (*c*) What economic groups other than shoe manufacturers are likely to be affected by the public's decision to wear buttoned shoes? Explain.

3. HOW goods and services are produced is very much influenced by the expectation of profit. (*a*) Under what circumstances might theater owners substitute counters and salesclerks for soda-, popcorn-, and candy-vending machines? (*b*) What factors might an insurance company consider before it replaced five clerical workers with one computer system? (*c*) What factors would a dress manufacturer take into consideration in deciding where to locate a new factory?

4. Critics have charged that the market economy (*1*) fails to provide goods and services that are needed yet are unprofitable and (*2*) imposes certain harmful effects, or "externalities," upon the public at no expense to those who caused them. (*a*) Explain these arguments. (*b*) Tell whether you agree or disagree with them and why.

5. Some observers maintain that the economic goals of the American people are impractical, unachievable, and inconsistent. They argue, for example, that economic efficiency and economic justice are frequently in conflict with each other. Explain, with examples to back up your point of view, why you agree or disagree with this statement.

SKILLS: Analyzing a Political Cartoon

Base your answers to the following questions on your knowledge from reading the text and on the cartoon on the next page.

1. Explain the meaning of the cartoon. In your explanation, make reference to the two buildings.

2. Each of the "pillars" in the cartoon has certain limitations. For example, private property rights are limited by eminent domain.

a. Explain how eminent domain limits one's right to own property.

b. Identify and explain *three other* limitations on the "pillars" of the U.S. economy.

CHAPTER 3

Demand, Supply, and Price

O V E R V I E W

"You mean you bought another watch?"
"I know, I already own two watches. But at the price, I simply couldn't pass this one up."

"I just took a job at Vendors Mart."
"Vendors Mart? That's a department store. I thought you were working for Gold Star Clothing."
"I was until Vendors Mart offered me twice as much as I was making at Gold Star."

"I'm looking for a new 18-speed bike."
"I thought you already owned one."
"I did. But Gloria offered me so much money for it that I had to sell it to her."

There are many reasons why people decide to make a purchase, get a job, or sell something. Whatever the reasons, one element that is always present is price. If the price is too low, sellers will not sell. If the price is too high, buyers will not buy. Prices play a crucial role in our economic system. To understand how a nation's economy functions, it is necessary to have some understanding of that nation's price system.

This chapter describes the forces that determine the price of a good or service. Economists call these forces "demand" and "supply." Our discussion will consider these two forces and explain how they interact to establish "market price."

DEMAND

Many people would like to own a sports car, wear designer clothes, or travel to distant lands. To an economist, these desires are merely wishes that have no economic significance. But if a person steps forward with the necessary amount and says, "I will pay $40,000 for a sports car now," the economist would identify this as *demand*. Demand is the desire to purchase a particular item at a specified price and time, accompanied by the ability and willingness to pay.

Demand Schedule

The quantity demanded varies with the price of an item. Suppose, for example, you surveyed a class of students to find out how many would purchase a slice of pizza for $2.50. Two hands might go up. If the price you quoted was $1.75, 23 hands might be raised. What you would find is that (up to a certain point) the lower the price, the greater the number of pizza slices students would be willing to buy. If we were to insert the data into a table, the *demand schedule* might look like this:

TABLE 3.1 DEMAND FOR PIZZA SLICES

At a price of	Number of slices students would buy
$2.75	1
2.50	2
2.25	6
2.00	12
1.75	23
1.50	45

Demand Curve

The demand schedule shown in the table can be illustrated with a *demand curve*. (See Figure 3.1 on page 50.) This is a line graph that shows the amount of a product that would be demanded at each price. The vertical axis represents price per unit, while the horizontal axis represents number of units, or quantity. In Figure 3.1, the demand curve D slopes downward and to the right. The points on the curve correspond to the demand schedule for pizza slices. A demand curve thus shows how much of a commodity will be sold at any given price.

🗲 The Law of Demand

The *Law of Demand* tells us that buyers will purchase more of an item at a lower price and less at a higher price. The reasons for this are that at a lower price (1) more people can afford to buy the product, (2) people tend to buy larger quantities of the product, and (3) people tend to substitute the product for similar items that are either more expensive or less desirable. Similarly, as the price of a product goes up, (1) fewer people can afford to buy the product, (2) buyers tend to purchase smaller quantities of the product, and (3) people tend to substitute cheaper products for the more expensive one. The Law of Demand can be generalized as follows: *Quantity demanded varies inversely with* (in the opposite direction to) *changes in price.*

In our example, the Law of Demand affected how many pizza slices would be sold at each price. As the price of the slices was reduced, more students demanded them. The lower price might also have attracted students who had not been planning to eat at that time. Others who would have purchased one slice at a higher price will now buy two or more at a lower price. And still others who had been planning to buy a sandwich or a burger after class might decide to eat pizza instead.

Storekeepers are well aware of the Law of Demand. That is why they lower prices when they want to clear out merchandise. Butchers know, for example,

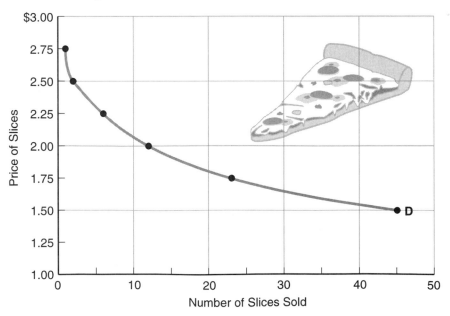

Figure 3.1 **Demand Curve for Pizza Slices**

that consumers who would not buy steak at $10 a pound will pay $5. They also know that while some consumers prefer steak, they also eat chicken, fish, and other foods. At $10 a pound, steak is more expensive than many other foods that consumers might purchase. But with steak at $5 a pound, the difference in price between steak and some alternative foods is less.

Principle of Diminishing Marginal Utility

Once you buy something, the money spent is no longer available for any other purchase. When we conducted our pizza-slice survey, we in effect made each member of the class ask herself or himself the question, "Do I want to give up some of my purchasing power in order to have a slice of pizza?" Anyone about to make any purchase must ask a similar question.

Why does a buyer choose one product instead of another? Assume, for example, that you have 75 cents with which you plan to buy either chewing gum or candy. After a few moments' consideration in front of the candy counter, you decide to buy the gum. Why gum and not candy? The economist would explain this choice in terms of utility: the measure of satisfaction one gets from the use of a good or service. When you chose the chewing gum, you decided that it would better satisfy your wants than a candy bar. In economic terms, the utility of chewing gum is greater than the utility of a candy bar.

Economists have devised the concept of *marginal utility* to help explain the spending patterns of consumers. Marginal utility is the degree of satisfaction or usefulness a consumer gets from each additional purchase of a product or service. The word "marginal" has several meanings in economics. In this case, it means "additional."

People will buy something if they expect the purchase to yield them more satisfaction, or utility, than something else. In the example of the pizza slices, many students are willing to buy a second, a third, or even a fourth slice if the price is low enough. But as the pizza is consumed, it becomes less satisfying. By the time the second or third slice is downed, the thought of still another slice has become less appealing. In economic terms, each additional slice has less utility than the preceding one. This phenomenon is summarized in the *Principle of Diminishing Marginal Utility,* which states: Each additional purchase of a product or service by a given consumer will be less satisfying than the previous purchase.

The Principle of Diminishing Marginal Utility applies to almost any product. One overcoat may be a necessity; two or three may be desirable; but what would persuade you to buy four or five? Each new purchase will be less satisfying than the one before. It will have less utility. You will be less willing to give up something else to buy an additional overcoat. You may still decide to buy another coat, but only at a lower price.

💢 Elasticity of Demand

The Law of Demand is clear: Fewer items are bought at a higher price than at a lower one. The Law of Demand, however, does not tell by how much the quantity demanded will increase or decrease at different prices. If the price of milk doubles, less milk will be sold. Similarly, if the price of steak doubles, consumers will buy less steak. Nevertheless, will sales of milk and steak fall by the same percentage? For example, if milk sales drop 20 percent as the price doubles, will steak sales also drop 20 percent as the price of steak doubles? Certainly not. The population as a whole can do without steak far more easily than it can do without milk. Even at the higher price, the demand for milk will be greater than the demand for steak, and the decline in steak sales will be far greater than the decline in milk sales.

If the prices of milk and steak drop by 50 percent, more of both products will be sold, in accordance with the Law of Demand. The percentage increase in steak sales, however, will probably be far greater than that of milk sales. The reason is that after consumers purchase what they consider a sufficient amount of milk, they are still willing to buy more steak. Of course, in this example we are referring to the population as a whole. Many individuals do not or cannot drink milk at any price. Some people avoid red meats such as steak, while others do not eat meat at all, at any price.

One way to measure the degree of demand is through the concept of *elasticity of demand.* This term describes the percentage change in demand (as measured by the dollar value of spending for an item) that follows a price change. The more demand expands or contracts after a price change, the greater the elasticity

Law of Demand. What factors will affect the demand for hot dogs at this stand?

TABLE 3.2 DEMAND FOR MILK AND STEAK					
	Price (P)	×	Units Sold (Q)	=	Total Revenue (TR)
Milk	$ 1.20		200		$240.00
	.60		350		210.00
Steak	$10.00		60		$600.00
	5.00		175		875.50

of the demand. The demand for most goods and services may be described as either relatively elastic or relatively inelastic. When a drop in the price of an item causes an even greater percentage increase in demand, we say that the demand for that item is relatively "elastic" (the demand has "stretched" a great deal). When a drop in price results in a decrease or only a small increase in demand, we say that the demand is relatively "inelastic." The same holds true for increases in price. Demand is considered elastic if a rise in price results in a large drop in demand, and inelastic if a rise in price results in a small drop in demand.

Elasticity of demand is measured by the amount that price changes affect total dollar sales. If a decrease in price of an item results in an increase in revenue, the demand for the item is said to be elastic. If a decrease in price results in a decrease in revenue, the item is said to be inelastic. Similarly, if an increase in price results in a decrease in total dollar sales, the demand is elastic; and if an increase in price results in an increase in revenue, the demand is inelastic.

Suppose that your local supermarket reduced the price of both milk and steak by 50 percent. Before the sale, milk was selling for $1.20 a quart and steak at $10 a pound. At those prices, the store sold 200 quarts of milk and 60 pounds of steak each day. At the sale prices, customers bought 350 quarts of milk and 175 pounds of steak per day. This information is summarized in Table 3.2.

Table 3.2 shows that total revenue from the sale of milk fell from $240 to $210 when the price of milk was reduced. This result indicates that the demand for milk is inelastic. Total revenue from the sale of steak, however, increased from $600 to $875. This increase shows that the demand for steak is elastic.

What Makes Demand Elastic or Inelastic?

When we question why some items are subject to elastic demand and others are not, we are really asking why price changes affect the purchase of some things more than of others. If one of the following four conditions is present, the demand for a good or service will usually be sensitive to price changes.

1. The item is considered a luxury. *Luxuries* are goods or services that consumers regard as something they can live without. Consumers are less likely to buy a luxury if the price is high. They will, however, consider buying one if the price drops enough. An item considered a luxury need not be costly in dollars. For example, a person with a modest income might consider fresh flowers, a steak dinner, and a taxi ride as luxuries. Also, what are considered luxuries by one person (for example, plane tickets, meals in restaurants, and expensive clothes) may be normal or even necessary expenses for someone else. If a product or service is considered a luxury by a large number of consumers, it will be subject to elastic demand.

2. The price represents a large portion of the family income. Buying an automobile or a home would represent a significant portion of most families' incomes. Therefore, a rise in the price of such items will discourage many consumers from buying them. Because of the greater utility of many costly items, however, a decrease in their price will cause a significant increase in sales.

3. Other products can easily be substituted for it. Because there are many less expensive substitutes for steak, many people will shift to chicken or some other meat if the price of steak goes up. Similarly, if the price of steel rises, manufacturers and builders will substitute other materials, such as aluminum or concrete. At present, though, there are no competitive substitutes for gasoline as a fuel for automobiles. Therefore, the demand for this fuel is inelastic. Our society is trying to develop alternative energy sources that pollute less and can be produced at competitive prices. Such products include natural gas, solar-powered cells, and battery-powered electric motors.

4. The items are durable. Furniture, appliances, and automobiles are relatively long-lasting. Since they are often major household items, many consumers purchase new ones if the prices are low enough. If prices remain high, however, people tend to "make do" with the old ones rather than replace them.

What Is the Significance of Demand Elasticity?

The elasticity of demand for a good or service is an important factor in many business decisions. Suppose, for example, that a local bus company whose fares are regulated by the government finds itself in need of additional funds. Should the company apply for a fare increase? The answer depends on the elasticity or inelasticity of demand for the bus service.

Table 3.3 shows two possible results of a 20 percent fare increase. If the demand for the bus service was elastic, a 20 percent fare increase might lead to a 25 percent reduction in riders and a decrease in earnings. If the demand for the bus service was inelastic, however, a 20 percent fare increase might lead to only a 15 percent loss in riders and an increase in earnings. In order for the bus company to decide whether or not to apply for the fare increase, someone (possibly an economist) has to estimate the degree of elasticity of demand for its service.

TABLE 3.3	DEMAND FOR BUS SERVICE		
	If the fare is	And the number of passengers is	Total revenue will be
Present	$1.00	10,000	$10,000
Elastic Demand	1.20	7,500	9,000
Inelastic Demand	1.20	8,500	10,200

What Economists Mean by an Increase or a Decrease in Demand

Certain events can make people more or less willing to pay a certain price for something than they once were. This change in willingness affects the demand for goods or services at all prices. If buyers are willing to buy more items at each price, we say that there has been an increase in demand. When buyers are willing to buy fewer items at each price than they once did, we say there has been a decrease in demand. To illustrate increased demand, consider the following situation.

> It is mid-July, and temperatures have been going above 90 degrees all week. Sally Simmons, a local fast-food vendor, tells us that on December 15, during a cold spell, ice cream cones that sold for $1.50 each found only 2 buyers. Now, she says, she is able to sell 9 cones a day at that price. Moreover, Ms. Simmons believes that she could sell as many as 30 cones at $1.10 each. She adds that if she reduced her prices to 70 cents each, sales would jump to 66 cones. (Some customers would consume more than one!) Let us look at a demand schedule for sales of ice cream cones on December 15 and on July 15, in Table 3.4.

This demand schedule can be plotted as a demand curve. (See Figure 3.2 on page 56.) D represents the demand on December 15, while D_1 represents the demand on July 15. We can see that when demand changes, the entire schedule shifts. Because the change in this case was an increase in demand, the curve shifted to the right. Had there been a decrease in demand, the curve would have shifted to the left.

TABLE 3.4	DAILY DEMAND SCHEDULE FOR ICE CREAM CONES	
	Number of cones people will buy	
At a price of	On December 15	On July 15
$1.70	1	6
1.50	2	9
1.30	6	18
1.10	12	30
.90	23	45
.70	45	66

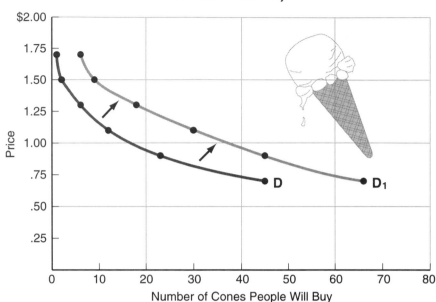

Figure 3.2 **Demand Curve for Ice Cream Cones (Increase in Demand as Reflected by a Shift in the Demand Curve)**

In the previous example, a rise in temperature caused an increase in the demand for ice cream cones. There are many other things that can cause a change in demand. What effect do you think each of the following situations would have on the demand for a given product?

1. an increase in the price of substitute products
2. an increase in most people's income
3. a change in the taste of buyers
4. the expectation that the price of the product will soon fall
5. the appearance of a new substitute product
6. the fear that the economy is about to go into a recession, one in which many firms fail and unemployment increases

 SUPPLY

Neil Simi, an economics teacher, opened the day's lesson with an experiment.

"Class, how many of you are wearing wristwatches?" Twenty-eight hands went up.
"You may have noticed this paper bag sitting on my desk," Mr. Simi continued. "This bag contains $100 in one-dollar bills. I will give this bag of money to any one of you in exchange for your wristwatch. Please raise your hand if you are willing to

sell me your watch for $100." The teacher counted the raised hands and wrote the number 24 on the chalkboard.

"Brenda," Mr. Simi said, "I noticed that you did not raise your hand. Don't you want to sell me your watch?"

"No, because it cost much more than $100 only a few months ago."

"I see," the teacher replied and then peered into the bag.

"Class," he went on, "I seem to have made a terrible mistake. I thought I had $100 in this bag. Actually, it looks more like $50. Let's start over again. Who would sell me his or her watch for $50?" Once again Mr. Simi counted the raised hands, wrote the total (15) on the board, and then looked into the bag. With feigned surprise, he took a smaller bag out of the paper bag.

"Oh, this is embarrassing," he said. "I thought I had only money in this bag, but I see I packed my lunch in it, too. I don't believe there's more than $20 here. Will anyone sell me a watch for $20?"

Five hands went up, and the number was duly noted.

Mr. Simi reached into the bag and started counting off bills. "Seven, eight, nine, ten! Well, it seems I have only $10 here. Does anyone want to sell his or her watch for $10?"

Only one hand was raised this time. The teacher placed the number 1 on the board.

"Bill," Mr. Simi said to the remaining seller, "it looks as if you have the only watch I will be buying today. Here is your $10."

"On second thought, Mr. Simi," said Bill, "I think I'll hold on to my watch. You can keep the $10."

Why did Bill suddenly refuse? Perhaps it was the name "Monopoly™" printed on the money that changed Bill's mind.

Mr. Simi's experiment demonstrated the economic concept of *supply*. Economists use the word "supply" to describe the amount of goods or services offered for sale at a particular price. As the price that Mr. Simi offered for a wristwatch went down, fewer watches were offered for sale. Just the opposite would have happened if Mr. Simi had offered $10 to start and had increased the price: More watches would have been offered for sale.

The dress shirts worn by members of the U.S. Army are produced by several different manufacturers in accordance with specifications prepared by the military. Let us assume that a survey was taken among the manufacturers to see how many shirts each could provide at various prices. The *supply schedule* prepared after all of the manufacturers had submitted their bids is shown in Table 3.5.

TABLE 3.5   SUPPLY SCHEDULE FOR ARMY SHIRTS

At a price of	Sellers will offer
$ 6	8,000
8	8,600
10	9,600
12	11,200
14	14,000

🔯 The Law of Supply

The examples of the wristwatches and army shirts both illustrate the Law of Supply. The *Law of Supply* states: The quantity of a good or service supplied varies directly with its price. That is, the number of units of something offered for sale increases as the price increases, and decreases as the price decreases. There are two reasons for this. First, existing producers will increase their output at the higher price. Second, new producers will be lured into the market by the higher prices. The Law of Supply will become clearer as you look at the supply schedule for in-line skates in the following example.

The supply schedule in Table 3.6 lists the number of in-line skates that manufacturers are willing to sell at the prices indicated. The schedule shows that at a price of $90, only 8,000 pairs of in-line skates will be offered for sale. At $270 each, however, 56,000 pairs will be offered. Why are sellers willing to offer so many more in-line skates at the higher price? One reason is that at a price of $270, manufacturers can afford to take on the extra help and pay for the overtime necessary to increase output to 56,000 pairs. Another reason is that manufacturers of related products such as skateboards and roller skates will find it worth their while to stop making those goods and start making in-line skates instead.

A supply schedule, like a demand schedule, can be plotted on a graph as a *supply curve.* In Figure 3.3, the supply curve S, which slopes upward to the right, summarizes the information contained in the in-line skate supply schedule for March 1.

🔯 Changes in Supply

Suppose that in-line skate manufacturers discovered they could turn out the skates in a way that was less expensive and quicker. This changeover in production methods would enable producers, large and small, to increase their production

▷ TABLE 3.6   SUPPLY SCHEDULE FOR IN-LINE SKATES ON MARCH 1

At a price of	Pairs sellers will offer
$ 90	8,000
120	20,000
150	30,000
180	39,000
210	45,000
240	52,000
270	56,000

Figure 3.3 **Supply Schedule for In-Line Skates on March 1**

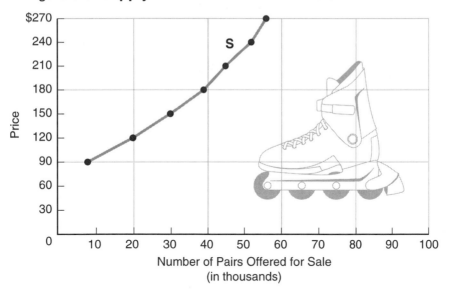

so that more skates would be available for sale at each price. The supply of in-line skates would increase. Table 3.7 summarizes such a possibility. If we plot this increase on a graph, the shift from the S curve to the S_1 curve will be to the right, as in Figure 3.4 on page 60.

Suppose that instead of a decrease in costs, the industry experienced an increase, such as one resulting from an increase in wages. What would happen then to the supply schedule and the supply curve?

Elasticity of Supply

Like demand, supply is subject to elasticity. The supply of some commodities is more sensitive to price changes than the supply of others. If a change in price

TABLE 3.7 SUPPLY SCHEDULE FOR IN-LINE SKATES ON OCTOBER 1			
At a price of	**(Percent Increase in Price)**	**Sellers will offer**	**(Percent Increase in Supply)**
$ 90	(0)	12,000	(0)
120	(33.3)	30,000	(150)
150	(25.0)	45,500	(50.0)
180	(20.0)	55,000	(82.7)
210	(16.7)	67,000	(82.1)
240	(14.3)	78,000	(85.9)
270	(12.5)	90,000	(86.7)

Figure 3.4 **Supply Schedule for In-Line Skates on October 1 (Increase in Supply as Reflected by a Shift in the Supply Curve)**

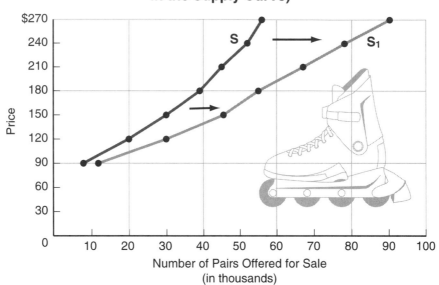

causes a larger percentage change in supply, the supply is said to be elastic. If a change in price produces a smaller percentage change in supply, the supply is said to be inelastic.

The supply of in-line skates in our example is elastic. It is elastic because as the price for a pair of skates increases from $120 to $150 (a 25 percent increase), the quantity of in-line skates offered for sale at that price increases by 50 percent.

Manufactured goods generally are subject to greater supply elasticity than goods provided by nature. In-line skate manufacturers might be able to increase their output by asking their employees to work overtime. Dairy farmers, however, could not expect such cooperation from their herds. Therefore, an increase in milk production would take longer to achieve than an increase in in-line skate production.

The amount of natural resources available is usually limited. While some resources, such as trees and wildlife, can eventually be replaced (through reforestation, conservation, and repopulation), these measures take many years. Some additional land can be made fit for farming by draining swamps or through irrigation. For the most part, though, we have to make do with the land we have. Minerals such as petroleum, iron, and copper also are subject to relatively inelastic supply. The output of these minerals is limited by the expense of the equipment needed to extract them, the size of the known deposits, and the uncertainty of discovering new sources.

HOW PRICES ARE DETERMINED

Our discussion of demand and supply has thus far concentrated on the number of items buyers and sellers are willing to consider at different prices. We have seen that the amount of goods and services that buyers and sellers are willing to exchange fluctuates with changes in price. What people are willing to do, however, is not always what they are able to do. You may be willing to buy a new, imported 18-speed bicycle for $50, but since no one is likely to sell you one at that price, you will probably not be able to buy it.

The price at which goods and services may actually be bought or sold is called the "market price." The following discussion describes how market price is determined.

Supply, Demand, and Market Price: Bringing It All Together

In describing how the forces of supply, demand, and price come together, we will be dealing with a model of *perfect competition*. Under perfect competition, the following conditions are assumed to exist:

● There are many buyers and sellers acting independently. No single buyer or seller is big enough to influence the market price.

● Competing products are practically identical, so that buyers and sellers of a given product are not affected by variations in quality or design.

● All buyers and sellers have full knowledge of prices being quoted all over the market.

● Buyers and sellers can enter and leave the market at will. That is, buyers are free to buy or not to buy; sellers are free to sell or not to sell.

Now let us see how prices of goods and services are set in the U.S. market system.

How Supply and Demand Determine Price

As price increases, the number of items offered for sale (supply) increases, but the quantity that buyers are willing to buy (demand) decreases. There is only one price at which demand and supply are equal. On a graph, this price is shown by the point where the demand and supply curves intersect. Because it is the price at which supply and demand are equal, the price at which goods are sold is sometimes called the *equilibrium price*. Because this price is established in the market, it is also called the *market price*.

Equilibrium Price. What part do supply and demand play in determining the price a store charges for sneakers?

To summarize: The price at which sales take place is the price at which the amount demanded is equal to the quantity supplied.

Table 3.8 shows the demand for in-line skates on March 1. If we add the supply schedule for this day, we will have Table 3.9. The demand and supply schedule in Table 3.9 shows that at a price of $150, the number of in-line skates offered by manufacturers is equal to the number that buyers are willing to buy. This information is illustrated graphically in Figure 3.5. Point M, which lies at the intersection of D and S, identifies the market or equilibrium price. The figure shows that this price is $150 and that 30,000 pairs of skates can be sold at this price. As long as demand and supply do not change, this is the only price at which all the skates produced can be sold. At any higher price, there will be sellers with leftover in-line skates that they can sell only by lowering the price. At a price lower than the market price, buyers unable to find any skates but willing to pay more will bid the price up until they too are satisfied. All sellers willing to sell at the market price or less will be satisfied, and so will all buyers willing to pay that price or more.

▷ **TABLE 3.8   DEMAND SCHEDULE FOR PAIRS OF IN-LINE SKATES ON MARCH 1**

Price	Demand
$ 90	48,000 pairs
120	36,000 pairs
150	30,000 pairs
180	24,000 pairs
210	17,000 pairs
240	11,000 pairs
270	7,000 pairs

TABLE 3.9	DEMAND AND SUPPLY SCHEDULE FOR PAIRS OF IN-LINE SKATES ON MARCH 1	
At a price of	**Buyers will take**	**Sellers will offer**
$ 90	48,000	8,000 pairs
120	36,000	20,000 pairs
150	30,000	30,000 pairs
180	24,000	39,000 pairs
210	17,000	45,000 pairs
240	11,000	52,000 pairs
270	7,000	56,000 pairs

What will happen to the buyers who will not pay more than $120 per pair of skates, and those sellers who will not sell for less than $180? The buyers will have to do without skates, and the sellers will be unable to sell their skates because the market price is too high for the buyers and too low for the sellers. At the equilibrium or market price, the "market is cleared"—that is, all possible sales are made. For any new price to be established, there has to be a shift in supply, demand, or both.

Effect of a Change in Demand on Market Price

Suppose that a panel of distinguished physicians announced that in-line skating was the key to good health and long life. Suppose also that this report received

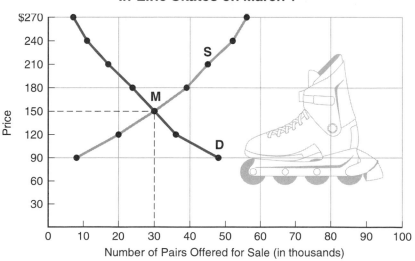

Figure 3.5 **Demand and Supply Schedule for In-Line Skates on March 1**

nationwide publicity and that prominent people in all walks of life were soon observed in-line skating to and from work and social activities. Many thousands of people might now be willing to pay more than in the past to take up the hobby. The demand for in-line skates would increase dramatically. The new demand schedule is illustrated by line D_1 in Figure 3.6. The new demand curve intersects the supply curve S at a higher point, M_1, and the new market price is $175.

Suppose, however, that the panel of doctors announced that in-line skating was found to be harmful to one's health. It is very likely that the demand for in-line skates would fall off, and the demand curve would shift to the left. In Figure 3.7, curve D_2, which intersects S at M_2, represents the new, lessened demand for in-line

Figure 3.6 **Increased Demand for In-Line Skates**

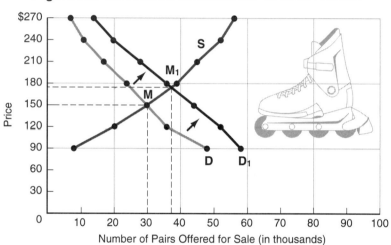

Number of Pairs Offered for Sale (in thousands)

Figure 3.7 **Decreased Demand for In-Line Skates**

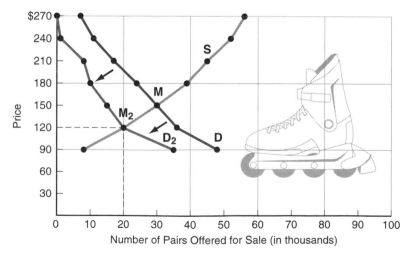

Number of Pairs Offered for Sale (in thousands)

skates. The curve shows that as demand decreases, market price also decreases. Common sense tells us that this will be so. Manufacturers must sell what they have produced. If fewer people want a product while its supply remains constant, suppliers must lower the price to attract buyers. We can express this principle in general terms: *Price varies directly with changes in demand.*

Effect of a Change in Supply on Market Price

How is market price affected if supply increases or decreases while demand remains constant? Earlier in the chapter, we described how an improved way of making in-line skates might result in an increase in supply. The effect of such an increase was to make more skates available for sale at every price and to shift the supply curve to the right. In Figure 3.8, S_1 represents an increase in supply. The new market price, M_1, is lower than the old price, M.

Suppose that the price of wheels rose sharply and there was a decrease in the supply of in-line skates. In Figure 3.9 on page 66, S_2 represents the new supply schedule. The curve has moved to the left, and M_2, the new market price, is higher than M. Again common sense tells us that if fewer items are available for sale, the price per item will increase.

The same principle applies to any product or service. If large quantities of diamonds were suddenly discovered and made available for sale, the price of diamonds would fall. When certain fruits and vegetables are in short supply, their prices rise. Thus, price increases when supply decreases, and price decreases when supply increases. In general terms: *Price varies inversely with changes in supply.*

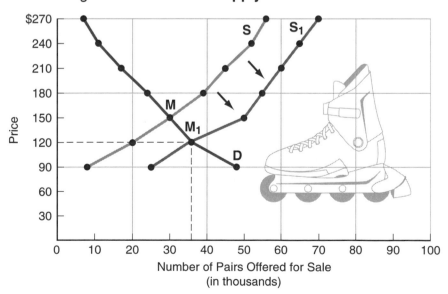

Figure 3.8 **Increased Supply of In-Line Skates**

Figure 3.9 **Decreased Supply of In-Line Skates**

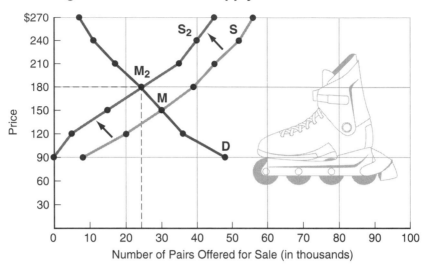

To What Extent Do Supply and Demand Affect Price?

So far, our discussion of market price has been based on a model of perfect competition in which price is determined entirely by supply and demand. The model has the following characteristics: (1) there are many buyers and sellers; (2) similar products are assumed to be identical; (3) all buyers and sellers have full knowledge of market conditions; and (4) buyers and sellers can enter and leave the market at will.

In an actual economy, however, these conditions are very seldom met. The supply of an item may be controlled by only one company or by a handful of firms. Similar products are often not identical. Even when they are virtually identical, advertising and other factors influence consumers to prefer one product over another. Buyers may not know that they can get the same or similar item for less under a different brand name or at the store around the corner. For these and many other reasons, the laws of supply and demand do not operate in real life the way they do in the model.

If perfect competition is a laboratory concept that rarely exists in real life, why do we discuss it? The reason is that in spite of its limitations, competition does give us an insight into some of the forces that control prices. Although in the actual economy we may never see all four conditions of perfect competition, we may see one or two. In those instances, supply and demand will affect prices. Prices are important because they keep the market functioning, and the market system is at the heart of our economy.

So far, we have discussed supply, demand, and price determination in an open, competitive market. Now let us take a look at what happens to supply and demand when government, not the market, sets prices.

WHEN GOVERNMENT CONTROLS REPLACE THE LAWS OF SUPPLY AND DEMAND

We have seen that the equilibrium price "clears the market." That is, the number of items offered for sale at the market price exactly equals the quantity demanded. Consequently, all buyers willing to pay the price will be satisfied, and no goods will remain unsold. Any price other than the equilibrium price results in either surpluses or shortages. That is, at a price higher than equilibrium, more goods will be offered for sale than buyers are willing to accept, thereby creating a surplus. Similarly, at a price lower than equilibrium, shortages will appear because there will be more buyers than there are sellers.

Sometimes governments attempt to control the market by imposing ceilings or floors on prices. A *price ceiling* sets a maximum price that sellers may charge for their products. A *price floor* guarantees sellers a minimum price for their products. The effects of price ceilings and floors are illustrated in Figures 3.10 and 3.11.

Figure 3.10 **Government Price Ceilings Result in Shortages**

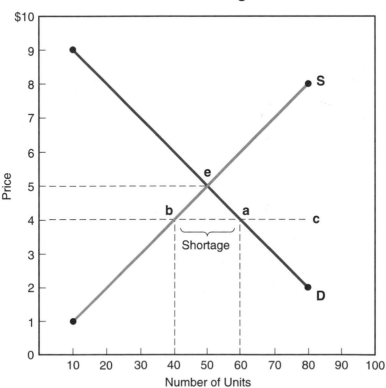

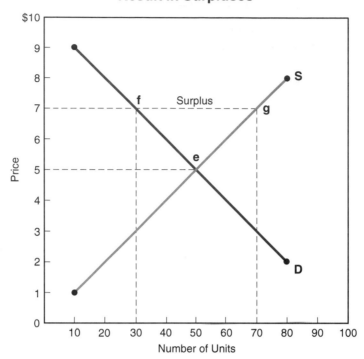

Figure 3.11 **Government Price Floors Result in Surpluses**

Price Ceilings

Before its collapse in 1991, the Soviet government set the maximum price of bread artificially low to keep consumers happy. In this illustration, the demand curve D and the supply curve S intersect at e (at a market price of $5). Government, however, has established a price ceiling at c ($4). At that price, buyers are willing to take the number of items at point a (60 units), whereas sellers supply only the number at point b (40 units).

The difference between the two points (60 − 40 = 20 units) represents the shortage of the product offered for sale at the government-set price of $4. Since there was not enough bread to go around at that price, lines formed outside Soviet bakeries where those at the head of the line got their bread, and those at the end had to do without. (For additional information on the economy of the Soviet Union, see Chapter 24.)

Price Floors

From time to time, the U.S. government has tried to help farmers by guaranteeing a minimum price on one or more of their crops. As a result, buyers had to

As the 19th century drew to a close, the world described by Adam Smith and other economists had undergone considerable change. The *Industrial Revolution* had transformed Britain from a primarily agricultural society into an industrialized one whose very survival was dependent on its international trade. Political power, which in Smith's day was totally in the hands of the landed aristocracy, was now shifting to the middle class of the world of business, industry, and finance.

In the world of economics, critics of classical theory asserted that it failed to reflect these changes. Others, whom we would now describe as "socialists" and "Communists," called for the replacement of the existing order with a new kind of economic system. The publication of *Principles of Economics* by **Alfred Marshall** in 1890 came as a tonic to the "silent majority" of the day who were looking for a restatement in modern terms of the theoretical basis of their economic order.

Alfred Marshall (1842–1924), whose work became a bible for what came to be known as "neoclassical" economics, was a member of the faculty of Cambridge University from 1885 until his death. He became a legend in his own time, and his lecture hall became the center of economic thought and education for the English-speaking world. Even before the publication of his *Principles,* it was said that at least half the professors of economics in Britain's universities had been his pupils. Marshall's influence spread even wider as universities in Britain and the United States made the *Principles* required reading. Not until the 1940s was the *Principles* supplanted by other works.

What Marshall had accomplished was a revitalization of the classical economics of writers like Smith by modernizing it and fleshing out areas of weakness in its theoretical framework. For example, Marshall developed the concept of elasticity of demand in order to explain price behavior.

For many years, too, classical economists had been debating whether supply or demand was the more important determinant of price. Marshall's introduction to his position on this issue is worth quoting as an example of his skill at slicing through complex issues with easy-to-grasp logic.

> We might as reasonably dispute whether it is the upper or the under blade of a pair of scissors that cuts a piece of paper, as whether value is governed by utility or cost of production (demand or supply). It is true that when one blade is held still, and the cutting is effected by moving the other, we may say with careless brevity that the cutting is done by the second; but the statement is not strictly accurate and is to be excused only so long as it claims to be merely a popular and not a strictly scientific account of what happens.

Although today's economic students are no longer required to read the *Principles,* Marshall's theories and methods are reflected in the works of all modern textbook authors and are part of the education of practicing economists.

pay at the price floor (or more) for the protected crop. Meanwhile, farmers could sell any or all of their unsold crop to the government at the floor.

Government-imposed price floors often result in surpluses. This is illustrated in Figure 3.11 in which we assume that the demand (D) and supply (S) curves intersect at equilibrium e (a market price of $5). But assume that the U.S. government has established a price floor of $7. At that price, buyers will take 30, while farmers will offer 70. The difference of 40 (70 – 30 = 40 units) is a *surplus*. Under its farm program, the U.S. government has had to assume the cost of purchasing, storing, and finding ways to dispose of surplus farm products. (For further information on U.S. agricultural programs, see pages 297–301.)

S U M M A R Y

Price is determined by the forces of supply and demand in a market economy. The quantity demanded varies inversely with the price, and this relationship can be indicated with a demand curve. Demand increases when prices fall and decreases when prices rise. The percentage change in the total value of spending that follows a price change is the elasticity of demand. An increase or decrease in demand at all prices is known as a shift in demand.

The quantity of a good or service supplied varies directly with price. More goods and services will be offered for sale as price increases, while fewer will be offered for sale as price decreases. A supply schedule can be indicated on a graph as a supply curve. The percentage change in the amount supplied brought about by a change in price is the elasticity of supply.

The price at which a sale takes place is the price at which the amount demanded is equal to the quantity supplied. This can be shown on a supply and demand curve as the point where the two curves intersect. Governments sometimes set limits to either supply or price. The price that is established may be higher or lower than the market price.

REVIEWING THE CHAPTER

BUILDING VOCABULARY

Match each item in Column A with its definition in Column B.

Column A

1. demand *e*
2. demand curve *C*
3. supply *G*
4. supply curve *B*
5. Law of Demand *F*
6. Law of Supply *H*
7. marginal utility *J*
8. elasticity of demand *I*
9. elasticity of supply *d*
10. market price *a*
   equilibrium

Column B

a. the price at which the amount demanded of a good or service is equal to the quantity supplied
b. a line on a graph that shows the number of a particular item that will be sold at each price
c. a line on a graph that shows the number of a particular item that will be purchased at each price
d. the extent to which supply changes following a change in price
e. the quantity of a product or service that would be purchased at a particular price
f. the idea that the quantity of a good or service demanded varies inversely with changes in price
g. the quantity of a good or service offered for sale at a particular price
h. the idea that the quantity of a good or service supplied varies directly with its price
i. the extent to which the dollar value of total spending changes following a change in price
j. the degree of satisfaction from each additional purchase of a product or service

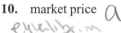

Diminishing marginal return –

UNDERSTANDING WHAT YOU HAVE READ

1. When the supply of a commodity increases while the demand remains the same, the market price will (*a*) rise (*b*) fall (*c*) stay the same (*d*) vary directly with the change in supply. homess wagner —> example de Bears

2. Which *one* of the following would probably lead to an increase in the demand for bricks? (*a*) an increase in the price of lumber, which can be used as a substitute for bricks (*b*) a decrease in the income of potential home builders (*c*) an increase in the wages of bricklayers (*d*) an increase in the price of bricks.

3. Which *one* of the following would *not* have the same effect as the other three on the amount of beef consumed? (*a*) a rise in the price of lamb (*b*) a fall in the price of beef (*c*) an effective advertising campaign on the part of pork producers (*d*) an effective advertising campaign on the part of beef producers.

4. When described in connection with supply and demand schedules, an increase in demand means that (*a*) the price will fall (*b*) buyers will take a larger quantity at all prices than before (*c*) the demand for the product has become more elastic (*d*) the demand curve slopes downward.

5. In an industry that has many competing firms, an increase in demand may be expected to result in (*a*) a decrease in production (*b*) no change in production (*c*) an increase in production (*d*) the elimination of inefficient firms.

6. The demand for a good is elastic when (*a*) total revenue increases with each decrease in price (*b*) total revenue decreases with each decrease in price (*c*) the demand curve shifts to the right (*d*) price changes have no effect on total revenue.

7. For which *one* of the following commodities is supply most elastic? (*a*) eggs (*b*) plastic toys (*c*) gold (*d*) corn.

Base your answers to questions 8–10 on Figure 3.12.

8. In the graph, AA represents (*a*) the supply curve (*b*) the demand curve (*c*) equilibrium (*d*) the market price.

9. In the graph, D represents (*a*) the supply curve (*b*) the demand curve (*c*) the demand schedule (*d*) the market price.

10. In the graph, BB represents (*a*) the supply curve (*b*) the demand curve (*c*) equilibrium (*d*) the market price.

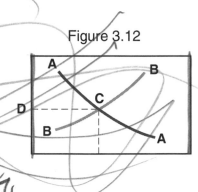

Figure 3.12

THINKING CRITICALLY

1. For *each* of the five possible events described below, tell (*1*) how the event would affect either the supply of or the demand for the italicized product and (*2*) how the event would affect the price of the product. (*a*) Yields decline as *corn* crop is hit by mysterious blight. (*b*) The wearing of *hats* is again becoming fashionable among men

in the United States. (*c*) Only two days are left to buy a *turkey* for Thanksgiving, and food markets have many unsold turkeys. (*d*) Manufacturers of *U.S. automobiles* show great interest in the rise in European wages. (*e*) Midwestern drought forces ranchers to rush their *cattle* to market.

2. Explain the difference in prices for *each* of the following pairs of goods in terms of the laws of supply and demand: (*a*) natural diamonds and zircons (human-made diamonds), (*b*) a loaf of bread baked today compared with day-old bread, (*c*) roses in January and roses in June.

3. A clothing store will usually reduce the price of smoke-damaged merchandise following a fire. Explain why some customers will buy this clothing even though it smells of smoke.

4. In Middletown, there were five bakeries and five florists. Last year, however, one firm bought out all the bakeries and another firm bought out all the florists. Both of the remaining companies have now decided to increase their prices. Which will be able to increase prices the most, the bakery or the florist? Explain.

SKILLS: Graphing Supply and Demand

Price	$16	14	12	10	8	6	4	2
Quantity	6	10	16	24	30	40	50	80

1. Construct a graph based on the data in the chart above. You may use graph paper for more precise plotting of points.

2. Does the graph show a demand or a supply curve?

3. Why does the curve slope downward?

4. On the same graph, construct another curve using the following:

Price	$16	14	12	10	8	6	4	2
Quantity	48	44	40	36	30	20	0	0

5. Does this curve represent supply or demand?

6. Why does this curve slope upward?

7. What is the equilibrium or market price?

THE ROLE OF BUSINESS

CHAPTER 4
The Business of Business

OVERVIEW

Perhaps the most distinctive feature of the American economic system is the extent to which the means of production are privately owned. In command economies such as North Korea and Cuba, the government owns a good proportion of the means of production. In the United States, 85 percent of the goods and services produced come from its 25 million privately owned business firms. These companies come in all sizes. Some, such as Wal-Mart, General Motors, and Microsoft, are classified as "big businesses." Each employs thousands of workers and has annual sales running into tens of billions of dollars. Big businesses tend to dominate their industries. Nine out of ten firms in this country, however, are classified as "small businesses." While definitions vary, firms with fewer than 500 employees fall into that category.

Washington Graphics is an example of a small business. A few years ago, Frank and Rose Washington decided that it was time to go into business for themselves. Both had worked for other people. Now they wanted to work for themselves so that they would be their own bosses and be able to earn more money.

By combining their savings and taking out a few loans, Frank and Rose were able to put together the $80,000 needed to buy a computer graphics company in Lincoln, Nebraska. They were not deterred by the fact that this company had fallen on hard times and had just recorded an unimpressive $100,000 in yearly sales. The purchase price provided the Washingtons with necessary equipment and a list of customers. They found other customers by joining the local chapter of the Minority Development Council, a group of minority businesspeople.

Under Frank and Rose's leadership, business boomed. The company created art designs and put these designs on all types of fabrics, including T-shirts, sweatshirts, caps, jackets, and bags. Within three years, annual sales at Washington Graphics had grown to more than $1.5 million.

In this chapter, we will see how U.S. businesses, both large and small, organize to produce and sell their products. As we read, we will learn about the principal forms of businesses—the sole proprietorship, partnership, and corporation—and the advantages and disadvantages of each. Finally, for those of you thinking of someday owning a business of your own, we will describe some of the things you will need to know before making that decision.

MINI-READING

Is Entrepreneurship for You?

Is entrepreneurship for you? For many Americans, owning a business of their own is the fulfillment of a dream. As with owning a car or a home, people often find personal satisfaction in owning their own business. If you ask them why they chose the entrepreneurial life, people are likely to speak of how much they like being their own boss and having the possibility of earning large profits and wealth if the business proves to be successful.

There are a number of risks that go with business ownership. As a business owner, one must have enough money available at all times to meet expenses. Employees need to be paid regularly, along with other creditors and one's suppliers. These expenses, along with taxes that business enterprises face, need to be met before one can clear any profits.

As the owner of a business, the happy responsibility for its success will be yours. But so too will the blame fall on your shoulders if it fails to meet its goals. In fact, you can never be entirely on your own because you need to satisfy your customers. If you do not, soon they will go elsewhere, and you will be out of business.

You should know, too, that business ownership is not for everyone. Some people are better suited to the demands of entrepreneurship than others. The **U.S. Small Business Administration (SBA)** suggests that before investing in a business, one should evaluate one's strengths and weaknesses by asking oneself the following questions:

- Am I a self-starter?

- How well do I get along with people having personalities different from my own?

- How good am I at making decisions?

- Do I have the physical and emotional stamina to run a business?

- How well do I plan and organize?

- Is my drive strong enough to stay interested in a difficult undertaking?

Some high school students might want to form a landscape company. Do you think young entrepreneurs can borrow enough or earn enough to buy the mower, the used truck, and other equipment?

THE SOLE PROPRIETORSHIP

Wilma Jones had been at her job for four years when she decided to use her savings to go into business for herself. She rented a store in her old neighborhood and set up a small grocery. Although she was able to hire a clerk to help wait on customers and stack the shelves, Jones was always busy. Since she was the owner, responsibility for the success of the business rested on her shoulders. She was there when the store opened in the morning and when it closed at night. She did all the ordering, kept the books, and often waited on customers. Because the business was hers alone, however, there were certain advantages. She did not have to share her profits with anyone. Moreover, she was her own boss.

The kind of business that Jones ran was a *sole proprietorship,* a business that is owned by one person.

Advantages of the Sole Proprietorship

There are *three* major advantages of this type of business organization.

EASY TO FORM.   The most important advantage of sole proprietorships is that they are easy to form. Aside from meeting some local license requirements, all Jones needed to do to start her business was open her doors and sell groceries.

"YOU'RE THE BOSS."   Another advantage of the sole proprietorship is the appeal of working for oneself. Although Jones might have found a job in another grocery store, she would not have been her own boss. As a proprietor, however, Jones is free to run the business her own way. She can try out her ideas on improving sales, and she does not have to take orders from others.

POTENTIAL PROFITS.   As the sole owner, Jones does not have to share profits with anyone. She knows that were she working for someone else, she would receive a wage that was more or less fixed. Best of all, there are no limits to the amount of profits a successful business can earn. Jones finds that possibility very attractive.

Because of its advantages over other forms of business organizations, about 72 percent of all firms in the United States are sole proprietorships.

Disadvantages of the Sole Proprietorship

The success or failure of this type of business falls on one person: the sole proprietor. The owner often has to work long hours and forgo vacations. Running a business can cut into one's time spent on recreation or with one's family. Other disadvantages of the sole proprietorship are:

Figure 4.1 **Types of Business Organizations**

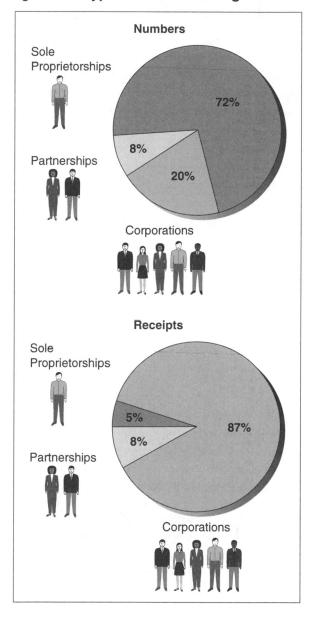

UNLIMITED LIABILITY. While there are no limits to the amount of profits that Jones might earn as the sole proprietor of her business, there are also no limits to the amount she could lose (that is, her *liability*). Economists describe this dire possibility as *unlimited liability.* Given that two out of three new businesses fail within four years of opening, you can see that the risk of loss is quite real.

LIMITED CAPITAL. Another disadvantage of the sole proprietorship is that the amount of capital (money) that the owner can raise is limited. That is, the most money that a proprietor can put into the business depends on the size of his or her savings and that person's ability to borrow.

LIMITED LIFE.   If Wilma Jones decides to go out of the grocery business (or is seriously injured or dies), the proprietorship will end. Thus, we say that sole proprietorships have a *limited life.* For that reason, it is often more difficult for proprietorships to borrow money than it is for other forms of business. Banks may be reluctant to lend to firms that may no longer exist in a few years.

 # THE PARTNERSHIP

Wilma Jones was growing tired of the long hours and responsibilities of her business. Even though she now had two people working for her, she still had to be there when the store opened in the morning and when it closed at night. Although business had been getting better, it was not getting any easier. One day, Fred Cruz, one of Jones's oldest and closest friends, dropped by to say hello. In recent years, Cruz had been working as a cook at a resort hotel. During the conversation, Cruz told Jones that he had saved some money with which he was hoping to open a small restaurant.

> "Hey, that gives me an idea, Fred," Jones exclaimed. "Why don't you come into business with me? The store next door is available. We could expand my store into there and add a take-out food section that you could run. We would own the combined businesses together as one partnership."
>   "You might have something there, Wilma," Cruz replied. "I was getting nervous about going into business on my own. This way we'd be able to help each other out."

After some further talk in which they worked out the details, Jones and Cruz drew up an agreement and formed a *partnership.* It replaced Jones's sole proprietorship. A partnership is a business organization owned by two or more persons, who are known as "partners." Partners may share the responsibilities and profits in any way they choose. Under the terms of Jones and Cruz's agreement, Cruz put up some cash, and the two agreed to share the profits equally. Soon, they began work on the store expansion. They put up a new sign in the window announcing the creation of the "C&J's Food Emporium."

Advantages of the Partnership

As with a sole proprietorship, there are several advantages to a partnership.

ADDITIONAL CAPITAL.   A principal advantage of a partnership over a sole proprietorship is that the available capital (that is, money) is increased by whatever amount the additional partners bring into the business. In this instance,

C&J's Food Emporium was able to expand because of the additional funds that Cruz invested in the business.

"Two Heads Are Better Than One."   Partners can share the problems and responsibilities that go with owning a business. Jones now may have more free time than when she was the sole boss. Partners may also bring special talents or skills into the firm. Fred Cruz's talents as a cook enabled the business to add a lunch counter to its operations.

Easy to Organize.   Finally, partnerships, like sole proprietorships, are fairly easy to organize.

Disadvantages of the Partnership

What are the negative aspects of partnerships?

Limited Life.   One disadvantage of the partnership is that its life is limited. When a partner dies or resigns, a new partnership must be created.

Partners May Disagree.   Another disadvantage of partnerships is the possibility of conflict among the partners. When partners disagree, the business is likely to suffer. In fact, studies have shown that disagreement among partners is a frequent cause of business failure.

Difficult to Sell.   It is often difficult to find a replacement when a partner wants to withdraw from a partnership. Besides the problem of finding someone willing to pay a fair price for a share in the company, the buyer and the price have to be acceptable to the other partner or partners.

Why do you suppose these two businessmen wanted to form a partnership rather than go it alone?

LIMITED CAPITAL.   The amount of capital that partnerships can raise is limited. That is, it is limited by the wealth of the partners, the business's earning power, and its ability to borrow.

UNLIMITED LIABILITY.   The principal disadvantage of the partnership can be summed up in two words: unlimited liability. This means that each partner or group of partners could be held personally liable for the debts of the business. Since there is no limit to the amount of money that a business could lose, the possibility of loss for each of the partners is similarly unlimited. Consequently, many people are reluctant to enter into partnerships because doing so would make them personally liable for the debts of the business.

Some time after forming their partnership, Jones and Cruz approached their former classmate and friend Yvette Miller to ask her for money to modernize their store. Miller agreed to invest $15,000 in exchange for a 10 percent share in the partnership. Because she was busy running her own dress shop, however, Miller would not have time to spend at C&J's Food Emporium. She made the investment with the understanding that she would be a "silent partner." Although she would get 10 percent of the profits, the management of the firm would be left to Jones and Cruz.

Unfortunately, the store soon fell upon hard times. Sales declined drastically. Unable to pay their debts, Jones and Cruz had to close their doors and go out of business. By this time, the company owed its creditors $20,000, and neither Jones nor Cruz had any money of his or her own. Yvette Miller, however, had about $25,000 in savings. Even though she was only a 10 percent partner, her status as a partner made her fully liable for its debts. The creditors were paid off by Miller, whose savings were reduced by $20,000.

▷ TABLE 4.1   FORMS OF BUSINESS ORGANIZATION

Form of Business	Advantages	Disadvantages
Sole proprietorship	Ease of formation "You're the boss" Potential profits	Unlimited liability Limited capital Burden of responsibility on owner Limited life
Partnership	"Two heads are better than one" Ease of formation Additional capital	Limited life Partners may disagree Difficult to sell Unlimited liability Limited capital

THE CORPORATION

We have seen that the advantages of the sole proprietorship and partnership are offset by a number of serious disadvantages for each. For that reason, many businesses turn to a third type of organization: the corporation.

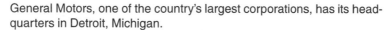

What Is a Corporation?

A *corporation* is a business organization licensed to operate by a state or the federal government. A corporation's license is called a *charter.* It gives the firm the right to do business and to issue a specified number of *shares of stock* (certificates representing ownership in a corporation). Anyone holding one or more shares of stock is a part owner of the corporation. If, for example, a corporation issues 1,000 shares of stock, anyone holding 100 shares owns 10 percent of the business. Those who own shares in a corporation are called *shareholders* or *stockholders.*

A unique feature of the corporation is its separation from the people who own it. Corporations can enter into contracts, sue or be sued, and pay taxes. For that reason, corporations are often described as "artificial persons." Thus, a musician who signs a contract with a recording company is, in a legal sense, entering into an agreement with the corporation rather than with the people who own it.

General Motors, one of the country's largest corporations, has its headquarters in Detroit, Michigan.

Let us return to the time when Cruz and Jones invited Miller to invest in C&J's Food Emporium. Suppose that instead of coming into the business as a partner, Miller had asked that the company be reorganized as a corporation. Under the terms of her proposal, Cruz and Jones would each keep 45 percent of the stock. Meanwhile, Miller would be given 10 percent of the stock in exchange for her $15,000 investment.

The partners liked Miller's proposal enough to ask their lawyer to apply for a charter from the state. After they obtained the document, they changed the sign over the store to read: "C&J's Food Emporium, Inc."

✍ Advantages of the Corporation

Why had Miller insisted on incorporating before she agreed to invest in the business? She did this because of the special advantages of the corporate form of business.

LIMITED LIABILITY.   Because the corporation is legally separated from those who own it, the shareholders cannot be held liable for its debts. Therefore, if the business fails, the most money that any shareholder can lose (that is, her or his liability) is limited to whatever she or he had paid for their stock. This *limited liability* is arguably the most important advantage of the corporation over other forms of business enterprise. For that reason, British corporations use the term *Limited* (abbreviated as *Ltd.*) to identify their corporations rather than our *Incorporated* (abbreviated as *Inc.*).

Returning to the tale of C&J's Food Emporium, Inc., let us again suppose that the company failed, leaving $20,000 in unpaid debts. Let us suppose, too, that Yvette Miller had $25,000 in her savings account. In this instance, her savings would be safe. The most that Miller could now lose is her original $15,000 investment.

Because the possibility of personal loss is limited, it is easier to interest people to invest in a corporation than in a partnership. This advantage is especially important to businesses that would like to expand. They can do so by selling shares of stock to the general public.

UNLIMITED LIFE.   Unlike businesses that end when the owners withdraw or die, corporations can go on forever. They have *unlimited life*. This situation makes it easier for corporations than for unincorporated businesses to borrow money for long periods of time.

EASE OF TRANSFER.   Buying in or selling out of a corporation is relatively easy. To buy, all one needs to do is find someone with stock to sell. To sell one's ownership in a corporation, all one needs to do is find a buyer for the shares that one owns.

⚡ Disadvantages of the Corporation

What are some of the disadvantages to forming a corporation?

DIFFICULTY AND EXPENSE OF ORGANIZING.   Organizing and operating a corporation is a complex process. It usually requires the services of a lawyer and an accountant—services that can add thousands of dollars to the cost of doing business.

DOUBLE TAXATION.   One of the reasons that people invest in a corporation is to receive *dividends,* profits that are distributed to shareholders. Like any other income, dividends are subject to *personal income taxes.* But even before dividends are distributed to shareholders, corporate profits are subject to *corporate income taxes.* (Various types of taxes will be discussed in Chapter 14.)

Many people have long argued that this *double taxation* is unfair. Nevertheless, except for the S-corporation (discussed below), double taxation remains as the major disadvantage of the corporate form of business enterprise.

⚡ S, the Corporation for Small Businesses

In an effort to aid certain small businesses, Congress added **Subchapter S** to the **Internal Revenue Code.** This law allows the owners of corporations with 75 or fewer stockholders to be taxed as though they were sole proprietorships or partnerships. Thus, owners of *S-corporations,* as the businesses are called, enjoy limited liability and the other advantages of the corporation while, at the same time, they avoid double taxation.

⚡ The Limited Liability Company (LLC)

The *limited liability company (LLC)* is the newest form of business organization. Like the S-corporation, a limited liability company combines advantages of the partnership with those of the corporation. LLC owners, who are called "members," are not personally liable for the debts of the business. Similarly, an LLC can sue or be sued and hold property in its name. Like a partnership, however, LLCs are easier to form than corporations and S-corporations, and their income is not subject to double taxation. That is, at year's end, an LLC's profits are "passed through" to its members as income liable for taxation. Unlike a corporation, the LLC itself has no income tax liability.

The principal disadvantages of LLCs are the following:

● *Limited life.* Like partnerships, LLCs may end with the death or withdrawal of one of its members.

> **TABLE 4.2   FORMS OF BUSINESS ORGANIZATION**

Form of Business	Advantages	Disadvantages
Sole proprietorship	Ease of formation "You're the boss" Potential profits	Unlimited liability Limited capital Burden of responsibility on owner Limited life
Partnership	Two heads are better than one Ease of formation Additional capital	Limited life Unlimited liability Partners may disagree Difficult to sell Limited capital
Corporation	Unlimited life Ease of transfer Limited liability	Double taxation Difficulty and expense of formation
S-corporation	Limited liability Unlimited life Ease of transfer No double taxation	Difficulty and expense of formation
Limited liability company	Limited liability No double taxation Ease of formation	May be difficult to transfer Life may be limited

- *Transferability.* Unlike corporations, whose ownership can be transferred through the sale of stock, no one can become a member of an LLC without the consent of a majority of the membership.

All in all, however, the advantages of the limited liability company so outweigh its disadvantages, that it is the fastest-growing form of small business ownership.

OTHER FORMS OF BUSINESS ORGANIZATION

Besides the more common sole proprietorships, partnerships, and corporations, we will look at other forms of business organizations, some of which are variations of the three major types.

🗲 Government-Owned Corporations

While most businesses in the United States are privately owned, some are owned and operated by a local or state government or by the federal government. One of the oldest and best-known government-owned corporations is the nation's largest power producer: the Tennessee Valley Authority. Founded by Congress in 1933, TVA provides flood control, agricultural and industrial development, and electric power for the 8.3 million people living in the Tennessee River Valley.

Atlanta's Metropolitan Area Rapid Transit Authority (MARTA) is a corporation owned by local government. It operates a regional bus and subway system. Similarly, the Pennsylvania Turnpike Authority and the U.S. Postal Service are examples respectively of state and federal government-owned corporations.

In many instances, government ownership developed because private interests were unable or unwilling to supply needed services. The reluctance of private utilities to provide electric service in some rural areas in the 1930s explains why the federal and state governments went into that business then.

THE TREND TOWARD PRIVATIZATION.　Since the 1980s, there has been some movement away from government ownership of businesses. The trend, known as *privatization,* seeks the transformation of publicly run businesses into privately operated and owned ones. In some states or communities, for example, privatization has led to the establishment of privately operated prisons and fire departments.

🗲 Not-for-Profit Corporations

The American Red Cross, the United Way, and the Boy Scouts of America are examples of *not-for-profit corporations.* So too are most other public service, charitable, and religious organizations. Unlike businesses that distribute profits to their owners, anything earned beyond costs by a not-for-profit business is put back into the organization to further its work. For this reason, not-for-profits are generally exempt from the payment of income taxes.

🗲 Cooperatives

Cooperatives (co-ops) are associations of individuals or organizations. Co-op members band together to buy or sell more efficiently than they could as individuals. The most common types of cooperatives in this country are consumer cooperatives, producer cooperatives, and cooperative apartment buildings.

A *consumer cooperative* is a retail business owned by some or all of its customers. Co-ops in which only members can make purchases sell their products at lower-than-average prices. Those that are open to the public usually have somewhat higher prices. They might distribute profits to their members in proportion to the amount of purchases each member makes during the year.

Producer cooperatives are organizations of producers who cooperate in buying supplies and equipment and in marketing their products. Ocean Spray cranberries, Sunkist oranges, and Blue Diamond almonds are well-known examples of products sold by producer cooperatives.

A *cooperative apartment building* is run by a corporation whose capital stock is owned by its tenants. As stockholders, co-op tenants receive many of the benefits normally associated with landlords, such as tax deductions and reduced rents.

How Large Corporations Are Organized

Corporations account for 87 percent of the business generated in this country. Although they vary in size from small, family-operated businesses to huge enterprises employing tens or even hundreds of thousands of workers, it is the largest firms that play the most important role in our economy. In one recent year, for example, the oil company ExxonMobil (with more than 100,000 employees and 700,000 stockholders) ran up sales totaling nearly $213 billion. That same year, the 500 largest industrial corporations accounted for $4 trillion in sales, or 40 percent of the nation's GDP.

Giant corporations like Exxon have organizational and operational problems quite different from those faced by smaller corporations. Although each of its 700,000 stockholders is a part owner of the company, it would hardly make sense for all of them to attempt to own the company. Instead, large corporations look to their officers and boards of directors to run the businesses on behalf of the shareholders.

OFFICERS.   The people who run a corporation are its *officers.* They are selected by the corporation's board of directors. Typically, officers include the president, a number of vice presidents, a secretary, and a treasurer (see Figure 4.2). The officers hire the personnel and conduct whatever operations are necessary for the functioning of the firm.

BOARD OF DIRECTORS.   Shareholders elect the *board of directors,* including its chairperson. Unlike political elections that follow the "one person, one vote" rule, shareholders are entitled to one vote for every share of stock they own. Consequently, a person with 25,000 shares of stock in a corporation in which 100,000 shares were issued is entitled to cast 25,000 votes (one quarter of the total).

Typically, the board of directors sets long-range goals for the corporation but leaves day-to-day operations to its officers. Two of the board's principal areas of concern are long-term financing and the distribution of profits. When,

Figure 4.2 **Organization of a Typical Corporation**

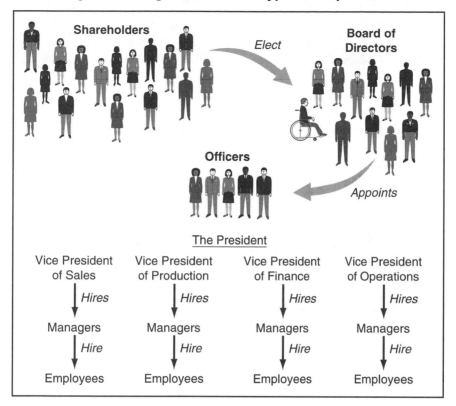

for example, the company needs additional funds for expansion, the board of directors decides whether to borrow the money or sell additional shares of stock. Similarly, the board decides how much of the firm's profits to distribute as dividends and how much to reinvest in the business.

The board also keeps shareholders informed of significant developments, prepares certain financial reports, and conducts periodic elections to seats on the board.

🔷 The Separation of Ownership and Control

Although giant corporations are owned by many stockholders, only a handful of stockholders own enough shares to be able to influence corporate policy. In a large corporation, control lies in the hands of those able to select the board of directors. Obviously, any individual or group holding more than 50 percent of a corporation's stock has absolute control because the individual or group can select the board of directors. More often than not, however, one can gain control with something less than 50 percent of the stock.

Boards of Directors' Governance Issues

Whether large or small, corporations are owned by their stockholders. Stockholders elect directors to represent them and protect their interests. Directors, in turn, are expected to hire executives to manage the day-to-day operations of the corporation. In recent years, events in the corporate world demonstrated that something was terribly wrong in the way boards of directors were carrying out those responsibilities.

In 2001, the energy giant Enron Corporation declared bankruptcy. In less than a year, the corporation's net worth plummeted from $80 billion to zero. Thousands of employees lost their jobs and their retirement benefits. Millions of stockholders were affected as Enron stock fell from a high of $89 to $1 per share. "Why," many people asked, "hadn't the board of directors done something to prevent the disaster?" Investigations by the U.S. Senate on the causes of Enron's collapse seemed to identify Enron's board of directors as part of the problem leading to the collapse. Among other things, the Senate report concluded that (1) the sources of Enron's problems extended back over a number years, (2) the company's directors knew about many of the problems, and (3) they should have done something about it.

As Enron's story unfolded, many wondered if the boards of directors of other giant corporations were failing their stockholders and, if so, why. Further investigations revealed that:

- In too many instances, the *CEO (chief executive officer)* of a corporation hired the directors. As a result, directors' first loyalty was to the people who hired them rather than the stockholders whom they represented. This seemed to be the case in 2000 when the Enron directors paid their top executives $750 million in compensation, of which $140 million went to the CEO. All that in a year when Enron's total net income was only $975 million.

- Allowing directors to have a financial stake in another firm with which the corporation does business raises conflict-of-interest questions. In one notorious example, 5 out of the 15 board members of one of the nation's largest poultry processors were hired by the company as paid consultants. Meanwhile, 7 others had lucrative contracts to provide the firm with aircraft, office space, and the like. Critics were quick to claim that the first loyalty of those directors could not have been to the stockholders whom they were supposed to represent.

As an outgrowth of the scandals in the corporate boardrooms, specific reforms have been proposed to eliminate the worst of the abuses. Among these are:

- separate the roles of the chairperson (who heads the board of directors) and the CEO (who heads the operations of the company).

- make it easier for stockholders to choose and replace directors.

- ban business deals between directors and the corporation.

- disclose how directors voted on important issues such as executive pay.

Many corporations have voluntarily incorporated these and other similar proposals into their bylaws. Others have not. For that reason, some critics say that it is time for government action on the issue.

How is it possible for an individual holding only a fraction of the total shares to control a corporation? The answer has to do with the use of proxies. A *proxy* is a written authorization by a shareholder giving another person the right to vote one's shares of stock at a shareholders' meeting. Most stockholders are reluctant to become involved in the details of a corporation. They do not know or care to know how the business functions. For this reason, they usually give their proxies to the present management when requested to do so. As long as management can gather enough proxies to control 50 percent of the votes cast, it can remain in power indefinitely.

Some people have criticized the fact that ownership and control in the large corporation are so widely separated. They argue that it is not right that individual stockholders are almost powerless to change the course set by management. Others, while conceding that individual stockholders have little, if any, control over their company, argue that this is as it should be. Modern-day businesses are so complex that only experts can make intelligent decisions pertaining to them. Thus, most people investing in a large corporation willingly turn over control of their investment to management in exchange for the opportunity to share in the profits and growth of the company. Sometimes, however, groups of stockholders get together in an attempt to oust management. While these undertakings are usually very difficult, they have on rare occasions been successful.

═══════ S U M M A R Y ═══════

The U.S. economic system is built on a foundation of some 25 million privately owned businesses. Most of these firms are organized in one of three ways: as sole proprietorships, partnerships, or corporations. The first is a business owned by one person, while a partnership is a business association of two or more owners. A corporation is a business owned by its stockholders. Since it is impractical for stockholders to maintain hands-on control of large corporations, they elect a board of directors to represent them. The board of directors, in turn, hires officers to manage the corporation.

Although corporations have important advantages over unincorporated firms, they are often too costly to organize for most small businesses. In recent years, however, the S-corporation and the limited liability company (LLC) have made it practical for small firms to enjoy many of the advantages of corporations at a more affordable price. Other forms of business organizations are government-owned corporations, cooperatives, and not-for-profit corporations.

Since the 1980s, a number of communities have transferred activities traditionally performed by government to private hands. This process, known as privatization, has resulted in a number of privately operated public schools, prisons, toll roads, utilities, and even fire departments.

REVIEWING THE CHAPTER

BUILDING VOCABULARY

Match each term in Column A with its definition in Column B.

Column A

D **1.** sole proprietorship
I **2.** partnership
G **3.** corporation
F **4.** S-corporation
A **5.** unlimited liability
B **6.** limited liability company
E **7.** dividends
J **8.** shareholder
C **9.** limited life
H **10.** charter

Column B

a. the status of being personally responsible for all the debts of a company
b. unincorporated firm that has many of the advantages of a corporation
c. the trait of a business that it will close upon the death of an owner
d. an unincorporated business owned by one person
e. profits that are distributed by corporations to shareholders
f. a type of business with fewer than 76 stockholders
g. a business chartered under state or federal law and owned by its shareholders
h. a government license to form a business
i. an unincorporated business owned by two or more persons
j. an owner of a corporation

UNDERSTANDING WHAT YOU HAVE READ

1. Which form of business organization is most numerous in the United States? (*a*) sole proprietorships (*b*) partnerships (*c*) corporations (*d*) cooperatives.

2. Which *one* of the following is the most attractive feature of the sole proprietorship? (*a*) the ease with which it can be organized (*b*) its ability to expand across state borders (*c*) the ease with which ownership can be transferred (*d*) its limited liability.

3. Which *one* of the following is a disadvantage of most corporations? (*a*) limited life (*b*) unlimited liability (*c*) limited capital (*d*) double taxation.

4. As a rule, who has voting rights in a corporation? Its (*a*) officers (*b*) stockholders (*c*) board of directors (*d*) employees.

5. Stockholders in a large corporation generally do not (*a*) receive a share of the profits (*b*) elect the board of directors (*c*) manage the everyday affairs of the business (*d*) own the business.

6. Limited liability, unlimited life, and a charter are characteristics of (*a*) sole proprietorships (*b*) partnerships (*c*) all businesses in the United States (*d*) corporations.

7. Which *one* of the following is true of a limited liability corporation (LLC)? A LLC (*a*) is the least expensive kind of business to organize (*b*) is not subject to the corporate income tax (*c*) is the only form of business organization that offers limited liability (*d*) is the only form of business organization that provides unlimited life.

8. "Do[uble tax]...fers to the fact that (*a*) corporations have to pay both state and fed[eral]...part of a corporation's earnings not distributed as dividends is sub[ject]...its taxes (*c*) corporations pay both income taxes and sales taxes (*d*)...ncome taxes on their earnings, and the earnings that they distribute...[s] dividends...[are su]bject to personal income taxes.

9. The [Girl Scouts of A]merica is an example of a (*a*) consumer co-op (*b*) sole proprietorship...corporation (*d*) government-owned corporation.

10. Wh[ich one of the fo]llowing is the best reason for owning a business of one's own? (*a*) I[t is the surest way] to a profitable future. (*b*) Entrepreneurship gives one the ability to ig[nore the competi]tion. (*c*) Most new businesses are financial successes. (*d*) Entrepreneurs are their own boss.

THINKING CRITICALLY

1. You have saved enough money to start a shoe-repair business in your neighborhood. A friend who has business experience suggests that you start your operation as a single proprietorship. Another experienced businessperson tells you to incorporate. Whose advice would you take? Explain your answer.

2. On graduation from electronic repair school, Harriet Zoltan opened a small shop as a sole proprietor. A few years later she was approached by an old friend, Bill Paseo, who offered to put $5,000 into the business in exchange for 50 percent interest. Zoltan agreed, and they formed the partnership of Zoltan and Paseo.

   a. Explain *three* factors that might have led Zoltan to start her business as a sole proprietorship.

   b. Explain *three* reasons why Zoltan might have been willing to take Paseo into the business.

3. Suppose, because of business losses, Zoltan and Paseo decide to call it quits. After selling all the tools, furnishings, and inventory in the shop, they are still $10,000 in debt. Bill Paseo tells Harriet Zoltan that he is broke because every penny he had was invested in the business. Harriet replies that all she has is the $10,000 in the bank— money that she has been saving to buy a new car.

   a. How much, and from whom, will Zoltan and Paseo's *creditors* (the people to whom the $10,000 is owed) receive?

   b. Suppose that instead of organizing as a partnership, Zoltan and Paseo had formed a corporation. How would you then answer question *a*?

   c. If Harriet and Bill had decided to incorporate, do you think that they should have formed an S-corporation? Explain your answer.

4. The stockholders are the owners of a corporation. However, giant corporations with thousands of stockholders have organizational and operational problems quite different from those faced by small, closely held corporations.

   a. What is the role of the board of directors in a large corporation? How are board members elected?

b. What is the function of the officers of a large corporation? How are the officers selected?

c. What is meant by separation of ownership and control in large corporations?

5. In a recent election for the board of directors of a large corporation, the efforts of a group to unseat the existing board failed. The reelected board stated that the election represented "corporate democracy in action." The losers said that the election simply demonstrated how difficult it is to defeat the "insiders." Explain both points of view.

SKILLS: Completing and Analyzing a Table

► TABLE 4.3   BUSINESS ORGANIZATIONS AND THEIR RECEIPTS

Number (thousands)	Percent of Total	Business Organizations	Receipts (billions)	Percent of Total
17,409		Sole Proprietorships	$ 918	
1,855		Partnerships	1,534	
4,849		Corporations	16,543	

1. Complete the table by calculating and filling in the percentages of total number and total receipts for each type of business organization. Use the information contained in the completed table and in the text to answer the following questions.

2. According to the table, how many sole proprietorships are there? Partnerships? Corporations?

3. Compare the earnings of those three types of business organizations. Which has the greatest earnings? The smallest?

4. How would you explain the fact that with such a small percentage of the total number of business firms, corporations account for such a large percentage of business earnings?

USING THE INTERNET

If you are thinking of someday starting a business of your own, a visit to the U.S. Small Business Administration's Web site is a good place to begin. There you can learn about what it takes to be an entrepreneur, how one might begin to organize a small business, and sources of financing available to small business owners. Interested? Like to know more? Great!

- Go to the SBA Web site at <<www.sba.gov/starting—business/startup/guide.html>>.

- Click on the first hyperlink: ASK YOURSELF, and bring up page 1. Try to answer the questions. If you can—well, who knows? One day you might really own a business of your own. Based on what you have read, explain why you think that entrepreneurship may or may not be for you.

- Now click on *Starting a Business* and, after reading through the suggestions contained in *Startup Topics,* see if you can describe a business that you might want to start up one day.

CHAPTER 5
Business Finance

OVERVIEW

Louise and Bob White formed Quail Hill Window Cleaning Service about a year ago. Working together, they washed windows of downtown stores, as well as of a number of private homes and apartments. Last weekend, Louise and Bob gathered their financial records together. They looked to see if the year's efforts had been worthwhile.

"So, what do you think?" Bob asked after all the results had been tallied.

"Darn good, I'd say. We've paid for our supplies and cleaning equipment, and never missed a payment on our truck loan."

"See, I told you the truck would be a good idea," Bob continued. "Now, if we could just afford to hire one or two helpers, we could take on more jobs and make more money."

"That's true, but what would happen if we hired a couple of people and business fell off?" Louise asked. "You miss a couple of payments on the truck loan, and it's bye-bye truck."

"You know what it boils down to, Louise? Money! If the cash keeps flowing, we'll be able to hire more workers and have more time for ourselves."

"And if it doesn't," Louise interjected, "Quail Hill will become a dead duck."

WHY DO BUSINESS FIRMS NEED MONEY?

We sometimes call money the "lifeblood of business." Like its red equivalent, the flow of funds enables business firms to meet their day-to-day obligations and to grow. If something were to interrupt the flow of money, the firm would wither and eventually die.

Businesses need money to:

- meet their everyday expenses, such as payroll, rent, and utilities
- replace and expand their *inventory* (the quantity of finished goods on hand and the materials used in their manufacture)
- expand and grow through the purchase of additional plant and equipment
- meet the interest payments on their debts.

Normally, funds needed to meet a firm's daily expenses come out of its *revenues* (that is, income from the goods or services that the firm sells). When revenues are not sufficient to meet a firm's needs, it resorts to one or more of the following:

- dips into its savings
- borrows money
- sells some more of its stock.

 # SHORT- VS. LONG-TERM FINANCING

When businesses run short of cash and need to finance operations, they may choose to use short-term financing to make up the difference. *Short-term financing* applies to loans that need to be repaid in less than a year. *Long-term financing* applies to loans and other financial strategies that are made for periods of a year or more. In most instances, businesses use long-term financing to pay for things like major renovations, new buildings, and expensive equipment.

Short-Term Sources of Funds

The most common forms of short-term financing are *trade credit* and *bank loans*.

TRADE CREDIT.   Business suppliers frequently give their customers 30 to 60 days to pay for their orders. This kind of payment delay, known as trade credit, is the most common type of short-term financing.

BANK LOANS.   Banks generally extend credit as a promissory note or a line of credit. A *promissory note* is a written promise to repay a loan, plus interest, at a specified date. A *line of credit* is a loan arrangement in which a bank allows a business to borrow any sum, up to a specified limit, whenever it needs the money. Terms of repayment are part of this arrangement.

Figure 5.1 **The Flow of Company Funds**

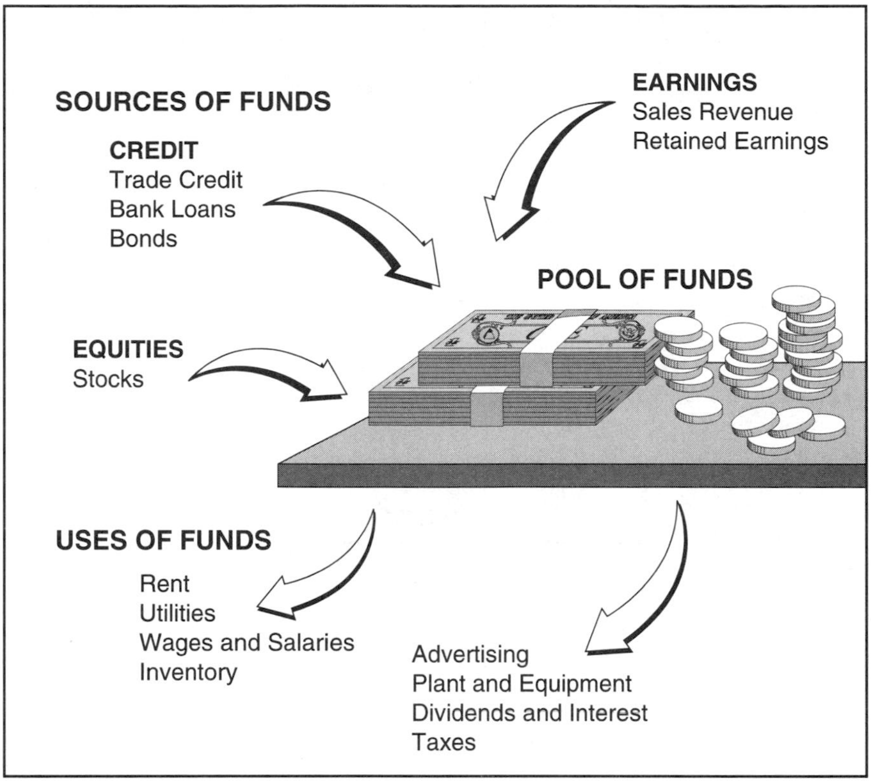

SOURCES OF FUNDS

CREDIT
Trade Credit
Bank Loans
Bonds

EARNINGS
Sales Revenue
Retained Earnings

POOL OF FUNDS

EQUITIES
Stocks

USES OF FUNDS
Rent
Utilities
Wages and Salaries
Inventory

Advertising
Plant and Equipment
Dividends and Interest
Taxes

RETAINED EARNINGS.   Profits that are not distributed to the owners of a business are called *retained earnings* or *undistributed profits.* Corporations rely on retained earnings as the major source for their new funds. A major advantage of retained earnings, compared to borrowing, is that they are interest free. Indeed, it is even possible for the firm to earn interest on those balances.

LONG-TERM SOURCES OF FUNDS

Corporations have *three* long-term financing sources available to them: long-term loans, bonds, and equity financing.

 Long-Term Loans

Long-term loans are most often used by business firms to purchase machinery and equipment. Long-term borrowers are usually expected to make periodic

CASE STUDY

Leverage in Action

Using borrowed funds to finance business operations is called *leverage.* Leverage can increase the rate of return earned on an investment. The following example illustrates this concept.

Last year, Frankie and Ernie each opened a newspaper stand at the local airline terminal. The two businesses, which competed with each other, were virtually identical. Both Frankie and Ernie (1) sold newspapers and magazines to airline passengers and (2) had invested $50,000 to start their business. There was a major difference between the two, however. Ernie paid cash to open his business, while Frankie put up only $5,000 of her own funds. Instead, she borrowed the difference at 15 percent interest. At the end of their first year, Frankie and Ernie reported their financial results as follows:

TABLE 5.1

Frankie's Investment		Ernie's Investment	
Cash	$ 5,000	Cash	$50,000
Loan (at 15%)	45,000	Loan	0
	$50,000		$50,000
First-Year Earnings			
Earnings	$15,000	Earnings	$15,000
Less interest payments	6,750	Less interest payments	0
Profit	$ 8,250	Profit	$15,000
Return on investment	$\dfrac{\$\ 8{,}250}{\$\ 5{,}000} = 165\%$	Return on investment	$\dfrac{\$15{,}000}{\$50{,}000} = 30\%$

By year's end, both Frankie and Ernie had earned $15,000. Since Ernie had no interest to pay, he kept his entire $15,000. This represented a return of 30 percent on his initial investment.

After paying the interest on her loan, Frankie was left with a profit of $8,250. In this case, however, the return was 165 percent on her investment!

As long as earnings exceed the cost of borrowing, leveraging increases the return on an investment. When they fall below that point, they magnify the loss.

Alas, second year earnings for both Frankie and Ernie fell to $5,000. Note how this affected the return on their investments.

TABLE 5.2

Frankie's Investment		Ernie's Investment	
Cash	$ 5,000	Cash	$50,000
Loan (at 15%)	45,000	Loan	0
	$50,000		$50,000

Second-Year Earnings			
Earnings	$ 5,000	Earnings	$ 5,000
Less interest payments	6,750	Less interest payments	0
Profit (loss)	($ 1,750)	Profit	$ 5,000
Return on investment	$(-)\dfrac{\$\,1,750}{\$\,5,000} = (-35\%)$	Return on investment	$\dfrac{\$\,5,000}{\$50,000} = 10\%$

By the end of the second year, both had earned $5,000. Since Ernie had no interest to pay, he kept the entire $5,000. This figure represented a return of 10 percent on his initial investment.

After paying the interest on her loan, Frankie was left with a loss of $1,750, or 35 percent of her investment.

payments over the life of the loan and pledge some form of collateral. *Collateral* is any item of value that the lender may seize should the borrower fail to make loan payments as promised. If, for example, the Alpha Shipping Company borrowed money to purchase a new truck, the truck could serve as collateral for the loan. If at a later date, Alpha failed to make its periodic payment on that loan, the lender could seize the truck.

One thing that sets a corporation apart from an unincorporated business is its ability to sell stocks and bonds. Unlike stocks (which represent ownership in a corporation), *bonds* are certificates issued in exchange for a loan. Thus, stockholders are part owners of a business, whereas bondholders are among its creditors.

Bonds

A bond is a kind of long-term IOU. It is a promise by a corporation or government to repay a specified sum (the *face value* of the loan, or *principal*) at the end of a specific number of years, along with annual interest.

CORPORATE BONDS. Since bonds represent a debt of a corporation, bondholders are among its creditors. If a company declares itself to be *bankrupt* (unable to pay its debts), it will pay off its bondholders and other creditors first. Then, if there is any money left, it may pay its stockholders.

Many investors assume that bonds are always safer investments than stocks. This is not always true. The safety of any security depends on the company that issues it. The common stock of a well-established, profitable corporation is likely to be safer than the bonds of a newly organized gold-mining enterprise that has yet to find any gold.

GOVERNMENT BONDS.   You may be familiar with the Series EE savings bonds issued by the U.S. government. The most popular of these bonds sells for $25. It pays $50 after being held for a number of years. Like corporate bonds, government bonds are evidences of debt. When we purchase a savings bond, we are lending money to the federal government. In exchange for the loan, the government promises to return our principal plus interest on a specified date. (We discuss bonds again beginning on page 105.)

All levels of government—federal, state, and local—sell bonds from time to time. Depending on the type of bond, methods of payment, interest rates, and denominations differ. All bonds are issued in exchange for a loan and thus represent a promise to repay the loan with interest.

⚡ Equity Financing

Equity financing refers to the sale by a corporation of shares of its stock as a means of raising capital. In terms of the total amount of money raised by corporations, equity financing is the least important source. In a recent year, for example, the sale of stock accounted for only 4 percent of the funds raised by corporations. To those corporations that rely on the sale of stock to finance their operations, however, equity financing is extremely important. It is important also to the millions of people who, for reasons described below, are buying or selling shares of stock.

You may have heard of *stock exchanges,* or stock markets, as they are also known. These are places where shares in the nation's major corporations are bought and sold. Daily newspapers, the Internet, and radio and television programs carry reports on the doings of the stock exchanges. The ups and downs of the stock market often mirror how investors, both at home and abroad, view economic conditions. For that reason, economists and others monitor stock market trends to help them assess the nation's mood. When the public is feeling good about the future, stock purchases increase and stock prices rise. When the public is feeling pessimistic, stock sales fall, along with stock prices.

STOCKS: COMMON AND PREFERRED.   Most stocks are *common stocks.* They entitle their owners to a voice in the selection of the board of directors. Holders of common stock may also share in the profits of the company whenever the corporation's board of directors decides to pay dividends.

Suppose that a corporation's directors set aside $3 million of profits for distribution to shareholders. If the corporation had sold 1 million shares of stock,

Common Stock Certificate. Why would someone want to own one of these certificates?

stockholders would receive $3 for every share they own. If the business were dissolved, holders of common stock would receive their share of whatever remained, if anything, after all debts had been paid.

While all corporations issue common stock, some also distribute *preferred stock*. Holders of preferred stock usually have no voting rights. They are, however, entitled to a fixed dividend whenever the board of directors votes to pay it. Holders of common stock cannot receive dividends until the holders of preferred stock have received theirs. In a similar situation, if the business fails, the holders of preferred stock are in line to share in its assets ahead of the holders of common stock. Some companies have stock that is "cumulative preferred." This term means that if a corporation fails to pay dividends during one year, it must make up the missed payments in the following years to owners of cumulative-preferred stock before common stockholders can receive any dividends.

The Miracle Lantern Company's motto, "If it works, it's a Miracle!" made the company a household name. The company has issued 100,000 shares of cumulative-preferred stock that pays annual dividends of $1 per share. In addition, it has issued 1 million shares of common stock. Two years ago, the company paid no dividends. The following year, the board of directors set aside $700,000 in profits for payment to stockholders. The company paid dividends to the cumulative-preferred stockholders of $2 per share: $1 for the current year and $1 for the previous year (when no dividends had been paid). That left $500,000, or 50 cents a share, available for distribution to the holders of common stock.

HOW CORPORATE STOCKS AND BONDS ARE SOLD TO THE PUBLIC

When a corporation needs to sell its stocks or bonds to the public, it usually goes to an *investment bank,* a bank that specializes in this kind of activity. The investment bank *underwrites* the issue: It buys the entire issue of some corporation's stocks or bonds and then sells the securities to the public at a price that will yield a profit. The corporation can use the funds it receives from the bank without any further concern over whether all the stocks or bonds are sold.

State and local governments also use investment banks to market their bonds. In contrast, the federal government sells its bonds through the Federal Reserve System, which is discussed in Chapter 17.

People who buy stocks and bonds from investment banks are free to sell them any time they choose. But neither the issuing corporation nor the initial *underwriter* (the investment bank involved) is likely to buy them back. Hence, there is a need for organized markets in which stocks and bonds may be sold. *Securities markets* fill much of that need. They provide a place where buyers and sellers can come together and instantly trade their stocks and bonds.

Securities Markets

The securities of the nation's largest corporations are generally traded in one of the stock exchanges. The largest of these are the **New York Stock Exchange,** the **American Stock Exchange,** and **NASDAQ.** All are headquartered in New York City. There are other exchanges in major cities around the country, but these are far the most important. Figure 5.2 on page 108 illustrates how exchange transactions are reported in a daily newspaper.

The New York Stock Exchange (NYSE) and the American Stock Exchange (AMEX) are the oldest of the three. The NYSE was created in 1792 in response to the U.S. government's need to repay its Revolutionary War debt. Meeting in a building on Wall Street in New York City, 24 brokers and other prominent business leaders agreed to trade securities on a common commission basis. At that time, only five companies offered securities for trade (three were government bonds, and two were bank stocks). Today, some 2,800 companies have their shares traded on the New York Stock Exchange.

Shortly thereafter, brokers meeting on the streets of New York began trading government and private securities on behalf of their clients. Because of those origins, the market was known as the "Curb Exchange"—a name that stayed with it even after it moved into its own 14-story building. In 1953, the Curb Exchange took the name of the American Stock Exchange. NYSE and

The New York Stock Exchange. How do sellers and buyers of stock find each other?

AMEX operate trading floors on which stocks and bonds are bought and sold through an auction system. Brokers, representing the buyers and sellers, call out their bids in an attempt to acquire or sell securities for their clients at favorable prices.

Established in 1971, NASDAQ (the National Association of Securities Dealers Automated Quotation system) is the newest of the three exchanges and the second most active. The shares of most companies not listed on the NYSE or AMEX are traded through NASDAQ. Unlike NYSE and AMEX, where trades take place on the floor of the exchanges, NASDAQ representatives exchange buy and sell orders through their own computer network.

Why do securities markets exist? One reason is that investors would not be willing to buy stocks or bonds if there were no easy way to sell them at a later date. Corporations would then find it extremely costly to find investors interested in buying their securities.

Another reason stock markets are needed is that they enable us to know the value of stocks. This knowledge is indispensable to investors who own or are thinking of buying stocks. Stock markets are also important to the economy as a whole. They serve to withdraw funds from areas where money is no longer needed and transfer these funds to areas where money is needed. Suppose for example, that the outlook for new car sales is poor at a time when there is an increasing demand for personal computers. During this time, the value of automobile industry stocks will probably decrease, while the value of computer industry stocks will increase. Firms in the computer industry will then have an easier time than auto firms raising new money through the sale of stocks.

NASDAQ is headquartered in this building in Times Square, New York City. Up-to-the-minute stock quotes flash across the front of the building.

💢 Brokerage Firms

People who want to buy or sell stocks or bonds usually must use the services of a *brokerage firm*. Brokers buy and sell *securities* (stocks and bonds) on behalf of their clients and receive a commission, or fee, for their work. When a customer places an order for a stock listed on an exchange, the broker relays the order to the brokerage firm's representative at the appropriate exchange. There the broker's representative meets with others who are trading the same security (or, if it is a NASDAQ listing, sends the order out through their wires) and buys according to the customer's instructions.

The price at which a security is bought and sold depends on the supply of and the demand for that security. If the demand for the security rises, its price will be pushed up. If the demand for the security falls, so too will its price. Similarly, if few people want to sell a security, the short supply will push prices up. If many want to sell, the oversupply will push prices down. Whatever the price, none of the money that changes hands after the first sale goes to the corporation that issued the security.

⚡ Why People Buy Stocks

Stock ownership in the United States is not confined to the wealthy. Data released by the Federal Reserve shows that members of nearly half of all U.S. households own stock. In addition, millions of Americans who have insurance policies or are participants in pension funds own stocks indirectly. The insurance companies and pension funds invest in stocks and bonds to build up their reserves of money. Why do so many people and institutions invest in the stock market? Most do so for one or more of the following reasons:

DIVIDENDS.   Each year, a corporation may distribute to its shareholders dividends, a part of the company's profits. Many individuals and institutions invest in stocks in order to receive these dividends, although the issuing of dividends is not as common as it once was.

CAPITAL GROWTH.   The value of a stock is not fixed. Instead it fluctuates with changes in supply and demand. Many people invest in stocks because they expect that in time these stocks will be worth more than what they paid for them. Such an increase in value is called *capital growth*.

This stockbroker uses the phone, written reports, and the Internet to do her work. What is the function of stockbrokers?

Why, you might ask, do stock prices go up and down? Stocks increase in value for a number of reasons. One reason is business performance. If a corporation's sales and profits increase, its value and the value of its stock will rise. The value of a stock also increases because of public expectations. If investors expect a corporation to do well, the demand for its shares will increase and so will the value of those shares.

Still another reason why individual stocks increase in value has to do with the value of stocks in general. At times when the stock-buying public is feeling optimistic about the economy, the prices of securities tend to rise. When they are feeling pessimistic about the economy, stock prices tend to fall.

SPECULATORS.   People who buy and sell stocks for the reasons listed above (for dividends and capital growth) are called *investors.* Another category of buyers and sellers of stocks are known as *speculators.* Unlike investors (who hope to share in a company's profits and growth over the long term), speculators hope to turn a quick profit.

Because the prices of stocks fluctuate from day to day, speculators can profit if they can correctly predict the price movements. Depending on whether they predict a rise or fall in prices, speculators will either "buy long" or "sell short."

BUYING LONG.   Speculators who believe that the price of a given stock will rise are called *bulls.* For that reason, a general rise in stock prices is known as a *bull market.* Bulls hope to profit from their expectation by *buying long*—that is, by buying the stock now and selling it later at a higher price. If the price of the security falls, however, bullish investors will lose money when they sell. Thus, when Enron—one of the nation's largest corporations—went bankrupt in 2001, many stockholders lost most or all of their investment.

> Clara Ferdinand is bullish on Xerxes, a computer software company whose stock is currently selling at a price of 24.5. (Stock prices are quoted in dollars and decimal percentages of a dollar.) Ferdinand bought 200 shares of Xerxes for $4,900 (200 × $24.50 = $4,900). Three months later, Xerxes shares had risen to 30.25, and Ferdinand sold. This left her with a profit of $5.75 per share, or $1,150 (less brokerage fees and taxes). Of course, if instead of increasing, the price of Xerxes stock had fallen, Clara Ferdinand would have lost money.

SELLING SHORT.   Speculators who anticipate that the price of a stock will soon fall are called *bears.* In order to profit on their prediction, bears sell the stock "short." That is, they sell a stock *that they do not own* by borrowing it from their broker. Then, when the price of the security falls as predicted, bears instruct their brokers to buy back the security at the lower price, and they pocket the difference.

> Frank Jones feels that the stock of Maypak Corporation is overvalued and that its price will soon fall. Jones does not happen to own any Maypak stock. Since he

expects its price to fall, it would not be profitable for him to buy the stock. So instead of actually buying Maypak stock, Jones borrows the stock from his broker.

Jones orders his broker to sell 100 shares of Maypak short at the current market price of 50.25. (Remember, he does not own any Maypak stock.) Jones's broker lends the stock to Jones, sells it for him, and credits Jones's account for $5,025. A week or so later, Jones's prediction proves correct. The price of Maypak falls to 43. Jones then orders his broker to settle his Maypak account. The broker withdraws $4,300 from Jones's account and uses the money to buy 100 Maypak shares (the number of shares that was "lent" to Jones) at the new, lower price of 43. Jones returns the 100 shares to his broker. This leaves Jones with a gross profit of $725. From this sum, the broker deducts brokerage fees, taxes, and a rental fee for the borrowed stock.

Of course, it is also possible to lose money in this kind of transaction. Indeed, in a short sale there is no limit to the amounts speculators can lose if they are wrong, because there is no limit to the prices to which their stocks could climb. For example, if the price of Maypak stock in the previous example had climbed to 80, Jones would have had to pay $8,000 for 100 shares for which he received only $5,025—a loss of $2,975.

THE ROLE OF THE BROKER.   Brokers act as intermediaries between bulls and bears and earn fees and/or commissions from each transaction. For every bull who is buying, there must be a bear who is selling.

MARGIN.   People may purchase stocks partly on credit, an action called *buying on margin.* In the past, though, too many people invested with stock bought on credit, and the stock market crashed. To prevent future crashes, the Federal Reserve Board sets the *margin* (percentage that a buyer has to put up in cash). Since 1934, the margin has fluctuated between 40 and 100 percent.

BUYING AND SELLING BONDS.   Like stocks, corporate bonds are usually bought and sold through brokers. As with stocks, the price is determined by how much buyers are willing to pay and how little sellers are willing to accept. Figure 5.3 on page 109 illustrates how bond market transactions are reported in a daily newspaper.

The price of a bond is influenced chiefly by two factors: its safety and its rate of return (interest). If the public has any doubts about the ability of the issuer of the bond to pay either the principal or the interest, the bond's price tends to fall. The price also tends to fall if the rate of interest of the bond is less than the rate of interest prevailing in the economy. For example, in order to sell a $1,000 bond that paid 4 percent interest at a time when the prevailing rate on other bonds was 8 percent, one would expect the price to be considerably less than $1,000.

Similarly, the interest paid on newly issued bonds reflects both how safe the investment is and current interest rates. The interest paid on bonds issued by a local electric power company (a safe investment) is likely to be less than that paid by a newly organized oil-drilling corporation (a risky investment, because the corporation's income depends on its ability to find oil).

PERSONAL ECONOMICS

Investing in Corporate Bonds

Like stocks, corporate bonds may be purchased or sold through brokers in securities markets like the New York Stock Exchange. The price at which bonds are traded depends primarily upon *risk* and prevailing interest rates.

Risk

Corporations that sell bonds as a means of raising capital promise to repay their face value at *maturity* (date at which a security is due to be redeemed), along with periodic interest payments until that date. Will the company issuing a bond be able to make its interest payments and repay the principal when due? The certainty with which these questions can be answered about a corporate bond affects the price at which a bond can be sold prior to its maturity. Other things being equal, the greater the risk, the lower the value of a bond. Because they are thought to be safer, bonds issued by well-known, financially stable corporations can usually be sold at higher prices than ones issued by lesser-known or unstable firms.

In assessing the relative safety of a corporate bond, it is also important to know if it is part of a secured or unsecured issue. *Secured bonds* (sometimes known as *mortgage bonds*) are backed by specific property that passes to the bondholder if the issuer cannot live up to its obligations. *Unsecured bonds* (sometimes known as *debenture bonds*) are backed by the good name of the corporation issuing them.

Bonds are analyzed and classified by bond-rating services according to how likely the issuers of the bonds are to repay the principal at maturity. **Standard & Poor's Corporation** and **Moody's Investors Service** are the best known of these services. Ratings at Baa (under Moody's) or BBB (under Standard & Poor's) and above are considered *investment grade.* Bonds below investment grade are sometimes called junk bonds. (See Table 5.3.)

In the 1980s, junk bonds were quite popular. People seeking to take over corporations offered these bonds as a way of obtaining the necessary capital. Investors were attracted to the high rates of interest that junk bonds were offering and were willing to take the risks involved in these securities. Today, some investment advisers still recommend the purchase of junk bonds to improve the performance of certain individuals' portfolios. In the financial section of newspapers, you can see these risky bonds advertised as "high-yield bond funds."

Interest Rates

Bond values vary inversely with the rise and fall of *interest rates.* The rate of interest is the cost of credit and is usually expressed as a percentage of face value that is payable annually. When interest rates rise, bond prices fall, when interest rates fall, bond prices rise. For example, a 5 percent bond with a face-value of $1,000 will pay $50 in annual interest. Suppose however, that interest rates were to increase to a point where bonds generally paid 7 percent in interest. In that event, the price of bonds paying $50 would have to be reduced to a point that would give buyers a 7 percent return on their investment.

A quick way to calculate how much a bond would sell for at various interest rates is to divide the dollar amount paid in interest by the selected rate. For example in order to earn 7 percent a bond that paid $50 in interest would have to sell for $714.29 (*because 50/.07 = $714.29*). At 4 percent, a similar bond paying $50 in interest would sell for $1,250 (*because 50/.04 = $1,250*).

TABLE 5.3   BOND RATINGS

Rating	Moody's	Standard & Poor's
Highest Quality	Aaa	AA
High Quality	Aa	AA
Upper Medium Grade	A	A
Medium Grade	Baa	BBB
Predominantly Speculative	Ba	BB
Speculative, Low Grade	B	B
Poor to Default	Caa	CCC
Highest Speculation	Ca	CC
Lowest Quality, No Interest	C	C

Since the 1980s, corporations raised huge sums through the sale of what came to be known as *junk bonds*. These are highly risky investments that offer extremely high rates of interest. Junk bonds are issued by companies with heavy debt or other financial problems. Their higher yields are necessary to compensate investors for accepting the risk that the company issuing the bond might not be able to repay its debts.

 Specialized Markets

Similar to securities exchanges, markets also exist for selling and buying commodities such as wheat, barley, rye, coffee, tin, and silver. If you examine the financial pages of your local newspaper, you will probably see these specialized markets listed. Because trading in these markets requires far more specialized knowledge than trading in the securities of large corporations, the specialized markets are not as popular with the public.

 SECURITIES AND EXCHANGE COMMISSION

The **Securities and Exchange Commission (SEC)** was created by an act of Congress in 1934. Its purpose is to protect the public against deception or fraud in the selling of securities.

 Caveat Emptor

The SEC does not say what it thinks of a specific investment, nor does it make recommendations as to the merit of one company's securities as opposed to another. Rather, it does what it can to protect the public by applying the principle of *caveat emptor*—"let the buyer beware." Caveat emptor suggests that,

How to Read Financial Tables

Figure 5.2 **How to Read a NYSE Table**

52-Week High	52-Week Low	Stock	Div	Yld %	P/E	Sales 100s	High	Low	Last	Chg
18.54	5.55	Avnet	...	...	dd	9900	18.48	17.68	18.41	+0.61
67.25	45.22	Avon	.84	1.3	28	24064	67.00	65.31	65.44	−1.30
27.75	23.00	AXIS Cap n	...	...	...	3342	24.00	23.25	23.42	−0.58
19.90	11.00	Aztar	...	...	11	2005	17.35	17.00	17.32	+0.29

B

52-Week High	52-Week Low	Stock	Div	Yld %	P/E	Sales 100s	High	Low	Last	Chg
47.90	31.22	BASF	1.54 e	3.3	...	711	46.94	46.56	46.65	+0.04
38.80	30.66	BB&T Cp	1.28	3.4	14	15270	37.60	36.96	37.46	+0.34
19.90	10.79	BBVABHIF	.75 e	4.1	...	3	18.11	18.01	18.11	+0.20
7.35	1.56	BBVABFrn	...	...	...	795	5.48	5.35	5.42	+0.23
23.84	15.17	BCE gs	1.20	...	...	2125	22.19	21.92	21.98	+0.02
24.10	18.25	BG Grp	.38 e	1.7	...	165	22.00	21.45	21.86	+0.15
14.60	9.37	BHP BillLt	.29 e	2.0	...	8667	14.60	14.25	14.42	+0.02
13.54	10.21	▲BHPBil plc	...	...	...	13	13.70	13.51	13.56	+0.14
25.00	13.02	BISYS	...	...	21	4414	19.25	18.97	19.10	−0.06
42.40	23.00	BJ Svc	...	...	37	23566	37.33	36.26	37.06	+0.06
24.50	9.20	BJs Whls	...	...	15	10483	22.32	21.78	22.12	+0.12
23.45	15.36	BKF Cap	...	...	dd	324	22.20	21.86	22.00	−0.01
20.80	10.85	BMC Sft	...	...	cc	25329	16.00	15.51	15.94	−0.19
29.75	21.84	BOC ADS	1.33 e	4.7	...	134	28.75	28.42	28.42	+0.24
45.40	34.67	BP PLC	1.67 e	4.0	16	29078	43.24	42.96	43.00	+0.12

Columns 1 and 2 list the highest and lowest prices at which the stock traded during the past 365 days (but not including yesterday). Prices are quoted in dollars and cents per share (note that .30 equals 30 cents). During the year, Avon Corporation ranged in price from $45.22 to $67.25 per share. The name of the company issuing the stock (Column 3) is followed by the annual dividend (Column 4), here $.84 per share. (Listings are of common stock unless the letters pf—meaning preferred—follow the stock's name.) Yield (Column 5) is the percentage return in the form of dividends due to an investor who purchased the stock at the day's closing price. Thus, $.84 (the annual per share dividend) is 1.3 percent of $65.44 (the closing price of one share of stock). Column 6, price-earnings ratio, is the number of times by which the company's latest 12-month earnings per share must be multiplied to obtain the stock's current selling price. (The PE ratio is 28.) In Column 7, the number of shares sold during the reported trading day is listed in hundreds (in this case, 24064 equals 2,406,400 shares). Columns 8–10 (High, Low, and Last) refer to the trading price range during the day. In this case, the high was $67.00 per share, the low was $65.31, and the closing price was $65.44. Change (Column 11) is the difference between this day's closing price and the previous day's closing price. Here the closing price of $65.44 was $1.30 less than the closing price on the previous day.

given the facts, individual investors should be allowed to judge for themselves whether the stocks or bonds of a given corporation are a good investment. For that reason, the SEC requires that publicly owned corporations publish certain financial information about their operations. Failure to do so, or making false or misleading statements, is punishable by fine, imprisonment, or both. It is then up to individual investors to evaluate the facts and decide for themselves if they

Figure 5.3 **How to Read a Bond Market Table**

Company	Cur. Yld	Vol	Price	Chg
CoeurDA 7$1/4$05	cv	1	101	+ $1/4$
CSFB 6$1/8$11	5.9	60	104	− $1/2$
CrwnCk 7$3/8$26	9.5	5	78	+15$5/8$
DR Hrtn 8s09	7.5	30	107	...
DelcoR 8$5/8$07	8.9	113	97$1/2$	− $1/4$
DevonE 4.9s08	cv	90	102$1/4$	+ $5/8$
DukeEn 6$7/8$23	6.9	20	100$1/2$	− $1/8$
DukeEn 7s33	6.9	10	101	...
FstData 2s08	cv	11	107$1/4$	+2
GBCB 8$3/8$07	8.3	18	100$1/2$	−1
GMA 6$5/8$05	6.3	40	105$1/2$	− $1/4$
GMA 6$1/8$08	6.0	17	102$1/2$	+ $1/4$
GMA dc6s11	6.1	25	97$1/2$	− $1/2$
GMA zr12	...	31	510$1/8$	−1$7/8$
GMA zr15	...	28	420	+2$1/2$
GoldmS 7$1/2$05	7.0	62	107$5/8$	...
Honywll zr07	...	30	86	...
Honywll zr09	...	45	74$3/4$	+ $1/4$
IBM 5$3/8$09	5.1	40	105$3/8$	+ $1/8$
IBM 6$1/2$28	6.3	5	103	+ $5/8$
JCP 6$3/4$25	6.9	25	98	−1
KCS En 8$7/8$06	9.1	148	97$1/4$	...
Lilly 8$3/8$06	7.2	33	115$7/8$	−1$1/2$

In Column 1, the name of the firm issuing the bonds (J.C. Penney Company) is listed in abbreviated form (JCP), followed by the bonds' rate of interest (6¾) and the year in which they mature (25, which stands for 2025). These bonds pay 6.75 percent of their $1,000 face value, or $67.50, in interest yearly. When they mature (come due) in the year 2025, the bonds will be worth $1,000 each (their face value) to their holders. Column 2 lists the current yield (Cur. Yld.), the rate of return on investment based on the purchase price. Newspaper quotations use the closing (or last) price in calculating the current yield. Since the closing price was $980.00 (from Price, in Column 4, explained below) and the bonds paid $67.50 in interest, the yield was 6.9 percent. Column 3 (Vol.) tells the number of units worth $1,000 in face value that changed hands. In this instance, 25 J.C. Penney bonds worth a total of $25,000 in face value (25 × $1,000) were sold. Closing bond prices are found by multiplying the published figures in Column 4 by $10. Thus, the closing price was $980 (98 × $10). Net change (Chg in Column 5) is the difference between the previous day's closing price and the closing price on the day reported. Here the closing price of 98 (or $980) was less than the closing price of 99 on the previous day.

want to invest in a company. If, for example, an oil company whose wells were dry informed the public of these facts, then those who lost money by investing in the firm would have no one to blame but themselves.

The SEC has also established guidelines to prevent individuals or groups from profiting from certain practices. For example, "insider trading," in which individuals with information about a company buy or sell its securities before the news is out, is against the law. Recently, the CEO of a major pharmaceutical company learned that the government had denied the company a license to sell a new drug. Knowing that when the public learned of the government's action the company's stock price would fall, the CEO sold his securities and advised friends and relatives to do the same. His actions resulted in his indictment for criminal violation of SEC rules and other federal laws.

FINANCIAL STATEMENTS: REQUIRED READING FOR INVESTORS

We have said that the sale of stocks and bonds of stocks can greatly affect both investors and the economy in general. For that reason, corporations are required by law to make certain financial information available to the general public. Investors can find this information in the corporation's prospectus and/or annual report. A *prospectus* describes the operations of a company that is issuing new securities. An *annual report* (which comes out once a year) provides financial information about a company whose securities are traded on an exchange.

The most important financial statements found in these documents are the balance sheet and the income statement.

BALANCE SHEET. Think of a balance sheet as a kind of snapshot of a firm's finances. We say "snapshot" because it presents a picture of a business at a particular point in time. Balance sheets summarize information concerning a firm's *assets, liabilities,* and *net worth.* Let us take a closer look at these accounts.

Assets. These are anything owned by a business that have a money value. Cash on hand or in the bank, plant and equipment, merchandise, and furniture and fixtures are all included in the assets section of a balance sheet.

Liabilities. These are the debts or other financial obligations of a company. The liabilities section of a balance sheet includes items such as unpaid bills and salaries, borrowed money, and mortgages on the building or equipment.

Net Worth. The difference between what a firm owns and what it owes is its *net worth,* or *owner's equity.* The concept may be stated as

$$\text{Assets} - \text{Liabilities} = \text{Net Worth}$$

For convenience, accountants *transpose* (transfer) liabilities from one side of the equal sign to the other when drawing up the balance sheet, in the following manner:

$$\text{Assets} = \text{Liabilities} + \text{Net Worth}$$

Table 5.4 illustrates a typical balance sheet.

INCOME STATEMENT. If we think of a balance sheet as a snapshot of the financial condition of a business, then the income statement is like a motion picture. This is because an *income statement* (also known as a *profit-and-loss statement*) summarizes financial activities of a firm over a period of time.

The principal purpose of an income statement (as in Table 5.5) is to show profitability. It does this by summarizing the items of (1) *income* and (2) *expense,* and by subtracting expenses from income to determine (3) *profit* or *loss.*

> **TABLE 5.4   SUNSHINE LAUNDERETTE BALANCE SHEET DECEMBER 31, 200–**

Assets		Liabilities and Net Worth	
Cash	$ 7,000.00	Accounts payable	$ 1,480.00
Machinery	12,200.00	Unpaid taxes	1,000.00
Supplies	350.00	Total liabilities	2,480.00
Truck	2,400.00	Owner's equity	19,470.00
Total Assets	$21,950.00	Total Liabilities + Net Worth	$21,950.00

> **TABLE 5.5   PRECISE STATIONERY COMPANY INCOME STATEMENT FOR THE YEAR ENDING DECEMBER 31, 200–**

Sales	$141,000.00	
Cost of goods sold	(–)84,500.00	
Gross profit on sales	$ 56,500.00	
Other income	750.00	
Gross income		$57,250.00
Operating expenses	$ 35,930.00	
Other expenses	240.00	
Gross expenses		$36,170.00
Net income		$21,080.00

Limitations of Financial Statements

Financial statements are useful, but they have certain limitations. Some of the more important limitations are

- Financial statements are a record of past events, not a forecast of the future. Past success does not guarantee a successful future.
- Financial statements may not reflect the changing value of money that results from inflation or deflation.
- Some of the data in the statement may be based on opinion, not on fact. For example, some firms assign a dollar value to their name on the theory that a good reputation often attracts customers. If that is the case, the company would be worth more than the total value of its assets. How much more shows up as "goodwill" in the asset section of the balance sheet. Whether goodwill is overstated, understated, or belongs there at all affects the accuracy of the balance sheet. The figure for "total assets" is supposed to give

some idea of what a firm would be worth if it were forced to *liquidate* (sell off its assets and go out of business). If as sometimes happens, however, inventory is valued at a higher price than it is really worth, it makes the firm appear to be more valuable than it really is.

S U M M A R Y

All businesses need money to meet their day-to-day expenses and to grow. They obtain their funds by dipping into savings, borrowing money from suppliers and banks, or selling stocks or bonds.

When people buy stocks in a corporation, they become part owners of that business and have votes on certain matters regarding the corporation. Bondholders, by contrast, are creditors of a corporation and have no voting rights. People often buy stocks and bonds through stockbrokers. Investors buy stock in expectation of periodic dividends and an eventual rise in value of the stock. The main appeal of bonds is the interest that they pay.

Investing in stocks and bonds of businesses is risky. Before investing in a corporation, one should read its financial statements. Moreover, one should not invest more than one can afford to lose.

REVIEWING THE CHAPTER

BUILDING VOCABULARY

Match each term in Column A with its definition in Column B.

Column A

1. retained earnings
2. inventory
3. bull
4. bear
5. equity financing
6. asset
7. investment bank
8. net worth
9. income statement
10. leverage

Column B

a. the use of borrowed funds to finance ownership of something

b. any item of value owned by a business

c. someone who buys stock expecting its price to rise

d. profits of a business that are not distributed to its owners

e. the sale of a corporation's stock as a means for the business to raise additional capital

f. a summary of the financial activities of a company over time

g. an institution that buys an entire new issue of a corporation's stock or bonds for resale to the public

h. someone who buys stock expecting its price to fall

i. the difference between what a firm owns and what it owes

j. the goods a business plans to sell and the materials used in their manufacture

UNDERSTANDING WHAT YOU HAVE READ

1. Corporations obtain most of the funds that they need for expansion from (*a*) the sale of stocks (*b*) the sale of bonds (*c*) short-term borrowing (*d*) their undistributed profits.

2. The holder of one share of stock in a corporation is (*a*) a creditor of the corporation (*b*) a debtor of the corporation (*c*) an owner of the corporation (*d*) an officer of the corporation.

3. The holder of a corporate bond is (*a*) a creditor of the corporation (*b*) a debtor of the corporation (*c*) an owner of the corporation (*d*) an officer of the corporation.

4. Preferred stock is like (*a*) a bond in that the dividends must be paid regularly (*b*) a bond in that the holder of the stock is a creditor of the corporation (*c*) common stock in that dividends increase as profits increase (*d*) common stock in that there may be times when the board of directors decides to pay no dividends.

5. A corporation pays a dividend on its common stock (*a*) every year (*b*) when the interest becomes due (*c*) whenever its board of directors votes to do so (*d*) whenever it earns a profit.

6. Which *one* of the following statements is true? (*a*) Every time people buy Microsoft stock, Microsoft receives money for new capital investment. (*b*) Preferred stock is always better than common stock. (*c*) The main function of the SEC is to prevent stockholders from losing money on stock purchases. (*d*) The higher the margin rate, the more difficult it is to buy stocks with borrowed funds.

7. To "buy on margin" means to (*a*) buy long (*b*) buy over-the-counter (*c*) buy stocks in the hope of selling at a profit in the near future (*d*) buy stocks with borrowed funds.

8. When a corporate security is registered with the Securities and Exchange Commission, this means that (*a*) the SEC has approved the security as a safe investment (*b*) certain financial information has been filed with the SEC (*c*) the SEC may act as a broker for the corporation (*d*) the public may inquire of the SEC as to its opinion of the advisability of purchasing the security.

9. All of the following information is contained in a balance sheet, *except* (*a*) assets (*b*) liabilities (*c*) net worth (*d*) total sales.

10. Which *one* of the following pieces of information is contained in a corporation's income statement? (*a*) net income (*b*) accounts payable (*c*) value of the firm's factory (*d*) total liabilities.

THINKING CRITICALLY

1. Explain why you agree or disagree with the statement, "The fortunes of the stock market mirror how the people of the United States view their economy."

2. What arguments can you give for and against buying each of the following securities: (*a*) common stocks (*b*) preferred stocks (*c*) corporate bonds (*d*) government bonds.

3. When they are not selling new issues, those who sell BellAtlantic, Gillette, and Sears Roebuck stocks on the New York Stock Exchange do not add new funds to these companies. Why, then, are the officers of these corporations concerned about fluctuations in the prices of their corporation's stock sold on the exchange?

4. Some people invest for dividends, while others invest for capital growth. Explain the differences between the two types of investing and the advantages and disadvantages of each to an investor.

5. Why is it important for the wise investor to carefully study a corporation's financial statements before investing in that corporation? What are the limitations to the information in a corporation's financial statements?

SKILLS: Understanding Stock Market Transactions

1. On January 12, the following transactions took place:

   - Robert Allison, convinced that Dr Pepper stock was undervalued, instructed his broker to buy 200 shares of it.

   - Margo Bromley, believing that Tenneco stock was undervalued, purchased 100 shares.

   - Patrick Chin thought that Wal-Mart was in for a bad year and ordered his broker to sell short 100 shares of its common stock.

   These transactions took place at the closing price for January 12:

   - Dr Pepper   12.75
   - Tenneco   97.5
   - Wal-Mart   35

   Three months later, Allison, Bromley, and Chin closed out their stock transactions at these prices:

   - Dr Pepper   18.5
   - Tenneco   90.25
   - Wal-Mart   70

   a. Identify the bulls and the bears in these transactions.

   b. How much money did each of the three speculators earn or lose? (Ignore commissions and taxes in calculating your answers.)

2. The Boswash Computer Company, Inc., has the following securities outstanding:

   - $1 million in 10 percent bonds, due 2009
   - 2 million shares of common stock

   Last year, the company's profits totaled $1.75 million after all interest payments had been made, including debt on the bonds. The board of directors voted to distribute $1 million to the common stockholders as dividends. (a) How much was paid in interest to the bondholders? (b) How much did a holder of 100 shares of common stock receive in dividends? (c) In connection with the bonds issued by the corporation, explain the meaning of "due 2009." (d) Suppose that next year Boswash Computer fails and the company is liquidated. After all the corporation's debts are paid, $1.2 million remains. How will this sum be divided?

EXPLORING CURRENT ISSUES IN ECONOMICS

The Issue: Is vigorous enforcement of stock market regulations in the public interest?

The Challenge: Use the resources of your library and/or the Internet to gather the data needed to write the essay described below.

Case in Point: On April 28, 2003, ten of the nation's biggest investment firms agreed to pay fines and other penalties totaling $1.4 billion. According to the Securities and Exchange Commission, the investment companies had lured millions of investors into buying billions of dollars worth of shares in companies they knew were unworthy of investment.

Public reaction to the decision was mixed, with some in favor of the SEC action and others opposed. Those supporting the government's prosecution of the case argued that since the brokerage houses had deliberately misled the public as a way of enriching themselves, they deserved to be punished. Indeed, some said that the fines should have been stiffer, while others wanted to see those involved in the fraud sent to jail.

On the other hand, some people argued that the action by the SEC and state agencies represented unwarranted government interference in the securities market. The public knows, they said, that there are no guarantees in the stock market, and consequently those who invest are aware of and willing to take those risks. It was therefore unrealistic to expect the government to conduct an investigation every time people lost money in the stock market.

There were ten investment firms involved in the SEC decision: Merrill Lynch, Credit Suisse, UBS Warburg, Bear Stearns, Piper Jaffray, Citigroup, Goldman Sachs, Lehman Brothers, Morgan Stanley, and Deutsche Bank.

The Essay: With reference to *one* of the investment firms listed above, write an essay in which you

- summarize the charges that were leveled against the firm and the evidence on which the charges were based

- explain why you agree or disagree with the appropriateness of the decision that was handed down by the SEC.

The following sources will provide the kind of information and differing points of view you will need to understand the issues and draw conclusions:

- the SEC Web site at <<www.sec.gov/litigation/complaints/comp18115.htm>> for detailed information related to the charges against each of the named investment companies

- the 4/28/03 edition of most major newspapers, which carried one or more stories about the event

- magazine articles like the following, which presented contrasting views about the events:

  "Criminalizing Capitalism," *Forbes,* 5/12/03 <<www.forbes.com>>.

  "Spitzer's Shakedown," *National Review,* 1/3/03 <<www.nationalreview.com>>.

  "The Investigation," *The New Yorker,* 4/7/03.

CHAPTER 6
Production and Productivity

OVERVIEW

"Oh, I remember when I was your age. Those were the good old days."

How often have you heard your grandparents or other older adults speak lovingly of times gone by as "the good old days"? To hear them tell it, the days of their childhood were full of simple pleasures and abundance.

Perhaps things were better for some at an earlier time. Today, though, most people in the United States are living longer and enjoying more goods and services than earlier generations ever did. We can illustrate this as follows.

- In 1914, the average factory workweek was 55 hours. Workers then were earning less than $16 per week (equivalent to approximately $239 today). Factory workers now work about 40 hours per week, for an average wage of $650.

- In the 1920s, it took an average factory worker more than 275 hours to earn enough to buy a clothes-washing machine and about 400 hours to buy a refrigerator. Today's factory worker earns enough to pay for a washing machine in about 23 hours and a refrigerator in about 30 hours.

- One hundred years ago, half the nation's population lived on farms. Today, less than 2 percent do so. Yet our farms are able to feed and clothe us, and much of the outside world as well.

- With a gross domestic product of $12 trillion, the United States is now the world's greatest producer of goods and services.

In this chapter, we will describe how increasing productivity and the ever-increasing production of goods and services have enabled the U.S. economy to become the world's wealthiest nation. As you read, you will learn about how business firms organize for production in order to maximize production, productivity, and profits.

WHAT IS PRODUCTIVITY?

Productivity can be defined as the output per unit of input. In economics, productivity measures the efficiency with which we produce goods and services. Productivity increases have enabled today's factory workers to produce more, in fewer hours, than did factory workers in years gone by. Similarly, increased farm productivity, has enabled 21st-century agricultural workers to produce more than ten times as much food as their 19th-century counterparts.

When productivity is growing, the nation's output of goods and services increases, and living standards rise. When productivity stagnates, so too does the well-being of the American people.

Measuring Productivity

Productivity is the efficiency of a factor of production, measured in terms of units of output for every unit of input. Batting averages, for example, measure a baseball player's productivity as a hitter. A ball player whose batting average is .300 has made three hits (output) for every ten times at bat (input). By comparison, a .200 hitter made only two hits for every ten times at bat.

Other measures of productivity might factor the amount of capital used to produce a firm's product, or farm acreage per unit of output. But the measure most frequently used to gauge economic efficiency is *labor productivity*. Labor productivity is expressed as the output per worker per hour.

Figure 6.1 **People Fed by One U.S. Farmworker**

Blair Chair Company manufactures folding chairs that are commonly used for picnics, barbecues, and other outdoor activities. The factory employs five workers and had been producing on average 160 chairs in an eight-hour day.

Under these circumstances, labor productivity at Blair Chair was four chairs per worker per hour. We arrived at this figure with the following two mathematical operations:

- 160 chairs ÷ 8 hours = 20 chairs/hour
- 20 chairs/hour ÷ 5 workers = 4 chairs/hour/worker.

Last week, executives of Blair Chair Company rearranged its plant's manufacturing process in the hope of making it more efficient. The experiment proved to be a great success. Using the new procedure, the same number of workers could produce 240 chairs in an eight-hour day, as compared to only 160 under the old method. This represented a productivity increase of 50 percent, as output per worker jumped from 4 to 6 chairs per worker per hour.

The new results were calculated as follows:

- 240 chairs ÷ 8 hours = 30 chairs/hour
- 30 chairs/hour ÷ 5 workers = 6 chairs/hour/worker
- 6 is 50 percent greater than 4.

 # PRODUCTIVITY IN THE UNITED STATES

Advances in productivity, that is, the ability to produce more with the same or less input, are a significant source of increased potential national income. The U.S. economy has been able to produce more goods and services over time, not by requiring a proportional increase of labor time, but by making production more efficient.

Bureau of Labor Statistics, 2003

In March 2000, the United States recorded the longest period of prosperity in peacetime history. Since 1991, business investment, profits, jobs, consumer spending, and other measures of economic progress all had shown an upward trend. While economists differ as to the reasons why the expansion occurred when it did, all agree that rising productivity was a key ingredient.

A nation's standard of living improves when the output of goods and services increases faster than its population. There are two ways output can increase: (1) by applying more resources (e.g., capital and labor) to production, and (2) by increasing the *productivity* (i.e., output per unit of input) of the factors of production.

U.S. productivity has been increasing at an average annual rate of 2 percent over the past century. This may not sound like a lot, but the compound effect of the increase results in a doubling of output every 35 years. In 1999, the economy produced 30 times the volume of goods and services than it did in 1899. It accomplished this with only 5 times as many workers. That it took 5 rather than 30 times as many workers to produce 30 times the output is a tribute to the enormous increases in productivity taking place over those years. Of course, growth rates can fluctuate up and down from year to year. Productivity rose at an average annual rate of only 1.4 percent from 1973 to 1995. But from 1995 to 2000, the average annual rate jumped to 3.1 percent. If that rate continued, the GDP would double in about 23 years.

U.S. productivity has been increasing because of

1. The quality of the labor force. The quality of the workforce (in terms of education and experience) has improved over the years. Since 1980, the average U.S. worker has been better educated and has more experience than his or her predecessors.

2. Increasing capital investment per worker. Labor productivity increases when workers have more capital (plant, equipment, etc.) to work with. Since 1995, business investment as a share of GDP has been increasing. This increase is often cited as a reason for the recent increases in labor productivity.

3. Infrastructure. The record shows that investment in *infrastructure,* such as roads, bridges, and airports, has contributed to the nation's growth.

4. Innovations. Since 1960, federal and private spending on research and development has averaged around 2.5 percent of the GDP. In dollar terms, this was more than the combined total spent by Japan, Germany, and France. One hundred years ago, the development of electric power and the internal combustion engine led to enormous increases in productivity. Many expect a similar result from modern innovations such as the computer, the Internet, and e-commerce.

Figure 6.2 **U.S. Productivity Growth Since 1973**

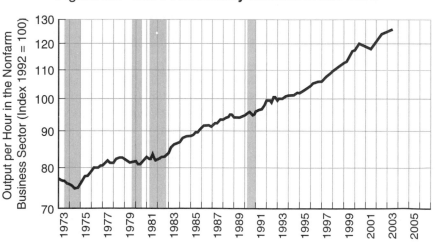

PRODUCTIVITY, PRODUCTION, AND PROBLEMS ON THE FARM

Since 1929, the number of people working on farms has shrunk by two thirds, yet output has increased by more than 60 percent. Or, to put it another way: In 1940, the average farmer produced enough to feed 12 people. Today, one farmer produces enough to feed 142. How is it possible for so many people to be fed by so few? The answers can be found in what some have described as the "miracle of American farm production and productivity."

The increase in farm productivity is the result of advances in science and technology. Highly specialized equipment performs tasks that until recently could be performed only by hand. As a result, modern farmworkers can cultivate far more acreage than their predecessors. Similarly, improvements in fertilizers, pesticides, and seeds have enabled farmers to increase their output per acre.

Profit Maximization on the Farm

Like all entrepreneurs, farmers strive to maximize profits. But unlike their non-farm counterparts who can control their output, advertising budgets, and selling price, farmers have little or no control over the supply of, demand for, and price of their products. Here are some of the reasons for the differences.

INELASTIC DEMAND FOR FARM PRODUCTS.   Although people will buy more farm products at a lower price than at a higher one, there is a limit as to how much any of us can eat (or are willing to buy) at a particular time. For that reason, the

How does this photo explain why the farm population declined in the 20th century?

demand for farm products is relatively inelastic. That is, the percentage change in the total dollar value of food demanded for farm products is less than the percentage change in price. For example, it is unlikely that your family will buy twice as much bread, milk, or lettuce if the prices for those products are reduced by half. Your family is likely to buy more bread, milk, and lettuce, but not enough to make up for the price decreases to farmers. For farmers, this means that in years when harvests are abundant and prices fall, so do their incomes.

INELASTIC SUPPLY.   When sales slump, manufacturers can reduce production by laying off workers and shutting down plants while, at the same time, maintaining prices. Similarly, when demand for their products increases, manufacturers can increase their output accordingly. Farmers do not have these options. Once their crops are planted or the size of their herds is established, there is little that farmers can do to increase or decrease production until the next season. For that reason, the supply of farm products is relatively inelastic.

As a result, farm prices often follow a boom or bust pattern. For example, with wheat prices unusually high at the end of a poor growing season, farmers are likely to increase their wheat acreage the following year. But if that year is also accompanied by good weather, yields will be higher than needed to satisfy demand, and prices will plummet.

Adding to their woes is the inability of individual farmers to affect prices. Wheat farmers have little choice but to plant as much as they can, even when prices are high. If they do not plant the wheat, the prices will fall anyway because individual production decisions do not affect market prices. By not planting, the farmers simply deny themselves a share of the wheat market.

Both the state and federal governments have enacted a number of programs to assist farmers. Some of them are described in Chapter 13.

ORGANIZING FOR PRODUCTION

As was discussed in Chapter 1, entrepreneurs bring together the factors of production in order to create a business enterprise. Since organizing and launching a business is costly, time-consuming, and difficult, one might ask, "Why do it? Why risk time, effort, and money in a venture that might very well fail?" While much can be said for the personal satisfaction to be found in creating a business, watching it grow, and being "one's own boss," none of this would be possible unless the enterprise was profitable.

Profits are the lifeblood of private enterprise. With profits, a business will succeed; without profits, it will die. Entrepreneurs do what they do (launch business ventures) in the hope that they will succeed and earn profits. Profits represent the difference between revenues and costs. For that reason, entrepreneurs try to combine the factors of production in such a way that they earn the greatest revenues at the least cost. Some of the things they need to consider in that effort are described in the following case study.

> Lucille Miracle is an entrepreneur. She gathered together a group of wealthy investors who, along with her, put up enough money to set up a factory to manufacture a line of lanterns. (Customers use these battery-powered lanterns outdoors at night to cast a strong beam of light.) The venture became known as the "Miracle Lantern Company."
>
> Lucille thought about the things she needed to get production under way. On a sheet of notepaper, she wrote:
>
> THINGS TO CONSIDER
>
> - Factory: should we rent or buy?
> - Machinery: given our budget, should we get the latest models (requiring a few highly skilled workers) or less complicated equipment (requiring a greater number of workers but who need not be so skilled)?
> - Raw materials: should we buy enough to carry us through for a few years or reorder from week to week?
> - Products: should we manufacture plastic and/or metal models? How many different models will we offer?
>
> After deciding which products to produce and where and how to produce them, Lucille remembered two more questions that needed to be added to her list.
>
> - Diminishing returns: when will they set in?
> - Economies of large-scale production: when will "bigness" become a disadvantage?

🌀 Law of Diminishing Returns

When we add additional factors of production such as workers or machinery, productivity usually increases. Eventually, though, we reach a point where the addition of inputs (in this instance, workers or machinery) has the opposite effect. That is, output per worker or machine begins to decline. Economists describe this phenomenon as the *Law of Diminishing Returns*. The following illustrates diminishing returns in action.

> With one worker, Miracle Lantern was able to produce 50 lanterns a day. By adding a second worker, total output grew to 110 lanterns. This increased output prompted the company to hire a third worker, with the result that 180 lanterns were completed. The production is summarized in Table 6.1.
>
> As additional workers were added, both the total number of lanterns produced (output per day) and productivity (output per worker) increased. Let us see what happened as the company continued to add workers to its production line.

TABLE 6.1   LANTERN OUTPUT WITH ONE TO THREE WORKERS

Number of Workers	Output per Day	Net Increase From Each Additional Worker	Output per Worker
1	50	50	50
2	110	60	55
3	180	70	60

The Miracle Lantern Company continued the experiment by adding a fourth, fifth, sixth, and finally a seventh worker to its production line. The results were tallied and assembled in Table 6.2.

We see from the tables that although the fourth worker increased total output from 180 to 240, average production per worker (productivity) remained unchanged at 60 lanterns. When the fifth worker was added, something different happened. Although total output continued to increase, output per worker declined to 56 units. This was Miracle Lantern Company's point of diminishing returns. Once diminishing returns began to set in, each additional worker added less to total output. Eventually, the continued addition of production workers resulted in negative returns. This occurred with the hiring of the seventh worker when total output fell from 300 to 280 for the day.

Diminishing returns set in because as more and more variable resources are added, less of the fixed resources are available for sharing. In the case of Miracle Lantern, as more workers (the variable resource) were added, less of the fixed resources (machinery, tools, floor space, etc.) was available to each worker. To put it another way: As more and more workers were added, the need to share machinery and tools resulted in a decline in productivity.

 # THE ECONOMICS OF "BIGNESS"

Maximum production under existing conditions at the Miracle Lantern factory was 300 units per day, as we can see in Table 6.2. To expand production beyond

 TABLE 6.2   LANTERN OUTPUT WITH FOUR TO SEVEN WORKERS

Number of Workers	Output per Day	Net Increase From Each Additional Worker	Output per Worker
4	240	60	60
5	280	40	56
6	300	20	50
7	280	−20	40

that would require additional resources, such as new or additional equipment or floor space.

In thinking about adding to its *capacity* (potential output), a firm must consider both the advantages and disadvantages of expansion or, as economists sometimes say, the *economies and diseconomies of scale*.

🗡 Advantages of Expansion

The principal reason for increasing a firm's output is to reduce unit costs or, to put it another way, to increase productivity. The following factors may contribute to increased output for larger companies.

DIVISION OF LABOR, OR SPECIALIZATION.   It is a rare factory worker who has a hand in the manufacture of a product from beginning to end. Were you to visit most large plants today, you would likely see workers involved solely in one or two stages of the total production process. For example, if you visited a plant that manufactured gasoline-powered lawn mowers, you might see one group of workers preparing motors for installation, a second group doing the electrical wiring, and a third overseeing the stamping and painting operations. Final assembly and packaging might be the responsibility of two other groups.

This breakdown of the total production process into a series of simpler tasks is known as *division of labor*. Among the many advantages of division of labor are the following.

- As the tasks that workers and management perform are simplified, on-the-job training becomes easier.
- Because the task has been subdivided, it is easier to perform. In a television assembly factory, only a highly trained worker is able to assemble an entire set. By dividing the tasks, however, the firm is able to hire less skilled workers at lower wages.
- Supervisory and management responsibilities may also be subdivided with specialization. Like other workers, supervisors and managers are able to attain a higher level of expertise in a few specialized tasks than they would if they were responsible for all production from beginning to end.

QUANTITY DISCOUNTS.   Frequently, large firms can obtain their raw materials at lower cost than small ones. Suppliers are especially eager to keep their biggest customers and may offer discounts for quantity purchases.

AVAILABILITY OF SPECIALIZED MACHINERY.   Large-scale production and the division of labor make more practicable the use of specialized machinery. Large firms can more easily afford to purchase such machinery. For example, large automobile companies can afford to buy very expensive laser equipment to weld joints on automobile body frames. A small firm, however, cannot afford to do so.

EASIER ACCESS TO CREDIT. Big businesses find it easier to borrow than do small ones. One reason is that the large firms are better known, and consequently lending institutions and the public are often more willing to lend them money. Also, their size makes them appear to be less of a risk. This access to capital funds makes it easier for large firms to expand their operations.

RESEARCH, DEVELOPMENT, AND BY-PRODUCTS. As businesses grow, they can afford to hire the best brains available to conduct elaborate research programs. Research has led to the development of many new products and methods of production. In addition, research leads to the discovery and development of by-products. These are goods produced along with the major items of production, often from materials that once were considered waste. For example, companies that process orange juice formerly discarded the orange peel. After industrial researchers discovered that orange peels could be made into fertilizer and feed, the juice industry began selling a profitable by-product. Big businesses are better able to invest in the equipment needed to produce by-products than are smaller ones. Large meatpacking companies, for example, have been able to produce glue, fertilizers, and soap by-products that smaller meatpacking firms could not afford to produce.

 # WHEN FIRMS GET TOO BIG

As a firm grows, it may pass the point where the economies of large-scale production (the economies of scale) are effective. It reaches a point of diminishing returns. That is, the increase in income resulting from the firm's expansion is less than its increased cost of operation (economists sometimes call this the *diseconomies of scale*).

Many of the giant firms in the United States—like General Motors, IBM, and General Electric—experienced the disadvantages of being too large in the early 1990s. General Motors, partly because of its size, had become inefficient and was spending more than many of its competitors to produce an automobile. In 1992, GM announced that it was going to reduce the size of its operations by closing plants and laying off workers. As a result of this downsizing and measures to reorganize and divide operations, GM once again became competitive. What GM and many other large companies realize is that they can expand only to the point where *unit production costs* (the average costs of producing an item) stop decreasing and begin to increase. This is the point where diminishing returns set in. In order to reverse this trend and bring down unit production costs, firms are likely to reorganize and divide operations. GM followed this course. By 1994, it had become a leaner but more profitable company.

CREATIVE DESTRUCTION

> Capitalism . . . is by nature a form or method of economic change and . . . never . . . can be stationary. . . . The fundamental impulse that sets and keeps the capitalist engine in motion comes from the new consumers, goods, the new methods of production . . . , the new markets, the new forms of industrial organization that capitalist enterprise creates. . . . This process of Creative Destruction is the essential fact about capitalism.
>
> *Joseph A. Schumpeter,* Capitalism, Socialism, and Democracy

Along with diminishing returns and the diseconomies of scale, giant corporations need to be aware of the implications of *creative destruction*. First described in 1942 by Harvard economist Joseph Schumpeter, "creative destruction" suggests that capitalism exists in a constant state of change in which innovation destroys established enterprises and yields new ones.

Problems arise when successful firms devote their energies to defending their old operations rather than adapting to change. Thus, typewriter manufacturers that failed to adapt to the age of the personal computer disappeared into the dustbin of history.

MINI-READING

How Creative Destruction Turned Things Around at General Electric

In the 20 years between 1981 and 2001, Jack Welch, CEO of General Electric, *divested* (sold off, or shut down) 117 of its business units. In their place, GE installed new lines of merchandise and services better suited to the needs of the 21st century. As Welch put it, in this new business environment "nothing is sacred," "change will be accepted as the rule, rather than the exception," and "paradox is a way of life."

Welch's policy proved spectacularly successful. Between 1981 and 2000, shareholders in similarly large corporations earned an annual return of 15 percent on their investment, compared to GE stockholders who earned 23 percent on theirs.

Costs, Revenues, and Profits in the Process of Production

The principal goal of any business firm is to earn profits. For that reason, when given a choice of two or more production alternatives, a firm will select the alternative that it believes will result in the largest profits for the company. Economists describe the efforts to earn the greatest profits as *profit maximization.*

In order to maximize profits, one of the first things a firm must determine is the best level of production. "Why," you might ask, "doesn't a firm simply produce all it can?" The reason is that although profits are likely to increase for a time as output is increased, eventually a point will be reached at which profits begin to decline.

The discussion that follows analyzes (1) the reasons why the level of production affects profits and (2) how economic analysis helps business managers determine the level of production that will give a company the greatest profits.

Recently, the management of Miracle Lantern Company became unhappy with company earnings. In an effort to increase profits, Miracle hired a firm of economic consultants to analyze its operations and make recommendations for improvements.

The consultants found Miracle's production process to be a fairly simple one. A specially designed machine at one end of the assembly line stamped out lantern cases. After that, a conveyor belt moved parts past workers who assembled and prepared the finished products for shipment. An office staff attended to administrative chores (payroll, advertising, sales, and so on).

As indicated by Table 6.3 (columns 1 and 2), output depends on the number of workers employed on the assembly line. With one worker, the factory could produce 200 units a week. With two workers, output increased to 500 lanterns, and so on until a maximum of 1,490 units were turned out by eight workers. Beyond that number, output declined.

Consultants determined that Miracle's capacity is 1,490 units. A plant's *capacity* is the maximum number of units it can produce in the short run. To an economist, a *short run* refers to a period of time during which a factory operates with existing equipment. A *long run* is a period of time during which any or all of the factors of production could vary. For example, a factory could enlarge its plant and/or buy additional equipment. Under such new circumstances, Miracle could increase production beyond its present capacity. This process, however, would take some time to accomplish.

Table 6.3 also illustrates the effect of the Law of Diminishing Returns. As we can see in column 3, the addition of the first, second, and third workers resulted in a net increase of 200, 300, and 400 units respectively. When a fourth worker was added, however, the increase in output diminished from previous increases. We can see, too, that the addition of a ninth worker marked the onset of negative returns, or losses.

At one point, the consultants examined Miracle's costs of production—both its fixed costs and its variable costs. *Fixed costs* are those that remain unchanged regardless of the number of units produced. These include rent, real estate taxes, and interest on loans. Miracle's fixed costs, those that the company had to meet whether it produced one lantern or a thousand, totaled $2,000 a week.

Variable costs are those that increase or decrease with the level of production. Variable costs include things like wages (because workers can be laid off when business is slow and rehired when it picks up again), raw materials, and electrical power to operate equipment. A detailed account of Miracle's variable costs, along with a number of other findings, is summarized in Table 6.4. Let us take a closer look at these figures.

(*continued on page 130*)

127

TABLE 6.3   COST, REVENUE, AND PROFIT POSSIBILITIES, MIRACLE LANTERN COMPANY

| Workers | Output | (Net Increase) | Total Fixed Costs | Total Variable Costs | Total Costs | Average Unit Costs | | |
| | | | | | | Fixed | Variable | Total |
Column 1	Column 2	Column 3	Column 4	Column 5	Column 6	Column 7	Column 8	Column 9
0	0	(0)	$2,000	$ 0	$2,000			
1	200	(200)	2,000	500	2,500	$10.00	$2.50	$12.50
2	500	(300)	2,000	1,000	3,000	4.00	2.00	6.00
3	900	(400)	2,000	1,500	3,500	2.22	1.67	3.89
4	1,150	(250)	2,000	2,000	4,000	1.74	1.74	3.48
5	1,275	(125)	2,000	2,500	4,500	1.57	1.96	3.53
6	1,375	(100)	2,000	3,000	5,000	1.48	2.22	3.70
7	1,450	(75)	2,000	3,500	5,500	1.38	2.41	3.79
8	1,490	(40)	2,000	4,000	6,000	1.34	2.68	4.02
9	1,480	(−10)	2,000	4,500	6,500	1.35	3.04	4.39

TABLE 6.4 COST, REVENUE, AND PROFIT POSSIBILITIES, MIRACLE LANTERN COMPANY

| Workers | Output | Total Fixed Costs | Total Variable Costs | Total Costs | Average Unit Costs | | | Marginal Costs | Price (Marginal Revenue) | Total Revenue | Profits |
Column 1	Column 2	Column 3	Column 4	Column 5	Fixed Column 6	Variable Column 7	Total Column 8	Column 9	Column 10	Column 11	Column 12
0	0	$2,000	$ 0	$2,000							
1	200	2,000	500	2,500	10.00	$2.50	$12.50	$0.60	5.00	$1,000	(−) $1,500
2	500	2,000	1,000	3,000	4.00	2.00	6.00	0.80	5.00	2,500	(−) 500
3	900	2,000	1,500	3,500	2.22	1.67	3.89	2.00	5.00	4,500	1,000
4	1,150	2,000	2,000	4,000	1.74	1.74	3.48	4.00	5.00	5,750	1,750
5	1,275	2,000	2,500	4,500	1.57	1.96	3.53	5.00	5.00	6,375	1,875
6	1,375	2,000	3,000	5,000	1.48	2.22	3.70	6.67	5.00	6,875	1,875
7	1,450	2,000	3,500	5,500	1.38	2.41	3.79	12.50	5.00	7,250	1,750
8	1,490	2,000	4,000	6,000	1.34	2.68	4.02		5.00	7,450	1,450

(continued on next page)

129

Column 2 shows *output*—the total number of units produced weekly by the workers listed in column 1. Total fixed costs are listed in column 3. Variable costs, averaging $500 per worker, are summarized in column 4. Total costs (column 5) represent the sum of the variable and fixed costs (listed in columns 3 and 4).

Columns 6, 7, and 8 list the *average unit costs* of production. These were calculated by dividing the fixed, variable, and total costs of production by the number of units produced at each level of input.

Thus far, all we have been looking only at has been the company's costs of production. As we have noted, however, a firm's primary goal is to earn a profit. Thus, the question uppermost in management's thoughts must be, "What level of production will yield the greatest profit?"

To answer that question, Miracle's consultants (and most economists) turn to *marginal analysis.* It is simply a way of looking at what happens to profits when a firm adds one more unit to the production process. In this instance, the consultants analyzed the effect of adding one more assembly-line worker on output, costs, and profits. As long as adding workers adds to profits, it pays to do so. When the point is reached where adding a worker results in a reduction in profits, however, this person should not be hired.

In fact, a company will increase production only as long as the revenue that production generates is greater than what it costs the company to produce the additional output. Economists say it this way: As long as marginal revenue remains greater than marginal costs, expanding output will add to a company's profits. *Marginal revenue (MR)* is the income from the production of one more unit. *Marginal cost (MC)* is the addition to costs resulting from the production of one extra unit.

Now we can answer the question, "What level of production will yield the greatest profit?" The answer is: *the point at which marginal revenue equals marginal cost.*

You can see this concept at Miracle Lantern Company. In Table 6.4, the price at which Miracle sells its lanterns is $5 each. (See column 10.) Since each additional lantern produced adds $5 to the firm's income, we can say that $5 represents the firm's marginal revenue. Its marginal costs, the costs of producing the *additional* lanterns, are summarized in column 9.

We know that the Miracle Lantern Company is in business to make money. We have also learned that the company can produce 1,490 lanterns with its present equipment. If the company can sell whatever quantity it chooses to produce up to its present capacity, what level of production would you expect management to target?

If you said 1,275 units, you would be correct, because at that level the firm would earn the greatest profit. Table 6.4 shows that at an output of 1,275 lanterns, marginal costs are $5 and marginal revenue is also $5, giving Miracle a profit of $1,875. Now suppose that Miracle increased production by hiring additional workers. What would happen to the company's profits? Table 6.4 shows that a sixth worker increases marginal costs to $6.67, while marginal revenue remains at $5. The result is that profits have not increased even though output and sales have. Adding still more workers will result in lower profits.

S U M M A R Y

The United States is able to produce so much because it is fortunate to have abundant resources. In addition, resources in the United States are used efficiently. Productivity, the ability to use resources, is measured in terms of units of output for every unit of input. Entrepreneurs try to combine the factors of production in order to earn the greatest profits. Often, increasing output results in increased productivity. At some point, however, diminishing returns set in. Profit maximization depends on the level of production and productivity. Economists use marginal analysis to determine the most efficient level of production in terms of maximizing profits.

REVIEWING THE CHAPTER

BUILDING VOCABULARY

Match each term in Column A with its definition in Column B.

Column A

1. capacity
2. variable costs
3. labor productivity
4. division of labor
5. economies of scale
6. Law of Diminishing Returns
7. fixed costs
8. marginal analysis
9. profit maximization
10. marginal revenue

Column B

a. the breaking down of production into simpler tasks
b. the maximum amount that can be produced in the short run
c. a reduction in the unit costs of doing business that results from increases in the size of operations
d. efforts to earn the greatest profits
e. a way of looking at profits when a firm adds one more unit to the production process
f. output per worker per unit of time
g. costs that increase or decrease with the level of production
h. describes the point beyond which adding variable inputs to fixed resources results in decreased productivity
i. the income from the production of one more unit
j. costs that remain unchanged regardless of the number of units produced

UNDERSTANDING WHAT YOU HAVE READ

1. As a result of our nation's increasing productivity, (*a*) most goods are cheaper than they were years ago (*b*) more goods are available per person than years ago (*c*) goods are made better by machine than they were by hand (*d*) output per employee per hour has decreased.

2. Before modernizing, the Chelsea Video Games Company employed 20 workers and produced 200 games a day. After modernizing, the company laid off 5 workers and is now producing 300 games a day. As a result of modernization, productivity at the Chelsea plant (*a*) doubled (*b*) increased by 50 percent (*c*) remained the same (*d*) declined.

3. Which *one* of the following is least likely to result in increased productivity? (*a*) efficient use of natural resources (*b*) employee training programs (*c*) improved machinery (*d*) working overtime.

4. When the point of diminishing returns is reached as workers are added to a production line, (*a*) total revenue will decline (*b*) output per employee will decline (*c*) total profits will decline (*d*) the factory should hire more workers.

5. The best way to increase productivity in a plant is to (*a*) employ all the factors of production more efficiently (*b*) keep hiring more workers (*c*) keep hiring more plant managers (*d*) increase output.

6. Which *one* of the following is an example of a fixed cost? (*a*) rent (*b*) electricity to power machinery (*c*) commission on sales (*d*) raw materials.

7. In industries with high overhead costs, increasing production tends to lower (*a*) return on investment (*b*) total variable costs (*c*) overhead cost per unit (*d*) total operating costs.

8. The Kilroy Bicycle Company has fixed annual costs of $100,000 and variable costs of $10 per bicycle. If output is increased from 5,000 to 10,000 bicycles per year, the total cost of producing each bicycle will be reduced from $30 to (*a*) $25 (*b*) $20 (*c*) $15 (*d*) $10.

9. Which *one* of the following is an example of a disadvantage to a company of getting too big? A company (*a*) goes out of business because of decreased demand for its product (*b*) becomes so large that it has to expand into new quarters (*c*) finds that it is spending more on new managers than it is earning in additional profits (*d*) is receiving more orders than it can fill.

10. When he became CEO of General Electric back in 1981, Jack Welch announced that he would prepare GE for the 21st century by selling off or destroying existing operations, and introducing new ones. As a result of those policies, GE grew at annual rate of 23 percent for the next 20 years. Such a program is known as (*a*) research and development (*b*) marginal analysis (*c*) creative destruction (*d*) personnel management.

THINKING CRITICALLY

1. After acquiring the equipment for the production of automobile batteries, a manufacturer hired one worker to operate it. This resulted in a day's production of 50 batteries. The next day, the manufacturer hired a second worker, and total output rose to 120 batteries. Continuing the procedure, the manufacturer found that three workers could produce 210 units. Eventually, the manufacturer hired a total of nine workers. Table 6.5 gives partial data on the company's productivity. (*a*) Complete the table. (*b*) At what number of workers did the operation reach the point of diminishing returns? (*c*) At what number of workers did the manufacturer reach negative returns? (*d*) What additional information would be necessary in order to determine how many workers the manufacturer should employ?

TABLE 6.5 AUTOMOBILE BATTERY PRODUCTION

Number of Workers	Output per Day	Output per Worker	Net Increase From Each Worker
1	50	50	50
2	120	60	70
3	210		
4	260		
5	300		
6	330		
7	350		
8	360		
9	351		

2. A manufacturer of motorcycle batteries has a plant capacity of 100,000 batteries per year. Overhead costs are $500,000 per year, in addition to which there are variable costs of $10 for each unit produced. Sales have been running at 50,000 units per year at a wholesale selling price of $25. Recently, a large mail-order department store offered to purchase an additional 50,000 batteries a year, which it would market under its own name. The store offered to pay the manufacturer $20 per battery. (*a*) Assuming that 50,000 units continue to be sold to the other customers at $25 each, should the manufacturer accept the offer? Explain. (*b*) Suppose that the department store offered to buy the entire output of 100,000 batteries at $15 per battery. Should the manufacturer accept the offer? Explain.

3. . . . *Rising productivity over most of the last 100 years has dramatically changed the face of the American economy in terms of living standards, the affordability of life's basic goods, and the range of goods and services Americans can buy.*

— Economic Report of the President, 2000

   a. What does rising productivity have to do with "the affordability of life's basic goods, and the . . . goods and services Americans can buy"?

   b. What effect is *each* of the following events likely to have on productivity? Explain your answers. (*1*) Owing to a recession, investment in new plant and equipment has decreased over the year. (*2*) The average worker today is better educated than those in his or her parent's day. (*3*) A dress manufacturer installs a sound system to play music during working hours.

4. One of the surest sources of productivity growth is technological change that results in tools and equipment that work faster or better than those they replace. Consider, for example, the impact on productivity that must have resulted from the introduction of the Universal Product Code (bar code), the personal computer, and the Internet.

   With reference to a business in your community, and *one* of the innovations mentioned above (bar code, computer, Internet), describe (*a*) how the firm uses the item, (*b*) how the same functions were accomplished in the years before the technology was developed, and (*c*) the impact of the innovation on the firm's productivity.

SKILLS: Working With Data in Tables

1. According to the data contained in Table 6.3 on page 128, (*a*) when did Miracle reach the point of diminishing returns? (*b*) what happened to average fixed costs per unit as output increased from 900 to 1,450 lanterns?

2. According to the data given in Table 6.4 on page 129, (*a*) how many workers would be needed to give Miracle the greatest profit? (*b*) what would happen to profits if output were increased from 900 to 1,275 lanterns per week? (*c*) what would happen to profits if output were increased beyond 1,275 lanterns per week?

3. What would Miracle Lantern Company have to do if it wanted to increase output while maximizing profits beyond 1,490 lanterns per week?

CHAPTER 7
Competition and Monopoly

O V E R V I E W

"I do not believe it. I don't care if she is my teacher."
"You don't believe what?"
"My economics teacher said that eggs and breakfast cereals are sold in different kinds of markets. C'mon—it just so happens that I work in a supermarket after school, and I know that we sell breakfast cereals and eggs. She's wrong. They're sold in the same market."
"You know what the problem is? You're talking about a store. She's talking about an economic market."

Perhaps some of us are also confused about the term "market." It might become somewhat clearer if we understand that a market is simply any place or process in which buyers and sellers exchange goods and services. For example, farmers, wholesalers, and retailers are engaged in the production and distribution of eggs—from hens to people—in the egg market. Similarly, those employed in the manufacture, storage, and sales of breakfast cereals comprise the market for breakfast cereals.

All markets are similar in one respect: they are made up of buyers and sellers. But the numbers of buyers and sellers (and their ability to control prices) differ from one market to another. In this chapter, we will discuss the range of situations between *perfect competition* (with its many buyers and sellers and a free flow of information) and *monopoly* (in which one supplier controls the entire output of a good or service). We will also discuss types of business combinations (past and present), laws that regulate business combinations and encourage competition, and some of the pros and cons of big business today.

TYPES OF MARKETS

In Chapter 3, we described perfect competition. In this largely theoretical situation, market price is determined exclusively by the forces of supply and demand. Although the concept of perfect competition provides a useful framework for understanding market situations, it does not describe most everyday buying and selling activities. The prices people pay for food, clothing, entertainment, and everything else that goes into daily living are not set in a fully competitive market. Instead, they are subject to some kind of competition.

The kinds of markets that exist vary all the way from perfect competition, in which there are many buyers and sellers, to monopoly, in which there is only one seller. A market in which there is a single buyer is known as a *monopsony*. For example, as the sole buyer of certain kinds of military hardware, the U.S. government exercises monopsony power in that market.

The term *market power* refers to the power of buyers and sellers to influence prices. In a perfectly competitive market such as the egg market, there are so many buyers and sellers that no one buyer or seller has the power to set the prices. However, in a market where there is one major producer of a product, sellers have considerably more market power.

Economists use the term *imperfect competition* to describe markets where there is neither perfect competition nor pure monopoly. Imperfect competition may be further subdivided into (1) monopolistic competition and (2) oligopoly. The following pages show the range of markets extending from perfect competition to monopoly.

Perfect Competition

In Chapter 3, we discussed how the interaction of supply and demand affects prices. The laws of supply and demand apply to the market structure only of perfect competition. All the following conditions must prevail in order for perfect competition to exist.

- There are many buyers and sellers acting independently. No single buyer or seller is big enough to affect the market price.
- Competing products offered for sale are virtually identical, so that buyers do not care from whom they buy.
- Buyers and sellers are fully informed about prices, quality, and sources of supply.
- Firms can enter and leave the market at will.

The market for eggs resembles perfect competition for the reasons just cited. In this market, there are many buyers and sellers; competing products are almost identical; buyers and sellers are well informed; and it is relatively easy to go into the egg business.

Those who sell in competitive markets are sometimes called *price takers,* because they accept whatever the market (equilibrium) price happens to be. They have no control over the price they receive for their wares. Once suppliers begin to exercise control over prices, imperfect competition exists. In that situation, it can be said that they are *price makers* rather than price takers.

Imperfect competition can take a variety of forms ranging from monopoly, in which there is only one supplier, through oligopoly, with a few competitors, and on to monopolistic competition with more competitors. As you read about types of markets, you will learn how and the extent to which each form controls the prices they receive for their products.

Monopolistic Competition

Most people who own motor vehicles are likely to prefer to use one service station over all others. The quality of the service, the location, or some other reason may account for their preferences and willingness, perhaps, to pay a little more for the service. What is true for service stations for some people may also apply to restaurants, shoe stores, grocery stores, and other local retail shops. That is, these businesses offer goods or services that are available elsewhere at similar (but not necessarily identical) prices.

Gas stations, groceries, and shoes are only a few of the goods and services sold under conditions of *monopolistic competition.* Monopolistic competition contains the following characteristics:

- product differentiation
- many sellers who produce similar products that the buyer believes differ in some qualities.

It is fairly easy to start a business selling haircuts, shoes, or groceries. For that reason, there are many of these businesses. Nevertheless, despite the competition (and the fact that the products or services they sell are nearly identical to those of their competitors), these sellers have some control over prices. In each of these examples, *product differentiation* gives suppliers the power to influence prices.

Product differentiation refers to whatever it is that gives buyers the impression that virtually identical products are different. Brand names, advertising campaigns, packaging, and the quality of services are the kinds of things that make one product more attractive to buyers than another virtually identical product. In addition, consumers may prefer one product over a similar product because of family tradition or personal loyalty.

As an example of product differentiation, consider aspirin. All aspirin manufacturers use the same general formula. For that reason, one brand is

When, because of product differentiation, consumers perceive some goods or services to be better than the competition, sellers of those items are able to charge more. How was Ivory differentiated from other brands of soap?

about the same as another. Yet supermarkets and drugstores regularly stock a half dozen or so brands of aspirins. The best-selling brand (let us call it "Brand X") is usually the most expensive. Brand X can charge more for its product because the public believes it to be a better aspirin than its competitors. Through advertising and packaging, the manufacturer has created a kind of monopoly for its product. It did this by convincing consumers that its product is unique and worth the higher price. Of course, what is true for aspirin is also true for other products with brand names.

⚡ Oligopoly

A market in which a few sellers produce all or most of the supply of a product is called an *oligopoly*. The breakfast food industry provides an example. A handful of large corporations dominates the industry. While it is fairly expensive to build a cereal-processing plant, it takes millions of dollars more in advertising and other expenses to persuade the public to try a new cereal product. Other industries dominated by oligopolies include those that manufacture

Joan Robinson

Joan Robinson (1903–1983) was one of Britain's and the 20th century's most influential economists. When she began her studies of the market system, economists generally believed that in the long run, trade would take place under conditions of "perfect (pure) competition." According to the theory of perfect competition, no individual buyer or seller could become big enough to determine prices. The lure of profits, economists assumed, would always attract competition and for that reason monopoly would not long survive.

Although the theory worked on paper, perfect competition simply did not exist in real life. Much of the world's trade was being carried on by giant monopolies and oligopolies, whose conduct did not match that of the perfect competition model.

Robinson demonstrated this disparity between theory and reality in *The Economics of Imperfect Competition* (1933). Joan Robinson wrote this book shortly after she joined the faculty of Cambridge University, where she had been a student. In outlining her theory of imperfect competition, Robinson argued that product differentiation and consumer preferences gave certain companies the ability to manipulate prices despite the presence of competing firms. In other words, under imperfect competition, giant firms gained monopoly-like powers.

In Robinson's view, monopolistic competition posed a threat to society as a whole. By restricting production in order to maintain unnecessarily high prices, monopolists deprived the public of the goods and services it might otherwise have enjoyed. Worse still, she went on, fewer goods and services resulted in fewer jobs, declining income, and less consumption. In other words, the end result would be economic recession. Robinson called for vigorous regulation of the economy by the national government as a way of preventing what she viewed as abuses of the market system.

Although many economists disagreed with her conclusions, Joan Robinson continued to work on the central economic questions of the day until her death. She helped explain John Maynard Keynes's economic theory (discussed in Chapter 18) in her *Introduction to the Theory of Employment* (1937), discussed overall economic growth in *The Accumulation of Capital* (1956), and also wrote *Economic Philosophy* (1962) and *Introduction to Modern Economics* (1973).

automobiles, chewing gum, electrical appliances, steel, cement, and aluminum. An oligopoly has the following characteristics:

- few sellers that produce almost identical products (such as the aluminum, steel, and chemical industries)

● few sellers that produce differentiated products (such as the industries that make automobiles, breakfast cereals, and soft drinks).

COMPETITION WITHIN INDUSTRIES DOMINATED BY OLIGOPOLIES.   Industries operating under conditions of oligopoly are usually dominated by a handful of giant producers. Executives in every firm know that if they cut prices, other firms in the industry will also reduce their prices. Therefore, all that cutting prices accomplishes is reducing everyone's profits. For that reason, oligopolies try to avoid price competition. Instead of relying on competition, prices for products of oligopolies are the result of *product differentiation* and, in some instances, *collusion* and *price leadership.*

1. Product Differentiation.   Industries that make cement, steel, or paper clips produce products that are virtually identical with those of their competitors. Thus, product differentiation is minimal. Still, USX Corp., for example, does try to convince buyers that its steel products are better than or different from those of its competitors. Other oligopolistic industries, such as those that produce electrical appliances, automobiles, and soft drinks, lend themselves better to product differentiation. Ford Motor Co. goes to great expense to convince the public that its automobiles are different from and better than those of DaimlerChrysler Corporation, General Motors, and foreign auto companies. Coca-Cola, Dr Pepper, and Pepsi do much the same in the soft drink industry, as do Maytag and General Electric in the appliance industry.

2. Collusion.   Since there are so few competing firms in an oligopolistic market, there is a great temptation to limit competition by setting prices and dividing the market among these few firms. (This is called *collusion.*) Agreements to limit competition, however, are illegal. Therefore, oligopolistic firms adopt strategies other than collusion to accomplish the same goal (to fix prices) and, they hope, evade prosecution. One such strategy is price leadership.

3. Price Leadership.   This term refers to a practice by which the most powerful company in an industry sets its price, and every other firm follows. Price leadership, like collusion, is illegal. As an example of price leadership, consider the following case involving eight airlines.

U.S. CHARGES 8 AIRLINES IN FARE-FIXING SCHEME

WASHINGTON, DC, Dec. 21, 1992. The Justice Department accused the country's 8 largest airlines with using their computerized reservation systems to fix air fares.

The complaint said that by listing future fare changes in the computer, other firms were able to follow suit while, at the same time, act as if it were their idea. Without admitting or denying the accusation, several airlines agreed to end the practice.

In the airlines case, the accused relied on computer ticketing systems to keep one another informed of when and how the price leader was revising its fares.

⚡ Monopoly

A monopoly is a firm that controls the entire supply of a good or service. The word also describes a market in which

1. there is a single supplier. As the only supplier, the firm controls both the supply and the price of a product.
2. there are no close substitutes for the product that the single supplier sells. This is the case, for example, with firms that provide local electrical service.
3. it would be extremely difficult for any other firm to enter the industry, for the following reasons:

High Costs. The costs of entering certain businesses are so high that it is extremely difficult for others to do so.

Exclusive Ownership of a Resource. Before the 1950s, the Aluminum Company of America (ALCOA) controlled virtually all the bauxite (aluminum ore) produced in the United States. This gave ALCOA a monopoly over the aluminum market for years.

Legal Barriers. These include patents, copyrights, and public franchises.

- *Patents*. Issued by the federal government, patents give the inventors of new products the exclusive right to market their inventions or sell the rights to them. Patents are enforceable in courts of law. In a 2002 court decision, for example, Intel (a computer chip manufacturer) was ordered to pay $150 million in damages to the Intergraph Corporation. The court found that Intel had incorporated design features in their chips that were protected by patents held by Intergraph.
- *Copyrights*. These give exclusive rights to authors, musicians, composers, and artists to reproduce and/or sell their works. The federal government grants patents and copyrights as ways of stimulating innovation, cultural achievements, and scientific progress. By placing limits on the number of years that patents and copyrights are in effect, however, the law prevents the subsequent monopolies from becoming permanent.
- *Public franchises*. These are licenses granted by governments to firms that allow them to do business within their jurisdictions. Public franchises create monopolies because they exclude other firms from competing with the franchisees.

Natural Monopolies

Certain industries require such an enormous investment of capital that one company operating alone can supply the entire market for its product at a lower cost per unit than two or more competing firms. Economists describe such an industry as a *natural monopoly*.

During the railroad construction boom of the 19th century, the Boston and Maine Railroad laid track and provided railroad service between Boston and Portland, Maine. The Boston and Maine kept a natural monopoly over that run. How? Because the cost of building track and acquiring equipment was so great that it discouraged other investors from laying more track and gathering the rolling stock necessary to compete with the Boston and Maine.

For a more modern example, think of cable television. In most communities, the cost of erecting or leasing poles and stringing wires to carry the cable signal to every home that wants to use the service simply does not lend itself to competition.

For that reason, cable television companies operate as monopolies in most small towns and in localized neighborhoods in larger cities.

Natural monopolies in industries regarded vital to a community's welfare are described as public utilities. Examples of public utilities include local electric, gas, and water companies. Localities authorize natural monopolies to operate in their communities by granting them a franchise, or exclusive license to do business.

Natural monopolies may be publicly or privately owned. Either way, they are subject to extensive regulation by government agencies. These regulatory agencies spell out the kinds of service that needs to be provided and the rates that can be charged. In exchange for the burden of government oversight, however, firms operating as public franchises can be secure in the knowledge that competing firms will be legally prohibited from entering the industry.

THE ECONOMICS OF MONOPOLY POWER

Large, unregulated monopolies have all but disappeared from the U.S. economy. *Monopoly power* remains, however. This term refers to the ability of a group of firms to behave as if they were one big monopoly. The exercise of monopoly power by big business has been a controversial issue for many years. In examining the problem of monopoly power, we will (1) explain what it is, (2) describe its impact on output and prices, and (3) summarize governmental efforts to regulate it.

Measuring Monopoly Power: The Concentration Ratio

Strictly speaking, a monopoly exists when there is only one seller of a good or service. As a practical matter, however, most large firms operate in markets in which there is at least some competition.

Monopoly power is directly related to a firm's control over supply. If two or three firms control nearly all of an industry's output, they have a great deal of monopoly power. Selling new automobiles, for example, is highly competitive. But because a relatively few big companies control the supply of new automobiles, they alone determine total output and, therefore, price. However, where there are many competitive firms (none of which controls a large share of the market), monopoly power is not a factor.

As a way of measuring the extent to which monopoly power exists in imperfectly competitive markets, economists devised the *concentration ratio.* This number is the percentage of an industry's total output produced by its four largest firms. (See Table 7.1.) If an industry consists of four or fewer firms, its concentration ratio is equal to 100. This number indicates a high degree of monopoly power. In contrast, industries with a concentration ratio of 10 or less are unlikely to have monopoly power.

Some economists define oligopoly as an industry with a concentration ratio of 50 percent or more (that is, one in which 50 percent of the industry's output is in the hands of four or fewer corporations). For example, even though there are some 22 manufacturers of breakfast cereals, the industry has a concentration ratio of 85 percent. In other words, the four largest producers of breakfast cereals account for 85 percent of the industry's sales. Only 15 percent of the market remains to be shared by the remaining 18 or so processors. We can say, therefore, that the breakfast cereal industry (1) falls within our definition of an oligopoly and (2) exercises considerable monopoly power.

Similarly, economists generally classify industries with a concentration ratio of 25 percent or less as monopolistically competitive markets. With more than 5,000 manufacturers and a concentration ratio of 6 percent, the women's dress industry easily falls into this category.

TABLE 7.1   COMPETITION IN SELECTED INDUSTRIES

Industry	Concentration Ratio
Sugar refining	99%
Cameras and film	98%
Razor blades	98%
Chewing gum	97%
Household refrigerators	94%
Electric lightbulb	90%
Breakfast cereals	85%
Men's and boys' shirts	19%
Book publishing	17%
Ready-mix concrete	7%
Women's dresses	6%
Machine shops	2%

"Concentration Ratios," U.S. Census Bureau

Concentration ratios can sometimes be misleading. For instance, one might think that the camera and film industry in the United States (with a ratio of 98 percent) has enormous monopoly power. This is not the case, though, because the figure excludes the powerful Japanese and German camera and film companies that sell in the United States. Because of these foreign firms, the camera and film industry in the United States is actually quite competitive.

Near the opposite end of the scale is the ready-mix concrete industry with a concentration ratio of only 7 percent. Although no ready-mix firm dominates the national market, more often than not producers have considerable monopoly power in their local communities. Why? The reason is that mileage costs make it uneconomical for a customer to buy concrete from distant suppliers.

EFFECT OF MONOPOLY POWER ON OUTPUT AND PRICES

Under perfect competition, individual sellers cannot affect the market price. Sellers have the choice of either accepting the going price for their product or service or staying out of the market. If, for example, a person owns 100 shares of AT&T stock and wants to sell them on a day when the market price is $85, that person would have the option of selling anywhere from 0 to 100 shares at $85 per share.

Output and Prices in Monopolized Markets

We have said that in perfectly competitive markets, sellers are "price takers." That is, they must either take the equilibrium price ($85 per share in the AT&T example) or drop out of the market. Under monopoly conditions, the opposite is true: Sellers are "price makers." That is, because they are the only supplier of a product, monopolists can charge any price they want along the demand curve and adjust their output accordingly. As with any demand curve, the quantity demanded declines as the price increases. This will become clearer as we discuss how monopolies maximize profits.

How Monopolists Maximize Profits

Unlike sellers in competitive markets who can sell only at the market (or equilibrium) price, monopolists can look at the demand curve for their product and choose any price that they want. Why? Because they are the only sellers of that good or service. Buyers have to pay their price, or do without. What price then will monopolists select? The one that is the highest that buyers are willing to pay? The lowest? Neither. Like all sellers, monopolists try to *maximize* their profits. That is, they strive to select the price and level of output that yield them the greatest profit.

ABC Pharmaceuticals, Inc., holds the patent and, therefore, a monopoly on the manufacture of Itchaway. Itchaway claims to be the nation's most effective treatment for athlete's foot. After an extensive market survey, ABC's economists prepared an analysis of the demand for Itchaway, along with a breakdown of production costs. Their findings are summarized in Figure 7.1 and Table 7.2.

After studying the results of the market survey and the production data, ABC's management selected a selling price of $3 per can. Why did management choose this price? Table 7.2 shows that ABC's maximum profit—$169,000—corresponds to a price of $3 per can. Since ABC Pharmaceuticals is a monopoly, management can set production at any level it chooses. In this example, management determined that an output of 125,000 cans will result in the greatest profits.

The following year, ABC's patent on Itchaway expired. Hundreds of new producers entered the market. We can see in Figure 7.2 that as new producers entered the market, the equilibrium price dropped from $3 to $2 per can. At a price of $2 ABC can sell 275,000 cans. The graph illustrates the point that output is usually lower and prices are usually higher in a monopoly market than in a perfectly competitive market.

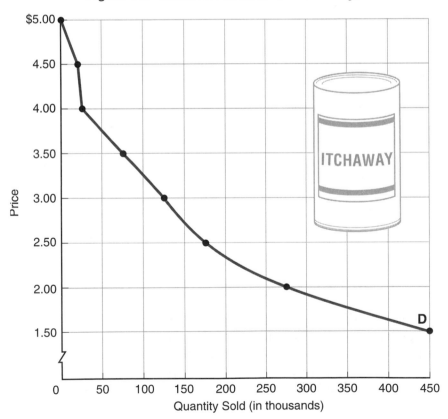

Figure 7.1 **Market Demand for Itchaway, I**

TABLE 7.2   ABC PHARMACEUTICALS PRICE-SALES ANALYSIS

At a price per can of	We could sell this number of cans	Gross income of	Minus costs of	Would leave us with a profit of
$5.00	5,000	$ 25,000	$ 60,000	−$ 35,000 (loss)
4.50	20,000	90,000	85,000	5,000
4.00	25,000	100,000	88,000	12,000
3.50	75,000	262,500	163,000	99,500
3.00	125,000	375,000	206,000	169,000
2.50	175,000	432,500	300,000	132,500
2.00	275,000	550,000	500,000	50,000
1.50	450,000	675,000	837,000	−$162,000 (loss)

Figure 7.2 **Market Demand for Itchaway, II**

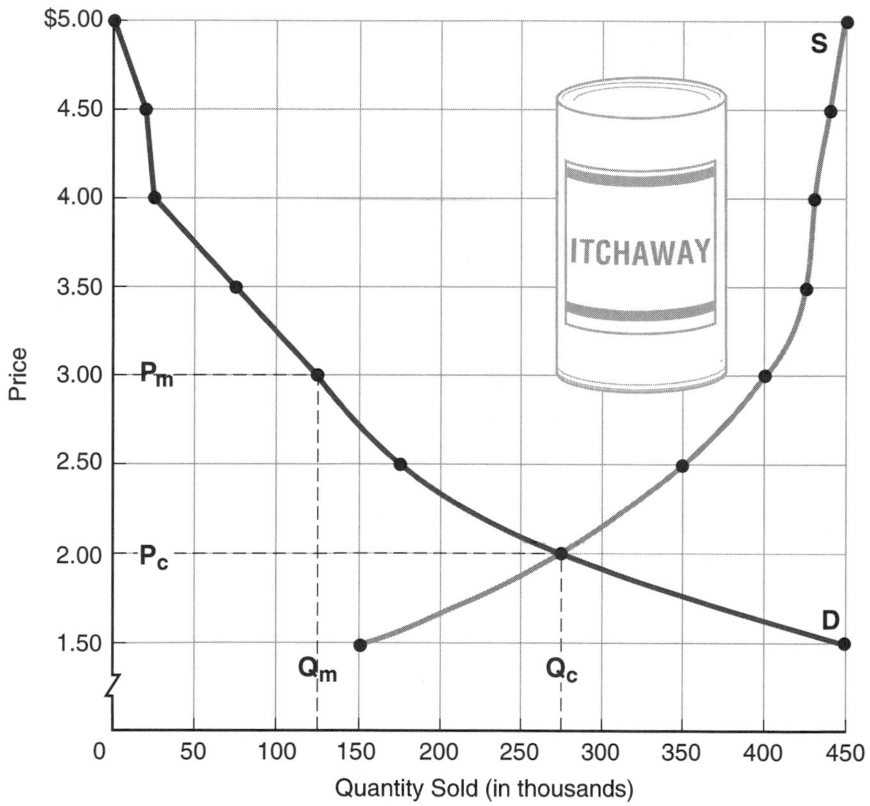

ABC Pharmaceuticals is a hypothetical company that we selected to illustrate how monopoly price is determined. A real-world example concerns a federal court's finding in a case against Microsoft Corporation.

MINI-READING

Maximizing Monopoly Profits at Microsoft

In 1999, a federal court found Microsoft, the world's largest software company, guilty of using its monopoly power to (1) limit competition and (2) harm consumers.

Competition was limited, the court said, because Microsoft was able to pressure computer manufacturers into buying and installing software programs in the computers that they sold—software that the manufacturers might not have wanted—or face the threat of not being licensed to install the popular Microsoft's Windows operating system in their new computers.

Consumers were harmed, the government argued, because its monopoly enabled Microsoft to impose a price nearly twice as high as it could have under competition.

The court put it this way: "a MICROSOFT study . . . reveals that the company could have (profitably) charged $49 for an upgrade to WINDOWS 98—but the study identified $89 as the *revenue-maximizing price,* and for that reason Microsoft opted for the higher price."

What did the court mean by the "revenue-maximizing price"?

BUSINESS COMBINATIONS, PAST AND PRESENT

An early form of business combination was the *pool,* an agreement between two or more firms to share the market for their products and to fix prices. A number of industries, including railroads, set up pools in the 1870s and 1880s, but pools became less popular in the 1890s. Since pools were created informally (and secretly), their agreements could not be enforced. If one or more member firms broke the rules by underselling the pool or invading another member's territory, the pool ceased to exist. Eventually, a new type of business combination emerged—the trust.

 ## Trusts

Standard Oil became the country's first *trust* (a large business monopoly whose shareholders place control of the firm in the hands of trustees). With its power to undersell other oil companies, Standard Oil was able to demand that independent firms sell out to them or face a price war they could not win. Most of these companies chose to sell. When they did, stockholders of the purchased companies turned their shares of stock over to the *trustees* of Standard Oil, the people who ran the corporation. In exchange, the former stockholders received "trust certificates" entitling them to a share of the profits in the form of dividends.

Oil was not the only 19th-century industry dominated by a trust. Trusts soon developed in other industries, including cottonseed oil, linseed oil, whiskey, sugar, lead, and ropes. By 1904, trusts controlled 50 percent or more of the production in each of 80 of the nation's largest industries. Public opposition to trusts soon resulted in actions by Congress and the courts. The **Sherman Antitrust Act** of 1890 and the **Clayton Act** of 1914 outlawed trusts that were "in restraint of trade." Rulings by several state courts made many trusts in their states illegal.

💨 Holding Companies

After trusts were declared illegal, *holding companies* became the most important means by which companies combined to reduce competition. A holding company is a corporation organized for the purpose of owning or "holding" a controlling interest in other corporations. Controlling interest is ownership or control of more than 50 percent of the voting stock of a corporation. In Figure 7.3, Companies A, B, and C are controlled by Holding Company X. If each company is worth $100,000 (as represented by 100,000 shares of stock at $1 per share), an investment of $50,001 (which we shall call $50,000) will give the purchaser control of the firm. With $150,000, therefore, Holding Company X will have acquired control of Companies A, B, and C.

Assume identical conditions for Holding Company Y and Companies D, E, and F, as shown in Figure 7.4 on page 148. We now have two holding companies, each with stock worth $150,000 that controls corporations whose value totals $300,000. Suppose now that another holding company is created and that it acquires control of Holding Company X for $75,000 and control of Holding Company Y for $75,000. Figure 7.5 shows that this new holding company, Z, has acquired control of corporations whose total value is $600,000.

We can see that control of Holding Company Z could be obtained with an investment of $75,000, and this would mean control of $600,000 worth of corporations. The technique of building up control of corporations through several levels of holding companies is called *pyramiding*. Companies X and Y,

Figure 7.3 **Holding Company X**

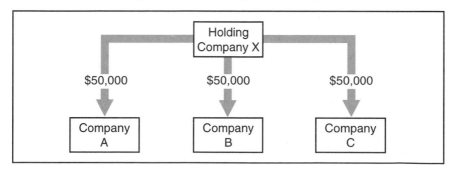

THE ROLE OF BUSINESS

Figure 7.4 **Holding Company Y**

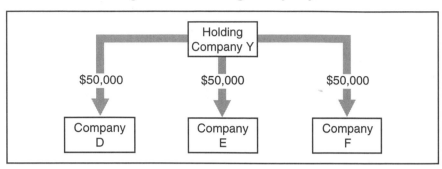

Figure 7.5 **Holding Company Z**

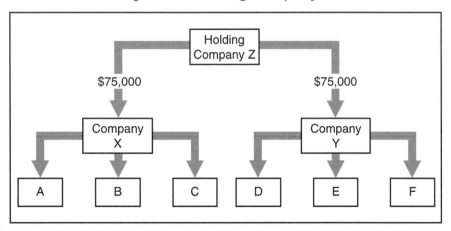

which control operating firms, are called "first-level holding companies." Company Z is called a "second-level holding company" because it holds control of first-level holding companies. In the case of public utilities, holding companies beyond the second level are illegal.

 Interlocking Directorates

When the same people sit on the boards of directors of several firms, these firms have *interlocking directorates*. In Figure 7.6, directors B, C, and D sit on the boards of Corporations X, Y, and Z.

While many kinds of interlocking directorates are illegal, others are legal and are used at times to coordinate the operations of two or more companies.

Figure 7.6 **Interlocking Directorate**

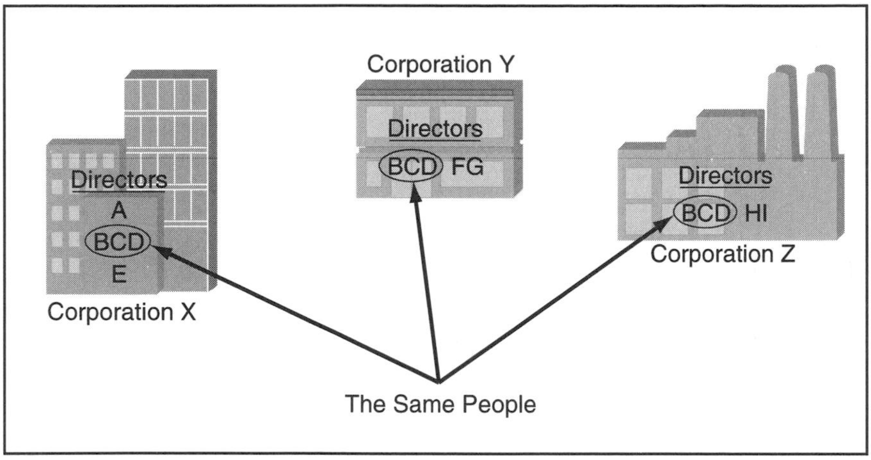

Corporation Y

Directors

BCD FG

Directors

A

BCD

E

Corporation X

Directors

BCD HI

Corporation Z

The Same People

Cartels

When independent firms formally agree to stop competing and work together to establish a monopoly, they have created a *cartel.* The two essential ingredients in a cartel are control of production levels and control of prices. By limiting production to an agreed, low level, the cartel creates a demand for a product. With increased demand, the price of the product goes up. This kind of collusion is generally illegal in the United States, but it is legal in most other countries. The world's best-known cartel is the **Organization of Petroleum Exporting Countries (OPEC)**. In the 1970s, OPEC was able to raise the world price of crude oil from $1.40 to $40 a barrel by severely limiting output.

Mergers

In recent decades, the most common form of business combination has been the *merger.* A merger occurs when one corporation absorbs another. The absorbed company may remain intact as a division of the parent firm or it may lose its identity completely. Sometimes an entirely new company is formed from a merger of two or more firms. Such was the case when the Lockheed Corporation and the Martin Marietta Corporation merged in March 1995 to form the Lockheed Martin Corporation. Mergers are generally classified as horizontal, vertical, or conglomerate.

HORIZONTAL MERGER.   In a *horizontal merger,* two or more companies engaged in the same line of business are brought under one management. The Lockheed Martin Corporation was an example of a horizontal merger because both Lockheed and Martin Marietta were producers of airplanes.

Figure 7.7 **Horizontal, Vertical, and Conglomerate Combinations**

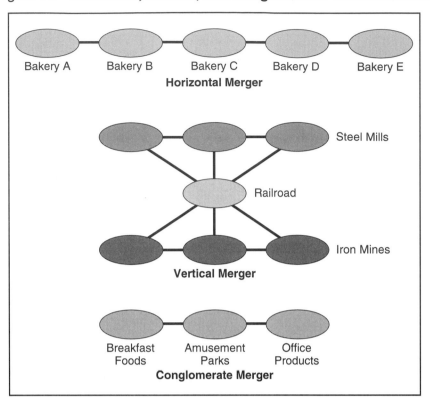

Horizontal mergers have been common in the banking industry in recent decades. One such merger occurred when the Fleet Financial Group (Fleet Bank) acquired NatWest Bank. NatWest had been a U.S. subsidiary of the National Westminster Bank of Britain. Another merger was that of J.P. Morgan & Co. with the Chase Manhattan Bank to form the company known as J.P. Morgan Chase & Co. Among other things, combinations like these serve to reduce competition and reduce overhead costs.

Competition is reduced because the firms that are combined were formerly contending with each other for business. Costs can be reduced because functions that were duplicated can now be combined. For example as a result of their merger with NatWest, Fleet hoped to trim 1,800 jobs and close 30 branches.

VERTICAL MERGER. In a *vertical merger,* two or more firms engaged in different stages of producing or marketing the same good or service combine under a single ownership. United States Steel, for example, owns its own iron mines, shipping companies, and steel mills.

CONGLOMERATE MERGER. A conglomerate merger combines companies producing unrelated products or services. For example, Philip Morris Companies owned one of the nation's largest tobacco firms and also owned the

Nabisco, Kraft, and Post food companies. (In 2002, Philip Morris's stockholders voted to change the corporation's name to the Altria Group.) Some businesspeople see conglomerate mergers as a way of spreading or cushioning the impact of hard times. When business is bad for one industry in a conglomerate, it may be better for another industry in the same conglomerate.

Other reasons for conglomerate mergers are to: (1) gain entry into a line of business at lower cost than if the acquiring company had to start fresh; (2) buy a company undervalued by the stock market at a bargain price; (3) take advantage of loopholes in the tax laws; (4) invest surplus funds; and (5) benefit from economies of size. Recent court decisions indicate that the federal government is more likely to approve conglomerate mergers than horizontal or vertical mergers because conglomerate mergers are least likely to reduce competition.

Downsizing

A major reason for business combinations is the expectation that the merged firms will be more efficient than the separate units. Often this is the case. Some businesses found out, however, that bigness is not always better and have broken up into smaller companies. For example, during the last years of the 20th century, UBS (Switzerland's largest bank) merged with SG Warburg (another bank) and PaineWebber (a large U.S. brokerage house). The new firm, calling itself UBS Warburg/UBS PaineWebber, saved money by firing workers whose jobs duplicated those of other workers in the enlarged firm. A business downturn during 2001–2003 forced the new firm to find ways to reduce the scope of its operations still further. As a result, the company in 2003 announced plans to lay off thousands more workers and assimilate all its operations under the UBS brand name.

Evolution of Federal Antitrust Legislation

We have seen that compared to perfect competition, imperfect competition leads to a less efficient use of resources and higher prices. For that reason, *antitrust laws* have been enacted to promote competition and limit the abuse of market power.

By the end of the 19th century, public opposition to "trusts" (as large industrial corporations were called) and their exercise of monopoly power led to demands for government regulation of businesses. Congress responded by enacting a series of antitrust laws. The most important of these were the following:

INTERSTATE COMMERCE ACT (1887).   This law restricted monopoly power of railroads by creating the nation's first regulatory agency, the **Interstate Commerce Commission (ICC)**. The ICC could sue railroads engaged in interstate commerce if it believed that the railroads refused to obey its regulations. The ICC continued to regulate the railroads and other means of transportation until 1996, when it was abolished by act of Congress. The ICC's duties were taken over by other federal agencies.

SHERMAN ANTITRUST ACT (1890).   The act declared that ". . . every contract, combination . . . or conspiracy in restraint of trade is illegal." It provided penalties for those who violated the law by conspiring to limit competition.

At first, the Sherman Act was weak, because

- it failed to specify exactly what constituted a "restraint of trade."
- it failed to create an agency responsible for administering the law.
- the U.S. Supreme Court in 1903 held that (1) only "unreasonable" trade restraints were illegal and (2) the law could be used to curb the power of labor unions as well as business trusts.

CLAYTON ANTITRUST AND FEDERAL TRADE COMMISSION ACTS (1914).   The laws sought to correct the weaknesses of the Sherman Act by

- describing specific practices as "restraints of trade"
- exempting labor unions from the provisions of the antitrust laws
- creating another regulatory agency, the **Federal Trade Commission (FTC)**. The FTC's responsibility is to promote competition, protect consumers, and enforce the antitrust laws. You will learn more about the work of the FTC on page 243.

ROBINSON-PATMAN ACT (1936).   This law sought to protect small stores from unfair competition by chain stores and other large retailers. The **Robinson-Patman Act** required wholesalers to offer the same discounts to both large and small retailers, unless the discounts could be justified by lower costs.

CELLER-KEFAUVER ANTIMERGER ACT (1950).   The **Celler-Kefauver Antimerger Act** prohibited mergers that would result in the creation of a monopoly.

Why Has Monopoly Power Been Restricted?

Except for legal monopolies (such as utilities), monopolies are outlawed in the United States. This prohibition has been the result of the following accusations against monopolies.

MONOPOLIES RAISE PRICES.   Prices are higher in industries in which monopoly power is exercised than they are in competitive markets. The only limitation on a monopolist's ability to set prices is the ease with which buyers can find substitute products. If the public can easily do without the product, demand will quickly fall as prices rise. If, however, the product is a necessity for which there are no adequate substitutes, buyers will be under greater pressure to pay the price asked.

"It's enough to make you believe in reincarnation!"

Renault, *Sacramento Bee*/Rothco Cartoons.

MONOPOLIES REDUCE OUTPUT AND LIVING STANDARDS. Monopolists set prices by adjusting output to match the demand for their product. Since monopoly prices are higher than prices would be in a competitive market, output is lower. In this way, monopolies reduce everyone's standard of living because fewer goods are available. When consumers must pay more for these goods, they have less money to spend on other things.

MONOPOLIES ARE INEFFICIENT AND WASTEFUL. Since monopolies do not have to worry about competition, they are under less pressure to reduce costs or to increase productivity. In this way, they waste human resources, capital resources, and natural resources.

MONOPOLIES ARE INSENSITIVE TO CONSUMER DEMAND. In a free market economic system, firms do their best to outperform the competition by giving consumers what they want, at the lowest possible prices. Where there is no competition, however, sellers can offer their wares to consumers on a take-it-or-leave-it basis.

ECONOMIC ISSUE

Government Regulations— Why the Controversy?

QUESTION: What do the airline, electric utility, and telecommunications (telegraph, cable, telephone, radio, and television) industries have in common?

ANSWER: All were government-regulated industries that have since been deregulated.

Certain industries require such a large investment of capital that one company operating alone can supply the entire market at a lower cost per unit than can two or more competing firms. For a local cable television company, for example, the cost of erecting or leasing poles and stringing wires to carry the cable signal to every home that wants to use the service is so great that it rarely makes sense for a second firm to duplicate the effort.

Natural monopolies in industries regarded vital to a community's welfare are described as public utilities. Examples of public utilities include local electric, gas, and water companies.

For many years, critics of regulatory agencies argued that by guaranteeing profits and supervising operations, government robbed regulated industries of the incentives needed to innovate and improve service, and to reduce prices. The solution, as they saw it, was to allow competing firms to enter the formerly protected markets. In time, the calls were heeded. Starting in 1978 and continuing through the 1990s, the airline, telecommunications, and electric power industries were deregulated. (*Deregulation* is the lifting of government regulations to allow for competition and the forces of supply and demand to function more freely.)

In each instance, opponents of deregulation warned that the removal of government oversight would result in poorer service, higher prices, and concentration of power in a handful of firms within the industry. By the early years of the 21st century, it appeared that both sides were partly right and partly wrong in their predictions. The controversy between those opposing deregulation and those in favor continues.

In the airline industry, competition has reduced operating costs and increased productivity. As a result, airline fares on many of the most popular (and competitive) routes have declined. But service into and out of the smaller and less popular destinations has become more expensive than it was before deregulation. This may be because so many airlines whose routes included small town America were bought out by the major airlines. Indeed, barely a third of the 292 U.S. airlines with passenger service in 1978 are still operating.

On the one hand, deregulation in the telecommunications industry has resulted in better equipment, improved services, and many more options for telephone, cable television, broadband (Internet), and satellite subscribers. On the other hand, local service is still run by monopolies that (in the absence of regulation) have made some of those services costlier than ever.

Prior to 1992, government regulated electric utilities. Typically, electric companies generated electricity and delivered it to their customers at rates determined by the regulating authority. That year, in response to the argument that competition among electrical generating companies would result in lower prices and more efficient use of energy, Congress enacted the **National Energy Policy Act**. It allowed out-of-town power companies to compete for the sale of electricity generated by them to local electric utilities.

Here again, controversy rages between supporters and detractors of deregulation. Those favoring deregulation point to Pennsylvania, where the cost of electricity to consumers decreased substantially.

Those opposed prefer to talk about California's experience with deregulation. There (according to the **Federal Energy Regulatory Commission**) suppliers of electrical power manipulated output in such a way as to create shortages, inflate prices, and inflict blackouts on consumers.

MONOPOLIES ENGAGE IN UNFAIR COMPETITION.   Monopolists prevent other firms from entering the market and destroy those already there. Powerful companies sell their products at a loss so as to force their competitors into bankruptcy. Then, with the competition eliminated, prices are restored to their original level or to a higher one.

MONOPOLIES HELP BRING ON RECESSIONS.   Monopolies are often guilty of *price rigidity*—the maintenance of prices at unnecessarily high levels even when demand is declining. But the only way to maintain prices in the face of falling demand is to reduce output. This often leads to job layoffs, unemployment, and recession.

MONOPOLIES THREATEN OUR POLITICAL SYSTEM.   Big companies (some of which are monopolies) spend millions of dollars on public relations, lobbying, and supporting politicians and political parties. In these ways, large firms seek (and sometimes get) the passage of national and state laws favorable to their special interests. Politicians who get financial support from big businesses may feel more indebted to these companies than to their constituents.

Is "Bigness" Necessarily Bad?

Some people believe that the antitrust laws may have gone too far in limiting the ability of U.S. firms to compete in global markets. Further, they argue, big is not necessarily bad. Their arguments are:

ECONOMIES OF SCALE.   The economies of scale resulting from mass production serve to raise the country's standard of living. Mergers often result in

What disadvantages of monopolies does this cartoonist illustrate?

Dredge © *Punch*/Rothco Cartoons.

reduced costs, increased productivity, and technological innovation. Thus, consumers benefit in terms of new and improved products at lower costs.

INTERNATIONAL COMPETITION. Antitrust laws impair the ability of U.S. firms to compete in international markets. These firms may be prosecuted and found guilty of violating U.S. antitrust laws for their activities abroad. Thus, U.S. antitrust laws put American firms at a disadvantage in competing abroad with foreign firms that do not have to worry about such laws.

Antitrust laws also curtail the ability of U.S. firms to compete with foreign companies in the United States. Although the courts penalize U.S. companies for growing too big, in some cases the foreign companies with whom they are competing are even bigger. Critics of antitrust laws argue that domestic firms should be as free to compete with foreign oligopolies as the foreign companies are free to compete with U.S. firms.

EXPENSE OF ANTITRUST WORK. Many of the antitrust cases prosecuted by the U.S. government cost too much, take too long, and should not have been started in the first place. These cases often continue for ten years or more, can cost millions of dollars to prosecute, and are sometimes dropped or end up with the government's defeat.

EFFECT ON CONSUMERS. Even when the government does win, it is not clear that the public benefits. As a result of an antitrust action in 1984, the nation's largest corporation, the American Telephone and Telegraph Company (AT&T), sold off its 22 local telephone companies. Some people argue that consumers are now paying more for their local telephone service than when it was all provided by AT&T.

BIG BUSINESS GROWTH IS NATURAL. The population of the United States, our government, and labor unions are all bigger than they were when the major antitrust laws were enacted. Moreover, these large power blocs offset the power of big business. For example, big labor unions limit the power of big businesses to set wage rates for workers in their employ. Thus, the powerful giant automobile, steel, and rubber industries must all bargain with equally powerful labor unions and with one another.

BIG BUSINESS BENEFITS SMALL BUSINESS. Small companies feed off the large companies and have actually increased in number rather than disappeared as a result of the growth of big business. For example, consider the vast number of auto dealerships, auto supply stores, and service stations that thrive because of the existing giant auto companies.

S U M M A R Y

In a theoretical situation of perfect competition, prices are set in the marketplace by supply and demand. Conditions of perfect competition rarely exist, and most markets fall somewhere between perfect competition and monopoly. This imperfect competition can be further divided into monopolistic competition and oligopoly. Oligopolists rely mainly on product differentiation to set prices. The ability of an oligopoly to set prices depends on its monopoly power in the market as measured by concentration ratio. The monopolist price is not necessarily the highest price a firm can get but is the price that will return the maximum profit.

Monopolists have resorted to various organizations to reduce competition, including trusts, interlocking directorates, cartels, holding companies, and mergers. Because of negative effects associated with monopoly power, Congress has passed antitrust laws to limit this power and to encourage competition. Some people argue, however, that large corporations help the economy and that antitrust laws may have gone too far in limiting the ability of U.S. firms to compete in a global market.

Government takes an active role in limiting the abuses of imperfect competition. Antitrust laws have been enacted to break up monopolies, to prevent monopolies from forming, and to prevent firms from engaging in practices that restrain competition.

REVIEWING THE CHAPTER

BUILDING VOCABULARY

Match each term in Column A with its definition in Column B.

Column A

1. monopoly
2. copyright
3. monopolistic competition
4. product differentiation
5. oligopoly
6. concentration ratio
7. antitrust law
8. natural monopoly
9. patent
10. deregulate

Column B

a. remove a government regulation
b. percentage of an industry's total output produced by its four largest firms
c. a market in which a single firm can satisfy demand more efficiently than competing firms
d. a market that has only one supplier
e. a market that has only a few suppliers
f. efforts to give buyers the impression that virtually identical products are different
g. a government grant of legal control over reproduction of a literary, musical, or artistic work
h. a market with many sellers offering similar products that the buyers believe differ
i. an exclusive right given to market an invention
j. an act that prohibits a business monopoly

UNDERSTANDING WHAT YOU HAVE READ

1. Prices are usually lowest for a product when it is produced by (*a*) only one company (*b*) many competing companies (*c*) a few very large companies (*d*) a public utility.

2. In setting their selling price, monopolists select the price that (*a*) will maximize their profit (*b*) is the highest price they can get for their product (*c*) is determined by consumer demand (*d*) is determined by both supply and demand.

3. Monopolistic competition takes place when (*a*) there are only a few buyers for a product (*b*) only two or three firms manufacture a product (*c*) many firms sell a similar product (*d*) there is no competition among firms selling similar products.

4. Product differentiation enables businesses to (*a*) charge more than they would under perfect competition (*b*) set prices as they would under conditions of monopoly (*c*) improve the quality of their product (*d*) produce products completely different from those of their competitors.

5. Patents and copyrights are similar in that both (*a*) provide government with important sources of revenue (*b*) are issued by the boards of directors of corporations (*c*) last forever (*d*) grant the holder a legal monopoly.

6. In its effort to expand, ABC Pharmaceuticals acquired the stores of two of its competitors in the manufacture of products for the treatment of athlete's foot. In this way, ABC Pharmaceuticals was building a (*a*) horizontal combination (*b*) vertical combination (*c*) conglomerate combination (*d*) circular combination.

7. Business was so brisk for ABC Pharmaceuticals that its management bought a box-manufacturing company. This purchase enabled ABC to manufacture its own packaging materials. The new company was a (*a*) horizontal combination (*b*) vertical combination (*c*) conglomerate combination (*d*) circular combination.

8. A few months ago, ABC Pharmaceuticals was acquired by one of the nation's largest producers of breakfast cereals. The new company was a (*a*) horizontal combination (*b*) vertical combination (*c*) conglomerate combination (*d*) circular combination.

9. Interlocking directorates are formed when one company (*a*) is absorbed by another (*b*) holds controlling shares of stock in other companies (*c*) has representatives on the boards of directors of competing firms (*d*) absorbs another company.

10. The federal government has attempted to regulate monopolies chiefly in order to (*a*) eliminate big business in the United States (*b*) reduce the number of public utilities (*c*) encourage competition (*d*) increase the number of small businesses.

THINKING CRITICALLY

1. In Elmwood, all music stores charge the same price for their CDs. Competition, however, is quite brisk, and the stores frequently advertise on the radio. (*a*) Since all the stores are charging the same prices for their merchandise, what techniques might each one adopt to differentiate its products and services from the others? (*b*) What kind of competition does this illustrate? (*c*) Advocates of other economic systems have argued

that it is wasteful for firms to compete in the sale of identical products. Give *two* arguments to counter this point of view.

2. Big businesses have developed a number of strategies to combine and coordinate the activities of what had formerly been independent firms. In the past, these strategies included pools and trusts and, more recently, holding companies and mergers.

   a. Explain how *each* of these business combinations may reduce competition and enable powerful firms to control prices and increase profits.

   b. How might it be argued that business combinations enable firms to increase their economies of scale, reduce their production costs, and thus reduce prices to consumers?

   c. Explain why you think that "big business" in the United States today is, or is not, too big.

3. Which *one* of the following involves the most efficient use of natural resources? Explain your answer.

   a. A city with one bus company.

   b. The same city with two bus companies providing service to the same neighborhoods.

SKILLS: Interpreting a Table

Refer to Table 7.1 on page 142 to answer the following questions.

1. (*a*) Identify the *three* industries with the greatest amount of competition among those listed. (*b*) Identify the *three* industries with the least amount of competition among those listed.

2. With reference to *one* of the industries you identified in question 1a, why do you think this industry is so much more competitive than others?

3. With reference to *one* of the industries you identified in question 1b, what would account for the lack of competition in this industry?

4. "Concentration ratios can be a misleading measure of competition or the lack of competition." Explain this statement.

EXPLORING CURRENT ISSUES

The **Telecommunications Act of 1996** deregulated the radio industry. The consequences of deregulation are still being debated. According to the critics, the deregulation has allowed a handful of economically and politically powerful corporations to gain control of the radio industry. In 2003, three companies owned half the radio stations in America. The largest of these, Clear Channel, operated 1,240 stations reaching 100 million listeners. Critics of this consolidation claimed that the American public was left with less diversity in programming and exposure to few, if any, political ideas that conflict with those held by the major operators.

Not so, said those who have favored the 1996 Act. They claimed that consolidation of radio stations led to more, not less diversity in programming. They pointed to towns like Atlantic City, New Jersey, where listeners could tune in to a selection of 14 formats (country, adult contemporary, top 40, rock, ethnic, etc.), up from 10 in 1996, and Little Rock, Arkansas, where formats increased from 11 to 14 between 1996 and 2003.

- Has the deregulation of radio benefited or harmed the nation?
- Where do you stand on this issue?

Before answering the question, you will want to learn more about the issue. You can do so on-line by using a search engine to uncover facts and opinions on the consequences of the deregulation of the radio industry. Or you might want to visit a library to consult magazine articles like the following:

- "Free the Airwaves," *Forbes,* April 15, 2002, p. 106.
- "Empire of the Air," *The Nation,* January 13, 2003, p. 28.

UNIT III

THE ROLE OF LABOR

CHAPTER 8
The Labor Force in Our Economy

OVERVIEW

Assume that you are about to graduate from high school and are planning to spend at least the next four years at a college. It is not going to be easy, and it is going to cost you and/or your family a lot of money. So you might think, "Will it be worth it? Will I be able to find work in my chosen field, and, if so, how much can I expect to earn?" Sure, you have heard of athletes signing multimillion dollar contracts, but what are your chances of earning anything like that?

As you think about the kind of a *career* (lifelong work) that you might want, it soon becomes clear that you need to become more knowledgeable about the world of work. You need to become more familiar with the overall labor market. In this chapter, we will discuss this market and how and why it is changing. We will discuss the forces that determine an individual's earnings. We will then examine what the best job opportunities are today and what they are most likely to become in the coming years. Finally, we will look further at what factors to consider in choosing a career.

 ## LABOR FORCE TRENDS

The *labor force* (sometimes called the workforce) is made up of all persons 16 years of age or older who are either working or looking for work. In 2004, the size of the labor force in the United States was approximately 148 million people, or about half the total U.S. population of 295 million people. Significant changes are taking place in the labor force, and present trends will probably continue for years. Since eventually you will likely enter the job market as a full-time employee, you may want to think about these changes as you plan your career.

The labor force changes as the country's population changes and as the kinds of work that people do change. As we examine how the population is changing, we will also study changes in the labor force and in particular occupations.

🌀 The U.S. Population Is Growing

As indicated in Figure 8.1, the U.S. population has been growing for a long time. As the country's population has grown, so, too, has its labor force. One reason is that an increase in population usually means that more people are looking for jobs. In addition, an increase in population often leads to the growth of the economy. As the economy grows, it creates more jobs.

The population of the United States is expected to increase by over 24 million during the 2000–2010 period. While this represents a slightly faster growth rate than during the previous decade (1990–2000), it is considerably slower than it was in the 1980–1990 period. Therefore, according to most estimates, as the population growth declines, the labor force growth rate will also decline from almost 18 percent during the 1980–1990 period to less than 12 percent in the period 2000–2010.

Along with the growth in the size of the labor force, we can expect to see an increase in the demand for goods and services. More people will want and need more things. The demand for workers is directly related to consumer demand for goods and services. Most likely, more workers will be needed to help produce the increased goods and services that consumers demand.

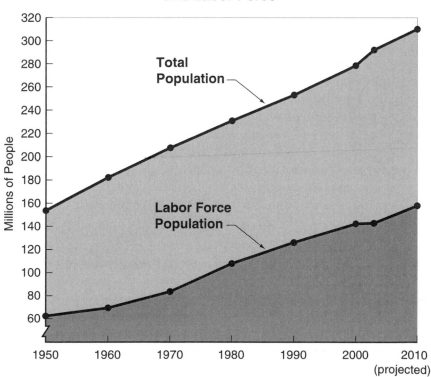

Figure 8.1 **Increases in Size of the U.S. Population and Labor Force**

⚡ The Population Is Getting Older

As the average age of the U.S. population gets older, so too does the average age of the labor force. The age group 55–64, for example, is expected to increase by 11 million persons over the 2000–2010 period. This increase is greater than for any other age group. It is anticipated that the participation of this age group in the labor force will increase from 12.9 percent in the 1990–2000 period to 16.9 percent in the 2000–2010 period. However, the young adult population, ages 16–24, is also expected to grow and by 2010 is projected to be 16.5 percent of the labor force. The 35–44 age group is the only group expected to decrease as a percent of the labor force. As a result, the larger group, ages 25–54, which represented 71 percent of the labor force in 2000, is projected to represent only 66.6 percent by 2010. The overall picture, therefore, is of an older population and an older labor force. At the same time, more young people age 16–24, including those just completing high school or college, will be working or looking for work.

Current estimates are that those 85 years and older will increase about four times as fast as the general population through 2010. This increase, in turn, is bound to add to the demand for workers in the health-care industry, already one of the fastest-growing industries in the economy. Individuals 85 and over are more likely to require medication and medical treatment than are younger persons. Some elderly will require institutional care. Doctors, nurses, health aides, and other health-care workers will be in greater demand to service the growing numbers of elderly persons.

EARLIER RETIREMENT AGE.   Although Americans are living longer, people are retiring at a younger age. The *median retirement age* (half fall above and half fall below this level) was 66.9 for men and 67.7 for women in 1950. It dropped to 62.7 for men and 62.9 for women in 1994, and it is expected to drop still further—to 61.5 for men and 61.0 for women—by 2010. Sometimes firms offer older workers early retirement, with benefits, in order to reduce the number of workers on their payroll, or to replace senior workers with young workers who receive lower salaries and fewer benefits.

Changes in retirement patterns of the population affect employment opportunities. As workers retire from the labor force, job opportunities open up for younger people.

⚡ The Population Is Becoming More Varied

Increasing numbers of women are members of the labor force. In 1979, 42 percent of the labor force was women. This percentage grew to 46 percent in 2000 and is projected to increase to 47.9 percent by 2010. In greater numbers than ever before, women have gained top management positions and jobs that once were considered almost exclusively "men's work."

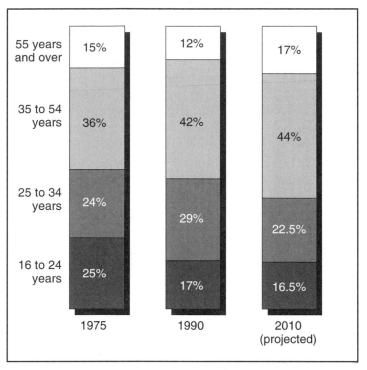

Figure 8.2 **Age Distribution of the U.S. Labor Force**

	1975	1990	2010 (projected)
55 years and over	15%	12%	17%
35 to 54 years	36%	42%	44%
25 to 34 years	24%	29%	22.5%
16 to 24 years	25%	17%	16.5%

Which age groups in the labor force are expected to increase between 1990 and 2010?

Nonwhite workers are also becoming a larger part of the labor force. Figure 8.3 on page 166 describes some projected labor-force changes.

 # THE LABOR FORCE BY OCCUPATION

The composition of the labor force may be examined in terms of the kinds of work that people do for a living. As the labor force has grown, occupations have changed. At one time, the terms white-collar worker and blue-collar worker were used to designate occupational categories. White-collar workers were those in the professional, technical, clerical, sales, and managerial categories. They got this name because in the 19th and early 20th centuries, it was customary for workers employed in those occupations to wear a white collar to work. Blue-collar workers were those who had craft, operative, and laboring jobs. Workers in those occupations customarily wore blue denim or a similar shirt to work. It eventually became apparent that these designations had become obsolete. Workers began to dress as they wished. Moreover, new, clearer categories

Figure 8.3 **Projected Shifts in the Racial Composition of the Labor Force**

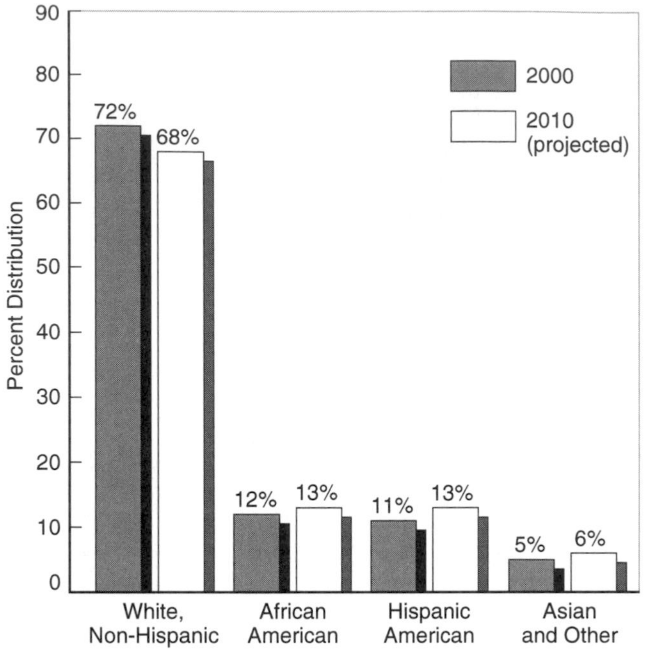

Source: U.S. Bureau of Labor Statistics

of workers became more popular. The Bureau of Labor Statistics currently uses the terms goods-producing industries and services-producing industries to categorize occupations.

Most New Jobs Are in the Services- Producing Industries

For some time there has been a shift from goods-producing industries to services-producing industries. Of the 22 million new jobs projected over the 2000–2010 period, 20.2 million (92 percent) will be in the services-producing industries.

Goods-producing industries include manufacturing, agriculture, forestry, fishing, and mining. The overall growth in this sector is projected to be approximately 1.8 million new jobs (8 percent) in the 2000–2010 period.

Services-producing industries include finance, insurance, and real estate; government; services (such as business, health, and social services); transportation, communications, and utilities; travel and hospitality; and wholesale and retail trade.

These trends are expected to continue. Services-producing industries will account for much of the job growth that is projected to the year 2010. They are

Figure 8.4 **Fastest-Growing Occupations, 2000–2010**

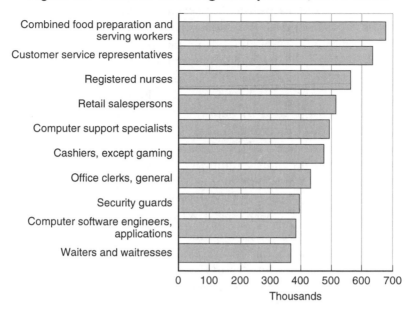

expected to provide almost nine out of ten new jobs by the year 2010. Farm-workers will remain a small part of the workforce.

In view of these trends, consider the following factors as you begin to make your plans for the future.

Occupations Are Changing

We know that in the past, some industries grew more rapidly than others. Very likely, some industries will grow more rapidly than others in the future as well. Figure 8.4 illustrates occupations where the largest numerical increases in employment are likely to be.

The Role of Technology

Technological revolution is a term used to describe the rapid changes in ways of producing goods and services. In recent decades, electronic machines have reduced the amount of human labor needed to produce an equal output. This revolution in technology is occurring worldwide. Examples of changing technology include the use of computers to perform many tasks in offices and the use of robots or other automated machinery in factories. Satellites, microwave equipment, and fiber optic wires allow people to communicate more rapidly with one another than before. You probably know many more examples of technological changes.

The technological revolution has resulted in both losses and increases in jobs.

LOSSES OF JOBS.   New technologies and work processes can improve the quality of workers' jobs as well as the services they provide. They can also eliminate jobs, render some skills obsolete, and dilute the services provided to the public. In automobile-manufacturing plants, for example, robots have replaced workers to weld, paint, and test automobile frames. Fewer autoworkers are now needed to build the same number of automobiles as before. In many factories, bottling plants, and oil refineries, similar changes have taken place. Automated machines operated by handfuls of technicians in each plant produce what had previously required hundreds of workers. In offices, automated phone systems, photocopiers, fax machines, and upgraded computers provide services to employers previously requiring hours and hours of human labor. Internet services speed up the processing of driver's licenses and car registration and unemployment claims and, in the process, require fewer government clerks than before. The increased use of ATM machines and Internet banking reduces the number of bank tellers required to handle customers.

In the period 1991–1995, the 400 largest U.S. corporations reduced employment by 4 million. General Motors and IBM, facing stiff competition and poor sales, restructured their organizations and introduced improved technology. These two giant firms were able to *downsize* by reducing the number of manufacturing plants, offices, and workers. For example, in the early 1980s, General Motors employed 369,000 people at 130 manufacturing facilities to make 4.5 million vehicles a year. After downsizing in the early 1990s, GM reduced its workforce to about 250,000 people at 120 facilities to produce roughly the same number of vehicles. Similarly, IBM went from 373,000 people at 34 manufacturing facilities to produce computers and computer software in the 1980s to 225,000 at 22 manufacturing facilities in 1995.

One of the proposed solutions to job losses caused by automation is to set up job-retraining programs. What is the cartoonist's view of these programs?

ROB ROGERS Reprinted by permission of United Features Syndicate, Inc.

As the U.S. economy improved during the period 1995–2000, layoffs averaged about 5.6 milliion workers a year. Faced with a recession in the United States in 2001, average annual layoffs increased to approximately 8.4 million.

GAINS IN JOBS.   While the technological revolution has displaced workers in some industries, it has created new jobs for other workers. Although 4 million jobs were lost among the 400 largest U.S. firms in the period 1991–1995, employment increased by 6 million nationwide in the same period. Many of these jobs were in new industries. The demand for highly specialized workers was so great in some industries that employers had difficulty filling jobs.

Highly trained people are needed to design computers and other automated machines. Other educated individuals are needed to develop the software that operates such complex equipment. And trained workers are needed to operate, maintain, and service computers and computer-operated equipment.

The Emphasis on Education Will Continue

The *educational attainment* (years of schooling) of the average worker has been increasing. In 1975, 67 percent of workers between the ages of 25 and 64 had completed only four years or fewer of high school. By 1990, this number had dropped to 53 percent. During the same period, workers with four or more years of college increased from 18 to 26 percent. High school graduates are more likely to go to college today than in the past. Whereas in 1970, 52 percent of high school graduates enrolled in college, 63 percent of high school graduates in 2000 enrolled in college. College graduates age 25 and over earn nearly twice as much as workers who do not go to college but stop after receiving a high school diploma. Education is essential to a high-paying job. Of the 50 highest paying jobs, all but two—air traffic controllers and nuclear power reactor operators—require a college education.

High school dropouts who manage to find jobs (unemployment rates are highest for this group) most likely earn the least. Also, they have the poorest opportunities for advancement. The slogan "It pays to stay in school" is true, as we can see in Table 8.1.

TABLE 8.1   WEEKLY EARNINGS AND UNEMPLOYMENT RATES BY EDUCATIONAL ATTAINMENT, 2000

Educational Attainment	Median Weekly Earnings	Unemployment Rate
College graduate	$1,342	1.8 percent
Some college	849	2.8 "
High school graduate	687	3.5 "
Less than high school	418	6.2 "

Even though an occupation is expected to grow rapidly, it may provide fewer openings than a slower growing but larger occupation. For example, *paralegals* (assistants to lawyers) is a category that is expected to increase by 33.2 percent between 2000 and 2010. Retail sales workers, by contrast, are expected to increase by only 12.4 percent in this period. Neverthe-less, in 2004, there were slightly more than 4 million retail sales workers and fewer than 60 thousand paralegals. Thus, a 12.4 percent increase in the retail trade came to more than 508,000 workers, while an 33.2 percent increase in paralegals came to only 19,900 workers.

 # WHY DO SOME JOBS PAY MORE THAN OTHERS?

If all people and jobs were exactly alike, there would be no differences in wages. We know, though, that the labor force is not homogeneous. People and jobs are different, and some jobs pay more than others. This is true for those in the same occupation as well as for individuals in different occupations. For example, some of the country's best athletes have become wealthy, while other athletes cannot earn a living at their sport. Newspaper accounts tell of multi-million-dollar contracts signed by the nation's outstanding football, baseball, basketball, and tennis players. We do not hear similar tales about outstanding volleyball, water polo, or badminton champions. Regardless of their ability, those athletes are unpaid or paid relatively little.

What is true of professional athletics applies to every other occupation as well: some workers get paid more than others. Why is this so? Why do physicians, lawyers, and engineers earn more, on the average, than secretaries, cashiers, and child-care workers? (See Table 8.2.) To explain these differences, economists refer to (1) the market forces of supply and demand and (2) nonmarket forces.

> **TABLE 8.2   MEDIAN WEEKLY EARNINGS BY OCCUPATION, 2001**

Lawyers	$1,398
Physicians	1,258
Chemical engineers	1,246
Aerospace engineers	1,142
Computer analysts	1,100
Rail workers	947
Aircraft mechanics	791
Secondary school teachers	774
Electricians	714
Secretaries	479
Waiters and waitresses	369
Janitors and cleaners	365
Apparel sales workers	336
Cashiers	299
Child-care workers	246

Source: Bureau of Labor Statistics

Market Forces in Action: How Supply and Demand Affect Wages

Every Sunday during the football season, millions of fans are glued to their television sets or are at stadiums watching their favorite professional teams compete. Professional baseball, basketball, soccer, tennis, golf, and hockey also have many fans. We can say that there is a great demand on the part of the public to see outstanding athletes perform. Yet only a tiny number of athletes are capable of making the grade in these sports. The supply of and demand for outstanding athletes create a market situation that pays high wages.

What is true for athletes also applies to other jobs and professions. Physicians earn more than emergency medical technicians, and plumbers earn more than individuals in retail apparel sales. We can use our knowledge of supply and demand (as described in Chapter 3) to explain these differences in earnings.

Figure 8.5 on page 172 compares the market for plumbers with the market for retail apparel sales workers. The supply of these salespeople is far greater than the supply of plumbers (as anyone knows who tries to find a plumber in an emergency). Because of the demand for plumbers, the average hourly wage paid plumbers is greater than that of retail apparel sales workers.

The hourly wage for plumbers in the illustration is around $18 per hour at point e, the equilibrium price. At this intersection, the supply of plumbers willing to accept $18 per hour is equal to the demand for plumbers at that wage rate. In the other part of the graph, we note that 38,000 individuals are willing to accept a wage of $8 per hour as retail apparel salespeople. At a wage above the equilibrium price (e_1), the demand for sales workers would be less than the

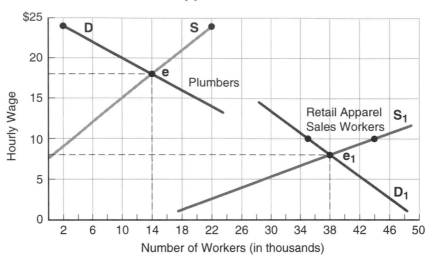

Figure 8.5 **Supply and Demand for Plumbers and Retail Apparel Sales Workers**

supply available. At a wage below the equilibrium price, not enough sales workers would be willing to work.

So far we have been discussing wage rates in the same terms used in Chapter 3 (supply and demand). Supply and demand as applied to people, however, requires further explanation.

What Factors Affect the Demand for Labor?

The term "demand for labor" is the number of workers that a firm will hire at a particular wage. This, in turn, depends on (1) the demand for the firm's products and services and (2) the productivity of each additional worker in the firm.

DEMAND FOR GOODS AND SERVICES.   If consumers buy less of a good or service, the demand for workers in that industry will decline. In the 1970s, for example, U.S. consumers switched from buying domestic-made television sets and radios in favor of those made in Japan. As a result, the number of workers that the U.S. consumer electronics producers were willing to hire at any price declined. Or, as economists might say, the demand for workers in the consumer electronics industry declined. This is illustrated graphically in Figure 8.6.

When consumers buy more of a good or service, the demand for workers who produce that item or service increases. Suppose that millions of people suddenly become fans of water polo. Increased consumer demand to follow the sport would lead to an increase in the demand for professional water polo players. Other things being equal, increased demand for players results in an increase in the wages paid to those athletes. In terms of supply and demand curves, we say that the demand curve shifts to the right.

Figure 8.6 **Effect of Reduction in Consumer Demand on Employment in Consumer Electronics Industry**

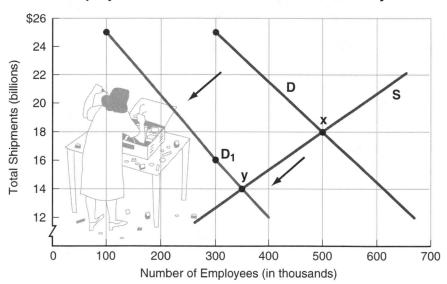

Fewer workers are needed to produce the smaller quantity of electronic goods. In this hypothetical illustration, consumer electronics industry output is represented by curve S. With consumer demand at levels represented by D, the industry employed 500,000 workers to produce and ship $18 billion worth of goods (see point x). When consumer demand declined from D to D_1, production fell to $14 billion, and the workforce was reduced to 350,000 (see point y).

The number of workers that a firm hires (or fires) depends on a firm's expected sales and output. As more goods and services are demanded, the demand for labor needed to produce those goods and services increases. As fewer goods and services are demanded, the demand for workers to produce these goods and services decreases. The demand for labor is called a *derived demand* because the demand for goods and services being produced (the primary factor) influences the number of workers employed (the derived or secondary factor).

PRODUCTIVITY.   The second factor affecting the demand for labor is the productivity of each additional worker hired. An employer can afford to pay a new worker no more than what the worker adds to the firm's income. For example, if the addition of one worker will add $60 in income per day, the employer can afford to pay that worker any wage up to $60 daily. (For this example, a worker's wage includes taxes, insurance, and all other expenses associated with hiring and keeping that worker.) A wage above that figure will result in a loss to the firm. If, because of improved technology, this worker was later able to produce $100 worth of additional income daily, the firm could then afford to pay a wage up to $100 per day.

Productivity sets only the upper limits to the amount of wages that workers are likely to earn. Employers try to pay workers much less than the increased

If you stop to think about it, almost half of your waking hours will be spent going to, returning from, or working at a job. That being the case, you will want to spend that time doing something you find satisfying. Moreover, the kind of occupation you have determines how much you earn. That, in turn, determines the kind of lifestyle you and your family can lead.

The job you want may or may not be there when you want it. Or it may be available but not close to your hometown. In addition, it is easier to find work when the economy of the country as a whole is doing well than when business conditions are poor. Given all of these factors, here are some ideas of how you should go about choosing your career.

First, decide what you want most out of your career. Is it money? Prestige? Helping people? Would you rather work with your hands or your head? Do you prefer working outdoors? Indoors? With people? Alone? What are your hobbies and other interests? Can they be transformed into an occupation?

Once you have put together your thoughts on these and other concerns, you should talk to your school guidance counselor. If one is available, you should also talk to a job counselor at a local counseling service. These trained specialists can help you to learn more about the careers that interest you.

Counselors can also help you match your abilities with possible careers. Knowing what your abilities are, though, is tricky. On the one hand, some people seem to be born with certain talents. On the other hand, a lot of what we call talent is really the result of hard work. A great athlete or musician must spend many hours learning and developing the skills that make that individual outstanding. So talent and skill (which together make up one's abilities) go together with effort. If you think you have a special talent, it is important that you develop it through education, training, and lots of hard work.

The amount of education and training you will need depends on the career you choose. Your first objective, though, is to finish high school. Then, you might continue with your education, go directly to work, or join one of the branches of the armed forces.

If you decide to continue your education, you might attend a two-year junior or community college, both of which offer programs leading to an associate's degree. You may want to go to a four-year college and receive a bachelor's degree, or to a trade or technical school to learn specific job skills.

Choosing the armed forces can open up other career choices to you. You might make the service a lifetime career or enter a training program in a specialty that you can follow in civilian life.

Entering the world of work will open up many other possibilities to you. Your first job need not be your final one. It might be merely a step up on a career ladder. In this first job, you might receive *on-the-job training* (learning a job by doing it). Or you may improve your skills by attending evening classes in subjects related to your field of interest. Remember, whatever your first job, it need not last forever. You may leave one job for another if you think the second one offers you greater opportunities. You might work for a while, then return to school or join the armed forces. After completing your education or your hitch with the armed forces, you might return to the world of work, preferably in your chosen career field.

There are many sources of information about careers. In addition to a school guidance counselor, your teachers at school may help you, particularly teachers in your field of interest. Do not forget those close at hand—your relatives, friends, and neighbors. Ask these people questions and listen to what they have to say. Pay particular attention to people who are already working in a field in which you are interested.

Private employment agencies and state employment offices provide good information about available job openings. Your state employment office may even offer free job counseling.

Finally, do a lot of reading. There are many books and magazines related to any number of careers. Become familiar with careers that interest you. Study the *Occupational Outlook Handbook,* a biannual U.S. government publication that describes some 250 occupations. For each one, it tells the nature of the work, working conditions, requirements for the job, number of jobs, job locations, typical salaries, and the *job outlook,* or chances of finding work in that occupation. Much information is also available to you elsewhere—on videos, CD-ROMs, and the Internet, and in books and magazines—concerning schools, colleges, job opportunities, and other career concerns. Choosing a career is not easy. It takes much time and effort, but your time and effort will be well spent.

value of the good or service that these workers produce. Suppose that in one week, a company with ten workers produces goods worth $4,000 more than the cost of raw materials, rent, and capital. The employer cannot afford to pay these ten employees more than an average of $400 each. The employer is certainly willing to pay them less than $400 because lower wages add to the company's profits.

Economists sometimes use the term *marginal productivity* to describe the value of the output of the last worker hired by a company. In theory, a company will add workers until the point is reached where the extra income added by the last worker hired is equal to the worker's wage. Economists express this by saying that workers will be hired until marginal revenue is equal to marginal costs—that is, until the value of the additional production is equal to the cost of the last worker hired.

The demand for labor varies inversely with wages. In other words, all other things being equal, more workers will be hired at a lower wage than a higher one.

Factors Affecting the Supply of Labor

By the term "supply of labor," we mean the number of workers available to perform a particular job at a specified wage. As is the case with goods, the supply curve for labor slopes upward. The number of workers increases as wages rise and decreases as wages fall. This is logical because as wages in one field increase, workers in other fields are attracted to it. If, for example, nurses in private hospitals are paid more than those in public hospitals, nurses will leave public service for the higher-paying private jobs. Similarly, if wages in one industry fall, workers in this industry will move to higher-paying jobs in other industries.

Wages alone cannot determine the total supply of labor in a particular field. Supply is subject to a number of other factors, including the following:

ATTRACTIVENESS OF THE JOB. Some jobs carry more prestige or are more appealing than other jobs paying similar salaries. Many people prefer office work to more strenuous jobs even though office work may pay less. Also, writers, actors, dancers, and artists tend to like their work so much that they often stay in their fields even though they could probably earn more money elsewhere.

Skills Required.   Only a limited number of people have the skills or talent required for certain jobs. No matter how well the job pays, for example, not everyone can become a professional singer or ballplayer.

Required Training.   Some occupations have much longer training periods than others. Young people who want to become physicians may have to spend an additional eight to ten years in school after they graduate from high school. Other professions and technical fields also require extensive training beyond high school. Many people, though, cannot afford the time or money necessary for this training. The greater the amount of training required for a particular job, the smaller the supply of workers available.

Worker Mobility.   The willingness of workers "to move to where the jobs are" is described as their *mobility.* Young adults who have no family responsibilities are more mobile than others. But most people want to stay in the community where they are living. Employers in certain parts of the country may find it difficult to hire enough workers. Merely raising wages slightly may not help attract workers to this region. People are naturally reluctant to leave their friends and families or move their children from one area to another.

During the 1999–2000 period, almost 5 million workers (3.7 percent of all those employed) moved out of state. About half of those workers moved to a different region of the country (the South and Southwest were the most popular destinations). Of those who did move, about one-third remained with their current employer.

The peak years in which workers move are ages 20–24. About 15 percent of this age group migrate each year, whereas by age 32, the rate is 10 percent and falls to only 5 percent by age 47. There is also a correlation between worker mobility and educational level, as shown in Table 8.3.

TABLE 8.3   U.S. MIGRATION RATES FOR WORKERS AGE 30–34, BY EDUCATIONAL LEVEL

Educational Level (years)	Moving Between Counties Within a State	Moving Between States
9–11	6.0%	3.8%
12	3.7	4.1
13–15	4.5	4.7
16	4.6	6.1
17 or more	6.1	7.7

✵ Nonmarket Forces in Determining Wages

While supply and demand—the so-called market forces—are major factors in determining wage levels, they are not the only ones. In some instances, other factors (or nonmarket forces) also have an impact. These include the following.

LABOR UNIONS.   When labor union negotiators and company management sit down to negotiate wages, the laws of supply and demand often fade into the background. Instead of supply and demand, the relative strengths of labor and management are likely to dominate the proceedings. If, for example, union members appear to be able to weather a long strike, they might extract a substantial wage increase from the employer. If, however, the workers appear as if they could not afford the loss of income from a work stoppage, the unions will be under pressure to keep their salary demands low.

Although labor-management negotiations are partly guided by nonmarket forces, both labor and management are still subject to the laws of supply and demand. Businesses must show a profit in order to survive. This factor places a limit on the amount they can pay in wages. Similarly, there is a bottom-line salary below which qualified workers will simply quit or (if not currently employed) refuse to apply for jobs. (The role of labor unions is discussed in more detail in Chapter 9.)

GOVERNMENT LEGISLATION.   Laws can affect wage levels. Regardless of the laws of supply and demand, employers must pay the minimum wage set by federal and state laws. Similarly, laws require that many workers must be paid higher, overtime rates whenever they work more than a maximum number of hours per week. Other laws limit the supply of labor by banning the employment of children in many industries and requiring that children attend school until they reach a certain age.

Civil rights laws and other government rules require that workers receive equal pay for equal work. The purpose of these laws is to prevent discrimination on the basis of race, age, religion, nationality, sex, sexual orientation, or disability. The extent to which such laws are enforced will, therefore, affect the job market and wages.

DISCRIMINATION.   Certain groups in this country earn more than others. Studies show that African-American and Hispanic-American men earn less than non-Hispanic white and Asian men, and that women earn less than men (see Table 8.4 on page 178). Although there are a number of reasons for these differences, discrimination is a major cause. *Discrimination* involves favoring one group over another in hiring, salaries, or promotion for reasons that have nothing to do with ability to learn and perform job skills. Discrimination in employment is a violation of both federal and state laws.

TABLE 8.4	MEDIAN WEEKLY EARNINGS BY RACE AND SEX, 2001	
	Male	**Female**
White	$694	$521
Black	518	451
Hispanic	438	385
Asian	533	324

GEOGRAPHY. Where people live and work affects their earnings because wages differ from one part of the country to another. This is shown in Table 8.5, which ranks the top five and the bottom five states according to average annual pay. The rankings may change from one year to the next. It is important to realize that just because one lives in a high-wage state (such as Connecticut) it does not mean that one is better off than someone living in a lower-ranking state. Remember, you are looking at average earnings in a state. There are workers in Connecticut, for example, who earn much less than the average earnings in that state. Furthermore, there are individuals in Montana who earn more than many workers in Connecticut. In addition, the cost of living in high-wage states is usually much higher than that of the low-wage states.

EDUCATION. People who have completed many years of school earn more, on the average, than those who have completed fewer years. How much more the better-educated ones earn is shown in Table 8.1 on page 169. Education is becoming increasingly important in our highly technological global economy. We have noted that most job growth is in the services-producing industries. However, within those industries are low-paying jobs such as working at the checkout counter at a supermarket and high-paying jobs such as being chemical engineers. We can conclude that it pays to get a good education.

TABLE 8.5	AVERAGE ANNUAL PAY OF WORKERS, BY SELECTED STATES, 2000	
Rank	**State**	**Annual Pay**
1	Connecticut	$42,653
2	New York	42,133
3	Massachusetts	40,331
4	California	37,564
5	Illinois	36,279
46	Oklahoma	25,748
47	Arkansas	25,371
48	Mississippi	24,392
49	South Dakota	23,765
50	Montana	23,253

George Danby for the *Bangor Daily News,* Maine.

S U M M A R Y

The labor force in the United States is made up of all those 16 years of age and older who are working or looking for work. As the population of the United States has changed, so too has the labor force. More women are entering it. The average age of the labor force is getting older, but workers are retiring earlier. Technological change has brought changes in the composition of the labor force. The services-producing industries is the fastest-growing sector. The percentages of services-producing industries workers in the labor force are increasing, while percentages of goods-producing industries workers are decreasing.

Some jobs pay more than others. The market forces of supply and demand help explain wage differentials. Wages are highest where the demand for workers' services is greatest and the supply of such workers is smallest. The demand for workers is influenced by the demand for the product or service the workers provide. The supply of workers is influenced by the skills, training, and education needed; the attractiveness of the job; and whether workers are willing to move to accept jobs. Wages are influenced by nonmarket forces, including labor unions, government laws, and location.

REVIEWING THE CHAPTER

BUILDING VOCABULARY

Match each term in Column A with its definition in Column B.

Column A

1. labor force
2. educational attainment
3. discrimination
4. goods-producing industry
5. derived demand
6. career
7. downsize
8. worker mobility
9. technological revolution
10. marginal productivity

Column B

a. the willingness of workers to move to where the jobs are
b. the added value of production by the last worker hired
c. one's lifelong employment
d. rapid changes in ways of producing goods and services
e. to make a company smaller
f. agriculture, forestry, mining, and manufacturing
g. the number of years of school completed
h. the favoring or slighting of someone because of the racial, religious, ethnic, or gender group to which the person belongs
i. the number of people 16 years of age or older working or looking for work
j. the demand for something that is caused by the demand for something else

UNDERSTANDING WHAT YOU HAVE READ

1. As soon as you take some action to find a job, you (*a*) have chosen a career (*b*) enter the labor force (*c*) must leave school (*d*) cannot change your mind about your job.

2. A striking change in the labor force in recent decades has been the increase in numbers of (*a*) farmworkers (*b*) manufacturing workers (*c*) service workers (*d*) laborers.

3. There is a growing demand for workers with (*a*) a lot of talent but little training (*b*) little education and training (*c*) more education and training (*d*) much physical strength.

4. Average yearly earnings are generally highest for (*a*) elementary school graduates (*b*) high school dropouts (*c*) high school graduates (*d*) college graduates.

5. The demand for workers in an industry tends to rise as (*a*) the supply increases (*b*) the demand for the goods produced decreases (*c*) the demand for the goods produced increases (*d*) productivity falls.

6. Employers will hire additional workers (*a*) until the point of diminishing returns is reached (*b*) until the value of the additional production is equal to the cost of hiring the last worker (*c*) so long as marginal costs are greater than marginal revenue (*d*) until production exceeds demand.

Figure 8.7 **Supply and Demand for Computer Analysts**

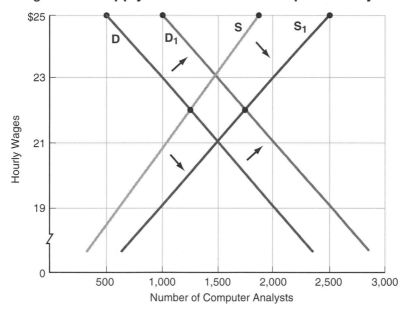

As the manager of a large firm, you are responsible for hiring computer analysts. Your company is willing to pay up to $22 per hour to the individuals you hire. Study Figure 8.7 and then answer Questions 7–10.

7. About how many computer analysts will be in demand at an hourly wage of $22 before demand increases to D_1? (*a*) 1,000 (*b*) 1,250 (*c*) 1,500 (*d*) 2,000.

8. About how many computer analysts are willing to work for $22 per hour? (*a*) fewer than 1,000 (*b*) 1,250 (*c*) 2,000 (*d*) 2,500.

9. What wage will you have to offer a computer analyst when the demand increases from D to D_1 but the supply remains the same? (*a*) $19 (*b*) $22 (*c*) $23 (*d*) $25.

10. A large number of computer analysts graduate from engineering school, causing supply curve S to shift to the right (S_1). As a result, the number of persons willing to accept $22 per hour will most likely (*a*) increase (*b*) decrease (*c*) remain unchanged (*d*) not enough information is given to determine this.

THINKING CRITICALLY

1. "The labor force changes as the country's population changes."

    a. Why should we be concerned about the population growth rate in the United States?

    b. How does an increase in the size of the population of the United States affect each of the following? (*1*) size of the labor force (*2*) demand for jobs (*3*) demand for goods and services (*4*) demand for workers.

    c. How may the aging of the U.S. population and the trend toward earlier retirements affect employment opportunities in the United States?

2. "The labor force in the United States is becoming more varied."

   a. How has the composition of the labor force changed?

   b. More young people than ever before will be working or looking for work. How will that affect you?

3. The technological revolution has brought about a considerable change in the composition of the labor force.

   a. How has the technological revolution affected the demand for labor?

   b. Explain why you are encouraged, or discouraged, by the impact the technological revolution has had on employment opportunities.

4. The market forces of supply and demand affect wages.

   a. Referring to Figure 8.6 on page 173, explain why the demand for labor is called a "derived demand."

   b. Why are wages related to productivity and, in particular, marginal productivity?

5. "Nonmarket forces affect wage payments in the United States." Select *three* of the following and describe how each has an impact on wages in the United States. (*a*) labor unions (*b*) government legislation (*c*) discrimination (*d*) geography (*e*) education.

SKILLS: Interpreting Double-Line Graphs

Study the graphs below and answer the questions that follow.

1. What was the average annual pay for workers in (*a*) Connecticut (*b*) Mississippi?

Figure 8.8 **Supply and Demand for Workers in Two States**

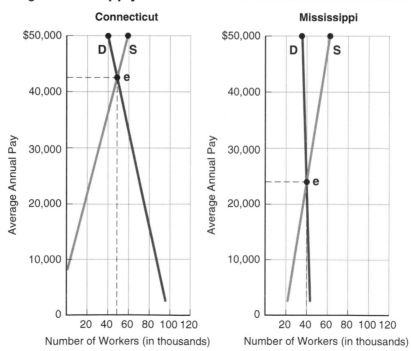

2. Explain why a shift in the demand curve to the right or the supply curve to the left would increase the average annual pay in Mississippi.

3. What factors might bring about a shift in the supply or demand curve for labor in Mississippi?

USING THE INTERNET

- The following are sources of information on population shifts, job opportunities, and occupations that are most likely to need workers: <<factfinder.census.gov>>; <<stats.bls.gov>>; <<armedforcescareers.com>>; <<bls.gov/oco/home.htm>>.

- To learn more about wages, hours, and employment by occupations, age, and gender, go to <<www.bls.gov>>.

- There are a number of Internet search engines to choose from when looking for a job. "Career Job Search—Guide to Internet Job Search" at <<www.e-careercenter.com>> provides a list of various job-search sites, hints on using the Internet to make your job search more effective, instructions on how to prepare a resume, and much more.

CHAPTER 9
Labor Unions in Our Economy

OVERVIEW

Some 15.8 million workers in the United States (about one worker in nine) belong to labor unions. Although this figure represents a decline from the peak years of the 1950s (when one in three workers belonged), labor unions remain a powerful force in the U.S. economy.

It was not always this way. Historically, unions in this country have long struggled to gain strength and recognition. Most business managers have viewed unions as a threat. After all, a major goal of unions has been to pressure employers to raise wages and improve working conditions. Such demands, when granted, have added to employers' costs. From the point of view of many workers, however, unions have been a necessity, especially in workplaces where wages have been low and working conditions poor.

In this chapter, we will discuss the history of labor unions in this country from the earliest labor organizations to the present. Then we will discuss some of the basic aims of unions, including wages, nonwage benefits, and working conditions. Finally, we will examine how unions negotiate with employers and what happens when such negotiations fail.

HIGHLIGHTS FROM THE HISTORY OF LABOR UNIONS

Labor unions existed even in the early days of the U.S. republic. These early unions were local *craft unions,* consisting of only a few members who worked in the same *craft* (skilled occupation). For example, workers in the print shops of Philadelphia joined together in 1786 to force employers to raise wages. In a similar manner, barrel-makers in Boston joined together, as did weavers in New York. Unions, however, were not yet organized on a national level, so that printers in New York and Boston did not help printers in Philadelphia when the latter were on strike.

The way unions negotiate an employment contract is known as collective bargaining. In *collective bargaining,* the union represents its members in negotiations rather than having each worker negotiate individually with the employer. Before the Civil War (1861–1865), unions were small, local, and poorly organized. They had great trouble persuading employers to negotiate with union representatives. Instead, employers usually dealt directly with each employee.

Rise and Fall of the Knights of Labor

Unions in the United States increased in size as a direct response to the increased size of businesses. After the Civil War, railroad companies spanned whole regions of the country and wielded enormous power. How could workers hope to bargain for better employment contracts from these corporate giants? One way was to organize unions on a national scale instead of on a local basis.

The first *national union* to achieve any real success was the **Knights of Labor,** which **Uriah Stephens** founded in 1869. Unlike earlier unions, the Knights did not build on the existing craft unions. Instead, it was "one big union." All workers, regardless of the kind of work they did, could become members. They could be skilled or unskilled. Neither race nor national origin became a consideration for membership in the Knights.

The Knights conducted several strikes against railroad companies, some of which were successful and resulted in wage increases for union members. By 1886, total membership in this national union had grown to an impressive 700,000. Then, however, the Knights were unfairly blamed for the Haymarket Riot in Chicago, which resulted in the deaths of at least seven police officers and one civilian. Because of the incident, the union's reputation was damaged, and it went into a period of decline. By 1889, the Knights of Labor had almost ceased to exist.

Rise of the American Federation of Labor

In 1886, a cigar maker named **Samuel Gompers** founded the **American Federation of Labor (AFL)**. It was not a union but a federation, or association, of existing craft unions. These craft unions (cigar makers' union, carpenters' union, wheelwrights' union, and so on) maintained their separate identities within the larger organization. Only skilled workers of a particular trade were eligible for membership in the craft union that represented that trade. Thus, only a skilled carpenter could belong to the carpenters' union, a skilled cigar maker to the cigar makers' union, and so on. An unskilled worker (such as a clerk or janitor) in a printing shop could not join the printers' union.

The AFL became the most successful labor organization of its time. Its membership grew steadily to a peak of almost 4 million in 1920. Gompers insisted that the AFL concentrate on economic issues such as higher wages, shorter hours, and better working conditions. When political candidates of

Figure 9.1 **Development of Labor Unions in America**

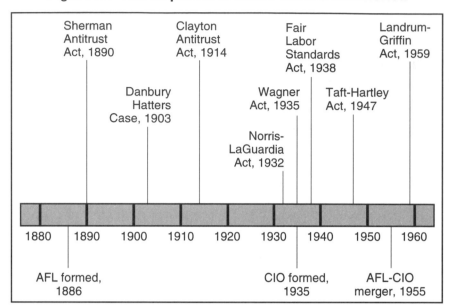

either major party (Republican or Democratic) offered to support the goals of the AFL, they, in turn, received the AFL's endorsement.

⚙ The Opposition of Business and Government

Despite the growth of the AFL, unions were still at a serious disadvantage in their dealings with powerful corporations. Before the 1930s, U.S. presidents and state governors tended to give more help to employers than to union organizers. Striking workers sometimes clashed with nonunion "strikebreakers" in battles outside factory gates. Government authorities would then send troops and militia to stop the violence by arresting union leaders. The presence of troops made it easier for business managers to crush strikes. In 1892, for example, unionized steelworkers called a strike against the Carnegie Steel Company mills at Homestead, Pennsylvania. The state governor responded to the resulting violence at Homestead by sending in state militia to restore order. This government action had the effect of breaking the strike.

In 1919, the AFL tried and failed to create a union in the steel industry. It began to organize steelworkers and called a strike. The steel companies, however, were able to keep their plants going with strikebreakers. The AFL's reputation was hurt after it ended the strike without gaining any benefits for the workers.

Before the 1930s, the courts' interpretation of federal laws tended to hurt unions and help businesses. In Chapter 7, we discussed how Congress passed the Sherman Antitrust Act in 1890 in order to regulate business monopolies. In 1903, though, the U.S. Supreme Court ruled that this law could apply to unions as well. The Court said that a striking union of hat makers in Danbury, Connecticut, had violated the restraint-of-trade provision of the Sherman Act. The Court ordered the union to pay damages to the hatmaking company. This interpretation of the Sherman Antitrust Act prevailed until 1914, when Congress passed the Clayton Antitrust Act. This law stated that unions were not combinations in restraint of trade and, therefore, were not subject to penalties under the Sherman Act.

Existing laws, however, still allowed courts to severely limit union activities by issuing injunctions. An *injunction* is a court order that directs a person or group to stop committing certain acts. From the 1890s until 1932, state and federal courts regularly issued injunctions to stop unions from carrying out strikes. Then Congress passed laws to make it more difficult for courts to issue such injunctions.

A New Deal for Labor

The laws that most dramatically improved the status of unions were enacted during the Great Depression in the 1930s. Near the close of Herbert Hoover's administration, Congress passed the **Norris-LaGuardia Anti-Injunction Act**

Mary ("Mother") Jones, left, helped organize coal miners and helped found the Industrial Workers of the World. Samuel Gompers, right, missed only one year between 1886 and 1895 as president of the AFL.

of 1932. This law limited the use of court injunctions in labor disputes. Franklin Roosevelt, who followed Hoover as President, thought that federal laws should protect and encourage unions. As part of his **New Deal** program, Roosevelt signed into law two acts of Congress that enabled unions to grow into extremely large and powerful organizations. One law was the Wagner Act of 1935 (also called the National Labor Relations Act). The other was the Fair Labor Standards Act of 1938.

- The **Wagner Act** helped change the balance of power between labor and management. It guaranteed all workers the right to organize and join unions and the right to bargain collectively. It defined unfair labor practices by management and created a **National Labor Relations Board (NLRB)** to enforce provisions of the law. The NLRB could conduct elections in a factory or other workplace to determine whether workers wanted to be represented by a particular union.

- The **Fair Labor Standards Act** established a national minimum wage of 25 cents per hour and a maximum workweek of 44 hours. (In a few years, the former would rise to 40 cents, while the latter would fall to 40 hours.) Workers who put in more than the maximum workweek were to be paid overtime at a rate one and a half times their normal hourly pay. Another provision of the act restricted the employment of children.

⚡ Rise of the CIO

Until the 1930s, unskilled and semiskilled workers in steel mills and other mass-production industries had been generally left out of the union movement. They could not join the AFL because they did not belong to any skilled trade group. The passage of the Wagner Act in 1935, however, made it possible for unions to organize all wage earners in an entire industry.

This was the goal of labor leader **John L. Lewis**, who in 1935 helped to form the Committee for Industrial Organization. At first, Lewis's group was only a committee within the AFL. It set out to found "vertical unions" in major mass-production industries. Such unions were to include all the workers within an industry regardless of the job they performed. For example, the autoworkers union would include those who worked on the assembly line as well as office workers, mechanics, janitorial staff—any worker within the industry manufacturing and delivering automobiles. The older "horizontal unions" grouped workers of similar skills, such as carpenters or cigar-makers. Quarrels between Lewis and leaders of the AFL caused Lewis to break away and create, in 1938, a new federation of industrial unions. This was the **Congress of Industrial Organizations (CIO)**.

The CIO and the AFL competed with each other for members, and so they became increasingly alike. Like the CIO, the AFL brought in many unskilled members; like the AFL, the CIO recruited some highly skilled workers. Factory workers often quarreled among themselves about whether to be organized by the AFL or by the CIO. To avoid these troubles, the great rivals decided in 1955 to merge into one organization—the **AFL-CIO.**

Federal Laws That Regulate Unions

Following World War II (1941–1945), Congress enacted several important laws designed to regulate unions.

TAFT-HARTLEY ACT, 1947.   This law limited the activities of labor unions in a number of ways. The **Taft-Hartley Act** (1) defined certain labor practices as "unfair" and (2) outlawed the closed shop but did permit the union shop. In both shops, all workers in a workplace must belong to the union that is recognized as their bargaining agent. In a *closed shop,* which had been legal under the Wagner Act, workers were required to be union members before they could be hired. But in a *union shop,* nonunion workers are permitted (and are required) to join the union after they have been hired. (3) The act also required that a union give a company 60 days' notice before going on strike. Moreover, in an industry that affects the national welfare, the U.S. president can request a court injunction delaying the strike an additional 80 days. (4) As an attempt to control union corruption, the law required union leaders to submit reports on union finances to the government.

LANDRUM-GRIFFIN ACT, 1959.   This law also sought to reduce corruption and to improve democratic procedures in unions. The **Landrum-Griffin Act** guaranteed workers the right to participate in the union's affairs and to elect their officers. The *embezzlement* (stealing) of union funds was made a federal offense.

RIGHT-TO-WORK LAWS.   Some 22 states, located mostly in the South and Midwest, have enacted *right-to-work laws.* These laws state that workers may hold jobs without being required to join unions.

THE DECLINING POWER OF LABOR UNIONS

By 1955, unions in the United States had gained tremendously in membership and power. There were 17 million union members then (compared to just 3 million members in 1930). Fully one-third of all nonagricultural workers in the United States belonged to a union in 1955. Unions' power has decreased in recent decades. By 1980, union membership had declined to 23 percent, and by 2004 it had fallen to 12.5 percent. When the millions of union members who work for federal, state, and local governments are excluded, unions represent only about 8 percent of private sector personnel.

Figure 9.2 **U.S. Labor Union Membership**

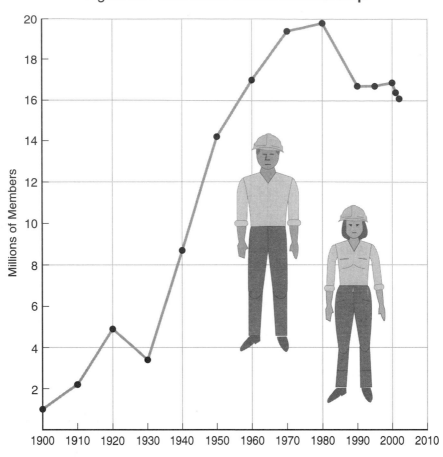

In view of what has been said, the percentage of workers belonging to unions has been declining since its peak in 1960. Total union membership, as shown in Figure 9.2, increased continually since the 1930s along with the increase in the size of the labor force. However, as the graph indicates, union membership declined in the period 1980–1990 and again more recently.

Although economists disagree as to the exact reasons for the decline, most would include the following: (1) the decline of mass-production industries, (2) automation, (3) global competition, and (4) the unpopularity of unions among some Americans.

Fewer Mass-Production Jobs

In the discussion of the labor force in Chapter 8, we learned that there has been a decline in workers in the goods-producing industries and an increase in workers in the services-producing industries. It was the workers in the mines, factories, and iron and steel mills—the goods-producing industries—who had flocked to the unions in the 19th and early 20th centuries. The number of goods-producing industry workers has been declining because mass-production industries have been declining. (*Mass production* is the making of a product in quantity, usually with machinery.) Today, there are fewer jobs in auto and textile plants in the United States and more jobs in insurance and financial services companies.

Although there are fewer factory jobs, office jobs continue to grow. Office workers have always been less likely to join unions, even though unions are spending much effort trying to organize them. An exception is in government employment, some of which involves office work. Union membership among government employees has grown dramatically in recent decades. While in the 1960s only about 10 percent of nonmilitary government workers belonged to unions, by 2002 this figure had grown to about 42 percent. Local government workers (teachers, police officers, and firefighters, for example) are the most highly unionized of all government employees, with about 47 percent of members belonging to a union.

Automation

The trend toward using more automated equipment to produce more goods with fewer workers is also contributing to the decline in union membership. *Automation* has resulted in the need for fewer mechanics and line workers, both groups that tend to join unions.

New techniques of production associated with automation have hurt government unions. Many services formerly performed by union employees are now automated. Citizens can renew licenses, pay their taxes, and obtain information all by the use of the Internet and automated phone-answering machines. Thus, there is less of a need for government employees.

Automation has made it easier for businesses to *outsource* tasks (have certain jobs done by employees of different firms), often by firms that are not unionized. In fact, many tasks are now outsourced to firms located in foreign countries. For example, animation work for television cartoon shows is often outsourced by U.S. companies to firms in the Philippines and India. Because many people living in these countries speak English, they are often hired to answer phones for U.S. mail-order firms and other U.S. companies. Many U.S. firms find it less expensive to have their data processing done abroad.

In some ways, new technology may provide opportunities for union growth. Unions use new technology such as the Internet to communicate with their members and spread their message to the general public. The International Association of Machinists solved its problem of trying to organize 119,000 ticket agents of United Airlines in 1999 by putting press releases, photos, testimonials from workers, and other information on its Web site. Unions also use the Internet to gather information about employers and investigate labor laws and court cases.

✡ Global Competition

As a result of increased foreign competition, some industries (such as consumer electronics, men's and women's clothing, and shoe manufacturing) have moved most of their production abroad. To remain competitive with foreign companies, many firms still located in the United States have sought to reduce their costs of doing business. Many unions have had to accept wage reductions, reduced benefits, and the introduction of labor-saving technologies as concessions to increased foreign competition. These retreats by labor unions have made the unions less attractive to workers.

✡ Unpopularity of Labor Unions Among Some Americans

Unions are not universally popular among workers. There are a number of reasons for this.

Americans pride themselves on their individualism, and some are wary of what they think might be an institution foreign to this American ideal. Many workers associate unions with collectivism and, therefore, alien to the American way of having individual workers negotiate their difficulties or needs directly with their employer. Furthermore, some American workers think that one day they might become the boss, and if that happens, they would not want to face the interference of a union.

Some workers believe that union dues are too high and that membership in a union does not provide enough benefits to offset these dues. Others do not want to belong to a union because they believe that union leaders are corrupt. They get this idea because some union officials have been found guilty of pocketing money that was supposed to be used for the benefit of all union members. Finally, union leaders today often lack the charisma of some labor leaders of the past (such as Samuel Gompers or John L. Lewis).

Unions have not been as popular in the South as elsewhere. Thus, many employers from the Northeast and the Midwest have moved operations to that part of the country (or abroad) to avoid having to deal with unions. In addition, many of these companies are offering their workers salaries and benefits comparable to those offered in unionized firms, thus making joining a union less attractive to workers. To counter this trend, unions have been trying, without much success, to organize workers in the South.

THE BASIC AIMS OF UNIONS

Labor unions have many goals. The major ones are higher wages, better working conditions, a union shop, job security, fringe benefits, and grievance machinery.

Higher Wages

Of primary concern to all unions are the so-called bread-and-butter issues of wages and hours. In presenting their demands for higher wages, unions usually rely on one or more of the following arguments:

PROFITS AND ABILITY TO PAY.   Unions believe that workers are entitled to share in a company's prosperity. Thus, unions frequently claim that large profits justify wage increases.

EQUAL PAY FOR EQUAL WORK.   If workers performing identical or similar jobs in other companies are earning higher rates of pay, union leaders argue that their members should be brought up to that level. This is fair, they claim, because if the job is worth so much to one company, it should be worth that much to another.

PRODUCTIVITY.   Union leaders argue that if the productivity of a group of workers is increased, those workers should share in the profits that often result from increased productivity.

RISING COST OF LIVING.   For the last five decades, U.S. consumers have experienced a general rise in prices. If prices continue to rise, workers' current wages will probably not be able to buy as much in the future as they can today. To protect their members against increases in living costs, unions frequently base their wage demands on expected changes in the price level. They may also ask for an *escalator clause* in their contract. This clause ties money wages to the cost of living in order to keep real wages constant. Thus, if the cost of living rises by 10 percent in the course of the year, wages automatically are raised by 10 percent. Often an escalator clause ties wage raises to a cost-of-living index such as the Consumer Price Index, discussed in Chapter 15.

Shorter Workdays and Workweeks

Just as unions have striven to increase their members' wages, they have sought to reduce the number of hours worked. This latter effort has been directed toward the reduction of both the number of hours worked each day and the number of days worked each week. Whereas in the early 19th century, the workweek in New England textile mills averaged 72 hours, the present-day nonfarm workweek averages about 35 hours. Unions claim much of the credit for this reduction in number of working hours.

Union Shop

During collective bargaining, a union attempts to gain more than improved wages and hours. Among its primary goals is the establishment of a *union shop,* a workplace where only union members can be hired. For its part, management prefers an *open shop,* one in which workers are free not to join the union. A compromise between the union shop and the open shop is the *agency shop.* Under this arrangement, nonunion workers are required to pay dues to the union as long as they work in the shop. These workers, though, do not have to join the union. In an agency shop, there are no "free riders," workers who do not pay dues to a union but who benefit from the gains won by the union. About 1.8 million workers are represented at their workplace by a union even though they are not union members.

Checkoff

Another contract provision commonly sought by unions is the *checkoff.* It provides that dues are deducted automatically from the workers' pay and sent on to the union. This provision helps the union stay financially solvent.

Union Label

Some goods for sale have a label that announces that the goods were made by union workers. Unions try to pressure employers to attach this union label to the goods they produce. Unions also try to induce the public to look for a union label before making purchases.

Job Security

One of the main objectives that workers expect union negotiators to achieve is *job security.* Union contracts usually provide that workers may not be dismissed without good reason. In anticipation of layoffs, most contracts provide that the workers with the most *seniority* (years of service) will be the last to lose their jobs. Unions have also tried to achieve a form of guaranteed annual wage. In some contracts, this takes the form of supplementary unemployment benefits, which are payments by the employer to laid-off workers.

 Fringe Benefits

Benefits not directly connected with wages or the job are called *fringe benefits.* They include items pertaining to health, welfare, vacations, and retirement. In recent years, fringe benefits have made up an increasing percentage of the total labor costs of employers. Many employers, for example, pay the cost of health insurance programs for their employees. Although the cost of this insurance does not appear in workers' pay envelopes, it nonetheless represents added income.

Grievance Machinery

Once a labor contract is drawn up and in force, disagreements may arise between the employer and union members over many issues. A worker may feel that a supervisor has been unfair. Management may claim that union members have not been living up to their responsibilities. Whatever the dispute, most labor contracts provide for *grievance machinery* (methods by which disputes can be resolved). This machinery usually involves hearings, with the right of appeal to a higher level. The final appeal under many union contracts is to an impartial arbitrator. Under the procedure of *arbitration,* an impartial third party, the *arbitrator,* hears both sides of the argument and renders a decision that is binding on both parties.

THE COLLECTIVE BARGAINING PROCESS

Before a shop is organized, there are usually some workers who would like to be represented by a union and others who are either uncertain or would prefer to remain independent. The situation may be further complicated if two or more unions are seeking to organize the same workers.

Achieving Recognition

Under the terms of the National Labor Relations Act, a union can ask the **National Labor Relations Board** to *certify* (approve) it as the official bargaining agent for a particular shop. If there is any objection, the NLRB is authorized to conduct an election to determine who, if anyone, should represent the employees. Having won a majority of the votes in such an election, a union is certified by the NLRB as the sole bargaining representative for its members. The employer is legally bound to bargain in good faith with that union.

🌀 Negotiating a Labor Contract

Once it has been designated as the exclusive bargaining agent, the union seeks to negotiate a *labor contract,* a written agreement between the employer and the union representing employees. The labor contract sets the conditions of employment (compensation, hours, and working conditions) and the procedure to be used in settling disputes.

Representatives of the union and management sit down to hammer out an agreement through collective bargaining. More than 90 percent of union contracts are drawn up entirely as a result of these kinds of discussions. There are times, however, when collective bargaining breaks down, and disagreements between employer and union members become difficult to resolve. Workers might go out on strike.

We read and hear more about strikes than about other types of union activities. They frequently become the focus of television newscasts and newspaper stories. This is understandable because strikes are more exciting news than labor agreements are. Nevertheless, peacefully negotiated agreements in the United States average about 300 a day, while fewer than 3,000 strikes take place in a year.

Negotiating a contract usually involves talks between the officials of a single company and a union. Sometimes, however, unions negotiate with more than one company at a time. Negotiating contracts normally follows one of these patterns:

LOCAL BARGAINING.   Where companies in a particular industry do not normally compete outside their own community, negotiating a contract usually takes place on a community basis. For example, retail food stores in Peoria, Illinois, do not compete with those in Columbia, South Carolina. Therefore, food merchants in those towns may negotiate separately with the local unions.

PATTERN BARGAINING.   In certain industries, a few very influential companies control major portions of the market. Whatever they do will probably be followed by the other firms. Consequently, unions first try to reach an agreement with the most influential company in an industry. United States Steel, General Electric, and Ford are typical of the companies with which unions negotiate in the expectation that the agreements reached will "set the pattern" for other companies in the industry.

INDUSTRYWIDE BARGAINING.   If one trucking company could sign a union contract in which its drivers were paid less than those working for other firms, this company would be in a position to undersell its competitors. This would not take place under industrywide bargaining, in which representatives of all firms negotiate one nationwide union contract for all firms in this industry. This kind of negotiation can benefit both management and unions. Management is

Everyone is pleased when management and workers agree on a new contract because the agreements are often the result of weeks or months of negotiating.

protected against unfair competition from companies having lower labor costs. Unions help keep competing firms in business, thus protecting the jobs of their members. (Note that an industrywide contract could include foreign companies that operate union shops in the United States.)

 # WHEN COLLECTIVE BARGAINING FAILS

Although the overwhelming number of union contracts are worked out through collective bargaining, there are times when this process fails to bring about an agreement between management and the union. When face-to-face negotiations break down, the choices that remain usually involve either intervention by a third party or the application of some form of "arm-twisting" by either management or the union.

How Unions Put Pressure on Management

In seeking to achieve their goals, labor unions may use a variety of tactics.

STRIKES.   A *strike* is a work stoppage for the purpose of gaining concessions from management. It is labor's most powerful weapon because of the financial penalties it imposes upon the employer. Of course, a strike also costs participating workers a loss in income. Striking workers often wonder whether the potential gains from a successful strike will outweigh the expenses of lost wages.

The amount of time lost because of work stoppages is far less than the public seems to believe. In a recent year, for example, the time lost because of strikes was less than 0.01 percent of the total time worked by all workers in the country. Indeed, as indicated by Figure 9.3, in only one year since 1945 has the working time lost because of strikes gone above 1 percent of the total. In this regard, union leaders remind us that the time lost because of strikes is tiny compared to the number of workdays lost through unemployment.

Despite the relatively light cost of strikes, certain industries are so closely related to the public interest that even the briefest stoppage can become intolerable. If, for example, a strike shuts off public transportation, garbage removal, or milk delivery, the public welfare is directly involved. Also, the U.S. economy is so specialized that, if one segment of it fails to function, many others will feel the pinch. A strike in the steel industry will eventually be felt by all industries that use steel. A tire strike will affect the production of all motor vehicles. A stoppage by dockworkers that shuts down the waterfront will inevitably leave its mark on many other industries and their workers. Thus, despite the relatively small number of strikes in the United States, their impact can be widely felt. Furthermore, because the public is often affected by strikes, it frequently adopts a hostile attitude toward the strikers.

Discussed first on page 189, the Taft-Hartley Act permits the federal government to obtain an injunction that can delay a strike for 80 days if the national welfare is involved. Of course, at the end of the 80-day period, the workers can

Figure 9.3 **Work Time Lost Because of Strikes Since 1945**

What two points of view are presented here?

Marty Lowe, from *The Wall Street Journal.*
Permission Cartoon Features Syndicate.

go on strike. When Congress passed the act in 1947, people hoped that during this "cooling-off period" the negotiating process would continue and a strike could be avoided. In extreme cases of national emergency, as during wartime, the government has seized and operated plants that were on strike. This is a last-resort measure that most lawyers feel is unconstitutional during peacetime.

PICKETING.   Picketing takes place when workers march outside a business carrying signs, usually to proclaim the existence of a strike. The objectives of picketing are to (1) discourage workers from entering the workplace and (2) arouse public sympathy and urge the public not to patronize the struck business.

BOYCOTT.   A union *boycott* is a refusal to buy goods or services from a company whose workers are on strike. Unions ask their members and their families to "spread the word" to boycott the struck company's goods. They may also call on the general public to cooperate in the action. The objective is to add to the financial pressures on the employer by reducing the company's sales. Because the pressure is being applied to the company being struck, this tactic is called a "primary boycott." The same pressure put on a company whose workers are not on strike (but which is doing business with the struck company), is called a "secondary boycott." If, for example, the workers of the Rifle Towel Company were on strike and they and others refused to buy Rifle towels, it would be a primary boycott. However, if the union ordered its members not to have any dealings with stores that sell Rifle towels, this would be a secondary boycott. Certain types of secondary boycotts have been made illegal by the Taft-Hartley and Landrum-Griffin acts.

SLOWDOWN.   When workers deliberately reduce their output in order to force concessions from their employer, this is called a *slowdown.* Since they are not on strike, however, workers can continue to receive their wages. During the

In the 1970s, Cesar Chavez (center) of the United Farm Workers Union organized a boycott of lettuce grown on nonunionized farms.

later months of 2002, West Coast dockworkers initiated a slowdown protesting management's proposed plans to introduce labor-saving technology. The shipping companies countered with a lockout, discussed on the next page.

POLITICAL ACTION.   Although labor has not organized its own political party, unions try to induce their members to support political candidates whose views the unions consider favorable. These activities are no different from those of business leaders who support political candidates. Also, like business leaders, unions lobby for the passage of laws that will strengthen their position.

ILLEGAL METHODS.   Unions have resorted to tactics that either were never legal or have since been declared illegal. Among the most common of these were the following:

1. **Secondary Boycott.**   This tactic was described on the previous page.

2. **Strong-Arm Methods.**   Unions have been known to hire thugs to coerce management into accepting their demands. The extent and nature of these ille-

gal activities were revealed in the investigations conducted in the 1950s by the McClellan Committee of the U.S. Senate. After considering the findings of this committee, Congress passed the Landrum-Griffin Act in 1959 (discussed on page 189).

3. Jurisdictional Strike.   Sometimes a dispute breaks out between two unions over which one has authority over a particular job. For example, should the worker who removes a part of a costume from the stage during a play be a member of the Costumers' Union or the Stagehands' Union? While at one time such disputes might have led to *jurisdictional strikes,* the Taft-Hartley Act of 1947 outlawed them as unfair labor practices.

How Management Puts Pressure on Unions

Most employers have accepted the idea of working with unions and have done their best to maintain cordial relations with them. Nevertheless, the occasional breakdowns in labor-management negotiations have led management to take certain steps against unions. The following are some of the more important management tactics.

LOCKOUTS.   A *lockout* occurs when management shuts down a workplace in hopes of forcing the workers to accept its terms. Although the effect is the same as a strike (in that work is suspended), management hopes it can better afford the temporary financial losses involved. In recent decades, the lockout has sometimes been followed by a permanent shutdown of operations and a move to a region of the country where unions are weaker. The possibility of such a move puts pressure on the union to come to terms. In October 2002, the Pacific Maritime Association (an association of shipping companies) instituted a ten-day lockout at 29 West Coast ports. Some 200 ships, carrying all sorts of items from auto parts to plastic toys and frozen foods, were lined up at ports waiting to take in or unload cargo. It was estimated that the cost of this work stoppage amounted to $2 billion daily and that the lockout was affecting businesses and consumers throughout the United States. President George W. Bush invoked the Taft-Hartley Act to end the ten-day lockout.

INJUNCTIONS.   Sometimes a court issues an injunction to halt a strike. The use of the injunction in labor disputes, however, is not common. It was sharply limited by the Norris-LaGuardia Act of 1932.

STRIKEBREAKERS.   One way for an employer to break a strike is to hire workers to replace striking union members. It is legal to hire *strikebreakers,* or "scabs," as the unions call them. Some states, however, require that employers tell these new employees that they have been hired to replace workers on strike.

The growing importance of economics and the influence of economists were given international recognition in 1969 with the award of the first Nobel Prize in Economic Science to Ragnar Frisch of Norway and Jan Tinbergen of the Netherlands. They were pioneers in *econometrics*. Economists in this field develop mathematical models that are used to describe and predict changes in the economy. Since 1901, the **Nobel Prizes** (which are financed out of the estate of the Swedish inventor of dynamite, Alfred Nobel) have been given for outstanding achievement in physics, chemistry, medicine, literature, and international peace. The award for economics was the first new category added since the creation of the prize. In 1979, the prize was shared by Theodore W. Schultz of the United States and Sir Arthur Lewis of Great Britain. Sir Arthur, the first black to win a Nobel Prize in Economics, studied the transition from agricultural to industrial society in developing nations.

TABLE 9.1 WINNERS OF THE NOBEL PRIZE FOR ECONOMICS

Year	Winner	Year	Winner	Year	Winner
1969	Ragnar Frisch	1982	George Stigler	1996	William Vickrey
	Jan Tinbergen	1983	Gerard Debreu		James Mirrlees
1970	Paul Samuelson	1984	Sir Richard Stone	1997	Robert C. Merton
1971	Simon Kuznets	1985	Franco Modigliani		Myron S. Scholes
1972	Sir John Hicks	1986	James Buchanan	1998	Amartya Sen
	Kenneth Arrow	1987	Robert Solow	1999	Robert A. Mundell
1973	Wassily Leontief	1988	Maurice Allais	2000	James J. Heckman
1974	Gunnar Myrdal	1989	Trygve Haavelmo		Daniel L. McFadden
	Friedrich von Hayek	1990	Harry Markowitz	2001	George A. Akerlof
1975	Tjalling Koopmans		Merton Miller		A. Michael Spence
	Leonid Kantorovich		William Sharpe		Joseph E. Stiglitz
1976	Milton Friedman	1991	Ronald Coase	2002	Daniel Kahneman
1977	Bertil Ohlin	1992	Gary Becker		Vernon L. Smith
	James Meade	1993	Robert Fogel	2003	Robert F. Engle
1978	Herbert Simon		Douglass North		Clive W.J. Granger
1979	Sir Arthur Lewis	1994	John Harsanyi	2004	Finn E. Kydland
	Theodore Schultz		John Nash		Edward C. Prescott
1980	Lawrence Klein		Reinhard Selten		
1981	James Tobin	1995	Robert E. Lucas, Jr.		

POLITICAL ACTIVITY.   By persuading the federal government and the states to pass laws that limit the power of unions, industry has tried to maintain a strong bargaining position. Unions point to states' right-to-work laws as examples of legislation favoring management.

PUBLIC RELATIONS.   Industries have founded or supported organizations such as the **National Association of Manufacturers** and the **Chamber of Commerce of the United States**. These groups have sought to present management's point of view to the public and have lobbied for laws favorable to management. In addition, some companies buy newspaper advertisements and time on radio and television to present their side of a labor dispute.

✦ Peaceful Ways to Settle Labor Disputes

There are a number of methods of settling disputes between labor and management that avoid strikes.

FACT-FINDING.   In some labor disputes, the government might appoint a *fact-finding board.* This board investigates the issues, makes a report, and, in many cases, suggests solutions. Its recommendations are not necessarily binding.

MEDIATION.   In *mediation,* a third party brings together the two parties in the dispute, listens to their arguments, and perhaps offers a solution. The compromise proposals suggested by the mediator, however, are not binding on either party. (This procedure is also called "conciliation.")

ARBITRATION.   As discussed earlier in the chapter, in the arbitration method of settling labor disputes, a third party gives a decision that is binding on both sides. Arbitration is rarely used to negotiate labor contracts. More frequently, it is used as the final step in the handling of a grievance arising out of the interpretation of an existing contract.

GRIEVANCE COMMITTEE.   Where workers are represented by a union, procedures for the handling of *grievances* (complaints) are spelled out in the labor contract. Union contracts provide for hearings in which workers air their grievances or in which management explains the reasons why it wants to discipline or dismiss a worker.

═══ S U M M A R Y ═══

Early labor unions in the United States were small, local, and associated with a particular craft. In the 19th century, the Knights of Labor organized skilled and unskilled workers on a national level into one big union. Later, the AFL created a federation of independent craft unions. In the 20th century, the growth of mass-production industries gave rise to the CIO, an organization of unions of all workers in the same industry. The AFL and CIO merged into the AFL-CIO in 1955. While unions were very powerful then, they have since lost much of their power, mainly because of the decline of the mass-production industries that were the major sources of union members.

Unions have as their basic aims higher wages, better working conditions, a union shop with a check-off provision, job security, fringe benefits, and grievance machinery. Collective bargaining is the process whereby the union negotiates a contract for its members. Both labor and management resort to various practices when collective bargaining fails. The strike is the primary weapon of unions, while the lockout is a powerful management weapon.

REVIEWING THE CHAPTER

BUILDING VOCABULARY

Match each term in Column A with its definition in Column B.

Column A	Column B

Column A

1. arbitration
2. collective bargaining
3. boycott
4. closed shop
5. craft union
6. mediation
7. open shop
8. injunction
9. strike
10. lockout

Column B

a. a court order to stop a certain action
b. the process of settling a dispute using nonbinding decisions of a third party
c. the process of settling a dispute using binding decisions of a third party
d. negotiations by representatives of a union and a company about the terms of a union contract
e. the shutting down of a business by management to keep workers off the job
f. a workplace in which only workers belonging to a specific union may be hired
g. the refusal to buy goods or services from a company
h. a union action against an employer to refuse to continue working
i. a union of skilled workers in the same trade
j. a workplace in which the employer is free to hire either union or nonunion workers

UNDERSTANDING WHAT YOU HAVE READ

1. Labor unions in the United States have as their main goal to (*a*) create labor unrest (*b*) prevent new technology from being introduced (*c*) improve workers' wages and working conditions (*d*) make conditions difficult for employers.

2. About what proportion of the U.S. labor force belongs to unions? (*a*) more than 75 percent (*b*) between 50 and 75 percent (*c*) between 20 and 50 percent (*d*) less than 20 percent.

3. Most labor contracts are arrived at as a result of (*a*) a strike (*b*) picketing (*c*) collective bargaining (*d*) arbitration.

4. The growth of the assembly line and mass-production industries led to the organization of the (*a*) Knights of Labor (*b*) AFL (*c*) CIO (*d*) National Labor Relations Board.

5. Labor legislation was most favorable to labor unions during the period (*a*) 1865–1910 (*b*) 1910–1930 (*c*) 1930–1945 (*d*) 1945–present.

6. The first law to guarantee the right of collective bargaining was the (*a*) Sherman Antitrust Act (*b*) Wagner Act (*c*) Taft-Hartley Act (*d*) Landrum-Griffin Act.

7. Which *one* of the following tactics might be used by union workers against management? (*a*) lockout (*b*) injunction (*c*) picketing (*d*) hiring strikebreakers.

8. Which *one* of the following tactics might be used by management against union workers? (*a*) slowdown (*b*) strike (*c*) boycott (*d*) lockout.

9. When a strike threatens the nation's health and safety, the president of the United States may (*a*) forbid the strike (*b*) request an injunction to halt the strike temporarily (*c*) impose a settlement (*d*) provide for government operation of plants threatened by the strike.

10. In which type of shop must workers join the union after being hired? (*a*) union shop (*b*) closed shop (*c*) open shop (*d*) agency shop.

THINKING CRITICALLY

1. The history of labor unions in the United States indicates several periods of growth. Select *one* of the following two periods: 1869–1920 or 1935–1955. Describe the labor unions and national organizations that developed during the period you selected and discuss the reasons for their growth.

2. Study Figure 9.4 and then answer the questions that follow:

Figure 9.4 **Balance Between Labor and Management in 1914, in 1946, and Today**

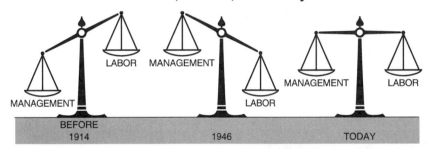

a. Give *three* arguments to show that labor was at a disadvantage in the years before 1914.

b. Give *two* arguments to show that in 1946 labor had the upper hand in its relations with management.

c. What events have taken place in the years since 1946 to help "restore the balance of power" between labor and management?

d. Explain why you agree or disagree with the idea that the balance of power has been restored.

3. Union power has decreased in recent decades. Some of the reasons given for this decline are (*a*) global competition, (*b*) the shift in types of jobs in the labor force, and (*c*) automation. Select any *two* of these reasons and explain, with examples, how each one chosen may have contributed to the decline in the power of labor unions.

4. In recent decades, there have been a number of strikes by public employees, such as teachers, sanitation workers, and air traffic controllers. In most instances, these strikes were in violation of U.S. antistrike laws. Do you believe that public employees in this country ought to have the right to strike? If your answer is "yes," explain why. If your answer is "no," suggest some procedures for settling disputes between government and its employees.

5. Assume that the union representing the workers in a large bakery has just signed a contract with management. (*a*) Explain under what circumstances the bargaining in this situation will be local, pattern, or industry-wide bargaining. (*b*) Summarize under the following headings some of the provisions that the agreement is likely to include: (*1*) union recognition (*2*) conditions of work (*3*) grievance procedures (*4*) wages (*5*) job security (*6*) fringe benefits (*7*) other provisions.

6. Some labor disputes are settled through arbitration. (*a*) Explain the meaning of arbitration. (*b*) Do you think that arbitration is a good method to settle labor disputes? Explain your answer.

SKILLS: Creating and Interpreting a Graph

1. Draw a line graph using the data given in the table below. Put dates on the horizontal axis and percentages on the vertical axis. Give the graph a title.

2. Do you find the graph to be more useful than, less useful than, or about as useful as the table in understanding the given data? Explain your answer.

3. What conclusions can you draw from reading this graph?

4. Compare your line graph to that of Figure 9.2, "U.S. Labor Union Membership." Explain how the graphs differ and why they differ.

5. Explain why it is possible for the percentage of workers belonging to unions to decline while total union membership increases.

▷ TABLE 9.2   UNION MEMBERSHIP AS A PERCENTAGE OF NON-AGRICULTURAL WAGE AND SALARY WORKERS

Year	Percent	Year	Percent
1950	31.5	1980	25.2
1955	33.6	1985	18.0
1960	31.4	1989	16.4
1964	29.5	1991	16.1
1966	28.8	1995	14.9
1968	28.4	2000	13.5
1970	28.0	2002	13.2
1978	23.6	2004	12.5

USING THE INTERNET

1. Check out the Web sites of some of the major union organizations, such as that of the AFL-CIO at <<www.aflcio.org>>; the American Federation of State, County and Municipal Employees at << www.afscme.org>>, and the United Auto Workers Union at <<www.uaw.org>>.

2. For more information on the backgrounds of the winners of the Nobel Prize in Economics, search their Web site at << www.nobel.se/economics/laureates>>.

3. The latest data on labor union membership can be found at FEDSTATS, which collects information from 70 federal agencies, at <<www.fedstats.gov>>.

4. For information on right-to-work laws, check out <<www.nrtw.org>> and <<www.right-to-work.org>>.

UNIT IV

PERSONAL ECONOMICS

CHAPTER 10
Personal Financial Planning

OVERVIEW

During your lifetime, you will probably be receiving an income. If so, you will have to decide how much of that income you will spend and how much you will set aside as savings and investments. How you use your income, savings, and investment opportunities will directly affect the quality of your life now and in the future. Consumer spending is important to the individuals who do the spending (that is, all of us) and also to the economy as a whole. The reason is quite simple. Consumers as a group buy more than two-thirds of all the goods and services produced and sold in the United States. What consumers do not spend, they save. That too is important to the whole economy. On a personal level, the ways in which you choose to save and spend will affect the quality of your life. Those who choose wisely might live better than those who do not.

In this chapter, we will discuss how you may prepare a financial plan to enable you to make the best use of your financial resources. Next, we will analyze the various factors that go into your decision to spend, save, or invest your money and how your decisions, together with those of all other consumers, affect the economy. Finally, we will take a close look at the various ways you can save or invest your money.

WHAT IS FINANCIAL PLANNING?

There is some concern that young people live for the present and do not give much thought to the future. The reality, however, is that at some point in time, the future *is* the present! As workers, producers, savers, and investors, we will all have at our disposal *financial resources* (money or assets that can be converted into money) in the form of income, savings, investments, and property.

Managing financial resources involves making decisions both for the present and for the future. It is helpful in this regard to have a financial plan.

A *financial plan* is like a road map to guide you toward your financial future. Your personal financial plan will take into consideration where you are now, where you want to be in the years ahead, and how you propose to get there.

Why Plan Ahead?

Should you spend your money now or save for the future? Some people never worry about tomorrow. They spend their money as fast as they receive it, sometimes even faster. Others worry too much about tomorrow. They deny themselves even simple pleasures for fear that they will have nothing in the future. Both are extreme views. You should plan for the future but not at the expense of losing out on the joys of living in the present. A good financial plan helps you to find the middle road so that you can make the most with what you have while preparing for future needs. Those who choose wisely will live better than those who do not.

Setting Financial Goals

You may have heard the saying, "If you don't know where you want to go, you won't know how to get there." The same applies to financial planning. Setting personal goals simply means that you identify what you would like to do in the

Buying a home is a major long-term goal for many people.

future. Many, but not all, of your goals will require that you spend money. For example, "I plan to go to the Senior Prom ten months from now, and I will need $500 dollars in order to be able to do so." A married person with a young child might think, "In 15 years, I will need $100,000 to pay college tuition costs for my child." Goals setting gives you targets to shoot at. It is basic to financial planning.

In the above examples, you may have noticed that the goals of the high school student were different from those of the young married person. You should expect your goals to change as you go through the various life stages of infancy, childhood, and teen, adult, and senior years. As your goals change, your spending patterns change. A teenager may be concerned with setting aside money for books, clothing, and school supplies. A young single adult may be thinking about getting married, setting up a home, and having children. A 35–45-year-old may want to plan to care for elderly family members, a child's education, or retirement.

In some ways, all consumers are alike. We buy to satisfy our wants and needs. In other ways, we are all different. Because we have individual tastes, wants, values and beliefs, we have different goals. Not every high school student is an athlete. Not every high school senior is concerned about going to the senior prom. Nor is every parent thinking about eventually sending his or her child go to college. Since the goals of two individuals may be different, they may spend and save differently.

SHORT-TERM GOALS.   Goals that you want to achieve in a year or less are called *short-term goals*. Saving money for the senior prom some ten months from now would be a short-term goal. Similarly the desire to purchase a DVD player and to enroll in a driver's education course (both of which can be paid for in a year or less) are short-term goals.

LONG-TERM GOALS.   Goals that would take you more than a year to achieve are called *long-term goals*. To pay for an automobile of your own or the cost of going to a good post-secondary school are the kinds of long-term goals that you, as a high school student, might be thinking about. On the other hand, some parents with children still in elementary school may be setting aside funds for their children's college expenses. This, too, is a long-term goal.

GOALS WORKSHEET.   Identifying your goals is the first step in financial planning. In thinking about your goals, it is useful to set time limits. A goals worksheet is a useful device to help you visualize what you want, what it will cost to get it, and how long it will take. The following "Goals Worksheet" is a shortened version of what your goals worksheet might look like.

A Goals Worksheet enables you to monitor and evaluate the progress of your short- and long-term goals. In the examples above, you know that you must save $50 per month for a period of ten months in order to have enough money to attend your senior prom. Or, if you want that used car, you must save $100 per month for 36 months. Are either of your goals realistic? To answer that question, there are a few more steps you must follow.

▶ GOALS WORKSHEET			
Short-Term Goals	**Cost**	**Completion Date**	**Savings From Income Needed per Month**
Example: Senior Prom	$500	10 months	$ 50
Long-Term Goals	**Cost**	**Completion Date**	**Savings Needed per Month**
Example: Used car	$3,600	36 months	$100

✳ Determine Net Worth

Before you can decide where you want to go, you should know where you are financially. That is, you should be able to list your assets, liabilities, and net worth. (These terms were introduced in Chapter 5.)

Assets (A) represent anything of value that you own. Your assets would include your cash on hand or in the bank, stocks and bonds, automobile, home, insurance policies, and the like.

Liabilities (L) represent anything you owe, including unpaid bills, borrowed money, credit card debt, payments owed on a motor vehicle, and a mortgage on a home.

Net worth (N) is the difference between what you own (your assets) and what you owe (your liabilities). In other words, $A-L=N$.

Assets, liabilities, and net worth are summarized in a financial statement known as a balance sheet. Balance sheets offer a kind of snapshot of one's finances at a particular point in time. With a balance sheet in hand, an individual or a family is better able to set realistic financial goals.

Table 10.1 illustrates the Hinkson family balance sheet as prepared on March 1 of this year. The family has purchased a $100,000 insurance policy on the life of the breadwinner. The family owns its home and an automobile. They purchased U.S. savings bonds and have other investments and savings. (Later in this chapter, we will discuss a number of these savings and investment choices.)

How realistic is it that *you* will be able to accumulate a net worth of more than $100,000? It is very realistic. It is entirely possible that by the time you reach the age of 35 or 40, you will already have a sizable estate or net worth. As demonstrated in the following Mini-Reading, $1,000 left untouched in the bank at an interest rate of 5¼ percent would be worth almost $13,000 after 50 years. Now let us suppose that you are 17 years old and instead of $1,000 you set aside $5,000 and continue to receive 5¼ percent interest. By the time you are 40 years of age and without investing another penny, your $5,000 will be worth $15,357.62. (If you were fortunate enough to have an investment that paid

> ### TABLE 10.1   HINKSON FAMILY BALANCE SHEET AS OF MARCH 1

ASSETS

Cash and equivalents

Checking accounts and money-market funds	$ 15,000
Savings accounts	1,500
Cash value of life insurance (discussed in Chapter 12)	43,000

Investments

Stocks	$ 4,200
Bonds	5,000
Mutual funds	7,350
Company 401(k) plan	28,000
Individual retirement plan (IRA)	16,000

Real estate (estimated current market value)

Residence	$145,000
Other properties	None

Personal property (estimated current market value)

Household furnishings	$ 6,000
Car(s)	13,400
Jewelry, furs	1,150

TOTAL ASSETS	**$285,600**

LIABILITIES

Credit card balances	$ 150
Charge account balances	825
Life insurance loans	6,000
Auto loans	10,800
Personal loans	None
Mortgage on primary residence	82,000
Other	None

TOTAL LIABILITIES	**$ 99,772**
NET WORTH	**$185,828**

10 percent, which is possible but not likely, your $5,000 would be worth $44,771.51.) So, it is not unreasonable to assume that by planning now you will be able to grow a fairly sizable estate by the time you are in your 30s and 40s. Is this just an empty dream or a possibility? That depends on you and whether you will be able to save and invest. But in order to save and invest, you need to know how to spend less than you earn. You have to budget wisely.

The Power of Compound Interest

Deposits in savings accounts have a mighty force working for them called *compound interest.* It is interest earned on an original deposit and on the interest already earned on that deposit. Suppose, for example, that you deposited $1,000 in a savings account that paid 5¼ percent interest compounded annually. At the end of the first year, your account would be credited with $52.50 in interest, giving you a new balance of $1,052.50. At the end of the second year, the 5¼ percent would be *compounded.* That is, it would be calculated on the basis of the new balance, with interest now amounting to $55.26. The additional dollars in interest may not sound like much now, but suppose that the deposit had been made by a 15-year-old who decided to leave the money in the bank until retirement at age 65. After 50 years of compounding at 5¼ percent, the $1,000 would have grown to $12,915.31. Compare this compounding process to calculating *simple interest,* a situation where interest is earned on the principal alone. In that case, the $1,000 would have grown to only $3,625 after 50 years.

Compound interest becomes spectacular at higher levels of interest. Suppose that instead of 5¼ percent, the account had paid 12 percent in compound interest. Then the $1,000 deposit would have grown to $289,001.90 in 50 years!

SPECIAL NOTE: Compound interest can be computed quite easily on some pocket calculators or computers. Simply add 1 to the interest rate; multiply this sum by the principal; and press the (=) key once for each year to be compounded. For example, suppose that you wanted to calculate the balance after seven years of a deposit of $800 in an account that pays 9.5 percent in compound interest. This process could be entered in a calculator as follows:

$$1.095 \times 800 \ = \ 876.00$$
$$= \ 959.22$$
$$= \ 1,050.35$$
$$= \ 1,150.13$$
$$= \ 1,259.39$$
$$= \ 1,379.03$$
$$= \ 1,510.04$$

The final readout is the correct balance: $1,510.04.

PREPARING A BUDGET

A *budget* is a financial plan that summarizes anticipated income and expenditures over a period of time. Our federal, state, and local governments prepare annual budgets (see Chapter 13). Most personal budgets, however, are planned on a monthly basis.

CASH FLOW.   Before Millie Hamilton prepares a monthly budget, she first takes stock of her *cash flow.* Cash flow presents actual income and expenditures. You want to keep track of the money coming in and how it is being spent. Millie compiles a cash-flow worksheet. This requires a little discipline on her part, but it is not difficult to do. She jots down every item that she purchases and its cost, including spending for carfare, lunch, snacks, movies, school supplies, club dues—everything. Next, she lists her sources of income for the month, whether it is from her earnings at her job or gifts of money. Adding up all of her expenses and subtracting this amount from her income lets her know if she is spending more, less, or the same as the income entering her household. If her income is greater than her expenditures for the month, she will have some savings.

With a knowledge of your cash flow, you are ready to prepare a preliminary budget consistent with your income and spending habits.

A budget consists of three sections: (1) *Current Monthly Income,* (2) *Current Monthly Expenses,* and (3) a *Financial Summary.*

CURRENT MONTHLY INCOME.   If you are currently working, you know that there is a difference between your *gross pay* and what you actually receive, that is, your *take-home pay.* Gross pay is the total before any deductions are made. Assume that you earn $7.50 per hour and you work 20 hours a week after school and on weekends. Your weekly pay, therefore, is $150 per week. You will not find $150 in your paycheck. Your employer must deduct federal income, Social Security, and Medicare taxes, and (in some states) state income taxes from your gross pay. There may be additional deductions for health insurance charges, pension contributions, and union dues. If these weekly deductions add up to $45, you take home only $105. Gross pay minus deductions equals take-home pay. Therefore, you would expect to have an income in January of $420 ($105 × 4 = $420). If your birthday is in January and you assume that you will receive a $25 each from your grandmother and a parent, you would include $50 in your anticipated income for January. Your anticipated January income would then equal $470 ($420 + $50 = $470).

CURRENT MONTHLY EXPENSES.   Some expenses, like carfare, rent, and payments on a loan, recur every month. In other words, they do not vary from month to month. They are *fixed expenses.* Other expenses (such as going to movies, buying pizzas, signing up for class trips, or spending for magazines, books,

Holding a part-time job will increase your monthly income.

DVDs, and the like) do vary from month to month. Such expenses are called *variable expenses.* Assume that your fixed expenses amount to $200 per month and that you planned variable expenses amounting to $180 for January.

FINANCIAL SUMMARY.   In this section, you list your total anticipated income ($420) and subtract your total planned expenses ($200 + $180 = $380). Note that you planned to have a *surplus budget.* A surplus occurs when spending is less than income. In your planning for January, you expect to have $40 available for savings ($420 − $380 = $40). You would have a *balanced budget* if your income of $420 were equal to your spending. In this case, you did not plan to have any savings. Without savings, you would not be able to achieve any goal you may have set for yourself.

At the end of the month, examine your actual income and expenditures (your cash flow). If you spent $450 during January, you had a *deficit budget.* Your expenses were greater than your income by $30 for the month. This deficit must be made up from previous savings or by borrowing. Budget planning does not end at the end of one month. Following the same procedure used for the month of January, you will plan a budget for February. Now you should consider why your budget went askew in January. You will do the same again in March and for each month for the rest of the year. Record the results of your actual income and spending and modify your budget as necessary to make it consistent with reality and your goals. For example, it is unrealistic to anticipate that you will win the state lottery and include the winnings in your budget estimate. It is equally unrealistic to plan to save $200 a month because that would leave you without any personal spending money.

In reviewing your budget worksheet, look at ways to reduce your variable expenses in order to eliminate deficits and increase surpluses. Perhaps you could pass up the pizza parlor or buy one fewer DVD. It should be clear that you must make choices and that these choices involve trade-offs and opportunity costs (discussed in Chapter 1). Your budget does not allow you both to save for the senior prom and to spend on a class ski trip in January. Whichever you choose will involve a trade-off. If you go on a ski trip, you will be trading it off against saving for the prom. If you save instead, you will be trading it off against the ski trip.

Every trade-off has a cost. The cost is the opportunity that was lost when one choice was made over another. The opportunity cost of saving for the prom was the lost satisfaction of going on a ski trip.

MONITORING YOUR PROGRESS.   You have set your goals and prepared a budget in which you put aside savings in order to achieve your goals. Financial planning, however, is a never-ending process. Now you must monitor your progress. Were you able to save as much as you had planned? If not, are there any variable expenses that you are able to cut back? Should you borrow money in order to achieve one of your goals, or can you dip into your assets? Perhaps your goals are unreasonable and you have to scale back a bit. In any event, assume that you are planning properly and your plans are working out as you

Figure 10.1 **Household Expenses for an Average Family**

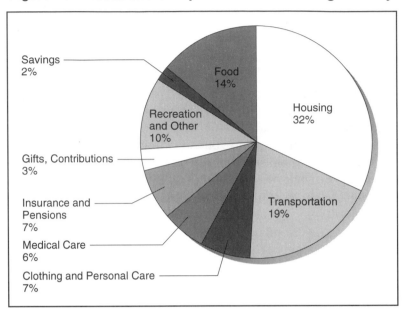

had anticipated. Now you want to know a little more about saving and investing your money. Your decision to spend or save is very important, not only to you but to the U.S. economy as well. Let us see why this is so.

CONSUMER SPENDING AND THE ECONOMY

In the discussion of the interdependence of economic society in Chapter 2, you followed a flow of money as it constantly passed back and forth among the public, business firms, and all levels of government. This "circular flow," as it is called, consists of consumer spending (C), business firm investments (I), and government spending (G).

The money that American consumers spend every year (the C in our equation) runs into the trillions of dollars. Indeed, more than two-thirds of the goods and services that make up our gross domestic product (*GDP*) is purchased by or for consumers. Business firms and government purchase the remainder (see Table 10.2). Total spending, or *GDP*, equals $C + I + G$. Consequently, even a small shift in consumer spending is likely to be felt by the entire economy. If consumers spend less, business firms will produce less, and they will need fewer workers. If consumers spend more, production and employment will increase. In 2002, for example, a 5 percent increase in consumer spending would have pumped an additional $365.18 billion into the circular flow ($7,303.7 \times .05 = \$365.18$). Naturally, a 5 percent decrease in consumer spend-

TABLE 10.2 GROSS DOMESTIC PRODUCT, 2002 (IN BILLIONS)	
Consumer Spending (Consumption)	$ 7,303.7
Business Spending (Investment)	1,593.3
Government Spending (Government)	1,549.2
GDP	$10,446.2

ing would have had quite the opposite effect. Total spending would have dropped by $365.18 billion (from $7,303.7 to $6,938.52 billion).

Looking at the circular flowchart (Figure 10.2), we can see that the money consumers spend does more than simply pay for the goods and services they buy. Those same payments are distributed as profits to businesses, as wages to

Figure 10.2 **The Circular Flow of the Economy**

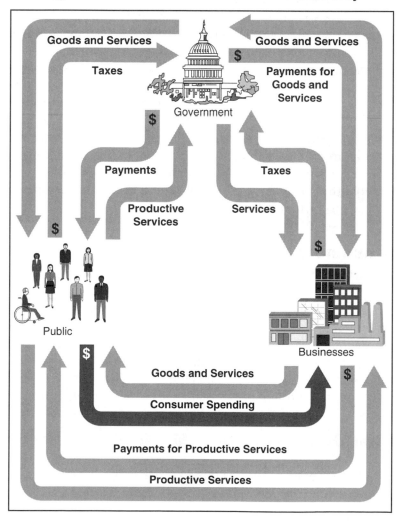

workers, and as taxes to government. Since consumer spending is so important to total spending, to earnings, and to production in the U.S. economy, it is no wonder that economists study why and how consumers spend and save their money.

The Economic Implications of Savings

In order for any society to increase its output, it must devote part of its production to the manufacture of capital goods and services. The automobile industry, for example, cannot increase its total output unless some companies build new machinery and tools. What is true for the automobile industry is true for all industries. New capital must be constantly produced to expand production and to replace equipment that has worn out.

To pay for capital investments, businesses might set aside part of their earnings in the form of savings, sell stock, or borrow. In other words, business investment is paid for out of the savings of businesses themselves or of others. Businesses might also borrow money from commercial banks, insurance companies, investment banks, or other financial agencies. These institutions in turn get their funds from people who put their money in these institutions.

Saving and investing are voluntary in our economy. No one tells consumers or businesspeople how much they may spend or save. Although the government may use its powers to influence these choices, the final decisions rest with individuals.

The sum total of millions of individual decisions whether to spend or save will ultimately affect the kind and quantity of goods and services produced. Savings are an important link in the economic process because savers, by giving up the opportunity to enjoy goods and services in the present, make possible increased production in the future.

Consumers Can Either Spend or Save Their Income

Consumers can do one of several things with their income: spend it, save it, or spend part and save the rest. In recent years, consumers have been spending about 95 percent of their *after-tax income* (income that remains after paying taxes). They have been putting the rest (about 5 percent) into savings. Economists describe the tendency to spend one's income as the *propensity to consume,* and the tendency to save a portion of one's income as the *propensity to save.*

What Determines How Much We Save or Spend?

Economists have identified five factors that determine how much consumers spend or save: income, wealth, interest rates, future expectations, and government policies.

What factors determine how much this consumer spends today at this store?

INCOME.   How much we spend or save is largely determined by how much money we have available to us. For low-income families, that sum depends on how much its members regularly receive. Members of low-income families are likely to spend everything they receive just to meet the costs of living. They save little or nothing. As a family's income increases, though, so too does the amount its members set aside as savings.

SOURCES OF INCOME.   People's sources of income are varied. Many people receive wages or salaries for the work they perform. Some also receive interest and/or dividends on their savings and investments. Those people who own businesses may earn profits. Retired people might receive pension payments from their former employers or regular Social Security payments from the federal government. The government supplements some people's incomes in other ways as well, including providing several types of welfare payments.

DISPOSABLE FAMILY INCOME.   More than any other factor, *disposable family income* (how much a family has left after paying personal taxes) determines how much a family spends or saves. In 1857, German statistician **Ernst Engel** concluded that as a family's income increases, the percentage of that income spent on food decreases. Moreover, the percentage spent on operating the household remains almost unchanged and the percentage spent on all other categories (luxuries, medical care, and personal care, for example) and on savings increases. These generalizations are known as *Engel's Law.*

WEALTH.   Wealth is not the same as income. *Wealth* is anything that has value (such as stocks, bonds, real estate, and savings). Income, by contrast, represents money that a family or individual receives (such as salary, sale of house, and dividends from stock). All other things being equal, the percentage of family income saved decreases as its wealth increases. This can be illustrated by the following example.

> Two young families, the Blues and Greens, each have two young children. Both families earn identical salaries and identical incomes, but the Blues recently inherited $250,000. Since the Greens do not have $250,000 to fall back on in case of need or emergency, they (more so than the wealthier Blues) are under pressure to save for the future. It is likely, therefore, that the Greens will save a larger percentage of their income than will the wealthier Blues.

INTEREST RATES.   A person or business usually pays interest for the use of someone else's money. Consumers who borrow money to finance a purchase have to pay interest on the loan. Similarly, banks pay interest to their depositors in exchange for the use of the money on deposit.

When interest rates are rising, it becomes more costly to borrow. Higher costs, in turn, discourage consumer spending, particularly spending by consumers who spend with borrowed money (e.g., use credit cards). But higher interest rates encourage saving simply because individuals are offered higher interest to put their money into a savings plan. As an individual puts more of her or his income into savings, less is available to spend.

Falling interest rates have the opposite effect: the propensity to consume increases, while the propensity to save decreases. As interest rates fall, it is

Why would knowing interest rates help determine whether this customer buys a new car?

cheaper to borrow. For example, if you have to pay back $8 in interest rather than $10, you would have an additional $2 to spend. In contrast, if your bank reduces interest rates on every $100 deposited, you would have less of an inducement to save your money in that bank. You might decide to spend your $100 rather than save it.

FUTURE EXPECTATIONS.   Consumers often base their decisions concerning how much to spend on what they feel about the future. When the general public is feeling good about the future, consumer spending tends to increase. When pessimism prevails, consumers tend to postpone some of their more costly purchases. These ideas are illustrated by the following dialogue.

> "My parents were going to buy a new car, but they didn't."
> "Oh, yeah, what happened?"
> "I don't know. Business is so bad that my dad figured the factory where he works might have to lay off workers next year."

GOVERNMENT POLICIES.   The use of government's power to tax and spend may also affect consumer spending and saving patterns. Tax increases tend to discourage spending by taking purchasing power away from consumers by an amount equal to the tax. Conversely, tax reductions stimulate spending by increasing take-home pay. Tax laws have also been used to encourage savings. For example, federal laws defer taxes on the interest earned from certain retirement savings accounts. (IRAs, or individual retirement accounts, and other retirement plans are discussed on page 229.)

Similarly, government programs such as Social Security, welfare, unemployment insurance, and veterans' benefits can either add to or take away from consumers' purchasing power. For example, the money spent by state governments to increase benefits for unemployed workers adds to the workers' purchasing power and to consumer spending. Conversely, by withholding or reducing welfare payments, food stamps, or unemployment benefits, the individuals who would have received these payments will have less to spend.

Defining Savings and Investments

Many people do not immediately spend all of their income. They try to set aside some amount for use at a later time. Income that is not spent is called *savings.* Some people use their savings to buy property that they believe will increase in value. This activity is called *investing.* The properties that people purchase while investing are called *investments.* Stocks, bonds, and mutual funds are some of the popular investments that we will discuss later in this chapter.

THE DECISION TO SAVE AND INVEST

Why do people set aside a portion of their income in savings and investments rather than spend it all? There are several reasons.

- *To prepare for the unexpected.* When an emergency (such as an accident, long-term illness, or the loss of a job) occurs, savings and investments can help soften the financial burden. That is what people mean when they say they are "saving for a rainy day."

- *To finance costly purchases.* Some purchases (such as automobiles, vacations, and computers) cost more than one's current income. Savings provide a way to afford those purchases.

- *For additional income.* Money set aside in savings accounts and investments typically earns a return in the form of interest or dividends.

- *For retirement.* Most people would like to retire when they reach a certain age. Probably they will be entitled to Social Security benefits. Some people are also entitled to receive benefits from their employer's pension plan. But all these benefits might not be enough to support the retired person. In order to be able to retire comfortably, an individual would be wise to establish another fund on which he or she can draw after retirement.

- *As a hedge against inflation.* The real value of assets or income shrinks with time as the purchasing power of the dollar declines. Thus, $100 set aside in a cookie jar in 1990 did not buy as much in 2005 as it would have in

Figure 10.3 **Economic Support for Retirees**

1990. If the $100 had been placed in a bank earning interest at 6 percent per year, 15 years later it would have amounted to almost $240. However, if the rate of inflation during these 15 years was greater than 6 percent per year, the $240 would have also bought less in 2005 than $100 could have purchased in 1990. Since the rate of inflation was actually about 3 percent per year during the period 1990–2005, savings earning 6 percent brought a net return (adjusted for inflation) of only 3 percent per year. But a net increase of 3 percent per year is preferable to a loss in purchasing power, which would have been the case if money had not been invested at a rate higher than the rate of inflation. From this example, we can conclude that it is wise to save or invest as a hedge against inflation.

Depending on earning money from a savings account is not usually considered the best way to hedge against inflation. Banks may pay interest for savings accounts at rates below the rate of inflation. Moreover, one may get a better return by investing in securities. Many people buy corporate stocks as a hedge against inflation because the value of stocks tends to rise during inflationary periods. Of course, the value of individual stocks might also fall during times of inflation (or any time). The *market risk* that the value of an investment will be low when one wants to sell is as much a concern to an investor as is inflation. The greater the market risk, however, the greater is the potential return.

Some people invest in *real estate* (land and buildings). They expect that land and building values will rise considerably faster than the rate of inflation. This was the case through much of the 1980s. Then in the late 1980s, the real estate market collapsed. Banks and insurance companies that had invested heavily in real estate suffered great losses.

Some individuals invest in objects of art or other collectibles. Prices of specific collectible items rise or fall in value depending on demand.

Evaluating Ways to Save and Invest

Banks and stock brokerage firms want consumers to entrust their money with them. In deciding which of the alternative savings and investment plans best suits their needs, wise consumers seek answers to the following questions.

How Safe Is It?   Some forms of savings are more secure than others. Money invested in U.S. savings bonds are as secure as the federal government itself. Similarly, bank deposits of up to $100,000 are insured by an agency of the federal government—the **Federal Deposit Insurance Corporation (FDIC)**. Congress created the FDIC so that even if a bank fails, its depositors will not lose their money.

What Are the Returns?   The *yield* (percentage rate of return) varies from one savings or investment instrument to another. The rate of interest one earns at a bank depends on the kind of account one opens, when one opens the account, and which bank one goes to. Corporate stocks and bonds offer the possibilities of earning more money than savings instruments. But both dividends and capital gains go up and down with the fortunes of the company that issued the stocks and bonds. Similarly, the interest offered by corporate bonds varies from one firm that issues bonds to another.

How Liquid Is It?   The ease with which a savings vehicle can be converted into cash is described as its *liquidity*. ATMs (automated teller machines) enable some bank depositors to withdraw limited amounts of funds at any time of any day. Slightly less liquid are bank savings accounts that can be withdrawn only during business hours. Some forms of savings require advance notice for withdrawals, while other types of savings must be left on deposit for a period of months or years before they can be withdrawn without a penalty.

Ways to Save and Invest

In this section of the chapter, we will discuss a number of saving and investment methods: savings accounts, certificates of deposit, bonds, U.S. savings bonds, stocks, and mutual funds.

Savings Accounts.   Commercial banks, savings and loan associations, mutual savings banks, and credit unions all offer one or more types of savings accounts. Savings accounts offer easy access to funds. But compared to other vehicles for saving (and compared to investment vehicles), they pay relatively low rates of interest. Some checking accounts called *NOW accounts* pay interest and thus can be considered a form of savings account. But the interest that these NOW checking accounts pay is always quite low.

Certificates of Deposit.   Since savings accounts pay so little in interest, it is advisable to leave in them only limited sums (say, the equivalent of two months' income). Additional savings (those that will not be needed until the distant future) are better invested in vehicles with higher rates of return. One such option is the *certificate of deposit (CD)*. A certificate of deposit is a time deposit that the depositor agrees to keep in a bank for a specified time. CDs offer higher rates of return than do savings accounts. While depositors can withdraw their money from savings accounts whenever the bank is open, CDs must be held for anywhere from 3 to 72 months before they can be cashed in without a penalty.

Bonds.   Bonds are long-term obligations issued by governments and private corporations. With most bonds, the issuer of the bonds repays the principal at the end of a specified period of time. It also makes periodic payments of interest to the bondholders. Interest paid by state- and local-government bonds is exempt from federal income taxes, as well as from state and local taxes. Interest

Certificates of deposit are offered with different rates of interest for different time periods. Several choices are presented on this chart.

CERTIFICATES OF DEPOSIT		
3 Month CD	0.71	0.71
6 Month CD	0.80	0.80
7 Month CD	1.00	1.00
9 Month CD	1.04	1.05
13 Month CD	1.19	1.20
15 Month CD	1.59	1.60
18 Month CD	1.59	1.60
2 Year CD	1.69	1.70
3 Year CD	2.23	2.25
4 Year CD	2.66	2.70
5 Year CD	3.15	3.20
7 Year CD	3.25	3.30
10 Year CD	4.11	4.20

APYs as of Nov. 4th

paid by federal bonds is exempt from state and local taxes but not from federal income taxes. (We discussed bonds in more detail in Chapter 5.)

Unlike bank deposits, corporate bonds and government bonds (with the exception of U.S. savings bonds) do not guarantee the return of principal before maturity. Maturity is the date at which the issuer of the bond promises to *redeem* (buy back) the bond at its face value. If a corporation or government agency is selling a bond that has a face value of $1,000 with maturity at 2009, it is promising to pay $1,000 to the owner of the bond in the year 2009.

U.S. SAVINGS BONDS.   A *U.S. savings bond* is a contract showing that money has been loaned to the Treasury of the United States. Buying these government-guaranteed bonds is an absolutely safe and liquid investment. The Series EE

This U.S. EE savings bond was purchased for $25, but it will be worth $50 on maturity.

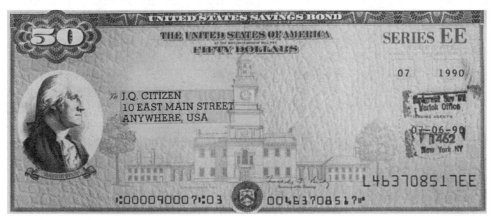

savings bonds are easily available for the small investor because they may be purchased for as little as $25 from many local banks. The bonds accrue interest until they are redeemed (cashed in) or they reach final maturity, whichever happens first. Series EE bonds are available in $50, $75, $100, $200, $500, $1,000, $5,000, and $10,000 denominations. The purchase price of each bond is 50 percent of its face amount. For example, a $100 bond costs $50. It will be worth $100 at its maturity.

The *original maturity* of a Series EE bond depends on the guaranteed minimum rate of interest at the time of purchase. For example, if the government guarantees a rate at the time of purchase of 4 percent, a $100 savings bond will have an original maturity of 18 years ($50 compounded semiannually at 4 percent equals $100 after 18 years). Series EE bonds held five years or longer earn interest on a market-based variable rate, which may be higher than the original rate offered (the minimum rate). It may never be lower than the minimum rate. Therefore, a Series EE bond may reach maturity before 18 years from issue (assuming an original rate of 4 percent). Savings bonds continue to earn interest (until they are redeemed) for up to 30 years from issue. Thirty years is the final maturity date.

Although buying U.S. savings bonds is a liquid investment, they must be held for at least six months after the issue date before they can be redeemed. The benefits of purchasing U.S. savings bonds include safety and the absence of fees for purchasing or redeeming bonds. U.S. savings bonds are exempt from state and local taxes. The U.S. government guarantees the bondholder both principal and interest. If a bond is lost, stolen, mutilated, or destroyed, it can be replaced free of charge.

COMMON STOCKS.   As discussed in Chapter 5, some people invest a portion of their savings in the stocks of publicly held corporations. Many of these stocks yield a return in the form of dividends. Investors who sell their stocks might also receive a *capital gain* if the value of these stocks has increased from the time they bought them.

There is considerable risk attached to stock ownership. A firm's ability to earn profits and grow directly affects the size of the dividend it can afford to pay and the value of its stock. The failure of the firm either to produce a profit or to grow could, therefore, result in financial loss to those who had invested in it.

If you do invest in stocks or bonds, it is advisable that you investigate before you invest. Learn what you can about the business in which you plan to invest your money. You also want to know what has been the company's past history and what are its prospects of future performance. (In order to better understand the finances of the business you are investing in, you may want to review Chapter 5, where we discussed the purchase of stocks and how to read corporations' financial statements.)

You can reduce your risks by *diversifying* your investment. Instead of putting all of your money into the stocks of one company, you may invest in a number of different companies, in both stocks and bonds, and in different types of industries. Whatever you do, remember that conditions change and even the best corporations sometimes perform poorly. Keep your eye on your investments!

MUTUAL FUNDS.   There are thousands of stocks and bonds from which to choose. Investors with much money to invest often look to professional securities consultants to assist them. Most consumers, however, have neither the funds nor the skills necessary to buy and sell securities on their own or to pay for the services of an investment adviser. For that reason, many people have turned to *mutual funds* as a way of diversifying their investments.

A mutual fund is a corporation that uses the proceeds from the sale of its stock to purchase the securities of other corporations. Mutual fund managers work with pools of funds running into millions (sometimes billions) of dollars. In this way, the mutual fund managers can spread the risk of investing over many securities. They can also afford to hire full-time analysts to manage their investments. Since most mutual fund managers will open accounts for $1,000 or less, they are within the reach of the average investor.

Valuable information about mutual funds (including past performances and ratings in terms of risk) is available from a number of sources. The following Web sites are updated daily: <<money.cnn.com/funds>>; <<www.morningstar .com>>; and <<www.valueline.com/ >>. For those who prefer to research print publications, there is *NoLoadFundX* (a monthly newsletter), *The Value Line Mutual Fund Survey* (a yearly publication), and *The Mutual Fund Buyer's Guide* (a paperback book).

IRAS AND 401(K) PLANS.   The federal government has authorized several methods to allow individuals to accumulate funds for retirement. An *individual retirement account (IRA)* can be set up by individuals with earned income. An individual has many investment options with an IRA. In fact, any one or combination of the savings and investment vehicles previously discussed may make up an IRA.

A *401(k) plan* is a pension plan run by an employer for employees that allows an individual employee to contribute regularly a portion of his or her paycheck into a special savings or investment account. Some employers also contribute to the account. For example, a company might agree to contribute 50 cents to every eligible employee's account for every dollar contributed by each employee. Investment options vary from plan to plan. Employees usually have some choices as to how to invest their retirement money.

Under 401(k) plans and some IRAs, income tax on part of the employees' salary and accumulating interest is deferred (delayed) until money is withdrawn from the retirement account. This means that earnings from these plans can grow without being taxed until retirement, when (presumably) one's income is less than when one is working. When withdrawals are made, taxes are levied only on the amount withdrawn each year.

Investing in Mutual Funds

There are many varieties of mutual funds. The most common are the money market, equity, and bond funds.

1. **Money Market Funds.** The managers of money market funds pool the savings of hundreds or thousands of investors to purchase short-term credit instruments, such as treasury bills and short-term promissory notes. (*Treasury bills* are credit instruments representing borrowing by the U.S. government to meet its current expenses. *Short-term promissory notes* are issued by individual corporations and government agencies in order to borrow working capital from banks.) The money market funds earn interest on these securities and distribute most of the interest to the investors. Money market funds are highly liquid. Investors can withdraw their money at any time without penalty. Money market funds, unlike savings deposits, are not insured against loss by the federal government.

2. **Equity Funds.** This type of fund consists of *portfolios* (groups of investments) of corporate stocks. Typically these stocks earn both dividends and capital gains, most of which are distributed to the shareholders by the managers of the mutual funds.

3. **Bond Funds.** As the name suggests, bond funds consist of portfolios of bonds. Managers of the bond funds periodically distribute to the investors most of the interest earned on these investments.

4. **Balanced Funds.** This type of fund is made up of portfolios of both stocks and bonds. By buying into such a fund, investors hope to gain the advantages of both stock and bond ownership.

Should You Put Your Savings in a Mutual Fund?

Like the stocks and bonds that the fund managers buy, the value of mutual funds fluctuates daily. For that reason, on any given day some people might find that the mutual fund shares that they own are worth less than when they first bought them.

Mutual fund managers charge for the services they perform. These charges add to the cost of purchasing a mutual fund. Some funds charge more than others. It is also true that some funds are better managed than others. For all these reasons, people thinking about investing in mutual funds should investigate and compare funds before making their decisions.

SUMMARY

A financial plan is a guide to one's financial future. It involves setting goals, examining one's assets and liabilities to determine one's net worth, and then making the necessary spending, saving, and investment decisions to achieve those goals. A budget summarizes anticipated income and expenditures for a period of time. Personal budgets are usually planned on a monthly basis.

The consumer is very important to the U.S. economy. Consumer spending represents about two-thirds of our gross domestic product. A decline in consumer spending can result in a decline in production and employment nationwide. An increase in spending can increase production and employment in the United States. Consumer savings are also important to the economy because they comprise the fund from which new capital investment is derived.

Consumers have a choice to spend or save their income. The consumers' propensity to spend is determined by income, wealth, interest rates, future expectations, and government policies. Consumers' propensity to save is influenced by such factors as the safety, return, and liquidity of the vehicle in which they put their savings. There are a variety of savings and investment choices available to consumers. Some of these include savings accounts, U.S. savings bonds, corporate stocks and bonds, mutual funds, and CDs.

REVIEWING THE CHAPTER

BUILDING VOCABULARY

Match each term in Column A with its definition in Column B.

Column A

1. certificate of deposit
2. maturity
3. liquidity
4. money market fund
5. mutual fund
6. compound interest
7. IRA
8. savings
9. disposable family income
10. wealth

Column B

a. a fund into which an individual annually deposits a limited amount to have money for retirement
b. the interest earned on the principal and on the interest already earned
c. a corporation that uses its stockholders' capital to buy securities of other firms
d. income that is not spent
e. the ease with which a form of savings can be converted to cash
f. an investment instrument in which the buyer agrees not to withdraw his or her deposit for a period of time
g. what a family has left after paying taxes
h. anything that has value
i. a vehicle that allows consumers to invest savings in short-term securities
j. the date at which a bond is set to be redeemed at face value

UNDERSTANDING WHAT YOU HAVE READ

1. A financial plan can best be compared to a (*a*) corporate balance sheet (*b*) road map (*c*) statement of net worth (*d*) mutual fund.

2. A budget summarizes (*a*) actual income and expenditures (*b*) anticipated income and expenditures (*c*) cash flow (*d*) short-term goals.

3. Most of the nation's output of goods and services is purchased by (*a*) consumers (*b*) business firms (*c*) state and local governments (*d*) the federal government.

4. Which *one* of the following forms of saving and investing offers the greatest liquidity? (*a*) savings account (*b*) corporate stock (*c*) real estate (*d*) certificate of deposit.

5. Which *one* of the following types of saving and investing would consumers be most likely to use if they were interested in growth? (*a*) savings account (*b*) NOW account (*c*) corporate stock (*d*) government savings bond.

6. Which *one* of the following forms of saving and investing offers the greatest degree of safety? (*a*) mutual funds (*b*) corporate stock (*c*) real estate (*d*) a government savings bond.

7. Which *one* of the following types of bond funds is most likely to return the highest yield? (*a*) government bond fund (*b*) municipal bond fund (*c*) high-quality corporate bond fund (*d*) "junk bond" fund.

8. A bond yields $100 yearly at 4 percent interest. What is its market value? (*a*) $1,000 (*b*) $1,500 (*c*) $2,000 (*d*) $2,500.

9. In February, you examine your actual income and spending for the month of January. This gives you a picture of your (*a*) net worth (*b*) cash flow (*c*) accumulated debt (*d*) accumulated savings.

10. Approximately how much would $1,000 invested at 4 percent compounded annually be worth in ten years? (*a*) $1,040 (*b*) $1,200 (*c*) $1,316 (*d*) $1,480.

THINKING CRITICALLY

1. "A financial plan is like a road map to guide you to your financial future."

   a. Explain the meaning of this statement.

   b. Explain why is it important to set goals when preparing a financial plan.

   c. Indicate whether you think each of the goals cited below is a short-term, medium-term, or long-term goal.

▷ FINANCIAL GOALS

Goals	Short-Term (less than 1 year)	Medium-Term (1–5 years)	Long-Term (5–10 years)
Education expenses			
Buy a car			
Buy a house			
Buy a vacation home			
Make home improvements			
Other large purchases			
Take a vacation			
Start a business			
Have children			
Retirement funds			
Provide for survivor			
Other			

2. What are the differences among net worth, cash flow, and a budget?

3. Prepare your weekly budget by completing the following chart.

Current Income		**Current Expenses**	
Earnings	_____	Transportation	_____
Allowance	_____	School supplies	_____
Gifts	_____	Lunches	_____
Other	_____	Entertainment	_____
		Other	_____
Total Income	_____	Total Expenses	_____

Financial Summary

Total Income	_____
Total Expenses	_____
(+ or −)	_____

4. Explain what is meant by the statement, "Savings are essential to the nation's economic health."

5. Compare the following kinds of savings and investment alternatives by describing their advantage in one column and their disadvantages in another: (*a*) savings account (*b*) certificate of deposit (*c*) money market fund (*d*) NOW account.

USING THE INTERNET

- Information about U.S. government securities (including savings bonds) is available at <<www.treasurydirect.gov>>. To help answer your questions before investing, the Securities and Exchange Commission makes available a number of publications which may be ordered at <<www.sec.gov>>. Another source is <<financialplan.about. com>>.

- You can take a "Reality Check" offered without charge at <<www.jumpstart.org/reality check>> to understand what you need to know about saving and investing to meet long-term goals.

- The Stock Market Game at <<www.smgww.org>> is sponsored by the securities industry and enables participants to discover the rewards and risks involved in decision-making, the sources and uses of capital, and other related economic concepts.

CHAPTER 11

Buying With Cash and Credit

OVERVIEW

Consumers are people like you, your family, and friends who buy goods and services for their own use. Sometimes we borrow in order to obtain the goods or services we want. In our market economy, we are blessed to have so much from which to choose. But the wide choice can make buying confusing. Merchants want us to buy what they have to sell. They use a variety of techniques to encourage sales. If consumers cannot pay for a purchase immediately, they can pay for it later. That is, they can buy on credit. Today, buying on credit is quite common. The results can either be beneficial or harmful.

In this chapter, we will discuss how to be a wise buyer. We will also discuss the advantages and disadvantages of advertising, sources of information and assistance available to consumers, and how to obtain and use credit wisely.

WISE BUYING

Budgeting, as discussed in the previous chapter, is an important tool in financial planning. Having a budget, however, does not guarantee that you are going to get the most for your money. Millie Hazami and her sister, Sue Witte, budget the same amount of money for daily family expenses. Nevertheless, Millie always seems to have more of everything in her home. The reason is that Millie is a better shopper than her sister.

It is not always easy to be a wise shopper. It takes a lot of work and planning. There are so many choices of products and services available that it is easy to become confused. Supermarket shelves, for example, are stacked high with all sorts of foods. And each category of food comes in a variety of brands. Moreover, these products come in different sizes and weights, with different packaging and prices. How can the shopper tell, for example, which can of peas is the best buy? What is true for canned peas is equally true for the thousands of other products sold in supermarkets and elsewhere. So how can you know what to buy? How can you become a wise shopper?

The following *four* steps can help you to shop wisely.

1. Know what you want and what you can afford. Fancy, new sports cars can sell for over $100,000. Simple, but practical, new cars can sell for under $20,000. When you are finished with school and get a full-time job, you may want to purchase the more expensive car but realize that you can afford only the cheaper one. Like it or not, you may have to settle for the less expensive model. Similarly, in choosing which restaurant to eat at or which item of clothing to buy (and in every other situation in which you have a choice among goods and services), you must be sensible about your purchases. Sometimes it is best not to make a planned purchase. It is as important to know what you can afford as to know what you want.

2. Plan ahead. Do not buy on impulse. Make a list of the things to buy and then shop around. Compare prices and brands. It is very common to find the product that you want selling at different prices at different stores. Buy only what you can use or store safely. It is foolish to buy what you do not need just because it is on sale. Why buy a lawn mower that is on sale if you do not have a lawn to mow? Does that sound way out to you? Perhaps, but the concept is correct. Check your own household for unused tools, equipment, kitchen utensils, and clothing that were bought just because they were on sale.

With impulse buying, you might find bargains, but you might also end up with items that you do not need.

3. Read labels, tags, and guarantees. A lot of valuable information is on a product's label. For many food products, labels must state the weight, ingredients, and nutritional facts about the product. In the case of canned peas, for example, it makes no difference which brand you buy if the cans are of similar ingredients, nutritional value, and weight. The wise buyer will buy the least expensive can of peas. Clothing labels state where the item was made, the materials used in its manufacture, and cleaning instructions. You should know that if a clothing item requires dry cleaning, it will be more expensive to maintain than a clothing item that is machine washable. Appliances such as hot water heaters, air conditioners, heat pumps, furnaces, boilers, refrigerators, and dishwashers have an *EnergyGuide label.* It provides an estimate of the yearly cost of operating the appliance and how that appliance compares in energy usage with competing products.

4. Save by watching for sales, specials, and clearances. You can save money by buying items on sale. Of course, as mentioned earlier, a sale item is not worth buying if you do not need it. Many stores run sales following Christmas and on some national holidays, such as Presidents' Day. By waiting to buy when these sales take place, you can enjoy considerable savings. Your local newspaper carries many ads announcing sales and discounts on various products. You may also see ads for "going out of business sales" or seasonal "clearance sales." Prices at such sales are often well below their nonsale prices. Newspaper inserts are often filled with store ads containing coupons. By redeeming these coupons for the products listed, significant savings are very often possible. In addition to sales items, you want to know more about items that are not on sale. One of the major sources of information about products and services is advertising.

 # ADVERTISING AND THE CONSUMER

Advertising consists of paid announcements (ads) that call attention to a product or service in the hopes of attracting customers. The purpose of advertising is to increase sales by creating demand for the advertised products. Consumers are confronted by advertisements day and night—over the radio, on billboards, on the Internet, in newspapers and magazines, on television, on flyers handed out or sent by mail, in store windows and movie theaters, and, it seems, almost everywhere. Can we trust these ads? Is advertising good or bad for consumers? Actually, it is a little of both. After examining the advantages and disadvantages of advertising, you can make up your own mind.

PERSONAL ECONOMICS

Reading Labels

Here are several types of labels that consumers should be familiar with.

The EnergyGuide Label

EnergyGuide labels can help consumers save money. In the long run, it is often cheaper to buy a more expensive model of an appliance if it is *energy efficient* (uses less energy than other, similar models). Let us compare the cost of buying and operating two refrigerators over a 15-year period (the average life of a refrigerator).

Refrigerator A sells for $850. Its EnergyGuide label indicates that A's yearly operating cost is $100. The second refrigerator, B, is priced at only $750, but its EnergyGuide label indicates that its yearly operating cost is $125. Which is the better buy? Refrigerator B costs $100 less to purchase but $25 more each year to operate. In four years, therefore, the energy-efficient model will cancel out the difference in the original purchase price ($25 × 4 = $100). After 15 years, the consumer would have saved $275 by purchasing the more expensive, energy-efficient model.

TABLE 11.1   COMPARISON COSTS OF TWO REFRIGERATOR MODELS

	Refrigerator A	Refrigerator B
Selling price	$ 850	$ 750
Energy cost	+	+
for 15 years	($100 × 15)	($125 × 15)
	$1,500	$1,875
Total cost after 15 years	$2,350	$2,625

The Nutrition Facts Label

The *nutrition facts label*, found on almost all food products (see photo on page 238), shows *four* important pieces of information:

- the weight or size of the package (in ounces, grams, or liters) and the number of servings in the package

- how many calories and nutrients in each serving (including the number of calories from fat, grams of fat, cholesterol, sodium, carbohydrates, vitamins, and fiber)

- the percentages of recommended daily values of fat, cholesterol, sodium, carbohydrates, protein, vitamins, and fiber the food contains

- the ingredients in the package (arranged in order of the quantity of each ingredient).

The Grade Label

The U.S. Department of Agriculture sets quality standards for various food products. Its inspectors periodically check meats, eggs, butter, and frozen foods of producers who agree to use the USDA grading system. These producers can use official labels that show the *grade* of the product. For example, butter graded AA is of top quality. For consumers contemplating the purchase of one of two competing brands of butter, it does not matter who produces the butter if both are labeled Grade AA.

Meats also are graded. Meats graded Prime are of top quality. Meats stamped Choice are as nutritious as Prime meats but are less expensive. Choice meats have less marbling (a way of distributing the fat) and, therefore, are less appealing to some consumers.

(continued on next page)

Examine the label on this can of soup. The can contains two servings based on a serving size of 245 grams per person. One serving of this vegetable soup provides 90 calories, of which 10 are from fat. The total fat content is 1.5 grams, or 2 percent of daily value based on a 2,000-calorie diet. This can of soup contains .5 gram of saturated fat and 5 mg. of cholesterol. It also contais 910 mg. of sodium per serving, or 38 percent of daily value. The soup is rich in vitamin A and C and also supplies moderate amounts of iron and calcium.

There is no difference in taste between a white egg and a brown one of equal size and grade. Only the shell color differs, and one does not normally eat the shell. Thus, customers should look at the grade of eggs in making such a purchase.

The Unit Price Label

For certain types of products, stores must show unit pricing information near where the products are displayed. The *unit price* tells the price of the product per unit of weight or unit of volume. For example, suppose you see two different cans of vegetable soup of different size and price, from two different producers. The 19-ounce can, which is labeled "family size," costs $1.71; the smaller can, which is labeled "economy size" and weighes 16 ounces, costs $1.60. Which can of vegetable soup is more economical? Mom's Vegetable Soup. The unit price of Mom's is $.09 per ounce, while the unit price of Dad's Vegetable Soup is $.10 per ounce. (See Figure 11.1.)

Unit pricing lets you know which bar of soap, box of cereal, container of detergent, cut of meat, and a host of other products cost the least in terms of unit of weight or volume. The product with the lowest unit price is always the least expensive.

Figure 11.1 **Unit Pricing for Canned Vegetable Soup**

✒ Techniques of Advertising

Advertisers rely on a number of techniques to create demand and to sell their products.

APPEALS TO REASON, NEED, AND INTEREST.   Perhaps you have seen an advertisement for an automobile that stresses the car's fuel economy and low-maintenance costs. The ad might show a young couple examining the car and looking in the trunk. This ad is appealing to the consumers' interests and need for a low-cost, practical automobile.

APPEALS TO VANITY.   Perhaps you have seen an advertisment for a luxury car that shows how glamorous the driver or passengers might appear to others. Driving the car might make one more important looking, or so the advertisement implies.

EXAGGERATIONS OR HALF-TRUTHS.   Have you seen product ads that say something like "Look and feel younger!"? The ads imply that using a product will create great changes in how one looks, how healthy one feels, or how happy one is. Very few of these products do all that they seem to promise. An ad may take one fact about a product and then exaggerate its importance.

APPEALS TO EMOTIONS.   All of us want to feel loved. And we all have fears. Advertisers play on these emotions. Have you seen ads showing an attractive young person with a clear complexion or lovely hair and with another, admiring person looking on? The suggestion of the ad is that if you too use the product advertised, you will be loved.

DESIRE TO CONFORM.   One of the most common appeals used by advertisers is based on the knowledge that almost everyone wants to be accepted by one's peers. The ads tell us to buy the same goods that our friends and other peers buy so that we will be accepted.

IDENTIFICATION.   An advertiser might claim that a well-known actor or other personality uses a product or service. Or this famous person might be doing the sales pitch. The advertiser is tying the product or service with the personality in order to get you to buy it. In real life, the famous personality might not use the advertised product or service, or even like it.

GETTING SOMETHING FOR NOTHING.   Watch out for ads that offer you something for nothing. Banks and department stores sometimes offer new customers "free gifts" for opening an account. Accept such offers only if you are planning on opening an account anyway. Otherwise, the value of the "free gift" may not be worth the costs or time involved in having these accounts. Watch out for offers of free trips or vacation stays. These offers are being sent to you to try to get you to listen to a sales pitch.

BRAND NAMES.   Advertisers try to develop loyalty to *brand names*. They want us to think that their product is somehow different from those of their competitors. We might hear commercials in the form of jingles, songs, or slogans that are repeated again and again. This advertising adds to the cost of the product. Consumers might be better off buy a competing product that does not have a brand name; instead, it might be a *generic product* (the same product but without a well-known name) or have the name of the store or chain of stores *(house brand)*.

BAIT-AND-SWITCH.   The advertising and sales tactic called *bait-and-switch* usually involves a store advertisement of a well-known product offered at a low price (the "bait") so as to attract customers. Once in the store, customers are "switched" by salespeople to a more expensive competing brand at a price that will earn the dealer a larger profit. Customers are usually told that the advertised product has been sold out.

Advantages of Advertising

You can learn a lot from an ad. You might be interested in buying a digital camera and then come across a newspaper ad for one. The ad might include a picture of the camera, its price, and other information you want to know. Ads also let you know about new products on the market or used ones that are available for sale. Automobile manufacturers always advertise their new model cars months before they are ready for sale. Knowing what products are available, where they are sold, and how much they cost can help consumers save time. Consumer can even shop and compare prices of products without leaving home! Many shoppers rely on the Internet in searching for and buying all sorts of products and services, including automobiles, cameras, computers, and even life insurance. Others prefer printed mail-order catalogs from which items may be selected and ordered by mail or by phone.

Advertising stimulates competition and results in lower prices to consumers. By reading, listening to, or watching ads, consumers can learn about similar products being offered for sale and their prices. The availability of information forces manufacturers to keep abreast of the competition by producing a better product at a lower cost to consumers.

Advertising stimulates demand and, in so doing, encourages large-scale manufacturing. As discussed in Chapter 6, this process enables manufacturers to produce goods at lower cost per item with potential savings to the consumer.

Advertisers pay for almost all of the programs that we watch on television or listen to over the radio. In fact, advertising provides the major source of income for magazines, newspapers, radio, and television. It provides important revenue for some Internet sites as well. Without advertising, the costs of pro-

What advertising techniques are used in these billboard ads?

ducing many of the entertainment events we are accustomed to would be much higher and, therefore, the events' ticket prices would be too expensive for the average consumer.

Disadvantages of Advertising

The purpose of advertising is to sell goods. Therefore, the advertiser is not always concerned with the best interests of the consumers. Wise consumers are aware that advertising might be misleading

It is expensive for firms to advertise. Naturally, the cost of advertising is added into the cost of producing the product or service that is being offered for sale. It has been argued, therefore, that the goods and services we purchase would be a lot cheaper if there were less spent on advertising. (Compare this argument with the arguments above claiming that advertising results in lower prices.)

Advertising brand names reduces competition. Competition works best when products offered for sale are interchangeable with and indistinguishable from each other. Through effective advertising, a company convinces some consumers that its brand-name product is different from competing products of similar ingredients and quality. For example, aspirin is a derivative of salicylic acid used for pain and fever. Yet many consumers will only buy aspirin manufactured by a particular company even though the aspirin sold by that company is no more effective than that manufactured by competitors selling for less. Since consumers believe that the various brands of aspirin are different (because of their brand names), it may be argued that the products are not engaged in pure competition. Remember that pure competition presupposes that the competitive products are indistinguishable from one another.

Some of the advantages and disadvantages of advertising have been discussed. The fact is, though, that advertising is part of modern living. The wise consumer, aware of advertising's strengths and weaknesses, uses it like any tool—with intelligence and caution.

ASSISTING AND INFORMING CONSUMERS

In discussing investments, we said to investigate before you invest. The same advice is valid when shopping for goods and services, borrowing money, or buying on credit. Although there are laws to protect consumers, it remains the consumer's responsibility to investigate carefully and to choose wisely.

Consumer assistance and information is available from government agencies and nongovernment organizations. Sometimes the assistance is given without the consumer's being aware of it. At other times, the consumer must take the initiative to get help and/or information.

Federal Agencies

There are more than 50 federal agencies that provide some form of protection and information to consumers. For example, the **Consumer Product Safety Commission** monitors the safety of some 15,000 kinds of consumer products and issues recalls of products deemed unsafe, such as clothing that might easily catch fire or toys that might be dangerous for toddlers. The **Food and Drug Administration (FDA)** protects consumers against dangerous foods, drugs,

The U.S. Department of Agriculture has approved the use of the label "Grade AA Large" for this package of eggs.

and cosmetics. This agency not only monitors products already on the market but also requires firms to prove that their products have been tested and are safe before they may be sold to the public. The **U.S. Department of Agriculture (USDA)** inspects and regulates the grading of meats, fruits and vegetables, frozen foods, and canned products. The **Federal Trade Commission (FTC)** monitors advertising and can take action against companies that issue false or misleading statements about their products or services. In addition to their monitoring and regulatory services, each of these government agencies provides a wealth of information in print materials or on the Internet.

State and Local Agencies

State and local governments also provide both protective services and information to consumers. For example, your local department of health may inspect sanitary conditions at local restaurants and cafeterias. Your state department of agriculture checks such things as the dating of milk and the labeling of processed meats at your local supermarket. Your teacher is licensed by the state, as are your community's doctors, nurses, hairdressers, and electricians. All states, and most localities, maintain an office of consumer affairs to assist consumers and to provide them with information.

Nongovernmental Consumer Service Providers

There are hundreds of various kinds of consumer service providers, such as consumer action groups, testing and rating organizations, and business and professional associations.

CONSUMER ACTION PROFESSIONALS.   Your local newspaper and television and radio stations may feature a "Consumers' Column" where a variety of products, health issues, and topics of interest to consumers are presented. Often, the columnist or media personality may act on behalf of someone who is having difficulty resolving an issue with a retailer. In addition, there are sites on the Internet devoted to helping consumers resolve complaints in such circumstances where the consumer, working alone, is unable to do so.

TESTING AND RATING ORGANIZATIONS.   Two well-known independent, non-profit national organizations devoted to testing and rating products are **Consumers' Research** and **Consumers Union**. These organizations test and rate products and publish their findings in magazines sold to the public (*Consumers' Research* and *Consumer Reports,* respectively). Neither of their publications carries advertising. This assures consumers that they are receiving an honest appraisal by experts whose evaluations are not influenced by advertisers. Suppose that you are interested in purchasing a DVD player. Searching at your local library, you might find an issue of *Consumer Reports* that contains an article devoted to DVD players. Such an article might compare a number of DVD players tested, indicating the pros and cons of each machine. It may then present a table evaluating each DVD player in terms of reliability, price, ease of operation, frequency of repair, sound and picture quality, and other technical aspects of the appliance. The article may also suggest a "Best Buy." This is not necessarily the best DVD player of the group being tested but the one that the experts consider the best value for the money. A more expensive DVD player may receive a higher rating, but because of its price it is not a "Best Buy."

Some testing organizations test but do not rate products. The **United States Pharmacopoeia** tests drugs and vitamins. The products it approves carry the *USP* mark. Electrical equipment that has been tested for fire and shock hazards by the **Underwriters Laboratories** carries the *UL* label. If you look at bottles of medicine in your medicine cabinet or the cords on your lamps, you will probably find stamped on the items (or printed on tags attached to them) the mark of these testing organizations.

BUSINESS AND PROFESSIONAL ASSOCIATIONS.   There are about 150 *Better Business Bureaus* sponsored by private industry and located in communities across the country. The purpose of the bureaus is to promote honest business practices. Consumers who feel that they have been misled or cheated in a transaction with some firm may bring the matter to their local Better Business Bureau. The Bureau will try to resolve the issue by contacting the firm on behalf of the consumer. The Bureau maintains a file of the various complaints made by consumers against companies doing business in their locality. Before buying or using the services of a business, consumers can contact the local Better Business Bureau to find out if there have been complaints lodged against that firm.

Many industries are organized into associations. To name just a few, there are: the **American Insurance Association**, representing more than 370 property and casualty insurance companies; the **American Textile Manufacturers Institute**, representing the textile firms that produce more than 80 percent of domestic textiles; and the **American Gas Association**, representing gas pipeline and utility companies. These and other industry associations set standards for their industry and provide all sorts of information to consumers, including the scheduling of speakers for consumer groups. Of course, though these associations may provide useful information to consumers, their main function is to act on behalf of their membership. Keep in mind that the interests of such organizations are not always the same as the interests of consumers.

Professionals such as doctors, dentists, accountants, lawyers, and teachers have their own associations. The **American Medical Association (AMA)**, the **American Dental Association (ADA)**, and the **American Bar Association (ABA)** are just a few examples. These groups try to keep the standards of their profession as high as possible. In turn, this benefits consumers who use the services of the members of the association. The AMA publishes technical papers and suggests medical procedures that meet with their approval. The ADA gives its approval to brands of toothpaste that meet its standards for products that are helpful in reducing cavities (look for it on your tube of toothpaste). The ABA often makes recommendations as to the qualifications of individuals seeking judicial appointment. Professionals who are members of these associations are expected to maintain the standards of the organization. If a professional is deemed in violation of such standards, the organization may remove the member. This would have the effect of forcing the professional to improve her or his work habits and then request reinstatement, practice outside of the organization's jurisdiction, or seek some other line of work. Removing a member is not an action that is lightly taken. For that reason, few professionals have actually been removed.

 # CONSUMER BORROWING

"Neither a borrower nor a lender be." Until about 75 years ago, most people would have agreed with the advice given by a character in Shakespeare's *Hamlet.* Borrowing by individuals was looked upon as a human frailty, one with terrible, long-term consequences. Attitudes have since changed drastically. The use of credit has become a way of life for millions of U.S. consumers (see Figure 11.2 on page 246). Despite credit's popularity, however, the excessive use of debt can cause personal hardship and unhappiness. For that reason, it would pay us all to learn how to use credit properly.

People use credit because it enables them to buy things now that they would otherwise have to forgo or delay buying until they had saved enough money. Consider the case of the young married couple who would eventually like to purchase their own appliances, car, and home. They calculate that by setting aside a portion of their income each week, they will have saved enough by the end of the year to buy the appliances they want. The car will take about three years more. But purchasing a home will take at least 20 years of saving. They decide, instead, to borrow the money to buy now the appliances, automobile, and home that they want.

A similar decision to use credit was made by a high school graduate who decided to take a student loan to pay for a college education. And two coworkers at an insurance company used credit to "fly now and pay later" for their two-week summer vacation in Europe.

Consumer credit also serves to keep up the high level of consumer spending on which our economy relies to stay healthy. It is likely that if buyers had to pay cash for everything, fewer goods and services would be purchased. Experience has shown that people spend far more in their lifetime when they are able to borrow against future earnings than when they have to pay out of past savings. We can see, therefore, that the availability of credit for consumers increases their total level of spending. This increase, in turn, benefits the economy as a whole.

Figure 11.2 **Consumer Credit Since 1930**

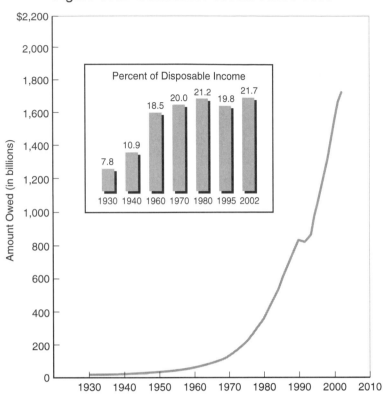

Credit, while usually costly, can sometimes save people money in the long run. One might, for example, find it less expensive to buy a car on the install-ment plan than to regularly rent one. Large families might find it less expensive to buy a washer and dryer on credit than to continue using coin-operated machines to do the family's laundry. When an item is on sale, it may pay to bor-row money to buy the item if the cost of borrowing is less than the savings from the sale.

Suppose that you want to buy a computer. Ordinarily, the computer you are interested in has a list price of $1,400. You do not have $1,400. You find out that at one store it is being offered at a sale price that is $120 less than its list price. But you have only $500. The salesperson says that you can borrow the remain-ing $780 at 8½ percent interest. That would cost you an additional $66.30 per year ($780 × .085 = $66.30). If you bought the computer on sale, borrowed the money and repaid the $780 within a year, you could be ahead by $53.70 ($120 − $66.30 = $53.70).

Of course, if you cannot repay your loan within the year, the cost of bor-rowing will evenually be greater than the amount saved at the sale. Would it be worth it in this situation to borrow the $780?

What would you do if the interest rate charged you was 15 percent? At that rate of interest, there would be no monetary advantage to your borrowing the

Figure 11.3 **Department Store Credit Application**

CREDIT APPLICATION
DUNHAM'S DEPARTMENT STORE

About you

	First	Middle	Last		Date of Birth	Mo.	Day	Year
Name								

Home Address — Street No. / City, Town / State / Zip / Years There / Own ☐ Rent ☐

Home Phone (Area Code) / **Monthly Rental or Mortgage Payment** / **Social Security No.**

Previous Address — Street No. / City, Town / State / Zip / Years There

Name of Close Relative — Name / Address / City / State / Zip / **Relative's Phone** (Area Code)

Present Employer — Name of Company / **Your Position**

Business Address — Street No. / City / State / Zip / **Business Phone** (Area Code)

Your capacity

Annual Salary / **Years There** / **Other Income**

Previous Employer / **Years There**

Your credit history (character) and collateral

American Express ☐ **Visa** ☐ **Mastercard** ☐ / Account No. / Exact Name of Account

Savings Bank / Account No. / Address of Bank

Checking Bank / Account No. / Address of Bank

Loan Reference

I hereby certify that all statements made are true and complete and submitted for the purpose of obtaining credit. I authorize you to check my credit and employment history.

Signature _____

Date _____

$780 and paying back the loan in a year. The total interest charged would be greater than the $120 you saved ($780 × .155 = $120.90).

What Kinds of Credit Are Available to Consumers?

Consumer credit is generally available in any or all of the following forms: installment plans, charge accounts, credit cards, personal loans, home mortgages, and home equity loans.

INSTALLMENT PLANS.   Some consumers use the *installment plan* (a method of buying something on credit with scheduled payments over time) to finance the purchase of expensive items, such as household appliances and motor vehicles.

At the time of sale, installment buyers are required to make a down payment and sign a contract. The contract will include the following:

● a statement showing the selling price of the item, the size of the down payment, all the finance charges that will be added to the selling price, and the total cost of the purchase after the charges are added to the selling price

● the number, amounts, and due dates of all payments

● the penalty for failure to make the regular payments on time.

CHARGE ACCOUNTS.   Most large department stores, as well as some smaller stores, offer *charge accounts.* With a charge account, title to the merchandise passes to the buyer in exchange for a promise to pay. Those who pay their charge account bills on time (usually within 30 days of the billing date) do not have to pay *finance charges.* Late payers, however, are subject to these additional fees.

Some stores provide special kinds of charge accounts for customers who prefer not to pay the full amount of their purchases within a month. These *revolving charge accounts* entitle buyers to repay a portion of the outstanding balance every month.

CREDIT CARDS.   The little plastic cards that so many people carry to pay for all kinds of goods and services—*credit cards*—came into their own in the 1960s and 1970s. These cards permit their holders to charge purchases at thousands of stores, restaurants, and hotels—both in the United States and abroad.

Why has the cartoonist shown credit cards stacked this way?

"SO FAR, SO GOOD"

—from *Herblock on All Fronts* (New American Library, 1980).

Many of the nation's banks offer credit cards through the MasterCard, Discover Card, and Visa programs. In addition, some large retail chains issue their own credit cards. Those considering getting a credit card should be aware of certain costs.

Annual Fees.   Some credit card companies require the card holder to pay an *annual fee*. Other credit cards do not have this cost.

Late Charges.   Credit card holders are billed monthly if something has been charged. If the card holder does not make at least the minimum monthly payment within a set number of days, the card holder is charged a *late fee*.

Interest Rates.   Those customers who do not pay the the whole amount on their bills are subject to a *interest charge* of about 1.5 percent of the monthly balance.

Consumers who want to obtain a credit card should engage in comparison shopping. Interest rates and annual fees vary from one issuer of cards to another. Do not necessarily accept the first offer of a credit card that you receive. And if you think that you will not be able to pay credit card bills on time, do not accept any offers. You can quickly get into more debt than you can pay. Moreover, your *credit rating* will suffer.

Even if you promptly pay the minimum required each month by your credit card company, you can get into financial difficulty. By paying only the minimum each month, your monthly balance keeps increasing and increasing. You could get to the point where you will never be able to pay off even the minimum because it gets so large.

In addition to credit cards (left), many banks issue *debit cards* (right). Although debit cards look like credit cards, they are different. While a credit card is a form of borrowing, a debit card is similar to paying with cash. To be more exact, it is just like writing a check. For example, suppose you purchase a jacket at a cost of $99.99 and pay for it with your debit card. Your bank is then charged $99.99. Since the money is withdrawn from your account at that bank, there are no interest charges. You may make purchases only up to the amount available in your account at the bank that issued you the debit card.

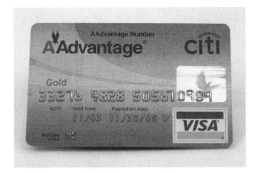 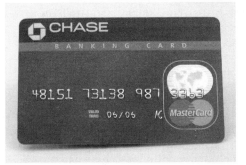

PERSONAL ECONOMICS

Shopping for Credit

It costs money to borrow money. Lenders charge interest on their loans. They may also levy charges to cover the cost of credit investigations, insurance, and other expenses. Since interest costs and other charges vary, it is wise to compare costs before deciding on a particular kind of financing. The U.S. **Truth-in-Lending Law** has simplified the task of comparing the cost of loans by requiring that lenders tell borrowers the *annual percentage rate (APR)* and the *finance charge* on their loans. The APR is the percentage cost of credit on a yearly basis. The finance charge is the total dollar amount one pays to use credit.

Suppose you decide to buy a used car that sells for $7,500. You have saved $1,500 for the down payment and plan to finance the $6,000 balance with a loan. The car dealer offers to arrange the financing, as do two of your town's banks. Each lender offers somewhat different terms, which are summarized in Table 11.2.

Which of these arrangements would be best for you? The lowest-cost loan overall is available at Bank X, where you will pay back a total of $7,279.20 on a loan of $6,000. You could, however, lower your monthly cost by taking a longer-term loan from Bank Y or from the dealer. These loans, however, would ultimately be more costly than one from Bank X. A loan from Bank Y would add nearly $450 more to the cost of the loan. A loan from the car dealer would cost almost $600 more than a loan from Bank X.

TABLE 11.2   CREDIT OPTIONS FOR A USED-CAR PURCHASE

Lender	Amount Borrowed	APR	Length of Loan	Monthly Payment	Finance Charge	Cost of Loan
Bank X	$6,000	13%	3 years	$202.20	$1,279.20	$7,279.20
Bank Y	$6,000	13%	4 years	$160.98	$1,727.04	$7,727.04
Car Dealer	$6,000	14%	4 years	$163.98	$1,871.04	$7,871.04

What Creditors Look For: The Three C's

Nobody has to lend you money. Creditors—the people in the business of making loans—have a right to expect to be repaid on schedule and in full for the use of their money. They also have the right to investigate applicants for loans in order to determine if they are good credit risks. Sooner or later, you are likely to need some kind of credit. Thus, it is wise to take steps to establish your creditworthiness before that need arises.

In looking into the qualifications of a person applying for a loan, credit investigators usually apply the *Three C's* test of creditworthiness: character, capacity, and capital. "Character" refers to the applicant's willingness to repay debts incurred, as indicated by a search of the applicant's *credit history* (a record of how an applicant has paid bills in the past). "Capacity" measures a person's ability to meet obligations when they fall due. It weighs current income and expected income against current and expected expenses. "Capital" refers to the financial resources (income and savings) behind the applicant's promise to repay the loan.

If you want to establish yourself as a good credit risk, a logical first step is to open savings and checking accounts in your own name. These accounts, plus a charge account at a local store, will provide you with several financial references when the need for them arises.

If you pay your bills on time and maintain a balance in your checking account, you will gain the reputation you are seeking: a person who is a good credit risk. In all likelihood, your record will be passed along to one or more credit bureaus. These institutions maintain files on virtually everyone who has ever used bank or charge account credit in the United States. Lenders pay these bureaus for information about the people who apply for loans. If your file indicates that you are a good credit risk, you are likely to get your loan. If it does not, you may be out of luck.

A company that gathers and sells credit information is called a *consumer reporting agency.* A credit report issued by one of these agencies lists all credit card accounts or loans you have, the balances, and how regularly you make your payments. It also shows if any action has been taken against you for unpaid bills. Your credit rating is then drawn from your credit report. Of course, it is desirable to have a good credit rating. Not only may you be denied credit if you have a bad rating, you may also be denied a job that you might apply for or even the chance to buy insurance.

It is important to see a copy of your credit report before you apply for credit, such as for a car loan or a credit card. Errors sometimes creep into credit reports. Someone with bad credit may have the same name as yours, or the information about you may be out of date. How can you find out about your credit rating? You can contact a consumer reporting agency. Three of these are:

Equifax
PO Box 105873
Atlanta, GA 330348
(800) 685–1111

Experian
PO Box 2104
Allen, TX 75013
(888) 397–3742

Trans Union LLC
Consumer Disclosure Center
PO Box 390
Springfield, PA 19064
(800) 916–8800

Federal Laws Protect Those Who Borrow or Want to Borrow

Creditors have the right to deny you a loan because you are a poor financial risk. Federal laws, however, prohibit lenders from turning you down because of your sex, race, disability, religion, national origin, marital status, age (provided that you are old enough to make a legal contract), or receipt of public assistance.

If you are turned down for a loan, the law requires that the lender notify you within 30 days and explain the reason. At your request, credit bureaus holding files on you must make the contents of those files available for your inspection. The credit bureaus must make corrections if you can show that the flles contaln any errors.

PERSONAL LOANS. Banks and other lending agencies make personal loans that are secured by a customer's general credit rather than by any specific merchandise. In such cases, the lender has a reasonable assurance that the borrower can repay the loan in periodic installments out of current income. If the lender is a bank in which the borrower has a savings account, the bank may extend a low-interest loan based on the balance in the depositor's savings account.

HOME MORTGAGES. A *home mortgage* is a loan to finance the single biggest investment in many people's lives: the purchase of a home. Mortgage loans are long-term loans, usually running from 15 to 30 years. *Collateral* (security) for the mortgage loan is the home that it finances. After making a sizable down payment, the new homeowner will pay equal monthly installments until the mortgage is paid in full. One portion of the payment is used to reduce the principal of the loan. The rest of the payment goes to pay interest on the outstanding balance. Most mortgages have a fixed interest rate.

In recent years, banks have also been offering *variable-rate mortgages.* Those who obtain such loans typically pay a lower rate of interest for the first year or so. If interest rates in general are rising, the bank will raise the rate of the variable-rate mortgage. This rate will come down again when interest rates in general decline.

Writing a Letter of Complaint

If you believe that you have been treated unfairly as a consumer, do not be afraid to complain. Store personnel are used to receiving complaints. The largest companies have people whose job it is to listen to your comments about their products or services and try to settle any complaints. Most of the time, all you need to do is return any defective merchandise or discuss your complaint with the store manager or person who waited on you. But if this method does not help you, make a formal complaint in writing.

Keep your letter of complaint brief and to the point. All you need are three paragraphs that do the following:

- Describe the item or service purchased. State what you bought, its model or serial number (if any), and the date and place of purchase.

- Clearly state the problem you have with the product or service. Present your complaint and tell what you have tried so far to do about the problem. Include the names of the business's personnel you have spoken to about the problem.

- Ask for satisfaction. State what you want done. Then state in your letter what further action you might take if you do not get satisfaction. Allow a reasonable time before taking further action.

You should enclose copies (not originals) of all receipts and documents (such as a manufacturer's warranty). Keep the originals and a copy of your letter for your own file. Your finished letter of complaint should look something like the letter below.

Figure 11.4 **Letter of Complaint**

> Your Address
> City, State, Zip Code
> Date
>
> Appropriate Person
> Company Name
> Street Address
> City, State, Zip Code
>
> Dear (Appropriate Person):
>
> I recently purchased a (name of product or service including model number). I made this purchase at (place, date, and other important details of the transaction).
>
> Unfortunately, (the product or service) has not performed satisfactorily because (state the problem). Therefore, I would like you to (state the specific action you want, such as "return my deposit" or "take back my purchase in exchange for undamaged goods"). Enclosed are copies (do not send originals) of my records of this transaction.
>
> I am looking forward to your reply and to a prompt resolution of this matter. Please contact me at the above address or by phone at (your telephone number).
>
> Sincerely,
>
> Your Name

HOME EQUITY LOANS.   Some people use their home as collateral in purchasing major consumer goods. This type of loan is a *home equity loan.* The term "equity" refers to the value remaining on a property after deducting the mortgage. If the fair market value of the home is $200,000 and the mortgage balance on this home is $125,000, then the owner has an equity in the home of $75,000 ($200,000 − $125,000 = $75,000). Assuming that the owner has no other legal claims on the property, the owner may borrow up to $75,000 on the equity.

Home equity loans are popular for two reasons. (1) Current federal tax laws allow deductions of 100 percent of the interest on home equity loans (up to $100,000) from the sum of one's total income in determining tax liability. (2) Home equity loans can be obtained at rates lower than the prevailing rates for other types of consumer loans. As with any type of loan, there are some disadvantages to the home equity loan. One must pay back the loan in a timely manner or risk losing one's home.

S U M M A R Y

There is an abundance and variety of products and services available to consumers. Advertising is an important part of our economic environment. Its purpose is to increase sales. It provides information, stimulates competition, and (by increasing sales) allows for such benefits of mass production as low prices. Advertising is a major source of income for newspapers, radio, and television and for those working in the advertising industry. Advertising can misinform. It is expensive and can lead to higher prices for products and services.

Information and help are available to consumers from government and nongovernment sources. Federal, state, and local laws and agencies; consumer groups; national business and professional associations; consumer magazines; seals of approval; and EnergyGuide labels are available to consumers seeking advice, information, or assistance.

Consumer credit is a form of borrowing. While credit enables consumers to buy and enjoy things now they would otherwise have to wait for, it may lure people into spending more than they can reasonably afford. Credit purchases usually are more expensive than paying with cash. The most common forms of consumer credit are home mortgages, credit cards, charge accounts, and personal loans. It is wise to shop for credit, pay bills on time to reduce finance charges, and maintain a good credit rating.

REVIEWING THE CHAPTER

BUILDING VOCABULARY

Match each item in Column A with its definition in Column B.

Column A	Column B
1. APR	*a.* paid announcements calling attention to one's product or service in hopes of attracting customers
2. mortgage	*b.* borrowing money to buy a home by pledging the value of that home
3. credit card	*c.* a method of purchasing credit with scheduled time payments
4. home equity loan	*d.* a pledge of property as security for a loan other than a mortgage
5. charge account	*e.* the percentage cost of credit on a yearly basis.
6. credit history	*f.* security on a loan
7. collateral	*g.* character, capacity, and collateral
8. installment plan	*h.* a customer's account at a business to which her or his purchases are charged
9. three "C's" of creditworthiness	*i.* a piece of plastic that allows a customer to buy goods or services and pay for them later
10. advertising	*j.* a record of all loans and purchases made using credit by one person

UNDERSTANDING WHAT YOU HAVE READ

1. The foolish shopper (*a*) buys whatever he or she wants (*b*) plans ahead (*c*) reads labels (*d*) watches for sales.

2. An EnergyGuide label (*a*) explains how many hours the appliance may operate in a day (*b*) evaluates different appliances and advises which is the best buy (*c*) indicates the yearly operating cost of an appliance (*d*) estimates the life expectancy of an appliance.

3. The purpose of advertising is to (*a*) stimulate competition (*b*) create demand (*c*) encourage wise buying (*d*) reduce manufacturing costs.

4. Which *one* of the following statements is true? (*a*) There is nothing to learn from an ad. (*b*) Watching ads is a waste of time. (*c*) Advertising may both stimulate and reduce competition. (*d*) Advertisers are always concerned about the best interests of the consumer.

5. The federal agency that monitors advertising is the (*a*) USDA (*b*) FDA (*c*) CPSC (*d*) FTC.

6. The Better Business Bureau is a (*a*) testing and rating organization (*b*) testing but not a rating organization (*c*) nationwide organization sponsored by private businesses (*d*) consumer cooperative organization.

7. Which *one* of the following is *not* a form of consumer credit? (*a*) charge accounts (*b*) installment plans (*c*) credit cards (*d*) debit cards.

8. Which *one* of the following statements about consumer credit is false? (*a*) It is available only in the form of personal loans. (*b*) It enables people to buy things now that they otherwise would delay buying. (*c*) It serves to keep up the high level of consumer spending in our economy. (*d*) While usually costly, it can sometimes save people money.

9. Unit pricing is a way of (*a*) grading eggs (*b*) comparing the cost of items per unit of weight or volume (*c*) applying price stickers to items for sale in a store (*d*) grading meat.

10. According to federal law, a person wanting to borrow may be denied a loan because she or he is (*a*) disabled (*b*) unmarried (*c*) an immigrant (*d*) a poor financial risk.

CRITICAL THINKING

Base your answers on what you have read in this chapter.

1. The American economy offers an abundance of goods and services to consumers.

   a. Why does this present a problem for consumers?

   b. They say that "you get what you pay for." Explain why you agree or disagree with this statement.

   c. Discuss how the consumer can obtain help or advice from governmental and nongovernmental sources.

2. There are many forms of credit available to consumers.

   a. Discuss *two* different types of credit instruments.

   b. Why is it said that credit can be a master or a servant?

SKILLS: Reading a Credit Card Statement

Examine the sample credit card statement below and answer the questions that follow.

Central City Bank	**CREDIT CARD STATEMENT**		**Send Payment To** Box 1234 Central City, NV

ACCOUNT NUMBER 4168–372–256	**NAME** Mary Nevins	**STATEMENT DATE** 6/13/04	**PAYMENT DUE DATE** 7/09/04

CREDIT LINE $1,500	**CREDIT AVAILABLE** $1,200	**NEW BALANCE** $300	**MINIMUM PAYMENT DUE** $20

REFERENCE	**SOLD**	**POSTED**	**ACTIVITY SINCE LAST STATEMENT**	**AMOUNT**
397ve56789		5/18/04	PAYMENT THANK YOU	− 285.50
475p12345	5/09/04	5/13/04	Sam's Supermarket	35.75
432198764	5/12/04	5/15/04	Belmont Restaurant	62.25
8E7654321	5/21/04	5/23/04	Ebony Mall	102.50
4321GH22	6/01/04	6/04/04	Central Computers	99.50

Previous Balance	285.50	**Current Amount Due**		300.00
Purchases	300.00	**Amount Past Due**		
Cash Advances		**Amount Over Credit Line**		
Payments	285.50			
Credits				

FINANCE CHARGES
Late Charges
New Balance 300.00

FINANCE CHARGE SUMMARY	**PURCHASES**	**ADVANCES**	For Customer Service Call:
Periodic Rate	1.45%	0.54%	1–800–XXX–XXXX
Annual Percentage Rate	19.80%	6.48%	For Lost or Stolen Card Call: 1–800–XXX–XXXX

Please make check or money order payable to Central City Bank. Include your account number on the front.

1. Explain the difference between (*a*) statement date and payment due date, (*b*) current amount due and minimum payment due, and (*c*) credit line and credit available.

2. What should you do if you believe that there is an error on your statement?

3. How would you report a lost or stolen credit card?

4. If you could afford to make only the minimum payment, how much would it be and how much will it cost you in interest? (If you want to calculate your costs for paying the total due in minimum payments, check out the Banking Tutor at <<www.practicalmoneyskills.com>>).

USING THE INTERNET

Information concerning products offered for sale over the Internet is provided at a number of Web sites.

- Information about the activities of the Better Business Bureau may be found at <<www.BBB.com>>.

- Cases involving misleading advertising and consumer fraud and information about the Federal Trade Commission are available at <<www.ftc.gov>>.

- Health topics are covered by the Department of Health and Human Services at <<healthfinder.gov>> or the Food and Drug Administration at <<www.fda.gov>>.

- Advice and information for the wise consumer are offered at <<www.italladdsup.org>>; <<www.chicagofed.org>>; and <<www.consumerworld.org>>.

- The Federal Consumer Information Center at <<www.pueblo.gsa.gov>> suggests consumer information in various formats such as pamphlets, books, audiotapes, and Internet Web sites.

- Services to protect consumers may be found at the Consumer Product Safety Commission's Web site at <<www.cpsc.gov>>. Among the many private, nonprofit organizations on the Web are Consumer Reports Online at <<www.consumerreports.org>>.

- You can gain practical money skills and learn how to read a credit card statement including all terms used in the statement at <<www.practicalmoneyskills.com>>.

CHAPTER 12

Personal Risk Management

OVERVIEW

By setting realistic goals and carefully investing their savings, Millie and John Hamilton have accumulated a sizable net worth. Millie is 37 years old, while John Hamilton has reached his 40th birthday. Millie and John were thinking how lucky they have been. They have both been healthy. Their daughter, Samantha, is a junior in college, and their son, John Jr., is a senior in high school. Both children are doing well and have never given Millie and John any scares other than the usual childhood diseases. But could something go wrong? John thought some more and then told Millie, "We have to sit down and plan for the future. We don't know what it will bring, but we sure can do our best to prepare for it. I want to know what we can do to protect all that we have worked and saved for." Millie agreed. In this chapter, we will discuss why the Hamiltons should consider the following items in their plans—and so should you!

- risk management

- estate planning.

Life is uncertain, and we all need to prepare as best we can to meet those uncertainties. We must also face the fact that we cannot live forever. What will happen to the assets and liabilities we accumulate through a lifetime? In this chapter, we will discuss health, property, liability, and life insurance as part of risk management and the importance of a will as part of estate planning.

Risk management involves identifying the perils that you and your family are exposed to and taking steps to reduce the monetary costs that may occur. Perils include accidents, illnesses, damages to one's property, being sued, and loss of life. Once you have identified the risks, you should try to eliminate or reduce them. Things like better door locks can reduce the risk of burglary. Smoke alarms can reduce injuries and deaths in case of fires. A healthful diet can reduce the risk of illnesses. Some risks, though, cannot be avoided or controlled. The financial losses incurred, however, can often be transferred to a third party by purchasing insurance.

 # INSURANCE

Insurance is a way of protecting oneself and others against money losses by sharing risks. Insurance cannot prevent adverse events from happening. Insurance will not prevent a forest fire from destroying a home, nor will it prevent automobile accidents. But insurance can help in facing the financial burdens that result from such occurrences.

Just as an umbrella protects you when it rains, insurance offers protection when a financial loss occurs. You buy an umbrella never knowing when it will be needed. Insurance works the same way. You purchase insurance never knowing when it will be needed.

Many people share risks by purchasing insurance from an insurance company. For example, suppose that you are one of the millions of Americans who purchase motor vehicle insurance. You pay yearly premiums to an insurance company even though you may never have an accident. However, if another person insured by the same insurance company does have a motor vehicle accident, the insurance company will probably be required to make some payment.

What Kind of Insurance Do You Need?

Good money management requires that you purchase insurance with the same guidelines you apply when making any major purchase. Ask yourself, "How does this purchase fit into my financial plan in terms of my needs and goals and what can I afford?" You buy insurance to fit your personal, individual needs. You do not buy motor vehicle insurance if you do not own a motor vehicle. Moreover, insurance needs vary with life cycles. A single teenager probably does not need to buy life insurance. But parents with children should consider buying it.

As we go through different stages of life, our insurance needs change. If we buy a motor vehicle and/or a home, we will need insurance to cover risks associated with these purchases. As we get older, our health declines, so we will then be more concerned with buying health insurance and perhaps nursing care insurance.

We rely on insurance of one kind or another to prepare for each foreseen and unforeseen peril. For almost every possible risk we face in life, there is insurance that we can buy to reduce the money losses that we may incur. Remember that insurance does not do away with the risks. It only reduces the dollar cost to us resulting from losses or *lawsuits* (legal actions in court).

The following table lists common risks and the insurance programs that are designed to reduce the financial losses that may result.

▷ TABLE 12.1   REDUCING FINANCIAL LOSS THROUGH INSURANCE

Risk	Type of Insurance
Loss of life	Life insurance, mortgage insurance
Accident	Accident insurance
Illness	Health insurance*
Loss of job	Unemployment insurance*
Old age	Social Security *
Auto accident	Motor vehicle insurance
Fire; theft	Homeowner's or renter's insurance
Lawsuit	Liability insurance

*Government programs protecting its citizens, such as Medicaid, Medicare, and Social Security, are discussed in Chapter 13, on pages 293–294.

BUYING INSURANCE.   Private (nongovernmental insurance) may be purchased through an insurance agent or directly from an insurance company (through the mail or on the Internet). A number of Web sites provide information about insurance companies, the policies they offer, and the costs of these various policies. Buying insurance should be approached as you would buy any other product—with caution. Your insurance policy is only as good as the company that issues it. An insurance company is a business, and like any other business it hopes to make a profit. Some insurance companies are well managed; others are not. As in any business, some companies are more reliable than others. There are several independent, reliable companies that rate and evaluate insurance companies. Among these are Moody's Investor Service, A.M. Best Company, and the Fitch's Insurance Group. (Their Internet addresses can be found on page 276.) The higher the rating an insurance company receives, the greater is the likelihood that the company will fulfill its obligations to its policyholders. Your state Insurance Department is another good source of information about insurance companies doing business in your state.

TYPES OF INSURANCE.   There are hundreds of different kinds of insurance policies, one to fit almost any risk. Ships on the high seas, oil tankers, factories, airlines, and many more business enterprises may be insured to cover all sorts of possible calamities. Among the countless possibilities, we will discuss three basic types of insurance of interest to consumers: (1) property and liability, (2) health, and (3) life insurance.

PROPERTY AND LIABILITY INSURANCE

Property and liability insurance today is a must for most Americans. It is required by law if you own a motor vehicle and required by a bank granting a home mortgage.

PROPERTY INSURANCE.   The term "property" refers to something one might own (such as jewelry, video camera, an automobile, a house or apartment, and all the items within a home). *Property insurance,* therefore, is insurance that provides financial protection against loss or damage to an insured person's property.

LIABILITY INSURANCE.   *Liability insurance* provides financial protection to the insured for damages or injuries to other persons or their property. Motor vehicle accidents happen all the time. Suppose you are driving and are involved in an accident. As a result, you damage another person's car or cause injury to the occupants of that car. In that case, you need financial protection to help pay the cost of the damages incurred.

Suppose you entertain at home and one of your guests slips on a newly polished kitchen floor and gets injured. Here, too, you need financial protection to pay the potential medical costs if your guest sues you for damages.

Motor vehicle insurance and homeowner's insurance are the two most common types of property and liability insurance purchased, so let us examine each in greater detail.

How does this photograph show the need people have for insurance?

✒ Motor Vehicle Insurance

Motor vehicle insurance provides the following coverage:

1. Bodily Injury Liability. *Bodily injury liability insurance* pays the financial costs resulting from any injuries or deaths sustained to an individual or individuals as a result of an accident involving an insured's automobile. The total amount that an insurance company will pay out depends on the amount of coverage purchased, which may be as little as $50,000 or as high as $1 million or more. Of course, the greater the amount of coverage, the more expensive is the insurance policy.

2. Collision Insurance. *Collision insurance* pays for damage caused to the vehicle of the insured. Collision insurance also covers damages caused by accidents that do not involve another vehicle. For example, hitting a deer on the highway or skidding and hitting a pole or guardrail are common accidents covered by collision insurance. Usually, there is an initial cost that is not covered, called the *deductible,* amounting to perhaps $250, $500, or $1,000. The greater the deductible your policy has, the cheaper is the cost of collision insurance. Since collision coverage is expensive, motorists have the option of reducing the costs of insurance by opting for a higher deductible. Some people with old cars have no collision insurance since the cost of the insurance over a few years may be greater than what the car is worth.

3. Property Damage Liability. This coverage applies to any damage caused by the insured person's vehicle to another vehicle or to the property of another person. Thus, in the event of an automobile accident, all or part of the costs of the damage to the other vehicle, or property, will be paid for by the insurance company of the insured.

4. Medical Insurance. This type of insurance covers the medical costs of anyone injured while riding in the insured individual's vehicle. The insured is also covered if injured while in another person's vehicle or if hit by a car while walking.

5. Uninsured Motorists. This coverage pays for injuries to the insured and members of the insured's family in cases where an uninsured motorist or a hit-and-run driver is legally responsible for the damages incurred. Uninsured motorists insurance is very important to have because an injured person is unlikely to collect from an uninsured motorist or a hit-and-run driver.

6. Comprehensive Coverage. This type of policy protects against financial losses from damages to a motor vehicle as a result of fire, theft, glass breakage, falling objects, riot, or hitting an animal.

7. No-Fault Insurance. Most states have laws that require one's own insurance company to pay each person's medical and hospital expenses no matter who was responsible for a motor vehicle accident. In some states, the no-fault law also applies to any income lost because of the accident.

💮 Homeowner's or Renter's Insurance

Every day somewhere in the United States, a homeowner or renter suffers a financial loss. It may have occurred because of a fire, flood, electrical or plumbing malfunction, robbery, or medical injury to an individual visiting or working in the residence. That is why homeowners and many renters purchase insurance. By paying a single yearly premium, they are able to insure their property against a wide variety of perils including fire, theft, and personal liability.

FIRE INSURANCE.   A standard fire insurance policy protects the insured only for damages to the home and its contents resulting from fire and lightning.

EXTENDED COVERAGE.   An *extended coverage* provision broadens the coverage to include damages from wind, hail, smoke, earthquakes, storms, explosions, riots, vehicles, and falling aircraft. The San Francisco area is subject to earthquakes. Storms, tornadoes, falling trees, and lightning are likely occurrences in many parts of the country. Homes in low-lying areas are subject to flooding, but separate flood insurance policies must be purchased to cover this catastrophe.

How would having a home insurance policy help this couple?

THEFT INSURANCE. Personal property owned or used by an insured is usually covered in a homeowner's policy against loss or theft anywhere in the world. The coverage is limited unless an additional premium is paid to cover specified items. Theft insurance may also be purchased separately from a homeowner's policy to cover specific items such as jewelry, furs, expensive paintings, musical instruments and, in fact, almost anything an individual considers valuable enough to insure.

With the increased use of credit cards and purchases over the phone or Internet, the problem of *identity theft* has become very serious. In cases of identity fraud, criminals assume the identity of the consumer for the purpose of gaining access to the consumer's accounts or obtaining and using credit in the name of the victim. Criminals gain access to a consumer's credit card number, bank account number, driver's license, or social security number. With this information, criminals can order merchandise and make purchases using the victim's credit card, withdraw funds from the victim's bank accounts, or make long-distance telephone calls. The victim may become aware of the theft only when refused a loan because of bad debts or informed of excessive telephone or credit card charges. Although federal law allows victims to seek restitution from the criminal perpetrator(s), actually obtaining such restitution is not a certainty. Therefore, insurance companies are offering identity theft insurance to compensate the insured victim for any losses and expenses incurred resulting from the identity theft.

PERSONAL LIABILITY INSURANCE. In addition to the standard and extended coverage homeowner's policies, many individuals purchase *personal liability insurance.* In the event that a visitor or someone working in the insured's residence has an accident and injury, personal liability coverage pays the legal costs and damages assessed against them up to the limits set by their policy.

Most people purchase a homeowner's or renter's policy that contains standard, extended coverage, and personal liability components. Of course, the greater the amount to be covered by insurance, the more expensive the policy is. However, the limit to how much a residence may be insured is determined by the insurance company based on the estimated value of the property to be insured. Thus a home valued at $100,000 cannot be insured for $500,000.

HEALTH INSURANCE

Health-care services are expensive and have been increasing steadily due to increasing demands by Americans on health-care providers and because of new and expensive medicines and procedures. Most Americans could not afford decent health care without some form of insurance. About 70 percent of Americans have some form of *private health insurance* (nongovernmental). Another

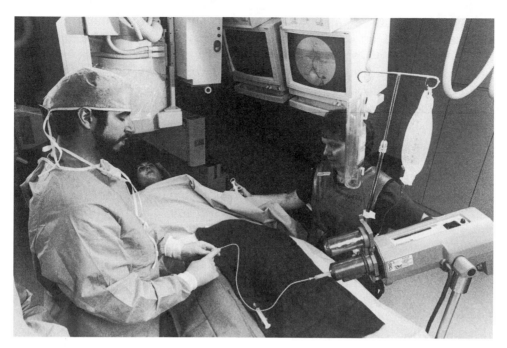

Without health insurance, one's medical bills can become quite high.

15 percent are covered by government health insurance programs. Most individuals (and their families) in the United States who have medical and hospital insurance receive their coverage through their workplace. That leaves about 15 percent (some 41 million Americans) without health insurance coverage. Two federal health insurance programs—Medicare and Medicaid—are discussed in Chapter 13, on pages 293–294. Here we will discuss private health insurance programs.

There are several reasons why so many people lack medical insurance. A primary reason is the cost of health insurance. A very few, such as young, healthy individuals or members of some religious groups, might think that they have no need for health insurance. However, the vast majority of the uninsured do not have health insurance because they just cannot afford it. As we have noted, health insurance in the United States is primarily an employment-based system. Most insured workers are insured through their place of work. The unemployed and workers whose employers do not offer health insurance often remain without health insurance. The number of persons entitled to Medicaid, a program that provides medical care and medicines for the poor, increases when unemployment in the U.S. increases. However, the vast majority of the uninsured are not the unemployed but low-income, hardworking individuals in our society. This group includes taxi drivers, waiters, gas station attendants, and others in low-paying jobs. Since health insurance is expensive, low-paid workers cannot afford it.

Medical insurance plans vary from one workplace to another. Plans also vary as to how much the worker must contribute (if anything) to the cost of the policy. Plans also vary as to which health-care providers the insured can see. Some plans require the insured to join a *health maintenance organization (HMO)*. By joining an HMO, an individual becomes a member of a group and must use the doctors and other medical providers in that group. Other, more expensive health plans allow an individual to choose one's physicians and other medical providers.

Health insurance programs basically provide coverage to pay all or parts of the cost of various medical and hospital expenses. The *surgical insurance* part of the policy will cover all or part of a surgeon's fee for necessary operations. The *medical insurance* portion of the policy will pay for the services of a doctor, other than for surgery, in the hospital, at home, or in the doctor's office. *Hospital insurance* will pay all or part of the costs incurred when confined to a hospital, other than surgical and doctor's fees. These covered costs are usually room and board, drugs and medication taken in the hospital, nursing care, the use of the operating room, and laboratory tests.

DISABILITY INCOME INSURANCE.   Closely related to health insurance policies are those providing for loss of income or other earnings because of extended illness or disability. This is called *disability income insurance.* According to the U.S. Census Bureau, nearly one in five Americans will become disabled for one year or more before the age of 65. Furthermore, nearly half of all home foreclosures are caused by unforeseen disabilities. It is easy to understand why disability income insurance is an important aspect of financial planning.

Disability income insurance is not to be confused with governmental disability insurance such as workmen's compensation or Social Security. Workers' compensation pays for a disability only if it is job-related. Government payouts for workers' compensation are low. Social Security provides disability benefits only if you qualify, if you are totally and permanently unable to do any job. It is based on your "covered earnings." Most disabled individuals applying for Social Security disability benefits are rejected.

Private, nongovernment disability income insurance provides monthly payments, up to a specified amount and for a specific time period, after a covered illness or injury occurs. However, the insurance must be purchased *prior* to the illness or injury. How much insurance you should purchase, of course, depends on how much money you will need to live on until you are able to return to work or eligible to receive other financial benefits such as retirement or Social Security income. The premium increases as the monetary benefit and the period of coverage increases. Do not buy more coverage than you can reasonably afford.

Employers, faced with higher health insurance costs, want to pass some or all of this increase on to their employees. Remember, an employer's contribution to health coverage is, in effect, a form of wage payment. As health coverage costs rise, so too does the cost of labor to the firm. The firm can pass these higher costs on to the consumer as higher prices or to the owners of the company as lower dividends. Or it can share the increased cost by increasing the workers' contributions.

Most medical insurance plans require a *co-payment* for each visit to a medical service provider. These co-payments have been rising in dollar figures. So too have the *deductibles* (the initial portion of a year's medical bills, not paid by an insurance company). Employees are being asked to pay an increasing percentage of the *premium* for health insurance. Some firms and health-care plans have been cutting coverage. For example, they may stop paying for mental health coverage or reduce the number of visits allowed per year to physical therapists.

LIFE INSURANCE

The main purpose of a *life insurance policy* is to offer some financial protection to the policyholder's beneficiary or beneficiaries. A *beneficiary* is an individual named in the insurance policy to receive some or all of the proceeds of an insurance policy. A life insurance policy provides for a specified amount of payment to the beneficiary on the insured's death. For example, Marie Wozlewki bought a $250,000 life insurance policy that named her husband, Jerzy, as beneficiary. In the event of her death, Jerzy would receive $250,000.

There are two basic forms of life insurance: (1) term-life and (2) straight-life.

Term-Life

Term-life insurance is strictly insurance. There is no savings factor added to it. *Term-life insurance* is in effect for a specific number of years (usually five), but it can be renewed at a higher premium at the end of each term. It is an ideal plan for someone who wants the maximum amount of life insurance protection at the minimum cost over a limited period of time.

Straight-Life

Straight-life insurance costs more than term, but it offers more. Assume that Marie's policy was a straight-life policy that provides that a stipulated sum of

Figure 12.1 **Dollar Value of Two Types of Life Insurance**

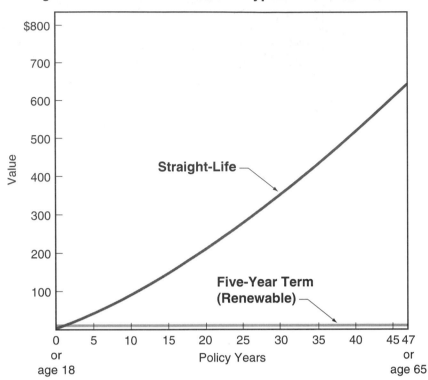

money, $250,000, will go to her husband, Jerzy, upon her death. In this illustration, life insurance acts as a safety net for Marie's beneficiary, Jerzy. Marie's insurance policy also serves as a means of forced savings. A *straight-life policy* consists of two parts: an insurance factor and a savings factor. Each year that Marie pays premiums, the savings portion of her policy increases in *cash value* equal to the accumulated savings plus any dividends that the insurance company pays on the savings portion. Marie may borrow against the cash value of her policy or cancel the policy and receive a cash settlement. Suppose that after 15 years of paying premiums, the cash value of the $250,000 policy is $42,875. Marie can then cancel the policy and receive a cash surrender value of $42,875.

In the example above, life insurance had two functions: savings and insurance. But the main purpose of life insurance is as a vehicle to protect one's heirs and not as a means of saving or investing. Could an individual just pay the insurance part of a premium and save or invest the savings factor elsewhere with a better return? Yes, and that is why many individuals prefer to purchase term rather than straight-life insurance.

Life insurance rates are higher for nonsmokers than for smokers and lower for females than for males. The reason is that nonsmokers are expected to live longer than smokers and females are expected to live longer than males. Therefore, nonsmokers and females will be paying premiums for a longer period of time before the insurance company has to make payments to a beneficiary. Insurance is a competitive business. Rates for similar policies vary among insurance companies and change from year to year. As with any major purchase, it is wise to shop around.

The following table is based on typical costs per $100,000 term-life and straight-life insurance policies for a male nonsmoker. Since rates vary from company to company and change frequently, the figures below are for comparative purposes only.

> **TABLE 12.2   SAMPLE ANNUAL COSTS PER $100,000 LIFE INSURANCE POLICIES FOR A MALE NONSMOKER**

Age	Term-Life	Five-Year Cost	Straight-Life	Five-Year Cost
Under 30	$ 36	$ 180	$206	$ 1,030
30–34	54	270	309	1,545
35–39	84	420	481	2,405
40–44	108	540	590	2,950
45–49	156	780	722	3,610
Total 20-year cost:		$2,190		$11,540

Abdul Hamid, a 25-year-old male, purchased a term-life insurance policy shortly after his wife, Tasha, gave birth to a baby girl. Abdul's policy cost $2,190 for 25 years of insurance. Had Abdul bought a straight-life policy, it would have cost him $11,540 over the same time period. So which policy is better? The potential payout for both is the same—$100,000. Now suppose that Abdul wants to stop paying the premiums and cancel the policy. He would receive nothing for his term-life policy. The straight-life policy, on the other hand, might have cash surrender value of perhaps $14,000 if he reinvested dividends earned on the policy over the 25-year period.

Suppose Abdul wanted to borrow $5,000 needed toward a down payment on a car. He could not borrow against a term-life policy, but he could borrow against a straight-life policy (probably at interest rates lower than he would pay for a similar loan from a bank).

Many young parents buy term insurance because it is so much cheaper in the early years. Look at Table 12.2. Between ages 35 and 39, it would cost Abdul only $84 each year for a $100,000 term policy. That amounts to a total of $420 for five years of insurance. A straight-life policy, on the other hand, would cost $481 each year for five years for a total cost of $2,405. The difference in the cost of these two policies is $1,985.

Suppose Abdul invests the $1,985 difference. Would he be better off after 20 years? We do not know. It depends on the soundness and returns of his investment. Furthermore, other needs may distract him from his investment program. Had Abdul purchased a straight-life policy, he would have no choice but to keep up his payments in order to keep his policy in force. Therefore, he is forced to save each year.

Remember, economics is all about making choices. Can you discipline yourself to save and invest regularly? Are you willing to risk your funds in an investment program of your own? If the answer is yes, you would be advised to buy a term-life policy. If you prefer playing it safe and know that you need to be forced to save, the straight-life policy is for you.

How Much Life Insurance Should You Buy?

How much you should buy depends on (1) how much you can afford and (2) how much you need.

AFFORDABILITY.   You might want to insure yourself for several million dollars. But few of us can afford to do so, and usually there is no need to do so. How much money you can afford to set aside for life insurance depends on many factors, such as income, spending habits, attitude, and motivation. The greater your income, the chances are the more you can afford to set aside for insurance. On page 221, we discussed Engel's Law, which demonstrated that an individual with a low income needs to spend a greater portion of that income on necessities and has little, if anything, left over to spend on insurance. It is equally true that even when individuals have similar incomes they may have different spending patterns. Some people like to believe that nothing will happen to them and that they will always be able to care for themselves and their family. They are not motivated to buy life insurance. At the same time, there are others who worry about providing for their family in the event of their death. Such individuals are willing to spend more for life insurance than is an individual who is less concerned.

THE NEED FOR LIFE INSURANCE.   The need for life insurance is different for different people. For example, if you are in high school, you probably do not need life insurance yet. On the other hand, a person who has young children does need life insurance, particularly if the individual is the main provider for the family. This person should ask, "What would my family need to maintain their current lifestyle without my income?" A surviving spouse with young children will need some source of income until he or she can get a job or the children can earn their own livelihood. In our senior years, when we are no longer the breadwinner of a family with children, we may want to provide only for our surviving spouse. Even then, however, we may want to leave an inheritance to our children or grandchildren. The decision whether or not to maintain a life insurance policy in this case is personal.

The greater your net worth, the less is your need for life insurance. Both the Spencer and Chu families estimate that they need a minimum of $80,000 per year to maintain their current lifestyles. Both Mr. Spencer and Mr. Chu are employed full time. Mrs. Spencer is a homemaker and, therefore, has no earnings. Mrs. Chu, on the other hand, earns $15,000 yearly at her part-time job at a real estate agency. The Spencers' net worth is minimal.

In the example above, how much insurance does each family need to maintain their current lifestyles in case the major breadwinner dies? Because the Spencers depend entirely on Mr. Spencer's earnings to maintain their lifestyle, they need life insurance that would provide an income of $80,000 yearly in the event of his death. The situation is quite different for the Chu family. They do not depend solely on Mr. Chu's earnings. Furthermore, in addition to Mrs. Chu's income, the family has stocks, bonds, real estate investments, and savings and pension benefits that yield about $25,000 annually. If we add Mrs. Chu's $15,000 salary to other income sources of $25,000, the family would have $40,000 yearly income even if Mr. Chu died. Therefore, the Chu family requires a life insurance policy sufficient to provide an additional $40,000 annually to maintain the family's current lifestyle on his death. In actuality, however, Mr. Chu might purchase a greater life insurance policy than Mr. Spencer because he can afford to do so. He would not want Mrs. Chu to have to depend on her earnings after his death, and he knows about the uncertainty of investment income.

 # ESTATE PLANNING

Estate planning is the sum of all the actions one takes to accumulate wealth to leave to one's heirs and to determine how to divide the estate among the heirs. It a subject many people, and certainly most high school students, do not think about. What is more, most people do not want to think about it. Whereas risk management deals with uncertainties, estate planning deals with a certainty— that someday each of us will die. We do not know how, when, or where it will happen, but it will happen. So what can we do about it? Throughout our living years, we will accumulate property, money, and personal items (such as jewelry, pictures, household furniture). Someone is going to get all that stuff when we are gone—perhaps a relative, a friend, or maybe even the government. Through proper planning, we can ensure that our wishes will be followed even when we are no longer here.

Life insurance policies, discussed earlier in the chapter, are part of estate planning. They provide for the distribution of benefits among the deceased's beneficiaries or heirs.

A lower-middle class family may have an estate value of several thousand dollars. An upper-middle class family may have one worth hundreds of thousands. Whatever its value, family members most likely want a plan to protect this valuable estate.

Estate planning is very complicated and often requires the assistance of professionals such as lawyers and accountants. Laws regarding estates vary among the states. There are also federal and tax laws regarding the dispostion of the assets of an estate. Furthermore, federal and state laws are modified from time to time. Therefore, the first thing to learn about estate planning is that you should seek professional help.

The Will

A *will* is a legal document that specifies how one's assets are to be distributed on one's death. An individual may legally prepare one's own will, but it is advisable to have a lawyer prepare one for you. The lawyer is familiar with a state's law concerning how an individual's assets may be distributed. A lawyer will know the law regarding the following questions: Is the individual married? What is his or her spouse entitled to? If there any children in this family, what are they entitled to? Despite state laws, though, there are questions that the individual drawing up the will must decide: How should whatever money or belongings that remain after one's death be distributed?

How does this photograph illustrate the importance of having a will?

Estate Taxes

Estate taxes are taxes on the asset value of an estate. Both federal and state governments may impose a tax on the estate of a deceased. Currently, such taxes are high, ranging from 37 percent to 55 percent. Unless you are wealthy, there is no need for alarm. In 2004, federal law exempted from federal taxes the first $1.5 million. In many states where there are high estate taxes, there are continued efforts to reduce them, increase the exemption, and even do away with estate taxes entirely. If you are wealthy enough that your estate is subject to tax, however, you will need a lawyer and an accountant who can show you how to legally reduce your tax burden.

So far, we have discussed estate planning in terms of the distribution of an estate on an individual's death. However, the value of an estate is built *during* the life of the individual. Therefore, estate planning must begin early. We have already discussed the importance of financial planning and long-term goals. As part of financial planning, provision should be made for savings, investing, and insurance. Over the years, these savings and investments accumulate and could amount to a sizable estate.

SUMMARY

Insurance is a way of protecting oneself and others against the financial losses that result from illness, accidents, death, fire, theft, and other risks. Insurance does not prevent loss; instead, it reduces the financial burden when a loss occurs. Life insurance may serve the additional function as a means of forced savings.

It is not unreasonable to assume that a high school student may accumulate a sizable estate during the next 50 years and, thus, may need to make plans for it. Estate planning consists of building up one's assets through careful saving, investing, and purchasing life insurance. Then it is necessary to provide for the distribution of those assets among beneficiaries and heirs. A will is a legal document that specifies how this should take place. The laws regarding wills, estates, and taxes are complicated, and this part of financial planning requires the professional assistance of lawyers and accountants.

REVIEWING THE CHAPTER

BUILDING VOCABULARY

Match each term in Column A with its definition in Column B.

Column A

1. a will
2. straight-life insurance
3. disability insurance
4. a beneficiary
5. cash value
6. term-life insurance
7. personal liability insurance
8. a deductible
9. no-fault insurance
10. estate planning

Column B

a. an initial portion of a year's medical bills, not paid by an insurance company

b. someone named to receive the proceeds of an insurance policy

c. a document specifying how one's assets are to be distributed after one's death

d. life insurance for a set number of years but that can be renewed, at higher costs

e. life insurance that also is a vehicle for forced savings

f. an amount equal to the accumulated savings and dividends of a life insurance policy

g. a policy to reduce the financial risk associated with being injured or becoming ill and not being able to work for a living

h. a policy that requires the insurance company to pay hospital and medical costs no matter who is responsible for an accident

i. a policy that pays the cost of damage or injuries to another person or their property

j. the sum of all actions one takes to accumulate wealth to leave to one's heirs and to determine how the estate is divided among the heirs

UNDERSTANDING WHAT YOU HAVE READ

1. Personal risk management is necessary because (*a*) our goals may be unrealistic (*b*) we may have invested only in stocks (*c*) life is uncertain (*d*) assets accumulate over a lifetime.

2. Risk management involves identifying risks that may occur and (*a*) taking steps to reduce the monetary costs that may result (*b*) avoiding accidents (*c*) staying on the job (*d*) reading the financial news every day.

3. Just as an umbrella protects us when it rains, insurance (*a*) reduces the risk of an adverse event happening (*b*) prevents adverse events from happening (*c*) helps individuals avoid accidents (*d*) protects an individual when a financial loss occurs.

4. Insurance companies are (*a*) all alike (*b*) well-managed organizations (*c*) not-for-profit institutions (*d*) businesses hoping to make a profit.

5. You should buy insurance (*a*) to fit your individual needs (*b*) to the limit the insurance company is willing to sell to you (*c*) strictly as an investment (*d*) according to the examples set by your neighbors or friends.

6. An individual's insurance needs change (*a*) according to the political party in power (*b*) on a monthly basis (*c*) as the individual's mood changes (*d*) as the individual goes through different stages of life.

7. Term-life insurance (*a*) is strictly insurance (*b*) is strictly savings (*c*) is more expensive than a straight-life policy for a young, male non-smoker (*d*) always maintains a high cash value.

8. The difference between property insurance and liability insurance is that (*a*) property insurance costs more (*b*) liability insurance is more expensive (*c*) property insurance, unlike liability insurance, provides financial protection against loss or damage to an insured person's property (*d*) liability insurance, unlike property insurance, provides financial protection against loss or damage to an insured person's property.

9. The two most common types of property and liability insurance are (*a*) motor vehicle insurance and homeowner's insurance (*b*) life insurance and health insurance (*c*) accident insurance and a will (*d*) life insurance and theft insurance.

10. An HMO is (*a*) another name for home health care (*b*) another name for the federal Medicaid program (*c*) a health maintenance organization (*d*) a health plan that allows the consumer unlimited choice regarding physicians.

THINKING CRITICALLY

Figure 12.2

1. a. Explain the meaning of the cartoon above.

   b. Explain why, if there are so many risks, individuals do not insure themselves against all possible risks.

   c. List *three* different types of insurance available to consumers.

   d. Select *one* of the three types of insurance you listed and explain why it may or may not be a necessary purchase for you.

2. Imagine that you are sitting around the family dinner table and you mention that you have been discussing risk management and estate planning in your economics class.

   a. Why might you bring up the topic of estate planning?

   b. Prepare a list of what you believe would be your major concerns to discuss with your family.

   c. How might you explain to your parents why a will is something that they should have if they do not already have one prepared?

USING THE INTERNET

The number of sites on the Internet relating to insurance and estate planning is endless. In fact, many people using the Internet see insurance ads pop up on the screen from time to time. In considering the "best buy" among competing insurance companies, the safest approach is to: (1) type "insurance" on an Internet search engine; (2) select one or more of the Web sites listed in your search and examine the information and what is being offered; and (3) check *one* of the following three insurance-rating companies: Moody's Investor Service at <<www.moodys.com>>; A.M. Best Company at <<www.ambest.com>>; or the Fitch's Insurance Group at <<www.fitchibca.com>>. See what, if anything, it has to say about the company or companies you are investigating.

GOVERNMENT AND THE ECONOMY

CHAPTER 13

The Economic Role of Government

OVERVIEW

In earlier chapters, we learned that the U.S. economic system of capitalism relies on market forces rather than on government to answer the WHAT, HOW, and WHO questions: WHAT goods and services should be produced? HOW should they be produced? WHO will receive the goods and services?

Despite the system's reliance on markets, there are times when the free enterprise system does not work. That is, there are market failures that prevent the price system from producing and allocating goods and services as efficiently as it should. In those instances, the public has come to look to government to perform the market's functions. One does not have to be a detective to find evidence of government's participation in the economy. Think, for example, of your daily trips to and from school. Although circumstances vary, it is likely that the roads you travel were constructed by government, the electricity you use is provided by or regulated by government, and the courses you take are prescribed by your state's education department.

In many ways, the economic behavior of government (local, state, and federal) is similar to the economic behavior of businesses and individuals. Government, too, must try to achieve its goals of obtaining the greatest amount of goods and services by using limited resources. The economic goals of government, however, are different from those of individuals and business firms. Whereas business firms and individuals are principally concerned with their own well-being, government needs to focus on the welfare of all its people.

In this chapter, we will learn more about the function of government in the U.S. economy. This will enable us to answer the following questions:

- What role does government play in the economy?

- Why have government's economic responsibilities been increasing over the years?

- What problems are created as a result of government's participation in the economy?

- How does a government's budget reflect its economic goals?

WHAT ARE THE ECONOMIC FUNCTIONS OF GOVERNMENT?

You know that government imposes and collects taxes. Indeed, the average family spends about 25 percent of its income on taxes. Business firms often spend a much greater percentage. The funds that government raises through taxation and borrowing are used to pay for the services it performs and will be described in Chapter 14. In this chapter, we will learn about the economic responsibilities of government. These include the following:

- safeguarding competition and the market system
- providing public goods and services
- correcting for harmful externalities, such as pollution
- maintaining economic stability
- redistributing income and wealth
- redistributing resources.

Safeguarding Competition and the Market System

Under ideal circumstances, the market system benefits us all. Competition and the quest for profits move producers to give consumers the goods and services they want. Since it is in the sellers' interest to meet or beat the competition's prices, it pays them to produce their products in the most efficient way they can. Thus, we can say that competition promotes the efficient use of scarce resources and the satisfaction of consumer wants.

The absence of competition has the opposite effect: Fewer goods and services are produced and prices rise. For these reasons, federal, state, and many local governments do what they can to promote competition and discourage those who try to restrict it. In Chapter 7, we discussed some of the antitrust laws that the federal and state governments have enacted. These laws prohibit efforts by individuals or firms to interfere with competition.

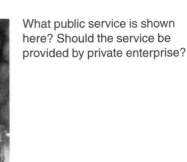
What public service is shown here? Should the service be provided by private enterprise?

🌀 Providing Public Goods and Services

Certain things would not be provided were it not for government. Economists describe goods and services provided mainly by government as public goods and services.

Public goods and services are available to everyone, whether they pay for them or not. Think of a local police force. Regardless of which residents of a community pay for it, police protection is available to everyone. Similarly, there is no way that the light from street lamps could shine only for those who pay for them. Since people will not normally pay for things they can enjoy for free, government often provides them. The alternative would be for people to do without the public good or service. While virtually everyone agrees that there are some things government should provide, there is considerable disagreement over the list of what those things should be.

🌀 Correcting for Harmful Externalities and Promoting Beneficial Ones

We have seen that within a market economy, the engine that drives supply, demand, and production is costs. Costs determine the price and quantity of an item that sellers will offer and buyers will take. But there are times when economic activities are taken at no cost to the producer, and others when benefits are received without cost to the consumer. Economists describe these as external costs (or more simply, externalities) because they are arrived at outside the marketplace, without reference to supply or demand.

Imagine a tractor factory whose coal-powered electrical generator spews harmful pollutants into the atmosphere. To the economist, both the coal that powers the generator and the air that carries off the smoky wastes are resources. To the factory operators, however, there is an essential difference between the two. Coal must be purchased before it can be burned. The atmosphere does not have to be purchased. The atmosphere is a natural resource belonging to us all. For that reason, the factory need not pay for it. Nor does it normally pay to clean the air it pollutes. That expense is usually borne by someone else, or by society in general.

Pollution, because of the damage it does to individuals and the environment, is a *harmful externality.* But not all externalities are harmful. For example, in many cities office buildings are erected with landscaped plazas and courtyards open to the public. Since those who use and enjoy the facilities did not pay for them, these features are described as *beneficial externalities.*

Externalities, both harmful and beneficial, are not affected by the laws of supply and demand. For that reason, it is usually left to government to discourage or eliminate the harmful ones and to encourage the beneficial ones. Government can discourage harmful externalities through regulation and taxation. Laws prohibiting harmful emissions or requiring the installation of emission controls are examples of how government regulations have been used to protect the public. Similarly, cigarette taxes and laws prohibiting smoking in public places are examples of how government uses its authority to protect the public from the harmful externality of secondhand smoke. Government efforts to promote or discourage economic activities are often controversial. Have our legislatures gone too far in their efforts to curb externalities they consider harmful, or not far enough? If, for example, it costs more to install antipollution devices than the value of the benefits they provide, one could argue that they were not worth

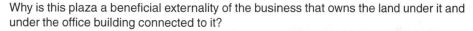

Why is this plaza a beneficial externality of the business that owns the land under it and under the office building connected to it?

the investment. Or if American firms are being priced out of the global market because the nation's environmental laws are much stricter than laws elsewhere, some other way to protect the environment might be called for. Moreover, where do we draw the line on restricting individual rights in order to protect the general welfare of everyone?

⚡ Maintaining Economic Stability

Economic stability describes a period in which there are only modest changes in the level of prices, employment, and business activity. History has shown that, without economic stability, we see unwanted increases in business failures, unemployment, and poverty levels.

Responsibility for maintaining economic stability has fallen largely to the federal government. In later chapters, we will discuss the kinds of things that the president, Congress, and the Federal Reserve Board do to maintain economic stability.

⚡ Redistributing Income and Wealth

Government conducts many programs specifically designed to help the poor and needy (such as Food Stamps and Medicaid). Since much of the money to pay for these programs comes from taxes paid by those better able to afford them, there is a redistribution of wealth from those paying taxes to those receiving benefits.

Some income redistribution programs generate beneficial externalities. An example is the federal job-training program that helps the unemployed get jobs. People with jobs pay most of the taxes that pay for this program. The unemployed, who are often poor, benefit from the program by learning skills that can lead to jobs. If they do get jobs, they can climb out of poverty and become taxpayers themselves.

⚡ Redistributing Resources

Resources used for one purpose cannot be used for another. Typically in years when the nation is expanding its military programs (as it does during times of war and national emergency), fewer funds are available for construction of playgrounds, hospitals, and highways.

Another example of a government program resulting in the redistribution of resources began in the 1960s when Congress voted to spend large sums on space exploration. When our best scientists are using their energies for the exploration of space, they are not available to study other problems. In other words, when government decides to spend its money in one way, the resources

When Does Government Regulation Become Too Much Regulation?

Ever since the Interstate Commerce Commission (ICC) was created in 1887, the federal government has used regulatory agencies or commissions to protect the public against many aspects of economic life. These agencies, now about 50 in number, make up what some have come to call the "fourth branch of federal government." (The legislative, executive, and judicial branches are the first three.) Some of the better-known regulatory agencies are the **Federal Communications Commission (FCC)**, the **Securities and Exchange Commission (SEC)**, and the **Consumer Product Safety Commission**.

While many people have praised regulatory agencies' work in protecting the public interest, other people (particularly in the business community) have complained that the agencies often go too far. Overregulation, they argue, increases the costs of doing business and leads to higher prices and lower living standards.

In response to these and other complaints, Congress has moved to deregulate a number of industries. With the **Air Transportation Deregulation Act** of 1978, for example, Congress removed price controls in the airline industry. The law also made it easier for people to form new airlines. In the years that followed, the federal government reduced its regulation of the banking, telephone, trucking, bus, and railroad industries.

More recently, opponents of regulatory agencies have sought to limit the effects of the **Clean Air Act**, the **Occupational Safety and Health Act**, and other key regulatory laws. After the Republicans gained control of Congress in the 1994 elections, they announced their intention to subject government regulation of businesses to *cost-benefit analysis.* This process involves weighing the numerical costs and benefits of a regulation. Experts would question laws, for example, that require paper mills to reduce their pollution of the air by acquiring new equipment to clean the mills' emissions. If experts could show that the cost of replacing present equipment outweighs the monetary value of the cleaner air (measured in reduced health-care costs, for example), the lawmakers might abolish the regulations.

Not everyone agrees with these proposals for cost-benefit analysis. Opponents of reduced regulation of business believe that there is no reliable way to measure the benefits of clean air and water and the safety of the food and toys we buy for our families. Furthermore, opponents of cost-benefit analysis proposals argue that the American people expect their government to safeguard the air they breathe, the water they drink, and the many other potentially harmful products they purchase, no matter the cost to taxpayers.

---

it consumes are no longer available to produce other goods and services. Thus, government directly affects how many of the nation's resources are used.

REASONS FOR THE GROWTH OF GOVERNMENT

Like a snowball getting ever larger as it rolls downhill, government's economic responsibilities have grown and grown and grown. For example, in 1929 spending by state and local governments and the federal government totaled $9 billion,

Figure 13.1 **Our Growing Local, State, and Federal Governments**

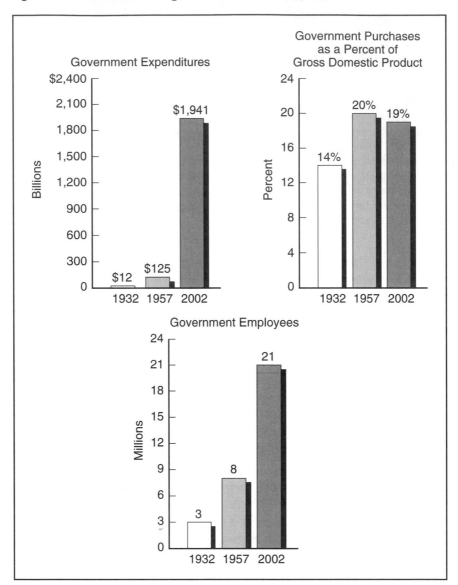

or less than 10 percent of that year's gross domestic product. Contrast this with 2002, when government purchased $1.9 trillion (or about 19 percent of that year's output of goods and services).

Government spending has grown over the years, especially since the 1930s when the federal government was fighting the Great Depression. Spending has grown in both real and actual dollars.

Table 13.1 illustrates government expenditures as a percentage of total national output (GDP). Note that the percentage of total government purchases

TABLE 13.1	GOVERNMENT PURCHASES AS A PERCENTAGE OF NATIONAL OUTPUT (GDP)		
Year	Total Government Purchases	Federal	State and Local
1930	10%	1.5%	8.5%
1935	11	3	8
1940	14	6	8
1945	46	41	5
1950	13	6	7
1955	19	11	8
1960	19	11	8
1965	19	10	9
1970	21	10	11
1975	20	8	12
1980	19	8	11
1985	19	8	11
1990	19	8	11
1995	19	7	12
2002	19	7	12

increased from 1930 to 1945, then decreased for a few years before increasing again. Since 1970, it has declined slightly. What is also interesting to note are the changes in the relative share of spending by the two levels of government. For example, federal spending was 41 percent of national output in 1945 (the year World War II ended), while state and local spending was only 5 percent that year. Compare those figures with the figures for 1970. We can see that the state and local government's percentage of spending increased while the federal government's percentage decreased. This trend has continued since 1970.

💢 Increase Military Spending

The United States assumed an immense financial burden in the 20th century by fighting four major wars and by undertaking the protection of the free world in the cold war. These costs were reflected in the nation's outlays for military hardware, military personnel, and other military expenses. When the cold war ended in 1991, military spending declined somewhat, but in the aftermath of the terrorist attacks of 9/11/01, the threats to world security from North Korea and other nations make it all but certain that defense spending as a share of GDP is likely to increase.

Population Growth

The United States has a much larger population now than it had a century ago. Since 1900, the population has grown from 76 million to more than 290 million. The increased population requires more schools, police, firefighters, roads, sewers, and prisons—in short, more of everything that government provides.

Rising Expectations

Thanks to the nation's enormous capacity to produce goods and services, people in the United States today expect to live better than earlier generations did. As a consequence, governmental expenditures for services have had to increase. Two-lane roads have been replaced by four-lane interstate highways in many areas. Government regulations require school districts to spend much more money on staff, equipment, and facilities than before. In these and other areas, citizens have come to expect more from their government.

Inflation

Since 1940, prices in general have increased ten times. Thus, the government has had to pay higher costs for all the services it provides. For this reason, a substantial amount of the greater expenditures of government results not from expanded services but from increasing costs.

CHANGING ATTITUDES TOWARD THE ROLE OF GOVERNMENT

Through most of the nation's history, people seemed to agree with the saying that "government is best which governs least." Accordingly, government was expected to furnish little more than protection from criminals and foreign enemies and a few goods and services that many people believed could not have been profitably provided by private enterprise, such as schools, postal service, and highways.

Attitudes toward the role of government changed dramatically in the 1930s. During the Great Depression of that era, unemployment and business failures achieved record highs. With the economy teetering on the brink of collapse, the public demanded that the federal government do something to revitalize the economy. From that time until recent years, government involvement in the nation's economic and social well-being continued to expand.

President **Lyndon B. Johnson** in his State of the Union Address in 1965 introduced his idea for a **Great Society** program. While Roosevelt's **New Deal** had been a response to an emergency—the Great Depression—Johnson was promising a better life for all at a time of general prosperity. President Johnson believed that poverty could be eliminated in the United States and that it was the responsibility of the federal government to take appropriate actions to achieve this end.

Earlier, in August 1964, Congress had given Johnson some weapons to begin his "War on Poverty." It passed the **Economic Opportunity Act**, aimed at eliminating the causes of poverty. The act established (1) the **Job Corps** in urban centers to provide vocational training for young adults, (2) the **Neighborhood Youth Corps** to provide jobs for young people, and (3) the **Work-Study Program** to give financial aid to needy college students. Other weapons in the War on Poverty included **Head Start** (a preschool program for underprivileged children), **VISTA** (**Volunteers in Service to America**—a domestic version of the Peace Corps), and **Manpower Development and Training** (a program to aid and retrain those workers displaced by machines).

Congress set up special redevelopment programs for specific regions of the country that were considered "pockets of poverty." For example, one program helped people in Appalachia, the coal-mining area of the Appalachian Mountains in the Eastern United States. Federal money was spent to build highways, sewage-treatment plants, hospitals, and vocational schools, and to restore lands scarred by mines.

Today, increasing numbers of Americans believe that government, especially at the federal level, has become too large, inefficient, and corrupt. These people want the state and local governments to take over from the federal government many responsibilities, including welfare programs, with few or no controls from Washington. They would also like to see many activities that government has been involved in taken over by private charities, religious institutions, community groups, and private enterprise.

Problems Associated With Government's Participation in the Economy

Just as markets occasionally fail or are unable to provide needed goods and services, the same can be said for government. People sometimes argue that government participation is a part of the problem rather than the solution. Critics most frequently cite the difference between incentives in the public and private sectors, and government waste as the reason why government programs often fail.

DIFFERENCE BETWEEN INCENTIVES IN THE PUBLIC AND PRIVATE SECTORS. Business firms strive to produce better products at the lowest cost because this will increase their profits. Similarly, consumers generally strive to get the most for their money and care for their property. Incentives like the profit motive and concern for one's standard of living are often absent in the public sector, where there is no need to operate at a profit. Legislators, on the other hand, feel a need to generate campaign contributions and get reelected.

GOVERNMENT WASTE.   Two frequent legislative tactics are logrolling and pork barrel legislation. *Pork barrel legislation* creates projects that benefit the voters in a legislator's home district. The process by which legislators support each other's proposals (in a kind of "you scratch my back, and I'll scratch yours") is called *logrolling*. All too often, it is argued, logrolling results in wasteful and unnecessary public projects. The watchdog committee Citizens Against Government Waste (CAGW) recently cited the following as examples of "pork" in public spending:

- $400,000 appropriation for a parking lot in an Alaskan town whose total population numbers 300
- a $110,00 National Science Foundation grant to study "The Modern Myth of the Mad Scientist," whose real purpose, said CAGW, was to give the researcher an all-expenses-paid trip to Germany
- a $1.5 million appropriation to refurbish a large, modern statue of a Roman god in Alabama.

The lack of financial incentives makes it less urgent for governments to think about the consequences of their actions, since no one (other than the general public) will lose money if the proposal results in harmful unforeseen consequences. Urban renewal programs that destroyed more homes than they created, highway projects that drove through and broke up old stable neighborhoods, and poverty programs that added to the nation's poor are often cited as examples of the consequences of the public sector's lack of financial incentives.

 # THE FEDERAL BUDGET

As discussed in Chapter 10, a budget is a financial plan that summarizes anticipated income and expenses. Like individuals and families, all levels of government rely on budgets to help them plan their income and expenditures. Think of the budget as a balance scale. When the planned income and expenses are equal, we say that the budget is balanced. When the expected income is greater than planned expenses, we say that the budget has a surplus. When anticipated income is less than the planned spending, we say that the budget has a deficit.

⚡ Establishing a Budget

A federal budget runs from October 1 of one year to September 30 of the following year. We call this 12-month period a *fiscal year.* The **Office of Management and Budget (OMB)** prepares the federal budget. This agency, which reports to the U.S. president, starts working on a budget about 15 months before the budget is to go into effect. This schedule enables the president to present a proposed budget to Congress each January, about nine months before the beginning of the fiscal year.

The budget that the president delivers to Congress is merely a recommendation. Congress has the power to make whatever adjustments it chooses in levels of income and spending. It might, for example, refuse to allocate funds for new programs requested by the president. It might decline to increase taxes as requested. Congress might increase spending for some program to levels much more than what the president asks for.

Once members of Congress have agreed on the changes they want, they put them into effect by passing a series of appropriation and revenue bills. Once passed, Congress sends them on to the president for his or her signature.

Since federal budgets are prepared in advance of the fiscal year, they are merely a forecast of what is expected to happen, not a summary of what actually occurs. This difference arises from several causes.

Figure 13.2 **Three Types of Budgets**

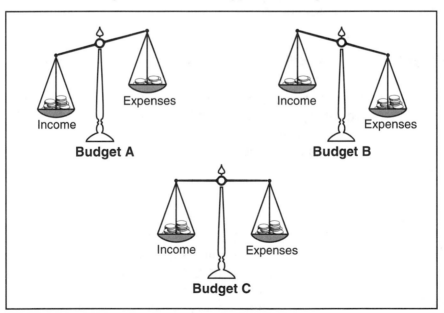

Which one of these three budgets is balanced? Which has a surplus? Which has a deficit?

▷ **TABLE 13.2 RECEIPTS AND OUTLAYS OF THE FEDERAL GOVERNMENT (BILLIONS OF DOLLARS)**

Year	Receipts	Outlays
1955	$ 65.5	$ 68.5
1965	116.8	118.4
1975	279.1	324.2
1985	734.1	946.4
2000	1,956.3	1,789.6
2004	1,922.0	2,229.3

In what year listed was the federal budget most nearly in balance? In what years was there a surplus? A deficit?

THE UNEXPECTED MAY OCCUR. Crises, such as the terrorist attacks of 9/11/01 and the U.S. military response in Afghanistan and elsewhere, require emergency appropriations to pay the cost of mobilizing troops and of assisting civilian populations caught in the middle of the fighting.

INCOME DEPENDS ON BUSINESS CONDITIONS. Unlike families living on fixed incomes, government income fluctuates. This happens because government tax revenues depend on the incomes of individuals and businesses. When times are bad, business and individual incomes decline, as do tax receipts. When times are good, the opposite occurs.

⚙ How Budgets Transform Goals Into Reality

The federal budget serves many purposes. Not only does it itemize expected revenues and intended expenses for the coming year, but it also is a plan for the future. What does the government plan to spend on each program, department, and agency? And how is it going to get the money to do all of this spending? Table 13.3 summarizes the principal items of income and expense in a federal budget. As we can see from the table, most of the federal government's income comes from taxes.

We will be taking a closer look at taxes in the next chapter. Meanwhile, let us examine the expense side (*outlays*) of the budget. The list of expenditures in the budget tells us much about what Congress and the president have agreed is important in a given year. Governments, like people, have limited resources. Agreement has to be reached among conflicting interests and groups as to (1) how much to spend, (2) what the money should be spent for, and (3) who will pay for this spending. Members of Congress often follow the wishes of their party leaders when they vote to spend or not to spend on various projects.

▷ TABLE 13.3   BUDGET OF THE FEDERAL GOVERNMENT, 2004

	Billions of Dollars	Percent of Total
Receipts		
Individual income taxes	$ 849.9	44.2%
Corporate income taxes	169.1	8.8
Social insurance taxes and contributions	764.5	39.8
Excise taxes	70.9	3.7
Estate and gift taxes	23.4	1.2
Customs duties	20.7	1.1
Other	38.5	2.0
Adjustment for shortfall	(−) 15.0	(−) 0.8
Total budget receipts	**$1,922.0**	**100.0%**
Outlays		
National defense	$ 390.4	17.5%
International affairs	25.6	1.1
Homeland security	28.0	1.3
General science, space, and technology	22.9	1.0
Income security	325.0	14.6
Health	246.6	11.1
Medicare	258.9	11.6
Social Security	497.3	22.3
Veterans' benefits & services	62.0	2.8
Education, training, employment, & social services	85.3	3.8
Commerce and housing credit	(−) 0.7	—
Transportation	63.4	2.8
Natural resources, environment, & energy	31.6	1.4
Community & regional development	17.1	0.9
Agriculture	20.8	1.0
Net interest	176.4	7.9
General government	20.5	0.9
Administration of justice	39.4	1.8
Undistributed offsetting receipts	(−) 81.6	(−) 3.6
Total budget outlays	**$2,229.3**	**100.0%**

Source: U.S. Budget FY 2004

The legislators, however, are looking ahead to the next election and must consider how their votes meet the needs and wants of their constituents.

By comparing the budget of one year with that of another, we can often identify those programs that seem to be growing in importance and those that may be falling out of favor. Let us see if we can detect any such trends by comparing the budget items in Table 13.3 with budget items of earlier years.

Figure 13.3 **National Defense as a Percentage of Total Outlays**

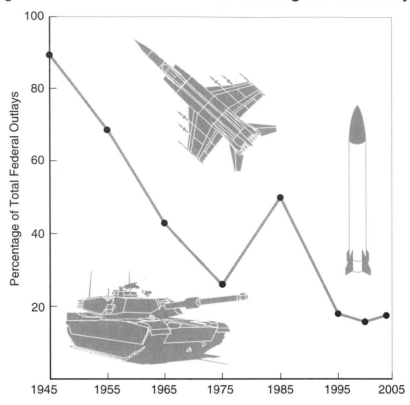

How do these expenditures reflect the nation's priorities?

NATIONAL DEFENSE.   National defense appropriations are used to support the activities of the armed forces. The level of defense spending often mirrors international conditions. During times of war or international tensions, defense spending tends to rise. When tensions decline, less money is appropriated for defense. From 1941—the year that the United States entered World War II—until 1973, national defense was the largest single item of expense in the U.S. budget. For many of these years, national resources were devoted to containing the military power and political influence of the Soviet Union.

Political and economic changes in Eastern Europe in the late 1980s led to a lessening of tensions between the Soviet Union and the United States. With the end of the cold war and the breakup of the Soviet Union in 1991, the threat of a global war had passed. People began to speak of a "peace dividend." They were expressing the hope that the nation could now reduce its defense outlays so dramatically as to enable the nation to spend more on other matters, such as social programs.

The War on Terrorism, coupled with other threats to global peace and security, make it likely that defense spending will have to be increased in the years ahead.

HOMELAND SECURITY.   In the aftermath of 9/11/01, Congress created the Department of Homeland Security, whose first priority is to protect the nation against further terrorist attacks. The new law brought the Coast Guard, Secret Service, Immigration and Naturalization Service, Federal Emergency Management Agency, and 18 other federal agencies under a single umbrella.

INTERNATIONAL AFFAIRS.   The United States plays an active leadership role in international affairs because national well-being depends, in part, upon events beyond its borders. Funding for these activities falls into four categories: (1) foreign economic and financial assistance, (2) military assistance to allies and other friendly nations, (3) administration and conduct of foreign diplomacy, and (4) foreign information and exchange activities. For many years, money budgeted for international affairs has remained between 1 and 2 percent of the total budgeted outlays.

INCOME SECURITY.   One of the major outlays in the federal budget is *income security,* or welfare. An example in this category is the **Food Stamp Program**. In 1956, outlays in income security made up 14 percent of the total budget. In the 1980s, though, the percentage grew much higher—to above 30 percent. By 2004, budgeted income security funds had dropped to about the 1956 percentage.

HEALTH CARE.   The federal government has been providing health services ever since 1798, when it created the **Public Health Service**. Now the largest health-care program is **Medicaid**, a program that provides medical care and

—Mike Smith/*Las Vegas Sun,* NV/Rothco.

What is the cartoonist saying about how this budget pie was sliced?

medicines for the poor. The federal government provides the states with a good share of the funds needed for Medicaid. Then the states are required to provide additional funds and administer the Medicaid program in their state. In 2004, the government budgeted $247 billion on Medicaid and other health-care programs. At 11.1 percent of total federal outlays, the health-care share of the budget was less than what it had been in 1990—14.1 percent.

MEDICARE.   Between 1970 and 2004, outlays for Medicare increased from $7 to $259 billion. **Medicare** is a federal health insurance program for people 65 or older and certain differently abled persons. There are two parts to the Medicare program. Hospital Insurance (Part A) helps pay for care of patients in hospitals and in skilled nursing facilities, as well as for home health care and hospice care. Medical Insurance (Part B) helps pay for doctors' services, hospital *outpatient* (relating to patients who do not stay overnight) services, hospital *inpatient* (related to persons who stay in a hospital) services, durable medical equipment, and a number of other medical services and supplies that are not covered by Part A of Medicare.

THE SOCIAL SECURITY SYSTEM.   Every month the federal government mails more than 45 million green checks to beneficiaries of the Social Security system. **Social Security** is the nation's basic method of providing a continuing income when family earnings are reduced or stop because of retirement, disability, or death. About nine out of every ten persons working today are covered. Coverage comes in a number of forms.

1. Retirement Payments.   Workers may start receiving retirement checks as early as age 62. Most people begin receiving benefits at age 65, but the standard age for receiving retirement checks is being raised gradually to 67.

2. Disability Payments.   These payments are sent to workers who become severely disabled before age 65.

3. Survivors' Benefits.   If a worker dies, payments go to dependent members of his or her family.

4. Health Insurance.   The two-part health insurance program called Medicare was discussed above. Although Medicare is part of the Social Security system, it has its own line in the budget.

5. Unemployment Insurance.   Most workers who have lost their job are entitled to receive *unemployment compensation.* These benefits, which vary from state to state, are paid out of a fund created by state payroll taxes on employers and by contributions from the federal government. Benefits run for a limited time only.

VETERANS' BENEFITS AND SERVICES. The government provides benefits to veterans and their families. It pays veterans for education, pensions, and health services. In recent years, this program has remained a small part of total outlays—about 2.5 to 3 percent. Many of the following budget lines have also maintained a constant proportion of the total budget.

EDUCATION, TRAINING, EMPLOYMENT, AND SOCIAL SERVICES. These programs help individuals who need to complete their education, acquire job skills, receive career counseling, or obtain assistance in child care.

TRANSPORTATION. The Department of Transportation is responsible for interstate highway planning, development, and construction; urban mass transit; railroads; aviation; and the safety of waterways, ports, highways, and oil and gas pipelines. Among the better-known agencies of this federal department are the Federal Aviation Administration, Federal Highway Administration, Federal Railway Administration, and U.S. Coast Guard. The cost of supporting all the activities of the Department of Transportation is accounted for in this budget category.

NATURAL RESOURCES AND ENVIRONMENT. Various federal programs attempt to curb pollution of the land, air, and water; conserve and develop minerals, timber, and other natural resources; and preserve natural areas, historic sites, and fish and wildlife stocks.

ENERGY. Funding for energy programs is designed to (1) protect the security and independence of the nation's energy supplies, (2) promote energy production and conservation, (3) develop renewable sources of energy, and (4) increase the safety of nuclear power and the long-term disposal of nuclear wastes.

COMMUNITY AND REGIONAL DEVELOPMENT. The federal government sponsors a number of programs that attempt to provide housing for the nation's poor. Other programs in community and regional development assist in creating business opportunities in economically depressed neighborhoods. Still other programs provide disaster relief and insurance.

AGRICULTURE. The major part of the money allocated to agriculture in 2004 was used to support the prices U.S. farmers receive for their products. Another area of the government's agricultural programs includes efforts to improve the production and marketing of farm products.

INTEREST ON THE DEBT. Interest is the cost of borrowing money. In recent decades, the money needed to pay the interest on the national debt has reached astounding proportions. Whereas in 1900 the public debt stood at $1.3 billion (or $16.60 for every man, woman, and child in the nation), by 2004 the total

ECONOMIC ISSUE

Privatizing Social Security?

One of the issues dividing Republicans (who generally supported the idea) and Democrats (who were opposed) during the 2000 presidential election year was the proposal to *privatize* Social Security. Although specifics vary, privatization is based on the idea that the funds withheld from workers' wages for the Social Security program should be available for private investment in stocks, bonds, or other personal investment programs.

Speaking on behalf of the proposal in 2002, President George W. Bush said, "At a time when older Americans have longer lives and more options than ever before, we need to ensure that they have access not just to a monthly check, but to personal wealth. . . . The generation of wealth should not be limited to a few in our society; it ought to be an opportunity for everybody."

This poster, found in U.S. post offices in the 1930s, promoted what was then the new Social Security system.

Another proponent asked, "Why should I, a relatively young person, be forced to pay into an antiquated retirement system that holds my money for years and gives me back peanuts when I am old? Virtually anyone could do better by investing the same money in long-term government bonds, or corporate stocks!"

What the proponents were saying was that in 2002, the average worker who retired after 45 years of employment got a monthly retirement benefit of $1,128. But if the same payroll contributions had been invested in a portfolio of stocks over the same period, it might have been worth $590,000, yielding a monthly income of $3,700.

Those opposed to privatization proposals argue the following:

- It is true that private investment and savings plans were likely to have enabled retirees to receive higher monthly returns than Social Security, but it was always the purpose of Social Security to supplement rather than replace savings programs.

- Not everyone enrolled in Social Security in the 45 years preceding a 2002 retirement would have been able to acquire a nest egg. Some would have died or been disabled during those years, and Social Security would have helped their families. Privatization proposals do not include provisions for such survivors.

- Over the years, corporate stocks can go down as well as up. In the year between March 2000 and April 2001, stocks declined by 28 percent. Those who retired that year and had invested everything in stocks would have had to make do with a nest egg that was worth 28 percent less than it had been the previous year.

- The funds withheld from workers for Social Security are not set aside in an account for these workers. Instead, they are used to pay the cost of benefits paid out to existing retirees and other beneficiaries. If Congress were to enact a privatization plan, it would immediately reduce the amount of funds available for present-day benefits.

Should privatization be introduced into the Social Security program? What do you think?

was more than $7 trillion (or $23,000 per person). Nearly all the $760 billion set aside for interest payments in 2004 was a result of this huge debt.

GENERAL SCIENCE, SPACE, AND TECHNOLOGY.   The goals of these federal programs are to (1) expand scientific knowledge through support of basic research in all fields of science, (2) promote technological innovation in industry, (3) develop a greater understanding of the solar system and physical universe through space exploration, and (4) develop and demonstrate practical, economic, and productive applications of space technology.

GENERAL GOVERNMENT.   The funds in this category are used to carry out the everyday business of government as it is conducted by the executive, legislative, and judicial branches.

ADMINISTRATION OF JUSTICE.   This category provides the funding needed to finance the activities of federal law-enforcement agencies (such as the FBI), the courts system, and correctional (prison, parole, and probation) programs.

A BRIEF HISTORY OF GOVERNMENT FARM PROGRAMS

Since the 1880s, when farmers first began to organize politically, federal and state governments have enacted numerous programs to aid the farmer. While the specifics of farm legislation have varied from one year to the next, they generally sought to exempt farming from the laws of supply and demand through the use of price supports, supply restrictions, and/or subsidies.

Price Supports

In the 1920s and 1930s, many farmers complained that the prices they were receiving for their products were too low. In response to those claims, the federal government introduced a program of price supports for some (but not all) of their products. With *price supports,* the government set a floor on the selling price of selected farm products by offering to buy these products at set prices. (Technically, the price supports involved a government loan to the farmers, but since the government often forgave the loans, the government's action was really a purchase.)

Because the value of money fluctuates, fixed prices were helpful for a limited time only. Suppose, for example, that the government put a floor of $1 per bushel for corn during a period when the value of the dollar declined by 25 percent. By the end of this period, the $1 per bushel price would have declined in purchasing power by 25 cents. For that reason, government support programs tried to protect purchasing power rather than prices. This was achieved through the concept of *parity,* the price for commodities that would give farmers the purchasing power that farmers had had during the years 1909–1914.

By way of illustration, let us assume that the average price of wheat between 1909 and 1914 was 50 cents a bushel. Also suppose that by 2004 the cost of living had increased by seven times. In those circumstances, it would have taken a wheat price of $3.50 a bushel in 2004 to equal its purchasing power in 1909–1914.

In most instances, the federal government supported prices at something less than 100 percent of parity. If in the above example government had chosen to support prices at 80 percent of parity, farmers would have been guaranteed $2.80 per bushel for their wheat that year ($3.50 × .80 = $2.80).

Because the floor set by government was usually higher than the equilibrium price, farmers produced more than they could sell. (See Figure 3.11 on page 68.) When this happened, the government stepped in to purchase and store the surplus products. Since storing farm surpluses was very costly, the government developed several programs to give the food away to the needy both at home and abroad.

Supply Restrictions

We have learned that price supports often created surpluses. The easiest way to increase agricultural prices without creating surpluses was to reduce the supply of farm products. *Supply restrictions* were carried out through strategies such as acreage control and import restrictions.

ACREAGE-CONTROL PROGRAMS.   In the 1930s, the federal government began paying farmers who grew certain crops to withhold a specified number of acres from planting. In this way, it was hoped, production of those crops would decrease and prices would rise. *Acreage-control* programs remained in effect until 1996, when they were abolished.

IMPORT RESTRICTIONS.   The supply of farm products may also be limited through *import restrictions.* The federal government can set a *quota* (limit) or outright ban on the importation of certain farm products. As a result, U.S. consumers will purchase more domestic farm products and reduce farm surpluses. Of course, U.S. consumers will have to pay a higher price for the protected products than would have been charged had there been no import restrictions.

One of the biggest beneficiaries of import quotas and price supports has been the sugar industry. The world price of sugar is about half of that paid to U.S. growers of sugarcane and sugar beets. Without the protection afforded by import quotas and support prices, sugar growing would all but disappear as an industry in the United States. Industrial users of sugar in the United States, such as soft drink and candy manufacturers, oppose supporting U.S. sugar growers. Since sugar is more expensive in the United States, U.S. manufacturers who use sugar in their products claim that they are at a competitive disadvantage with overseas producers of similar products.

Subsidies

Direct government payments to producers of certain goods or services are called *subsidies*. The U.S. government has used subsidies to assist farmers in a variety of ways. In one program, for example, the federal Department of Agriculture reimbursed farmers for a portion of their fertilizer expenses.

Farming Today

Changing conditions prompted many Americans in the 1990s to call for a revision of the government's agricultural policies. Congress in 1996 passed a new law that aimed (over a seven-year period) to reduce drastically the extent of

Figure 13.4 **Changes in U.S. Farming**

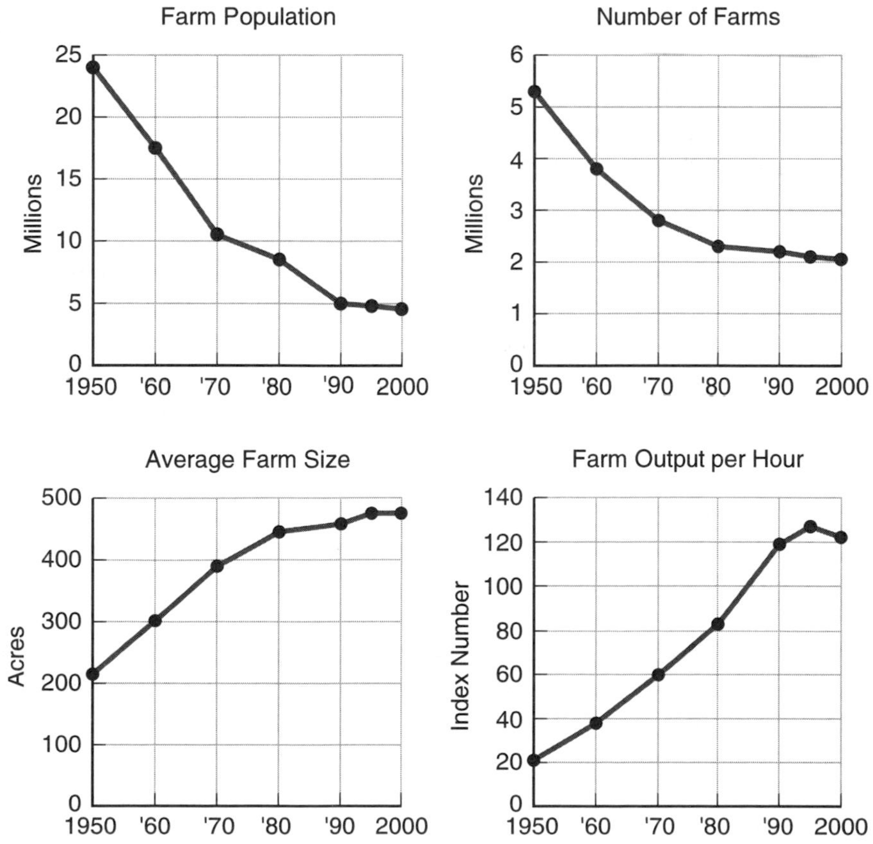

government intervention in farming. Instead, "market forces" (supply and demand) would determine what farmers got for their products. What were the circumstances that prompted the federal government's new agricultural policies?

BUDGET DEFICITS. By the early 1990s, the national debt had climbed to record levels. By way of slowing the growth of debt, legislators from all political camps called for balanced federal budgets. As a first step, many in Congress called for a reduction in the size and scope of spending on federal agricultural programs.

AGRICULTURE'S DECLINING CLOUT. When 25 percent of the population lived on farms, farmers (and the people who did business with them) had much political clout. Today, less than 2 percent of the population lives on farms, and farming accounts for less than 2 percent of the GDP.

GROWTH IN INTERNATIONAL TRADE. Productivity gains in agriculture fueled enormous growth in exports. In the 1930s, only 8 percent of U.S. wheat was exported; now 20 to 30 percent of this crop is exported. Similarly, corn exports have gone from less than 2 percent of production to more than 25 percent. But exports are greatest in a climate of free trade, which means fewer restrictions on the importation of foreign agricultural products and reduced levels of price supports given to products sold abroad.

THE AVERAGE FARMER IS NO LONGER POOR. In the 1930s, farmers earned about one-third less than other Americans. Then price-support programs were instituted that had the effect of raising the incomes of farmers. Now U.S. farm households have incomes better than the U.S. average.

FARM PROGRAMS BENEFIT THE WEALTHIEST FARMERS. Two-thirds of government farm benefits have gone to the largest 18 percent of farms—even though their average income is triple that of the typical U.S. household.

ENVIRONMENTAL CONCERNS. The environmental costs of farming have increased. Modern farmers use more artificial fertilizers and pesticides, which often run off the soil and pollute waterways. The pollutants also enter underground sources of drinking water. Agricultural expansion has also been a major cause of wetlands losses. Wetlands protect regions against floods, help purify water, and provide important places for wildlife to live.

INTERNATIONAL CONCERNS. High farm price supports make American farm products cheaper than those produced in the developing nations. Exporters in poor developing nations cannot compete with these depressed prices in the world market, contributing to their continued poverty and instability.

Efforts to take the government out of farming ended when Congress enacted the Farm Act of 2002. The new law restored subsidies and trade restrictions, created new price-support programs, and expanded existing ones. Critics charged that the new law was a "farm states welfare bill" whose real purpose was to help the **George W. Bush** administration win control of Congress and repay the agribusiness interests for their political support. Price-support advocates replied that protection was needed because foreign nations were supporting their farmers, thereby making it difficult for U.S. farmers to compete in overseas markets. Indeed, the argument continued, European nations paid far more in subsidies to their farmers than did the U.S. government to its farmers.

 # STATE AND LOCAL FINANCES

When economists speak of "state and local governments," they are referring to well over 80,000 units. In addition to the 50 states, these include some 3,000 counties, 19,000 municipalities, 17,000 townships, 15,000 school districts, and 30,000 special districts.

Where the Money Comes From

Income, sales, and property taxes provide large shares of revenues to state and local government. Their largest single source of money, however, is the federal government. State and local governments look to *grants-in-aid* to finance their operations. Grants-in-aid are funds given by a higher government (such as the federal government) to a lower one. Grants-in-aid may be *unconditional*—they can be spent in any way the recipient government sees fit. More frequently, grants-in-aid are *conditional,* which means that they must be spent for a particular purpose.

Suppose, for example, that a city needs additional street lighting at a time when federal grants are available only for waste disposal or rapid transit projects. In those circumstances, the city will have to finance a street lighting project out of its own funds. Meanwhile, it could also apply for federal funding of one of the other projects. Federal aid to state and local governments in 2004 totaled $394 billion.

States and localities seek additional revenue to meet expanding needs from sources other than those previously cited. Note in Figure 13.5 that sources other than income, sales, and property taxes and federal grants accounted for more than 19 percent of state and local revenue in a recent year. You may have heard about the "other taxes" and "fees and misc." that your state or locality imposes. You may have even complained about the costs of these other taxes and fees. These fees are collected as a percentage of bridge tolls, admissions to museums, fees for automobile licenses, fees for registration of documents, and fees for parking in a public garage.

Figure 13.5 **Combined State and Local Government Budgets, 2000**

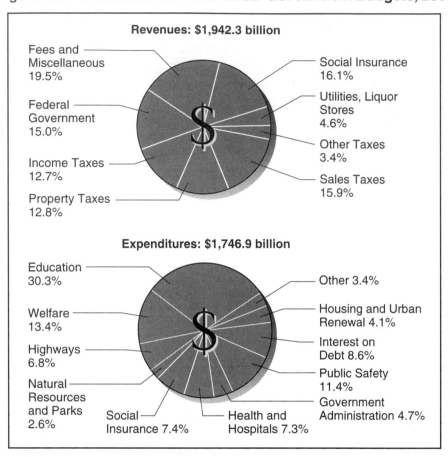

Revenues: $1,942.3 billion

- Fees and Miscellaneous 19.5%
- Federal Government 15.0%
- Income Taxes 12.7%
- Property Taxes 12.8%
- Social Insurance 16.1%
- Utilities, Liquor Stores 4.6%
- Other Taxes 3.4%
- Sales Taxes 15.9%

Expenditures: $1,746.9 billion

- Education 30.3%
- Welfare 13.4%
- Highways 6.8%
- Natural Resources and Parks 2.6%
- Social Insurance 7.4%
- Health and Hospitals 7.3%
- Other 3.4%
- Housing and Urban Renewal 4.1%
- Interest on Debt 8.6%
- Public Safety 11.4%
- Government Administration 4.7%

States and municipalities can raise money in other ways as well. They can sell bonds. They can issue traffic and parking tickets. Some states run lotteries or authorize gambling establishments in order to raise revenues.

How State and Local Governments Spend Their Money

Thirty cents out of every dollar spent by state and local governments goes for education. Programs that aid the needy, unemployed, and differently abled are the next largest category of expenses. As you might expect, road construction and repair of roads and public transportation networks make up a fair percentage of total state and local expenditures.

States and localities have found it increasingly difficult to balance their budgets. Many state and local officials blame their problems on so-called *unfunded mandates*. These are programs and services that one level of government requires a subordinate level to provide but that get little or no funding from the higher level. The following are examples of unfunded mandates.

- In 1989, Congress forced the states to provide Medicaid to pregnant women and their children up to age six in families with incomes below 133 percent of the official poverty line. In 1990, the federal government required states to extend Medicaid coverage to all poor children under the age of 19. As a result of mandates such as these, Medicaid soon made up nearly 20 percent of state government spending.

- Congress forced states to allow longer and heavier trucks onto highways within their borders. This rule added to the state's costs in road maintenance because the larger trucks cause more wear on the highways.

- Federal law now requires that mass-transit systems modify their equipment to achieve "total accessibility for the handicapped." Local governments that operate buses, subways, and trains find that this requirement has added greatly to their expenses.

Some local governments have been especially hard hit by unfunded mandates. Columbus, Ohio, for example, was ordered to clean up some discarded solvents at a municipal garage. Columbus officials calculated that this federally mandated task would add $2 million to the city's projected expenses. Many small communities that have volunteer firefighters have been faced with new federal requirements regarding these volunteers. The federal government has required towns to apply the same standards to volunteer firefighters that they apply to paid, professional fire departments. With required physical examinations, individual face masks, hazardous material-training programs, and the like, Indiana's Wayne Township spent more than $2 million to bring its volunteer force up to standard. This was almost half of the local government's annual budget.

In 1995, Congress enacted a law making it more difficult for the federal government to impose rules on states and localities without providing federal money to pay for them.

In a related matter, some political leaders have urged that control over social, environmental, and safety programs be transferred to the states (and, in some instances, to charities and other private organizations). This transfer to the states could be accomplished, they say, through more use of *block grants*— sums of money that the federal government grants to the states to achieve broad policy goals. But they want these block grants to have no strings attached so that the states would have freedom to decide how to spend these grants. States, for example, would be free to use transportation block grants to fund whatever road-building or mass-transit projects they preferred. States could set their own environmental standards and set their own rules for eligibility for Medicaid and welfare funds.

This method would contrast with current methods whereby the federal government gives the states funds for specific programs with strict guidelines as to how these funds are to be used. The current methods involve much paperwork, which (the reformers claim) is very time-consuming and wasteful. Critics of federal programs say that states and localities know best how to solve state and local problems. They say that federal programs do not work, waste money, and often make beneficiaries lazy.

Opponents of this trend toward less federal control have raised several points.

- Along with eliminating federal controls, Congress is providing less money for affected programs. This means either that the state or local governments must raise more funds or that the programs will become weaker or be eliminated. Critics of block grants see dangers for a society that has weaker environmental laws, provides less money and health care for the poor, and spends less on building and repairing roads, bridges, and water and sewage systems.

- Problems caused by pollution and the destruction of wildlife often require national rather than state or local solutions. How, for example, could block grants prevent the destruction of forests in the Eastern part of the country by emissions from Midwestern factories?

- What evidence is there that state and local governments will be more efficient, less wasteful, and more honest in administering programs than the federal government has been?

- Those who favor continuing federal control of many programs argue that without federal regulations and controls, there would be disparities from state to state on how well government helps its citizens.

- In response to suggestions that private charities take over some of the welfare responsibilities from the federal government, critics of this idea say that private charities are not wealthy enough or large enough to do the job.

The sides are clearly drawn. Whether the states should, or could, replace the federal government in many tasks is likely to be a matter of debate for years to come.

S U M M A R Y

Government (federal, state, and local) plays important roles in the U.S. economy. Through antitrust laws, government attempts to safeguard competition and the market system. It provides public goods and services and corrects for harmful externalities. Government is concerned with maintaining economic stability. Through programs designed to help the poor and needy, government redistributes wealth.

The federal government's role in the economy grew for awhile for the following reasons: increased military spending; increases in the U.S. population; increased demands for government services; and increased costs of these services. The roles of state and local governments in the economy have been growing even faster. State and local governments together purchase more of the nation's output of goods and services than does the federal government.

The federal government and state and local governments have budgets. A budget tells us about a government's economic goals by indicating how much it will spend on various programs. By comparing budgets from year to year, we can see which programs have grown in importance and which have declined.

REVIEWING THE CHAPTER

BUILDING VOCABULARY

Match each item in Column A with its definition in Column B.

Column A

1. beneficial externality
2. harmful externality
3. economic stability
4. price supports
5. fiscal year
6. unfunded mandate
7. subsidy
8. block grant
9. parity
10. income security

Column B

a. a form of federal aid to state and local governments
b. a harm caused by an economic activity that is paid for by society as a whole
c. a government program that aids farmers by guaranteeing minimum prices for their products
d. government benefits to help the aged, differently abled, and unemployed
e. a payment by the government to individuals or businesses
f. for the federal government, the period from October 1 of one year to September 30 of the following year
g. a benefit of an economic activity that is paid for or enjoyed by society as a whole
h. a period of modest changes in the level of prices, employment, and business activity
i. a price that gives farmers the same purchasing power from the sale of crops that earlier farmers had had during the years 1909–1914
j. a program or service required by one level of government of a lower level and that the lower level has to pay for

UNDERSTANDING WHAT YOU HAVE READ

1. Approximately what percentage of the gross domestic product is accounted for by government spending today? (*a*) 5 percent (*b*) 10 percent (*c*) 19 percent (*d*) 25 percent.

2. "Spending large amounts on the space program means that less money is available to spend on other areas of the economy." This statement illustrates the (*a*) superiority of government-sponsored programs (*b*) laws of supply and demand (*c*) effect of government spending on the allocation of resources (*d*) law of diminishing returns.

3. A government's budget is a (*a*) summary of the money that was spent in previous years (*b*) statement of expenditures and income that took place during the preceding year (*c*) plan of income and expenses for the year to come (*d*) law to prevent the government from spending more than it earns.

4. According to Table 13.1, "Government Purchases as a Percentage of National Output (GDP)" on page 285, total government purchases of the nation's GDP was greatest in (*a*) 1930 (*b*) 1945 (*c*) 1970 (*d*) 2002.

5. Approximately how large is the federal debt per capita? (*a*) $1,000 (*b*) $4,000 (*c*) $10,000 (*d*) over $20,000.

6. State and local governments spend the most on (*a*) roads and highways (*b*) food stamps (*c*) education (*d*) public safety.

7. When the government expects that its income will be more than its expenditures, the budget will be described as (*a*) balanced (*b*) showing a deficit (*c*) having a surplus (*d*) allocated.

8. Which *one* of the following is not an economic responsibility of government? (*a*) redistributing income (*b*) maintaining economic stability (*c*) safeguarding competition (*d*) solving the problem of scarcity.

9. Which *one* of the following is an example of a government regulatory agency? (*a*) Consumer Product Safety Commission (*b*) Department of Homeland Security (*c*) Post Office (*d*) Federal Bureau of Investigation.

10. Those who favor transferring some of the authority of the federal government to the states and localities would most likely advocate (*a*) another War on Poverty (*b*) martial law (*c*) more unfunded mandates (*d*) more unconditional block grants.

THINKING CRITICALLY

1. Two speakers are discussing government spending and the U.S. economy. With which speaker would you agree the most? Explain your answer.

   Speaker A: "The U.S. government has to decide what it wants to do first: balance the budget; eliminate poverty and homelessness in the country; or stop the spread of political tyranny abroad."

   Speaker B: "With a ten-trillion-dollar GDP, the U.S. government can do anything it wants, provided it stops wasting its resources."

2. "That government which governs best, governs least" summarizes a popular attitude held by many Americans during the 19th century. Then the U.S. government was relatively small, and its involvement in the economy was also relatively small. Since the beginning of the 20th century, however, the federal government has played a much larger role in the nation's economy.

   a. With reference to *three* events or developments that have taken place after 1900, show why the role of the government in the economic life of the nation has expanded.

   b. In your view, was this expansion of governmental activities necessary? Explain your answer with at least *two* examples.

3. Study the data in Table 13.1, page 285.

   a. Summarize the changes that have taken place in total government expenditures as a percentage of GDP since 1930.

   b. Compare the growth of state and local government purchases of the nation's output of goods and services with that of the federal government since 1970.

4. Social Security, Medicare, and Medicaid have all been causes of concern to economists and politicians. These programs, called *entitlements* because people are entitled to them if they meet certain qualifications, are major expenditures, which continue to rise each year. Many beneficiaries (and potential beneficiaries) fear that the programs will run out of money and their benefits will be cut. Discuss why you agree or disagree with each of the following proposals: (*a*) Taxes should be increased to fund these programs. (*b*) Benefits should be cut across the board. (*c*) Beneficiaries with higher incomes should receive lower benefits than poor beneficiaries.

5. The federal government has set up two major health-care programs: Medicaid and Medicare. Briefly describe each program, pointing out how Medicaid differs from Medicare.

SKILLS: Interpreting a Table

Study the "Budget of the Federal Government" on page 291. Based on the data in Table 13.3 and information given in the text, answer the following questions.

1. What was the major source of revenue for the federal government?

2. What was the major outlay of the federal government?

3. Which was greater, receipts from social insurance taxes and contributions or combined expenditures for Social Security and Medicare?

4. Was the federal budget a balanced budget? Explain.

5. What percentage of the federal budget went to pay interest? Why was this figure so high?

EXPLORING CURRENT ISSUES IN ECONOMICS

In 2003, the states of New York, New Jersey, and Connecticut settled a lawsuit they had brought against the Virginia Electric and Power Company (now Dominion Virginia Power). The suit alleged that the company had violated certain provisions of the federal **Clean Air Act** by making major modifications to its plants without installing pollution-reducing devices. The plants' emissions, said the plaintiffs, worsened smog in the New York, New Jersey, and Connecticut metropolitan areas.

Under the settlement, the company agreed to spend $1.2 billion over the next decade to reduce emissions of sulfur dioxide and nitrogen oxide by 70 percent at six plants in Virginia and two in West Virginia. It will also pay for a variety of environmental projects, such as installation of solar energy devices on municipal buildings in New York and filters on New Jersey Transit buses that spew diesel pollution in both states.

1. How could emissions from power plants in Virginia and West Virginia affect the people in New York, New Jersey, and Connecticut?

2. "The problem leading to the Virginia Electric case was an example of a harmful externality." Explain this statement.

3. As an economist pointed out at the time, ". . . the settlement agreed to between the States and Virginia Electric resulted in the creation of one or more beneficial externalities." Explain this statement.

4. Why is it left to government, rather than to the laws of supply and demand, to deal with externalities?

CHAPTER 14
Taxation

OVERVIEW

". . . but in this world nothing can be said to be certain, except death and taxes."

—Benjamin Franklin

Benjamin Franklin had it right: Taxes are a fact of life. They are also quite costly. Tax collections by the federal, state, and local governments came to $3 trillion in 2000. That averaged out to roughly $11,000 for every man, woman, and child living in the United States that year.

The previous chapter dealt mainly with how governments spend money. This chapter focuses on taxes and taxation. Here we will discuss (1) why governments levy taxes, (2) the kinds of taxes people pay, (3) various standards for a good tax, and (4) proposals to strengthen the tax system.

WHY TAXES?—THE FUNCTIONS OF TAXATION

It is not news that few people want to pay taxes. The American colonists' objection to British taxes was one of the reasons for their revolution against the British government (1775–1783). In 1794, farmers in Pennsylvania who objected to a federal tax on whiskey staged a violent protest that came to be known as the "Whiskey Rebellion." If so many people have been against taxes, why do governments tax? The purposes of government taxation are several.

To Pay for the Costs of Government

The principal reason that governments levy taxes is to pay for the costs of governing. In the previous chapter, we learned that the federal government spends billions of dollars on national defense, Social Security, and other programs. State and local governments spend billions more on police, education, roads, public buildings, and other matters. Someone must pay for all these federal, state, and local expenditures. That someone is primarily the taxpayer. About 82 percent of federal income and 50 percent of the income of state and local governments come from taxes. Not surprisingly, as the responsibilities and costs of government have increased over the years, so too have taxes increased.

To Redistribute Wealth

Taxes redistribute wealth by taking money from some people and giving it to others. For example, the Medicaid program pays medical bills of poor people. Much of the funding for the Medicaid program comes from taxes collected by the federal government. These taxes are collected largely from people who have more money than the Medicaid recipients. In contrast, the poor people who are Medicaid recipients generally pay little or no tax. Other examples of tax money being used to redistribute wealth are food stamps and welfare payments. Again, the taxes paid by those who benefit from these programs are relatively minor compared to taxes paid by those with higher incomes.

To Promote Certain Industries

Some taxes, such as tariffs, are designed to benefit certain industries. A *tariff* is a tax on goods entering the country from a foreign country. The purpose of tariffs can be to raise money for the government, to raise the cost of imported goods, or to do both. We call this tax a *protective tariff* when its major purpose is to raise the cost of imports. The tariff is protective of an industry in the United States because it tends to make foreign imports more expensive than similar U.S.-made products. In this way, the tariff promotes U.S. industries. For example, suppose that Sally Smith in her Connecticut factory produces shirts that sell for $16 each. Sam Huong obtains similar shirts from a factory in Taiwan and sells them in the United States for $15 each. An import tax of 10 percent on shirts will protect Sally Smith's market in the United States. Ten percent of $15 is $1.50. An imported shirt that might otherwise sell for $15 will now cost the U.S. consumer $15 + $1.50, or $16.50. The tariff makes it possible for Sally Smith (a U.S. producer) to undersell Sam Huong (an importer).

To Influence Consumer- and Business-Spending Patterns

The level of taxation affects the amount of money individuals and business firms spend or invest. Assume that an individual with taxable earnings of $30,000 is taxed 15 percent on that salary. Fifteen percent of $30,000 is $4,500. Thus, after taxes are subtracted from $30,000, the individual will have $25,500 left to save, spend, or invest ($30,000 − $4,500 = $25,500). Now suppose taxes are increased to 30 percent. Thirty percent of $30,000 is $9,000. After paying these taxes, the individual would only have $21,000 to save, spend, or invest ($30,000 − $9,000 = $21,000).

Whenever government increases taxes, individuals and business firms have less to save, spend, or invest. Conversely, when government lowers taxes, individuals and business firms have more money to save, spend, or invest. There are times when it would be helpful to the economy if everyone spent less and saved more. At other times, the economy would become healthier if everyone spent more and saved less. In Chapter 19, we will describe how the federal government uses its power to tax to influence levels of spending and saving.

Local governments try to attract new business firms to their communities by offering to excuse them from paying local taxes for a time. A local government might, for example, offer to excuse a firm from paying all or part of its real estate taxes for ten years just for locating that business in the community. The business firm benefits by the amount saved in not paying real estate taxes. When the business locates in the community, it creates jobs and more taxpayers. It also increases the amount of money circulating in the local economy, thereby helping other businesses as well.

To Discourage Certain Behaviors

Taxes designed to discourage what some members of society consider to be improper or unhealthy behavior are often known as *sin taxes*. A government might impose these taxes on products that it wants to discourage people from using, such as alcohol and tobacco. Imposing federal and state taxes on these products substantially increases the cost of these products for the consumer.

THE FEDERAL INCOME TAX

The *individual* (or *personal*) *income tax* is the principal source of revenue for the federal government. It is also perhaps the tax with which most people in the country are familiar.

The income tax is the nation's only *progressive tax*. Such a tax is one that takes a larger percentage of the earnings of high-income individuals than of low-income ones. The progressivity of the federal income tax is demonstrated in the following table.

> **TABLE 14.1   TAX RATE SCHEDULES, 2003**

	If TAXABLE INCOME		The TAX Is			
			THEN			
	Is Over	But Not Over	This Amount	Plus This %		Of the Excess Over
Schedule X— Single	$ 0	$ 7,000	$ 0.00	10%		$ 0
	$ 7,000	$ 28,400	$ 700.00	15%		$ 7,000
	$ 28,400	$ 68,800	$ 3,910.00	25%		$ 28,400
	$ 68,800	$143,500	$14,010.00	28%		$ 68,800
	$143,500	$311,950	$34,926.00	33%		$143,500
	$311,950	—	$90,514.50	35%		$311,950

As you can see, in 2003 single individuals with $7,000 in taxable income were liable for a 10 percent or $700 income tax. At higher income levels, the tax rate increased until it reached that year's maximum tax rate of 35 percent. Thus, those with $14,000 in income paid $700 *plus* 15 percent on earnings in excess of $7,000. At earnings over $28,400 the tax rate on the additional income rose to 25 percent. From there it went to 28 percent on amounts over $68,800; 33 percent on amounts over $143,500, and 35 percent on income in excess of $311,950.

Some Americans go to a commercial tax preparer to help them fill out their tax forms and file them with the IRS. If the preparer gives one a quick refund on the income tax withheld, then the tax preparer is loaning this money and will often charge a high rate of interest.

THE INCOME TAX IN OUR DAILY LIVES

Much of the responsibility for maintaining the income tax system is left to individual taxpayers. All taxpayers are expected to keep records, report income, calculate their taxes, and make payments. These tasks are made easier by the fact that employers must regularly withhold income taxes from their employees' wages. The employers, in turn, must forward the collected taxes to the **Internal Revenue Service (IRS)**, the federal agency that collects income taxes. Self-employed persons (and others with non-wage income) are required to estimate their tax liability for the coming year. They then pay that amount to the IRS in four equal installments during the year.

We have seen that the amount of income taxes one pays depends upon the tax rate and the individual's *taxable income.* The key phrase here is "taxable income," because whatever one earns or receives in the course of the year is more than one's taxable income. There are three reasons for this: (1) some forms of income are excluded from taxation, (2) certain exemptions and deductions can be taken against one's income, and (3) some individuals are entitled to tax credits.

INCOME NOT SUBJECT TO TAXATION.   Not all income is subject to taxation. Depending on one's family status, the first $7,000 to $14,000 of earnings is exempt from federal income tax. So too is interest earned on state and municipal bonds and welfare benefits. Other forms of income, such as inheritances and Social Security payments, while largely exempt from income tax liabilities, may be taxable in part.

REGRESSIVE TAXES.   *Regressive taxes* are ones that take a larger fraction of the income of low-income people than of high-income people. Sales and excise taxes (discussed on pages 317 and 320) are examples of regressive taxes.

EXEMPTIONS AND DEDUCTIONS.   Taxpayers are entitled to reduce their taxable income with an *exemption* for each of their dependents, including themselves. In 2003, the exemption was $3,050 per person. Thus, a couple with three dependent children was entitled to take $15,250 in exemptions (because three children plus two adults equal five exemptions. $3,050 × 5 = $15,250). One effect of these exemptions is to allow the lowest-income families (for example, a family of five with an income under $15,250) to avoid paying any income taxes. Also, large families are given a tax break (because they have more exemptions than a small family).

All taxpayers can reduce their taxable income by choosing to use the so-called *standard deduction.* In 2003, a married couple filing a joint return could claim a standard deduction of $9,500. The standard deduction for an

In IRS offices, specialists and computers check all tax returns for errors as part of the processing of returns.

individual that year was $4,750. The amount of the deduction usually increases from one year to the next.

Certain expenses can be used to reduce the amount of taxable income still further. Instead of using the standard deduction, some taxpayers may choose to *itemize* (list) deductions on Schedule A, Form 1040. On this form, amounts paid for state and local taxes, real estate taxes, mortgage interest, charitable gifts, and medical expenses may be deducted from one's taxable income.

INCOME TAX CREDITS.   After reducing one's earnings to eliminate those items not subject to tax, a taxpayer calculates his or her income tax liability. This too may be reduced if the taxpayer is entitled to certain *tax credits*. These credits are offered for two purposes: (1) to promote certain activities and (2) to help specific groups of individuals.

Education Credit.   This entitles taxpayers to deduct tuition costs of up to $2,000 for the first two years of post-secondary school for themselves or their dependents.

Earned Income Tax Credit.   Low-income taxpayers may qualify for the earned income tax credit (EITC). The EITC reduces the amount of income taxes owed and could result in a refund check. Many taxpayers who qualify for EITC may also be eligible for free tax preparation and electronic filing by participating tax professionals and volunteers.

Elderly and Disabled Tax Credit.   Taxpayers 65 years of age or older and persons retired on permanent and total disability may be entitled to a reduction of up to $1,125 of their income taxes.

🌀 Opinions Differ on the Income Tax

People who favor the personal income tax stress its progressive character and the effect it has on income distribution. By taking more from the wealthy and less from the poor, the income tax helps break down income differences. Also, the argument continues, the tax does not harm the economy because enough people, after paying this tax, are left with the purchasing power they need to buy the goods and services produced by the nation's industries.

Almost all taxpayers agree that existing income tax laws are too difficult to understand and need to be simplified. Moreover, too many people are able to avoid paying the tax. Other criticisms of the personal income tax are the following.

FAVORS THE RICH AT THE EXPENSE OF THE POOR.   Income earned from wages and personal effort was taxed as high as 91 percent in the 1950s, 70 percent in the 1960s, and 50 percent in the 1980s. By 2003, the top rate had fallen to 35 percent. At the same time that the tax rates on high-income earners were declining, rates on taxpayers in the lowest income bracket increased from 11 percent (prior to 1987) to the present 15 percent. Moreover, the argument continues, wealthy individuals can afford to hire lawyers, accountants, and other specialists to structure their finances in such a way as to lower their taxes. As a result, the actual percentage of income wealthy individuals pay on all their income— taxable and tax-free—is much less than it appears. The current personal income tax is less progressive than it once was.

DISCOURAGES INVESTMENTS.   Some critics of the personal income tax say that it is harmful to the economy because it lacks enough deductions, exemptions, and credits that would promote individual investments in private enterprises. They want more tax advantages for investors, like those for people purchasing municipal bonds. For example, these critics would like to lower or remove the tax on capital gains—the money one gains by selling a stock, bond, or piece of property at a price higher than what one originally paid for it. Critics of capital gains taxes claim that more people would buy investments if the capital gains tax was much lower or was abolished.

 OTHER FEDERAL TAXES

In addition to the individual income tax, the federal government imposes other major taxes, including the corporate income tax, excise taxes, estate and gift taxes, and Social Security and Medicare taxes.

TABLE 14.2	INDIVIDUAL INCOME TAXES COLLECTED BY INCOME CATEGORY		
Adjusted Gross Income	Taxes Collected (billions)	Percent of Total Collections	Tax as a Percentage of Adjusted Gross Income
Less than $7,000	$ 1.1	.03%	1.0%
$7,000 to $14,999	7.7	1.05	3.2
$15,000 to $24,999	18.7	3.38	5.6
$25,000 to $29,999	18.7	3.38	8.4
$30,000 to $39,999	43.1	5.89	9.6
$40,000 to $49,999	47.7	6.39	10.7
$50,000 to $74,999	110.3	15.08	11.9
$75,000 to $99,999	80.2	10.97	14.5
$100,000 to $199,999	126.3	17.27	17.8
$200,000 to $499,999	99.5	13.61	24.6
$500,000 to $999,999	51.3	7.01	29.0
$1,000,000 or more	121.9	16.67	28.8

Source: Statistical Abstract of the United States, 2002

How might the data in the table above be used either to support or oppose criticisms of the personal income tax?

 Corporate Income Tax

About 9 cents of every dollar raised by the federal government comes from the income tax on corporations. Like the individual income tax, the *corporate income tax* is based on a simple principle: Taxes on net profits increase proportionately with the size of these profits. Defining what constitutes net profit can become complicated, however, and frequently requires the services of accountants and lawyers.

The corporate income tax has received the following criticisms.

- The corporate tax subjects the owners of corporations (the stockholders) to double taxation. In the first instance, profits are subject to the corporation income tax. Then if dividends are distributed out of what remains, these are again subject to taxation when shareholders file their personal income tax returns.

- The corporate tax discourages economic growth because the money taken by government might have been used by corporations to expand their production.

- Some or all of the corporate income tax is passed on to consumers in the form of higher prices. If this happens across the country, the cost of living rises, what we call inflation.

Figure 14.1 **Sources of Federal Income**

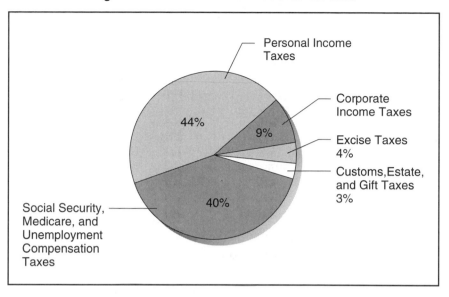

Those favoring the corporate tax argue that the government is able to tap a source of revenue that might otherwise avoid taxation. Since corporations do not have to distribute all their profits, were it not for the corporate income tax, money that the corporations retain would not be taxed.

Moreover, corporations enjoy many benefits the cost of which they should share. For example, the law treats corporations as if they were people. This gives them legal protection they would not have if they were unincorporated. Other laws protect some corporations from foreign competition and directly or indirectly subsidize their operations. With all that they receive from the government, the argument goes, it is only fair that they share in its costs.

🌀 Excise Taxes

Taxes levied on the manufacture or sale of particular goods and services are called *excise taxes*. These taxes account for four cents out of every dollar collected by the federal government. Those who pay an excise tax usually pass its cost along to the final consumer. If competition is strong or the product is subject to relatively elastic demand, however, producers are likely to absorb some or all of the excise tax themselves.

Politicians are frequently attracted to excise taxes because most people are unaware that they are paying them. While many items are subject to an excise tax, nearly three-fifths of the government's excise receipts come from taxes on alcoholic beverages, gasoline, and tobacco. These are mass-consumption goods on which poor families spend a larger percentage of their incomes than do wealthy families. Excise taxes are thus likely to be regressive.

🌀 Estate and Gift Taxes

The *estate tax* is levied on a person's property at the time of death. Most people are not affected by federal estate taxes because the law exempts the first $1.5 million from taxation.

The *gift tax* was created to prevent wealthy persons from giving away their property so that their heirs would escape paying estate taxes. Thus, gifts in excess of specified limits are subject to federal taxation.

Recently, efforts have been made to eliminate the estate tax. Those favoring abolition make the following points.

- Being able to pass on wealth to one's children is a strong incentive to save. Estate taxes, which reduce inheritances, discourage savings and investment. This is serious, the argument continues, because savings and investment are needed to add to the nation's stock of plant and equipment.

- The complexity of the estate tax law is such that tax experts are routinely able to provide clients (who can afford their services) with programs that minimize the tax paid by their estates. In the late 1990s, for example, estates worth between $2.5 million and $5 million had a higher average tax rate than those worth more than $20 million.

- The tax often forces the breakup of small family businesses and farms when children who inherit them cannot afford to pay the estate tax.

Those who favor keeping the estate tax argue that

- The multimillionaires on whom the estate tax falls represent the wealthiest 2 percent of the population. For this group, the estate tax is affordable and fair.

- The law was enacted as a way to prevent the creation of an upper class, whose claim to privilege and power comes from inherited wealth.

- It is only fair for the government to take a portion of the estates of those with great wealth and use it for the common good.

🌀 Social Security and Medicare Taxes

The Social Security and Medicare taxes are payroll taxes designed to pay the costs of the Social Security and Medicare programs. About 33 cents out of every dollar received by the federal government comes from these taxes. Wage earners and their employers both pay the same percentage of the workers' salaries into the Social Security system. The Social Security tax is sometimes described as an income tax in reverse. This is because it taxes income only under a certain limit ($87,000 in 2003). There is no income limit for the Medicare tax.

The Flat Tax—Should It Replace the Graduated Income Tax?

Much of the controversy surrounding the federal personal income tax results from the complex loopholes, deductions, credits, and incentives that have crept into the system. Most of these features, whose purpose is to reduce taxes, would be eliminated by the *flat tax,* a proposal that has attracted considerable attention. Simply stated, a flat tax applies a single rate—20 percent is one suggestion—to all incomes above a certain level. Depending on the proposal, few or no deductions or exemptions would be permitted. Since people would be taxed on a greater amount of their earnings, tax rates could be significantly lower than they are now. A flat-rate system, its supporters claim, would discourage many existing schemes (some legal, some not) to avoid paying taxes. Filing income taxes would become much simpler. Some reformers suggest that the form could fit on the back of a postcard.

Wealthy individuals whose income places them in the top tax brackets often support the idea of a flat tax. For them, the sharp reduction in tax rates offered by a flat tax would more than offset the loss of deductions contained in the present law.

Opposition to the flat-tax proposal comes from people or groups who benefit directly from the deductions and loopholes in the present laws. Charitable organizations, for example, fear losing income if contributions are no longer tax deductible. State and local government officials worry about what would happen to their borrowing ability if the interest on their bonds was no longer exempt from taxation. (For many investors, tax exemption is the principal reason why they buy state and local bonds.) Similarly, those in the real estate industry foresee a decline in home sales and construction if mortgage interest payments can no longer be deducted from taxes.

Others fear that the elimination of exemptions for dependents would work a hardship on large families with wage earners in lower income brackets. In addition, many homeowners feel threatened by the potential loss of the deductions for interest on mortgage payments and property taxes that would be part and parcel of a flat tax.

By permission of Mike Luckovich and Creators Syndicate, Inc.

STATE AND LOCAL TAXES

State and local governments impose a variety of taxes. Among the more important of these are the following:

✦ Sales and Gross Receipts Taxes

> "How much do I owe?"
> "Let's see now. The items you bought add up to $15.65. The tax on that amount is $1.25. So the total bill is $16.90, please."

Everyone who lives in a state or community that has a sales tax will recognize this dialogue. State and local governments levy *sales taxes* on the value of certain retail sales of goods and services. These taxes are usually computed as a percentage of the sales price and added to that price. The firms that sell the taxed goods and services are responsible for collecting and forwarding the taxes to the state or local government.

Certain states and communities also levy *gross receipts taxes* on businesses. These taxes are calculated as a percentage (usually a fraction of 1 percent) of a firm's receipts from wholesale as well as retail activities. A business may or may not pass on gross receipts taxes to its customers. When these taxes are passed on to consumers, however, the buyers are unlikely to be aware that they paid the taxes.

Sales and gross receipts taxes are the principal sources of income for many states. Sales taxes are popular with the states because they are easy to collect and administer, and because they yield much money. Sales taxes are often regressive in that they impose a heavier burden on the poor than on the rich. In order to make the sales tax less regressive, many states and localities exempt from the tax certain necessities, such as food, medicine, and rent.

✦ Property Taxes

As we saw in Figure 13.5 on page 302, property taxes are a major source of income to state and local governments. These taxes fall into two categories: *real property taxes,* which are levied on buildings and land; and *personal property taxes,* which are levied on expensive items, such as jewelry, furniture, securities, clothing, and automobiles. Of the two, the tax on real property is by far the more widespread.

In administering the real property tax, the locality *assesses* (officially evaluates) each taxpayer's holdings. The community's total *assessment* (official evaluation) serves as the basis for setting the real property tax rate. Thus, if the community needs $1 million in revenue for the coming year and the total assessed valuation of all the taxpayers' holdings is $100 million, the tax rate for that year will be 1 percent.

The real property tax rate is usually applied uniformly throughout a community regardless of a taxpayer's ability to pay. It is, therefore, often particularly regressive. For example, if two families live in identically assessed homes, they will both pay the same tax. It is possible, however, that one of the two families is much wealthier than the other. The tax is more of a burden to the less wealthy family than to the wealthier one. The tax can cause hardships for elderly people who own their own home but have limited income. Therefore, some communities give the elderly with low incomes a break on their property taxes.

Critics of both real and personal property taxes point out the absence of a uniform method of assessing property. As a result, some property may be overvalued and some undervalued. In general, studies have shown that smaller real properties are more likely to be overvalued than larger properties. This again tends to make the tax regressive. In addition, personal property is easy to hide and therefore may go unassessed and untaxed.

Some critics also complain that the real property tax discourages home improvements because improvements increase the value of property and, therefore, the homeowners' taxes.

User Taxes

Taxes that are imposed on people who use a product or service are called *user taxes*. This category includes gasoline taxes, license and registration fees for motor vehicles, hunting and fishing license fees, and highway and bridge tolls. Highway and bridge tolls pay for the maintenance and construction of roads and bridges. State gasoline taxes help finance the construction and repair of roads and bridges. Hunting and fishing license fees pay for programs that manage wildlife.

Personal Income Taxes

Most states and some localities impose personal income taxes that are similar in concept to federal personal income taxes. These taxes currently account for about 25 percent of the tax dollars raised by the states and 6 percent of the funds raised by localities.

Inheritance Taxes

State *inheritance taxes* are similar to the estate taxes levied by the federal government.

Tax Loopholes and the Underground Economy — A Drain on Us All

"Where'd you get the nice tan?"

"Bermuda. We opened our new 'company headquarters' there—saves us a bundle in taxes."

"I can paint your apartment next week, but remember, I expect you to pay me in cash."

"Working for tips is great—you collect $100 and report $50."

"Isn't that illegal?"

"Of course, but who's to know?"

The income tax rate on corporate profits is 35 percent. If corporations actually paid that much, tax collections would have totaled an estimated $308 billion in 2002. But actual tax collections amounted to only $136 billion that year. What happened to the rest? Tax breaks and "loopholes" in the tax law enabled corporations to avoid paying the other $172 billion. Microsoft, for example, paid no taxes in 1999, despite the fact that the corporation earned $12.3 billion in profits that year. And GE, America's most profitable corporation, paid only 11.5 percent of its $50.8 billion earnings in income taxes during the 1995–2000 period.

One of the more costly loopholes is *offshore tax shelters*. These enable corporations to avoid paying U.S. income taxes simply by opening an office and reincorporating in certain foreign countries. Some of the most frequently used offshore shelters are located in Bermuda, Gibraltar, Madeira, and Seychelles. While incorporating offshore in no way affects how a firm operates its business, it can save the company millions of dollars in taxes. According to a report issued by the **Office of Management and Budget**, offshore tax schemes enabled corporations to avoid paying between $20 billion and $40 billion in a recent year.

Another source of leakage in tax collections is the *underground economy*. Unlike corporations

that take advantage of legal loopholes in the tax code, participants in the underground economy evade the payment of taxes by breaking the law.

Who are these income producers in the underground economy? Some are hardened criminals whose unlawful activities will land them in jail once they are caught. More common, however, are people from many walks of life who have found ways to conceal from the government the financial details of their otherwise legal activities. Shopkeepers who fail to ring up cash sales and professionals who fail to report cash payments fall into this category. So too do those who fail to report their tips or who trade one thing of value for another and fail to report the transactions.

How large is the underground economy? There is no way to know for sure, but government economists have arrived at some estimates that are astonishing. By assuming that all underground activity relies on the use of cash, they have compared the amount of currency required to conduct the reported volume of business with the amount actually in circulation. The excess of cash provides the basis for estimates that run anywhere from $700 billion to $1,050 billion per year. That figure would put the total value of the U.S. underground economy at something more than the GDPs of Turkey, Greece, Iceland, New Zealand, Norway, and Portugal combined.

"What," you might ask, "has all this got to do with me? Why should I care if some people or corporations are getting away with not paying taxes?"

There are some very good reasons for being concerned. For one thing, if all taxpayers paid their fair share, the tax burden on the rest of the country would be less. Moreover, the underground economy gives government planners and others a distorted picture of the economy. For example, the federal government relies on certain data when deciding whether to increase or decrease the nation's money supply. If, because of the $700 billion or more in the underground economy, the government erred in its economic planning, a recession that might otherwise have ended will continue.

1. When she heard that her company was planning to reincorporate in Bermuda, one worker said, "I pay my own taxes, but I don't want also to pay the taxes of companies that pretend that they are moving to Bermuda." Explain the statement.

2. What is meant by the term "underground economy"?

3. Why is the underground economy sometimes described as a "drain on us all"?

4. "Any estimate of the amount of money circulating in the underground economy will always be more a guess than a fact." Explain this statement.

5. How does the underground economy complicate the government's job of monitoring our nation's economy?

6. Why are tax loopholes such as offshore tax shelters sometimes described as "corporate welfare"?

7. What do you think should be done, if anything, about the underground economy? Explain your answer.

Payroll and Business Taxes

Collected in a variety of forms by state and local governments, *payroll taxes* and other business taxes are often used to finance unemployment insurance programs, as well as health, disability, and retirement programs.

Corporate Income Taxes

Some states and localities impose taxes on corporations that do business in their jurisdiction. These corporate income taxes are similar to the corporate taxes levied by the federal government.

Unincorporated Income Taxes

To raise money from businesses that are not corporations (and thus do not pay corporate income taxes), some states and localities impose the *unincorporated income tax*. This name comes from the fact that sole proprietorships and partnerships are not incorporated businesses.

Grants-in-Aid Programs

As discussed in Chapter 13, grants-in-aid are sums given for a specific purpose by the federal government to states and localities, or by states to localities. Though not a tax, a grant is a very important source of income. In 2000, federal grants-in-aid totaled $292 billion, or about 15 percent of the total receipts of the states and localities.

Grants-in-aid provide another example of how the power to tax can be used to redistribute income. The grants usually go to areas that are in need. For example, federal grants-in-aid have been given to states to help them set up child-care centers, provide unemployment insurance, and aid the handicapped. Grants-in-aid programs can also stimulate states to take action in fields that they had neglected in the past. Through "matching provisions," the federal government gives aid to the states only if the states also make matching appropriations. The **Interstate Highway Act** set up a program of this kind by matching $9 of federal funds for every $1 of state funds appropriated for the construction of interstate highways.

States also have grants-in-aid programs. They give financial aid to their cities, counties, townships, and special districts. In recent years, most of this assistance has been for education.

 # IS THE TAX SYSTEM WORKING WELL?

People frequently complain about the taxes they pay. Government spending has reached record high levels, and taxes have risen to keep up with the increased government spending.

Criticisms of Our Tax System

For some time now, critics of our tax system have claimed that (1) it has not raised enough revenue, (2) it is too complex and inefficient for its own good, and (3) too many people are able to evade paying taxes. Some people believe that certain groups are not paying their fair share of taxes and that other groups are being taxed too much. Virtually all people in the United States would like to see improvements in the country's tax policies. Therefore, the existing tax structure is a subject of continuous study and discussion.

What Are the Ingredients of a Good Tax System?

In his *Wealth of Nations* (1776), British economist Adam Smith set forth three standards for judging a nation's tax system. To this day, economists refer to these standards in their evaluation of taxes.

FAIRNESS. The first standard Smith set forth was that taxes should be fair and that taxpayers should believe the taxes are fair. For this reason, Smith called for governments to require the payment of taxes in proportion to one's income.

CLARITY AND CERTAINTY.   Everyone should be able to understand what the rate of the tax is and how the tax is to be paid. Smith felt that people would be more willing to pay their taxes if they knew what was expected of them. If, by contrast, the tax was whatever the tax collectors felt like charging (as was frequently the case in 18th-century Europe), people would be tempted to avoid it.

SIMPLICITY AND EFFICIENCY.   If the cost of collecting a tax was more than what was collected, there would not be much point to levying the tax. Taxes should be easy to collect, difficult to evade, and inexpensive to administer.

To this list of Smith's standards, modern economists have added what they consider another essential ingredient of any tax system: flexibility.

FLEXIBILITY.   Taxes should adjust to economic conditions. In times of general prosperity, people can afford to pay taxes that at other times might be a hardship. Business taxes that at one time are reasonable might at another time (and at the same rate) be oppressive.

Ideally, taxes should adjust themselves automatically to the state of the economy. In reality, however, few taxes are able to do this. The income tax leans in the right direction. When business activity booms and people's earnings increase, the people's and businesses' income taxes increase automatically. Similarly, during periods of recession and business decline, the amounts paid in taxes are automatically reduced because people are earning less.

🔥 Fairness in Taxation

Everyone agrees that taxes need to be "fair." But what makes a tax fair? Or to put it another way: Who should pay taxes? And how much? Responses to these questions usually involve one of two principles of taxation: (1) benefits received and (2) ability to pay.

BENEFITS-RECEIVED PRINCIPLE.   The suggestion that taxes ought to be paid by individuals in proportion to the benefits they receive from the government is called the *benefits-received principle*. A gasoline tax whose proceeds are used to finance the construction and maintenance of highways is an example of a benefits-received tax. Why? Because the tax is paid "at the pump" by motorists who will directly benefit as roads are improved.

Benefits-received taxes are limited in usefulness. For example, a tax whose proceeds will be used to aid people living in poverty could not be financed by the poor. Nor could public education function well if its costs were borne only by those with children attending public schools.

ABILITY-TO-PAY PRINCIPLE.   The most widely supported principle of taxation is that people should be taxed in accordance with their ability to pay. This *ability-to-pay principle* suggests that those who earn more should pay more in taxes, and those who earn less should pay less, regardless of the benefits they receive from government programs.

Progressive, Regressive, and Proportional Taxes

We discussed progressive and regressive taxes earlier. Depending on people's income levels, the two taxes take different proportions of their incomes. In contrast to these two, a tax that requires all persons to pay the same percentage of their total income in taxes is a *proportional* tax.

PROGRESSIVE TAXES.   When the percentage of income paid in taxes increases as one's income increases, the tax is said to be progressive. As we discussed earlier, the federal personal income tax is a progressive tax.

REGRESSIVE TAXES.   Regressive taxes take a larger fraction of one's income as income decreases and a smaller fraction as income increases. Sales and excise taxes are examples of regressive taxes. We can illustrate how regressive a sales tax is in the following example:

> The sales tax on a new automobile is the same regardless of whether one earns $20,000 or $200,000. Suppose, for example, that the sales tax on a new car is $1,000. One thousand dollars is 5 percent of the earnings of a person whose yearly income is $20,000, whereas it is 1/2 percent of the earnings of a person earning $200,000. Since the individual with the lower income pays a higher percentage of that income in sales taxes than does the individual with a higher income, the sales tax is said to be regressive.

"Hutchins, what on earth gave you the notion that we want the rich to get poorer and the poor to get richer?"

What issue of taxation is the cartoonist raising?

PROPORTIONAL TAXES.   Taxes that take the same share of one's income at all levels are *proportional*. By way of illustration, suppose that everyone was subject to an income tax rate of 20 percent. In those circumstances, an individual earning $15,000 would pay $3,000 in taxes, while a person with $150,000 in earnings would pay $30,000. Some people argue that this is a fair tax because it takes ten times as much in taxes from someone earning ten times more in income. Others, however, cite Engel's Law (first discussed in Chapter 10) to show that proportional taxes discriminate against low-income families.

Ernst Engel, a 19th-century German economist who pioneered in studies of consumer behavior, developed a theory that came to be known as Engel's Law. It states that the proportion of family expenditures for necessities (basic food, clothing, and shelter) increases as income decreases, while the proportion of expenditure for luxuries (expensive clothes, furs, cars, jewelry, expensive houses, and so on) decreases as income decreases. Thus, a family of four earning $15,000 a year might have to spend 90 percent of its income on food, clothing, and housing. That would leave it with only $1,500 for life's luxuries. In those circumstances, a $3,000 tax takes all the funds a family has for luxuries plus $1,500 of the money the family needs to buy necessities.

By contrast, a family earning $150,000 might need to spend only 30 percent of its income for the same necessities. The remaining 70 percent (or $105,000) could be spent on luxuries. For this family, a $30,000 tax would simply reduce the funds they had available for savings or luxuries from $105,000 to $75,000.

The Social Security program is financed in part by a kind of proportional tax. All workers pay the same percentage (7.65 percent) of their income, up to a certain limit. Earnings above that limit are not subject to the Social Security tax.

TAX INCIDENCE: WHO REALLY PAYS A TAX?

CUSTOMER: "Gee, that's a nice pair of jeans. Let's see, they're my size, and they're on sale for $15. I've got $15. I'll take them."

CASHIER: "Yes, that's a nice pair of jeans. That will be $16.20, please."

CUSTOMER: "I think you're mistaken, these jeans were marked down to $15. Oh, I forgot—you also charge sales tax."

CASHIER: "Hey, we don't charge the sales tax, we just collect it. The extra $1.20 goes to the state."

In many instances, those who pay taxes to a government can pass the cost along to someone else. Sales tax laws require merchants to put aside a percentage of their sales and send this amount on to the state or local government. But these sales taxes are really paid by customers, who find the tax added to their bills.

The process of transferring the burden of a tax from those on whom it is levied (in many cases, the merchants) to another individual or business is known as *shifting*. The *incidence* of a tax refers to those on whom the burden of a tax finally falls. Thus, one might say, "The incidence of a sales tax is shifted from retailers to their customers."

🗡 Direct and Indirect Taxes

Taxes can be classified as either direct or indirect.

DIRECT TAXES. Taxes that are levied on people and that cannot be shifted are called *direct taxes.* Examples include income taxes (which are levied on people's earnings and other income) and inheritance or estate taxes (which are levied on heirs).

INDIRECT TAXES. Taxes that can be shifted to others are called *indirect taxes.* Such taxes are usually levied on goods and services rather than on people. Excise taxes, sales taxes, and tariffs are indirect taxes because the person or company on whom the tax is levied can shift the burden on to another. A real property tax is usually a direct tax. It becomes indirect, however, when a government taxes a building owner who in turn passes the tax on to the renters in the building in the form of higher rents.

Although sales taxes are added to the posted prices of goods and services, excise taxes and tariffs are not. Instead, the latter two taxes are already included in the selling price. Thus, a Peruvian sweater selling for $40 may include a

Rates

Up to 1 hour	11.81
Up to 2 hours	16.03
Up to 3 hours	17.72
Up to 12 hours	19.41
Max to 24 hrs or O'nite	23.63
Suv's/Vans addl	8.44

18½% Parking tax extra

What does this sign tell us about the shifting and incidence of taxes on parking a car?

$5 tariff in its selling price. The wholesaler who imported the sweater from Peru recovered the $5 by adding it to the price she charged the retailer. For his part, the retailer shifted the tax along to the consumer by including the $5 tariff in his selling price.

Taxes that are included in the selling price of an item without the buyer's knowing about them are often described as *hidden taxes*.

The Effects of Tax Incidence

The question of tax incidence is one of the first things legislators consider when thinking about changing tax laws or introducing new taxes. Suppose, for example, that Congress wanted to levy an excise tax on wheat. Before enacting such a law, however, the lawmakers would want to investigate the incidence of the new tax. For example, they might ask one or more of the following questions.

- Will the tax be passed on to consumers in the form of higher bread prices?
- Will farmers absorb the tax with lower profits?
- Will millers and bakers absorb the tax by reducing their profits or by requiring their employees to absorb some or all of the tax in the form of reduced wages?
- What effect will the tax on wheat have on the market for substitute products, such as rye or oats?

=========   S U M M A R Y   =========

The federal, state, and local governments all impose taxes. Taxes are necessary in order to pay for the many government services, such as police, armed forces, schools, roads, health care, and welfare programs. As government expenditures increase, government income to meet these increasing costs must also rise.

Although taxes are the main source of income for governments, taxes have other uses. They may be used to redistribute wealth in our economy. They may be used to promote certain industries. Taxes are sometimes passed to influence consumer and business spending.

The major tax of the federal government is the personal income tax. Social Security taxes, Medicare taxes, and corporate income taxes are also principal sources of federal income. State and local governments rely on revenue largely from sales and property taxes, and to a lesser extent from personal and corporate income taxes. Another major source of revenue for states and localities is grants-in-aid.

When considering the fairness of a tax, one might discuss the benefits-received and the ability-to-pay principles. One should also consider whether a tax is progressive, regressive, or proportional. Finally, whether a tax is direct or indirect is important in evaluating it.

REVIEWING THE CHAPTER

BUILDING VOCABULARY

Match each term in Column A with its definition in Column B.

Column A	Column B
1. ability-to-pay principle	*a.* a tax whose burden cannot be shifted
2. benefits-received principle	*b.* a federal tax levied on a person's property at the time of death
3. progressive tax	*c.* a tax that takes a larger proportion from low-income people than from high-income people
4. proportional tax	*d.* a tax whose burden can be shifted
5. regressive tax	*e.* a tax designed to discourage certain behaviors
6. assessment	*f.* the idea that taxes should be paid by those who benefit from the way the money will be spent
7. indirect tax	*g.* the idea that people who are best able to afford to pay taxes should pay more than others
8. direct tax	*h.* a tax whose rate increases as the taxpayer's income increases
9. "sin tax"	*i.* a tax with a single rate that is applied to all income above a certain level
10. estate tax	*j.* the official determination of the value of property

UNDERSTANDING WHAT YOU HAVE READ

1. Last year, A earned $5,000, B earned $50,000, and C earned $500,000. Under the terms of a special tax passed that year, A paid $50, B paid $500, and C paid $5,000. What kind of tax did they pay? (*a*) regressive (*b*) progressive (*c*) proportional (*d*) none of these.

2. Suppose that instead of paying the taxes described in question 1, A paid 10 percent of income; B paid 25 percent; and C paid 50 percent. The tax would now be described as (*a*) regressive (*b*) progressive (*c*) proportional (*d*) none of these.

3. Suppose that instead of the taxes described in questions 1 and 2, the government announced that all families would have to pay the same tax, $100, regardless of income. Such a tax would be (*a*) regressive (*b*) progressive (*c*) proportional (*d*) none of these.

4. Which *one* of the following types of revenue is based on the benefits-received principle? (*a*) income tax (*b*) sales tax (*c*) property tax (*d*) bridge and highway tolls.

5. The property tax is regressive because (*a*) it is old-fashioned (*b*) it is based on assessed valuation, not income (*c*) the rich pay heavier taxes on their homes than the less wealthy (*d*) property assessors do not allow for changes in the cost of living.

6. In the United States, taxation is used to accomplish all of the following, *except* to (*a*) redistribute income (*b*) reduce purchasing power (*c*) discourage the consumption of specific goods (*d*) promote the purchase of a particular brand of merchandise.

7. Which *one* of the following is the best example of an ability-to-pay tax? (*a*) income tax (*b*) sales tax (*c*) property tax (*d*) bridge and highway toll.

8. The process of passing taxes on to others is called (*a*) incidence (*b*) shifting (*c*) buck-passing (*d*) a nuisance tax.

9. A tax that cannot be passed along to someone else is called (*a*) an indirect tax (*b*) a direct tax (*c*) an excise tax (*d*) a tariff.

10. Assume that the sales tax is 8½ percent. How much would you have to pay to purchase an item selling for $100? (*a*) $185.00 (*b*) $108.50 (*c*) $100.85 (*d*) $85.00.

SKILLS: Completing a Federal Income Tax Form

Most people who have a job and/or receive interest income must file a federal income tax return. Moreover, it can be to people's advantage to fill out a tax return to see if they qualify to receive a refund from the Internal Revenue Service. The law requires that employers withhold a portion of their employees' wages in each pay period and send these sums to the government. When individuals file their returns, they calculate how much they owe in taxes on the previous year's income. The difference between the amount withheld and the amount owed is either returned to the taxpayer (if there is an overpayment) or paid to the government (if the amount withheld is not sufficient to cover the total amount of taxes owed).

Although preparing an income tax return can be complicated, it is usually a simple matter for single people with part-time jobs. In most instances, the return that they use will be the 1040EZ form. (See Figure 14.2.)

In 2003, Jean LaRue had a part-time job at a local supermarket. In the course of the year, Jean earned $9,240 at the supermarket and paid $1,050 in withholding taxes. Jean also had a savings account that paid $275 in interest.

Write the numbers 1–12 down the left side of a blank piece of paper. Put your answers to the following instructions on this paper instead of writing in Figure 14.2.

1. Enter Jean's wages on line 1.

2. Enter the interest Jean earned on her savings account on line 2.

3. Since she received no unemployment compensation, put nothing on line 3.

4. Add lines 1, 2, and 3. This is Jean's *adjusted gross income.* Enter this amount on line 4.

5. Like all taxpayers, Jean is entitled to a deduction from her adjusted gross income. The amount of that deduction depends on whether or not she can be claimed as a dependent on her parent or guardian's return. Since her parents can claim Jean as a dependent, she will check the "Yes" box on line 5, and complete the worksheet on the back of the 1040EZ form. In accordance with the instructions written on the back of the 1040EZ form, Jean received a standard deduction of $4,750. Enter this amount on line 5.

6. Enter the total earnings subject to tax (line 4 minus line 5) on line 6. This is Jean's *taxable income.*

7. Enter the amount of federal income tax withheld on line 7.

Figure 14.2 **1040EZ Federal Tax Form**

Department of the Treasury—Internal Revenue Service

Form
1040EZ

**Income Tax Return for Single and
Joint Filers With No Dependents** (99) **2003**

OMB No. 1545-0675

Label

(See page 12.)

Use the IRS label. Otherwise, please print or type.

Your first name and initial	Last name
JEAN	LA RUE

If a joint return, spouse's first name and initial | Last name

Home address (number and street). If you have a P.O. box, see page 12. | Apt. no.
1563 MAIN STREET

City, town or post office, state, and ZIP code. If you have a foreign address, see page 12.
OGDEN, UT 84403

Your social security number
000 : 00 : 0000

Spouse's social security number

▲ **Important!** ▲

You **must** enter your SSN(s) above.

Presidential Election Campaign (page 12) ▶

Note. Checking "Yes" will not change your tax or reduce your refund.

Do you, or your spouse if a joint return, want $3 to go to this fund? . . . . . . ▶

	You	Spouse
	☑Yes ☐No	☐Yes ☐No

Income

Attach Form(s) W-2 here.

Enclose, but do not attach, any payment.

1 Wages, salaries, and tips. This should be shown in box 1 of your Form(s) W-2.
Attach your Form(s) W-2. 1

2 Taxable interest. If the total is over $1,500, you cannot use Form 1040EZ. 2

3 Unemployment compensation and Alaska Permanent Fund dividends
(see page 14). 3

4 Add lines 1, 2, and 3. This is your **adjusted gross income.** 4

Note. You **must** check Yes or No.

5 Can your parents (or someone else) claim you on their return?
Yes. Enter amount from ☑ worksheet on back.
No. If **single,** enter $7,800.
☐ If **married filing jointly,** enter $15,600.
See back for explanation. 5

6 Subtract line 5 from line 4. If line 5 is larger than line 4, enter -0-.
This is your **taxable income.** .... ▶ 6

Payments and tax

7 Federal income tax withheld from box 2 of your Form(s) W-2. 7

8 **Earned income credit (EIC).** 8

9 Add lines 7 and 8. These are your **total payments.** .... ▶ 9

10 **Tax.** Use the amount on **line 6 above** to find your tax in the tax table on pages
24–28 of the booklet. Then, enter the tax from the table on this line. 10

Refund

Have it directly deposited! See page 19 and fill in 11b, 11c, and 11d.

11a If line 9 is larger than line 10, subtract line 10 from line 9. This is your **refund.** ▶ 11a

▶ b Routing number ☐☐☐☐☐☐☐☐☐ ▶ c Type: ☐ Checking ☐ Savings

▶ d Account number ☐☐☐☐☐☐☐☐☐☐☐☐☐☐☐☐☐

Amount you owe

12 If line 10 is larger than line 9, subtract line 9 from line 10. This is
the **amount you owe.** For details on how to pay, see page 20. .... ▶ 12

Third party designee

Do you want to allow another person to discuss this return with the IRS (see page 20)? ☐ **Yes.** Complete the following. ☑**No**

Designee's name ▶ | Phone no. ▶ ( ) | Personal identification number (PIN) ▶ ☐☐☐☐☐

Sign here

Joint return? See page 11.
Keep a copy for your records.

Under penalties of perjury, I declare that I have examined this return, and to the best of my knowledge and belief, it is true, correct, and accurately lists all amounts and sources of income I received during the tax year. Declaration of preparer (other than the taxpayer) is based on all information of which the preparer has any knowledge.

Your signature *Jean LaRue*	Date 3/25/04	Your occupation RETAIL CLERK	Daytime phone number (000) 000-0000
Spouse's signature. If a joint return, **both** must sign.	Date	Spouse's occupation	

Paid preparer's use only

Preparer's signature ▶	Date	Check if self-employed ☐	Preparer's SSN or PTIN
Firm's name (or yours if self-employed), address, and ZIP code ▶		EIN	
		Phone no. ( )	

For Disclosure, Privacy Act, and Paperwork Reduction Act Notice, see page 23.

Cat. No. 11329W

Form **1040EZ** (2003)

TABLE 14.3   PARTIAL TAX TABLE

At least	But less than	Single	Married, filing jointly
$4,650	$4,700	$468	$468
4,700	4,750	473	473
4,750	4,800	478	478
4,800	4,850	483	483
4,850	4,900	488	488
4,900	4,950	493	493
4,950	5,000	498	498

8–9. Leave line 8 blank since Jean is not eligible for an earned income tax credit. Bring down the amount on line 7 to line 9.

10. The amount of tax Jean owes on her taxable income is found in the tax table accompanying the 1040EZ instruction booklet. Determine Jean's tax from Table 14.3. Enter the amount of tax Jean owes on her taxable income on line 10.

11–12. Calculate the difference between Jean's total tax payments (line 9) and the amount you entered on line 10. Enter this amount—either a refund or an amount owed—on the proper line (either line 11 or line 12).

Great! You have completed Jean's 1040EZ tax form. Note that the preparer must sign and date the return. When it is time for you to fill out a tax form, be sure to read the declaration that you are asked to sign.

EXPLORING CURRENT ISSUES IN ECONOMICS

We pay taxes because they are a necessary part of government *and we are required to do so by law.* We are not, however, required to do things that would increase our tax liability. When individuals and businesses take lawful steps to minimize the taxes they pay, their actions are described as *tax avoidance.* While tax avoidance is legal, tax evasion is not. Deliberately failing to report income and improperly claiming deductions are examples of the crime of *tax evasion.* Tax evasion may be punishable by a fine and/or imprisonment.

Tax avoidance involves making use of "loopholes" in the tax law to reduce one's liability. While deductions for things like charitable contributions and medical expenses are very straightforward and easily identified, individual and corporate income tax laws have many complex provisions. For that reason, businesses and wealthy individuals often hire tax attorneys and accountants to identify strategies they can employ to minimize their taxes.

In the aftermath of the collapse of Enron and other giant corporations in 2001, Congress investigated the causes and consequences of those financial disasters. In a 2003 report on its findings, the **Joint Congressional Committee on Taxation** said that between 1996 and 2000, Enron had used loopholes in the tax law in such a way as to (1) deceive the public into believing that the company was operating at a profit and its stock was a good investment, (2) enable it to report losses to the Internal Revenue Service (IRS), and (3) enrich their highest paid executives.

This was accomplished, the committee explained, through the use of *stock options*. Stock options give the holder the right to buy a specified amount of stock over a specified period of time at a specified price. When the option price is less than the market price of the stock, option holders can make a profit. Options may be bought and sold much the same as other corporate securities.

While the details of the scheme are beyond the scope of this text, we can tell you that (1) the value of the options given as payment to its top executives was directly related to the value of Enron's stock, and (2) the company did not have to include the options as a business expense on its financial statements, but (3) they could use them to reduce the taxable income reported to the IRS.

As a result of this strategy, between 1996 and 2000 the following happened.

- Enron was able to report more than $2 billion in profits to its stockholders while at the same time claim $3 billion in losses to the IRS.

- As a result of the rosy profit reports, the price of Enron's stock remained high. This enabled those in top management (who held large blocks of stock and were aware of the corporation's financial troubles) to enrich themselves by selling out before the public was informed.

- The tax losses enabled Enron to avoid paying any federal income tax during those years.

In December 2001, the Enron Corporation filed for bankruptcy. Shortly thereafter, its stock became worthless. This was especially hard on its 25,000 employees whose retirement funds and savings were, for the most part, invested in Enron stock.

In the aftermath of their investigation, the Joint Committee on Taxation recommended that certain changes be made in existing tax laws. These included the following:

- Simplify existing laws to make it more difficult for companies and individuals to use the law to avoid paying taxes.

- Declare illegal (with heavy penalties) many current tax avoidance schemes to discourage those who think they have nothing to lose by claiming business deductions.

- Make tax consultants who accept and incorporate in their reports information from their clients that they know to be untrue liable (along with their clients) for the fraud.

1. In what way would each of the committee's recommendations make the tax laws fairer than they are at present?

2. How did Enron and others use stock options to minimize taxes and reward corporate officers?

MONEY AND BANKING

CHAPTER 15
Money in Our Economy

O V E R V I E W

We are all interested in money. We use money to buy the things we want. We save money for things we want in the future. Almost anything we have of value we measure in money. Without money, the economy as we know it could not function. Why is this so? What is money?

In this chapter, we will discuss these matters. We will also discuss the following questions:

• What kinds of money do we use in the United States?

• How is currency produced and distributed?

• How do we measure the nation's money supply?

• What is the relationship between interest rates and the money supply?

• Why does the value of money fluctuate?

 WHAT KINDS OF MONEY DO WE USE?

In Chapter 1, we discussed how money can be anything that is generally accepted in payment for goods and services. We also noted that there were times in U.S. history when any number of things (such as seashells, furs, and beads) were used as money. But that was then, and this is now. When people speak of money today, they are usually referring to currency (paper currency and coin), checkable deposits, and traveler's checks. There are, however, other forms of money, which we will describe shortly. Meanwhile, let us take a look at these most common kinds: currency, checkable deposits, and traveler's checks.

💱 Currency

Currency is money issued by the federal government. Any other person, group, or organization attempting to produce money is guilty of *counterfeiting* (the serious crime of creating an unauthorized currency).

There are two kinds of currency in use in the United States: coins and paper currency.

COINS.   As discussed in Chapter 1, the federal government produces pennies, nickels, dimes, quarters, and half-dollars primarily for the convenience of making change. In addition, it produces a small number of coins worth $1 that are useful in some coin-operated machines.

PAPER CURRENCY.   Virtually all the paper currency in circulation today is in the form of *Federal Reserve notes*. These notes are issued by the 12 regional banks of the Federal Reserve System (discussed in Chapter 17, page 385). The photo below portrays a typical $20 bill. We can identify it as a Federal Reserve note by the name that appears on the top line and in the black seal, and by the green serial numbers.

Immediately below the black seal are the words certifying that the note is "... legal tender for all debts...." Federal Reserve notes are printed by the Bureau of Engraving and Printing of the Department of the Treasury. The bureau's name does not appear on the notes, but the Department of the Treasury's green seal is located to the right of the portrait of Andrew Jackson, the nation's seventh president.

This Federal Reserve note was introduced in 2003 with special coloring to hinder counterfeiting.

How Currency Is Produced and Distributed

Did you ever wonder how the paper currency and coins that you have in your pocket are produced? One of the more fascinating visits that you can make in Washington, D.C., is to the **Bureau of Engraving and Printing**. There you can see the elaborate process by which our paper money is printed. Although the **United States Mint** also has its offices in Washington, you will not be able to see any coins being produced there because coins are *minted* (manufactured) elsewhere—at mints in Philadelphia and Denver. In addition, mints in San Francisco and West Point produce coins for collectors as well as medals.

The Bureau of Engraving and Printing does everything it can to prevent counterfeiting. Each feature of a bill (such as the portrait, lettering, and ornamental scrollwork) is prepared by a separate engraver. Engravers cut the individual features of a note's design into steel dies. These are assembled in a series of operations into plates for use in the printing process. The bureau uses distinctive, specially produced paper and manufactures its own inks according to secret formulas.

The question that might well come to mind at this point is, "How do these coins and paper money get into the hands of the public?" This is accomplished by the nation's banks, which act as intermediaries between the government and the public in the distribution of the currency. Individuals obtain currency from their banks either by cashing checks or making withdrawals from their accounts. "Well," you ask, "how do banks get the currency?"

Just as individuals maintain bank accounts on which they can draw when they are in need of funds, so too do the commercial banks. Commercial banks keep their "savings," or *reserves,* in the Federal Reserve bank in their district. Whenever a private commercial bank runs short of currency, it can draw on its account with the Federal Reserve and replenish its stock. The

Federal Reserve banks get their supplies of coins and paper money from the Treasury Department's Bureau of the Mint and Bureau of Engraving and Printing.

The Bureau of Engraving and Printing designs, prints, and finishes a variety of security products, including Federal Reserve notes, U.S. postage stamps, and Treasury securities.

On rare occasions, you might come across *United States notes,* bills issued by the Treasury Department. They have red serial numbers, a red seal, and the name "United States note" printed at the top. United States notes had their origins as the "greenbacks" that the Union (the North) began issuing during the Civil War (1861–1865). The federal government still prints and circulates a small quantity of these notes.

Currency and coins comprise about half of the money supply. Then, where does the rest of the money people use to make payments come from? The answer is very simple: checks. Most transactions are paid for with some kind of *checkbook money.*

Checkable Deposits

Although we tend to think of paper currency and coins as money, they represent only a fraction of the total money in circulation. Indeed, if the nation's total currency supply were equally divided, it would come to only $1,400 for every person in the country. Most transactions are paid for by check. Technically, checks are orders written by individuals or firms directing banks to pay specified sums to their legal holders. People who have money on deposit in accounts that offer check-writing privileges can order banks to make payments. These accounts are known as "checkable" ones or, more familiarly, as checking accounts. Accounts with check-writing privileges are also available from mutual savings banks, savings and loan associations, and credit unions.

Most checkable accounts (over 50 percent of the total) are held in demand deposits in the nation's commercial banks. A *demand deposit* is a deposit in a bank that promises to pay on demand an amount of money specified by the customer who owns the deposit. Unlike demand deposits, which pay no interest, some checkable accounts offer interest on part or all of the balance in the account. The best-known interest-bearing checking account is the *negotiable order of withdrawal (NOW)*. (A fuller discussion of banking services can be found on pages 363–366.)

Traveler's Checks

Travelers typically do not like to carry large sums of money with them, yet they might have difficulty cashing personal checks far from home. For that reason, some people purchase *traveler's checks,* which are widely accepted both at home and abroad. Traveler's checks are issued by a few large banks and certain specialized firms (such as American Express and Thomas Cook) and can be purchased at most banks. Since traveler's checks are as usable as checkable accounts, they are included in Federal Reserve data as a component of the money supply.

TABLE 15.1 MONEY SUPPLY, 2003 (BILLIONS)	
Paper currency	$ 620.4
Coin	43.1
Demand deposits	315.8
Traveler's checks	7.7
Other checkable deposits	292.1
Total money supply	$1,279.1

Source: Board of Governors, U.S. Mint

The money supply of the United States on a typical day in 2003 is summarized in Table 15.1.

MONETARY STANDARDS IN UNITED STATES HISTORY

We have seen that any number of things can be (and have been) used as money. Grains, shells, glass, stones, arrowheads, furs, and precious metals have all been adopted at one time or other for that purpose. Whatever commodity or definition a society chooses to use for its money is known as its *monetary standard.*

From its earliest days until 1900, the United States was on a *bimetallic monetary standard.* Two metals—gold and silver—served as the basis for our monetary system. The value of the dollar was expressed in terms of specific quantities of gold and silver. A dollar could be exchanged for either of those metals.

From 1900 until 1933, the United States was on the *gold standard.* This meant that the dollar was defined in terms of gold (about $21 for one ounce of gold) and that the government stood ready to buy or sell gold at this price. Under terms of the gold standard, institutions or individuals could convert their gold at any time into dollars, or they could convert their dollars into gold at the official price.

During the Great Depression of the 1930s, most of the world (including the United States) went on a modified gold standard. While the value of the dollar and other currencies continued to be based on gold, individuals and private institutions could no longer own that precious metal. In the United States, people were directed to convert their holdings of gold in the form of coins, bullion, or certificates into paper dollars, or face jail terms. The government also raised the official price at which it would buy gold from $21 to $35 an ounce.

Gresham's Law

In the 16th century, English financier **Sir Thomas Gresham** observed that when two (or more) kinds of money having the same nominal value circulate, the one considered more (or most) valuable is hoarded and disappears from circulation. Since that time, the principle that cheap money drives out expensive money has been known as *Gresham's Law*.

During and immediately following the Revolutionary War (1775–1783), American colonists saw Gresham's Law in action. People saw their silver and gold coins as having value and hoarded them. Soon this metallic money all but disappeared from circulation. To pay for goods, the colonists spent the distrusted paper dollars that were issued by the Continental Congress.

In the late 1950s, the rising world demand for silver as an industrial metal began pushing up its price. By the 1960s, prices had risen to the point where U.S. coins were worth more in terms of their silver content than of their face value. Once again, Gresham's Law swung into action as silver-based coins and currency began to disappear from circulation. More and more people chose to hoard their dimes and quarters (or sell them to metals traders) rather than use them for money.

Gresham's Law also affected paper currency during this period. In the 1950s and 1960s, U.S. paper currency consisted mostly of Federal Reserve notes and, to a lesser extent, of *silver certificates*. Unlike holders of Federal Reserve notes, holders of silver certificates had the right to exchange them for silver from the U.S. Treasury Department. Soon silver certificates disappeared from circulation. The public either hoarded them or sold them to speculators for more than their face value.

As more and more silver certificates and coins disappeared from circulation, Congress moved to eliminate silver from the money supply. Between 1965 and 1970, that metal was replaced by an alloy of copper and nickel in all coins except pennies. Moreover, Congress authorized the Treasury Department to stop redeeming silver certificates. As one economist put it, "Congress finally moved to repeal Gresham's Law."

Foreign governments could either buy or sell dollars at this price, and the Federal Reserve System was required to hold some gold as a reserve (backing) for the dollars it circulated.

This modified gold standard came to an end in August 1971 when the United States announced that it would no longer sell its gold for dollars even to foreign governments. In the United States, gold is now treated like any other commodity (such as wheat, rubber, or tin). Both private individuals and the federal government may buy or sell gold at will at a price determined in the marketplace. The U.S. government no longer guarantees to buy back dollars for gold at a set price, as was the case when the United States was on the gold standard. The U.S. dollar is no longer backed up by gold or any other precious metal. U.S. currency has value because the government says it has value—that is, by fiat—and because people are willing to accept the dollar for payments. Economists call this system a *paper money standard* or *fiat currency standard*.

In the absence of precious metals on which to base its value, today's U.S. dollar is often measured in terms of its purchasing power. But purchasing power is subject to change. Sometimes it increases, and sometimes it decreases.

MEASURING THE NATION'S MONEY SUPPLY

A proper supply and flow of money is vital to the survival of the economy. For that reason, economists closely follow the total quantity of money in circulation and the number of times it changes hands (its rate of flow). It is not easy, however, to accurately determine the rate of flow of money. To make matters worse, economists use several definitions when discussing the money supply. Let us now consider some of the problems in defining money supply and some of the compromise solutions reached.

▷ TABLE 15.2 MONEY SUPPLY AND ITS COMPONENTS, 2003 (BILLIONS)

M1		
Currency	$ 663.5	
Traveler's checks	7.7	
Demand deposits	315.8	
Other checkable deposits	292.1	
Total M1		$1,279.1
M2 = M1 +		
Money market deposit accounts and reserve deposits	$2,802.9	
Small denomination deposits (under $100,000)	873.7	
Money market mutual funds	930.1	
		$4,606.7
Total M2		$5,885.8
M3 = M2 +		
Large time deposits	$ 815.1	
Large money funds	1,196.7	
Other funds	670.9	
		$2,682.7
Total M3		$8,568.5

Source: Federal Reserve Board of Governors

Figure 15.1 **Measures of the Money Supply**

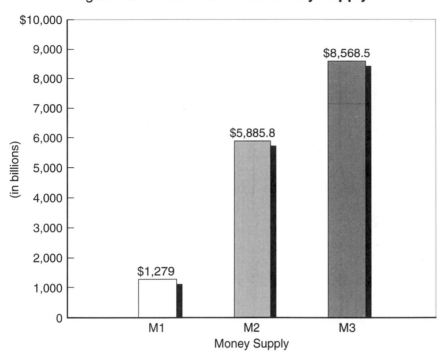

There is no question that paper currency and checkable accounts are generally acceptable in payment for goods and services, and so they fall within our definition of money. Problems arise, however, over the status of other assets that are easily converted into cash. For example, a shopper cannot walk into a store, plunk a bankbook down on the counter, and ask the clerk to wrap up an article worth $100. The shopper could, however, withdraw $100 from a bank savings account and pay for the item a short time later. People with money market accounts at a bank can quickly withdraw whatever they need to make a purchase by simply writing a check. At many banks, though, a service charge is made for each check drawn from a money market deposit account. Some people buy (from a broker) money market mutual funds that have check-writing privileges. Most of these funds require that checks drawn on an account cannot be below a specified dollar value, for example, $500. (Money market mutual funds were discussed in Chapter 10, page 230.)

Since assets such as government bonds, bank savings accounts, and money market funds are so easily converted to cash, economists include them in their definition of money supply. Because some forms of money can immediately be used to make a purchase, while others might take a day or two (or longer) to convert to cash, economists apply three different measures of the money supply to distinguish one from the others. These are M1, M2, and M3.

M1

M1 measures that portion of the money supply most easily used as a medium of exchange. This includes paper currency and coins, checking accounts, and traveler's checks. M1 is the measure most frequently referred to by economists and others when they discuss the money supply.

 M2

By adding savings accounts, money market funds, money market deposit accounts, certain bank reserves, and small certificates of deposit (CDs) to M1, we arrive at M2. These additions are less easily converted into cash than those included in M1.

 M3

M3 is the total of M2 plus large denomination certificates of deposit (CDs) ($100,000 or more), Eurodollars, and other large funds. The additions require a little more time to convert to cash than M2 does.

 # THE VALUE OF MONEY FLUCTUATES

"No, sir, a dollar just isn't worth a dollar anymore."

"You're telling me? Do you know what I just paid for a pack of chewing gum? I mean, chewing gum!"

"Don't tell me about chewing gum. When I was your age, we could buy a whole pack of gum for a dime, and when Grandma was your age, she bought a pack for a nickel."

"A nickel? I heard a comedian on a talk show last night say that prices are so high these days that even a nickel costs a quarter."

When people complain that "a dollar isn't worth a dollar anymore," they are not suggesting that there is something less than 100 cents in every dollar. What they are really saying is that most things cost more than they once did. We see, therefore, that although there will always be 100 pennies and four quarters in a dollar, what people will be able to buy with their money (its purchasing power or value) will fluctuate (move up or down).

Economists describe a period of generally rising prices as inflation. The value of the dollar falls during periods of inflation because it buys less than it once did. On rare occasions in the past, the United States experienced periods of generally falling prices, or *deflation.* Since during a period of deflation the dollar can buy more than it once did, its value is said to *increase.*

Measuring Purchasing Power With Index Numbers

When we speak of rising and falling prices, we are referring to the general price level rather than to prices of one or two goods or services. Those who measure changes in the price of goods and services often express the results of their findings in terms of an *index number.*

An index number expresses percentage change from a base year. The index number most frequently used to measure changes in the value of the dollar is the *Consumer Price Index (CPI)*. The CPI assigns a value of 100 to the average of prices from 1982 to 1984. In 2004, the CPI had reached 184. That meant that prices had increased by 84 percent between the base years and 2004 (because 184 − 100 = 84).

Sometimes the value of money is expressed in terms of its *purchasing power*. This is a way of expressing the cost of living in terms of dollars and cents. Thus, if the cost of living has doubled since the base years, one would say that the value of the dollar stands at $.50. Or, to put it another way, it would now take $20 to purchase what could have been purchased for $10 during the base period. Table 15.3 and Figure 15.2 illustrate what happened to the value of the dollar after 1950.

How Inflation Affects the Economy and People's Lives

Although money increases as well as decreases in value, there has not been a long-term period of deflation since the 1930s. Inflation, however, has been a fact of life for as long as most people can remember. With the exception of 1949 and 1955 (years when living costs actually declined), consumer prices

TABLE 15.3   CONSUMER PRICES AND PURCHASING POWER SINCE 1950

Year	Consumer Price Index (1982–1984 = 100)	Purchasing Power of Dollar (1982–1984 = $1)
1950	24.1	$4.15
1960	29.6	3.37
1970	38.8	2.57
1980	82.4	1.22
1990	130.7	.77
2000	170.0	.58
2003	183.0	.53

Figure 15.2 **Purchasing Power of a 1982 Dollar in Selected Years**

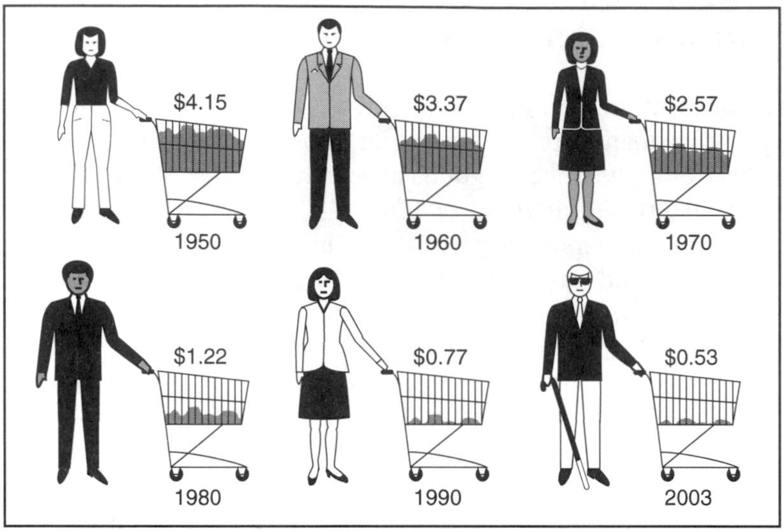

have risen in every year since 1939. Prior to 1965, however, the annual cost of living increase was rarely more than 1.5 percent. People grumbled about rising prices, but most Americans seemed to accept a modest inflation rate as the price of economic growth and relative prosperity. Beginning around 1965, however, inflation began to accelerate. Consumer prices increased at a 4 percent annual rate between 1965 and 1970, and this rate increased by 7 percent per year from 1970 to 1975 and by 9 percent from 1975 to 1980. In 1974, the nation experienced its first "double-digit inflation" (when the cost of living increased by 11 percent). Double-digit inflation struck again in 1979 and in 1980, when the inflation rate reached 13.5 percent.

In its more extreme forms, inflation can wreck an economy and even an entire society. The experiences of Germans in the years following World War I (1914–1918) stand as a terrible example of the consequences of runaway inflation. In 1913, the year before the war began, 4 *marks* (the German unit of currency) could be exchanged for a dollar. By 1923, it took 4,000,000,000,000 (that is, 4 trillion) marks to buy a dollar. The cost of living in Germany had increased a trillion times. So, for example, the price of a pound of butter had climbed to 1.5 million marks and that of a loaf of bread to 200,000 marks. Newspapers printed photographs of people with wheelbarrows and baby carriages on their way to the market to buy bread. Why the wheelbarrows and carriages? To carry the money needed for their purchases.

Not everyone is adversely affected by inflation, however. Depending on their circumstances, some people may actually profit from it. Here is a summary of inflation's likely impact on a variety of people in your community.

EFFECT ON SAVERS AND INVESTORS. For a wide variety of reasons, people set aside a portion of their incomes as savings. Some save for a "rainy day" when

Germany was beset by inflation in the 1920s. This woman in Berlin used German currency to light her stove because the money was almost worthless.

the unexpected will put special demands on the family purse. Others save for a new car, a musical instrument, or a college education. Whatever our reasons, we all would like to feel that our savings are secure and are earning a good return in the form of dividends or interest. If the cost of living increases at a rate higher than the return on our savings, however, the money we withdraw will be worth less than it was when we deposited it. Suppose, for example, that in 1979 Yvette deposited $1,000 in a savings account that paid 6 percent interest. Two years later, in 1981, she withdrew the deposit along with $123.60 in accumulated interest, for a total of $1,123.60.

"Not bad," she thought. "I put in $1,000 and got back $1,123.60. Not bad at all."

But wait. The inflation rate during those years averaged 12 percent a year. This means that in 1981 it took $1,254 to buy as much as $1,000 bought in 1979. But Yvette, the saver, received only $1,123.60 in principal and interest. She was, therefore, worse off by about $130.

Because money loses its purchasing power during inflationary times, people with surplus funds frequently look for investments that will increase in value as fast as or faster than the cost of living. Among the most popular hedges against inflation have been real estate, gold, and precious gems. For similar reasons, rare postage stamps, antiques, and works of art have also enjoyed popularity as vehicles for anti-inflationary investment.

Keep in mind, though, that there are no guarantees accompanying investments in "inflation hedges." Many people discover that when the time comes to sell, their so-called inflation hedges are worth less than their initial costs.

EFFECT ON PEOPLE ON FIXED INCOMES.   The income from some pension plans is fixed, meaning that affected retired people receive the same amount of pension payments each year. Those who depend on such "fixed incomes" for financial support suffer during periods of inflation. When prices go up, there is nothing that people on fixed incomes can do but spend less.

The income from annuities is also fixed. *Annuities* are funds purchased from insurance companies for a fixed sum in order to provide income at a later time. With one kind of annuity, this money (with accumulated interest or dividends) provides for payments beginning at an agreed-upon date (usually when one plans to retire) and continuing until the owner of the annuity dies. An annuity differs from life insurance, which pays the beneficiary at the time of the insured person's death.

In recent years, Social Security benefits have risen automatically with rises in the cost of living. This relationship means that as the Consumer Price Index increases, so too do Social Security payments. There is no guarantee that this federal policy will continue, however. Social Security income may become fixed.

EFFECT ON BUSINESS FIRMS.   The extent to which individual firms are affected by inflation depends on a firm's ability to cover its increased costs. Suppose, for example, that as a result of an inflationary trend, a firm is able to raise its selling prices by 20 percent without any loss in its volume of sales. If, at the same time, the firm's costs of doing business have increased by less than

What does inflation do to the cost of living?

Sean Miller, *The News and Observer*/Rothco.

20 percent, it will be better off than it was before the inflation began. If the increased cost of doing business cannot be offset by higher prices, however, the firm will be hurt by the inflation.

EFFECT ON PEOPLE WHO OWE MONEY.   *Debtors* (people who owe money) generally profit from inflation if the value of the money they repay is less than the amount of their loans. Suppose that you had borrowed $1,000, which you promised to repay in two years. Suppose also that inflation averaged 10 percent per year over those two years, for a total of 20 percent. You would be able to repay your $1,000 loan with dollars that had the purchasing power of only $800 (because 20 percent of $1,000 = $200; $1,000 − $200 = $800). As one economist aptly put it, "It's rather like borrowing steak and repaying the loan with hamburger."

You may recall from your study of U.S. history that certain groups, such as farmers, traditionally favored inflationary, or "cheap-money," policies. The farmers relied heavily on borrowed funds to finance their businesses. Moreover, they saw inflation as a means of easing their burden of debt because they repaid their loans with money that had less purchasing power than when they took out their loans. During some recent decades, though, many farmers suffered from inflation when the cost of borrowing increased even faster than the cost of living.

EFFECT ON PEOPLE WHO LEND MONEY.   Lenders can be hurt by inflation for the same reason that borrowers may profit: The value of the money that lenders lend is worth more than the value of the money that borrowers repay. Lenders can, and frequently do, protect themselves from the impact of inflation by putting that cost into their interest rates. For example, if the average cost of a loan was 20 percent over a period of time when the inflation rate was 8 percent, lenders would continue to earn a profit.

WHAT ARE THE CAUSES OF INFLATION?

Economists offer a number of reasons why we have inflation. Virtually all of these reasons fall into one of two categories: demand-pull and cost-push.

Demand-Pull

Demand-pull inflation occurs when the demand for goods and services outpaces the economy's ability to produce them. In this situation, prices will necessarily increase. One economist described demand-pull as a situation in which "too much money was chasing too few goods."

What, you may ask, is the source of all this excess demand? One source is the federal government. It sometimes spends more than it earns in taxes and other revenues. The effect of excess spending is that the public has more money and greater purchasing power than it had before the government acted.

The government also has the power to increase the money supply through the Federal Reserve System. The Fed issues virtually all the paper money that passes through our hands. If, as a result of Federal Reserve policies, the supply of money is increased fast enough, the excess demand that results will lead to a general rise in prices. (Fed policies are discussed in more detail on pages 435–439.)

The federal government, though, is not the only source of demand-pull inflation. Changes in the spending habits of individuals and business firms can also result in "too much money chasing too few goods." A classic example of this process followed the end of World War II (1941–1945). Although U.S. personal income was high during the war, production was geared toward military goods. As a result, there were few consumer goods for Americans to buy. Since savings were viewed as both practical and patriotic, most people set aside a portion of their earnings toward the day when consumer goods would again become more readily available. After the war ended, Americans rushed to buy new appliances, cars, and homes as fast as they became available. As a result, consumer prices, which had risen by only about 10 percent during the four war years, quickly escalated by an additional 30 percent over the following three years.

Still another source of demand-pull inflation is a psychological factor that is sometimes called "public expectations." If consumers and managers of business firms believe that prices will be rising in the near future, they may rush to buy today what they might otherwise have postponed buying until a later time. Ironically, if a large enough section of the public acts on this expectation, the prophecy will be fulfilled. Why? Because the rising demand will lead to an increase in prices.

Cost-Push

Not all inflation can be explained as "too much money chasing too few goods." The inflation of 1979–1981, for example, saw prices increase at a record rate at a time when U.S. industries were operating at barely 80 percent of capacity and one worker out of fourteen was out of work. In other words, people did not have "too much money." The U.S. economy could have produced many more goods and services if there had been more demand. And yet the country experienced inflation. Economists use the term *stagflation* in describing an economy experiencing inflation at the same time as its resources are heavily underuti-

Barter as a Response to Inflation in Argentina

Stella Lomas has little idea how much she will earn each week. Four months ago, the 36-year-old mother of four lost her job. Now she works long hours making pizza at a market in a working-class neighborhood on the outskirts of Buenos Aires, Argentina. But Stella does not sell her pies—she swaps them.

"A friend told me about this place three months ago, and I've been cooking pizzas here ever since. You can trade anything here—food, things for the house, clothes for the kids," says Stella as she works the dough to feed a line of hungry customers.

The economy of Argentina had been in decline since the 1990s. By 2003, one in five Argentines was unemployed, and half the population was living in poverty. Making matters worse, the country suffered an inflation in which the *peso* (Argentina's currency) lost nearly three-quarters of its value. That meant an Argentine bank account worth the equivalent of $2,000 in 2002 was worth only $500 in 2003.

In response to the economic disaster, some 300,000 Argentines have turned to barter (*trueque* in Spanish), and the number is growing. The trend has been so successful that the Argentine government now looks on *trueque* as a cushion for the jobless. Typically, sellers exchange their wares in locations similar to American flea markets that are run by independent barter clubs.

As is the case with most barter markets, matching buyers and sellers can be a problem. For that reason, the government has allowed barter clubs to issue a kind of currency known as *créditos*. At first, these paper coupons (available in denominations of 1, 5, 10, and 20) were considered legal tender only within the confines of the barter markets. Since 2002, however, the government has allowed a limited number of businesses outside the markets to accept them in payment.

lized, as was the case during 1979–1981. According to economists, the cause in this and some other recent rising price spirals was *cost-push inflation*. This name describes the run-up in prices that results as sellers raise their prices because of increases in their costs.

Cost-push inflation occurs because large segments of the nation's economy do not operate under conditions of pure competition. Thus, some labor unions can achieve wage increases without increasing their members' productivity. And producers in certain key industries have the power to increase prices even though shortages do not exist.

Management and labor are frequently at odds as to which is the first cause of a period of cost-push inflation. Management is likely to charge that the principal cause of inflation is unions' demands for wage increases that outrun productivity. In the absence of additional output, businesses must offset higher wage costs with price increases. For their part, unions are likely to argue that their wage demands are merely efforts to make up for increases in the cost of living. "Don't blame us," unions might say. "Businesses raised their prices first."

Some liken the question to the age-old puzzle about which came first, the chicken or the egg. Without attempting to settle the argument, we can say that the *wage-price spiral* has led to a series of inflationary price increases in the past and is likely to do so again in the future.

In recent decades, the type of cost-push inflation that has been most troublesome is known to economists as *commodity inflation.* This term identifies run-ups in the prices of certain key commodities as the source of general price increases. The most dramatic example of commodity inflation in the 1970s took place in the petroleum industry. Foreign suppliers operating through the **Organization of Petroleum Exporting Countries (OPEC)** were able to use their monopoly power to push prices from less than $4 a barrel in 1973 to $40 in 1980–1981. As the price increases radiated out to gasoline and other petroleum by-products, the inflationary spiral seemed to affect virtually every one of the U.S. economy's goods and services.

 # MONEY AND CREDIT

When she reached the checkout counter, Lucy paid for her groceries with a credit card.

The Murphys got the good news yesterday: The bank approved their auto loan. They expect delivery on their new car some time next week.

When Herschel picked out a shirt and tie in the men's department, he charged the purchase to his store account.

The transactions described above share something in common—they took place without any of the monies included in M1, M2, or M3. They were paid for instead, with credit.

While they are not money, credit cards, bank loans, charge accounts, and other forms of credit enable people to purchase the things they want. According to some estimates, about one-third of consumer purchases are in the form of credit. For that reason, the availability of credit, along with the money supply, affects business activity, the level of prices, and the economy in general.

The most important single factor affecting the use of credit is its cost. The cost of a loan is expressed in the rate of interest prevailing at the time of the loan. Interest is the price that one pays for the temporary use of someone else's funds. The return lenders or savings depositors receive is in addition to the principal value of their loan or deposit.

Real vs. Nominal Interest Rates

It is no secret that the principal value of a loan declines during a period of inflation. Although this might be great for borrowers who will be repaying less (in terms of purchasing power) than they borrowed, it is not a happy thought for lenders. Why would anyone be willing to lend money in inflationary times? The answer has to do with interest and interest rates.

Creditors lend money in order to earn interest on their loans. If lenders believe that a period of inflation is approaching, they can protect themselves against the loss of purchasing power of their loan by charging a higher rate of interest than they would have if there were no inflation.

> Frank Needsdough asks Marcia Rich to lend him $10,000. Frank and Marcia agree that in the absence of inflation, 4 percent would be a fair return on a one-year loan. That is, Frank would pay Marcia $10,400 at the end of the year for the privilege of having $10,000 today.
>
> But these are inflationary times, and Frank and Marcia anticipate that prices will have risen by about 6 percent by the end of the year. At that rate, the $10,000 that Marcia loaned Frank would have a purchasing power of only $9,400 at the end of the year.
>
> "There is no way," Marcia thought, "that I would lend money at 4 percent in these inflationary times. But if I could add 6 percent to the 4 percent that I was willing to take without inflation, the 10 percent interest would give me a fair return."
>
> At 10 percent, Frank would need to pay $1,000 in interest in addition to the $10,000 he borrowed at the end of the year. Since he recognizes that the $11,000 would have the same purchasing power at the end of the year that $10,400 has today, he agrees to the terms and borrows the money.

In the example above, Frank repaid a $10,000 loan plus 10 percent or $1,000 in interest. Economists would describe the 10 percent as the nominal interest rate. The *nominal interest rate* is the percentage return, as stated in the agreement, on a loan, bank deposit, or bond. However, because of the 6 percent inflation over the course of the year, the purchasing power of the interest on the $10,000 loan was equal to $400 at the beginning of the year. Economists would describe the $400 increase in purchasing power that the lender Marcia earned over the year as the *real interest rate.*

In summary, the nominal interest rate is the annual percentage amount earned on a sum that is loaned or deposited. The real interest rate is the actual percentage change in purchasing power that a borrower pays a lender. Real interest can be calculated by subtracting the inflation rate from the nominal interest rate.

The level of interest rates affects the economic decisions of individuals, businesses, and governments. Individuals thinking of buying a new car or home often base their decision on the cost of the loan they will need to make that purchase. Similarly, business firms thinking of expanding or replacing equipment or machinery compare the cost of financing those moves with the return on the same funds if they were placed in interest-bearing investments. The effect of those decisions on the nation's economic well-being will be described in later chapters.

S U M M A R Y

Money can be anything that people are willing to accept in payment for goods or services. Long ago, money replaced the barter system and is now used in all societies. Money provides a medium of exchange, a measure of value, and a store of value.

The principal kinds of money used in the United States are paper currency, coins, and checkbook money. Paper money and coins are issued by the federal government and distributed by the Federal Reserve System and the nation's banks. Checkable accounts constitute the largest share of the nation's money supply.

Depending on its liquidity (the ease with which an asset can be sold or converted to cash), the money supply is expressed in terms of M1, M2, and M3. M1 is the total amount of currency, checkbook money, and traveler's checks in circulation on a given day. M2 adds individual savings accounts, money market funds, and small CDs to the M1 total. M3 includes large deposits and CDs along with the M2 total.

The value of money changes. Inflation is a rise in the prices of most goods and services. Deflation is the opposite of inflation. Inflation hurts some groups of people more than others, but continued inflation hurts the economy as a whole. The purchasing power of the dollar is measured by the Consumer Price Index (CPI), which compares one year's prices to prices in a base year.

The level of economic activity at any given point in time is a reflection of the money supply and the availability of credit. How and why money and credit affect economic activity, and the strategies government uses to influence those outcomes, are the subjects of later chapters.

REVIEWING THE CHAPTER

BUILDING VOCABULARY

Match each item in Column A with its definition in Column B.

Column A

1. demand deposit
2. stagflation
3. demand-pull inflation
4. Consumer Price Index
5. deflation
6. cost-push inflation
7. Gresham's Law
8. M1
9. M2
10. M3

Column B

a. M1 plus individual savings deposits, small CDs, and money market funds
b. a rise in the level of prices caused by an increase in demand
c. the total of all currency, checkbook money, and traveler's checks in circulation on any given day
d. a checking account
e. a rise in price level caused by increases in costs of doing business
f. M2 plus large CDs and other large funds
g. a period of both recession and inflation
h. a general decline in the price level
i. a series of index numbers that shows the percentage change in prices from a base year
j. the idea that cheap money tends to drive good money out of circulation

UNDERSTANDING WHAT YOU HAVE READ

1. During the Revolutionary War, many American colonists spent their paper money, which had been issued by the Continental Congress, and hoarded their metallic currency. This activity was an illustration of (*a*) barter (*b*) legal tender (*c*) Engel's Law (*d*) Gresham's Law.

2. Harry loaned Kari $5,000 payable at the end of the year plus 12 percent interest. At year's end, Kari repaid Harry with a check in the amount of $5,600. Meanwhile, the cost of living had increased by 4 percent. What was the real rate of interest Harry earned on his loan? (*a*) 4 percent (*b*) 8 percent (*c*) 12 percent (*d*) 16 percent.

3. When the price level increases because "there is too much money chasing too few goods," economists describe this as (*a*) spiraling deflation (*b*) demand-pull inflation (*c*) cost-push inflation (*d*) push-pull inflation.

4. During periods of inflation, the value of the dollar (*a*) decreases (*b*) remains the same (*c*) decreases for a while and then increases (*d*) increases.

5. The purchasing power of the dollar (*a*) tells us the price of a good or service (*b*) is the same as the foreign exchange rate of the dollar (*c*) compares the value of the dollar in one period with its value in another period (*d*) never changes.

6. If the Consumer Price Index today stands at 125, this means that (*a*) prices have risen by 125 percent this year (*b*) prices have risen by 25 percent this year (*c*) there has been a decrease in the cost of living (*d*) the cost of living has increased by 25 percent since the base period.

7. An increase in average weekly income does not result in a higher standard of living if it is accompanied by (*a*) increased purchases of consumer goods (*b*) increased private investment (*c*) rising prices (*d*) increased productivity.

8. Which group generally finds inflation advantageous? (*a*) banks with 80 percent of their deposits invested in mortgage loans (*b*) retired workers living on pensions (*c*) investors whose holdings are mostly in bonds (*d*) farmers repaying long-term debts.

9. Traveler's checks and demand deposits are described as M1 because they (*a*) are closely connected with banks (*b*) can easily be converted into cash (*c*) can be used as legal tender (*d*) can be used as security for loans.

10. In totaling the value of the nation's money supply, which of the following items would *not* be included? (*a*) paper currency (*b*) demand deposits (*c*) traveler's checks (*d*) corporate stocks and bonds.

THINKING CRITICALLY

1. During the early Roman era, the merchants of Rome frequently traveled beyond the empire's borders to trade with other peoples. Summarize the trading difficulties that probably arose in the barter economies they encountered.

2. During World War II, U.S. prisoners of war used cigarettes as a form of money. Cigarettes were used to purchase anything that was for sale in the prison camps. We have discussed, however, that money should possess the qualities of durability, portability, divisibility, uniformity, ease of recognition, and scarcity. In terms of these six criteria, discuss the advantages and disadvantages of cigarette money in this prison economy.

3. Throughout history, the most popular form of money has been gold.

a. Give *three* reasons why gold has been such a popular form of money.

b. What would happen to the value of gold if people discovered that it could easily be made at home from inexpensive materials? Explain your answer.

c. Suppose that a nation's money supply consisted of copper, silver, and gold coins, and paper currency. Also suppose that the worldwide value of gold began to increase dramatically. Explain what holders of gold could be expected to do with their gold coins.

4. Exactly what constitutes the nation's money supply has been a matter of disagreement among economists and among government officials.

a. Define what money is.

b. Why do economists and others have difficulty measuring the nation's money supply?

c. What difference does it make how much money is in circulation at any particular time?

d. Explain the differences among M1, M2, and M3.

SKILLS: Interpreting a Table

Study Table 15.3 on page 345 and then answer the following questions.

1. (*a*) What information is given in column 2, "Consumer Price Index"? (*b*) What is meant by the notation "1982–1984 = 100"?

2. What information is given in column 3?

3. Explain how the price changes indicated in the table affected each of the following:

   a. a schoolteacher who retired on a fixed pension in 1980.

   b. a couple who sold their home in 2003 that they had purchased in 1970.

   c. a family with two children with money invested in a savings account starting in 1980.

   d. a farmer who borrowed money for a new tractor in 1990 that had to be repaid by 2003.

USING THE INTERNET

- The following Web site contains stories about *trueque* clubs: <<www.businessweek.com/magazine/content/01_20/b3732172.htm>>.

- For further information on the U.S. Mint, log on to its Web site at <<www.usmint.gov>>.

CHAPTER 16

Banks and Banking

O V E R V I E W

Most people have or will have a bank account. It might be a savings account or a checking account or both. Those who have bank accounts take for granted that a bank will accept their money for safekeeping and that they can withdraw this money from their accounts whenever they want. We are all familiar with checks. Probably all of us have received a payment for something by check. We hardly give it a thought when we accept a piece of paper with a promise to pay a certain amount. If we open a checking account, we have a mechanism for making payments as well as a place to hold our money. Banks serve other purposes besides offering checking and savings accounts. People and businesses borrow from banks—actions that are very important in keeping our economy growing. Moreover, banks provide many other services, such as selling traveler's checks and renting out safe-deposit boxes.

In this chapter, we will discuss the services that banks provide. We will also discuss

- the origins of banking

- the difference between commercial banks and thrift institutions

- how banks do business

- how banks create money

- how we keep our banks safe.

THE ORIGINS OF BANKING

As money replaced the barter system in the ancient world, the development of banking inevitably followed. History's earliest written records indicate that the people of ancient Babylonia (in what is now Iraq in Western Asia) developed an early form of currency and banking. The units of Babylonian currency were the shekel, mina, and talent. A shekel was roughly equal in value to a half ounce of silver. A mina equaled 60 shekels, and a talent equaled 60 minas.

As early as 2000 B.C., wealthy private citizens and priests of Babylonia granted loans and held funds for safekeeping. Records show that depositors in this ancient culture could draw on their balances held for safekeeping by writing a *draft* (a kind of check). Like bankers today, Babylonian bankers charged interest on their loans. Government regulations, however, imposed severe penalties on those who charged more than the legal limit.

Scientists have found similar evidence of banking in studying the ancient civilizations of India and China and the Mayan, Aztec, and Incan civilizations. As trade and commerce increased in these cultures, certain individuals and families held funds of others for safekeeping. They also made loans and, in some cases, exchanged one country's coins for another country's. Our story of banking will stress developments in Western Europe, because U.S. financial institutions are largely of Western European origin.

With the expansion of trade during the late Middle Ages, several large banking houses were established in Italy, Germany, and the Netherlands. Taking the lead were the Italians, who developed elements of banking as early as the 13th century. At that time, European trade was centered in the Mediterranean and was dominated by the Italian city-states of Genoa, Venice, and Florence. In time, the Italian bankers extended their operations to France, the German states, and England. In these places, they made loans; invested in hotels, shipping, and the spice trade; and financed military campaigns. The Italian bankers developed some of the practices of modern banking. They accepted deposits, made loans, and arranged for the transfer of funds. They are also credited with developing double-entry bookkeeping and selling insurance on cargo being shipped by sea.

Modern banking came to England in the 17th century through the efforts of the London *goldsmiths* (people who make articles of gold for a living). Because there were no police departments in those days, the goldsmiths had to provide for their own security. Then, because goldsmiths had this protection, other merchants eventually offered to pay the goldsmiths to hold their gold and other valuables for safekeeping. In exchange for their deposits, the merchants were issued receipts entitling them to the return of their property on demand.

At first, merchants looked upon the goldsmiths' shops as a kind of safe-deposit box or warehouse. They expected to get back the same bag of gold that

The development of modern banking began in Italy in the 13th century. On the right side of the painting, a man makes a deposit. On the left, a banker shows customers the ledger books.

they had left on deposit. In time, however, those merchants who held goldsmiths' receipts accepted the idea that it really did not matter which gold they got back as long as it was of equal value to the amount deposited. Then other merchants—those who did not have gold on storage with the goldsmiths—began to accept the goldsmiths' receipts in payment for goods and services. When that happened, goldsmith receipts became a kind of paper currency.

Somewhere along the way, the goldsmiths discovered that they did not need to keep all of the gold on reserve. It was unlikely that all their customers would withdraw their deposits at the same time. It followed, therefore, that the goldsmiths could add to their profits by setting aside a portion of the deposits as a reserve and lending out the rest. This simple assumption—that depositors would not withdraw all their money at the same time—has provided the foundation on which banking has rested from the goldsmiths' time down to the present.

To attract additional deposits (and thus add to their profits), goldsmiths began to pay interest to their depositors. Of course, in order to earn a profit, the interest the goldsmiths paid on deposits had to be less than what they charged for the loans.

Banking as developed by the goldsmiths was a primitive institution, serving the interests of the wealthiest people in Europe. Nevertheless, the practices that the goldsmiths developed provided the basis for our modern banking system.

Like the goldsmiths, today's bankers accept deposits and make loans. When things go as planned, banks earn more in interest on their investments and loans than they pay on deposits. When things do not go well, the opposite occurs: Banks earn less interest and suffer losses.

MODERN BANKING

Did you ever visit a bank and wonder what all those people were doing there? Most customers in a bank are making deposits to or withdrawals from their savings or checking accounts. Others may be applying for loans, purchasing certificates of deposit, or paying utility bills. Then there are those who have come to the bank to visit their safe-deposit boxes or buy foreign currency, money orders, traveler's checks, or bank drafts. Some banks maintain trust departments for those who want the banks to manage their wealth. For example, a person might name a commercial bank as trustee of an estate. While that person is living, the bank invests the client's money and, in some cases, pays that person's bills. Upon the individual's death, the bank distributes his or her money and property in accordance with the terms of a will.

Modern banks offer so many services that it is little wonder that they have been called "financial supermarkets." Banks that directly serve the public fall into two categories: commercial banks and thrift institutions (or "thrifts").

Commercial Banks

With some $7.2 trillion in assets, *commercial banks* are the nation's most important financial institutions. One reason for their dominance is that they provide business firms with checking accounts. Although the thrifts offer checking accounts to individuals and nonprofit organizations, they are prohibited from extending them to business firms. Consequently, virtually every business firm has a checking account with a commercial bank.

The second reason for the dominance of commercial banks is that they make high profits by extending loans to businesses. Commercial banks also grant loans to consumers to purchase motor vehicles, appliances, and homes, and to remodel homes.

Thrift Institutions

The term *thrifts* refers to three types of institutions: savings and loan associations, mutual savings banks, and credit unions.

SAVINGS AND LOAN ASSOCIATIONS.   The largest of the thrifts in terms of assets are the *savings and loan associations (S&Ls)*. A savings and loan association is interested primarily in home financing. Therefore, virtually all its loans are in the form of long-term mortgages. A *mortgage* is a loan that is secured by the property that was purchased with the borrowed money. Interest is paid to depositors out of the earnings generated by the S&Ls' loans and other activities.

While the services offered by savings and loan associations are not as

Figure 16.1 **Number and Assets of Banking Institutions**

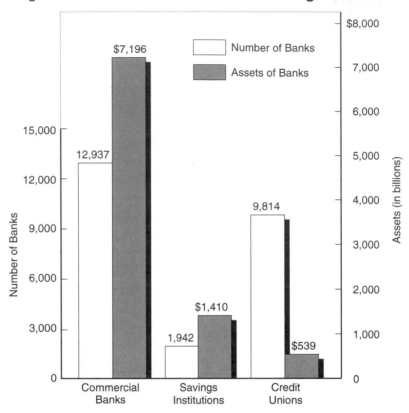

extensive as those offered by commercial banks, they go well beyond simple savings and home-loan activities. As part of their array of financial services, many S&Ls now offer interest-bearing checking accounts, credit cards, and individual retirement accounts as well as traveler's checks, government bonds, and consumer loans.

MUTUAL SAVINGS BANKS.   Depositors in a *mutual savings bank* are part owners of the bank. Theoretically, this gives them a voice in the management of the bank and a claim against its assets in the event of its liquidation. In practice, mutual savings banks are operated by professional managers with very little direction from their depositors.

The principal function of mutual savings banks is to accept deposits and use those funds to make loans. Depositors entrust their savings to these banks for safekeeping and for income, which is paid in dividends and interest.

In recent years, mutual savings banks have entered into competition with commercial banks by offering many of the services that were once the commercial banks' alone. For example, mutual savings banks now offer both regular and interest-bearing checking accounts to individuals and nonprofit organizations. Although the bulk of their lending is still in the form of long-term real estate

A customer cashes a check
at his credit union.

mortgages, they also offer short-term consumer loans, financial services (such as investment and retirement accounts), credit cards, and safe-deposit boxes.

CREDIT UNIONS.   Some 70 million Americans are members of the nation's more than 12,000 *credit unions.* Like mutual savings banks, credit unions are owned by their depositors. But unlike mutual savings banks, credit unions limit membership to those who belong to a particular group, such as workers at a business establishment, members of a labor union, or employees and students of a university.

Credit unions accept savings deposits from members, who thereby become entitled to borrow when the need arises and, in some cases, open checking accounts. Credit unions are nonprofit organizations. This status reduces operating costs and exempts credit unions from taxes. It also enables credit unions to pay higher rates of interest on their deposits and charge less for their loans.

 THE BUSINESS OF BANKING

As discussed in Chapter 5, everything of value owned by a business is known as an asset. Anything that it owes is a liability. Since a bank owns the loans and investments it makes, they are assets. Bank deposits, by contrast, represent money loaned to a bank by its depositors. Therefore, deposits represent liabilities. The difference between a bank's assets and its liabilities is its net worth.

A financial statement that summarizes assets, liabilities, and net worth is known as a balance sheet. Table 16.1 represents the balance sheet of the New City National Bank on June 19 in a recent year.

TABLE 16.1	NEW CITY NATIONAL BANK BALANCE SHEET JUNE 19, 200–

Assets		Liabilities and Net Worth	
Cash in vault	$ 200,000	Demand deposits	$ 6,200,000
Reserve account	1,600,000	Time deposits	4,200,000
with Federal		Total deposits	$10,400,000
Reserve Bank		Net worth	2,800,000
Loans	8,200,000	**Total**	$13,200,000
Securities	2,800,000		
Building and fixtures	400,000		
Total	$13,200,000		

Assets

The assets of the New City National Bank totaled $13.2 million. These assets consisted of the following:

CASH IN VAULT. A *vault* is a protected storage area. Bank vaults hold the bulk of the bank's cash (some cash is kept in the tellers' drawers), securities, and other valuables. Thus, *cash in vault* represents the money the bank has on hand to use. Banks need to keep a quantity of currency and coin on hand to meet the needs of their customers. The amount of cash in vault fluctuates from day to day with changes in public demand for paper currency and coins.

RESERVE ACCOUNT WITH FEDERAL RESERVE BANK. Bankers know that on any given day, some people will withdraw funds, while others will make deposits. By the day's end, a bank may have a net increase in deposits, or it may have a net decrease. Either way, it is evident that a bank needs to keep only a fraction of its total deposits on hand to meet withdrawal demands. The rest can be used to make loans or investments.

This simple assumption—that only a fraction of a bank's depositors will want to withdraw their funds at any point in time—is the basis for what is known as *fractional reserve banking*. Secure in the knowledge that they need keep only a fraction of their deposits "on reserve" to meet withdrawal demands, banks can generate income by lending or investing the balance.

How much of its deposits a bank holds depends on the *reserve ratio*. This ratio is the percentage of deposits that banks are required by law to hold on reserve. Suppose, for example, that a bank held $100 million in deposits, and the reserve ratio was 15 percent. In that case, the bank would be required to set aside $15 million in reserves. It could lend or invest the balance—$85 million.

Banks keep most of their reserves in special accounts at a district Federal Reserve bank. (We will study the Federal Reserve System in Chapter 17.) As indicated by its balance sheet, New City had some $1.6 million in its reserve account. Taken with the $200,000 cash in its vaults, the bank held a total $1.8 million in its reserves.

LOANS.   Loans are classified as assets because they are owned by the bank and represent obligations payable to the bank. Most of a bank's profits are earned from its loans. In addition to business loans, banks lend money to consumers to help finance major purchases, such as automobiles, major appliances, and real estate. New City had $8.2 million in loans outstanding on June 19th.

SECURITIES.   Banks cannot afford to allow funds for which they can find no borrowers to lie idle. Instead, banks invest those sums in relatively safe, interest-bearing securities, such as government bonds. New City's investments totaled $2.8 million that day.

BUILDING AND FIXTURES.   The premises in which New City National Bank conducts its business was estimated to be worth $400,000.

Liabilities and Net Worth

In a balance sheet, the sum of the liabilities and net worth equals assets. (Balance sheets were described in Chapter 5.)

DEMAND DEPOSITS.   Deposits are a bank's principal obligations. As discussed in Chapter 15, demand deposits are those that can be withdrawn at any time, such as checking accounts. Deposits in New City's checking accounts totaled $6.2 million.

TIME DEPOSITS.   Another term for savings accounts is *time deposits*. Such funds are usually left in banks for longer periods of time than demand deposits. Savings deposits are subject to advance notice of withdrawal, but as a rule they are available to customers whenever they choose to withdraw them. They are a liability of a bank because they represent funds owed to depositors.

NET WORTH.   The difference between a bank's assets and its liabilities is its net worth. In the case of New City, this amounted to $2.8 million.

HOW BANKS CREATE MONEY

When a bank grants a loan, the funds are usually deposited in the borrower's checking account. Since checks are a form of money, the loan represents an addition to the nation's money supply created by the lending bank. For example:

John Spratt owns a small toy store. In anticipation of the next Christmas shopping season, Mr. Spratt would like to add to his inventory of toys and games. He figures that if he can borrow $25,000 before the end of June, it will enable him to get his buying done well in time for the Christmas shopping rush, which begins in November.

Mr. Spratt discussed his problem with Nancy Hubbard, the lending officer at New City National, his local bank. Ms. Hubbard and other bank officers have been doing business with Mr. Spratt for many years. Confident that he will be able to sell his merchandise and pay off his loan, they approved his request.

Meanwhile, Spratt was happy that he would have the capital he needed that summer. For its part, the bank was also pleased because it needs to make loans in order to earn a profit.

On June 15, Spratt signed a *promissory note* (a legal IOU) at the New City National Bank in the amount of $25,000. As stated on the note, the principal was payable in eight months at an interest rate of 10 percent. Meanwhile, the bank credited Spratt's checking account with $25,000.

The moment that Spratt's account was credited for his loan, the nation's money supply increased by $25,000. Why? Because demand deposits are a form of money, and that sum did not exist until the bank granted the loan and credited the account.

Eight months later (on February 15), Spratt wrote a check in the amount of $26,667 to repay his loan. Of this total, $25,000 was the principal amount of the loan, while $1,667 represented the interest.

Interest is expressed as the rate per year. The equation for calculating interest (I) is:

$$I = P \times R \times T$$

where P = principal (amount borrowed)
           R = rate (of interest per year)
           T = time (in years or fractions of years)

Spratt's interest was calculated as follows:

$$I = \$25{,}000 \text{ (principal)} \times {}^{10}\!/_{100} \text{ (interest rate)} \times {}^{8}\!/_{12} \text{ (period of the loan)}$$
$$= \$1{,}666.67 \text{ (interest)}$$

🗲 Reserve Requirements and the Money Supply

We have seen that banks create money as the loans they grant are added to their demand deposits. There are, however, limits to the amount of money an individual bank can create. The amount of money that an individual bank can create is limited by its deposits and the reserve ratio. The *reserve ratio* is that percentage of a bank's deposits that must be held on reserve. For example, if the reserve ratio were 15 percent, and a bank held $1 million in deposits, it would be required by law to limit its loans (and ability to create money) to $850,000 while holding at least $150,000 on reserve.

By way of illustration, assume that at the very moment a new bank opened its doors, Mary Perkins walked in to open a checking account. As her first transaction, Mary deposited a check for $10,000 that she had just received from

Figure 16.2 **Promissory Note**

$25,000.00	Monroe, UT	June 15, **20** 04

Eight months **AFTER DATE**   I   **PROMISE TO PAY TO**

THE ORDER OF _____ New City National Bank _____

Twenty-Five Thousand and 00/100 _____ **DOLLARS**

PAYABLE AT _____ New City National Bank _____

FOR VALUE RECEIVED WITH INTEREST AT ___ 8% ___

DUE February 15, **20** 05   _John Spratt_

the City Central Insurance Company for damages to her home caused by recent floods. The deposit will appear on the bank's balance sheet as follows:

ASSETS		LIABILITIES	
Reserves	$10,000	Deposits	$10,000

When these events took place, the reserve ratio was 20 percent. This means that the bank had to add at least $2,000 (20 percent of $10,000 = $2,000) to its reserves. The remaining $8,000 was available for loans.

As luck would have it, the very next customer to enter the bank, John Scope, president of Scope's Hardware, applied for and was granted an $8,000 business loan. Mr. Scope needed the money to improve dock facilities at his hardware store. The amount ($8,000) was credited to the firm's checking account and was reflected in the bank's balance sheet as follows:

ASSETS		LIABILITIES	
Loans	$ 8,000	Deposits	$18,000
Reserves	$10,000		

Let us pause for a moment to see what happened.

Acting on a fundamental assumption of banking—that not all depositors will ask for their money at the same time—the bank lent the bulk of its first customer's deposit. Reserves still totaled $10,000 because, for the time being, no withdrawals had been made. Scope's Hardware has a credit of $8,000 in its checking account, which it will soon spend. Deposits, which totaled $10,000 before the loan, are now $18,000, even though no one brought in an additional

Using an ATM at a store may cost you more than using one at a bank where you have an account.

$8,000. Where did the additional $8,000 come from? It appeared when the bank granted the loan. Could the bank have loaned $9,000? No, because the reserve ratio at that time was 20 percent. (The bank could have loaned $9,000 if the reserve ratio had been 10 percent.)

We see, therefore, that an individual bank can expand deposits by an amount equal to its *excess reserves* (the reserves held by the bank over and above its required reserves). But that is not the end of the story. As the borrowed money is spent and redeposited, the funds continue to travel through the nation's banking system, and as they do, they expand still further.

How the Banking System Expands Deposits

Scope's Hardware, the business that borrowed the $8,000, paid Hickory Dock, Inc., that amount to improve its dock facilities. Hickory Dock deposited the check in its account at a second bank. The second bank's balance sheet reflects the $8,000 deposit as follows:

ASSETS		LIABILITIES	
Reserves	$8,000	Deposits	$8,000

The first bank's balance sheet now looks like this:

ASSETS		LIABILITIES	
Loans	$8,000	Deposits	$10,000
Reserves	$2,000		

The second bank is now able to lend out an additional $6,400 (80 percent of $8,000). When added to the borrower's (of the $6,400) checking account, the loan will be reflected with the following additions to the bank's balance sheet:

ASSETS		LIABILITIES	
Loans	$6,400	Deposits	$14,400
Reserves	$8,000		

Just as the original loan moved on to a second bank, this second loan could be deposited in a third bank, which could then lend up to $5,120 of the $6,400 deposited (80 percent of $6,400 = $5,120). Theoretically, this loan could move through the banking system until the last cent was set aside in reserve. At this point, a total of $40,000 would have been lent as a result of the initial $10,000 deposit, and total deposits would have expanded to $50,000. Note that although no one bank lent out more than its excess reserves, the banking system as a whole expanded deposits by five times the original deposit. Table 16.2 summarizes the progress of the $10,000 deposit as it moved through the banking system.

From this discussion, you can see that the reserve ratio affects the money supply. If, on the one hand, the ratio were 25 percent, then an initial deposit of $10,000 could have been expanded to only $40,000. On the other hand, a 10 percent reserve ratio would have permitted the deposit to expand to $100,000. In the next chapter, we will see how the government uses the reserve ratio as a tool to keep the money supply healthy.

When Deposits Contract

Just as a cash deposit can lead to an expansion of deposits through the banking system, so the withdrawal of funds can have the opposite effect. If a bank has no excess reserves and some money is withdrawn, it has to replace the reserves either by calling in loans or selling securities. If the funds that are withdrawn

TABLE 16.2   PROGRESS OF $10,000 THROUGH THE BANKING SYSTEM

Bank	Deposits	Required Reserves	Loans
First	$10,000.00	$ 2,000.00	$ 8,000.00
Second	8,000.00	1,600.00	6,400.00
Third	6,400.00	1,280.00	5,120.00
Fourth	5,120.00	1,024.00	4,096.00
Fifth	4,096.00	819.20	3,276.80
Sum of remaining banks	16,384.00	3,276.80	13,107.20
Total	$50,000.00	$10,000.00	$40,000.00

from one bank are placed in another, then the banking system as a whole does not lose. However, if the money is not deposited in another bank, then the total of all deposits in the economy is reduced. If the reserve ratio is 20 percent, then total deposits are reduced by $5 for every dollar withdrawn.

KEEPING OUR BANKS SAFE

The Great Depression of the 1930s was the most dreadful period in U.S. economic history. For many, the most psychologically painful memories of those times were the numbers of people without jobs and the many failed banks. During the worst of those times, in 1933, 25 percent of the labor force was unemployed and half the nation's banks failed. Let us think about what it must have been like to learn that the bank in which one's life's savings had been deposited had failed.

Failure of a savings institution meant that the bank could no longer meet withdrawal requests from its depositors. Later (perhaps months later, perhaps years later), depositors might receive a fraction of their savings. Some received 10 cents on the dollar, others received nothing. With so much to lose if one's bank failed, even the faintest rumor of trouble resulted in lines of depositors hoping to withdraw their money before disaster struck.

Widespread bank failures destroyed public trust in the banking system. They also left people fearful of spending or investing their money. This fear and uncertainty was bad for business. In addition, high unemployment levels made the situation even worse because people without jobs did not have money to save and invest, and little money to spend.

Deposit Insurance

To restore confidence, one of the first efforts of newly elected President Franklin D. Roosevelt was to get Congress to pass laws concerning *deposit insurance.* Thus, in 1933, Congress set up the **Federal Deposit Insurance Corporation (FDIC)**. The following year, Congress created a similar organization, the **Federal Savings and Loan Insurance Corporation (FSLIC)**, to insure people's deposits in savings and loan associations.

Eventually, the FDIC and FSLIC guaranteed deposits in insured banks and S&Ls for up to $100,000. Funding for the insurance came from the insured institutions, which paid a percentage of their deposits to the insuring agencies. Secure in the knowledge that even in the event of bank failures their deposits were safe, people regained their confidence in the banking system. Events in more recent years, however, again raised questions about the ability of banks and thrifts to protect their depositors.

THE THRIFT CRISIS.   In the 1980s, disaster struck the nation's banks and thrifts. Bank failures, which had averaged fewer than 3 per year between 1943 and 1974, reached 42 in 1982, 120 in 1985, and 203 in 1987! Even harder hit was the savings and loan industry. In 1988, one in three S&Ls was losing money, and one in six was in danger of folding.

A principal cause of the problem was the sharp increases in interest rates that had taken place during the early 1980s. The increases forced the S&Ls and other thrift institutions to pay higher and higher rates to attract deposits. Meanwhile, most of the thrifts' investments were in the form of long-term real estate loans. Since the loans had been made before the interest rate run-up, the thrifts received much lower interest payments than those for more recent loans. The thrifts' income from these loans did not keep up with rising costs. Many of the savings institutions were either barely breaking even or losing money. In an effort to increase their profit margins (and knowing that insurance would protect their depositors from loss), the thrift institutions made many risky loans.

Through it all, the nation's depositors were not worried, since they had been told that federal deposit insurance guaranteed their savings accounts. What the public failed to understand, though, was that the funds held in deposit insurance reserves were limited. With losses running so high, neither the FDIC nor the FSLIC had enough in its reserves to guarantee the deposits of all the failed institutions. That left it to the federal government to come up with the billions of dollars needed to guarantee the threatened savings accounts. By 1995, this need amounted to about $200 billion. More than a thousand thrift institutions had to close or merge with one another.

As a first step toward resolving the crisis in the thrift industry, Congress enacted the **Financial Institutions Reform, Recovery, and Enforcement Act (FIRREA)** of 1989. The principal goals of the act were to (1) bolster the enforcement powers of the agencies that regulate thrift institutions and (2) strengthen the deposit insurance programs. In addition, the FSLIC was dismantled and replaced by the FDIC, which is now responsible for all deposit insurance programs.

Some critics of FIRREA complained that the law did not do enough to eliminate the sloppy banking practices that got the thrifts into financial trouble in the first place. Others argued that the real cause of the thrift crisis was deposit insurance. Deposit insurance, they explained, lulls depositors into accepting poor banking practices because savings are guaranteed. Moreover, the argument continued, when savings are insured, bankers are almost encouraged to engage in reckless ventures with their customers' money.

 # GRAMM-LEACH-BLILEY ACT OF 1999

With the enactment of the Glass-Steagall Act of 1933, the U.S. government prohibited banks, insurance companies, and securities brokerage firms from getting into one another's business. These restrictions were enacted because Congress blamed the Great Depression partly on collaboration among those institutions to promote overvalued securities and real estate. Photos of bread-lines peopled by those who had lost their life's savings in banks that had failed filled the newspapers. Glass-Steagall erected a kind of wall between banks, insurance companies, and brokerage firms. The law kept one type of business from doing the business of the other two types of businesses.

For decades, the strict separation of financial markets was maintained. Then with the introduction of computers, ATM machines, electronic funds transfers, and money market funds, the face of banking changed. Moreover, foreign banks with branches in the United States were free to offer their clients brokerage, insurance, and other financial services. This competition, it was argued, put U.S. banks at an unfair disadvantage. By the 1990s, the demand for lifting the Depression-era restrictions on banking and other financial services prompted Congress to enact the **Gramm-Leach-Bliley Act of 1999.**

The new law allowed banks, brokerages, and insurance companies to merge their activities. It enabled, for example, Citibank (a bank), the Travelers Group (insurance companies), and Salomon Smith Barney, Inc. (a securities broker-age house) to combine into a single new conglomerate known as Citigroup.

Critics of the law were quick to predict that dire consequences would follow the repeal of the 1999 act. "Why give banks and brokerage houses the opportunity to repeat the kinds of mistakes of the past that led to the Great Depression?" they asked.

The Gramm-Leach-Bliley Act has also been criticized for allowing financial corporations to exchange and sell personal, health, and financial information relating to their clients. For example, a financial supermarket like Citigroup can access its clients' health records through their Travelers Insurance subsidiary, its brokerage records through Salomon Smith Barney, and its banking information through Citibank.

In its defense, proponents of the Gramm-Leach-Bliley Act point out that the public's privacy is protected. They say this because the law requires that before personal information can be bought or sold, individuals need to be notified in writing about the corporation's "privacy policy" and the steps they can take to ensure this privacy. But, say critics, the notice is usually buried in such fine print that few, if any, clients ever read or acted on the information.

 ELECTRONIC MONEY

Every day, approximately $3 trillion changes hands in payment for the goods and services in the United States. That averages out to something around $16,000 per capita. While almost all of the transactions (97 percent) are paid for in cash or checks, the dollar value of those transactions represents only a tiny portion of the total (see Figure 16.3). That is, of the $3 trillion that changes hands daily, only $360 billion of those payments are made in cash or by check. The rest, $2,640 billion in payments, is made through electronic funds transfers.

Electronic funds transfer (EFT) refers to the transfer of funds between accounts via electronic data systems. Virtually any individual or entity (business firm, government agency, not-for-profit corporation, etc.) that has a financial account can send or receive funds through some form of EFT.

Millions of private employers and government agencies now use one or more EFT systems to transfer wages directly into the bank accounts of their employees. Employers like the system because it eliminates the need to produce and deliver paychecks or cash. Employees benefit because the possibility of theft or other loss (such as might happen after being paid by check or cash) are virtually eliminated.

EFT transactions can be in any one of a number of forms. Two of the most familiar are the bank card and the Automatic Clearing House (ACH) system.

1. Bank cards. Credit cards, debit cards, and automated teller machine (ATM) cards are all different types of *bank cards*. Bank cards are primarily used to facilitate retail sales.

● *Credit cards* entitle the holder to purchase goods and services and obtain cash up to a specified limit. Credit cards may be of two types: those issued

Figure 16.3 **How Goods and Services Are Paid for in the United States**

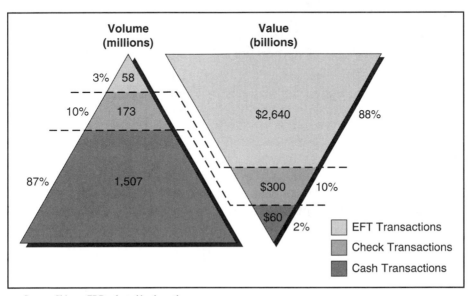

Source: Chicago FRB, adapted by the author.

by stores and other firms, and those issued by banks (like Visa and Master-Card). Credit cards and their use are discussed further on pages 248–249.

- *Debit cards* look like credit cards but function differently. While a credit card is a form of borrowing, a debit card is similar to paying with cash. Debit cards are used to take money out of one's checking or savings account at the time of a sale. Since money is withdrawn from your account, there are no interest charges. But you may make purchases only up to the amount available in your checking or savings account at the bank that issued you the debit card.

- *ATM cards* enable bank depositors to activate automated teller machines. These specialized computer terminals allow consumers to make cash deposits and withdrawals.

2. Automatic Clearing House (ACH). The ACH enables individuals and corporations to use their bank accounts to make direct payments and receive direct deposits.

- *Direct payments* enable consumers to pay their bills electronically. With direct payments, people authorize companies to deduct money from their checking or savings accounts. Typically these arrangements are made to pay recurring charges such as for telephone service and mortgage payments.

- *Direct deposits* enable employers to deposit wages into their employees bank accounts instead of distributing paper checks on payday.

Internet Banking

Some banks provide *Internet banking* services for their customers who have a personal computer. These customers are able to conduct much of their banking activities simply by connecting to the bank's Web site via the Internet.

For example, an Internet banking customer is able to access account information, pay bills, transfer funds, and find out if a check has cleared. Better still, he or she can do all these things and more from the comfort of home at any hour of the day or night. Before signing on for these services, however, customers should know that the Internet is a public network, and for that reason, some of the customers' personal information may be shared with other businesses. And it is possible that a hacker might get inside a bank's network and access customers' account information.

Maintaining a Checking Account

Many consumers continue to pay for their purchases with cash or its equivalent—checks. When paying for a purchase with a check, it is important to know how to properly write the check. Someday you may want to open a checking account, or you may already have one. The following explanations will help you to write and endorse checks, and to record transactions.

About Checks

A check is a written order directing a bank to pay a specified sum of money to a designated person or institution. The person making the demand has money deposited in the bank with the understanding that the bank will follow his or her orders.

There are three parties to a check: (1) the person writing the check, or *drawer;* (2) the bank on which the check is drawn, or *drawee;* and (3) the person to whom the check is payable, or *payee.*

Maureen Kane purchased a pair of in-line skates from Mort's Sports, Inc. She paid for the purchase by check, as illustrated in Figure 16.4.

About Endorsements

Endorsements pass title to a check on to another party. Mort's Sports will deposit Ms. Kane's check in Mort's Sports's bank account after endorsing it on the reverse side, as indicated in Figure 16.5.

(continued on next page)

Figure 16.4 **A Typical Check**

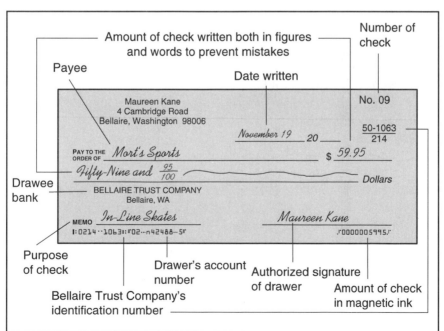

Figure 16.5 **Restrictive Endorsement**

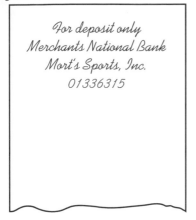

For deposit only
Merchants National Bank
Mort's Sports, Inc.
01336315

In addition to transferring ownership, an endorser guarantees that he or she will make good on a check if there is something wrong with it.

Endorsements can be made in a variety of ways. Figure 16.5 illustrates a *restrictive endorsement.* Such endorsements describe how the funds are to be used. In this instance, Mort's Sports has passed title to the check on to its bank with the understanding that the funds will be deposited in its account.

In Figure 16.6, Maureen Kane has simply signed her name on the reverse of a check written to her. This action is known as a *blank endorsement.* Such an endorsement transfers title to a check to anyone holding the check.

In Figure 16.7, Maureen has used a *full endorsement* to transfer a check made out in her name to her brother Arlo. Such an endorsement transfers title to a check to a specific party.

Keeping Records

One needs to know the amount of money in one's account before writing a check. Banks do not normally honor a check unless there are sufficient funds to cover it. For that reason, people with checking accounts need to maintain accurate records of both the deposits they make and the checks they write.

Banks simplify the task of record keeping for checking accounts by providing their depositors with a *check register.* Figure 16.8 illustrates how Maureen Kane recorded transactions in her checking account.

Figure 16.6 **Blank Endorsement**

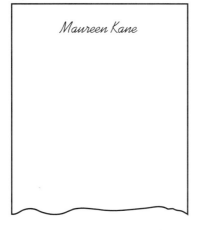

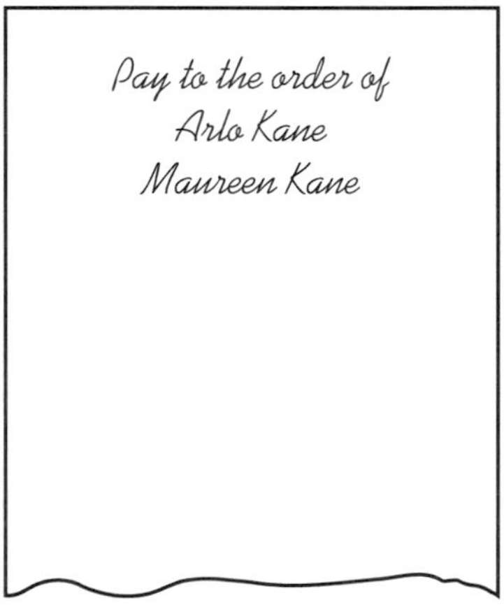

Maureen Kane

Figure 16.7 **Full Endorsement**

Pay to the order of
Arlo Kane
Maureen Kane

Figure 16.8 **Check Register**

No.	Date	Issued to or Description of Deposit	Amount of Check				Amount of Deposit		Balance Forward 672	31
108	11/17	To Myra Maple	25	15					− 25	15
									647	16
	11/18	Deposit Paycheck					358	49	+358	49
									1,005	65
109	11/19	To Mort's Sports	59	95					− 59	95
									945	70
110	11/20	To CASH	98	36					− 98	36
									847	34

S U M M A R Y

The origins of banking can be traced back to ancient times. Certain individuals or families accepted money for safekeeping, made loans, charged interest, and exchanged foreign and local coins. Commercial banks today make loans and provide checking accounts to both businesses and individuals. Moreover, they offer many other services to their customers, including savings accounts and safe-deposit boxes.

Thrift institutions include savings and loan associations, mutual savings banks, and credit unions. The thrifts offer to individuals many of the same financial services offered by commercial banks, but they are mainly depositories for savings and a place for individuals to obtain home mortgages and other loans. Unlike commercial banks, they do not offer services to businesses.

Banks earn money by making loans. When a bank grants a loan, the loan fund is deposited in a checking account. Since checking accounts are a form of money, the loan adds to the nation's money supply. The amount of money that an individual bank can create is limited by its deposits and the amount the bank must keep in reserves (the reserve ratio). The higher the reserve ratio, the less money the bank can create.

Bank failures during the Great Depression of the 1930s led to the creation of two federal agencies to insure deposits—the FDIC and the FSLIC. In 1989, Congress strengthened the deposit insurance system and dismantled the FSLIC, making the FDIC responsible for all federal deposit insurance programs.

REVIEWING THE CHAPTER

BUILDING VOCABULARY

Match each item in Column A with its definition in Column B.

Column A

1. blank endorsement
2. commercial bank
3. savings and loan association
4. restrictive endorsement
5. electronic funds transfer
6. direct deposit
7. cash in vault
8. reserve ratio
9. mutual savings bank
10. drawee

Column B

a. a check endorsement that restricts how funds are to be used
b. a savings institution owned by depositors
c. the percentage of deposits a bank is required by law to hold to meet withdrawal demands
d. the bank on which a check is drawn
e. money that a bank has on hand to use
f. a business that provides both individuals and business firms with checking accounts and loans
g. an arrangement whereby a paycheck or other regular source of income is automatically put into one's checking account
h. a business that mainly provides home mortgages
i. the movement of money electronically
j. a check endorsement that transfers title to anyone holding the check

UNDERSTANDING WHAT YOU HAVE READ

1. Which *one* of the following is not classified as a thrift institution? (*a*) commercial bank (*b*) credit union (*c*) mutual savings bank (*d*) savings and loan association.

2. The principal characteristic of a commercial bank is that it (*a*) lends money for home mortgages (*b*) provides businesses with checking accounts and loans (*c*) sells traveler's checks (*d*) sells stocks and bonds.

3. The major source of income for banks is (*a*) service fees charged on their deposit accounts (*b*) fees from the sale of government bonds (*c*) income from services such as safe-deposit boxes, life insurance, and notary fees (*d*) interest earned on their loans.

4. The section of a balance sheet in which a bank's deposits are summarized is the (*a*) capital stock (*b*) assets (*c*) liabilities (*d*) net worth.

5. Lila Gallo borrowed $10,000 from her bank to build up the inventory of her stationery store. The loan was payable in six months at 12 percent interest per year, which the bank deducted in advance. How much money did Lila actually receive? (*a*) $10,000 (*b*) $8,800 (*c*) $9,400 (*d*) $9,600.

6. Most bank reserves are kept in (*a*) the vaults of other banks where they can earn interest (*b*) a Federal Reserve bank (*c*) miscellaneous investments so as to earn income (*d*) very safe, long-term government bonds.

7. With a reserve ratio of 25 percent and deposits of $4 million, what is the total amount of money that a commercial bank is permitted to lend? (*a*) $3 million (*b*) $8 million (*c*) $1.6 million (*d*) $1 million.

8. The Federal Deposit Insurance Corporation guarantees (*a*) all funds deposited in all financial institutions (*b*) funds deposited in commercial banks only (*c*) funds of any depositor who buys a special insurance policy (*d*) deposits of up to $100,000 in all banks and thrift institutions in the United States.

9. Which *one* of the following statements about bank loans is true? (*a*) Most are offered without cost to bank customers. (*b*) They add to the nation's money supply. (*c*) Banks try to lend as little money as possible, because in doing so, they reduce their reserves. (*d*) Loans are usually the least important part of a bank's business.

10. In terms of dollar value, most payments in the United States are made with (*a*) cash (*b*) checks (*c*) electronic funds transfers (*d*) currency.

THINKING CRITICALLY

1. The origins of banks and banking can be traced way back in history.
   a. Describe *three* functions of a modern bank that can be traced back to activities performed by individuals and families in ancient civilizations.
   b. Describe *three* major practices developed by London goldsmiths that have been incorporated into modern banking.

2. Briefly describe the *three* types of thrift institutions.

3. Suppose that banks were required to keep 100 percent of their deposits on reserve. How would banking differ from the way it is currently practiced in the United States?

4. The expansion of bank loans affects the nation's money supply.
   a. Explain how a bank loan creates money.
   b. Explain why the amount of money that an individual bank can create is limited by its deposits and the reserve ratio.
   c. Explain, with reference to Table 16.2, how it is possible for the banking system as a whole to expand money by several times the amount of excess reserves in the system.

SKILLS: Analyzing a Balance Sheet

The balance sheet of the Third National Bank for December 31 is summarized in Table 16.3 on page 380. (*a*) Explain the meaning of each of the balance sheet entries (numbered 1–8). (*b*) In the week after December 31, cash deposits that were kept on hand increased by $10 million. In addition, the bank increased its loans by $7 million, all of which was credited to deposit accounts. Create a new balance sheet that shows the changes that took place as a result of these transactions.

▷ **TABLE 16.3   BALANCE SHEET, THIRD NATIONAL BANK
                 DECEMBER 31, 200–**

Assets		Liabilities and Net Worth	
(1) Cash in vault	$ 7,500,000	(6) Deposits	$24,000,000
(2) Reserves	12,500,000	(7) Capital stock	5,500,000
(3) Loans	9,750,000	(8) Surplus and profits	10,000,000
(4) Securities	8,500,000	**Total**	**$39,500,000**
(5) Other assets	1,250,000		
Total	**$39,500,000**		

READING FOR ENRICHMENT

We have seen that corporations seeking to raise money through the sale of stock often do so through the services of an investment bank (discussed in Chapter 5, page 100). Investment banks underwrite the entire issue of stocks and resell the stocks to the general public at a higher price. After this initial public offering, brokerage firms handle all further purchases and sales of stocks and bonds.

Prior to 1999, federal law prohibited brokerage houses and banks from acting as investment bankers. This policy ended with the enactment of the Gramm-Leach-Bliley Act. One of the brokerage houses entering into investment banking at the time was the nation's largest, Merrill Lynch.

Over the next several years, problems developed for the new investment banks/brokerage houses. In 2002, the Attorney General of New York State accused several firms of deceiving their customers into purchasing stocks the brokerage houses knew to be overvalued. Merrill Lynch was one of the firms accused and was fined $100 million. As revealed in thousands of pages of documents, Merrill stock analysts were expected to give positive recommendations for companies whose business its investment banking division was seeking. One of the most revealing aspects of the case was a series of interoffice e-mail letters in which Merrill analysts described the stocks the company was publicly recommending as "junk," "disaster," and worse.

In the aftermath of the scandal, some called for the abolition of the Gramm-Leach-Bliley Act and the restoration of the kinds of regulations that had existed before 1999 under the Glass-Steagall Act. Others defended the rules under the Gramm-Leach-Bliley Act, saying that the fact that Merrill Lynch had been so heavily fined proved that the problem was not with the law but with the actions of individuals. Moreover, they went on, times had changed so much since the 1930s (when Glass-Steagall had been enacted) that there was no way the nation could go back to the rules then in place.

1. Explain the argument advanced by those calling for a "restoration of Glass-Steagall."

2. Identify and explain *two* of the changes in banking and brokerage that led Congress to replace Glass-Steagall with Gramm-Leach-Bliley.

3. In your opinion, should investment banking, commercial banking, and securities brokerage be legally separated? Briefly explain your answer.

CHAPTER 17

The Federal Reserve System

OVERVIEW

Bankers assume that on most days deposits will more than offset withdrawals. That being the case, banks need to set aside only a portion of their deposits to satisfy withdrawal demands. Banks are free to use the rest of the deposits to make investments and loans. On the rare occasions when withdrawals exceed deposits and vault cash begins to run low, banks can replenish supplies by drawing upon their reserves at their Federal Reserve District Bank. Although the banking system works well enough today, it did not in the years before 1913. That was the year Congress created the Federal Reserve System.

In this chapter, we will discuss the role of the Federal Reserve System in our economy. We will also discuss these questions:

- Why did U.S. leaders decide that there was a need for the Federal Reserve System?

- How is the Federal Reserve System organized?

- What does the Federal Reserve System do?

 HISTORICAL BACKGROUND

The chief weakness of the banking system in the United States prior to 1913 was the lack of a central bank. A *central bank* is a national institution that has the responsibility for (1) supervising every other bank in the country, (2) controlling the volume of bank credit, and (3) regulating the money supply. A central bank deals mainly with other banks and the national government rather

Before the creation of the National Banking System, state banknotes such as this one were common.

than with the general public. That is why central banks are referred to as "bankers' banks."

Before 1913, the United States lacked a central bank but had a *National Banking System*. This was a system of federally chartered banks (still not quite a central bank) authorized to issue notes backed by U.S. government bonds. It was created by Congress in the **National Bank Act** of 1863.

Federally chartered banks were allowed to issue national banknotes worth up to 90 percent (later changed to 100 percent) of the amount of government bonds they held. Each federally chartered bank was required to redeem its own notes in gold or silver. These notes were uniform in design, and they were sound because they were backed by government bonds. By the end of the Civil War, in 1865, state banknotes were no longer in circulation. The United States had, for the first time, a uniform currency.

Weaknesses of the National Banking System

Despite the new system, in the years following the Civil War the nation experienced a number of financial panics (in 1873, 1884, 1893, 1903, and 1907). Many people blamed the national banking system for these panics. They pointed to the following *four* weaknesses in the system.

INFLEXIBILITY OF BANK CREDIT.   Banks could lend only up to the limit permitted by their reserves. Once that limit was reached, new lending stopped. There was no central agency to help banks that needed more cash to lend or to provide additional reserves. Thus, credit became tight.

INELASTIC MONEY SUPPLY.   The amount of national banknotes was relatively fixed. The National Banking Act provided no mechanism for increasing the money supply when more money was needed or reducing the money supply when less money was needed.

INEFFICIENT SYSTEM OF CLEARING AND COLLECTING CHECKS. Clearing checks under the National Banking System was inefficient and slow. It often took weeks to clear checks drawn against out-of-town banks. A check *clears* when payment is made to the final recipient of the check and the check is deducted from the account of the person who wrote the check. (In the last chapter, we discussed how this process of clearing checks may now be completed much more quickly.)

THE UNCONTROLLED SYSTEM OF REDEPOSITED RESERVES. Before 1913, it was the custom for small-town and rural banks around the country to deposit their reserves in big city banks that offered high interest rates. Naturally, the big-city banks used the deposits of the other banks to extend loans.

Problems arose during hard times when business activity declined. With their profits falling, business firms around the country withdrew their funds from local banks to meet expenses. Other business firms, unable to repay their bank loans, were forced into bankruptcy. As word spread about the heavy withdrawals and business failures, nervous depositors lined up to withdraw their savings. This compelled the smaller banks to call on the city banks to return some or all of their reserves.

The city banks, though, were soon in much the same fix as the country banks. Whenever bank depositors believe that their bank is unable to convert their deposits into cash, there can be so many withdrawals that the bank's cash reserves are depleted. Large withdrawals by many depositors at the same time is called a *run on a bank*. During a run, the bank might refuse to pay out currency. This happened in 1907 as many banks suspended payments and then collapsed. Historians refer to this breakdown of the banking system as the **Panic of 1907**. As banks suspended payments, various substitutes for currency came into use and, in fact, many people had to resort to barter to acquire the things that they needed.

In the wake of this panic, Congress began an investigation of the U.S. banking system. Its study concluded that to avoid future panics, the country needed (1) an elastic currency and (2) a central bank.

An *elastic currency* is one that expands and contracts with the needs of business. For example, suppose that Sally Jones needs money to meet the operating expenses of her furniture store in Texas. Jones goes to her bank—the National Bank of Amarillo—for a loan and receives cash. Jones's bank sends the promissory note that Jones signed to a central bank. The central bank accepts the note (for a fee) and gives the National Bank of Amarillo cash. When Jones repays her loan to the National Bank of Amarillo, this bank (1) returns the currency to the central bank and (2) buys back Jones's promissory note. Thus, cash is available when it is needed by business (when Jones receives cash) and withdrawn when it is no longer needed (when Jones returns the cash).

The congressional study of 1907 found that nearly all countries that had an elastic currency also had some form of central banking. Created by a federal government, a central bank (1) provides banking services to the government and to private banks, (2) supervises private banks, and (3) coordinates the nation's supply of money and credit. Although other major nations had long recognized its advantages, the United States was without a central bank from 1836 until 1913.

 ORGANIZATION OF THE FEDERAL RESERVE SYSTEM

Congress created the Federal Reserve System with the enactment of the **Federal Reserve Act** of 1913. Commonly known as the **Fed**, the **Federal Reserve System** functions as this nation's central bank. The Fed is composed of a Board of Governors located in Washington, D.C., and 12 Federal Reserve District Reserve Banks, each serving a different geographic region. Congress chose a decentralized system that was unlike the central banks set up in other countries because it wanted to (1) avoid placing too much power in the hands of a single bank and (2) meet the special needs of the regions.

Each District Reserve Bank is owned by the member banks in its district. All of the member banks are required to purchase the stock of its District Reserve Bank. Control of the Federal Reserve System remains, however, in the hands of the federal government. The district banks earn a profit every year. They do this because they acquire, in the course of their operations, large quantities of income-producing government securities.

The organization of the Federal Reserve System can be compared to a pyramid (see Figure 17.1). At its highest point is the seven-member Board of Governors. Below this board are the 12 Federal Reserve District Banks and their 25 branches. At the base stand the approximately 20,000 depository institutions that make up the bulk of the system.

The Board of Governors

The **Board of Governors** supervises the many activities of the Federal Reserve System. In addition, the board establishes and oversees the nation's *monetary policies*—that is, the Fed's programs to regulate the country's supply of money and credit. The seven members of the Board of Governors are appointed by the president of the United States, subject to the consent of the Senate. The term of their appointment is 14 years. The chairperson of the board is appointed from among the members by the president for a four-year term.

Figure 17.1 **Structure of the Federal Reserve System**

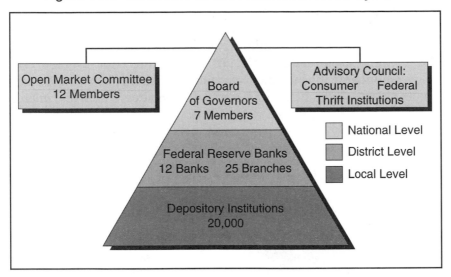

💢 The District Reserve Banks

The 12 District Reserve Banks are "bankers' banks" in that they are primarily concerned with servicing the member banks within their districts. All but two of the District Banks maintain branches, each of which meets the needs of member banks in its particular part of a district.

💢 Depository Institutions

Businesses that hold deposits are known as *depository institutions*. Approximately 20,000 in number, these include commercial banks, savings and loan associations, mutual savings banks, and credit unions. Depository institutions are an integral part of the nation's monetary system. Their activities can result in an expansion or a contraction of the money supply. For that reason, depository institutions are subject to federal regulations by the Fed and other government agencies.

💢 The Federal Open Market Committee

The **Federal Open Market Committee (FOMC)** is the most important policy-making group of the Fed. It directs the purchase and sale of government securities, thereby affecting the nation's supply of money and credit. Members of the Open Market Committee include the seven members of the Board of Governors and five of the twelve District Reserve Bank presidents.

Other Committees

With so many complex responsibilities, the Federal Reserve looks to a number of other committees to undertake major tasks. Among these is the **Federal Advisory Council**, a 12-member committee of bankers that meets several times a year to advise the Board of Governors on matters of current interest.

FUNCTIONS OF THE FEDERAL RESERVE SYSTEM

The Federal Reserve System has several key functions.

The Fed Supervises Individual Banks

Every day somewhere in the United States, one or more Federal Reserve examiners are going over the books or examining the procedures of a local bank. The examiners visit local banks to ensure that the banks conduct their business in a safe and legal manner. The Fed also supervises banks to ensure that consumers are treated fairly when they borrow money from the banks. The Fed oversees the nation's banking system in the following ways.

DISTRICT BANKS HOLD THE NATION'S RESERVE.   In the last chapter, we discussed how banks are required by law to keep a percentage of their deposits in reserves. The percentage of deposits a bank is required to keep in reserves is called the reserve ratio. Banks hold their required reserves either as cash in their vaults or as deposits in the Federal Reserve Bank in their district. If withdrawal demands are more than what a bank's reserves can handle, the bank can borrow additional funds from their District Reserve Bank.

SUPPLIES THE NATION'S CURRENCY AND COIN.   All new money printed or minted by the U.S. Treasury is put into circulation by the Federal Reserve System. The paper currency issued by the Fed consists of Federal Reserve notes. The public's need for money changes from day to day. More cash is needed during the days before holidays and weekends (and during the summer) than at other times.

The Fed introduces paper currency and coin to the public through the banking system. Banks maintain accounts at the Federal Reserve Bank in their district. As supplies of currency and coin run low, local banks order additional amounts from their District Bank. After a holiday, local business firms deposit excess cash in local banks. As local banks deposit the excess funds to their

Figure 17.2 **Districts of the Federal Reserve System**

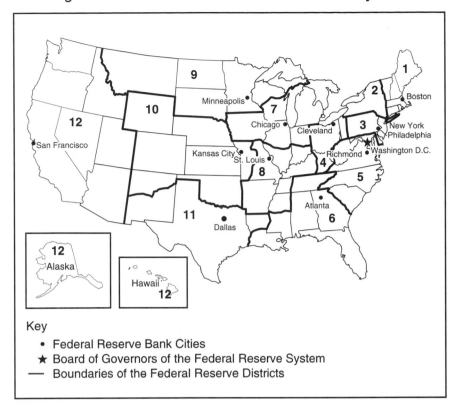

What is the number of the Federal Reserve District in which you live?

accounts at their District Bank, the cash finds its way back to the Federal Reserve System.

In the above example, we see how the Federal Reserve System provides an elastic currency, that is, one that expands and contracts with the needs of business. Currency that is made available for a holiday season is withdrawn when the currency is no longer needed.

THE FEDERAL RESERVE SYSTEM CLEARS CHECKS. The volume of checks written annually in this country has run to something like $74 trillion. Nearly all of these are submitted to the District Reserve Banks for clearance and collection. The following describes the system for check clearance used during most of the 20th century.

> Suppose that Brown gives Jones a check for $100 drawn on the First National Bank of Middletown, New York, in which Brown has an account. Jones deposits the check in the People's National Bank of Newburgh, New York, which is located in the same Federal Reserve district as Middletown. Jones's account is credited with $100.

At this point, we see that the People's National Bank of Newburgh has given Jones $100 in exchange for a check. It now wants to get its money back by presenting the check to the First National Bank of Middletown for payment. This could be accomplished by mailing the check to Middletown. However, this would hardly be a practical procedure since the First National Bank probably receives hundreds or thousands of checks from dozens of banks on any business day. The paperwork involved in settling with each bank individually would be staggering. Instead the bank sends the check to the clearinghouse at the Federal Reserve Bank in its district. Here the account of the People's National Bank of Newburgh is credited with $100, and the amount is deducted from the account of the Middletown bank. The check is then forwarded to Middletown, where the bank deducts the sum from Brown's account and sends Brown the canceled check.

ELECTRONIC FUNDS TRANSFER. The process just described worked fine for many years. Now, however, with billions of checks going through the system every year, the Fed uses an electronic system, the Automatic Clearing House facilities (described in Chapter 16, page 374).

The Board of Governors meets in this building in Washington, D.C.

The Fed Is a Banker for the U.S. Government

The Fed maintains the world's largest bank account—that of the federal government. Virtually all government checks are drawn on accounts maintained by the government at the District Reserve Banks. Similarly, most tax receipts are deposited into those accounts. The District Banks also sell and redeem government securities such as Treasury bills and U.S. savings bonds.

MONETARY POLICY AND THE FED

Since the price level (P) is determined by the amount of money (M) and the quantity of goods (Q), it follows that increasing or decreasing M or Q will affect prices. But the decision to produce goods and services in the U.S. economy is mostly in private hands. For that reason, government efforts to influence the economy usually focus on the money supply. By way of achieving its goals, the Federal Reserve System has a number of "tools" it can apply to regulate the supply of money and credit. These tools are (1) the reserve ratio, (2) the discount rate, and (3) open market operations.

Reserve Ratio

The business of banking involves the receiving of deposits and using those funds for investments and loans. We know, however, that banks must keep a portion of their depositors' funds on hand as reserves to meet their withdrawal demands. Bank reserves are held in accounts at the local District Reserve bank. Required reserves are expressed as a percentage of a bank's deposits that is known as the reserve ratio (first discussed in Chapter 16). Amounts over those minimums are known as excess reserves.

Reserve ratios are established by the Board of Governors of the Federal Reserve System. When the Board increases the reserve ratio, a bank's ability to lend is decreased because the bank must keep a larger share of deposits on hand. When the reserve ratio is reduced, the bank's ability to lend is increased. For example, with $100 million in deposits and a reserve ratio of 15 percent, the Second National Bank will be free to lend up to $85 million (100 percent − 15 percent = 85 percent or .85. Therefore, $100 million × .85 = $85 million). The remaining $15 million will be held on reserve in its account at a District Federal Reserve Bank, or in its own vaults. Now assume that the Fed increases the reserve ratio to 20 percent. Second National will then have to limit its loans to $80 million (80 percent of $100 million), thereby reducing its lending ability by $5 million.

The Equation of Exchange

There are times when the economy as a whole could benefit from an increase in the money supply. There are also times when less money and credit are needed. The relationship between the money supply and prices is summarized in the *equation of exchange.* An understanding of the principles contained in the equation will help you understand what the Fed is trying to achieve when it moves to increase or decrease the money supply. The equation is written as

$$MV = PQ$$

where M = money supply
V = velocity
P = average price paid for goods and services
Q = quantity of goods and services produced

The equation of exchange simply states that the total amount of money spent to buy the GDP is equal to the total amount received by sellers. That $5 bill you use to rent a video is given in change to another customer, who uses it to buy groceries. In similar fashion, the $5 continues to duck in and out of circulation, and by year's end, the $5 has changed hands 100 times. To find the total spending by all Americans over a year, multiply the money supply (M) by the number of times those funds were spent (V). As for the economy as a whole, total spending is equal to MV.

The dollar value of the goods and services purchased in the economy in a year is equal to the number of goods and services produced by the economy (Q) multiplied by the average price (P) paid for these goods and services. But the dollar value of all the goods and services produced by the economy in the course of the year is the gross domestic product (GDP). Therefore, PQ is the same thing as GDP, or $PQ = GDP.$

We can write the equation of exchange ($MV = PQ$) in terms of price: $P = MV \div Q.$ (We arrive at this new formula by dividing both sides of the original equation by Q.) The new formula tells us that the average price is equal to the money supply (M) multiplied by the *velocity* (V—number of times those funds were spent), divided by the number of goods and services produced in the country (Q).

By applying the formula P (in millions of dollars) = MV ÷ Q, you can predict what will happen to average prices when (1) the supply of goods and services changes and (2) the money supply changes. Now test yourself by answering the following questions. (Assume that velocity remains the same.)

1. What is the average price when $M =$ $1 million; $V = 10$; and $Q = 100,000$?

2. What happens to the average price when Q doubles? When Q declines by half?

3. What will happen to the average price if the money supply is increased from $1 million to $2 million? If the money supply is decreased to $500,000?

4. Since the Fed controls the nation's money supply, how can it apply those powers to affect average prices in the U.S. economy?

The effect of a change in reserve requirements is magnified as deposits travel through the banking system. In Chapter 15, we saw how a reserve ratio of 20 percent enabled a deposit of $10,000 to expand to $50,000 as it traveled through the banking system. We also noted that if the required reserve ratio was increased to 25 percent, a $10,000 deposit could be expanded to only $40,000.

The impact of changes in the required reserve ratio is reflected in the *deposit multiplier*. It tells the number of times deposits can be increased by the banking system for every dollar in reserves. The deposit multiplier is equal to 100 divided by the reserve ratio. For example, with a reserve ratio of 25 percent, the deposit multiplier is 4 (because $100 \div 25 = 4$). A new deposit of $1 million could potentially add $4 million to bank deposits and the money supply. Now suppose that the reserve ratio were reduced to 10 percent. The deposit multiplier would then go up to 10 ($100 \div 10 = 10$) and a new deposit of $1 million could add as much as $10 million to bank deposits and to the money supply.

The Fed can use its power to establish reserve ratios to increase or decrease the money supply. By increasing required reserves, the ability of banks to lend money is reduced, thereby reducing the money supply. When the reserve ratio is decreased, the opposite occurs.

⚡ The Discount Rate

When their reserves run low, member banks can replenish them with loans from their District Federal Reserve Bank. At one time, the interest on these loans was *discounted* (deducted in advance). Although loans are no longer discounted, the interest charged by District Banks on loans to member banks is still referred to as the *discount rate*. This rate is determined by the Fed.

Like any business, banks must make a profit in order to survive. For that reason, they need to charge more for the money they lend to their customers

Alan Greenspan is the Chair of the Federal Reserve's Board of Governors. What is the cartoonist saying about him?

M. Thompson/Rothco.

than those funds cost to borrow from the Fed. The discount rate that banks pay to the Fed is reflected in the interest rate that banks charge their customers. Thus, if the discount rate is 5 percent, a bank might charge its customers 5¼ percent. If the discount rate were to increase to 5¼ percent, the banks might charge their customers 5½ percent.

Since banks and other lenders adjust their loan rates to meet changes in the discount rate, the Fed can regulate the economy by making changes in the discount rate. For example, if the Fed wants to increase the money supply, it can do so by reducing the discount rate. Similarly, by increasing the discount rate the Fed can reduce the supply of money and credit.

💷 Open Market Operations

We have seen that the principal business of banks is to put to use the funds they receive from depositors and other customers in loans or other financial activities. We have also noted that the ability of banks to invest is limited by the need to hold a portion of their deposits on reserve to meet the needs of their customers. How much must be held in reserve is determined by the reserve ratio as established by the Federal Reserve System.

The most important of the Fed's monetary tools are *open market operations.* These operations involve buying and selling short-term government securities by the Federal Open Market Committee. Its goal is to raise or lower short-term interest rates.

- When the Fed *buys* securities, its payments are usually deposited in the sellers' bank accounts. This action increases bank reserves, thereby making more money available for the bank to loan. The Fed gets individuals and institutions to sell securities to it by offering whatever price is necessary to convince holders of securities to sell.

- When the Fed *sells* securities, the payments it receives reduce the balances in the buyers' accounts. This action reduces bank reserves, thereby decreasing the amount of money the banks can loan. The Fed gets individuals and institutions to buy securities by lowering the asking price of the securities it wants to sell so as to make these securities attractive to buyers.

We know that the lending power of banks is limited by the requirement that they maintain adequate reserves. When reserves are reduced, the lending power of banks is reduced. When they increase, the opposite occurs. Therefore, when the Board of Governors decides that it is time to increase the money supply, it may do so by ordering the FOMC to buy securities in the open market. When the Fed decides that it is time to reduce the money supply, it can do so by ordering the Open Market Committee to sell securities.

Like changes in the reserve ratio, the effect of open market operations is magnified by the deposit multiplier. (The deposit multiplier, you may recall from page 391, is equal to 100 divided by the reserve ratio.) For example, with a reserve ratio of 20 percent, the deposit multiplier is 5 (because $100 \div 20 = 5$). In those circumstances, the purchase of $100 million in government securities by the Open Market Committee could add as much as $500 million to the money supply.

For similar reasons, the sale of securities by the FOMC has the opposite effect on the money supply. The sale can shrink bank deposits and reduce the money supply by the deposit multiplier.

We will learn more about open market operations and monetary policy in Chapter 19.

S U M M A R Y

The Federal Reserve System is the central bank of the United States. Established in 1913, the Fed regulates the banking system, provides for an elastic currency, manages the nation's money supply, and protects its financial system.

The Federal Reserve System consists of 12 District Banks, each one in a different part of the country. A seven-member Board of Governors supervises the 12 Federal Reserve District Banks, which in turn supervise the nation's depository institutions. The Federal Reserve System serves as the central bank of the country. The Fed issues paper currency (Federal Reserve notes) and places into circulation all new money printed or minted by the U.S. Treasury. Member banks maintain accounts at their district bank. They can withdraw cash from their accounts as needed and return cash to the accounts when the funds are no longer needed.

Of all its functions, however, the Fed's ability to regulate the supply of money and credit—known as its monetary policy—is its most important. It derives this power from its power to set reserve requirements and the discount rate and conduct open market operations. How the Fed applies monetary policy in the pursuit of full employment and stable prices will be described in Chapter 19.

REVIEWING THE CHAPTER

BUILDING VOCABULARY

Match each item in Column A with its definition in Column B.

Column A

1. run on a bank
2. elastic currency
3. monetary policy
4. equation of exchange
5. depository institutions
6. discount rate
7. central bank
8. open market operations
9. deposit multiplier
10. clearing of checks

Column B

a. the process whereby a bank deducts the amount of a check from the account of the person who wrote it
b. the Fed's programs to regulate the country's supply of money and credit
c. the number of times deposits can be increased by the banking system
d. large withdrawals by many depositors at the same time
e. the interest rate the Fed charges member banks
f. a national institution that supervises other banks in a country
g. currency that increases or decreases in response to needs of business
h. banks, savings and loan associations, and credit unions
i. $MV = PQ$, where M equals the money supply, V equals velocity, P equals the average price paid, and Q equals the quantity of goods and services produced
j. the buying and selling of government bonds by the Fed

UNDERSTANDING WHAT YOU HAVE READ

1. Central banks are "bankers' banks" because they (*a*) deal mainly with banks and the national government (*b*) are located in large cities (*c*) deal primarily with the general public (*d*) are chartered by the states.

2. The Federal Reserve System was created in (*a*) 1789 (*b*) 1836 (*c*) 1863 (*d*) 1913.

3. Where are bank reserves kept? (*a*) entirely in the bank vault (*b*) partly in their own vault and the remainder at any other larger bank (*c*) entirely in a central bank (*d*) partly as cash-in-vault and the remainder at their Federal Reserve District Bank.

4. When output (*Q*) cannot be increased, an increase in the money supply (*M*) will result in (*a*) decreased output (*b*) lower prices (*c*) higher prices (*d*) greater price stability.

5. Which *one* of the following determines the maximum amount of money a commercial bank can lend? The amount that the bank has on hand of (*a*) reserves (*b*) Treasury bonds and notes (*c*) cash in its vault (*d*) gold and silver.

6. The Federal Reserve System acts as a fiscal agent for the U.S. government by (*a*) supervising the collection of income taxes (*b*) maintaining a part ownership in all the nation's commercial banks (*c*) receiving deposits and making payments on the government's behalf (*d*) printing all the nation's paper money.

7. Monetary policy refers to the Federal Reserve System's power to (*a*) provide currency to commercial banks (*b*) supervise the practices of the member banks (*c*) regulate the nation's supply of money and credit (*d*) clear checks.

8. When commercial banks expand the value of the loans they make, the effect on the economy is (*a*) a reduction in the money supply (*b*) an increase in the money supply (*c*) an increase in interest rates (*d*) a lowering of bank reserves.

9. All of the following are used by the Fed to expand or contract the country's money supply, *except* (*a*) open market operations (*b*) raising or lowering the discount rate (*c*) increasing or lowering the reserve ratio (*d*) raising or lowering taxes.

10. Federal Reserve notes are (*a*) interest-bearing securities (*b*) redeemable upon demand in gold (*c*) paper currency issued by the Fed (*d*) manufactured with an elastic consistency.

THINKING CRITICALLY

1. Explain why the National Banking System was unable to respond to the public demand for currency and credit during the Panic of 1907.

2. The amount of money that individuals and business firms can spend depends in part on how much they can borrow.

   a. How does availability of credit affect business activity?

   b. When would the economy as a whole benefit from an increase in the supply of money and credit?

   c. When would the economy as a whole benefit from less money and credit?

3. The Federal Reserve System controls the supply of money and credit in the U.S. economy. Explain how each of the following actions taken by the Fed will affect the supply of money and credit.

   a. lowering reserve requirements of member banks

   b. raising the discount rate

   c. buying securities in the open market.

4. "Bank reserve requirements affect the size of the nation's money supply."

   a. Prove this statement by showing the effect on the money supply of an increase in the reserve ratio from 10 percent to 20.

   b. Describe the effect on the money supply if a person withdrew $100,000 from a commercial bank account and buried it in his or her backyard. For purpose of illustration, assume a reserve ratio of 25 percent.

SKILLS: Working With the Reserve Ratio and the Deposit Multiplier

1. Complete the table below by filling in the missing data. Note that the deposit multiplier is equal to 100 divided by the reserve ratio. The maximum expansion of the original deposit is equal to the deposit multiplier multiplied by the amount of the excess reserves in bank.

2. Using data in the table, explain what action you would recommend to the Fed if you wanted it to (*a*) expand bank deposits (*b*) reduce bank deposits.

3. Explain why an increase in bank deposits increases the money supply, while a decrease in bank deposits reduces the money supply.

4. What conclusions can you infer from your answer to question 2 concerning the relation between the reserve ratio set by the Fed and the supply of money in the U.S. economy?

Reserve Ratio (Percent)	Deposit Multiplier	x	Excess Reserves in Bank	=	Maximum Expansion of Deposits
10	$100 \div 10 = 10$		10 × $ 100,000	=	$1,000,000
10			$1,000,000	=	
12.5			$ 100,000	=	
20			$ 100,000	=	
			$ 100,000	=	$ 100,000
25				=	$4,000,000

USING THE INTERNET

To learn more about the functions and structure of the Federal Reserve Board, visit one of the following Web sites.

- <<www.rich.frb.org/pubs/frtoday/structure.htm>>
- <<www.federalreserveeducation.org>>
- <<www.ny.fed.org>>
- <<www.frbatlanta.org>>
- <<www.bos.frb.org>>
- <<www.chicagofed.org>>
- <<www.federalreserve.gov>>

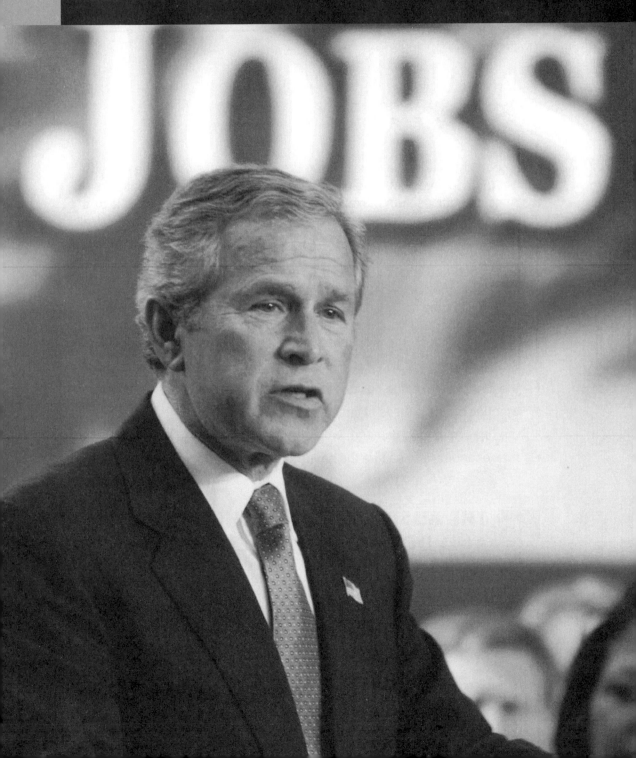

UNIT VII

MANAGING THE ECONOMY

CHAPTER 18
Our Fluctuating Economy

OVERVIEW

Both good times and bad have marked the economic history of the United States. In good times, jobs are plentiful, stores are busy, and the nation's factories and offices hum with activity. In bad times, just the opposite is true. Jobs are scarce, business is slow, and machines stand idle. The rise and fall of prices, production, consumption, employment, and investment is called the *business cycle.* Fluctuations in economic activity are not new. Economists have long debated what to do about them. Some believe that the economic fluctuations in the business cycle are governed by automatic forces with which government should not tamper. Other economists believe that intelligent government efforts to control economic fluctuations are both possible and desirable. After reading this chapter, you will understand why economic fluctuations occur. You will be able to explain each of the following:

- the four phases of the business cycle
- theories on the causes of business cycles
- the relation among demand, employment, and prices
- how economists measure the nation's economic performance.

THE BUSINESS CYCLE: THE UPS AND DOWNS OF THE ECONOMY

The periodic ups and downs in the level of economic activity are collectively known as the business cycle. Figure 18.1 summarizes fluctuations in economic activity since 1905. The straight horizontal (0) line depicts what statisticians determine would have been an average level of activity during those years. The jagged line indicates the extent to which actual economic activity was above or

Figure 18.1 **United States Business Activity Since 1905**

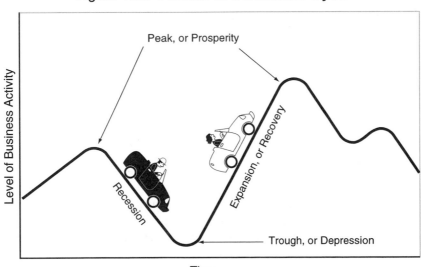

Business cycles are tracked and dated by the **National Bureau of Economic Research (NBER)**, a private, not-for-profit organization.

below the norm. For example, the jagged line is considerably below the horizontal (0) line during the Great Depression and well above that line during World War II.

The graph also shows that although no two cycles have been identical in either duration or intensity, there has been a consistent up-and-down pattern through the years. Economists studying business cycles have identified four phases through which each cycle passes: (1) contraction or recession, (2) trough, (3) expansion or recovery, and (4) peak. We will take a closer look at each of these phases, which are illustrated in Figure 18.2.

Figure 18.2 **Phases of a Business Cycle**

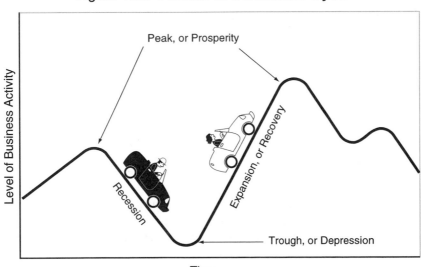

⚡ Contraction or Recession

During a *contraction,* economic activity goes into a decline. Consumers buy fewer goods and services. Retailers and wholesalers cut back on their orders, and the pace of manufacturing slows. As business goes into a decline, workers are laid off. The fall in earnings further reduces consumer spending and business profits. The NBER defines a *recession* as a "... recurring period of decline in total output, income, employment, and trade usually lasting from six months to a year. ..." Rather than wait for the NBER to officially proclaim the start of a recession, economists and government agencies say that the economy is in a recession if real GDP declines for two consecutive quarters.

⚡ Trough

Sooner or later, a contraction or recession will bottom out into what is described as the *trough* of the cycle. When a contraction or recession is mild and short-lived, the trough is reached before the levels of unemployment and business shrinkage become serious. At other times, a recession might reach great depths and extend for a long period of time. Such a recession is known as a *depression.* The most famous depression was the *Great Depression* of the 1930s. A more recent recession began in March 2001, some months before the terrorist attacks of 9/11/01.

⚡ Expansion or Recovery

As the economy advances out of the trough of the business cycle, it begins its period of *expansion.* When feelings of optimism spread, consumer spending (along with production and other business activity) increases. As more and more workers find jobs, the increase in earnings fuels still more spending by consumers and businesses.

When the expansion follows a contraction severe enough to have been classified as a recession, it is called a *recovery.*

⚡ Peak

The *peak* is the highest point in the roller-coaster-like ride of the business cycle. Increasing sales prompt firms to expand operations and reopen idled or underutilized factories. At the peak, the economy may get close to its capacity. When that happens, shortages of productive factors or goods and services may lead to generally higher prices. On November 26, 2001, the NBER announced that the most recent business cycle peak had been reached in March of 2001,

The Great Depression

Values have shrunk to fantastic levels; taxes have risen; our ability to pay has fallen; government of all kinds is faced by serious curtailment of income; the means of exchange are frozen in the currents of trade; the withered leaves of industrial enterprise lie on every side; farmers find no markets for their produce; the savings of many years in thousands of families are gone. More important, a host of unemployed citizens face the grim problem of existence, and an equally great number toil with little return. Only a foolish optimist can deny the dark realities of the moment.

—Franklin D. Roosevelt, *Inaugural Address,* March 1933

President Franklin D. Roosevelt chose these words to describe the economic crisis in which the United States then found itself. He hardly exaggerated. With 13 million workers unemployed (representing one out of every four persons in the labor force), 4,000 banks failing, other business failures at an all-time high, and production at its lowest point since 1900, times were hard indeed.

The Great Depression of 1929–1939 profoundly disturbed economists. Some explanation had to be found for those awful years. True, swings from good to bad times were nothing new. You may have heard about Joseph's Egypt and the seven fat and seven lean years. Those economic fluctuations, though, were brought about by obvious physical causes, such as droughts and plagues. No such cause could be identified for America's miseries in the 1930s. Although the production of goods and services had fallen by one-third from 1929 to 1933, the nation's capacity to produce was at an all-time high. Why then should a nation rich in resources and technology be so stricken? What remedial measures could be taken to restore the prosperity of the 1920s? What could be done to prevent the recurrence of such a depression?

In seeking the answers to these questions, economists tried to develop a better understanding of economic forces and their impact on human well-being. Several theories of the causes of economic fluctuations were formulated, along with steps that might be taken to keep them under control. The quest for answers to those questions did much to shape current thinking about (1) macroeconomic problems (economic problems that affect the economy as a whole) and (2) what government could, and should, do to solve them.

and that the country was now in a recession. The expansion, which lasted ten years, was the longest in modern history.

THEORIES ON THE CAUSES OF BUSINESS CYCLES

For as long as economists have been aware of the periodic ups and downs of the economy, they have searched for reasons to explain and predict them. **W. Stanley Jevons**, a noted British economist, created quite a stir in 1878 with his announcement that business cycles were caused by sunspots. These dark patches on the sun, Jevons believed, affected global weather patterns, which in turn had a direct influence on crops. Worldwide crop failures raised food prices, lowered living standards, and triggered recessions and depressions. It was an interesting idea, but the science of astronomy later proved that Jevons's theory had little basis in fact.

External Causes

Since Jevons's day, there has been no shortage of theories and explanations for the causes of business cycles. The most widely accepted explanations focus on two categories of causes—external and internal. *External causes* are those that are generated by events outside the economy. Sunspots would be an example of an external cause of fluctuation in the business cycle—if the sunspots theory were true. Other (more realistic) examples of external causes fall into the categories of innovations and political events.

INNOVATIONS.   Some economists have suggested certain innovations as principal causes of fluctuations in the economy. The shift from hand labor to machine labor in the textile industry, a process that opened the Industrial Revolution in 18th-century England, and growth of railroad systems in 19th-century America are cases in point. Similarly, the introduction of the "horseless carriage" (the automobile) in the early 1900s and the computer in the 1950s changed the direction of the U.S. economy.

Because innovations involve new ways of doing things, the theory goes, they require investments to pay for new capital (plant and equipment). These new investments put additional income into the hands of businesses and their employees. This income leads to additional business and consumer spending, which in turn stimulates expansion and prosperity. In time, the expansion fostered by the innovations comes to an end, leading to a leveling off of business activity, a contraction in consumer spending, and (possibly) a recession.

POLITICAL EVENTS.   Major political events, such as a war or an economic boycott, can so affect a nation's economy as to reverse its course. In 1973, for example, an *embargo* (refusal to sell something) on oil shipments to the United States by some Arab countries caused a sharp increase in petroleum prices and triggered an economic recession.

Perhaps the most dramatic case in recent years has been the War on Terrorism which began with the attacks of 9/11/01. The destruction of the World Trade Center and a portion of the Pentagon awoke the United States to the dangers of foreign-sponsored terrorism and triggered U.S. military responses in Afghanistan and a full-scale war on Iraq. The cost of the military response to the terrorist threats has yet to be determined. Similarly, the cost of the increased security measures to protect the nation from domestic terrorism and the loss of business in certain industries (such as travel and tourism) remain to be tallied.

National Guard troops joined Metropolitan Transit Authority troops in patrolling train stations and the subway system in New York City after the September 11, 2001, terrorist attacks on the World Trade Center and the Pentagon.

Determining exactly when a business cycle has reached a turning point is anything but an exact science. This was illustrated by the NBER's announcement in the fall of 2001 that the country's economic expansion, which had begun back in 1991, had come to an end in March of 2001. The NBER also indicated that, in all likelihood, the recession had been triggered by the terrorist attacks of 9/11/01.

"But," people asked, "if the recession began in March 2001, why blame it on an event that took place six months later?" The NBER replied, "Before the attacks, it is possible that the decline in the economy would have been too mild to qualify as a recession. The attacks clearly deepened the contraction and may have been an important factor in turning the episode into a recession."

 # INTERNAL CAUSES

Internal causes of fluctuation in business cycles relate to factors within the economy that are likely to trigger either an expansion or a contraction of business activity. Some of the more widely held theories on internal causes are described below.

🪷 Psychological Factors

If businesspeople believe that conditions are going to improve, these beliefs will lead to a series of events that will make the prophecy come true. For example, if in the expectation of increased sales most firms increase their investment in new plant, equipment, and merchandise, their actions will add to employment and personal income. With more to spend, consumers will, in fact, spend more, thereby stimulating additional business investment and personal income. Thus, as the economy expands, businesspeople will enjoy the fulfillment of their prophecy.

If, on the contrary, businesspeople believe that the future will be bleak, firms are likely to reduce production and lay off workers. This belief, too, could become a self-fulfilling prophecy. For with reduced employment, consumer spending will decline and businesses will continue to contract.

Psychological theory can also be applied to behavior patterns of consumers. When they believe that hard times are approaching, consumers are likely to

Figure 18.3 **Where Are We Going From Here?**

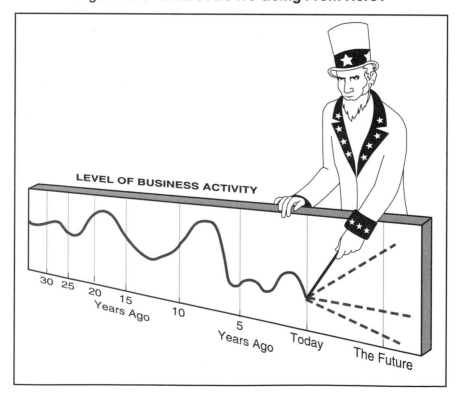

postpone major purchases and spend less money. The business community then has to reduce the level of its operations. As unemployment increases and personal income declines, the recession gains momentum. Consumers witness the fulfillment of their prophecy. Consumer optimism, in contrast, will have the opposite effect. Increased spending triggers increased business activity, employment, and earnings, and the business cycle swings into its recovery phase.

Underconsumption

A situation in which consumer expenditures lag behind output can be classified as *underconsumption*. According to the theory of underconsumption, recessions result when consumer expenditures lag behind the production of goods and services. As unsold inventories increase, business firms reduce their output and lay off workers. With unemployment on the rise, consumption (consumer spending) declines further, more workers lose their jobs, and the recession deepens.

MEASURING THE NATION'S ECONOMIC PERFORMANCE

Good drivers know that they need to look from time to time at their vehicle's dashboard gauges. By monitoring speed, fuel supply, and engine performance, drivers can often prevent trouble before it occurs. Just as motorists keep an eye on their dashboard instruments, so do economists and others monitor the nation's economic performance.

Although there is no such thing as an "economic dashboard," there are *economic indicators* (sets of data about the performance of a segment of the economy) that economists rely on to help them monitor the business cycle. Best known and most widely published of these is the gross domestic product (first discussed in Chapter 2). In addition to the GDP, there are dozens of other economic indicators. Let us take a look at some of them.

Economic Indicators

As a matter of convenience, economists place economic indicators into three categories: (1) leading, (2) coincident, and (3) lagging indicators.

LEADING INDICATORS.   These economic indicators move ahead of the economy. We see *leading economic indicators* going up or down some time before we see the peak or trough of the business cycle. Economists have discovered that soon after an increase in the construction of new homes, the entire economy seems to improve. Similarly, an increase in employment in manufacturing is likely to

The ideas of economists and political philosophers are more powerful than is commonly understood. Indeed, the world is ruled by little else. Practical men, who believe themselves to be quite exempt from any intellectual influences, are usually the slaves of some defunct economist.

In these words from the final pages of his most famous work, *The General Theory of Employment, Interest, and Money,* **John Maynard Keynes** (pronounced Kaynz) correctly anticipated the impact of his own writings on later generations. Keynes's *General Theory* now stands with Smith's *Wealth of Nations* and Marx's *Kapital* as one of the most influential statements of economic philosophy in the modern age.

Keynes was born into academic surroundings in Cambridge, England. His father was an economist at Cambridge University, and his mother was one of its first women graduates. At Cambridge, Keynes was considered Alfred Marshall's most brilliant student. (Marshall is discussed on page 69.) After graduation and a brief stint with the British civil service, Keynes joined the Cambridge faculty.

He left the university in 1915 to undertake a successful career in the British Treasury. In 1919, Keynes attended the Paris Peace Conference that followed World War I. His dismay with the direction in which those talks were taking led him to resign his post in protest. Keynes warned that the reparations the Allies were imposing on Germany would bankrupt the country and force it to take up arms again. As the chief British representative to the Bretton Woods Conference following World War II, Keynes helped shape the course of international trade for decades.

His *General Theory,* published in 1936 during the Great Depression, heralded what has come to be known as the "Keynesian Revolution." Prior to the appearance of his *General Theory,* most economists held that, left to its own devices, the economy would achieve *equilibrium* (a state of balance) at full employment. This theory was in accord with the ideas of French economist **Jean Baptiste Say** (1767–1832), who had suggested that supply creates its own demand, that is, whatever the economy produces will be purchased. Moreover, prices will seek whatever level is necessary to bring about this supply-demand relationship and full employment. If there is unemployment at any point in time, it exists only because wages are too high. In such circumstances, market forces can be expected to drive wages down to whatever level is necessary to enable employers to hire all those willing and able to work. Naturally, it follows from Say's reasoning that the worst thing a government can do is to interfere with the economy, for that prevents market forces from restoring a full-employment equilibrium.

In the 1930s, however, many people concluded that Say's theory simply did not work. Millions of workers then were unable to find jobs, while factories lay idle for want of orders. Similarly, farm products rotted unsold in the midst of worldwide hunger. Keynes pointed out that the economy had indeed reached equilibrium, but it had done so at a point well below full employment. There simply was no self-correcting mechanism that would, in the short run, put people back to work.

"Perhaps not," said many economists. "But in the long run, the system will come into balance and unemployment will disappear."

"Perhaps" Keynes is said to have replied, "but in the long run, we are all dead."

The key ingredient in Keynes's analysis was "aggregate demand." This refers to the total of goods and services that would be purchased by all elements in the economy (consumers, business, and government). There is, he argued, a level at which aggregate demand will support full employment. Anything below that level will simply result in equilibrium at something less than full employment. Aggregate demand at levels higher than full employment will trigger inflation.

The challenge, then, in times of unemployment and idle capacity was to find ways to increase aggregate demand. Keynes's solution called on governments to "prime the pump" of consumer spending and business investment through certain taxing and spending policies.

This proposal was a revolutionary break with the *laissez-faire* thinking of the time, which vigorously opposed government intervention in economic affairs. Indeed, Keynes ignited a controversy that continues to this day between those who favor government participation and those who oppose it.

One of those influenced by Keynes's ideas was President Franklin D. Roosevelt. His New Deal program marshaled the resources of the U.S. economy in an unprecedented effort to fight the Great Depression. Following World War II, the Employment Act of 1946 made the participation of government in efforts to stabilize the economy part of the overall economic policy of the United States. Significantly, in 1970 President Richard Nixon explained that he was favoring a tax cut as a way of fighting that year's recession by saying that, "We are all Keynesians now."

be followed by an upturn in business in general. By contrast, a decline in new housing or manufacturing is often a sign that the economy as a whole will soon decline. Indexes of building permits, factory employment, and new orders for manufacturing of consumer goods are some of the more closely followed leading indicators. As a matter of convenience, ten of these components are combined into a single *index of leading economic indicators*.

COINCIDENT INDICATORS. These indicators move up and down along with the economy. *Coincident economic indicators* let one know where the economy is in the business cycle. The *industrial production index* (which measures changes in output in the nation's factories, mines, and utilities) is a closely followed coincident indicator. So too are employee payrolls, GDP, and personal income. (Personal income is discussed on page 414.) The individual indexes are summarized in a single *index of coincident indicators*.

LAGGING INDICATORS. Measurements that seem to move behind general economic trends are *lagging economic indicators*. They reach their highs and lows later than the business cycle. So, for example, an increase in the average duration of unemployment tends to follow the beginning of a recession. That is, the length of time that workers remain unemployed does not decline until the

407

recovery is well under way. Like the individual leading and coincident indicators, lagging indicators are summarized and compiled into a single index—the *index of lagging indicators.*

✳ The Gross Domestic Product

Best known of the economic indicators, the gross domestic product is the one most frequently reported on and talked about. The GDP, you may recall, is the value of all the goods and services produced in the United States in a single year. To better understand this vital statistic, let us take a closer look at how it is calculated. Statisticians tally the gross domestic product by using either the (1) expenditures approach or (2) income approach.

GDP: THE EXPENDITURES APPROACH.   The total output of goods and services (GDP) is purchased by consumers, business, and government, and by international buyers of U.S. goods and services. Economists often state this mathematically as

$$GDP = C + I + G + X$$

where
- C = consumption
- I = investment
- G = government purchases
- X = net exports

This way of calculating GDP is called the *expenditures approach,* which is illustrated in Table 18.1.

Personal Consumption Expenditures.   This category is made up of all consumer spending. *Personal consumption expenditures* include *durable goods* (long-lasting items, such as automobiles, refrigerators, and furniture), *nondurable goods* (quickly consumed items, such as food, clothing, gasoline, and medicine), and services (such as medical care and recreation). Personal consumption expenditures typically account for about two-thirds of the GDP. (In 2002, personal consumption expenditures of $7,303.7 billion divided by a GDP of $10,446.2 billion equaled 69.9 percent.)

Gross Private Domestic Investment.   The statistic *gross private domestic investment* constitutes the sum of spending by businesses for new equipment, construction, and changes in business inventories of raw materials, partially finished goods, and finished goods. Gross private domestic investment amounted to $1,593.2 billion in 2002.

▷ TABLE 18.1 PURCHASERS OF THE GDP, 2002 (BILLIONS)		
Personal consumption expenditures		$ 7,303.7
Gross private domestic investment		1,593.2
Government purchases		1,972.9
Exports	$1,014.9	
Imports	– 1,438.5	
Net exports		– 423.6
Gross domestic product		$10,446.2

Government Purchases of Goods and Services.   In 2002, government purchases accounted for less than 20 percent of the GDP ($1,972.9 ÷ $10,446.2 = 18.8 percent). *Government purchases* is the sum of spending by all levels of government—federal, state, and local—for such things as national defense, income security, interest on debt, health care, highway construction, and much more. (The importance of government spending was discussed in Chapter 13.)

Net Exports of Goods and Services.   We have discussed that GDP measures U.S. production of goods and services. But not all the goods and services purchased by consumers, businesses, and government are produced in the United States. Nor, for that matter, are all the purchasers of U.S. goods and services living in the United States. *Imports* represent U.S. purchases of foreign goods and services, while *exports* represent U.S. products and services sold to foreigners. The difference between those two items is carried as *net exports*. Net exports is included (along with consumption, investment, and government purchases) in the final GDP tally. (If imports are greater than exports for a year, then the number is negative.) In recent years, imports have been greater than exports. This was the case in 2002 when exports totaled $1,014.9 billion, while imports amounted to $1,438.5 billion. The difference (– $423.6 billion) was included as net exports in the GDP of that year.

GDP: THE INCOME APPROACH.   We have just calculated the GDP by tallying the money spent by consumers, businesses, and government for the goods and services produced in the United States in a given year. We called this method the "expenditures approach." There is another way to calculate GDP, however—the *income approach*. In using this method, we identify the recipients of those expenditures and then tally all these receipts to find the GDP. In other words:

EXPENDITURES	=	GDP	=	INCOME
(total spent on year's output)		(total market value of goods and services)		(total income received by those in the production process)

Table 18.2 summarizes the amounts received as income by the recipients of the GDP in a recent year.

Compensation of Employees.   Most of the income flow goes to employees in the form of wages, salaries, and other benefits (health insurance, retirement plan, etc.). In 2002, employee compensation totaled nearly $6 trillion.

Proprietors' Income.   This figure is the profits earned by owners of the nation's unincorporated businesses. In 2002, proprietors' income totaled $757 billion.

Corporate Profits.   This figure shows what corporations earned in a year. In 2002, corporate profits came to $787 billion.

Rental Income.   This category includes payments to landlords for the use of property, *royalty payments* to individuals (such as inventors and songwriters) for the use of their creative works, and payments to corporate holders of patents and copyrights. Rental income added some $142 billion to the GDP in 2002.

Net Interest.   Most businesses borrow money, and some lend it. The term *net interest* represents the difference between the total interest received and that paid out by the business sector in a given year. In 2002, net interest was about $684 billion.

Capital Consumption.   This category, also called "depreciation," represents sums that businesses have to set aside to replace plant and equipment worn out in the course of producing the GDP. Depreciation is largely a bookkeeping entry and does not actually represent a current income flow. Funds set aside for depreciation will enter the flow of income as they are spent for new investment. In 2002, capital consumption was some $1,628 billion.

▷ **TABLE 18.2   GROSS DOMESTIC PRODUCT, 2002 INCOME FLOWS (BILLIONS)**

Compensation of employees	$ 5,977.4
Proprietors' income	756.5
Corporate profits	787.4
Rental income	142.4
Net interest	684.2
Capital consumption	1,627.9
Indirect taxes	470.4
Gross domestic product	$10,446.2

Indirect Taxes. The sales and excise taxes that we pay for our purchases are not kept by the businesses collecting them. Instead, they are passed on to the federal, state, and local governments. In 2002, indirect taxes totaled $470 billion.

MEASURING GDP CAN BE DIFFICULT. The gross domestic product is the primary measure of U.S. production. In using GDP, economists have to (1) find a way to tally the millions of goods and services going into the GDP without counting the same item more than once and (2) make it possible to compare GDP from one year to the next without having to worry about fluctuating dollar values. The solutions to these two problems are found in the concepts of *final goods* and constant dollars.

Why Only Final Goods Are Included in the GDP. In order to avoid counting the same product more than once, only the final price of an item is included in the GDP. See the example below.

Last year, the Warm Sweater Company spent an average of $10 in materials and labor to produce each sweater. The company sold its sweaters to wholesalers for $15 each. Retail stores paid $21 apiece for the sweaters, which they sold to consumers for $40. How much did Warm Sweater add to the GDP for every sweater it produced last year?

If your answer is $40, you are correct. In the example above, the $10 paid by the manufacturer, the $15 paid by the wholesaler, and the $21 paid by the retailer are all included in the price paid by consumers. Therefore, only the final price—$40—is added into the GDP.

A woman shops at a consignment store. Why are sales of used clothing such as these not included in the GDP?

Used goods are also not included in calculating the GDP. Suppose, for example, that after a month or so you decide that you no longer like your Warm Sweater and sell it to a friend for $15. That sum would not be added to the GDP because, like other used goods, it adds nothing to the nation's wealth.

CONSTANT DOLLARS: CORRECTING FOR CHANGES IN THE PRICE LEVEL. In Chapter 15, we discussed how the value of the dollar (in terms of what it can buy) is subject to change. A dollar may not buy as much in one year as it did in the previous year. For that reason, comparisons of the GDP from one year to the next can be misleading.

By way of illustration, suppose that in two successive years, the nation's output of goods and services was identical. The number of cars, computers, haircuts, and everything else that goes into the GDP remained exactly the same. Suppose, too, that during the second year prices rose by 10 percent. GDP the first year was $8 trillion. Since output the second year was identical to the first, the 10 percent increase in prices pushed the GDP up to $8.8 trillion. We see then that although the GDP increased by $800 billion, because of the effect of inflation the nation's output of goods and services did not increase at all!

Economists eliminate the effects of inflation on the GDP through the use of *constant* rather than *current* dollars. *Current dollars* reflect the price or value of goods and services at a particular time. *Constant dollars* indicate what the GDP (or anything else) would be if the purchasing power of the dollar had not changed from what it was in a base year. The United States currently uses 1996 as the base year in its national income accounts.

> In 1996, Product X sold for $100. Ten years later, prices had increased by 20 percent, and Product X was selling for $120. Economists say that while the current dollar price of Product X was $120, in constant dollars its price was $100. Why $100? Because the 20 percent increase in the price of Product X is canceled out by the 20 percent decrease in the value of the dollar.

The GDP in current and constant dollars for a number of years are summarized in Table 18.3.

PER CAPITA GDP AND ITS USES. *GDP per capita* is often used to compare productive output and living standards of two or more nations. (*Per capita* means "per person.") Other things being equal, the nation with the greater GDP per capita will have more goods and services available for its citizens. Per capita GDP is found by dividing a nation's GDP by its population.

LIMITATIONS OF THE GDP. Although the GDP is the most talked about measure of a nation's economic activity, it has its limitations. Two of the most serious defects of the GDP are its failure to include transactions that take place outside the market economy and its inability to measure the economic well-being of the nation in qualitative terms.

| | TABLE 18.3 GROSS DOMESTIC PRODUCT FOR SELECTED YEARS | |

Year	Current Dollars (billions)	Constant Dollars (billions, 1996 dollars)
1959	$ 507.4	$2,300.0
1964	834.1	2,822.7
1969	985.3	3,543.2
1974	1,501.0	4,061.7
1979	2,566.4	4,870.1
1984	3,932.7	5,477.4
1989	5,489.1	6,568.7
1994	7,054.3	7,337.8
1999	9,131.9	8,778.6
2002	10,446.2	9,439.9

   1. Failure to Include "Nonmarket" Economic Activities. The GDP is supposed to represent the total value of all goods and services produced by the economy, but a large chunk is not included. For example, homemakers who spend their days caring for children, cleaning their home, and cooking for their family are performing services whose value is not included in the GDP. Meanwhile, the services of paid housekeepers, cooks, cleaning service workers, and other household help are included. Similarly, the earnings of gardeners are included in the GDP, whereas the value of the labor performed by those who take care of their own gardens and lawns is not.

   In addition, there is an entire category of illegal and unrecorded economic activity that is not included in the GDP. Known as the "underground economy" (discussed in Chapter 14), these transactions include narcotics sales and illegal gambling, as well as purchases, sales, and employment that people fail to report to the government.

   2. Failure to Measure Economic Well-Being. Although the GDP tells us whether total output is increasing or decreasing, it does not tell us anything about the quality of that output. So, for example, $1 billion worth of cigarettes and $1 billion worth of grain receive equal value in the GDP totals, even though the former product may be harmful to people's health.

   Similarly, the production of things that we all want often leads to the production of harmful by-products that we do not want (such as pollution). In these circumstances, GDP counts the "good things," but it does not include the "bad things." When increased factory output leads to a greater quantity of goods and services, these totals are included in the GDP. If, however, the output creates a greater amount of environmental pollution, the cost of that pollution is not reflected in the GDP.

TABLE 18.4	GROSS DOMESTIC PRODUCT OF SELECTED COUNTRIES, 2002	
	Total GDP (millions)	Per Capita GDP
United States	$10,082,000	$36,300
China	6,000,000	4,600
Japan	3,555,000	28,000
France	1,540,000	25,700
Spain	828,000	20,700
Turkey	468,000	7,000
Poland	368,100	9,500
Sweden	227,400	25,400
Greece	201,100	19,000

Source: *CIA World Factbook*

OTHER NATIONAL INCOME ACCOUNTS. Three other measures of income often reported on by the news media are national income, personal income, and disposable personal income.

National Income. You might recall that earnings come in a variety of forms. Employees earn salaries and wages, property owners earn rent, corporations earn profits, and many people earn money in other forms, such as interest and dividends. The total of all these earnings is included in that part of the gross domestic product known as the *national income*. In 2002, national income came to $8,347.9 billion.

Personal Income. The total of income received by individuals and families before they pay their income taxes is *personal income*. In 2002, this totaled $8,929.1 billion. In addition to wages, dividends, interest, and rent, some people received *transfer payments*. These are government payments to individuals in exchange for which no goods or services were produced. Social Security benefits and unemployment compensation are examples of transfer payments. Table 18.6 summarizes the sources of personal income.

TABLE 18.5	NATIONAL INCOME, 2002 (BILLIONS)
Compensation of employees	$5,977.4
Proprietors' income	756.5
Corporate profits	787.4
Rental income	142.4
Net interest	684.2
National income	**$8,347.9**

TABLE 18.6   PERSONAL INCOME, 2002 (BILLIONS)

Wages and salaries	$5,003.8
Other labor income	610.6
Proprietors' income	756.5
Rental income	142.4
Personal dividend income	433.8
Personal interest income	1,078.5
Transfer payments	1,288.0
Less: Personal contributions for social insurance	−384.5
Personal income	**$8,929.1**

Disposable Personal Income.   Individuals' income remaining after personal income taxes have been paid is called *disposable personal income.* In 2002, people in the United States paid $1,113.6 billion in income taxes. That left them with a total $7,815.5 in disposable personal income ($8,929.1– $1,113.6 = $7,815.5).

AGGREGATE DEMAND, FULL EMPLOYMENT, AND THE PRICE LEVEL

The nation's total output of goods and services—its gross domestic product— is purchased by three principal groups: consumers, producers, and government. (For purposes of this discussion, we have included net exports with business spending.) As discussed earlier, economists refer to the total sum as "aggregate demand." In this chapter, *full employment* refers to the total amount of goods and services that the economy could produce if its resources (machines, equipment, factories, labor, etc.) were fully employed. The level of aggregate demand as compared to that of full employment goes a long way toward explaining why the economy is undergoing a period of recession, expansion, or inflation.

For example, during periods of recession, aggregate demand declines so that the spread between it and full employment increases. As factories, stores, and offices close, workers are laid off and total income falls.

The reverse happens during periods of recovery. At these times, consumer, business, and government demand is greater than current production levels. Producers expand their activities, leading to more employment, increased purchases of raw materials, and expanded production facilities.

As aggregate demand increases, it may exceed the capacity of the economy to satisfy it. If the nation's factories, shops, and workers are fully employed,

Aggregate Demand and Full Employment

Figure 18.4 illustrates the economic importance of aggregate demand and its relationship to full employment. In this hypothetical illustration, we have assumed that with its resources fully employed, the economy will be able to produce $10 trillion worth of goods and services at current prices.

In Case I, aggregate demand stands at $9 trillion. This level leaves the nation with unused capacity in the form of idle plants, shops, and, of course, workers. Economists refer to the $1 trillion spread between the actual GDP and its potential as the *recessionary gap*. How would you describe economic conditions under Case I?

In Case II, aggregate demand exactly equals the economy's ability to produce at full employment. How would you describe economic conditions under Case II?

In Case III, aggregate demand is running at $12.5 trillion. This level is 25 percent greater than the economy's ability to produce at full employment. Economists refer to the $2.5 trillion spread as the *inflationary gap*. How would you describe economic conditions in these circumstances?

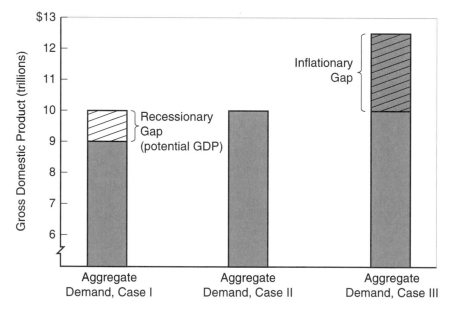

Figure 18.4 **Aggregate Demand and Its Significance**

increased spending will not add to employment or production. With "too much money chasing too few goods," prices will probably increase. Conversely, a reduction of aggregate demand in those circumstances is likely to lead to lower prices rather than to a reduced output of goods and services.

In its efforts to stabilize the economy and promote its growth, the federal government seeks to adjust aggregate demand at levels sufficient to keep the economy fully employed without promoting inflation. Toward that end, economists spend a great deal of time studying the gross domestic product and its components in an effort to discover ways to turn the government's dream into a reality. As recent history has shown, much remains to be done before that goal can be achieved. Nevertheless, a number of significant discoveries have been made.

ECONOMIC FLUCTUATIONS MAY BE CUMULATIVE

Frequently, economic fluctuations feed upon themselves: Expansion creates further expansion, and recession results in more recession. One explanation for these effects can be found in the multiplier.

The Multiplier

Two weeks ago Friday was your lucky day. You received a birthday gift of $1,000 from your Uncle Louis. You had no difficulty deciding what to do with the money. You put $200 in the bank and spent the remaining $800 on the digital video camera equipment you had wanted to buy for a long time. WAM Electronics, from which you bought the camera, used $640 of your money to have its storefront painted and banked the rest. Meanwhile, painter Paul Carmino used $512 of the $640 he received for his work to pay for a week's vacation in the woods. The remaining $128 went into Carmino's money market fund.

Let us freeze the action right here because something interesting has been happening. Uncle Louis's $1,000 gift has already led to total spending of $1,952 (because $800 + $640 + $512 = $1,952). Moreover, let us assume that as the process of spending and saving goes on, people will continue to spend 80 percent of their additional income. If this happens, another $3,048 in income will be generated. This will bring the total amount of spending begun by Uncle Louis's $1,000 to $5,000. Economists refer to the increased national income generated by additional spending as the *multiplier effect,* or simply the *multiplier.* Since in this instance total spending was increased to $5,000, the multiplier is said to have been 5. ($1,000 × 5 = $5,000.)

The size of the multiplier depends upon the public's inclination to spend. If, on the average, people spend 75 percent of any additional income that comes their way, the multiplier will be higher than if their inclination to spend or, as the economists put it, their *marginal propensity to consume* were only 50 percent.

Suppose, for example, that a state government plans to build a new length of highway at a cost of $1 million. As the work progresses, the sum will be disbursed to workers, suppliers, contractors, and others. Also suppose that during the course of construction the marginal propensity to consume is 50 percent.

Accordingly, the recipients of the $1 million in construction funds will spend $500,000 of that amount and save the rest. Those receiving the $500,000 will then spend half that amount, as will those receiving the $250,000, and so on down the line until there is nothing remaining to be spent. By that time, some $2 million will have changed hands. Since the $2 million is twice the original $1 million, the multiplier is 2.

Had buyers been willing to spend three-quarters of their additional income, the multiplier would have been 4, and the $1 million that went into building the highway would have added $4 million to national income.

The multiplier also works in reverse. A decrease in spending reduces total income by a multiple of the amount of the reduction. Thus, if total spending decreased by $50 billion when the multiplier was 3.5, national income would decline by $175 billion.

Aggregate Demand and the Government

While the amount spent by consumers and businesses is the result of millions of private decisions, government spending can be planned and controlled so that it benefits society as a whole. For example, when the economy is functioning at less than full employment, the government can increase its spending in order to increase aggregate demand. Similarly, the government can deliberately cut back on its spending to reduce aggregate demand during a period of inflation. In either case, the government's efforts are aided by the multiplier, which magnifies the impact of the increase or decrease in spending.

The government can also affect aggregate demand through its power to tax. Tax increases reduce the ability of consumers and business to spend, while tax cuts have the opposite effect. In Chapter 19, we will take a closer look at these and other techniques available as part of the U.S. government's efforts to regulate the economy.

The Paradox of Thrift

"A penny saved is a penny earned."
—Benjamin Franklin

Paradox: a statement that is seemingly contradictory or opposed to common sense and yet is perhaps true.   —*Merriam-Webster's Collegiate Dictionary*

We have mentioned that when the economy is producing at a level below its capacity, any increase in spending results in a still greater increase in output. But suppose that, instead of increasing its spending, society as a whole applied Benjamin Franklin's advice and increased its savings. Since more savings would reduce total spending, the multiplier would decrease production by an even greater amount. This sequence would add to unemployment, reduce earnings,

(*continued on page 421*)

The Multiplier and the Accelerator

When the economy is operating at something less than full employment, small changes in spending by consumers (consumption) or businesses (investment) lead to much larger changes in production and employment. The multiplier and the accelerator effect (or more simply, the accelerator) help us to understand why this is so.

As people earn additional income, they can do one of two things with their earnings: spend it or save it. We have seen that the marginal propensity to consume (MPC) describes the public's inclination to spend. Economists express the MPC as a fraction of an additional dollar of income that people would spend on additional goods and services. Thus, a marginal propensity to consume of .8 indicates that $100 of additional income would increase spending by $80. The balance of $20 (or .2) would go into savings.

Economists describe the public's willingness to save as the *marginal propensity to save (MPS)*. Since income not spent is considered to be savings, it follows that MPC + MPS = 1, or 1 − MPC = MPS.

Lola Montes has been promised a $2,000 raise in her yearly salary. She will spend $1,800 of that amount on buying clothes and put the rest into a bank. Since $1,800 is 90 percent of $2,000, we see that Lola's MPC is .9 and that her MPS is .1. (Remember that MPC plus MPS equals 1.)

The Multiplier

The multiplier is expressed mathematically as the *reciprocal* (reverse the numerator and the denominator of a fraction) of 1 minus the marginal propensity to consume. That is:

$$\text{multiplier} = \frac{1}{1 - \text{MPC}}.$$

But since 1 − MPC = MPS, the multiplier can be expressed as the reciprocal of the marginal propensity to save, or $\frac{1}{\text{MPS}}$.

If, for example, the marginal propensity to consume were 90 percent, the multiplier would be 10 because

MPC = .90; therefore MPS = 1 − .90 = .10.

Since the multiplier is equal to the reciprocal of the marginal propensity to save, the multiplier in this example would be $\frac{1}{10}$, or 10.

If, however, people were spending less so that the MPC were 80 percent, the multiplier would be 5 because: MPC = .80; MPS = (1 − .80) = .20; and the reciprocal of .20 equals $\frac{1}{20}$, which equals 5.

The Acceleration Principle

The *acceleration principle* states that small changes in the demand for consumer goods generate a much greater change in the demand for investment goods (and inventory) needed for the production of these goods. If the demand for consumer goods increases, there is a much greater demand for investment goods. And if the demand for consumer goods decreases (or remains the same), there is a much greater decrease in the demand for capital goods.

The *accelerator* describes the effect of changes in spending on business investment (the purchase of new plant and equipment). Consumer demand has a great impact on this investment in capital goods. As consumer demand increases, a point will be reached when business firms need to purchase additional equipment, build new plants, or add to their existing facilities in order to increase output. The significance of the acceleration principle is that it explains why changes in consumption lead to proportionately greater changes in investment. Table 18.7 demonstrates this effect by examining the impact of changes in lawn mower sales on the industry that makes engine blocks for power lawn mowers.

In our example, each lawn mower is fitted with one engine block. Assume that 100 milling machines are needed to manufacture 100,000 lawn

(continued on next page)

mower engine blocks and that 10 milling machines wear out each year and must be replaced.

According to the table, 100,000 mowers were sold in 2001 and 2002. The engine blocks for these mowers were manufactured with the help of 100 milling machines, but 10 of these milling machines had to be replaced each year. Therefore, as indicated in the table, there was no increase in the number of milling machines in either 2001 or 2002 from the previous year even though 10 replacements were purchased in each of these two years. What happened in 2003 when lawn mower sales increased to 110,000 units? The engine-block milling-machine industry needed 110 machines to produce 110,000 engine blocks. The industry had to purchase 20 additional machines in 2003

to meet the demand for 10,000 more engine blocks. Why was this true? Because 10 milling machines were needed as replacements plus 10 additional milling machines are needed to produce 10,000 additional engine blocks.

How does the increased demand for lawn mowers in 2004 and 2005 affect the milling-machine industry? In 2004, 120 milling machines are needed to produce 120,000 engine blocks. The industry already has 110 milling machines. Therefore, 20 additional milling machines (10 for the added production and 10 as replacements) are needed. But 20 milling machines are all that is needed in 2004. Thus, the number of milling machines purchased in 2005 is the same as in 2004.

TABLE 18.7   IMPACT OF LAWN MOWER SALES ON THE ENGINE-BLOCK MILLING-MACHINE INDUSTRY, 2001–2005 (HYPOTHETICAL)

Year	Mowers Sold (Consumption)	Milling Machines Required	Additional Machines Purchased	Percent Change From Previous Year
2001	100,000	100	10 (replacements)	0
2002	100,000	100	10 (replacements)	0
2003	110,000	110	20 (10 replacements + 10 additional)	+ 100
2004	120,000	120	20 (10 replacements + 10 additional)	0
2005	120,000	120	10 (replacements)	− 50

In 2005, the demand for lawn mowers is 120,000, the same as it was the previous year. How many additional milling machines are needed to meet this demand? Only the number of machines needed to replace the worn-out milling machines (10 in our illustration). As a result, the production of milling machines in 2005 declines by 50 percent from 20 in 2004 to 10 in 2005 (20 − 10 = 10; 10 ÷ 20 = 50 percent). In our illustration, even though consumer demand remains unchanged, the impact on a capital-goods industry is severe. Capital-goods industries (such as the milling-machine plant in our example) need an ever-increasing demand for consumer goods just to remain stable. But like everything else, consumer demand fluctuates. When it does, it triggers still wider swings in capital-goods industries.

Interaction of the Multiplier and the Accelerator

Just as two or more members of the same family can pass a cold back and forth in a cycle of illness,

so can the multiplier and the accelerator feed on each other. Thus, a recession will be aggravated, and economic expansion will be promoted.

As a result of the multiplier effect, a small increase in spending increases total income by a greater amount. This effect generates an even greater increase in investment as producers respond to increased consumer demand. The investment increase generated by the accelerator leads to another round of additions to income, spending, and multiplier effects, and the economy continues to climb toward prosperity, full employment, and (if the trend continues) inflation.

On the downside, a leveling off of consumer demand results in a still greater decline in the capital-goods industries. The reduction in investment and the decline in income that result lead to a reduction in consumer spending. National income is reduced by a multiple of the initial reduction in spending, and the recession picks up momentum.

and compel some people to dip into their savings in order to survive. In other words, by increasing its savings, society as a whole would have less to save. But, as everyone knows, an increase in savings is frequently a desirable course for individual families to follow. But if society as a whole did the same, it would reduce the amount available for savings. This concept, which defies the commonsense proposition that saving is a worthy activity for every individual, is described by economists as the *paradox of thrift.*

 ## THE BUSINESS CYCLE IN FOREIGN LANDS

Like the United States, all modern nations go through the ups and downs of business cycles. Although the timings of the turning points in the cycles of foreign lands do not exactly match those of the United States, they are closely related. This is because we now live in a global economy in which the economic fortunes of all nations are closely entwined with one another. The global economy is the subject of Unit VIII.

=========   S   U   M   M   A   R   Y   =========

Aided by the multiplier and the accelerator, the business cycle feeds on itself. As consumer demand declines, business cuts back on production and reduces its labor force. The resulting worker layoffs reduce consumer demand still further, and the recessionary process worsens. At its extreme, uninterrupted recession has led to widespread unemployment, poverty, and depression. On the recovery side, business expansion increases earnings. This, in turn, fuels demand and price increases, which can lead to inflation.

The economic behavior of consumers and business firms feeds the ups and downs of the business cycle. Government, though, has the ability to moderate those swings. It does this through the application of its monetary and fiscal powers. Monetary powers relate to government's ability to regulate the money supply. Fiscal powers come from its ability to tax and spend. In the chapters that follow, we will describe how the federal government uses its monetary and fiscal powers to regulate the economy for the common good.

REVIEWING THE CHAPTER

BUILDING VOCABULARY

Match each item in Column A with its definition in Column B.

Column A

1. business cycle
2. recessionary gap
3. trough
4. recovery
5. peak
6. multiplier
7. accelerator
8. economic indicator
9. national income
10. personal income

Column B

a. the expansion phase of a business cycle
b. a set of statistics about the performance of a sector of the nation's economy
c. the effect of increased spending on national income
d. ups and downs in the level of a nation's economic activity
e. the total income received by all individuals before they pay income taxes
f. the lowest point in a business cycle
g. the total of incomes earned by individuals and businesses in the production of the GDP
h. the upper turning point of a business cycle
i. the effect of changes in consumer spending on investment
j. the amount by which aggregate demand falls short of the total needed to sustain full employment

UNDERSTANDING WHAT YOU HAVE READ

Figure 18.5

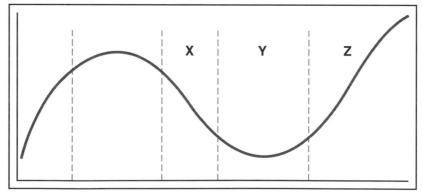

Questions 1–3 are based on Figure 18.5.

1. Phase X represents the (*a*) peak (*b*) trough (*c*) recovery (*d*) recession.

2. Phase Y represents the (*a*) peak (*b*) trough (*c*) recovery (*d*) recession.

3. Phase Z represents the (*a*) peak (*b*) trough (*c*) recovery (*d*) recession.

4. Which *one* of the following groups accounts for almost all purchases of the nation's total output? (*a*) government, business, and farmers (*b*) business, consumers, and government (*c*) households, consumers, and business (*d*) government, consumers, and foreign buyers.

5. When is the economy most likely to operate at less than full employment? (*a*) during periods of inflation (*b*) when there are shortages of unskilled labor (*c*) when total spending is falling (*d*) when consumer spending is increasing.

6. Shortly after Labor Day, George bought a brand-new Young City kayak at the Acme Water Sports Shop's end-of-the-season sale for $400. The list price on the boat prior to the sale had been $650. Acme Water Sports had purchased the kayak from Young City at the wholesale price of $325. It cost Young City $230 to build each of their kayaks. How much did the kayak that George purchased add to the Gross Domestic Product (GDP)? (*a*) $230 (*b*) $325 (*c*) $400 (*d*) $650.

7. Economists refer to the sum total of consumption, investment, and government spending as (*a*) the multiplier (*b*) the acceleration principle (*c*) the sunspot theory (*d*) aggregate demand.

8. If aggregate demand declines as compared to the productive capacity of the economy as a whole, which *one* of the following events is likely to occur? (*a*) Employment will increase. (*b*) The growth rate will decline. (*c*) Prices will rise. (*d*) Tax receipts will increase.

9. Changes in the level of spending by any sector of the economy (consumers, businesses, or government) will be magnified in their effect upon the total economy. One explanation for this is contained in (*a*) the Law of Diminishing Returns (*b*) Engel's Law (*c*) the theory of the multiplier (*d*) the innovation theory.

10. The size of the multiplier is directly affected by (*a*) government spending (*b*) business spending (*c*) business inventory (*d*) the marginal propensity to consume.

THINKING CRITICALLY

1. In comparing the economies of two nations, economists frequently use per capita GDP figures. (*a*) Why is per capita GDP rather than total GDP used? (*b*) What other indicators are important in comparing economies?

2. In the midst of a deep recession, the president of the United States calls on the nation's consumers to "spend their way" out of the slump. What does the president mean?

3. Assume that the nation has just reached the bottom of a long recession. Summarize the probable effect of the recession upon: (*a*) prices, (*b*) wages, (*c*) employment, (*d*) investment, and (*e*) profits.

4. In its efforts to stabilize the economy, the federal government frequently attempts to influence the level of aggregate demand.

   a. Explain how government may affect aggregate demand by reducing taxes.

   b. Explain how government may affect aggregate demand by reducing government spending.

c. Explain how the multiplier and the accelerator can magnify the impact of government efforts.

SKILLS: Analyzing a Line Graph and a Bar Graph

Answer the following questions based on your analysis of Figure 18.1 (page 399) and Figure 18.4 (page 416).

1. How would you describe generally the levels of economic activity in the United States in the period since 1905?

2. How would you describe specifically the levels of economic activity during World War I, World War II, the Korean War, and the Vietnam War?

3. During periods of war, workers and industries are fully employed and consumer demand is strong. Which example in Figure 18.4 corresponds to these periods of war—Case I, Case II, or Case III? Explain your answer.

4. Why is there a recessionary gap in Case I, Figure 18.4?

5. Which years in Figure 18.1 correspond to Case I? Explain your answer.

QUESTIONS FOR RESEARCH AND EVALUATION

Economists and others often consult statistical indicators of business activity as a way of seeing where the economy is and where it might be heading. Some of these, the coincident indicators, tend to change with the business cycle. Others, the leading indicators, tend to change prior to similar changes in the business cycle, while the lagging indicators occur sometime after the actual events.

1. Listed on the next page are some of the most widely followed economic indicators in each of the categories. With respect to *one* indicator in *each* category, explain

   a. the nature of the information contained in the indicator

   b. why it serves as either a leading, lagging, or coincident indicator.

2. Of the three indexes of economic indicators, the index of leading economic indicators is the most widely followed. How would you explain its popularity as compared to the other two (index of lagging economic indicators and index of coincident economic indicators)?

3. "While economic indicators are useful in describing the status of the business cycle today, one must apply them with caution when predicting the future." Explain this statement.

Leading Economic Indicators:
Average weekly hours of production workers in manufacturing
Average weekly initial claims for unemployment insurance
Manufacturers' new orders for consumer goods adjusted for inflation
Stock prices, 500 common stocks
New building permits for private houses
Index of leading indicators

Coincident Economic Indicators:
Employees on nonagricultural payrolls
Real personal income (i.e., income in constant dollars)
Industrial production
Manufacturing and trade sales

Lagging Economic Indicators:
Average duration of unemployment
Manufacturing and trade inventories
Ratio of consumer installment credit to personal income
Commercial and industrial loans outstanding

USING THE INTERNET

The NBER's findings can be found on the Web at <<www.nber.org/cycles.html>>.

CHAPTER 19
Managing the Nation's Economy: Monetary Policy

OVERVIEW

The eyes of the financial world and much of the nation were on Washington, D.C., that day. Alan Greenspan, Chairman of the Federal Reserve Board of Governors, was scheduled to appear before a congressional committee inquiring into the state of the economy. Mr. Greenspan was expected to reveal at the hearing what changes, if any, the Fed was planning to make in interest rates. Especially interested in learning the news were industries directly affected by the Fed's decisions, such as real estate, manufacturing, foreign trade, and securities.

In Chapter 17, we learned that the Federal Reserve System is empowered to regulate interest rates and the supply of money and credit. The application of these powers to achieve certain economic goals is known as monetary policy. In this chapter, we begin with a discussion of the goals of U.S. economic policy. Next, we discuss the challenges presented by the problems of unemployment and inflation. We conclude the chapter with a description of the ways the Federal Reserve System uses its monetary powers to solve those economic problems.

THE GOALS OF ECONOMIC POLICY

The closest thing to a formal statement of the nation's economic goals may be found in the Employment Act of 1946. The law made the federal government responsible for maintaining economic stability by promoting what it described as ". . . maximum employment, production, and purchasing power."

The act also created a Council of Economic Advisers. This three-member body (1) studies economic conditions, (2) recommends courses of action to the president, and (3) assists in the preparation of an annual *Economic Report of the*

President. A chairperson represents the Council in its dealings with the public and the president, attends all meetings of the Cabinet, and leads the Council.

Since maximum employment, maximum production, and maximum purchasing power are the prescribed goals of economic policy, let us take a closer look at what each of those terms mean and how monetary policy may be used to achieve them.

MAXIMUM EMPLOYMENT

The **Bureau of Labor Statistics (BLS)** of the U.S. Department of Labor is responsible for tracking and reporting on employment and unemployment. Among the most widely followed data compiled by the BLS are the size of the labor force and the unemployment rate. As discussed in Chapter 8, the labor force consists of everyone 16 years of age or older who has a job or (though unemployed) is ready, willing, and able to work. The *unemployment rate* represents the number unemployed as a percent of the labor force. Suppose, for example, that at a time when the labor force stood at 146 million, 8,400,000 workers were unemployed. In those circumstances, the unemployment rate would be 5.8 percent (because 8.4 ÷ 146 = .058, which is 5.8 percent).

Of all the problems associated with recession and depression, rising unemployment and the loss of jobs may be the most serious. Most families have financial obligations (such as monthly rent, doctors' bills, car payments, taxes, and the like) that need to be met whether they hold a job or not. For them, unemployment remains a threat to their savings and plans for the future. Added to this is the embarrassment and psychological stress that often accompany job loss. For many workers, this is the most difficult part of being unemployed.

A job seeker is assisted at the Illinois Employment and Training Center in Arlington Heights in 2003—a time when the national unemployment rate was 6.1 percent.

The Employment Act of 1946 committed the federal government to doing what it could to promote "maximum employment." Note, however, that "maximum employment," or "full employment" as it is more commonly described, does *not* mean that everyone willing and able to work will find a job. Most economists believe that some level of unemployment is inevitable and acceptable.

Promoting Maximum Employment

By way of promoting "maximum employment," economists have sought to identify the causes of unemployment and to design solutions based on their findings. Unemployment usually falls into one of four categories: *seasonal unemployment, frictional unemployment, structural unemployment,* and *cyclical unemployment.* Since the nature of each differs from the others, each requires a separate set of solutions.

SEASONAL UNEMPLOYMENT.   You probably know that many jobs need filling during the summer as the number of people on vacation increases. Similarly, the Christmas shopping season creates a demand for workers needed to help in fulfilling the demands of shoppers. Then, as summer turns to fall (or the Christmas shopping season ends), most of those workers who were hired to meet seasonal needs are laid off. Another example is the construction industry in the Northern states. More often than not, the winter months are too cold for outdoor work to continue; for that reason, many construction workers are laid off at that time.

Seasonal unemployment refers to just that—unemployment brought on by the status of work in certain industries at particular seasons of the year. In calculating its employment data, the BLS usually adjusts its data to account for seasonal variations. Suppose that unemployment usually increases by .3 percent during the weeks following the Christmas shopping season. In that case, BLS will seasonally adjust its unemployment data at that time of the year by subtracting .3 percent from the final results.

FRICTIONAL UNEMPLOYMENT.   When is unemployment not unemployment? When it is *frictional unemployment.* The term describes the status of workers who have left one job and are soon likely to find another. The jobs these workers are seeking are available, and it is only a matter of time before they will be employed again. Since frictional unemployment is a normal (and often voluntary) event, some economists allow for it in their definition of full employment. Exactly how many workers are frictionally unemployed at any time is uncertain. Most economists, however, agree that frictional unemployment of 4–6 percent of the labor force is a reasonable estimate. For that reason, if unemployment stands at 5 percent, economists say that the nation is "fully employed."

Since frictional unemployment is seen as a normal economic condition, the federal government has not done much to reduce it. Most states maintain

Figure 19.1 **Unemployment Rates for Selected Groups**

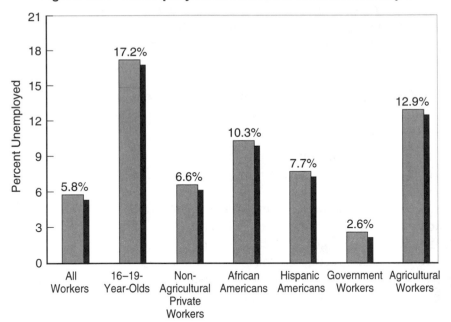

offices that assist both employers and employees in job placement. But unemployment levels vary from state to state. There can be a shortage of workers in a few states at the same time that there are high levels of unemployment in other states. To deal with this problem, a nationwide network of state job service agencies has been set up. It is designed to reduce frictional unemployment by speeding up the process by which people find jobs (and employers find workers) in states other than their own.

STRUCTURAL UNEMPLOYMENT.

> "Yes, I remember when I was your age, you had to talk to a *teller* in a bank before you could withdraw money. And the elevators in department stores were run by elevator operators."

Unlike frictional unemployment, *structural unemployment* refers to workers who have lost their jobs because of changes in technology, consumer preferences, or the movement of job opportunities from one region to another. These workers (like elevator operators and bank tellers) are not likely to be rehired in the near future at the types of jobs they had before. Meanwhile, it is possible that plenty of job vacancies exist for workers skilled in the new technologies that replaced the old (like computer programming and electronics).

Structural unemployment is caused by changes in the nature or location of employment opportunities. It may occur in certain parts of the labor force when new technology makes certain skills obsolete, as when farmhands are replaced by automatic harvesting machinery, and clerical workers are replaced by computers. Or structural unemployment may occur on a regional or sectional basis, as when much of the textile industry left New England for the South in the 20th century. The reduction of structural unemployment is extremely difficult and costly. At the least, it requires

- retraining workers whose skills are no longer in demand
- moving people to where the jobs are or enticing industry to move into areas of high unemployment
- changing the social values of those who would discriminate against others because of their race, age, religion, sex, or disability.

CYCLICAL UNEMPLOYMENT.   Unemployment that follows the business cycle by increasing during recessions and decreasing during periods of recovery is called *cyclical unemployment.* As the demand for goods and services decreases, for instance during recessions, business firms lay off workers. The opposite happens when the economy recovers: Consumer demand increases and businesses hire additional workers to meet the increased demand. In its efforts to reduce cyclical unemployment, government uses its fiscal and monetary powers to bring recessions to an end and restore aggregate demand to maximum employment levels. Government may also try to soften the impact of unemployment by extending unemployment insurance to workers who have been temporarily laid off.

 # MAXIMUM PRODUCTION

As discussed in Chapter 6, entrepreneurs try to combine the factors of production (land, labor, and capital) in order to earn the greatest profits. From the standpoint of the individual firm, *maximum production* is the level at which the entrepreneur or executive believes that it is no longer profitable to add more workers, land, or capital to the production process. In Chapter 6, we learned that this comes at the rate of output where marginal revenue equals marginal costs.

While business owners can fairly easily figure out their own maximum production levels, economists in the federal government have much difficulty discovering when the level of maximum production has been reached on a national level. They try to find out when the economy is producing the most goods and services of which it is capable. For that purpose, economists assume that rising employment levels lead to increased output. When that happens, increasing demand (relative to supply) leads to higher prices. Thus, economists generally assume that maximum production has been reached when further increases in employment bring on inflation.

MAXIMUM PURCHASING POWER

Most people want to feel that the money they set aside in savings will be able to buy as much in the future as it can today. That is, they hope that the purchasing power of their dollar will remain more or less constant. Consumers achieve *maximum purchasing power* when the general price level is maintained so that the purchasing power of the dollar remains stable. Assume that you have been saving up to buy a good dirt bike. When the time comes, you expect to be able to find something you like for about $1,500.

Experience tells us, however, that over time, some decrease in the value of the dollar and some increase in prices are more or less likely. If that proves to be the case when you are ready to buy, you might have to spend more than $1,500.

 # THE PROBLEM OF INFLATION

Inflation has been described as "the cruelest tax of all." It is "tax-like" because the payment imposed by inflation cannot be escaped. Inflation is "cruel" because it affects mostly those who can least afford its costs, such as people on fixed incomes. In Chapter 15, we discussed the causes of inflation and different

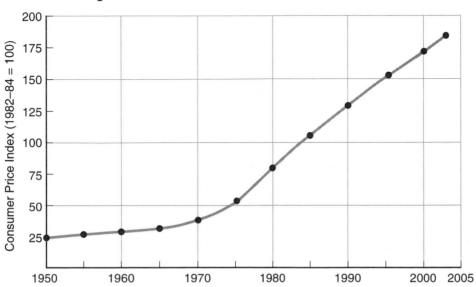

Figure 19.2 **Consumer Price Index Since 1950**

types (demand-pull and cost-push). In this chapter, we will concentrate on what the government does about inflation.

⚡ Fighting Inflation

Controlling or eliminating inflation has been a goal of the federal government ever since World War II. Most of this effort has been aimed at the principal causes of inflation: demand-pull and cost-push.

CURING DEMAND-PULL INFLATION.   Efforts to cure demand-pull inflation can have both positive and negative effects.

First, the Good News.   Demand-pull inflation can be moderated with monetary and/or fiscal policies. On the monetary side, the Fed can use its powers (described later in this chapter) to slow the rate of growth of the money supply.

Fiscal policies are the responsibility of the president and Congress, and include the powers to spend and tax. Any combination of reduced spending and increased taxes reduces the spending power of consumers and businesses. With less to spend, demand falls, along with prices.

And Now the Bad News.   While reductions in consumer and business demand take the pressure off price increases, reduced demand is likely to add to unemployment. This effect follows because with declining sales, business firms tend to lay off workers and reduce inventories. As unemployment rates increase, sales decline still further because unemployed workers have less money to spend.

The relationship between the inflation rate and unemployment can be represented graphically by a *Phillips Curve*. It was named in honor of **A.W. Phillips**, the British economist who developed it. In Figure 19.3, unemployment increased from 1 percent of the labor force to 10 percent as the inflation rate fell from 12 percent to 2 percent.

Another piece of bad news concerning the fight against demand-pull inflation has to do with the Fed's tactic of raising interest rates. This Fed action places a special burden on industries that rely heavily on borrowed funds, such as housing construction. Since virtually all housing is built at least partly with borrowed funds (in the form of mortgages), efforts to raise interest rates make borrowing more difficult. As a result, many people are unable to buy new homes because they cannot obtain or afford mortgages. Meanwhile, as the number of new housing plummets, building contractors, suppliers, and construction workers experience a reduction in earnings.

CURING COST-PUSH INFLATION.   While monetary and fiscal policies can fight demand-pull inflation by cooling aggregate demand, they are not effective against the cost-push variety of inflation. To fight cost-push inflation, government applies what are known as *incomes policies*. These policies seek to stem

Figure 19.3 **Phillips Curve**

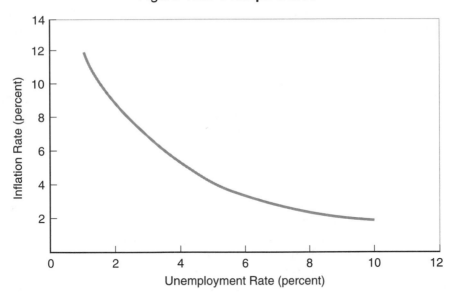

the wage and price increases associated with cost-push inflation with one or more of the following: voluntary controls, direct controls, antitrust laws, and aiming at inflation from the "supply side."

Voluntary Controls.   In the 1970s, presidents Nixon, Ford, and Carter called on labor leaders and heads of industry to limit voluntarily their respective wage demands and price increases. The government issued guidelines for what it considered proper percentage increases. These efforts to obtain self-regulation generally failed. Many company executives and labor leaders were fearful that even if they followed the presidents' requests, others would not, and these others would benefit.

Direct Controls.   During World War II and parts of the Korean and Vietnam wars, the federal government imposed wage and price controls across the country. These controls established maximum prices on many items and also fixed wages. Direct controls were generally effective during World War II because that war was a popular one and the U.S. public supported controls then. During other, less popular wars, however, controls have not been so well received. Many Americans regard price and wage controls as inconsistent with a democratic society and a free enterprise system. These controls are also very costly to administer because thousands of people have to be hired to enforce them.

Antitrust Legislation.   Cost-push is most likely to occur in those industries in which management or labor is so strong that it can dictate prices. For example, if a powerful union forces an industry to grant union workers a 10 percent wage increase, businesses in that industry very likely will increase prices by at least 10 percent, which can add to inflationary pressures. Similarly, a monopolistic firm may try to maximize profits by limiting output and raising prices. By contrast, in a competitive environment prices are less likely to increase and the pressure of inflation is reduced. That is why the government tries to control the powers of both labor and management through antitrust laws.

Aiming at Inflation From the "Supply Side." Market price, you might recall from Chapter 3, is a function of both demand and supply. In the 1970s, a group of economists suggested that price increases could be limited even if the output of goods and services were increased. As these economists saw it, the biggest hindrances to increased output were federal taxes, which were so high that they discouraged investment and production. Their key to reducing inflation was to reduce taxes. The increase in take-home pay that would result from reduced taxes, they reasoned, would enable consumers to increase both their spending and savings. The increased spending would then encourage businesses to expand. Meanwhile, the increased savings would add to the pool of funds available for investment. As investment increases, so too does output, that is, the supply of goods and services. As you know from your study of the laws of supply and demand, all other things being equal, an increase in supply results in a decrease in prices. Thus, the supply-siders concluded, reducing taxes would result in reducing inflation, because it would stimulate investment, increase output, and lower prices. The ideas proposed by these economists, named *supply-siders,* created a sensation. Previously, a tax cut had been regarded as a way to increase, not decrease, prices.

According to the cartoonist, what does a low unemployment rate lead to? Do you agree with this view? Explain.

Interest in supply-side economics as a recession-fighting tool was renewed following the 2000 election of George W. Bush as President. (A feature on supply-side economics can be found in Chapter 20, beginning on page 456.)

FIGHTING INFLATION IN THE 1980S.   The federal government used a combination of monetary policy and supply-side techniques to combat a very serious inflation in the early 1980s. Results of the effort were mixed. By limiting the growth of the money supply (monetary policies) and reducing taxes (a supply-side strategy), cost-of-living increases were slowed to the lowest rate in nearly 20 years. Unemployment, however, climbed to nearly 10 percent of the labor force, its highest level since the Great Depression. By 1989, though, the unemployment level had declined to 5.3 percent.

 # MONETARY POLICY

As discussed in Chapter 17, the efforts of the Federal Reserve System to stabilize the economy by regulating the supply of money and credit are called "monetary policy." The availability and cost of credit affect both the money supply and business activity. When loans are easily obtained, spending increases (along with the money supply, business activity, and prices). When loans are harder to come by, the opposite occurs: Sales decline (along with the money supply, business activity, and prices).

The Tools of Monetary Policy

You might recall from the description of the WHO, WHAT, and HOW questions in Chapters 1 and 2 that the allocation of goods and services was decided by the price of those items as determined by the laws of supply and demand. Like shoes and haircuts, the availability of credit and money is also affected by its price. The price of loanable money is known as "interest."

When interest rates are low, the public finds it easier to purchase homes, and firms are more likely to invest in plant and equipment. When interest rates are high, individuals and firms are less inclined to borrow and spend.

The Federal Reserve System relies on these facts to limit the harmful effects of inflation and recession. It does this by using its monetary tools to increase or decrease interest rates. You might recall that the most important of these tools are reserve requirements, the discount rate, and open market operations.

RESERVE REQUIREMENTS.   A major part of a bank's income comes from the interest it earns on the loans of its depositors' money. Banks, however, cannot lend unlimited sums. Instead, they are required to keep a percentage of their

The FOMC increases and decreases the federal funds rate by buying and selling government securities. How it does this and the effect of those actions are summarized in the following flow chart:

When the FOMC Eases	**When the FOMC Tightens**
Fed *buys* government securities from a firm that deals in them.	Fed *sells* government securities to a firm that deals in them.
↓	↓
It pays by *crediting* the account that the dealer's bank has at the Fed.	It pays by *debiting* the account that the dealer's bank has at the Fed.
↓	↓
The bank in turn *credits* the dealer's account.	The bank in turn *debits* the dealer's account.
↓	↓
The banking system has *more* funds to lend.	The banking system has *fewer* funds to lend.
↓	↓
Downward pressure on the *federal funds rate*—i.e., the interest rate banks charge each other for overnight loans.	*Upward* pressure on the federal funds rate.
↓	↓
Influences other interest rates in the economy—which also go *down.*	Other interest rates in the economy also *rise* as a result.
↓	↓
Gives the economy a *boost.*	*Slows* the economy and curbs inflation.

—From "You and the Fed: Tools of Monetary Policy," <<www.newyorkfed.org/pihome/educator/fed/tools.html >>.

🧭 Monetary Policy in Action

Depending on economic conditions, monetary policies generally follow one of three scenarios.

SCENARIO 1: THINGS ARE GOING WELL.   With full employment and price stability, the Fed tries to maintain the present state of affairs. It does this by allowing the money supply to grow at exactly the same rate as the growth of the GDP.

SCENARIO 2: THE ECONOMY IS IN A RECESSION.   With unemployment on the increase and business activity in a decline, the Fed might adopt an *easy-money* *policy* (that is, it might increase the money supply). This policy allows the money supply to grow faster than the GDP and stimulates aggregate demand.

In a recession, the Fed could (1) reduce reserve requirements to increase the lending power of the banking system, (2) lower the discount rate to enable member banks to charge lower interest rates for loans and, it is hoped, stimulate borrowing, and (3) direct the Open Market Committee to buy securities. When the Fed buys securities, the sellers of the securities deposit the proceeds in their accounts (adding to the deposits held by banks and increasing the banks' lending capacity).

SCENARIO 3: INFLATION THREATENS.   With prices increasing at an unacceptable rate, the Fed is likely to follow a *tight-money policy* (that is, slow the growth of the money supply). This policy (1) slows the rate of increase in the money supply to something less than the increase in the GDP and (2) dampens aggregate demand.

With its trusty monetary tools, the Fed in inflationary times could be expected to do one or more of the following:

Increase Reserve Requirements.   By requiring that local banks hold a larger portion of their deposits on reserve, the lending ability of banks is reduced, along with the money supply.

Raise the Discount Rate.   Since in borrowing from the Federal Reserve System, higher rates cost local banks more, they have to increase the interest rates they charge their customers. This increase, in turn, discourages borrowing, slows the growth of the money supply, and reduces aggregate demand and prices.

Direct the Open Market Committee to Sell Securities.   When the Open Market Committee sells government bills, bonds, and notes to the public, the payments from the sales of these securities are received by the Federal Reserve System. The sales reduce bank reserves, the lending ability of the banking system, and the money supply.

▷ **TABLE 19.1   MONETARY POLICY SUMMARIZED**

Recession and High Unemployment	Inflation and Full Employment
1. Lower the reserve ratio	1. Raise the reserve ratio
2. Buy securities	2. Sell securities
3. Lower the discount rate	3. Raise the discount rate
4. Lower margin requirements	4. Raise margin requirements

✳ Monetary Policy Has Its Limitations

We have described how the Fed uses its monetary tools to regulate the economy. How well the Fed can achieve its goals depends on a number of factors, the most important of which are:

- the ability of the Fed to forecast trends and time its responses
- the business cycle
- new banking laws
- the global economy.

FORECASTING AND TIMING DIFFICULTIES.   The success of monetary policy depends on how quickly and accurately the Fed recognizes economic trends. Though economists are able to describe in general terms how well or poorly the economy is doing, no one has discovered how to predict the future of the economy with certainty. If economists cannot be certain, how can the Fed know exactly how much to raise or lower the money supply? Furthermore, there is a time lag before monetary policies impact on the business community. In retrospect, some economists might argue that monetary measures came too soon, too late, or were not necessary to begin with.

THE BUSINESS CYCLE.   Monetary policy is least effective at either end of the business cycle. During the depths of a recession, the Fed will lower interest rates. This action alone, however, may not be enough to overcome fears created by a period of job layoffs and business failures. For that reason, business and consumer spending may remain at low levels despite the reduced costs of loans.

Similarly, as the business cycle climbs toward the upper reaches of a recovery, the effectiveness of monetary policy wanes. In these times, we can expect the Fed to increase interest rates so as to (1) discourage loans, (2) slow the growth of the money supply, and (3) lower prices. But with business prospects looking good (as they do during peak recovery periods), firms will continue to borrow and expand on the theory that increased sales will more than offset the higher costs of money. When this happens, prices will continue to rise despite the Fed's efforts to reverse the trend.

NEW BANKING LAWS.   There was a time when consumers placed the bulk of their savings in bank accounts, and the interest offered by savings institutions was limited by law. More recently, however, Congress gave banks the right to determine the interest they would pay depositors.

While the deregulation of interest rates has allowed banks to become more competitive, it has also made the banks less responsive to policy shifts by the Federal Reserve System. For example, in the days before deregulation, the Fed could direct the banks to reduce the interest rates they paid on their deposits as a way of discouraging savings. Today, however, bankers need not follow the lead of the Fed if, in their opinion, it would be more profitable to do otherwise.

TABLE 19.2	UNITED STATES INTERNATIONAL TRADE (IN BILLIONS)	
	1974	**2002**
Exports of goods and services	$148	$ 972
Imports of goods and services	137	1,664

THE GLOBAL ECONOMY.   As indicated in Table 19.2, U.S. participation in the global economy has grown enormously over the years. One result of this trend is that individuals and governments in foreign lands hold many more dollars than they once did. As we will discuss in Chapter 23, the U.S. dollar holdings by individuals and governments abroad has an effect on prices in the United States. But as we have seen, prices directly affect the level of economic activity. The problem is that while the Federal Reserve Board has a great deal of control over the supply of dollars in this country, its ability to regulate how dollars in foreign hands are used is limited. For that reason, the increasing involvement by the United States in the global economy has lessened the ability of the Fed to regulate the value of the dollar, the level of prices, and the business cycle.

S U M M A R Y

The federal government has the responsibility of maintaining maximum employment, maximum production, and maximum purchasing power. It attempts to do so by maintaining appropriate levels of aggregate demand. When aggregate demand equals the economy's ability to produce, the economy is at full employment. When aggregate demand is below this capacity, a recessionary gap exists. By contrast, an inflationary gap occurs when aggregate demand is greater than the economy's capacity to produce.

During periods of recession and inflation, the government attempts to correct imbalances in aggregate demand through the use of fiscal and monetary policies. The Federal Reserve System administers the country's monetary policy. It regulates the nation's supply of money and credit by virtue of its power to regulate reserve requirements, the discount rate, and open market operations. In the next chapter, we will discuss fiscal policy.

REVIEWING THE CHAPTER

BUILDING VOCABULARY

Match each term in Column A with its definition in Column B.

Column A

1. frictional unemployment
2. fiscal policy
3. structural unemployment
4. federal funds rate
5. easy-money policy
6. tight-money policy
7. cyclical unemployment
8. supply-sider
9. Phillips Curve
10. income policies

Column B

a. a graph illustrating the tradeoff between inflation and unemployment
b. the status of workers who lose their jobs because of insufficient demand for goods and services
c. the interest that banks charge one another for loans of federal funds
d. the use of the federal government's taxing and spending powers to regulate the economy
e. the status of workers who lose their jobs and are soon likely to find a similar one
f. the status of workers who lose their jobs because of changes in the nature or location of job opportunities
g. a Fed policy to expand the money supply
h. government policies to control wage and price increases
i. a Fed policy to slow the growth of the money supply
j. someone who believes that production is the key to reducing prices and increasing employment

UNDERSTANDING WHAT YOU HAVE READ

1. The statement that the federal government has the responsibility to use its powers to promote stability, growth, and maximum employment is contained in the (*a*) U.S. Constitution (*b*) Employment Act of 1946 (*c*) Social Security Act of 1935 (*d*) National Labor Relations Act.

2. When certain jobs disappear in one region and reappear in another, the unemployment that results is referred to as (*a*) normal (*b*) structural (*c*) cyclical (*d*) frictional.

3. Unemployment is likely to increase when (*a*) aggregate demand is high (*b*) there is a period of moderate inflation (*c*) the demand for goods is less than the economy is capable of producing (*d*) the economy is experiencing a recovery in the business cycle.

4. Which step might be taken to stimulate business activity during a recession? (*a*) lower the discount rate (*b*) increase margin requirements (*c*) decrease spending for public works (*d*) raise corporate income tax rates.

5. An increase in average weekly income does not result in a higher standard of living if it is accompanied by (*a*) increased purchases of consumer goods (*b*) increased private investment (*c*) rising prices (*d*) increased productivity.

6. Monetary policies are administered by the (*a*) Treasury Department (*b*) U.S. president (*c*) Federal Reserve System (*d*) Congress.

7. The term *open market operations* refers mainly to (*a*) speculation in stocks and bonds by members of the stock exchange (*b*) the purchase and sale of government securities by Federal Reserve Banks (*c*) adjusting the discount rate by Federal Reserve Banks (*d*) regulation of margin requirements by the Federal Reserve's Board of Governors.

8. A major effect of the lowering of reserve requirements for member banks by the Board of Governors of the Federal Reserve System would be (*a*) a decrease in margin requirements for stock purchases (*b*) a decrease in the supply of checkbook money (*c*) an increase in commercial bank loans (*d*) an increase in "tight money."

9. When the Federal Reserve raises the discount rate, member banks usually raise their interest rates because (*a*) as members they must go along with the wishes of the Federal Reserve (*b*) they are required to do so by law (*c*) it will now cost them more to borrow the funds that they will be lending out (*d*) they want to take the opportunity to increase their volume of loans.

10. The use of monetary policy to combat inflation has been criticized because it (*a*) calls for additional government spending (*b*) places too heavy a reliance on the Treasury Department (*c*) calls for higher taxes (*d*) discriminates against certain industries, such as the home building trades, that rely most heavily on consumer borrowing.

THINKING CRITICALLY

1. The federal government has been given the responsibility "to use all practical means . . . to promote . . . maximum employment, production, and purchasing power."

   a. Briefly explain maximum employment, maximum production, and maximum purchasing power.

   b. Should the government manage the economy? Explain your answer.

2. Inflation may be of the *demand-pull* or *cost-push* variety.

   a. Explain the meaning of each type of inflation. Which do you think is easier for the government to deal with—demand-pull or cost-push inflation?

   b. Why might workers oppose government measures to combat inflation?

3. Occasionally, the assertion is made that "full employment is not possible without inflation."

   a. Explain the meaning of this statement.

   b. Do you agree with it? Why or why not?

4. Assume that the nation has entered a period of recession and that the Fed has decided to use its monetary tools to deal with the problem.

   a. Explain *three* ways the Fed could use its monetary tools to reverse a recession.

   b. Assume that the tools used to reverse the recession worked and the economy seems to be heading for an inflationary period. Explain *three* tools the Fed could use to reduce inflationary pressures in the economy.

   c. Why is it difficult for the Fed to know when to implement corrective measures?

SKILLS: Researching and Writing About Economic Problems

During a period of inflation, the Fed is likely to adopt monetary measures to reduce aggregate demand. Efforts to reduce demand, however, are also likely to lead to increased unemployment.

1. Research in annual reference books such as *Economic Report of the President, Statistical Abstract of the United States,* and *World Almanac* for statistics on unemployment rates and inflation rates in recent years. Then find current unemployment and inflation rates in a newspaper or magazine or on the Internet.

2. Survey adults in your community (including some who are currently working or who own a business) on the subject of unemployment and inflation. Ask each adult whether he or she thinks either inflation or unemployment is a major problem in the United States today (and if so, why it is a problem).

3. Based on your results from SKILLS activities 1 and 2, write a short essay telling whether you think that the Fed should tighten money and credit at this time.

USING THE INTERNET

- Current and past editions of the *Economic Report of the President* can be viewed online at <<w3.access.gpo.gov/eop/>>.

- The latest Bureau of Labor Statistics data are available at <<www.bls.gov/>>.

CHAPTER 20

Managing the Nation's Economy: Fiscal Policy

OVERVIEW

Some of the most important efforts to manage the economy involve the application of fiscal policies. Fiscal policy refers to the use by the federal government of its powers to tax and spend to affect the level of economic activity. Fiscal policies are often described as *countercyclical* because they attempt to reverse (or counter) the course of the business cycle. That is, in times of recession, fiscal programs seek to slow and/or reverse the economic decline. Similarly, in inflationary times, fiscal policies could be designed to reduce aggregate demand.

In this chapter, we describe how fiscal policy can be used to affect the level of economic activity. We explain why fiscal programs are more difficult to apply than monetary policies. The chapter concludes with a discussion of deficit spending, the national debt, and the controversies swirling around those issues.

FISCAL POLICIES

We encounter examples of fiscal policies whenever we hear members of Congress or the president talking about the benefits of tax cuts or spending cuts (or tax increases or spending increases). Those who apply fiscal policies are seeking either to increase or to decrease aggregate demand. You may recall that aggregate demand is equal to the total spending of consumers (C), business (I), and government (G), or simply $C + I + G$. Consumer spending depends on the size of consumer income and the marginal propensity to consume. Because the marginal propensity to consume is fairly constant, consumer spending rises or falls mostly due to increases or decreases in consumer income. Business spending is far less predictable. The level of business spending is affected by many variables, such as the expectation of increased sales, anticipated price changes, tax laws, and government regulations.

Changing the level of government spending (*G*) while other components remain constant directly affects aggregate demand. An increase in government spending leads to an increase in aggregate demand when *C* and *I* are constant. Similarly, a decrease in government spending has the opposite effect: Aggregate demand declines.

The power to tax gives governments indirect influence over aggregate demand. When taxes are reduced, both consumers and businesses have more to spend, and their spending increases aggregate demand. Tax increases have the opposite effect. With less to spend, *C* and *I* fall along with aggregate demand.

The multiplier magnifies changes in aggregate demand. All other things being equal, with a multiplier of 5, an increase of $1 billion in government spending increases aggregate demand (total spending) by $5 billion. Consider the following hypothetical situation.

Assume that government economists have determined that at full employment the economy could produce $4 trillion in goods and services. Also assume that aggregate demand is running at $2.8 trillion, at a time when the multiplier is 4. In these circumstances, the recessionary gap will be $1.2 trillion (because $4 trillion − $2.8 trillion = $1.2 trillion).

In an effort to close the gap and end the recession, Congress votes (and the president approves) spending increases totaling $200 billion and tax reductions of $100 billion. This adds $300 billion to aggregate demand. Better still, since in our example the multiplier is 4, the $300 billion increase in purchasing power increases aggregate demand by $1.2 trillion ($300 billion × 4), and eliminates the recessionary gap.

"Free gifts to every kid in the world? – Are you a *Keynesian* or something?"

Limitations of Fiscal Policies

Political leaders have found that there are limitations to fiscal policies.

Forecasting and Timing Difficulties. The success of fiscal programs depends on how quickly and accurately the government is able to recognize economic trends. One problem is that business trends cannot be measured with absolute accuracy. Though economists are able to describe in general terms how well or poorly the economy is doing, no one has discovered how to predict the future of the economy with certainty. Assume, for example, that we are in a recession. Who can really say that tomorrow will not bring an upward turn? If that happens and recovery sets in before the government recognizes the shift, any effort to increase total demand (such as a tax cut or a spending program) could prove to be inflationary.

The sometimes agonizingly slow pace of the democratic process creates an additional problem. In many instances, Congress takes so long to act that necessary legislation is passed too late to achieve its fiscal goals.

Political Considerations. During periods of recession, the government might lower taxes and increase spending. These actions can be quite popular politically because voters almost always favor lower taxes, and many persons benefit directly from government spending. A problem arises, however, during periods of boom and inflation when opposing actions are called for—higher taxes and decreased spending. Members of Congress do not like to associate themselves with higher taxes. Nor is it politically helpful to reduce or eliminate spending programs that benefit the constituents back home. For this reason, fiscal policy is more popular when it is used to combat recession than when it is used against inflation.

Inflexibility of the National Budget. Ideally, government spending should increase during periods of recession and decrease during inflation. Currently, however, about 60 percent of the budget goes for interest on the national debt, national defense, and entitlements for the elderly. Interest payments on the national debt must be paid as a matter of law. The nation's security has the highest priority, and for that reason defense expenditures are rarely reduced from one year to the next. *Entitlements* are benefits for which people qualify automatically, by virtue of their age, income, or occupation. Social Security is an entitlement. So too are medical programs such as Medicare and Medicaid, civil-service and military pensions, and unemployment insurance. Unlike other budgetary programs, whose sizes are limited by the amount of money appropriated to meet them, the costs of entitlements cannot be controlled. If Congress appropriates $1 billion to build a highway, no more than that amount will be spent. But when, for example, it authorizes unemployment benefits, it can set no limit on the money that will ultimately flow from the Treasury. The government is legally obligated to provide benefits to anyone who can prove that he or she is eligible.

The political popularity of entitlement programs makes them virtually impossible to terminate. That leaves lawmakers with only a fraction of the total budget that they can manipulate to stabilize the economy.

LACK OF COORDINATED FISCAL POLICIES.   In the best of all possible worlds, state and local governments would mesh their budgets with that of the federal government so as to launch a coordinated attack on the nation's economic woes. In practice, the opposite is likely to take place.

During periods of inflation, state and local tax receipts increase, as does spending by the state and local governments. Increased spending, though, is the opposite of what is called for by fiscal theory. During times of inflation, state and local governments should decrease their spending so as to reduce total demand.

During recessions (when tax receipts are on the decline), states and localities often reduce their levels of spending. But in times of recession, fiscal theory says, government spending should be increased as a way of increasing aggregate demand. More government spending, in turn, would lead to increased spending by consumers and businesses.

Although state and local governments might like to increase their spending during hard times, they face major obstacles. Unlike the federal government, states and localities do not have the power to print money. Indeed, in many states balanced budgets are required by law. Moreover, states often find it more difficult to borrow during recessions. This leaves them with little choice other than to do their heaviest spending during times when their economies are flourishing. Unfortunately, inflationary periods can be just such times.

🌀 Discretionary and Automatic Fiscal Policies

Fiscal policies can be either discretionary or automatic.

Tax and spending programs initiated by the president and Congress to regulate the level of economic activity are known as *discretionary fiscal policies.* They are "discretionary" because they are enacted as Congress (often with the prodding of the president) deems necessary—that is, at the option (or discretion) of Congress.

Another kind of fiscal program automatically kicks in as needed without congressional action. Known as *automatic stabilizers,* these taxes and expenditures increase and decrease as needed to steady the economy. Three of the best-known automatic stabilizers are unemployment insurance, welfare programs, and the income tax.

UNEMPLOYMENT INSURANCE.   Under terms of the federal Social Security Act, every state has an unemployment insurance program. *Unemployment insurance* provides regular payments for a limited number of weeks to qualified workers who have lost their jobs. Funding for these state-administered programs comes from employment taxes paid by employers.

During recessions, when many workers are laid off and aggregate income is reduced, the number of people receiving unemployment insurance payments automatically increases. This helps to offset the income losses of unemployed workers. At the same time, the tax burden on employers is lessened because, with fewer workers, the employers' unemployment tax bills are reduced. In these ways, additional funds (through increased unemployment benefits and reduced taxes) are automatically pumped into the economy exactly when they are needed most.

During the recovery phase of the business cycle, the opposite happens: Employment increases and unemployment payments automatically decrease. At the same time, tax collections for the state unemployment programs are increased.

WELFARE.   Welfare programs provide both financial and in-kind assistance to poor individuals and families. *Financial assistance* comes in the form of cash payments. *In-kind payments* come in the form of goods or services (such as food) rather than money. Certain payments to welfare recipients fall somewhere in between in-kind payments and financial assistance. For example, *food stamps* can be used in much the same way as money. But unlike money, which

Workers collect unemployment compensation when they are laid off. How does this help the economy to recover from a recession?

may be used to purchase almost anything, food stamps may be used to purchase only food products. Some communities make rent payments directly to a welfare recipient's landlord; other communities give poor families a monthly rent allowance. Whatever the form of welfare payment, the economic impact is the same. Welfare payments tend to increase aggregate demand.

Like unemployment benefits, welfare payments increase during downswings in the business cycle because more people apply for welfare as jobs become scarce. Also, as with unemployment benefits, welfare payments decline during recoveries because jobs become more plentiful. Thus, welfare programs automatically add to aggregate demand during recessions and shrink aggregate demand during expansions.

INCOME TAX PROGRAMS.   The federal government and some state and local governments impose income taxes. Income taxes have an automatic stabilizing effect because the amount that individuals and corporations pay varies with their earnings. During periods of expansion when business activity, employment, and prices are on the increase, earnings increase. This results in an increase in income tax collections. Increased tax payments dampen the ability of businesses and individuals to increase their rate of spending, and thereby automatically keep a lid on the boom.

The opposite takes place during a recession. As incomes fall, so too do income tax payments. Reduced income tax payments leave consumers and business firms with an increasing share of their income that they can spend. Any increased spending, of course, helps to restore aggregate demand.

 # THE DEBT AND THE DEFICIT

The United States is in debt because the federal government often spends more than it earns. The *deficit* (difference between income and expenditures) is made up through borrowing. When the government borrows to pay for its expenditures, the process is known as *deficit financing*. In 2004, for example, estimated budget receipts totaled $1,922 billion, but expenditures ran to $2,229 billion. The additional borrowing necessary to cover the $307 billion deficit brought the *national debt* (the total that the government owes) up to about $4.2 trillion.

How much is a trillion dollars? Statisticians tell us that it would take a stack of $1,000 bills 67 miles high to reach that sum. Put another way, a $4.2 trillion debt divided equally among every man, woman, and child in the United States amounts to roughly $15,000 per person.

The United States has spent more than it has earned in 43 out of the last 50 years. Why does the United States often spend more than it has earns? Is there something ominous about an ever-increasing national debt? Or are there sound economic reasons for deficit financing, and if so, what are they?

🗲 Why Is the National Debt So High?

The national debt is as high as it is because the government has run a deficit in all but seven of its last 50 budgets. The two principal causes of deficit spending have been wars and recessions. Since 1776, the U.S. government's wartime economic policy has been to spend whatever was necessary to win wars and to worry about paying for them later. As a result of the Civil War (1861–1865), the U.S. debt topped $1 billion for the first time. U.S. participation in World War I (1917–1918) brought the national debt up to what was then the unheard-of total of $27 billion. Participation in World War II (1941–1945) added $200 billion to the total.

During the Great Depression of the 1930s, the U.S. government for the first time used its powers to tax and spend to fight a recession. Remember that fiscal solutions to the problems created by a recession call for increasing aggregate demand through tax reductions and/or increased government spending. Government expenditures for New Deal programs such as the Civilian Conservation Corps (CCC), the Works Progress Administration (WPA), the Tennessee Valley Authority (TVA), and the Social Security System added $30 billion to the national debt.

The largest increase in the national debt—some $2 trillion—occurred during the Ronald Reagan and George Bush administrations (1981–1993). During that time, however, the debt explosion was not war related. It was brought on instead by efforts to fight the recession of 1980–1982, by the massive tax cuts of 1981–1984, and by heavy defense spending throughout the 1980s. The debt continued to rise during the early years of the Bill Clinton administration (1993–1997), but during its final years (1998–2001) the nation ran a surplus.

Annual budget surpluses turned to annual deficits during the George W. Bush administration (2002 and thereafter). In looking for the reasons why the nation shifted back to deficit financing in 2002, the following are most frequently cited.

- A recession that began in March of 2001 and a long-term decline in stock prices caused a sharp decline in federal tax revenues.
- The 9/11/01 terrorist attacks caused a major increase in defense spending.
- Tax cuts that were enacted shortly after President George W. Bush took office in 2001 reduced federal income to a point well below expenditures.

🗲 How Large Is the National Debt?

When we speak of the national debt, we are talking about the bonds, notes, and other securities issued by the federal government when it borrows money. In 2004, this totaled $4.2 trillion.

Is a $4.2 trillion debt too large? To a young person whose only income is a $20-a-week allowance, even a $200 debt might seem unmanageable. If that person has a part-time job with a weekly income of $90, however, he or she might be able to carry a $200 loan. Similarly, for a family with an annual income of $25,000, a $15,000 auto loan could be out of reach. Those with an income of $50,000 might not find such a loan burdensome. In order to answer the question whether a $4.2 trillion debt is too large, we might consider the ability of the nation to carry such debt. Study Figure 20.1 to see what debts the country has carried in the past.

At the end of the Second World War in 1945, the GDP stood at $212 billion. That year's national debt was $235 billion, or 111 percent of the GDP. The debt declined somewhat in the five years after the war. After 1950, the national debt again continued to climb, but the debt as a percent of GDP declined. This happened because the economy grew at a much faster rate than the debt. In 1980, for example, the national debt of $712 billion represented only 26 percent of that year's GDP of $2.8 trillion. The rapidly growing budget deficits of the 1980s peaked in 1995. From 1996 until 2001, the national debt as a percent of GDP again declined. Since then, the national debt as a percent of GDP has been on the increase.

 Who Bears the Burden of Federal Government Debt?

Economists often analyze the burden of government borrowing in terms of its opportunity costs. The opportunity cost of a federal bond issue is expressed in terms of the goods and services that the nation had to forgo because of the issue.

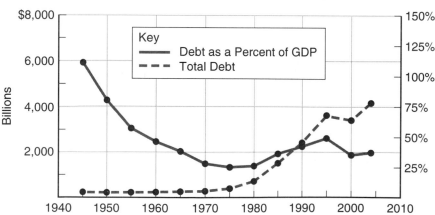

Figure 20.1 **Trends in Federal Debt Held by the Public**

INTERNAL DEBT.   Suppose that at a time when the economy was fully employed, the government chose to finance a $10 billion naval program with borrowed funds. Suppose, too, that the debt was an *internal debt*—that is, the money was borrowed from institutions and citizens of the United States. Since there was full employment, some shift out of civilian production would have to occur in order to build the warships and other items wanted by the U.S. Navy. In other words, the opportunity cost of the naval-building program would have been the $10 billion worth of civilian goods that would have to be postponed.

EXTERNAL DEBT.   While 89 percent of the national debt is held by U.S. individuals and institutions, the remainder is held by foreigners. This latter category is called an *external debt.*

Loans from foreign sources (that is, the external debt) might impose a burden on future generations of Americans, or they might not. An external national debt does impose a burden on future generations in the following example: Taxes collected in the future from U.S. residents (to make the interest payments on those foreign loans) will go to foreigners. In addition, when at some time in the future foreigners who hold U.S. government bonds choose to redeem them, dollars will flow out of the United States.

External debts may also benefit future generations of Americans in the following way: When government spending is financed by foreign loans, it enables the United States to obtain goods from abroad without reducing domestic production. This situation occurs because if the government does not borrow from foreign sources, it will would have to borrow from internal sources. And as discussed in Chapter 18, government borrowing through its sales of government securities reduces aggregate demand, which in turn reduces domestic production.

 # THE DEBATE OVER DEFICIT FINANCING

Deficit spending and the national debt have been controversial issues throughout U.S. history. At one extreme, there are those who argue that the national government should *never* spend more than its income. At the other extreme, there are those who argue that the government should spend as much as it needs without regard to how much (or how little) income it is generating. The opinions of most Americans, however, fall somewhere between those two extremes. What follows are the arguments most often heard on each side of the debate.

⚡ The Arguments Against Deficit Financing

One often hears the following arguments on the national debt:

THE GOVERNMENT IS SETTING A POOR EXAMPLE.   "If I continue to spend more than I earn, sooner or later I'll be unable to pay my debts, and I'll be forced into bankruptcy. Now, the same is true for a business and for the federal government. . . ." Statements such as this one are often used to criticize deficit spending. Many Americans believe that the federal government is living beyond its means by borrowing year after year. They feel that eventually the government will have to face the consequences and pay all its debts, as individuals and businesses have to do. Otherwise, they say, it will go bankrupt or stop operating.

INTEREST PAYMENTS ON THE NATIONAL DEBT ARE GETTING OUT OF CONTROL. A large national debt requires heavy interest payments. In 2004, interest payments were about $176 billion, or 8 percent of the yearly budget. Critics of high debts fear that this percentage could easily grow to a point where taxpayers could never repay the debt.

THE BURDEN WILL BE ON FUTURE GENERATIONS.   "The money that the federal government borrows has to be repaid by somebody. You know who that somebody will be? Our children and grandchildren, that's who. We're making future generations pay for our excesses." This is a frequent argument. The debts we contract today will add to the tax burden of future generations. Americans today pay about 31 percent of their gross income to taxes (local, state, and federal). Most Americans already think that this percentage is too great. They worry that when their children become taxpayers, the burden may be even greater.

The Federal Government Is Too Large.   Many Americans think that the U.S. government is too large. Some say it is inefficient and bureaucratic. A leaner government, they believe, would work more efficiently and also save money. Other critics of the federal government dislike certain of its policies, whether environmental laws, foreign aid, or other programs. Some Americans want many of the powers that the federal government now has turned over to the states. Such a transfer would shrink the size of the federal government.

Americans who want a smaller government usually support a balanced federal budget and a reduction in the national debt. They see the reduction of budgets for the various federal departments and agencies as a quick way to reduce the size and/or power of the U.S. government.

Budget Deficits Cause Inflation.   Many people believe that there is a direct relationship between budget deficits and inflation. If inflation is to be kept under control, they say, the government must balance its budget. At a time of full employment of the nation's productive resources, deficit spending adds to the money supply. There is more money competing for the same quantity of goods and services. Thus, prices simply have to go higher. We can see this by using the formula $P = MV \div Q$, introduced in Chapter 17. P (prices for goods and services) equals M (the amount of money in circulation) times V (how many transactions a dollar makes in a period of time) divided by Q (the quantity of goods and services our nation produces). Thus, if Q remains unchanged and M increases, P will increase.

Borrowing Redistributes Income Unfairly.   Interest payments on the national debt are mostly financed out of income tax receipts. Since the largest holders of government bonds and notes are financial institutions and wealthy individuals, the effect of interest payments going to these institutions and individuals is to transfer wealth from middle-class taxpayers to wealthier ones. Those who believe this say that if the government did not have to make interest payments, more money would be available to provide services to those in need, or to reduce taxes for middle- and low-income individuals.

Controlling Deficits Will Help Curb Waste.   Many spending items passed by Congress can be viewed as wasteful in the sense that they serve a relatively small number of people or businesses. Members of Congress have

Supply-Side Economics

The efforts of the federal government to stabilize the economy were for many years based on the theories of British economist John Maynard Keynes (featured on pages 406–407). Keynes identified fiscal and monetary policies as keys to both ending recessions and bringing inflation under control. According to Keynes, in times of recession the federal government should use its monetary and fiscal powers to increase aggregate demand (spending by consumers, business, and itself). In times of inflation, said Keynes, the government should use its monetary and fiscal powers to reduce aggregate demand and thereby reduce spending and bring down prices.

Keynesianism worked well enough during those years in which either a recession or a rise in the price level was troublesome. In the 1970s, however, the United States was experiencing both recession *and* inflation. Economists coined the term *stagflation* (for economic stagnation plus inflation) to describe those times. Few economists could suggest how the government could deal with both problems at the same time.

There was, though, one group of economists (including **Arthur B. Laffer** of the University of Southern California and **Paul Craig Roberts** of the Institute for Political Economy) who claimed to have found a solution to the dilemma. These were the "supply-siders," so-called because they saw production (i.e., supply) as the key to ridding the nation of stagflation. If production were increased, they argued, prices would have to come down. Meanwhile, the additional investment in new equipment and enterprises would put the unemployed back to work, increase personal and business earnings, and bring the recession to an end.

Unfortunately, in the supply-siders' view, there were three obstacles to increasing production:

- taxes that were so high that they discouraged investment in new plants, equipment, and business enterprises.

- government-sponsored welfare programs that discouraged individual initiative. Why, the supply-siders asked, would people look

for work if they knew that they could get as much money simply by going on welfare?

- government regulatory agencies whose rules were so narrow that they discouraged innovation and creativity.

The supply-side economists proposed these remedies:

- Reduce taxes, particularly for those in the upper-income brackets. This reduction would leave businesspeople and others with additional after-tax income, which could be invested in productive enterprises. Moreover, rich people would have greater incentive to earn more money.

- Reduce government spending for social programs so as to limit assistance to just the "truly needy." This provision would encourage the "less needy" to find jobs.

- "Get government off the backs of business" by reducing the number and powers of the regulatory agencies. Fewer government regulations would result in less work for business owners and managers and, thus, lower costs for businesses.

Critics of supply-side economics said that the tax proposals would enrich only the wealthy, create budget deficits, and add to the national debt. There was no guarantee that people with additional after-tax income would actually invest the money in business enterprises. Supply-siders were also accused of being indifferent to the needs of the millions of people in the United States sorely in need of government assistance. And some critics said that supply-siders were wrong in their assessment of the value of regulatory agencies.

Interest in supply-side economics was rekindled with the 2000 election of George W. Bush as President. With the nation in the midst of its first recession in ten years, the President called for dramatic tax reductions as a way of turning the economy around. These ideas were summarized in the *Economic Report of the President, 2003,* in which he said:

"Lowering tax rates and moving more Americans into the lowest tax bracket will help our economy grow and create jobs. . . . We will end the unfair double taxation of corporate income received by individuals. By putting more money back in the hands of shareholders, strengthening investor confidence in the market, and encouraging more investment, we will have more growth and job creation. These steps will allow Americans to keep more of their own money to spend, save, or invest. . . ."

1. (*a*) What is stagflation? (*b*) Why do the supply-side economists believe that production (or supply) is the key to fighting stagflation? (*c*) Compare the Keynesian approach to correcting a recession to that advocated by supply-side economists.

2. With respect to the following, explain the policies favored by supply-side economists and their reasons for those policies: (*a*) taxes, (*b*) welfare programs, and (*c*) the regulatory agencies.

3. (*a*) Summarize the information contained in the Laffer Curve, Figure 20.2. (*b*) Why do supply-side economists use the Laffer Curve to support their positions?

4. Critics of supply-side policies say that they (*a*) discriminate against the poor, (*b*) favor the rich, and (*c*) lead to record deficits in the federal budget. Evaluate *each* of these criticisms.

Figure 20.2 **Laffer Curve**

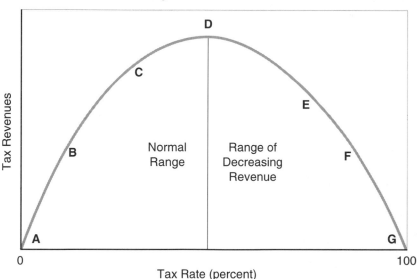

*Cut taxes yet increase revenues? Absolutely, argued Arthur Laffer, who demonstrated the proof of this seeming paradox with a graphic model, the now famous **Laffer Curve**. At point A, the income tax rate is zero; consequently, the government earns no revenue. As tax rates are levied and increased at B, C, and D, government revenues also increase. But something happens beyond point D: People begin to find taxes so high that they look for other uses for what had been their working time. Some people will work fewer hours, some others may drop out of the labor force, while still others may look for ways to hide all or part of their income from the tax authorities. At point E on the scale, revenues are less than they were at C and D. At F, revenues are the same as they were at B. At 100 percent (G), revenues are again back to zero, since no one would work if all earnings were taken in taxes.*

Laffer concluded from this study that as long as taxes remained within the normal range, increased rates of taxes would earn the government additional income. But beyond that lay a region of decreasing revenue. Within that broad range, government could increase its income tax revenue only by reducing tax rates.

traditionally proposed spending laws that benefit only certain people and businesses in their districts. Sometimes these proposals become law because lawmakers gain support for their proposals by promising to support those of their colleagues. If passed, such spending laws are called *pork-barrel legislation* (or sometimes just *pork*). If lawmakers become serious about passing a balanced budget, the argument goes, then pork-barrel legislation will become more difficult to pass (and there will be less government waste).

The Arguments in Favor of Deficit Financing

Many economists believe that deficit financing can be a useful tool of government at certain times. Moreover, they believe that a large national debt is not all that dangerous. Can a large debt bankrupt the nation? Does government borrowing impose an unfair burden on future generations? Let us look at these questions separately.

A Large Debt Will Not Bankrupt the Nation.   Bankruptcy occurs when an individual or business can no longer pay its debts. The federal government, however, is not likely to go bankrupt because existing debt can be refinanced over and over again. Furthermore, the federal government has the power to tax and print money. No private individual or business can do this. In other words, the federal government can increase taxes or print as much money as it needs to meet its obligations. Of course, there is a possible danger if taxes are raised too high. Taxpayers might get angry and vote lawmakers out of office. Moreover, if too much money is printed, the result might be severe inflation.

Future Generations Will Benefit From Today's Debts.   Many economists concede that the debts we contract today will add to the tax burden of future generations. But, the economists say, these debts can also benefit future generations. They will benefit when they use the roads, bridges, schools, and hospitals that are now being built using borrowed money. They will benefit from the debt if deficit financing is used to fight a recession. They will benefit from current peacekeeping operations if these actions prevent a greater war.

Nevertheless, the same logic that justifies deficit financing during recessions would also call for balanced budgets during times of full employment and stable prices. Balanced budgets during these times help to stabilize the economy. A budget in balance would neither increase nor decrease aggregate demand and, therefore, would not contribute either to an inflationary gap or to a recessionary gap.

Inflation Is Not Always Bad.   Most economists agree that budget deficits fuel inflation during times of full employment. At other times (such as during a recession), however, economists see a role for deficit spending. By reducing taxes and/or increasing spending, budget deficits can be increased. But such a policy also pumps additional funds into the economy, thereby stimulating production and employment.

For similar reasons, economists often call for *budget surpluses* as a way to fight inflation. A budget surplus is created when expenditures are less than receipts. In order to create a surplus in the federal budget, Congress would need to enact some combination of tax increases and/or spending reductions. But tax increases and spending reductions are politically unpopular. Given the increase in military spending to fight the War on Terrorism, budget surpluses are not likely to occur in the foreseeable future.

GOVERNMENT BORROWING IS AN ECONOMIC FACT OF LIFE.   Many economists recognize that government debt is a necessity, since certain programs cannot be paid for with the income that a government takes in during the course of one year. The basic facilities on which the nation's economy, commerce, and industry depend are known as its *infrastructure.* All of the following are considered inventory of the infrastructure: highways, aircraft control systems, armed forces bases and equipment, and space exploration equipment. Since each of these can be expected to last for many years after production or construction, some economists think that it is appropriate for the federal government to spread their costs over time by borrowing to finance them.

On a local level, infrastructure includes roads, water and sewage systems, schools, hospitals, and police and fire stations. Local governments often borrow to pay for these facilities.

 # BUDGET DEFICITS IN RECENT HISTORY

Budget deficits have been a way of life for the United States in recent decades. As illustrated in Table 20.1, with the exception of the four years between 1998 and 2001 (when the budget earned an annual surplus), deficits have been the order of the day. Meanwhile, the national debt went from $1.5 trillion in 1985 to $4.2 trillion in 2004. Not surprisingly, the nation's debt and the annual budget deficits that added to it have gotten the attention of the financial community and generated a debate over what, if anything, should be done about the supposed problem.

In an effort to legislate a balanced budget, Congress in 1985 enacted the **Gramm-Rudman-Hollings Act**, which called for year-by-year reductions in budget deficits and, by 1993, a balanced budget. The act's goals were not met (see Table 20.1) and the law was allowed to expire. The reasons for Gramm-Rudman-Hollings's failure were both political and economic. In terms of politics, U.S. representatives and senators feared the wrath of their constituents if they approved the kind of spending cuts and tax increases necessary to reduce the deficit. In terms of economics, the country was going through a recession in

TABLE 20.1	BUDGET DEFICITS AND SURPLUSES SINCE 1985 (MILLIONS OF DOLLARS)

Year	Deficit (unless otherwise indicated)
1985	$ 212,334
1986	221,245
1987	149,769
1989	152,481
1990	221,384
1991	269,169
1992	290,403
1993	255,100
1994	203,169
1995	163,900
1996	107,330
1997	22,600
1998	+ 69,200
1999	+ 125,200
2000	+ 236,400
2001	+ 127,300
2002	157,800
2003	374,000
2004	307,400*

1998–2001 indicated as surpluses.

*estimates

the early 1990s. Fiscal policy during recessions normally calls for some combination of tax reductions and increased government spending. Following the Gramm-Rudman-Hollings guidelines (that is, increasing taxes and/or reducing spending) might well have added to the economic decline.

The debate over budget deficits was renewed with vigor in the aftermath of the conclusion of the second U.S. war with Iraq, in 2003. With the nation in the midst of a recession and the war's costs yet to be calculated (but certainly to be in the hundreds of billions, an ongoing War on Terrorism added to all the "normal" expenses of running the U.S. government. President George W. Bush renewed his call for tax cuts. One thing on which everyone agreed was that the immediate effect of tax cuts at this time would be to increase the national debt. Was it appropriate to reduce taxes at such a time? On this question, the "experts" differed.

Those supporting the President argued that given the recession, a tax cut would serve as a stimulus to restart the economy. They also argued that as a percentage of GDP, the deficits were less than they had been in the 1980s. More important, many businesses were operating considerably below their capacity. If these businesses were presented with the opportunity to keep more of their profits (because of a tax cut), production and employment levels would increase, the recession would be brought to an end, and the economy would return to a healthy rate of growth.

Tax cut opponents argued that as a percentage of GDP the deficits were too high. More important, they said, a growing deficit increases the need of the government to borrow. But, particularly in times of recession, the amount of funds available to lend is limited. That being the case, the government with its risk-free bonds crowds out the private sector in the competition to attract investors. This situation, in turn, threatens to push interest rates up to much higher levels.

𝌗 What Does History Tell Us About the Effect of Tax Increases and Tax Cuts?

Some say, "Not very much." Consider the following.

WHAT WAS PREDICTED.   In 1982, President Reagan called for, and Congress enacted, large tax cuts that substantially added to the budget deficit. Some of the nation's leading economists at that time predicted that the durability of an economic expansion was going to be significantly limited by the huge deficits in the federal budget.

WHAT REALLY HAPPENED.   What followed was an economic expansion of almost eight years, starting in late 1982, along with a 4.3 percent annual growth rate and a 160 percent rise in the stock market.

WHAT WAS PREDICTED.   When in 1993 President Clinton called for (and Congress enacted) a major tax increase, some in Congress predicted that the tax increase would kill jobs, lead to a recession, and increase the deficit.

WHAT REALLY HAPPENED.   Instead, what followed was the longest economic expansion in U.S. history, a 2.5 percent annual rise in productivity, a budget surplus, and a jobless rate of only 3.9 percent.

S U M M A R Y

Some efforts to manage the economy involve the application of fiscal policies. This term refers to the federal government's use of its powers to tax and spend so as to affect the level of economic activity and the level of aggregate demand.

Fiscal policies are often described as "countercyclical" because they attempt to reverse (or counter) the course of the business cycle, That is, in times of recession, fiscal programs may seek to slow and/or reverse the economic decline by increasing aggregate demand. Similarly, in times of inflation, fiscal policies can be designed to reduce aggregate demand and bring down prices.

In this chapter, we describe how tax and spending programs may be used to affect the level of economic activity. We also explain why fiscal programs are more difficult to apply than monetary policies. The chapter concludes with a discussion of deficit spending, the national debt, and the controversies surrounding those issues.

REVIEWING THE CHAPTER

BUILDING VOCABULARY

Match each item in Column A with its definition in Column B.

Column A

1. countercyclical
2. automatic stabilizer
3. discretionary fiscal policy
4. national debt
5. in-kind payment
6. internal debt
7. external debt
8. deficit financing
9. infrastructure
10. pork-barrel legislation

Column B

a. basic facilities on which a nation's economy depends
b. the total of all money owed by the federal government
c. the money the federal government owes to U.S. institutions and citizens
d. laws that benefit mostly people in a legislator's home district rather than the general public
e. reversing the actions of cyclical trends
f. an action that the federal government may use to regulate the economy
g. the paying for government spending by borrowing
h. loans to the federal government from foreign institutions and people
i. a government program that automatically compensates for changes in the business cycle
j. the giving of a good or service by a government

UNDERSTANDING WHAT YOU HAVE READ

1. Discretionary fiscal policies (*a*) depend on the skills of the Federal Reserve System for their success (*b*) are more effective during periods of inflation than during recessions (*c*) call for the adjustment of interest rates on loans to businesses (*d*) require accurate forecasting and timely application to be effective.

2. Which *one* of the following is the *best* example of an automatic stabilizer? (*a*) an increase in government spending (*b*) an increase in taxes on tobacco products (*c*) unemployment insurance (*d*) a drug plan for senior citizens.

3. The federal government's fiscal policies differ from its monetary policies in that its fiscal policies are concerned mostly with (*a*) taxing and spending (*b*) reserve ratios and discount rates (*c*) economic stability in the short run (*d*) the management of "checkbook money."

4. Fiscal tools have been more effective during recessions than during periods of inflation because (*a*) people like to see the government reduce its spending (*b*) Congress finds it is easier to reduce taxes and increase spending than to adopt the opposite course of action (*c*) the Open Market Committee finds it easier to buy bonds than to sell them (*d*) a tax increase is relatively easy for the president to obtain.

5. An increase in government spending during periods of full employment would most likely result in (*a*) price increases (*b*) unemployment (*c*) increased production (*d*) increased employment.

6. Government spending that creates a deficit in the federal budget is most desirable when (*a*) business profits are too high (*b*) the cost of living has gone up (*c*) there is rapid expansion in private spending (*d*) there is a threat of a depression.

7. Which statement is true of the national debt? (*a*) Over 85 percent was borrowed from U.S. institutions and citizens. (*b*) It declined after 1945 as a percentage of the GDP. (*c*) It has passed the $4 trillion mark. (*d*) All of the above.

8. The burden of the public debt on taxpayers increases when (*a*) interest rates fall (*b*) both the public debt and the population are increasing at the same time (*c*) the size of the debt is increasing proportionately more rapidly than national income (*d*) national income is increasing and prices are relatively stable.

9. Who holds the largest portion of the national debt of the United States? (*a*) foreign governments (*b*) U.S. citizens and private institutions (*c*) foreign private institutions and businesses (*d*) the U.S. government.

10. Those who favor balanced budgets argue that deficit financing (*a*) distributes wealth more equally (*b*) sets a good example for individuals (*c*) fuels inflation (*d*) will benefit future generations at the expense of current taxpayers.

THINKING CRITICALLY

1. Assume that the nation has entered a period of inflation and that the federal government has decided to bring fiscal tools to bear upon the problem. (*a*) Explain two fiscal policies that the government might adopt to reverse the trend. (*b*) List and explain *three* built-in stabilizers that would automatically serve to slow down inflation.

2. Events in the early 2000s showed that neither monetary nor fiscal policies can guarantee full employment, a stable dollar, and economic growth. Identify and explain *four* reasons why monetary and fiscal policies may fail to achieve their goals.

3. The national debt was $4.2 trillion in 2004, bringing the average debt to about $15,000 for every man, woman, and child in the country. This huge amount of debt has sparked a bitter controversy. Some people regard the debt as an evil that should be reduced and eventually eliminated. Others argue that the debt is necessary to the nation's economic health. Identify and explain *two* arguments advanced for *each* point of view.

4. A Balanced-Budget Amendment has been proposed as a measure that would eliminate future deficits.

   a. Prepare a chart indicating the pros and cons of a Balanced-Budget Amendment.

   b. Using the information you gathered in your chart, explain why you favor or oppose such a constitutional amendment.

SKILLS: Interpreting a Statistical Table

▶ TABLE 20.2 TRENDS IN FEDERAL DEBT HELD BY THE PUBLIC (BILLIONS)

Year	National Debt	Debt as a Percent of GDP
1945	$ 235	111%
1950	219	80
1955	227	57
1960	237	46
1965	261	38
1970	283	28
1975	395	25
1980	712	26
1985	1,508	36
1990	2,412	42
1995	3,604	49
2000	3,410	35
2004*	4,166	37

*estimate

Study Table 20.2. Based on the information in the table and your reading in this chapter, answer the following.

1. Describe what has happened to total debt since 1945.

2. Describe what has happened to total debt as a percent of GDP since 1945.

3. In which year shown was debt as a percent of GDP the greatest? The lowest?

4. How do you explain why total debt was higher in 1975 than it was in 1950 while debt as a percent of GDP was lower in 1975 than it was in 1950?

5. Explain why you believe that the size of the total debt is or is not a serious problem today.

USING THE INTERNET

The U.S. Budget is available at <<w3.access.gpo.gov/usbudget>>.

CHAPTER 21

Economic Growth and the Quality of Life

OVERVIEW

Economic growth—the ever-increasing output of goods and service—may be society's oldest economic goal. It is hardly a surprising goal since the dream of a better tomorrow seems to be part and parcel of the human condition. For that reason, economists have long studied and written about the process of economic growth. Moreover, every U.S. president in modern times has supported policies and programs to promote growth.

In recent years, however, questions have been raised about some of the basic assumptions of economic growth. As evidence of the relationship between production and environmental decay continues to mount, some people question whether society can afford to pay the price of growth. The controversy has yet to be resolved.

In this chapter, we will discuss aspects of economic growth, including

- what this growth is

- why growth is important to our economy and to the global economy

- the ingredients of economic growth

- the role of government in promoting growth

- the debate between those who would limit economic growth and those who advocate few restrictions on it.

WHAT IS ECONOMIC GROWTH?

Economic growth refers to an increase in the output of goods and services over time. It is most commonly measured in terms of changes in the dollar value of

TABLE 21.1   U.S. GROSS DOMESTIC PRODUCT, 1959–2002 (CURRENT AND CONSTANT 1996 DOLLARS)

	CURRENT		CONSTANT	
	Total (billions)	Per Capita	Total (billions)	Per Capita
1959	$ 507.4	$ 2,806	$ 2,300.0	$12,721
1964	834.1	4,613	2,822.7	15,612
1969	985.3	4,790	3,543.2	17,275
1974	1,501.0	7,318	4,061.7	19,803
1979	2,566.4	11,271	4,870.1	21,388
1984	3,932.7	15,730	5,477.4	21,910
1989	5,489.1	21,956	6,568.7	26,275
1994	7,054.3	32,373	7,337.8	31,472
1999	9,274.3	32,955	8,733.2	31,032
2002	10,446.2	36,525	10,300.0	36,014

the gross domestic product (GDP). All other things being equal, if the GDP in one year is greater than that of the preceding year, we could say that economic growth has taken place. But all other things are not necessarily equal. We know, for example, that the value of the dollar is constantly changing. If the GDP increases by 5 percent in a year in which the purchasing power of the dollar declines by 10 percent, fewer goods and services are actually produced that year. For that reason, economists prefer to use GDP as expressed in *real GDP* (or constant dollars). This method eliminates yearly changes in the value of the dollar from the measurement of economic growth.

Population change is another variable affecting economic growth. While real GDP enables us to compare the economy's total output of one year with that of another, it does not tell us much about living standards. For example, if the population increased by 10 percent while the GDP was increasing by 5 percent, there would be fewer goods and services available per capita (for every person). Thus, despite the increase in output, living standards as measured by per capita GDP would decrease. For that reason, economists developed a second gauge of economic growth: *real GDP per capita*. This measure eliminates both fluctuations in the value of the dollar and population differences as factors in comparing the output of one period of time with that of another.

We can now refine our definition by saying that economic growth is the increase over time in real GDP per capita.

WHAT IS THE IMPORTANCE OF ECONOMIC GROWTH?

In the 18th century, English economist **Thomas Malthus** (discussed on pages 472–473) predicted that the world's population would outgrow the food supply. He believed that many people would starve to death unless wars and diseases killed them first. His theories have not yet proved correct. The world's population has increased tremendously since the 18th century, along with tremendous growths in food supplies. What has happened is that the productive capacity of industrialized nations has increased at a rate faster than the increase in population. Economic growth has made this possible. In many of the developing countries, however, economic growth has not increased at a faster rate than the increase in population. Thus, the dire predictions of Malthus are of real concern in these countries. (The many obstacles to growth in the developing nations are discussed in Chapter 25.) Economic growth has been largely responsible for the following: (1) higher living standards, (2) high employment levels, (3) income security, and (4) a strong national defense. We will discuss each topic.

Figure 21.1 **Real Gross Domestic Product (Annual Rates of Change)**

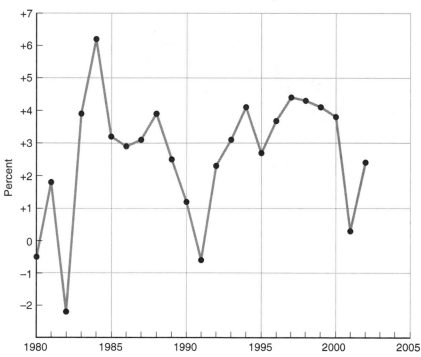

How does this graph illustrate economic growth? Which year or years shown do not show growth?

Higher Living Standards

Economists attribute the improved living standards in the industrialized nations of the world over the past 200 years to economic growth. As we said, economic growth is an increase in goods and services per capita over a period of time. Whenever real GDP per capita increases, there is more of everything to go around. This increase in goods and services resulted in higher living standards in the past and is likely to do so in the future as well.

High Employment Levels

If we are to maintain high employment levels, our economy must grow. We must create new businesses to compensate for the ones that are cutting back on numbers of employees and those businesses that are folding. The economy must expand to create more than a million new jobs each year.

Income Security

Economic growth enables the nation to maintain its Social Security system and programs to assist the needy, such as food stamps. Millions of Americans depend on these programs. The United States spends hundreds of billions of dollars each year on income security and poverty programs. Without economic growth, the country would have difficulty funding these programs.

Strong National Defense and Homeland Security

Because of its tremendous output of goods and services, the United States has been able to build a powerful national defense force and still meet its other needs. From the late 1940s until 1991, the United States was considered the leader in the free world's confrontations with the Soviet Union and its allies. Now that this cold war has ended, U.S. leaders believe that they still need to maintain heavy spending on national defense. They fear that instability in various regions of the world such as the Middle East might endanger U.S. interests. They also fear that several unfriendly nations are developing nuclear, biological, and chemical weapons and are promoting terrorism.

September 11, 2001, may be considered a turning point for the United States. Terrorists, assumed to be associated with al Qaida, a group led by Osama bin Laden (a Saudi-born exile living in Afghanistan), hijacked four American airliners. They crashed two planes into the Twin Towers of the World Trade Center in New York City and one into the Pentagon near Washington, D.C. The fourth plane was forced to crash in Pennsylvania when the passengers overcame the hijackers. All persons aboard these planes died, along with some 3,000 more in New York City and Washington, D.C. Subsequently, the United States established a Department of Homeland Security and began spending billions on maintaining the nation's security against further terrorist attacks.

Economic growth has made it possible for the United States to maintain its leadership role in world politics. The United States provides high levels of economic assistance to countries in various parts of the world. It participates in numerous UN-sponsored peacekeeping missions. In recent decades, for example, the United States sent armed forces to help restore order in Somalia, Haiti, Bosnia, and Kosovo. The United States joined other UN forces in 2001 to rid Afghanistan of its Taliban leadership and the al Qaida terrorist forces there. Strong resistance remains in Afghanistan. Meanwhile the United States is helping Afghanistan develop democratic institutions, a police force, and an army.

Figure 21.2 **Real GDP and Real GDP per Capita in 1959, 1979, and 2002 (Constant 1996 dollars)**

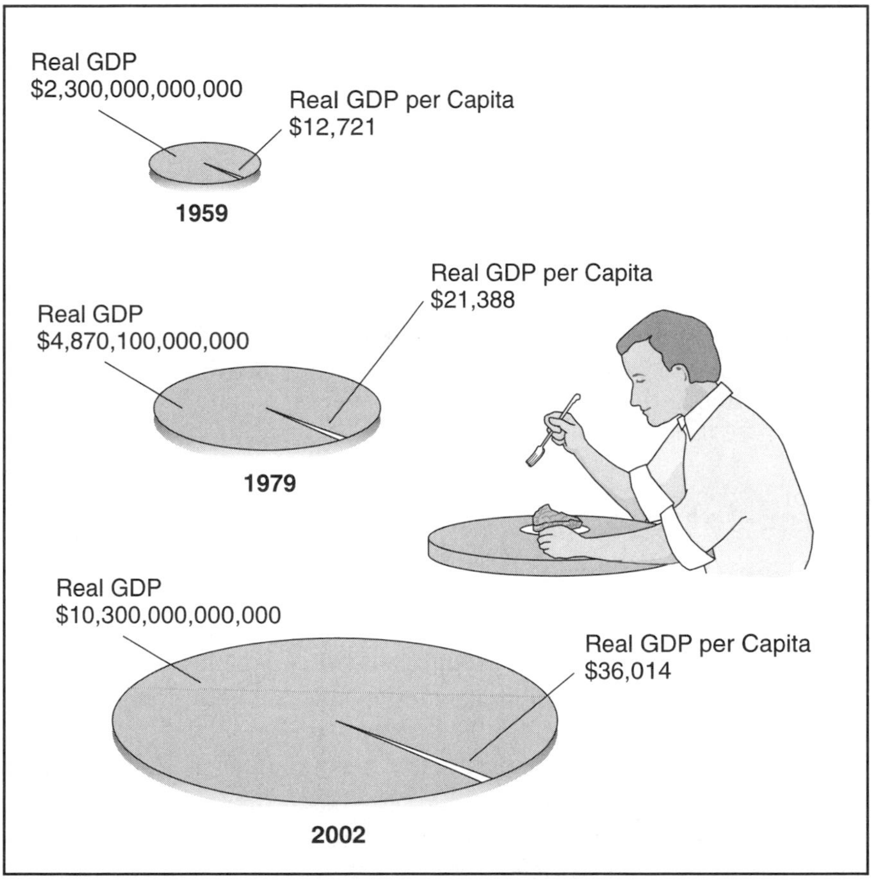

Real GDP
$2,300,000,000,000

Real GDP per Capita
$12,721

1959

Real GDP per Capita
$21,388

Real GDP
$4,870,100,000,000

1979

Real GDP
$10,300,000,000,000

Real GDP per Capita
$36,014

2002

As economic growth (the pie) increases, the size of the "slice of pie" each individual receives also grows. How might an increasing real GDP per capita in a country affect the quality of life in that country?

In March 2003, the United States, Great Britain, and Australia led a coalition of nations in what was called "Operation Free Iraq." One of the justifications given by President George W. Bush was to enforce UN resolutions ordering Iraq to destroy its *weapons of mass destruction (WMD),* which include nuclear, biological, and chemical weapons. France, Germany, Russia, China, and many other nations opposed war as a method of settling this issue and instead proposed continued negotiations and UN inspections. Unable to reach an agreement with its UN co-members, the coalition forces attacked Iraq and overthrew the regime of Saddam Hussein. In its place, the United States pledged to bring a new, democratic government to the Iraqi people. Meanwhile, U.S. troops in Iraq have become almost daily targets of shootings and bombings by Iraqis opposed to the U.S.-led invasion and occupation.

Some economists believe that it is possible for the United States to wage war away from its shores and defend its borders without seriously reducing living standards at home, but only if it has an expanding economy. They feel that the United States can borrow more money for only a limited period of time. They maintain that U.S. national defense demands increased U.S. economic growth in the years ahead.

WHAT ARE THE INGREDIENTS OF ECONOMIC GROWTH?

Like any good recipe, it takes a number of ingredients to produce economic growth. These are (1) an ever-increasing ability to produce goods and services, (2) expanding demand, and (3) a favorable business climate.

Ever-Increasing Productive Capacity

Economic growth requires a long-term increase in real output per person. There is a limit, however, to the amount of goods and services the economy can produce at any point in time. Exactly what this limit is depends on the economy's supply of productive resources and society's ability to use them—that is, its *productive capacity.*

As discussed in Chapter 6, productive resources such as raw materials, labor, management, and capital are limited. Once these resources are fully employed, output cannot be increased unless a new supply of resources is made available or new and more efficient production techniques are applied. Therefore, in order to stimulate or continue economic growth, our nation must be able to increase its ability to produce more goods and services. Thus, an ever-increasing productive capacity is essential to economic growth.

Expanding Demand

Regardless of what the economy is capable of producing, actual production depends on how much consumers, businesses, and governments are willing to buy. The total of this willingness to buy is called aggregate demand. To stimulate economic growth, aggregate demand needs to be maintained. In chapters 19 and 20, we discussed how the federal government attempts to do this.

Favorable Business Climate

Economic growth is more likely to occur in a climate favorable to businesses. Among the more important features of such a favorable business climate are the following.

POLITICAL STABILITY.   Businesses are more likely to flourish in *politically stable* countries, nations whose rulers come to power through legal means and whose governments are capable of maintaining order. In such an atmosphere, businesses are more inclined to accept the costs and risks of business expansion. In a politically unstable atmosphere, by contrast, businesses are less likely to accept the costs and risks of expansion and growth.

GOVERNMENT CONCERN FOR THE NEEDS OF BUSINESS.   There is much that government can do to assist businesses and thereby promote economic growth. We will discuss these measures on pages 473–475.

A WILLINGNESS TO SAVE AND INVEST.   Capital formation—the acquisition of tools, machinery, and plants—is essential to increasing productivity and stimulating growth. This capital cannot be acquired, however, unless there is a sufficient amount of money in the economy available for investment. Often this money comes from individuals who save and invest their money. Some societies are so poor that people cannot afford to save any money. The funds that should be set aside to invest instead are used to clothe, house, and feed people. Frequently, those few people with money available to invest prefer to do so abroad, where the financial returns are more certain. Other rich individuals may choose to use their wealth to acquire houses or luxuries, neither of which add to a nation's productive capacity.

GOVERNMENT AND ECONOMIC GROWTH

The federal government has a special role to play in fostering economic growth. It does this by using its powers to (1) influence aggregate demand;

Thomas Robert Malthus

Adam Smith and many other writers of the 18th century saw a world in which natural forces were working everywhere to benefit humanity. Indeed, the underlying justification for *laissez-faire* policies was to allow people to do what, in Smith's words, ". . . is advantageous to the society." In 1798, however, a work titled *An Essay on the Principle of Population* was published in Great Britain. Written by Thomas Robert Malthus, an English minister, its views served to mark economics as the "dismal science."

Malthus's central thesis was that a population always increases more rapidly than the food supply. With not enough food to go around, large sections of the population are doomed to go hungry or starve. The reason for this dilemma, Malthus explained, is that the population increases in a *geometric progression* (a sequence of numbers in which the ratio of one number to its predecessor is always the same, such as 2, 4, 8, 16). For example, a married couple (two people) might have two children; each of these two children might have two children, increasing the number at this generation of the family to four. The next generation might have eight; the following gener-

ation, 16; and so on in geometric progression. The amount of available land and the quantity of seed, fertilizer, and labor applied to it, in contrast, limit the food supply. Although the total food supply could be increased in time, it would do so in an *arithmetic progression,* (for example: 2, 4, 6, 8, 10; or 1, 2, 3, 4, 5). Figure 21.3 illustrates the Malthusian theory.

With population increasing at a faster rate than the food supply, there comes a time when the number of people is greater than the amount of food available to feed them. What happens once the population outstrips the food supply? Malthus foresaw a "season of distress" when shortages of food would push prices so high that many people would go hungry or starve. Malthus predicted that in the wake of the famine, disease, and war that would surely follow, fewer people would marry, and, as a consequence, the birthrate would decline. Meanwhile, an abundant supply of cheap labor combined with high food prices would encourage farmers to increase their output. In time, therefore, the supply of food would be equal to the needs of the population, and marriage rates and birthrates would return to normal. And then what? Population growth would once again surpass the food supply, and the dreary cycle would be repeated.

Was Malthus correct? Is Earth doomed to a perpetual state of overpopulation? Are famine, disease, and death unavoidable consequences?

History at first seemed to refute Malthus's predictions. Using the biological and technological advances of the Industrial Revolution, farmers in Canada, Australia, New Zealand, the United States, and Europe were able to provide more than enough food for their populations. Meanwhile, changing social attitudes in the industrialized nations slowed population growth. These two developments enabled the industrialized nations to escape Malthus's predictions.

But many of the nonindustrialized countries around the world have not been so fortunate. The world's population increased from 5 billion in 1987 to over 6 billion today. It is expected to

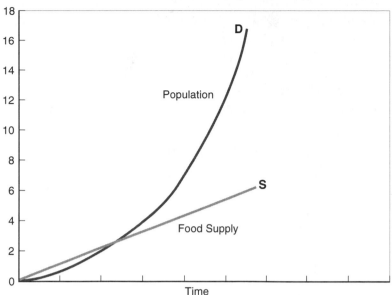

Figure 21.3 **Food Supply and Population Growth According to Malthus**

increase to 9 billion by 2050 and hover around 10 billion by the end of the century. Most of this growth will take place in the poorest, nonindustrialized countries. No doubt malnutrition will prevail there, and some famines will break out.

Some 200 years ago, Malthus wrote, "The power of population is infinitely greater than the power in the earth to produce subsistence for man." Do you think that Malthus's viewpoint is valid today?

(2) promote employment; (3) support research, education, and job training; and (4) promote savings and investment.

Influencing Aggregate Demand

Through various means, the federal government strives to maintain a healthy balance among business demand, consumer demand, and government demand. John Maynard Keynes (discussed in Chapter 18) argued that the key ingredient in growing the economy was aggregate demand (the collective spending by all elements of the economy). If the economy is to grow, aggregate demand must keep pace with its productive expansion.

Promoting Employment

Full employment has been a goal of the federal government for more than 50 years. Government advances this goal by stimulating business activity, promoting the education and training of the workforce, reducing discrimination in the workplace, and helping unemployed workers find jobs.

Government officials do not expect that every person willing and able to work will be able to find a job. Instead, the government tries to keep unemployment rates down to between 4 and 6 percent. In fact, some economists believe that if the unemployment rate were to get too low (say, below 5 percent), workers would be in demand and could command higher wages. If this happened all over the country, these economists think, then high rates of inflation might result.

Supporting Research, Education, and Job Training

Increasing productivity is a key to economic growth. As output per worker increases, total national output is likely to follow. One source of increased productivity comes from the invention of new machines. Another results as businesses develop new and improved ways of producing goods and services. From its earliest days, the federal government has stimulated inventions and innovations. In some instances, government has been directly involved in research and development projects, such as the NASA space program. The Defense Department grants money to some businesses doing research that might have applications in the area of national defense. Indirectly, government fosters research by awarding patents and by granting tax concessions to businesses for research and development projects.

Government aids all levels of education to help provide an educated workforce. There are some 40 different federal programs devoted to job training or to job placement assistance. The **Employment Training Administration (ETA)** is a major federal agency in this regard. The idea behind all of these programs is to increase the productive capacity of people to bring them, or keep them,

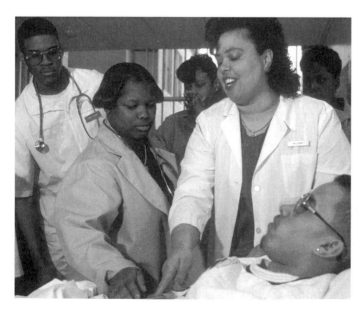

These young adults are enrolled in a job-training program that is government funded and that may help them get better jobs.

out of poverty. The **Job Corps**, which provides vocational training to young adults, is one such program. Another federal effort is the **Welfare to Work Act**, which provides grants to states for local job-training programs for welfare recipients who are having difficulty getting work.

Promoting Savings and Investment

In Chapter 14, we discussed the progressive income tax and proposals for a flat tax. According to the proponents of a flat tax, progressive income taxes tend to discourage savings and investment because those with the highest incomes (and thus the ones who would most likely save the most) are the ones who have to pay the highest rates of taxes. In contrast, a flat tax would encourage savings among the wealthy because it would reduce taxes for members of this group. According to some proposals for the flat tax, the government would not tax income from savings, investments, or capital gains, but it would tax income from wages and salaries. The lower taxes resulting from enacting a flat tax would encourage wealthy people and businesses to save and invest. Of course, there are good arguments against the flat tax and in favor of the progressive income tax.

In Chapter 20, we discussed supply-side economics. Supply-side economists believe that reducing taxes is the best way to increase incomes. As we have already discussed, the savings of individuals and families are the source of investments and capital formation that business firms need to expand. Anything the government can do to increase incomes in the United States encourages individuals to save more and, thus, allows business firms to invest more. We know that taxes take income away from individuals and businesses. Thus, lowering taxes results in increased income to individuals and businesses. This additional income becomes available for spending, savings, and investment, and grows the economy. Therefore, supply-side economists emphasize the importance of tax reductions for economic growth.

Trickle-down economics is a term used by its opponents to describe supply-side economics. According to the theory of trickle-down economics, tax benefits to the rich help everyone because they encourage rich people to save and invest more of their incomes, which will grow the economy. Eventually, according to the trickle-down theory, the not-so-rich will benefit from the growing economy with an increase in employment. However, there are economists who disagree with this theory. They doubt that additional tax-favored retirement accounts, tax-free dividends, tax-free savings accounts, an end to the inheritance tax, and lower business and income taxes will contribute to economic growth. On the contrary, these economists argue, such tax benefits will remain with those who already have money. The rich, they suggest, rather than saving and investing their additional incomes, will shift much of their savings from taxable to nontaxable accounts and, very likely, invest outside the United States. They conclude, therefore, that supply-side economics, which benefits the rich, impedes rather than promotes economic growth. A reduction in federal tax revenues, these economists believe, will result in a budget deficit and necessitate a cut in federal spending, which will lead to cutting social services to working people and the poor. Meanwhile, state governments, facing declining tax revenues and required by law to balance their budgets, will also be forced to reduce social services, health services, and funding for education. Cities and towns will be hit even harder. They will receive less funding from the federal and state governments. Tax revenues will decline as employment and incomes in cities and towns decline. Thus, contrary to supply-side economists who favor tax reductions at the top, opponents favor increased government spending in order to increase aggregate demand and put money in the hands of working people and the poor. These groups are more likely to spend their increased incomes, which would stimulate investment and contribute to growth.

Government has other ways to increase savings and investing. If capital gains taxes were decreased, individuals would likely invest more. If corporate taxes were lowered, businesses would likely invest more. Finally, businesses are likely to invest more when interest rates (the costs of borrowing) are low. As discussed in Chapter 19, the federal government has ways of influencing these interest rates. In sum, government policies can do much to promote savings and investment.

ECONOMIC GROWTH AND THE ENVIRONMENT

We have heard numerous praises of economic growth. But economic growth also has its critics. These critics caution that growth has been a principal cause of the depletion of our natural resources and environmental decay.

Depletion of Natural Resources

The ever-increasing output of goods and services, which we call "economic growth," consumes inputs of human, capital, and natural resources. Some of these resources are said to be "renewable" because, although consumed, they can still be replaced. Lumber is a renewable resource because cleared forests can be replanted. So too are fish and other wildlife renewable resources because they can reproduce. With proper management, reduced animal and plant populations can be returned to higher levels.

Nonrenewable resources (such as petroleum, coal, and copper) are those that cannot be replaced once they have been consumed. Given the absolute limit in the supply of any nonrenewable resource, one day its supply might be exhausted. How long the depletion process takes depends on the available supply and the rate at which the resource is consumed.

Supplies of renewable resources could also be exhausted if society fails to apply the kind of conservation techniques required to preserve them. In the early 1990s, for example, stocks of striped bass (an important sport and food

Here some forested areas have been been totally cleared of trees for commercial reasons. Clear-cutting of forests is not environmentally sound because the lack of tree roots leads to soil erosion and the degradation of streams and rivers.

fish) all but disappeared from East Coast waters because of the pollution in Chesapeake Bay and the Hudson River. In the Northwest today, industrial development along the Columbia River threatens the salmon fishing industry with extinction. Oceans around the world, too, are experiencing dramatic losses in fish populations. Greenpeace International estimates that 69 percent of the world's fish stocks are either overfished or depleted. This organization and others urge international cooperation to limit fishing around the world.

Given the relationship between economic output and pollution, some critics of continued economic growth have suggested that there should be *zero economic growth*. That is, the GDP should increase only enough to accommodate population growth. This zero economic growth, they say, would reduce pressure on the environment and protect global supplies of natural resources.

Is Economic Growth to Be Blamed for Environmental Decay?

Pollution is not a new phenomenon. First-century Romans, 15th-century Parisians, and 19th-century Londoners all complained about the foul wastes created by animals, households, and industries of their time. Never before, however, have the problems and dangers of pollution reached the point that they have today.

At one level, littered parks and highways are unsightly and deprive us all of the enjoyment they might otherwise provide. More serious is the air and water pollution that causes illness and even death. We know, for example, that prolonged inhalation of certain minerals and dusts (such as coal and asbestos) can cause lung disease and cancer.

Most ominous, however, are those forms of pollution that threaten the survival of the planet itself. A case in point is the *greenhouse effect,* possibly created when carbon emissions from numerous automobiles, factories, and power plants combine with water in the atmosphere. The effect creates a layer of carbon dioxide around the globe. This layer acts as a kind of giant greenhouse. A garden greenhouse allows the sun's light rays to come in and then be reflected out, while holding in the sun's heat. On a global basis, the warming created by the greenhouse effect threatens to change climate patterns. One possible effect of global warming is an increase in the number of violent storms and periods of drought. Another possible effect is the melting of the polar ice caps. If the polar ice caps melted, the action would release so much water that ocean levels would rise, flooding many of the world's coastal communities.

Scientists disagree whether or not human activities are creating a greenhouse effect that will lead to global warming. For example, consider the arguments presented below.

GLOBAL WARMING DOES NOT PRESENT A DANGER.   Some people believe that there is no convincing scientific evidence that human release of carbon dioxide, methane, or other greenhouse gases is causing or will, in the foreseeable future, cause catastrophic heating of the Earth's atmosphere and disruption of the Earth's climate. Moreover, they claim, there is substantial scientific evidence that increases in atmospheric carbon dioxide produce many beneficial effects upon the natural plant and animal environments of the Earth.

GLOBAL WARMING IS AN ENVIRONMENTAL CATASTROPHE.   Other people warn of an environmental catastrophe. They claim that global warming is a particularly ominous example of humanity's insatiable appetite for natural resources. During the last century, we dug up and burned massive stores of coal, oil, and natural gas, which took millions of years to accumulate. Our ability to burn up fossil fuels at a rate that is much faster than the rate at which they were created has upset the natural balance of the carbon cycle. The threat of climate change arises because one of the only ways the atmosphere can respond to the vast quantities of carbon being liberated from beneath the Earth's surface is to warm up. Critics of continued reliance on fossil fuels believe that the world's ecosystems and social structures are threatened by climate change. Burning fossil fuels such as oil, coal, and gas is the single biggest contributor to this human-made problem.

✖ The Kyoto Accords

In an effort to address the threat of climate change, delegates from many countries held an environmental conference in Kyoto, Japan, in 1997. The delegates passed *accords* (set of agreements) that would require the industrialized nations of the world (Canada, Russia, Japan, the European Community, the United States,

What mistakes do you think the man in the back seat of the vehicle was talking about?

and some others) to reduce CO_2 and other greenhouse gas emissions by about 7 percent below the 1990 emission level by the years between 2008 and 2012. Developing nations would not have to make these reductions.

THE UNITED STATES REJECTS THE KYOTO ACCORDS. The U.S. delegation sent by President Bill Clinton signed a modified version of the Kyoto Accords in November 1998. The U.S. Senate, though, has never ratified the accords. Moreover, after George W. Bush became President in 2001, he rejected the Kyoto Accords on the grounds that it was unworkable and unnecessary. His advisers had a number of arguments:

● The economic impacts of implementing the accords would be disastrous.

● The U.S. economy was slowing down early in 2001. The White House Council of Economic Advisers projected that by 2010, the U.S. GDP would fall by $1–$2 billion annually under Kyoto. The U.S. Department of Energy projected a much higher decline, adding that all energy costs would nearly double.

● Consumer prices for energy usage would rise and the impact of higher energy costs and compliance costs on the coal and auto industries would be severe.

● Increased energy regulation and compliance costs would cause (*a*) industry to move to developing countries; (*b*) plant closings (including all primary aluminum smelters), a 20 percent reduction in the output of petroleum refiners, the closing of between 23 percent and 35 percent of the cement industry; (*c*) job losses (including 100,000 jobs in the domestic steel industry); and (*d*) imports displacing domestic production in industries such as paper production.

- Greenhouse gas concentrations would increase anyway, even if all nations— not just the industrial countries—cut their greenhouse gas emissions as much the Kyoto Accords required of the United States. By abiding by the Kyoto Accords, it was estimated that carbon dioxide concentrations would reach 602 parts per million rather than 655 parts per million by 2047. The difference with or without the restrictions imposed by the Accords would be negligible. At best, the planet would be cooled by less than 0.2°C, and the U.S. contribution to this negligible cooling would be less than 0.05°C.

U.S. proponents of the Kyoto Accords answer these arguments as follows.

- We owe it to future generations to take the necessary measures to preserve and protect the environment regardless of costs.
- Claims of a trade-off between jobs and the environment are completely without substance. Very few shutdowns of manufacturing plants have resulted from environmental protection. More job losses in the United States are the result of corporate downsizing, competition from imports, and slowdowns in the economy.
- The *pollution haven effect* (the result of industrial firms relocating to poor countries to take advantage of lax environmental regulation) has seldom been observed. Pollution-control costs are only a small portion of total business costs. The vast portion of U.S. investments in manufacturing facilities has been in other developed countries, not in the developing countries. If high-polluting companies move to developing countries, it is not because pollution controls are less stringent. Instead, the reason is that wages are much lower in the developing countries.
- The great majority of economywide studies show a small positive effect of environmental regulation on overall employment. Job losses in the mining and logging industries have been more than made up by the increase in jobs in industries providing substitute products for timber and minerals and in sport fishing and other tourist industries.
- Plant shutdowns often occur because of the shift from goods-producing to services-producing industries in the United States and not so much because of the increased costs of pollution controls.

The position of the United States to "go it alone" is seen as a sign by the international community that the United States is not ready to cooperate with the international community when it feels that its self-interests are endangered. On the other hand, the United States presents very strong arguments in support of its position opposing the accords. The United States, it should be pointed out, was in the forefront in legislation to protect the environment, such as the Clean Air Act passed in the 1970s, which imposed strict technological standards to protect the quality of air and water in the United States.

🎇 Economic Growth Has Its Defenders

Those who say that economic growth should be allowed to follow whatever course the market dictates remind us that throughout history there have been those who predicted doom and gloom in every period of change. In each instance, they point out, humankind found a way to overcome the threat. For example, Thomas Malthus, who predicted that world population growth would outstrip the food supply, has thus far been proved wrong. Malthus failed to foresee that a technological revolution would increase farm productivity and that millions of acres of new farmland would be opened in the Americas and elsewhere.

In the same way, we are unable today to predict what discoveries later generations will make to solve their problems. Furthermore, the defenders of economic growth argue, we are a long way from exhausting supplies of natural resources. They say that new sources will be found or new technologies developed by industries when needed. Another important argument is that industries provide jobs, and that jobs and people are more important than the existence of certain species of plants and animals.

A major concern, as indicated in the debate over adoption of the Kyoto Accords, is the effect economic growth will have on air pollution and, in turn, climate change. A number of economists have proposed that there is a relationship between air pollution and income per capita of countries and that it is characterized by an inverted U-shaped curve called the *Environmental Kuznets Curve*. Measures of pollution are on the vertical axis, while income per capita of countries over time are on the horizontal axis.

At early levels of development, countries typically have low income per capita and low levels of air pollution. Environmental quality deteriorates as nations become industrialized and improve their income per capita. Air pollution is a by-product of manufacturing and other industries. When nations develop even more into a service economy, income per capita increases even more. But service economies do not contaminate the air so much because there are fewer manufacturing plants. Economists conclude, then, that economic growth will, for a while, contribute to air pollution by encouraging manufacturing and industrialization. Eventually, however, economic growth will bring about less air pollution as society moves from goods-producing industries to services-producing industries.

🎇 A Middle Ground

Somewhere between the two positions (unlimited economic growth and zero growth) lies a middle ground occupied by those advocating what they call *sustainable economic growth.* Advocates of this theory argue that every generation should pass along a stock of "net resources" to future generations. Net resources include natural resources, along with knowledge, technology, and physical and human capital. Thus, if part of a forest is harvested to build a school, the actions are considered sustainable growth because future generations will benefit from the school building.

Those who support growth say that a growing economy makes it possible to improve living standards for the poorest segments of society as well as for the wealthy. The wiser course, their argument continues, is to pursue economic growth while at the same time to seek ways to avoid the dangers that accompany the growth. Robert Solow, who won the Nobel Prize for Economics in 1987, put it this way:

> My real complaint about the Doomsday school (those who predict the worst) is that it diverts attention from the really important things that can actually be done to make things better. The end of the world is at hand—the earth, if you take the long view, will fall into the sun in a few billion years anyway, unless some other disaster happens first. In the meantime, I think we'd be better off passing a strong sulfur-emissions tax, or getting some Highway Trust Fund money allocated to mass transit, or building a humane and decent floor under family incomes, instead of worrying about the generalized "predicament of mankind."
>
> —"Is the End of the World at Hand?" *Challenge,* March 1973

There are measures that can be supported by both critics and defenders of economic growth. Even though reputable scientists disagree as to the dangers of global warming, all agree that greater research should be devoted to improving the accuracy of climate data and the effects of pollution. We are only beginning to recognize the potential of alternative energy sources such as wind and solar energy, hybrid fuel systems for motor vehicles, solar voltaic cells, fuel cells, and more efficient engines. Alcohol (a nonpollutant produced from corn) or hydrogen produced from the air (abundant in supply and a renewable resource) can be major components of the energy source for motor vehicles. Thus, our dependence on petroleum, a polluting and nonrenewable source of energy, would be considerably reduced. Methane gas, a by-product in landfills, can be harnessed as an energy source. Experimentation in converting coal into a gaseous product that is less polluting than burning soft coal in power plants shows promise as a viable, cost-effective energy source. We can also do a lot more in investigating into the use of geothermal energy and tidal power.

Nevertheless, we do not have to wait for more research to provide us with future ways to preserve our environment. Everyone can do something right now. For example, we know that fluorescent bulbs use less energy than incandescent light bulbs. We can turn our thermostats down at night and set them at moderate temperatures during the day. Electric lights should be turned off when not in use. Mass transit can, in many cases, be used instead of our automobiles. All communities should have recycling programs for paper, glass, and plastic.

S U M M A R Y

Economic growth is the increase in output of goods and services over time. Its most useful measurement is in terms of real GDP per capita. Economic growth helps the nation improve its living standards, maintain high levels of employment, continue its income security programs, and maintain a strong national defense.

Economic growth requires an ever-increasing productive capacity, expanding demand, and a favorable business climate. Government can contribute to economic growth in many ways. It can influence aggregate demand; promote employment; support research, education, and training; and encourage savings and investment.

Some people criticize economic growth as having a negative impact on the environment. They say it helps deplete nonrenewable resources, causes pollution, and adds to the greenhouse effect. Others argue that these environmental concerns are either unfounded or exaggerated, and that new resources and new technologies will be found to meet our needs. Those favoring economic growth argue that people's livelihoods are more important than the environmental concerns expressed. In between unlimited growth and zero growth are those who favor sustainable growth, which would provide for economic progress while still showing concern for the environmental impact of such progress.

REVIEWING THE CHAPTER

BUILDING VOCABULARY

Match each term in Column A with its definition in Column B.

Column A

1. zero economic growth
2. Environmental Kuznets Curve
3. sustainable economic growth
4. WMD
5. greenhouse effect
6. productive capacity
7. pollution haven effect
8. geometric progression
9. trickle-down economics
10. arithmetic progression

Column B

a. nuclear, chemical, and biological weapons
b. the idea that every generation should pass on a stock of net resources to future generations
c. the trapping of the sun's heat by atmospheric gases
d. no increase over time in real GDP per capita
e. the idea that if the wealthy are given tax breaks, then they will spend more, thereby stimulating the economy and creating more jobs for the less wealthy
f. a way of illustrating the relationship between air pollution and per capita income of countries
g. the result of industrial firms relocating to countries with lax environmental laws
h. a sequence of numbers in which the ratio of one number to its predecessor is always the same
i. a sequence of numbers in which the difference between any number and its predecessor is constant
j. the amount of goods and services that the economy is able to produce at a given time

UNDERSTANDING WHAT YOU HAVE READ

1. Economic growth may be defined as an increase in (*a*) personal income (*b*) population (*c*) the value of goods and services produced per person (*d*) the money supply.

2. If the population of a nation grows at the rate of 5 percent per year while production increases at the rate of 4 percent, (*a*) living standards are likely to increase (*b*) living standards are likely to decrease (*c*) living standards will remain the same (*d*) inflation is inevitable.

3. Which of the following is the most reliable measure of economic growth? (*a*) total GDP in current dollars (*b*) GDP per capita in current dollars (*c*) total GDP in constant dollars (*d*) GDP per capita in constant dollars.

4. According to Table 21.1 on page 466, real GDP per capita increased during the period 1989–2002 by (*a*) $1.2 billion (*b*) $3,732 (*c*) $545 million (*d*) $9,739.

5. Figure 21.2 on page 469 demonstrates that (*a*) economic growth varies directly with population growth (*b*) real GDP per capita varies directly with real GDP (*c*) real GDP per capita increases as long as GDP increases (*d*) economic growth cannot occur if there is an increase in population.

6. Economic growth may be expected to provide a nation with all of the following, *except* (*a*) more consumer goods and services per citizen (*b*) the ability to continue aiding foreign nations (*c*) more unemployment (*d*) the ability to reduce poverty at home.

7. All of the following are necessary ingredients in economic growth, *except* (*a*) increased productive capacity (*b*) reduction of aggregate demand (*c*) stable government (*d*) a highly motivated workforce.

8. Savings are important to economic growth because (*a*) when everyone saves, there is less wasteful spending (*b*) savings provide investment capital that can be used to increase future production (*c*) consumers can use their savings to buy the things they really need (*d*) when savings are ample, the government can afford to reduce its expenditures.

9. Advocates of zero economic growth favor (*a*) an increase in the GDP (*b*) a reduction in the GDP (*c*) a freeze in real GDP per capita (*d*) a rapid increase in real economic growth.

10. If aggregate demand declines while the nation's productive capacity is unchanged, (*a*) economic growth will decline (*b*) economic growth will increase (*c*) prices will increase (*d*) unemployment will decline.

THINKING CRITICALLY

1. "Economic growth refers to an increase in the output of goods and services over time."

   a. Explain the meaning of this statement.

   b. In describing economic growth, economists most frequently speak of "per capita GDP in constant dollars." Summarize the reasons why this phrase is preferable to the phrase "total GDP in current dollars."

c. "GDP per capita as expressed in constant dollars is not a perfect measurement of the nation's economic health for there are things that are important to economic well-being that are not reflected in the GDP." Explain this statement and then tell why you agree or disagree with it.

2. "The dream of a better tomorrow seems to be part and parcel of the human condition."

   a. What benefits can economic growth offer the nation as a whole?

   b. How does its economic growth put the United States in a position to help the world's developing nations?

   c. Show why *each* of the following has been a necessary ingredient in U.S. economic growth: (*1*) increasing productivity, (*2*) increasing aggregate demand, and (*3*) political and social stability.

3. Some economists of the 18th century such as Adam Smith believed that natural forces were working to benefit humanity. On the other hand, the views of Thomas Malthus served to mark economics as the "dismal science."

   a. What did Malthus say that seemed to suggest a pessimistic view for the future of humanity?

   b. Compare and contrast how Malthus's predictions have worked out in the industrialized and the nonindustrialized countries.

   c. Malthus wrote some 200 years ago that, "The power of population is infinitely greater than the power in the earth to produce subsistence for man." Do you think that Malthus's viewpoint is still valid today? Explain your answer.

4. "One of the key ingredients in economic growth is investment."

   a. Explain this statement.

   b. Identify and explain *two* steps that the government might take to promote investments.

   c. Why is the shortage of investment capital more of a problem for developing countries than for the world's developed ones?

5. The Kyoto Accords of 1997 called for measures by the more developed countries to slow down or stop global warming. Most nations of the world have approved the accords. The U.S. Senate has refused to do so.

   a. Explain the arguments in favor of ratifying the Kyoto Accords.

   b. Explain the arguments put forth by U.S. leaders opposing ratification of the Accords.

   c. Why do you think that the U.S. Senate should or should not ratify the Kyoto Accords?

SKILLS: Interpreting a Statistical Table

Refer to Table 21.1 on page 466 and answer the questions that follow.

1. What evidence in the table proves that during the period 1959–2002, economic growth took place in the United States?

2. The current GDP per capita in 1959 was $2,806. How do you explain why GDP per capita in constant dollars in that year amounted to $12,721? Which figure do you think helps more in explaining economic growth during the period? Explain your answer.

3. Total GDP in current dollars increased from $507.4 billion in 1959 to $10,446.2 billion in 2002. This was an increase of more than 20 times. However, GDP per capita was only 13 times greater during this period. Why is the percentage increase in per capita GDP less than the percentage increase in total GDP during the period 1959–2002?

4. What evidence is there that economic growth slowed down during the period 1994–1999?

USING THE INTERNET

- Data and research papers relating to economic growth may be found at the World Bank Internet site at <<econ.worldbank.org/programs/macroeconomics>>.

- The supply-side arguments for economic growth are presented by the National Center for Policy Analysis at <<www.ncpa.org/iss/i_econgrowth.html#supply>>.

- Arguments against unlimited economic growth are discussed in a paper by Charles Siegel, "The End of Economic Growth," at <<www.preservenet.com/endgrowth/EndGrowth.html>>.

- The Alliance for Energy and Economic Growth argues for the need for continued growth to meet energy needs at <<www.yourenergyfuture.org>>.

- Greenpeace, a major environmental organization, warns of the dangers of global warming at <<www.greenpeace.org>>.

- Also check the Environmental Protection Agency Web site at <<www.epa.gov>>.

UNIT VIII

THE GLOBAL ECONOMY

CHAPTER 22
International Trade

OVERVIEW

In September 2000, in Prague, Czech Republic, 8,000 demonstrators were met by 11,000 police and 5,000 military troops using tear gas and water cannons as 14,000 delegates attended a World Bank and IMF meeting.

In 2001, some 200,000 demonstrated in Genoa, Italy, against a G8 Economic Summit meeting to discuss free trade. In the same year, protesters tried to prevent a World Trade Organization Ministerial Conference in Doha, Qatar, where free trade agreements were negotiated.

The IMF and World Bank meeting in April 2002 in Washington, D.C., was another target of antiglobalization protesters.

In September 2003, in Cancun, Mexico, thousands of people, many of them farmers, protested against the World Trade Organization meeting there.

Why do meetings of the World Bank, the International Monetary Fund, and the World Trade Organization inflame such passions?

We are all active participants in the U.S. economy. We consume goods and services, and many of us have jobs as well. We rarely think, however, that we are also part of a much larger unit: the *global economy.* This economy includes the economies of all nations of the world. In this century, nations are increasingly interdependent. Many of the goods and services that we consume come to us either in part or in their entirety from foreign lands. Similarly, people in the rest of the world look to the United States for many goods and services.

Consider the case of a candy bar that can be purchased over the counter at a local store. Suppose that the candy bar is one of the chocolate-coated varieties with almonds. On examining the paper and aluminum foil wrapper, we see that a *multinational corporation,* a giant firm that operates its business in two or more countries, produced the candy bar. As for the paper, it was manufactured from wood pulp produced in Canada. The aluminum foil was made of bauxite mined in Jamaica and processed in a U.S. factory. Sugar, the principal ingredient in the candy bar, was produced out of Filipino cane, while the chocolate had its origins in cacao beans that were grown in Ghana. The almonds came from southern Italy. In the candy-making process, many cargo ships brought the ingredients to the United States. One of these ships, built in a Japanese shipyard for a Greek company, sailed under Liberian registry with a mainly Indonesian crew. In view of these facts, why, then, are there demonstrations against international organizations discussing trade?

In this chapter, we will discuss the global economy and why trade takes place between nations. We will explore why international trade promotes economic specialization and how specialization increases total world output. We will then discuss the evolution of U.S. trade policy and some of the current problems in global trade. Finally, we will also examine the arguments for and against *globalization* (the reduction of barriers to trade and labor migration among nations).

 # ECONOMIC SPECIALIZATION

Two hundred years ago, British economist Adam Smith wrote that the wise head of a household will never attempt to make at home that which can be bought outside the home for less. Smith went on to explain that it made more sense for people to work at whatever they do best, and to use their earnings to buy the things they want.

Smith's advice for households and individuals to specialize in some economic activity applies equally well to localities and to nations. Consider, for example, trade between New York State and Kansas. Much of the clothing sold in Kansas is made in New York, just as many of the wheat products consumed in New York have their origin in Kansas. The reason is that, among other things, New York has extensive facilities for the manufacture of clothing and a large, experienced labor force. Meanwhile, Kansas has the necessary soil, climate, capital, and labor to produce wheat. For similar reasons, West Virginia is a major producer of coal; Florida, of citrus fruits; and California, of semiconductors.

As with states, nations tend to specialize in the production of certain goods and services. Brazil concentrates on the production of coffee beans; Honduras, on bananas. Japan has a sizable electronics industry, while the United States produces much of the world's computer software. Meanwhile, U.S. airlines and British insurance companies provide further examples of the kinds of service exports that are concentrated in certain countries.

Nations specialize in the production of certain goods and services for a number of reasons. These are related to the uneven distribution of resources, absolute and comparative advantage, and political considerations—topics that we will now discuss.

⚙ Uneven Distribution of Resources Around the Globe

Just as individuals differ in size, strength, talent, and ability, so do nations and regions differ in their resources. These differences (which limit the kinds of economic activities in which nations can successfully engage) include climate, factor supply, and demand.

CLIMATE.   The effect of *climate* (the pattern of weather in a place over a long time) on the economy of a nation is usually apparent. Because of its climate, certain goods cannot be grown in the United States and, thus, have to be imported. The cacao beans that are used in many candy bars are imported from Africa. Coffee is another example of a product that needs to be imported. Coffee is produced in large quantities in Brazil (among other places) because the moderate temperature and heavy rainfall of certain regions of Brazil favor its growth. Rubber trees, also not grown in the United States, require a damp, hot climate, as in Indonesia.

Some crops can be grown in only parts of the United States. Citrus trees need frost-free areas, such as Florida, while grains thrive in cooler climates, as in the Great Plains of the United States. Many fruits and vegetables rely on the alternating cool-damp, hot-dry type of Mediterranean climate, as in California.

Coffee beans are harvested by hand, because not all the beans on a plant ripen at the same time. This coffee plantation is in Colombia.

Certain services are economically viable only in specific areas. For example, the terrain and cool climate of mountainous areas are most conducive to skiing, while warm beaches encourage tourists seeking sun and sand.

In recent years, climatic factors have lost much of their former importance in determining the course of a nation's economy. Clothing manufacturers now use synthetic fibers as substitutes for natural products (such as silk and cotton) that can be produced only in certain climates. Farmers now grow new types of wheat with a very short growing season in regions formerly considered too cold for wheat production. Some farmers now grow quality tomatoes year round under climate-controlled conditions in hothouses. Similarly, farmers in Israel and elsewhere with arid climates have developed elaborate irrigation programs that enable agricultural activities even in desert regions. Climatic factors, however, still continue to affect international trade. The costs of maintaining an artificial climate to develop certain industries are prohibitive. For this reason, nations generally continue to produce goods and services for which their climate and geography are most suitable.

FACTOR SUPPLY. The factors of production (land, labor, capital, and management) are not equally distributed around the world or even in most countries. This distribution helps explain, for example, why some parts of our country tend to specialize in the production of farm products, while other areas lean toward manufacturing. Texas, with its ample supply of land in relation to its population, can afford to allow cattle to roam over thousands of acres of range. Illinois, in contrast, is more densely settled. Its major city, Chicago, has many industries, including food-processing facilities and factories that manufacture machines.

On the international scene, too, the factors of production are unevenly distributed. Argentina and Australia are similar to Texas in that the ratio of people to land is relatively low. As a result, these nations can engage in extensive cattle and sheep grazing. By contrast, Great Britain and Japan, with their relatively concentrated populations, have developed manufacturing industries that rely on ample supplies of labor and capital.

The quality of labor also varies from one nation to another. Japan, the United States, and the nations of Western Europe have relatively more skilled labor than other nations. These countries are therefore able to support industries requiring highly trained workers and complex technology. Many developing nations (such as Pakistan, China, and Mexico) are still developing their labor resources.

Capital in the form of plant and equipment (and money to invest in plant and equipment) is also unevenly distributed throughout the world. The countries with the highest concentration of capital per worker tend to have the greatest productivity. Abundant capital enables these nations to concentrate on producing goods that lend themselves to mass production. For this reason, Sweden (with a relatively small population) was able to develop an automobile industry. For the same reason, Japan (with little or no iron ore) is competitive with the rest of the world in producing finished steel. Meanwhile, countries with limited industrial capacities, such as Belize, Ghana, and Sri Lanka, must emphasize preindustrial activities such as farming. In recent decades, however, business firms have been investing capital and establishing factories in less developed countries in order to take advantage of low labor costs.

Management, too, is a vital ingredient in production. Those nations that lack an adequate supply of industrial-managerial talent tend to concentrate on the production of agricultural goods. This concentration explains, in part, the difficulties that many less developed nations have in industrializing. These nations are short of managerial personnel and, therefore, have to either delay their programs or recruit managers from abroad.

DEMAND.   Even if a wondrous genie were to provide Sierra Leone, Honduras, and Nepal with automotive factories overnight, it is unlikely that many cars and trucks would be produced in these countries. The relatively small and poor populations of those lands could not afford to buy enough of the output to take advantage of the economies of scale. (It is more likely that foreign automotive companies might establish factories to manufacture some automotive parts in some of these countries.) Mass production can proceed only if there is a market for its output. The need for a market explains why only a small handful of nations produce commercial aircraft. Usually only a nation with markets large enough to support an aircraft industry can afford to have one. To get around this problem in Western Europe, groups of nations formed consortiums to produce airplanes (for example, the Airbus, produced by a group of European nations).

Absolute Advantage and Comparative Advantage

When one nation can produce a good or service at a lower cost than another, the former is said to have an *absolute advantage* in that item. Therefore, nations would do well to specialize in the production of those things in which they have an absolute advantage. Furthermore, they should use the surplus from the sale of these things to buy other goods and services from nations that have absolute advantages in different items. Consider the examples of trade between the United States and Indonesia and trade between the United States and Bolivia. We know that Indonesia has an absolute advantage in producing spices, Bolivia has an absolute advantage in producing tin, and the United States has an absolute advantage in producing transportation equipment. Thus, the United States buys spices from Indonesia and tin from Bolivia, and sells its transportation equipment to both countries.

Under certain circumstances, however, it pays for a nation to import goods and services from abroad even though they could be produced more cheaply at home. The principle of *comparative advantage* helps explain why this is so.

Developing nations often have some heavy industries. This steel foundry is located in Helwan, the hub of Egypt's steel industry.

First stated early in the 19th century by the English economist **David Ricardo** (featured on pages 496–497), the *Law of Comparative Advantage* may be summarized as follows: If two nations have different opportunity costs in the production of two goods or services, the nations should (1) specialize in the one in which their opportunity costs are lower, (2) leave the production of the other item to the other country, and (3) trade with each other. The concept of comparative advantage might be more easily understood if we consider the following example.

Lisa McBride, MD, is deluged with paperwork. Dr. McBride is an excellent typist, a skill she learned as a college student. Nevertheless, she is considering hiring a part-time typist to ease her burden. She estimates that the typist would be paid $75 a day and would be needed two days a week.

At the same time, Dr. McBride knows that she could probably handle all the typing work herself in somewhat less than two days' time and thereby save the expense of a typist—$150. But she also knows that each hour that she would spend typing would be an hour that she would lose in earnings as a medical doctor. Dr. McBride estimates that she could earn ten times a typist's salary by attending to her medical practice on the days she would devote to typing.

Should the doctor do her own typing or hire a typist? What do you think?

Economists would recommend that Dr. McBride hire the typist. They would explain the logic of this choice in terms of comparative advantage and opportunity costs. Opportunity costs, you may recall, are the amount of goods and services one must forgo to obtain more of something else. To Dr. McBride,

	TABLE 22.1 COMPARATIVE ADVANTAGE I		
Product	**United States**	**Japan**	**Total Dollar Output**
Bulldozers	3 × $100,000	2 × $100,000	$500,000
DVD players	1,000 × $200	1,200 × $200	$440,000
Total	$500,000	$440,000	$940,000

the opportunity cost of doing her own typing is the loss of income from one- or two-day's medical practice. These earnings are far greater than the $150 salary she would have to pay the typist for two days' work. Since the opportunity cost of doing her own typing is greater than that of attending to her practice, we say that the physician has a comparative advantage in medicine even though she enjoys an absolute advantage in both fields (she can both type and practice medicine better than the typist).

To illustrate how the Law of Comparative Advantage applies to nations, suppose that the United States is more efficient than Japan in the production of both DVD players and heavy earth-moving equipment, such as bulldozers. Even if the United States were able to produce both products more cheaply than Japan, it would pay the United States to produce the bulldozers and buy the DVD players from Japan. The reason for this is that the United States has a greater margin of efficiency over Japan in producing heavy equipment than it does in producing DVD players. The opportunity cost to the United States of producing DVD players would be the cost of diverting resources from producing heavy equipment.

To make this imaginary situation simpler, suppose that bulldozers and DVD players are the only two items each nation produces and that no other country produces these items. With a given quantity of land, labor, and capital, the United States can produce three bulldozers and 1,000 DVD players, while Japan can produce two bulldozers and 1,200 DVD players. Suppose further that a bulldozer sells for $100,000 and a DVD player sells for $200.

In this example with equal factor inputs, the United States produces $300,000 worth of bulldozers and $200,000 worth of DVD players. Japan pro-

	TABLE 22.2 COMPARATIVE ADVANTAGE II		
Product	**United States**	**Japan**	**Total Dollar Output**
Bulldozers	6 × $100,000	0	$ 600,000
DVD players	0	2,400 × $200	$ 480,000
Total	$600,000	$480,000	$1,080,000

duces $200,000 worth of bulldozers and $240,000 worth of DVD players. Now let us suppose that the United States produces only bulldozers and Japan produces only DVD players.

Both nations profit when the United States specializes in producing bulldozers and Japan produces only DVD players. Total output increases from three to six bulldozers ($500,000 to $600,000) in the United States and from 1,200 to 2,400 DVD players ($440,000 to $480,000) in Japan. World output, therefore, increases by one bulldozer and 1,200 DVD players or, in terms of dollars, by $140,000 ($1,080,000 − $940,000). We may conclude that international trade and specialization increase total world output.

In terms of opportunity costs, both the United States and Japan gain by specializing in the production of those goods in which they are most efficient—the one in which they have a comparative advantage. Both Japan and the United States can use their gain to produce additional goods and services, thereby raising the standard of living in each nation. It therefore follows that if all countries produce those things at which they are most efficient, the world's output will be raised to the greatest possible level. Thus, everyone's living standards will rise.

🔥 Political Considerations

Despite the benefits of international trade, the decision to trade or not to trade is sometimes based on political rather than economic reasons. At one time, Cuba was our leading source of sugar and a major market for our exports. Then after the Cuban revolution of 1959, Communists came to power there. Because of Cuba's Communist policies (including Cuba's nationalization of many industries), the United States stopped trading with that nation. Also for political reasons, the United States has virtually no trade with North Korea and Iran.

By contrast, we sometimes go out of our way to trade with some other nations simply because we want to support their governments. When the Polish Communist government was preparing to introduce democratic reforms in the 1980s, the U.S. government encouraged private U.S. banks to make loans to Poland. When Mexico was in great financial difficulty in 1995, President Bill Clinton issued an executive order making $20 billion in credit available to the Mexican government. For decades, our government has encouraged U.S. businesses to trade with South Korea but prohibited trade with North Korea. For many years, trade with the Chinese Nationalist government on Taiwan was encouraged, while trade with the Chinese Communist government on the mainland was prohibited. U.S.-Chinese trade policy changed in the 1970s after more normal diplomatic and trade relations were established between the United States and mainland China. Today, China is the United States' fourth largest trading partner (see Figure 22.2).

David Ricardo

The economic order first described by Adam Smith was studied and enlarged upon by those we now refer to as economists of the classical school. Second only to Smith in importance among classical economists was David Ricardo (1772–1823). The son of an affluent London stockbroker, young Ricardo opened his own brokerage firm and was so successful that by the time he was 35 he was able to retire a rich man. In later years, Ricardo went on to become a large landholder and member of the British Parliament. His most important work, *The Principles of Political Economy and Taxation,* is generally regarded as the best theoretical statement of classical economics.

Two topics that received special attention in *Principles* were income distribution and economic growth. Income, Ricardo said, was distributed to owners of land, workers, and business owners in the form of rents, wages, and profits, respectively. Left to their own devices, owners of businesses would expand their operations to the fullest in order to earn the greatest profits. This investment (business spending) would create jobs for workers, whose wages would be pushed up to whatever level was required to attract the needed supply into the labor market. With their wages rising, workers could afford to marry and have families. In that way, they would create their own competition by adding more people to the labor force. The addition of these new workers would push down wages to the point that workers would earn only enough to survive.

Meanwhile, the population growth would have encouraged farmers to open their less productive land to cultivation. This would increase food prices and, of necessity, wages, since workers had to be paid enough to survive. Unfortunately for the entrepreneurs, wage increases would have to come out of their profits. For their part, entrepreneurs could be expected to expand their operations as best they could through their investment in additional capital. This would lead them to employ additional workers at still higher wages, and the cycle would be repeated.

What a dismal picture Ricardo painted! Here were workers, bound to a life of bare subsistence by what came to be called the "iron law of wages," doomed because of their propensity to have children. Here, too, were entrepreneurs standing by helplessly as rising food prices pushed up the wages they had to pay at the expense of their hard-earned profits. Only the landlords seemed to benefit, for as the population grew, so too did the prices they could charge for their crops and the rents they earned on their lands.

One way out of the dilemma for the business owners (there was no way out for the workers, in Ricardo's view) was to bring down food prices by importing less expensive grain from other European countries. Unfortunately, this remedy could not be applied because the landowning nobility, whose primary source of income was from agriculture, controlled Parliament. To protect themselves from foreign competition in the early 19th century, these landowners sponsored a series of laws (the so-called **Corn Laws**) that levied high taxes on grain entering Great Britain. The effect of these taxes was to make the price of imported grain higher than the price of British grain.

In the midst of this dilemma, Ricardo's work provided the theoretical ammunition needed by the middle class, which wanted these laws repealed. What Ricardo did was to introduce the Law of Comparative Advantage. This theory, which is often cited by economists in defense of free trade, states that under certain circumstances two nations can benefit from trade even if one of them produces everything at lower costs than the other. In a well-known example, Ricardo demonstrated that it was to the mutual advantage of Great Britain and Portugal for Britain to export wool to Portugal and to import Portuguese wine in return, even though Portugal could produce both wool and wine at lower cost. Over the years, the political strength of the British middle class grew so that by 1846 it was able to bring about the repeal of the hated Corn Laws.

The passage of time has made obsolete much of what Ricardo had to say about the economy. Nevertheless, later economists employed many of his theories and methods as the starting point for the development of their own ideas, and his place in history is assured.

BARRIERS TO WORLD TRADE

From what we have said thus far, you might think that nations would be eager to promote international trade and take advantage of the benefits of specialization and comparative advantage. We know, however, that all nations, including our own, have imposed restrictions on imports, and sometimes on exports. In the discussion that follows, we will examine ways governments apply these restrictions.

Tariffs

The most common form of restriction on foreign trade is the tariff. As we learned in Chapter 14, a tariff is a tax placed on imported goods. The importer usually adds all or part of this tariff to the selling price of the goods. If this tax brings the price of the item to a point where it is more expensive than an identical domestic product, consumers may hesitate to buy the imported item. In this instance, the duty is described as a protective tariff, because it serves mainly to protect the domestic industry from the competition of foreign goods.

Tariffs designed primarily to raise money for the government are called *revenue tariffs*. With this type of tariff, the increased price resulting from the duty is still lower than that of the same goods produced at home. Suppose, for example, that sweaters imported from Scotland sell here for $50 each and similar sweaters produced in the United States sell for $65 each. A tariff of 10 percent would raise the price of the imported sweater by $5 (from $50 to $55). The Scottish sweater, however, would still be cheaper to buy than the one produced in the United States. In this example, the U.S. government receives $5 per sweater as a result of the revenue tariff imposed.

Tariffs are also classified by the way they are computed. A *specific tariff* assesses a certain amount of money per unit, such as $2 per ton. An *ad valorem tariff* is expressed as a percentage of the value of the goods.

Importers of items such as these rolls of fabric from Brazil have to pay an import tax, or tariff.

⚡ Quotas

A *quota* is a limit on the quantity of a particular good that may enter a country in a particular year. Once that limit is reached, no more of the product may be imported until the following year. The U.S. government, for example, has set a quota on imported sugar and Japanese cars. In fact, every nation in the world today has quotas, in one form or another, on goods or services entering from another nation. Regional trading blocs, discussed later in this chapter, remove quotas among member nations but retain import restrictions on goods from nonmember countries. One such trading bloc, the European Union, limited the import of Japanese cars into the European market in 1995 to a little over 1 million units. The Japanese overcame quota restrictions on the import of their cars by establishing plants in Europe. The output from these plants is free of quota restrictions.

⚡ Currency Controls

In order to import goods from a particular country, the importer usually must pay in that country's currency. Thus, for example, a Moroccan importer most likely pays in euros when buying French perfume. By limiting the amount of foreign currency that importers may buy, a government can limit trade with other nations.

Foreign Government Interference With Trade

Sometimes called the "invisible tariff," *administrative red tape* refers to the practice followed by some governments of making the process of importing so complicated that it discourages foreign businesses from attempting to sell their goods. By requiring the filing and processing of complicated forms, governments can discourage trade as effectively as they can by levying a protective tariff.

Export Controls

Export controls are another way to restrict trade. Certain kinds of goods cannot be sold unless an export license is first obtained. In this way, strategic materials such as high-technology weapons can be prevented from reaching specific nations. Moreover, the United States today forbids or severely restricts trade with a few nations, including North Korea, Iran, and Cuba.

Collaboration Among Firms

In addition to trade restrictions imposed by governments, large companies in a country can get together to control the home market and keep out foreign competition. In Japan, this arrangement is called the *keiretsu*—a closely knit corporate network of firms somewhat similar to interlocking directorates. *Keiretsu* is discussed in greater detail in Chapter 24.

EVOLUTION OF OUR TRADE POLICY

In studying the history of our nation, we find that trade policies played important roles. Before the American Revolution (1775–1783), Great Britain closely regulated the trade of its American colonies. The British Parliament passed laws that required colonists to export their raw materials only to British ports. It prohibited the manufacture of certain goods in the colonies. Moreover, it required that imports and exports be carried only in British or colonial ships, and not in ships of rival powers, such as Spain or France. A major purpose of these laws was to enable the colonial power, Great Britain, to have a *favorable balance of trade*—an excess of merchandise exports over imports. This concept is part of *mercantilism,* a doctrine popular in Europe from the 16th through the 18th centuries. According to mercantilism, the wealth of a nation can be measured by the amount of gold and silver it possesses. A favorable balance of trade increases this wealth because colonists pay for the home country's exports with gold and silver. Thus, these precious metals pile up in the home country.

Other European countries also followed mercantilist policies. Great Britain, France, and other nations resorted to protective tariffs and other restrictions to limit imports. These powers also did whatever they could to help domestic industries compete for foreign markets in order to increase exports.

After the United States won its independence from Great Britain, the new U.S. leaders had to concern themselves with trade issues. In 1791, Secretary of the Treasury **Alexander Hamilton** issued his *Report on Manufacturers* in which he recommended that the U.S. government take steps to develop the country's industries. Specifically, Hamilton urged Congress to offer cash payments to those who would start new industries or improve existing ones. He also wanted Congress to levy protective tariffs against competing foreign products. In an early application of Hamilton's advice, Congress in 1798 awarded a contract for 10,000 *muskets* (a type of heavy rifle) to the then-struggling young inventor **Eli Whitney**. While Congress could have bought muskets from manufacturers outside the United States, the deliberate government effort to help Whitney enabled this U.S. manufacturer to perfect his production methods. Whitney helped set up one of the country's first mass-production industries—musket making.

Tariffs have provoked many political battles through the course of U.S. history. During the War of 1812, newly started industries (sometimes called *infant industries*) developed in the United States. U.S. laws prohibiting trade with Great Britain during the conflict protected these industries. After the war ended in 1815, the British again began selling their manufactured goods in the U.S.

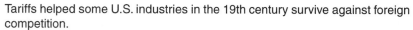

Tariffs helped some U.S. industries in the 19th century survive against foreign competition.

market. They could sell at prices much lower than those of comparable American-made goods. Owners of U.S. industries that had developed during the War of 1812 (such as New England cotton mills, Pittsburgh iron foundries, and wool producers in Vermont and Ohio) cried for protection against British and other foreign manufacturers. So in 1816, Congress passed the country's first protective tariff.

Nevertheless, U.S. industries continued to clamor for even higher protective tariffs. Through the rest of the 19th century, the protectionists generally had their way. U.S. tariff rates were raised in 1824, and again in 1828. From 1832 to 1857, tariffs were lowered slightly, but they remained mostly protective.

The tariff issue was a major cause of sectional conflict between the Northern and Southern states before the Civil War. Since most U.S. industries were concentrated in the North, many Northerners insisted on tariff protection. People in the South, which was largely agricultural, feared that high U.S. tariffs would lead to retaliation by the nations of Europe. This would mean that tariffs would be raised on U.S. exports, thereby making it more difficult to sell Southern cotton and tobacco abroad. In addition, Southerners often preferred to buy less expensive, European-manufactured goods over competing goods manufactured in the Northern United States. If tariffs were raised, then European-manufactured goods would become more expensive.

Protectionism reached its peak in the early 1930s during the Great Depression. In an effort to protect domestic jobs and increase sales by reducing foreign competition, Congress passed the **Hawley-Smoot Tariff Act** of 1930. It raised duties to an all-time high. Instead of promoting U.S. industries, though, Hawley-Smoot nearly destroyed them. Because foreign nations were no longer able to sell to the United States, they lacked the dollars to buy U.S. products. Thus, U.S. exports declined drastically. Moreover, the high U.S. tariffs so outraged our trading partners that many retaliated by raising their own tariffs. High foreign tariffs thus led to a decline in U.S. exports (particularly of farm products and machinery) and increased unemployment and business failures.

The protectionist trend was reversed after the 1932 landslide election of President Franklin D. Roosevelt and a Democratic-controlled Congress. In 1934, Congress passed the **Reciprocal Trade Agreements Act**. This law permitted a U.S. president to lower tariffs by up to 50 percent for imports from any nation that granted similar concessions to the United States.

The Act contained a *most-favored-nation clause.* Briefly, this clause said that each signatory nation would extend to the other the same preferential tariff and trade concessions that it may in the future extend to nonsignatories. Suppose, for example, that the United States and Japan sign a most-favored-nation clause as part of a trade agreement. If the United States later grants Indonesia a tariff reduction that is lower than its trade agreement with Japan, the United States is required to grant Japan (as a "most-favored-nation") the same favorable tariff terms given to Indonesia. If Japan, in turn, grants a trade concession to Germany, the United States (as a "most-favored-nation") is entitled to the same treatment that Japan gives to a nonsignatory (Germany).

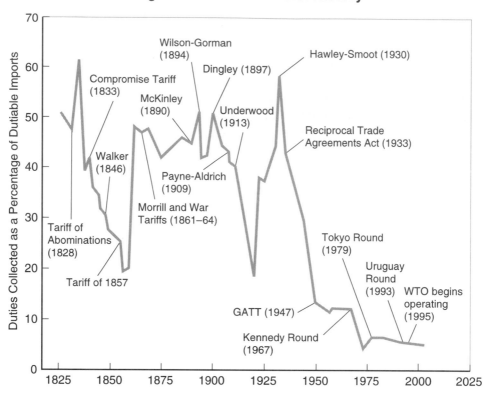

Figure 22.1 **Tariffs in U.S. History**

𝄢 The General Agreement on Tariffs and Trade (GATT)

After World War II ended in 1945, the United States and the other victorious powers vowed to avoid one of the mistakes of the past by promoting trade among nations. Toward that end, 23 of the world's trading nations created the **General Agreement on Tariffs and Trade (GATT)** in 1948. The organization grew to 128 members by 1995.

Unlike the Reciprocal Trade Agreements Act, which provided for *bilateral* (two-nation) negotiations, GATT established the machinery for *multilateral* (many-nation) negotiations. Some nine "rounds" of negotiations dismantled the tariff barrier system of the 1930s. As a result, tariff levels by 1995 were far lower than they had been half a century before.

𝄢 World Trade Organization (WTO)

The signatories to GATT formed the **World Trade Organization (WTO)**, which began operating in early 1995 with 140 members. (It has since grown larger.) This oversight body enforces trade agreements made by its members. All members pledge to reduce tariffs and eliminate import quotas. The WTO protects patents, trademarks, and copyrights. If a conflict arises between member countries on trade matters, any member can appeal the matter to the World Trade Organization for settlement.

One of the keys to the WTO's early success has been its ability to handle trade disputes among its members. Under its rules, if one WTO member nation accuses another of unfair trade practices, the nations are expected to attempt to settle the dispute among themselves. If that fails, the WTO can be asked to decide the matter. Then, if found to be guilty of an accusation, the offending nation has to mend its ways or face trade sanctions.

For example, in 1995 when the WTO was first organized, panels were formed to investigate

- Canada's complaints about French restrictions on the Canadian scallop trade
- charges brought by the European Union, Canada, and the United States against Japan for levying tariffs on imported alcohol
- Venezuela's complaints about U.S. rules restricting pollutants in gasoline.

That same year, three other disputes were settled even before a WTO panel had met. Supporters of the WTO took this as a sign that fear of losing a WTO case often prompts nations that violate trade rules to mend their ways. More recently, in 2002, the European Union brought an action before the WTO

Cancun, Mexico, September 2003. The WTO has been a target of demonstrations around the world. These farmer/demonstrators believe that the WTO renders judgments on global trade practices that favor corporate interests and further globalization. Whereas the purpose of the WTO is to make international trade less restrictive, critics believe that large corporations with international investments perpetuate social injustice, mismanage the natural resources of developing nations, and cause ecological damage.

01234

5678901234567890

against the United States for giving tax breaks to U.S. companies. The European Union (EU) alleged that the tax breaks gave the U.S. companies an unfair advantage and, therefore, constituted an unfair trade practice. The U.S. Congress provided a tax break that benefited companies such as Caterpillar, Inc., and Boeing Company. The EU appealed to the WTO, alleging that the tax break was, in effect, a subsidy to the U.S. firms and, therefore, an unfair trade practice. The EU threatened to impose tariffs on a wide range of U.S. goods. The WTO authorized the sanctions, declaring the U.S. tax breaks illegal.

The European Union and Other Regional Trade Groups

Tariffs and other trade barriers have long been some of the major sources of friction between nations. The search for a permanent peace in the years following the Second World War led many Western Europeans to look for ways to eliminate these barriers. A *regional trade agreement*, they argued, might lessen tensions among Western European nations. In addition, they believed that a free trade agreement would increase living standards of all nations that participated in the agreement. Thus, Western Europeans took a number of steps that eventually led to the present-day **European Union (EU)**.

HISTORICAL BACKGROUND.   The European Union had its origins in 1951 when France, Italy, West Germany, Belgium, the Netherlands, and Luxembourg created the European Coal and Steel Community. The purpose of this organization was to increase productivity in the member countries by reducing tariffs and other barriers to trade in the coal and steel industries. Coal and steel production increased dramatically, thereby encouraging the six nations to expand the range of their cooperation.

This was achieved in 1957, when the six nations signed the Treaty of Rome. The agreement created the **European Economic Community (EEC)**, whose principal aims were to (1) preserve and strengthen peace; (2) create a region in which the free movement of goods, people, services, and capital was guaranteed; and (3) provide for some kind of political unity. Membership in the EEC (or as it was soon popularly called, the **Common Market**) grew to 12 in number after the United Kingdom, Ireland, Denmark, Greece, Spain, and Portugal joined.

The Common Market later became known as the **European Community (EC)** and is now (with 25 members) known as the "European Union (EU)." In 1968, the EU eliminated tariffs among member nations, and for a time, their economies flourished. But a number of nontariff barriers to trade continued to slow the movement of goods across national borders. For example, member states were subject to differing sales and excise taxes, along with differing safety and health standards on machinery and agricultural products. Moreover, European nations subsidized some of their domestic industries.

The European Union's Parliament meets in Strasbourg, France. All members of the EU have representatives in this legislative body.

THE EUROPEAN UNION TODAY AND TOMORROW.   Today, goods, workers, and capital can easily cross borders between any two EU member nations. The countries have established uniform trade regulations and manufacturing standards. To further the goal of economic integration, a central bank was established and a single European currency, the *euro,* was issued by the EU's central bank in 2002. The euro replaced the currencies of 12 EU nations. By eliminating virtually all remaining trade barriers, the EU managed to weld its membership into a single market. With both a combined population and a GDP larger than those of the United States, the EU constitutes one of the world's largest and wealthiest markets.

EFFECTS OF THE EUROPEAN UNION ON THE UNITED STATES.   As long as EU markets remain open to all nations (including nations that are not members of the EU), integration benefits U.S. firms for the following reasons:

● The absence of physical barriers among EU countries (such as border controls for goods, services, and workers) reduces transportation bottlenecks and other costs of U.S. firms doing business in Europe.

● The uniformity of trade regulations makes it easier to achieve economies of scale in production and distribution. Previously, for example, Great Britain and Germany had different requirements for importing cars. In order for U.S. manufacturers to sell automobiles to both countries, U.S. workers had to assemble cars differently for each country. Now with one

Figure 22.2 **TOP PURCHASERS OF U.S. EXPORTS AND SUPPLIERS OF U.S. IMPORTS, 2002 (billions of dollars)**

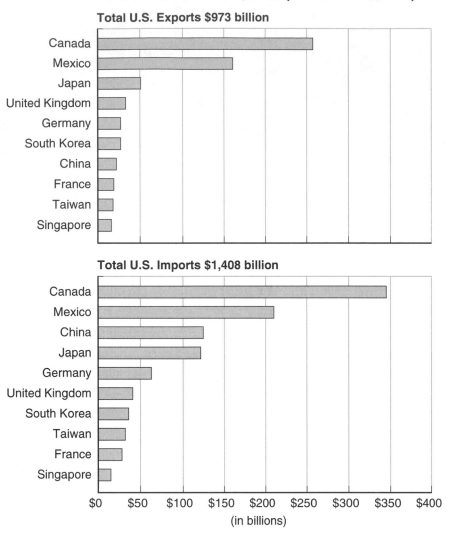

Which of the top trade partners of the United States are members of the EU?

standard in all EU countries, the U.S. manufacturer need produce automobiles to meet only the one standard requirement.

- Subsidiaries of U.S. firms based in any EU country have the right to buy and sell goods and services throughout the EU. Thus, General Motors, for example, has trade access to the EU equal to that of its European competitors because it has full or partial ownership in three European automobile companies.

NAFTA—The World's Largest Free-Trade Zone.   The **North American Free Trade Agreement (NAFTA)** links the United States, Canada, and Mexico in the world's largest free-trade zone. In 2002, about 43 percent of total exports from the United States went to Canada and Mexico, and those two nations accounted for almost 40 percent of all U.S. imports (see Figure 22.2). Under the terms of NAFTA, which went into effect in 1994, all tariffs (and most non-tariff barriers) will be lifted by by 2009. In the absence of trade barriers, goods can move between the Yukon and the Yucatán as they can now move between Los Angeles and Sheboygan, Wisconsin.

There has been some heated opposition to NAFTA by American labor unions and environmental and antiglobalization groups. One political opponent of the agreement, **Ross Perot**, stated his opposition rather colorfully by saying that there would be "a giant sucking sound" as jobs and businesses fled the United States and Canada for the cheaper resource markets of Mexico. It was argued that Mexican laws prohibiting child labor and environmental polllution are either not in place, are weak, or are not strictly enforced, thus reducing operating costs of manufacturing. In fact, a number of U.S. plants have moved to Mexico and, initially, some U.S. workers did lose their jobs. Even though many of these workers were able to find new jobs, usually the new ones were at lower wages than they had previously earned. During NAFTA's first year, for example, the U.S. Department of Labor estimated that more than 42,200 U.S. jobs had been lost due to NAFTA. Finally, opponents of NAFTA argued that the richer U.S. and Canadian firms operating in Mexico would unfairly impede industrial development in Mexico.

Defenders of NAFTA responded by saying that NAFTA was not the reason that U.S. plants had left the country. In some industries, high costs of production in the United States and lower production costs in some other countries were the factors that influenced U.S. companies to go elsewhere. They argued that if U.S. plants had not moved to Mexico, they would have moved their facilities to low-wage countries in Asia or elsewhere. Since U.S. plants were going to leave anyway, NAFTA defenders reasoned, it was to the advantage of the United States that the plants relocated nearby in Mexico. They said that these plants not only gave jobs to Mexican workers but also stimulated Mexican industries that service and supply American-owned factories. Defenders also argued that environmental protection procedures are more strictly enforced in the American-owned plants in Mexico than would be the case without American influence.

The movement of U.S. plants to Mexico does not always result in a loss of jobs for American workers. The Key Tronic Corporation, which manufactures computer keyboards in Spokane, Washington, laid off workers and moved their plant to Ciudad Juárez, Mexico. Because of the lower manufacturing costs there, Key Tronic was able to lower the prices of its products and increase sales. Since the Key Tronic computer keyboard assembled in Mexico uses some components that are made in plants near Spokane, overall employment around Spokane rose to keep up with the increased demand for the component parts.

Zenith Electronics manufactures television picture tubes in Illinois and sends them to Mexico for assembly into television sets. These sets, in turn, are shipped back to Texas for distribution in the Eastern United States. Some 1,300 new jobs have been created in the United States by this procedure (not all at Zenith Electronics). McDonald's, the U.S. food chain, has nearly 200 restaurants in Mexico. The company ships beef from the United States to Mexico, thereby increasing the demand for U.S. beef and benefiting U.S. cattle ranchers.

The elimination of artificial barriers to trade has benefited all three nations. In the absence of trade barriers, the law of comparative advantage has enabled the United States, Canada, and Mexico to allocate their resources more efficiently. NAFTA has already resulted in more jobs, more trade, greater output, and higher living standards throughout North America. In fact, U.S. trade with Canada and Mexico has increased to a greater extent than has U.S. trade with the rest of the world. Whereas U.S. exports to Canada and Mexico amounted to about 34 percent of total U.S. exports in 1994, they increased to 43 percent in 2002. Similarly, imports from Canada and Mexico increased from 26 percent of total U.S. imports in 1994 to almost 40 percent in 2002, making these two nations the major trading partners of the United States.

OTHER REGIONAL TRADE BLOCS.   The European Union and NAFTA are examples of regional trade blocs. Others are in operation in Latin America, Africa, and Asia. The most significant of these are the following.

- The **Caribbean Community and Common Market (CARICOM)** links most of the Caribbean islands (plus Belize and Guyana) in a kind of common market. CARICOM is working toward the elimination of trade barriers among member states.
- The **Central American Common Market** promotes trade links among Guatemala, Honduras, El Salvador, Nicaragua, and Costa Rica. Although the bloc has proclaimed its intention to eliminate trade barriers between its members, many quotas and other obstacles remain.

INTERNATIONAL TRADE IS GLOBAL

At one time, international trade was conducted by sellers of goods or services produced in one country to business firms in foreign lands. For example, a U.S. firm might produce automobiles in the United States to be sold to dealers in other nations. Since the end of the Second World War in 1945, however, international trade has become increasingly global. That is, more and more of it is being conducted as if national boundaries hardly existed at all. U.S. automobile manufacturers have production facilities in many nations outside the United States, including Canada, Mexico, Brazil, Great Britain, and Thailand. Japanese

Figure 22.3 **Total Exports of All Nations Since 1960**

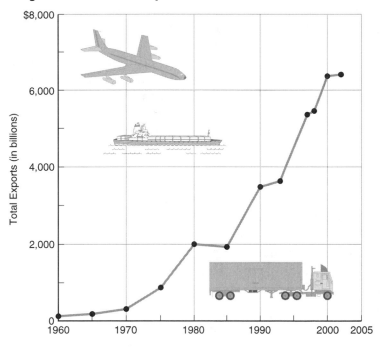

Why have exports generally grown since 1960?

automobile manufacturers also have plants in many nations, including a fair number in the United States and Ireland.

Much global trade today is in the hands of *multinational corporations (MNC)*. It is not unusual for one multinational corporation to have factories in many countries, be owned by shareholders in two or more countries, engage in research and development projects in several countries, and employ key executives of various nationalities. The world's multinational corporations, about 40,000 in number, account for two-thirds of the world's trade in goods and services.

🗲 The Rise of Multinational Corporations

There are several reasons why multinational corporations have grown so much since the end of World War II.

BARRIERS TO INVESTMENT AND TRADE HAVE BEEN FALLING. We have seen how regional trading blocs and international agreements like NAFTA, the European Union, and WTO have promoted trade among nations. By eliminating or reducing financial and investment barriers and tariffs, international trade has become much more profitable than it once was. Profitable trade and the ability to invest and build facilities in foreign countries have contributed to the growth of multinational corporations.

TELECOMMUNICATION AND TRANSPORTATION COSTS HAVE TUMBLED. An electronic revolution has made it possible for people to communicate or witness events anywhere in the world. At one time, it was expensive and time-consuming to deliver a portfolio of pictures and plans from, say, one part of Asia to a remote corner of Latin America. Such an operation today can be accomplished in moments at a cost of a few dollars. Reduced shipping and communication costs have promoted the growth of multinational corporations. Thus, even though the multinational corporation Asea Brown Boveri has some 120,000 employees in 100 countries, operating units can easily communicate among themselves and with headquarters in Zurich, Switzerland.

IT IS EASY TO MAKE PAYMENTS IN INTERNATIONAL TRADE. In an earlier chapter, we discussed money as the lifeblood of business. By making the movement of funds from one country to another as easy as a transfer of funds from Miami to Minneapolis, the breath of life has been pumped into all forms of global trade. The ease by which funds are transferred globally facilitates the operations of multinational corporations. Asea Brown Boveri, for example, can readily transfer funds between its operating units regardless of where in the world they are located.

Why Do Large Firms Become Multinational?

We have described how technological changes and the lowering of trade barriers made it possible for business firms to operate globally. But why would a firm want to become a multinational corporation? Or, to put it another way, what is in it for them? Corporations go global (or multinational) for a number of reasons, including to: (1) avoid protective tariffs and quotas and (2) reduce costs.

AVOIDING PROTECTIVE TARIFFS AND QUOTAS. Shortly after its creation in the 1950s, the Common Market levied an 18 percent tariff on farm equipment imported from nations that were not Common Market members, including the United States. As a result, U.S. firms that manufactured farm equipment were kept out of the Common Market. In order to get around the tariff, one U.S. farm-equipment manufacturer, John Deere, built a number of production facilities in Western Europe. Farm equipment produced in John Deere's Western European factories and sold in Western Europe were not subject to a tariff and, therefore, could more easily compete with farm equipment produced by Western European competitors.

Similarly in 1991, when NutraSweet (a brand name of a popular sugar substitute) was hit with high Common Market duties, its parent company, Monsanto (a U.S. corporation) entered into a joint venture with Ajinomoto (a Japanese corporation) to build an artificial sweetener plant in France. As multinationals, the U.S. and Japanese corporations were able to sell their products in Western

Asea Brown Boveri (ABB) is a multinational corporation. It was created out of the merger of two of the world's largest electric-power equipment manufacturing companies: ASEA of Sweden and Brown Boveri of Switzerland. After its creation in 1988, ABB acquired a number of large companies worldwide. The company is headquartered in Zurich, Switzerland, and is led by a German chief executive. Despite the company's origins, its official language is English and its accounts are kept in U.S. dollars.

Europe almost as easily as their European competitors. By forming multinationals, corporations are able to enter markets that discriminate against firms from certain countries. For example, Japanese firms have often discriminated against Canadian companies in favor of U.S. ones. So Northern Telecom (a Canadian telecommunications company), which has subsidiary companies located in the United States, conducts business with Japan through its U.S. subsidiaries rather than through Northern Telecom's main office in Canada.

REDUCING COSTS.   Corporations become multinationals to move their operations abroad as a way of reducing production costs. In the 1980s, Nike, an Oregon-based footwear company, closed the last of its U.S. plants and moved all production to its factories in South Korea. The shift enabled Nike to reduce labor costs from an average of $6.94 per hour that it was paying its U.S. production workers to something under 50 cents per hour. Then in the 1990s, Korean wages increased. Therefore, Nike closed its Korean operations and set up new ones in Indonesia, where the going rate for shoe workers was $1.03 per day.

Company	Home Country	Revenue
1. Wal-Mart Stores	United States	$246,525
2. General Motors	United States	186,763
3. ExxonMobil	United States	182,458
4. Royal Dutch/Shell Group	Netherlands/United Kingdom	179,431
5. British Petroleum	United Kingdom	178,721
6. Ford Motor	United States	163,871
7. DaimlerChrysler	Germany	141,421
8. Toyota Motor	Japan	131,754
9. General Electric	United States	131,698
10. Mitsubishi	Japan	109,380

TABLE 22.3   THE WORLD'S TEN LARGEST CORPORATIONS (MILLIONS OF U.S. DOLLARS)

Source: *Fortune's Global 500,* 2003

ECONOMIC ISSUE

Today's Debate on Globalization

The efforts of both the WTO and the IMF have generated widespread and sometimes violent antiglobalization protests in Seattle, Prague, Davos, New York, and elsewhere. The protesters, a coalition of antipoverty campaigners, environmentalists, trade unionists, and anticapitalist groups, see globalization as a threat. The proponents of globalization, on the other hand, see it as a means to further democracy, progress, and prosperity worldwide. At the heart of the issue lies the question of which course—protectionism or free trade—is more likely to increase jobs, raise living standards, and improve the quality of life.

The History of Globalization

The term *globalization* was coined in the 1950s to express the fact that the world is joined in a single global marketplace. Economies that were once separated by a variety of barriers to trade are now linked in a network of economic inter-

actions involving trade, finance, and production. Many corporations are multinational.

National economies have become more integrated with one another through trade, finance, production, and treaties. For example, incorporating the benefits of the comparative advantage of alternative production sites, semiconductor chips may be designed in India, while the basic wafers for the chips are produced in the United States, cut and assembled in Malaysia, and tested and shipped from Singapore. The capital needed for these various activities may come from investors and banks all over the world.

Globalization has resulted in the economic integration of rich and poor nations. It is thought by some to promise increased gains for both sides. Others fear that the integration of capital results in greater inequalities, dislocation in the poorer countries, and environmental hazards worldwide. Arguments for and against globalization are, in some ways, similar to arguments for and against protection or free trade.

Arguments Against Globalization

- Globalization has not benefited all people equally. The gains made by the more developed countries of the world have been at the expense of less developed countries.

- The fall of protectionist barriers has led to insecurity in the workplace. Goods imported from abroad are made by foreign workers. Had those same goods been purchased from U.S.-based manufacturers, U.S. workers would have made them.

- Imports tend to keep down wages of workers in the developed countries. To justify paying lower wages, U.S. employers often tell their workers that their work can be done by foreign workers who are willing to work at a fraction of the going U.S. wage.

- Globalization leads to unfavorable trade balances. When imports are greater than exports, the net outflow of dollars results in higher prices and interest rates.

- National cultures and identities are threatened by globalization. Contributing factors are the spread of satellite TV, international media networks, and increased personal travel. Western fashions, music, customs, and foods are replacing those of the local ones. Holywood movies are watched in theaters and on television sets around the world.

- Globalization threatens democracy. Huge multinational companies are becoming more powerful and influential than many democratically elected governments. The largest of the multinationals are larger than most nations measured in terms of GDP for countries and revenue for corporations. Of the 100 largest economic entities, 51 are corporations and 49 are nation-states. The interests of the corporate shareholders take priority over those of the community. Corporate power, antiglobalization groups argue, is restricting individual freedom.

- Multinational corporations disregard the environment in their drive for increased profits. The smoke from factories and nuclear plants and the residue from industrial wastes pollute the air, water, and soil and contribute to global warming.

- Trade barriers promote economic development by protecting "infant industries." Newly developed industries should be given time to grow and become efficient. These new industries grow only if the government keeps foreign competition out of the country.

- The free, unfettered movement of financial assets from more developed to less developed countries may lead to instability. There is a tendency for the underregulated and undercapitalized banks in less developed nations to gamble with their funds recklessly. Then, when creditors call in their loans, financial panic sets in. This occurred in Mexico in 1994; in Indonesia, Malaysia, the Philippines, and South Korea in 1997; and in Argentina in 2000.

- Certain industries are so vital to a nation's defense that their preservation is a matter of national security. For many years in the United States, foreign petroleum was subject to a protective tariff to guarantee the existence of the domestic oil industry and, thus, ensure adequate oil supplies in wartime. For similar reasons, the U.S. shipbuilding industry has been supported through direct subsidies and regulations requiring that only U.S.-owned ships carry certain goods destined for export. Those in favor of supporting the U.S. shipbuilding industry believe that the nation's fleet of merchant ships should be ensured in the event of a national emergency.

Arguments in Favor of Globalization

- Globalization gives consumers more choices. It has resulted in rising living standards and a growth in international travel.

- Globalization promotes information exchange, which can lead to a greater understanding of other cultures.

- International trade allows each country to concentrate on its most efficient activities. Two nations gain more from an exchange of goods than if both produced the same items on their own. The United States sells cars to Europe and imports cars from Europe. The United States could produce European-style cars but finds it more profitable to produce its U.S. models and sell some of them to Europe to finance the import of European cars.

(continued on next page)

- Because of labor-cost differences, certain goods can be produced more cheaply in some countries than in others. Therefore, the United States exports expensive, high-technology goods to Asia in return for inexpensive labor-intensive goods imported from Asia. Both regions gain from the exchange. U.S. industries with well-paid workers do compete in international markets because of high worker productivity and capital-intensive production techniques. Thus, U.S. machinery, transportation equipment, and office systems are major export items, and U.S. workers in those industries are well paid even by U.S. standards.

- Globalization and free trade raise living standards. With a given amount of money, consumers purchase more goods at lower prices. Imposing tariffs and other restrictions forces domestic consumers to purchase domestic goods at higher prices.

- The need to protect infant industries in the less developed countries is a weak argument against globalization. These countries share in global production when multinational enterprises operate in them. Automobiles, for example, are produced at multisite operations. The labor-intensive part of the production process is often assigned to a site in a less developed country.

- Income inequalities within more developed countries and between more developed and less developed countries are not the result of globalization. Less than 5 percent of U.S. workers are in competition with low-skilled workers in emerging markets. That is too small a percentage to explain the growth in inequality of income distribution in the United States. Changes in technology favor highly skilled workers over low-skilled workers and may better explain income inequalities in the United States, as well as in developing countries.

S U M M A R Y

International trade is the exchange of goods and services among people and institutions of different countries. This trade takes place because nations differ in factor resources. A nation has an absolute advantage when it can produce more of a product or service with the same amount of resources than another nation. A nation has a comparative advantage when it can produce a product or service at a lower opportunity cost than another nation. International trade promotes greater specialization, which in turn increases total world output. Global economic interdependence has been accelerated by technological changes.

Nations establish trade barriers to restrict the free flow of goods, services, investments, and people. These barriers include tariffs, quotas, currency controls, administrative red tape, and export controls. Free trade among nations raises worldwide living standards in the long run. But in the short run, some groups are likely to be hurt by international competition. Arguments in favor of trade barriers include the quest for a favorable balance of trade, the need to protect U.S. workers from lower-paid foreign workers, the need to protect U.S. "infant industries," national security, and the fact that tariffs are a source of revenue.

Tariffs have been an issue throughout the course of U.S. history. At first, protectionism dominated U.S. tariff policy. Then in 1934, the Reciprocal Trade Agreements Act provided for bilateral negotiations to reduce tariffs between the United States and any nation that would grant similar concessions to it. In 1948, the United States and 22 other nations signed the General Agreement on Tariffs and Trade, which provided for multilateral negotiations to reduce trade barriers. In 1995, GATT created the World Trade Organization. There are also a number of regional trading communities, such as the European Union and NAFTA. These associations provide for various degrees of barrier-free trade among member nations.

There are arguments for and against globalization. At the heart of the issue lies the question of which course—protectionism or free trade—is more likely to increase jobs, raise living standards, and improve the quality of life.

REVIEWING THE CHAPTER

BUILDING VOCABULARY

Match each item in Column A with its definition in Column B.

Column A	Column B
F **1.** global economy	*a.* a newly developed industry
G **2.** multinational corporation	*b.* having to do with two nations
I **3.** absolute advantage	*c.* a treaty provision requiring a signatory to extend the same preferential trade terms to other signatories that it extends to a nonsignatory
J **4.** Law of Comparative Advantage	
A **5.** infant industry	*d.* an excess of merchandise exports over imports
C **6.** most-favored-nation clause	*e.* a tax on imports calculated as a percentage of their value
E **7.** *ad valorem* tariff	*f.* the combined economies of all nations
B **8.** bilateral	*g.* a business firm that operates in two or more countries
D **9.** favorable balance of trade	*h.* having to do with many nations
	i. a situation whereby a nation can produce a good or service at a lower cost than another nation
H **10.** multilateral	*j.* the idea that a nation should produce products and services in which its opportunity costs are lowest and import all other goods and services

UNDERSTANDING WHAT YOU HAVE READ

1. The global economy refers to the economies of (*a*) all of the nations of the world (*b*) the Western nations of Europe and the Americas (*c*) the Common Market (*d*) the World Trade Organization.

2. An argument in favor of globalization is that (*a*) national cultures and identities tend to disappear (*b*) it increases the power of multinational corporations (*c*) trade barriers promote economic development (*d*) it allows each nation to concentrate on its most efficient activities.

3. An argument in opposition to globalization is that it (*a*) raises world living standards (*b*) favors the more developed countries at the expense of less developed nations (*c*) gives consumers more choices (*d*) results in a rise in prices of consumer goods.

4. A protective tariff is most effective in (*a*) allowing a nation to make the best use of its economic resources (*b*) increasing the export of goods to foreign nations (*c*) safeguarding the interests of particular domestic industries (*d*) raising the national standard of living.

5. Which *one* of the following has an effect different from that of the other three? (*a*) reciprocal trade agreements (*b*) import quotas (*c*) currency controls (*d*) protective tariffs.

6. Who ultimately bears the cost of a tariff? (*a*) the retailer (*b*) the government of the exporting country (*c*) the importer (*d*) the consumer.

7. If the United States abolished its tariffs, what would be a probable result? (*a*) There would be fewer job opportunities in U.S. exporting industries. (*b*) The U.S. standard of living would be considerably lowered. (*c*) Some workers in currently protected industries would lose their jobs. (*d*) Most farmers would be hurt.

8. From 1816 until the 1930s, U.S. tariff policy could best be described as (*a*) one of free trade (*b*) protectionist (*c*) reciprocal (*d*) nonexistent.

9. All of the following have brought about the reduction of tariffs among nations, *except* the (*a*) World Trade Organization (*b*) General Agreement on Tariffs and Trade (*c*) Hawley-Smoot Tariff Act (*d*) European Common Market.

10. An economic common market has all of the following advantages, *except* that it (*a*) lowers trade barriers among its member nations (*b*) allows workers from one member nation access to jobs in other member nations (*c*) permits nonmember nations unlimited trading advantages (*d*) develops economic policies for the economic advantage of all its members.

THINKING CRITICALLY

1. Economists frequently cite the Law of Comparative Advantage to show why nations should engage in international trade.

   a. State the law.

   b. Explain what happens when nations specialize in certain products and engage in international trade to obtain other products.

   c. Why is it *not* possible for one nation to have an absolute advantage in the production of all goods and services?

2. A U.S. appliance manufacturer in Peoria, Illinois, recently told a friend, "When Japanese manufacturers undersell my food mixers, I have to lay off some of my workers. What's more, the profits that I lose because of this foreign competition and the salaries that my former workers lose are lost forever from the U.S. economy. The only answer to this problem is to raise tariffs on Japanese goods."

   a. Should U.S. appliance manufacturers be protected against foreign competition that undersells them here? Give *two* arguments to support your point of view.

   b. Why would the Peoria manufacturer be unlikely to use these arguments against a competitor in Denver?

   c. Study Figure 22.1 on page 502. Select *two* periods in which the United States imposed high tariffs. Discuss the circumstances at that time and why, under those circumstances, you believe that the United States was or was not justified in protecting domestic producers.

3. The European Union represents both a triumph and a challenge. On the one hand, the EU provides a large, unified market for U.S. manufacturers and capital investors. On the other hand, the EU has become a formidable competitor in U.S. markets. (*a*) Why is the European Union an important market for the United States? (*b*) How has the EU become a "formidable competitor in many U.S. markets"?

4. Globalization and multinational corporations are a fact of modern economic life. Using the arguments on pages 512–514 as a guide, prepare an article for your school newspaper in which you discuss the arguments for and against globalization.

USING THE INTERNET

- The International Monetary Fund (IMF) discusses "Does Globalization Lower Wages and Export Jobs?" at <<www.imf.org/external/pubs/ft/issues11/index.htm>>.

- Links to organizations, institutions, and individuals trying to stop, slow, or reform globalization are provided at <<globalization.about.com/cs/antiglobalization/>>.

- Foreign trade statistics can be found at <<www.census.gov>>. Click on "Foreign Trade."

- The official Web site of the World Trade Organization is <<www.wto.org>>; that of the European Union is <<www.europa.eu.int>>; that of the World Bank is <<worldbank.org>>; that of the International Monetary Fund is <<imf.org>>; and that of the United Nations Development Program is <<www.undp.org>>.

CHAPTER 23

Financing International Trade

OVERVIEW

"Hey, welcome back. How did your Latin American vacation go?"

"It was fantastic. I just loved visiting all those countries and seeing the sights. But wherever we went, we had to use a different kind of money: cruzeiros, sucres, pesos. I had some time understanding prices."

United States citizens traveling abroad soon learn that they have to exchange their U.S. dollars for the money of the country they are visiting. Stores, restaurants, and hotels in other countries often do not accept U.S. dollars. To them, the dollars are foreign money. On their return home, tourists from the United States can convert their unspent foreign money back into U.S. dollars. Individuals and firms doing business in countries other than their own also must exchange the currency of their country for the currencies of the nations in which they do business.

In this chapter, we will study exchange rates and how the rate of exchange of one currency for another is determined. We will learn how gold was once used in settling international accounts, how payments in international trade are made today, how these payments are recorded, and the importance of balance of payments accounts.

EXCHANGE RATES

How much local currency people from the United States receive for their dollars in the countries they visit depends on the exchange rate. The *exchange rate,* or *rate of exchange,* is the price of one currency in terms of another. If, for example, you had been visiting Mexico on April 14 in a recent year, you might have learned that a dollar was equal to about 11 pesos on that day. Or, to put it another way, one peso equaled about \$.09 (1 ÷ 10.61 = .09). Table 23.1 on page 520 summarizes the exchange rates of the world's principal currencies on one specific day—April 14—in a recent year.

Like stocks and bonds, the prices of foreign currencies are constantly rising and falling. Indeed, because of its resemblance to the rising and falling motion of a ship at sea, economists often describe the process as *floating exchange rates*. An exchange rate table usually summarizes exchange rates at the close of a business day. Rates can vary from one day to the next and sometimes from morning to afternoon.

Exchange rates play a crucial role in international trade. Suppose that the rate of exchange for Norwegian kroner was to change from 7.33 kroner to the U.S. dollar to 10 kroner to the dollar. This change would make Norwegian goods less expensive to Americans because Americans would be able to buy more kroner for their dollars. As a tourist in Norway, for example, Americans could buy a 300-kroner sweater for only \$30 with the latter exchange rate (300 ÷ 10 = 30). Meanwhile, dollars and U.S.-made goods would become more costly to Norwegians.

To illustrate this, let us assume that at the old rate of exchange, Norwegians could have purchased a \$200 cellular telephone for 1,466 kroner (200 × 7.33 = 1,466). At the new exchange rate of 10 kroner to the dollar, the same telephone would cost 2,000 kroner (200 × 10 = 2,000).

Figure 23.1 **Floating Exchange Rates**

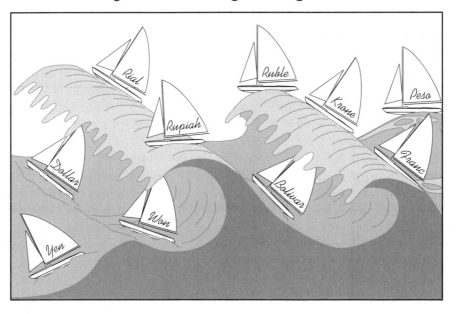

 TABLE 23.1 FOREIGN EXCHANGE RATES, APRIL 14, 200–			
Country	Foreign Currency	How Much One Unit of Foreign Currency Equals in U.S. Dollars	How Much $1 U.S. Equals in Foreign Currency
Argentina	(Peso)	.35	2.87
Australia	(Dollar)	.60	1.67
Brazil	(Cruzeiro)	.31	3.19
Britain	(Pound)	1.57	.64
Canada	(Dollar)	.69	1.45
Chile	(Peso)	.001	721.00
China	(Yuan)	.12	8.28
Denmark	(Krone)	.145	6.92
Euro Zone	**(Euro)**	**1.087**	**0.92**
Egypt	(Pound)	.17	5.90
Hong Kong	(Dollar)	.13	7.80
India	(Rupee)	.02	47.35
Japan	(Yen)	.0083	120.80
Mexico	(Peso)	.09	10.61
Norway	(Krone)	.14	7.33
Russia	(Ruble)	.03	31.27
South Korea	(Won)	.0009	1,123.80
Sweden	(Krona)	.12	8.45
Switzerland	(Franc)	.72	1.38
Taiwan	(NT$)	.03	34.81
Venezuela	(Bolivar)	.0006	1,596.00

Calculate the cost in dollars of a Norwegian sweater selling for 325 kroner.

What Determines the Rate of Exchange?

Why on the same day is the Japanese yen worth about $.001, the British pound $1.57, and the Mexican peso $.09? Why are exchange rates constantly "floating" up and down? And why do currencies sometimes plunge? An understanding of the laws of supply and demand helps answer these economic questions.

THE DEMAND FOR A NATION'S PRODUCTS AND ITS CURRENCY. Like securities in a stock exchange, the price of one currency in terms of another varies directly with changes in demand. Other things being equal, an increase in the demand for yen increases its price in terms of dollars and other currencies. Similarly, a decrease in the demand for Japanese currency has the opposite effect, that is, the value of the yen in terms of dollars and other currencies falls. The main reason that people outside of Japan would want to own yen is to buy Japanese goods. In other words, the demand for yen depends on the demand for Japan's goods and services. Therefore, if the demand for goods made in Japan increases, the need

A foreign currency trader in Seoul, South Korea, looks at the value of the U.S. dollar in terms of the Korean won.

to pay for those imports increases the demand for Japanese currency. The increased demand for Japanese goods and Japanese currency would also be followed by an increase in the price of the yen in foreign exchange markets.

THE SUPPLY OF A NATION'S CURRENCY. Like demand, changes in the supply of a currency in foreign exchange markets affect the currency's exchange rate. Other things being equal, an increase in the supply of won reduces the price of this South Korean currency in foreign exchange markets. A decrease in the supply of won has the opposite effect—that is, the price of won increases in foreign exchange markets.

The supply of a country's currency in foreign exchange markets depends largely on that nation's imports. Suppose, for example, U.S. firms import many goods and services from South Korea. When U.S. companies purchase goods or services from South Korea, payment has to be made in won. The U.S. dollars used to purchase the Korean currency will increase the supply of dollars in foreign exchange markets and, other things being equal, push down the price of the U.S. dollar.

Similarly, if South Koreans import fewer goods and services, the supply of won in foreign exchange markets will decline. As the supply of won falls, it

▷ **TABLE 23.2   EFFECT OF CHANGES IN SUPPLY AND DEMAND ON THE PRICE OF A FOREIGN CURRENCY**

As Demand for South Korean Goods	Supply of Won	Price of Won
Decreases	Increases	Falls
Increases	Falls	Rises

What makes the supply of won increase? What makes the price of won rise?

becomes more costly to exchange foreign currency for won. Meanwhile, South Koreans find it less costly for them to import goods and services because of the increased purchasing power of the won.

⚡ How Payments Are Made in International Trade

A department store in the United States orders sweaters from a French manufacturer at a price of 10,000 euros. The exchange rate for euros at the time is $1 = .92 euro. The U.S. store manager writes a check for $10,869.57, which she deposits with a local bank. The local bank purchases 10,000 euros (10,869.57 × .92) in the foreign exchange market and provides its customer with a check for that amount. The importer sends the check to the French company, which deposits the check in its bank account and ships the sweaters. The French bank now has a check from a U.S. bank promising to pay 10,000 euros to the French bank.

Meanwhile, a French music store orders $10,869.57 worth of CDs from an exporter in the United States. In similar fashion, the manager of the French music store writes a check for 10,000 euros and deposits the check at the store's bank. A local bank uses the funds to purchase $10,869.57 (10,000 ÷ .92) in the foreign exchange market, and provides the French business firm with a check for that amount. The music store sends the check to the U.S. exporter in return for the CDs. The U.S. exporter deposits the check in its local bank.

Figure 23.2 summarizes these transactions. We can see that

- the dollars used to purchase euros exactly equal the euros used to purchase dollars. Consequently,
- supply of, demand for, and the exchange rate of the currencies of the two countries remains the same, and
- exports enable nations to acquire foreign exchange.

THE GOLD STANDARD

From 1870 to 1971, foreign exchange rates hardly moved at all. *Fixed exchange rates* were the order of the day because the world's currencies were tied directly or indirectly to gold. This "tie" to gold gave the international monetary system its name: the *gold standard*. Nations on the gold standard agreed to exchange their currencies for a fixed amount of gold.

One of the advantages of the gold standard was that it made for stable and easily calculated exchange rates. During the 1930s, for example, the U.S. gov-

Figure 23.2 **The Process of Foreign Exchange**

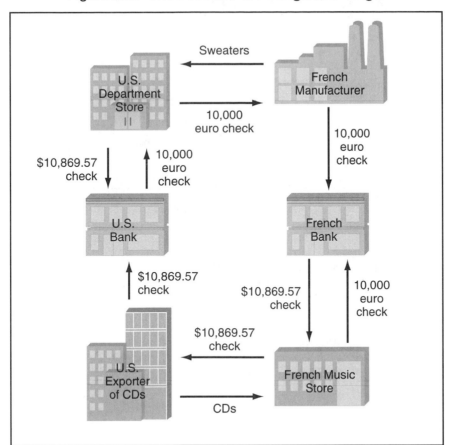

ernment converted its currency at the rate of 23.22 grains of gold to the dollar. At the same time, a British pound (£) was convertible into 113 grains of gold, or 4.87 times as much as the U.S. dollar (113 grains of gold ÷ 23.22 grains = 4.87). For that reason, the exchange rate between the pound and the dollar was £1 = $4.87.

In theory, the gold standard also served to keep international trade in balance. That is, no country could export more than it imported for very long because importers made payment in either gold or a currency convertible into gold. Exports increased the supply of gold of the exporting country. Since the money supply was tied to gold, an excess of exports served to increase the money supply as its supply of gold increased. As discussed in Chapter 15, prices increase (all other things being equal) as the money supply increases. Under the gold standard, therefore, an excess of exports brought about an increase in prices in the exporting country.

The larger the quantity of gold in the United States, the greater was the quantity of dollars placed in circulation. We can see how that worked from the

Figure 23.3 **The Gold Standard in Action**

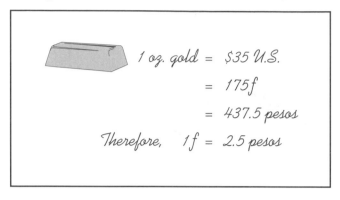

1 oz. gold = $35 U.S.

= 175f

= 437.5 pesos

Therefore,   1f = 2.5 pesos

In the 1960s, the Mexican peso was pegged (i.e., fixed) at 12.5 to the U.S. dollar, while the French franc was pegged at 5 to the dollar. Since the dollar was convertible to gold at 35:1, 175 francs was equal in value to an ounce of gold (because 5 × 35 = 175). Similarly, it took 12.5 × 35, or 437.5 pesos to equal an ounce of gold. Can you explain why one franc equaled 2.5 pesos?

following example. Assume that the U.S. government converted dollars into gold at the ratio of 23.22 grains to the dollar and that the U.S. Treasury held only 23.22 grains of gold. Under these conditions, the Treasury could have printed only one $1 bill or coin. Now assume that the Treasury had 1,000 times that quantity of gold (23,220 grains instead of 23.22). Then $1,000 in bills and coins could have been issued.

Under the gold standard, an excess of exports over imports resulted in an inflow of gold. The inflow of gold, in turn, increased the export nation's money supply. But an increase in the supply of money resulted in price increases in the exporting country. Higher prices in the exporting country tended to discourage exports and brought the favorable trade balance to an end. (Remember that in Chapter 3 we discussed how demand varies inversely with price.)

Suppose that U.S. firms had ordered 10,000 cashmere sweaters from British firms at a cost of £10 per sweater. Under the gold standard, Great Britain would have received 11,300,000 grains of gold. (113 grains of gold per £ × £10 = 1,130 grains of gold per sweater. 10,000 sweaters × 1,130 = 11,300,000 grains of gold.) The additional gold in the British treasury would have increased the money supply in Great Britain. All other things being equal, an increase in the money supply in Great Britain would result in a rise in British prices. Assume that prices of cashmere sweaters increased from £10 to £11 each. At the higher price, U.S. firms would have ordered fewer cashmere sweaters from the British. The net result would have been that British exports would decline. As exports declined, so would the inflow of gold to Great Britain.

Countries whose imports exceeded their exports lost gold because their imports had to be paid for in gold. In our example, the money supply in the

United States declined because gold was leaving the United States and going to Great Britain to pay for U.S. imports of sweaters. Prices in the United States declined, as we can see from the formula $P = M \div Q$. (P = price; M = money supply; and Q = GDP.) If we assume that M in the United States fell from \$100 billion to \$50 billion and Q remained the same at \$100 billion, P would have fallen from \$1 (100 ÷ 100) to \$.50 (50 ÷ 100). Lower U.S. prices would have attracted foreign buyers to purchase goods from the United States. As U.S. exports increased (assuming imports remained unchanged), a more favorable trade balance would have resulted.

Here is a summary:

- A nation with a favorable trade balance experienced an inflow of gold.
- An inflow of gold increased the nation's money supply.
- Increases in the supply of money caused price increases.
- Higher prices resulted in a reduction in that nation's exports.
- The nation with an unfavorable trade balance experienced a gold outflow.
- A reduction in a nation's supply of gold reduced the nation's money supply.
- A decrease in the supply of money resulted in price declines.
- Lower prices brought about an increase in exports.
- Increased exports resulted in an inflow of gold.

Weaknesses in the gold standard led to its downfall. Most serious of these was the inability of nations to manage their money supply. In Chapter 19, we discussed how countries rely on monetary policy (changes in the money supply) to regulate their economies. This was not possible in countries where the money supply was directly tied to gold. Under the gold standard, the money supply depended on how much gold a nation possessed. In many instances, the output of privately owned gold mines had a greater impact on a nation's economy than government actions did. An increase in gold output from a private mine would bring about an increase in the money supply and a rise in prices at a time when the government might have wanted to reduce inflationary pressures.

Suppose a nation wanted to increase its money supply in order to encourage price increases. Under the gold standard, the nation could increase its money supply only if it increased its supply of gold. The need to manage the economies of many nations and the difficulty in doing so while tied to the gold standard became apparent during the Great Depression of the 1930s.

The 1930s was a period of worldwide depression and hardship. In efforts to fight the effects of the Depression, nations printed currency in quantities greater than their gold supplies could support. Unable to acquire enough of the precious metal to redeem their currencies, the nations simply abandoned the gold standard. In the absence of gold to compare the value of one currency with another, international trade slowed drastically.

World trade almost disappeared for an additional reason—the disruption caused by World War II (1939–1945). In 1944, the powers that were winning the war called a conference for the purpose of restoring order to international trade. The rules that they drew up took their name from the town where they met—Bretton Woods, New Hampshire.

⚡ The Bretton Woods System (1944–1973)

Toward the end of World War II, representatives of 44 nations met at the **Bretton Woods Conference**, in New Hampshire, to plan the restoration of world trade. As a first step, the conference delegates hoped to re-establish a system of fixed exchange rates. We have seen that this was a simple matter in the days when nations relied on gold to back their currencies. But during the war (as Allied countries bought arms to win the conflict), most of the world's gold supplies went in payment to the United States.

It was left, therefore, to the delegates at Bretton Woods to find something other than gold on which to base exchange rates. They found it in the U.S. dollar. With most of the world's mined gold supply in its vaults, the United States guaranteed to continue to exchange dollars presented by foreign countries for gold at the rate of $35 per ounce. Meanwhile, nations without a gold supply agreed to swap their currencies for dollars at a fixed rate of exchange. By relying on the gold-supported dollar, nations continued to base the value of their currencies on gold without actually owning any of the metal.

One of the essentials to the success of the old *Bretton Woods system* was the ability of nations to offer dollars in exchange for their currencies. Since foreign countries could not print dollars, the only ways they could acquire dollars was by (1) exporting goods or services, (2) borrowing the funds, or (3) receiving dollars as gifts. Under the Bretton Woods system, it was possible for a nation to run short of dollars. In fact, this situation happened to many nations. Running short of dollars, in turn, made it difficult for these nations to import the capital (machinery, fertilizers, etc.) they needed to produce goods for export. With little to export, countries found it all but impossible to maintain stable exchange rates based on the dollar. For that reason, the Bretton Woods conferees also created the **International Monetary Fund (IMF)**.

The International Monetary Fund is a specialized agency of the United Nations. Its principal goal is to enable nations to obtain the foreign exchange necessary to conduct international trade. For that reason, the IMF lends dollars and other currencies to countries as needed. The countries that borrow are expected to repay the loan within a stated time.

For as long as the United States was able to exchange gold for dollars, the Bretton Woods system of fixed exchange rates worked well. In the 1960s, however, the U.S. gold supply began to diminish. U.S. trade deficits with Japan and Western European countries led to a flow of dollars into these countries. Then, as these countries redeemed their dollars for gold, U.S. supplies of the metal decreased.

Delegates from many countries met at the Bretton Woods Conference in 1944. Here U.S. Secretary of the Treasury Henry Morgenthau, Jr., addressed the opening meeting.

The End of the Bretton Woods System

In August 1971, President **Richard Nixon** announced that the United States would no longer exchange dollars for gold. This action was an attempt to devalue the dollar. (*Devaluation* is the reduction in value of a nation's currency in terms of foreign currencies.) U.S. leaders hoped that a cheaper dollar would stimulate U.S. exports, discourage imports (because a cheaper dollar would make imports more expensive to U.S. buyers), and thereby slow the outflow of dollars. The Bretton Woods agreement, however, prohibited devaluating a nation's currency. Thus, President Nixon had unilaterally canceled the Bretton Woods system.

For a time, the United States and other industrial nations tried to maintain the dollar at a fixed rate of exchange with other currencies. By 1973, this effort, too, had failed. Since they were no longer able to maintain fixed exchange values of currencies, the United States and the world's other industrialized nations announced their intention to allow their currencies to *float* (find their own values in relation to one another in the marketplace). The era of fixed exchange rates was over; the era of floating rates had begun.

Floating Exchange Rates

Floating exchange rates are determined in accordance with the laws of supply and demand in foreign exchange markets. The mechanics are much the same as that in which securities are priced in stock exchanges. Demand for a nation's currency comes from the desire of foreigners to obtain a country's goods and services or invest in a country's securities. Supply is derived from the desire of that nation's citizens to import the goods and services and invest in the securities of others. As the demand for Japanese goods and services increases, so too will the demand for the Japanese currency to pay for them. If, at the same time, there is no change in the pattern of Japanese imports, the price of the yen is likely to rise.

In the mid-1990s, both Germany and Japan were experiencing large favorable trade balances. Consequently, the price of German marks and Japanese yen increased relative to other currencies. By contrast, the value of U.S. imports from Germany and Japan exceeded the value of U.S. exports. The supply of dollars in foreign hands increased, and the value of the dollar (relative to the mark and the yen) declined: Although the U.S. dollar was falling against the mark and the yen, it was increasing in value relative to the Mexican peso and the Canadian dollar. This increase occurred because the United States was exporting more to Mexico and Canada than it was importing from those countries during this period.

Although foreign exchange markets function without government direction or supervision, nations monitor them to prevent their own currencies from fluctuating so widely that problems are created at home. They do this by buying or selling their own currencies as the circumstances dictate.

Special Drawing Rights

The flow of U.S. spending abroad increased dramatically during the years of U.S. participation in the Vietnam War (1965–1973). This mostly military spending was taking place at a time when U.S. imports were increasing. Consequently, foreign nationals had many dollars—more than they were willing to keep. The international currency markets went from a dollar shortage to a dollar glut. In 1968, in an effort to relieve the pressure on the dollar, the IMF created *Special Drawing Rights (SDRs)*. The SDRs represented an attempt to provide another reserve currency for international trade that could substitute for gold and dollars. SDRs were created out of a pool of foreign exchange deposited by 16 major nations that belonged to the IMF. SDR balances were credited to the member nation, which could then use them in place of dollars or gold to settle accounts with other countries.

The International Monetary Fund no longer buys and sells gold in exchange for foreign currencies. Instead, SDRs have become the primary asset that countries will accept in payment for their goods and services.

ECONOMIC ISSUE

Devaluation—The Cure for Economic Ills?

Some people suggest that floating exchange rates provide a remedy for certain economic problems. They want the U.S. government to devalue its currency as a way to increase exports and reduce imports. Devaluation would make the dollar less expensive in terms of foreign currencies. By reducing the value of the dollar, U.S. goods and services would become less expensive to foreigners. This situation, it is claimed, would increase exports and reduce the deficit in our balance of trade.

All economists agree that, other things being equal, a cheaper dollar would stimulate exports of both goods and servies. Most economists, however, agree that this stimulation of exports would work only in the short run. In the long run, a devaluation of the dollar would have little or no effect on foreign trade.

- With the dollar worth less in terms of foreign currencies, people in the United States would have to pay more for imported goods and services.

- Since many imported goods and services go into the manufacture of U.S. products, sooner or later domestic prices would also rise.

- Rising prices would, in turn, lead to demands for wage increases, still further price increases, and the return of exports to approximately the same level as they had been before the devaluation.

In the long run, say most economists, exchange rates are merely a reflection of a nation's competitive strength and productivity. The key to increasing exports is to produce goods and services that other nations want and at prices they can afford.

RECORDING INTERNATIONAL TRADE: BALANCE OF PAYMENTS

International trade involves the buying and selling of goods and services by nations. With few exceptions, payments are made in U.S. dollars or other currencies. Nations collect and summarize their international transactions in a financial statement known as the *balance of payments*. In the United States, the responsibility for preparing its balance of payments falls to the **Department of Commerce**.

Imports of goods and services flowing into the country are recorded on one side of the scale, exports on the other. As for payments, you might recall from Chapter 22 that sellers in international trade expect to be paid in their local currencies. That is, U.S. merchants expect to receive U.S. dollars for their wares; Japanese sellers expect to receive yen; French vendors, euros; and so on. For that reason, payments for U.S. exports are shown as U.S. dollars, while payments for imports are shown as foreign exchange.

Since U.S. imports and exports of goods and services are rarely, if ever, equal in a given year, additional funds need to be moved to bring the payments into balance. For the first 25 or so years following World War II, the United States exported far more than it imported. Payment differences were settled with capital movements in the form of loans, investments, or gifts from the United States to foreign lands. In recent years, the opposite has occurred: U.S. imports of goods and services have outstripped exports. Differences have been made up in the form of capital movements into the United States from abroad. Examples of these capital movements are foreign investments in U.S. corporations, in real estate, and in U.S. government bonds and notes.

Published quarterly by the U.S. Department of Commerce, the *U.S. Balance of Payments* summarizes such financial transactions between the United States and the rest of the world. Table 23.3 illustrates a recent balance of payments statement. Let us study its major components and see how the transactions are brought into balance.

💱 Current Account

Most, but not all, international trade involves the import and export of goods and services. The *current account* summarizes those activities in the sections headed (1) goods, services, and income and (2) unilateral transfers.

GOODS, SERVICES, AND INCOME.   We will discuss each of these topics separately.

1. Goods. When people think of foreign trade, most picture the exporting and importing of goods (also called "merchandise"). And well they might, for trade in goods constitutes over half of all global trade.

Imports of merchandise are paid for with foreign exchange and are recorded as an *outflow of funds*. Thus, when Tom Terrific's Toyota Agency imported $200,000 worth of automobiles, the company paid for the shipment with Japanese yen, which it purchased from its bank. The $200,000 payment was included in the $1,146 billion outflow in the merchandise imports account for the year.

Merchandise exports generate an *inflow of funds*. When, for example, a Venezuelan manufacturer purchased a $75,000 knitting machine from a U.S. firm, the sum was included in the $718.8 billion recorded in the U.S. Balance of Payments statement.

As long ago as the 16th century and continuing on and off almost to the present day, economists focused on the relationship between merchandise imports and exports. They called this relationship the balance of trade. In their view, a favorable balance of trade occurred when merchandise exports were greater than imports. An unfavorable balance of trade described a time when merchandise imports were greater than exports. (See pages 499–500 for a discussion of these ideas.) Most economists today do not attach a great deal of

TABLE 23.3 U.S. BALANCE OF PAYMENTS, 2001 (BILLIONS OF DOLLARS)

	Inflows	Outflows	Net
Current Account			
GOODS, SERVICES, AND INCOME			
Goods			
Merchandise exports	$ 718.8		
Merchandise imports		$1,145.9	
			−427.2
Services			
Military	12.2	15.2	
Travel	73.1	60.1	
Passenger fares	18.0	22.4	
Other transportation	28.3	38.8	
Royalties and fees	38.6	16.3	
Other services	108.9	57.4	
Total Services	**279.3**	**210.4**	+ 68.9
Income			
Income on foreign investments	126.0		
Foreign income on U.S. investments		260.8	
Other receipts from abroad	151.8		
Government income on assets abroad	5.9		
Government payments on foreign assets in the United States		8.5	
Total Income	**283.8**	**269.4**	+ 14.4
UNILATERAL TRANSFERS			
Government grants and pensions		17.3	
Private remittances		32.1	
			− 49.5
Capital Account			
U.S. ASSETS ABROAD			
U.S. Government assets		4.9	
Private assets		365.6	
Total		**371.0**	
FOREIGN ASSETS IN THE UNITED STATES			
Foreign government assets	5.2		
Other assets	747.6		
Total	**752.8**		
STATISTICAL DISCREPANCY	11.5		
Totals	**$2,046.2**	**$2,046.2**	

importance to this balance of trade in goods. Instead, they prefer to study the entire balance of payments as a way of getting a more complete picture of a nation's strengths and/or weaknesses in the global economy.

2. Services. Since goods can be seen and felt, they are often referred to as "visible." But there are other items of value in international trade that can be neither seen nor touched. These "invisible" imports and exports are generally described as "services." Roughly 25 percent of U.S. trade with the rest of the world is in the form of services. Table 23.3 summarizes the principal service transactions. An explanation of these transactions follows.

Military.   Payments by foreign governments to the U.S. government to train their armed forces are treated as exports of services. Similarly, payments by the U.S. government to foreign governments for allowing it to establish bases in their countries are included in this category as imports of services.

Although, strictly speaking, the purchase and sale of military hardware represents the exchange of goods (not a service), the U.S. Department of Commerce includes these transactions in this category.

Travel.   Foreign tourists visiting the United States spend money for food, hotel accommodations, sightseeing excursions, and a host of other items. The money spent by these tourists has much the same effect on our balance of payments as do U.S. exports. Both represent inflows of foreign funds to the United States.

Similarly, the money spent by Americans traveling in foreign lands is recorded as outflows of funds in the Travel section of the U.S. balance of payments.

Passenger Fares.   By reading Table 23.3, we can see that in 2001 Americans spent some $22 billion in fares to travel on foreign airlines, ships, and the like. That same year, foreigners spent about $18 billion in fares on U.S. carriers. Like other imports, Americans' spending as passengers on foreign carriers was recorded as an outflow of funds. Meanwhile, foreign passengers using U.S. carriers represented an export of services. These transactions were recorded as an inflow of funds in the balance of payments.

Other Transportation.   The cost of shipping merchandise imports and exports is reflected in this category. Foreign use of U.S. ships results in an inflow of funds. Meanwhile, the cost of shipping U.S. exports on foreign ships, planes, railroads, and trucks results in an outflow.

Royalties and Fees.   *Royalties* are payments for the use of creative works. Royalties paid to U.S. musicians, publishers, film companies, and the like by foreign users of their materials represent exports of services and are recorded as inflows of funds. Royalties and other fees paid by Americans to foreign sources are treated as imports.

3. Income. U.S. investments in foreign corporations, real estate, or other assets generate income. Depending on the type of investments, the income will be in the form of interest, dividends, and rents. The income is summarized as an inflow of funds in the balance of payments statement. Similarly, foreign investments in U.S. assets generate an outflow of funds from the United States to foreign lands.

As indicated by Table 23.3, both private investors and governments are included in the income category.

Unilateral Transfers.   In most instances, funds are transferred in payment for a good or service. This is not true of *unilateral transfers,* one-way trans- actions in which funds are simply given as gifts or foreign aid. The information

Figure 23.4 **International Trade and the Balance of Payments**

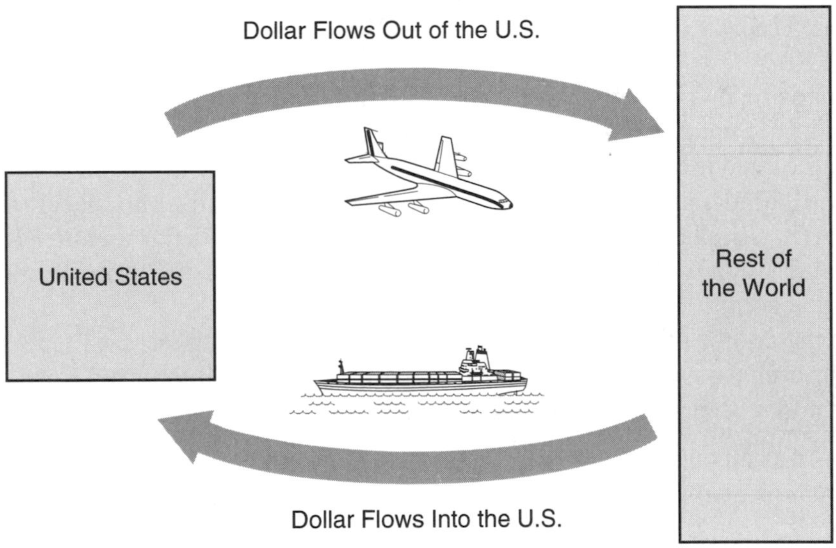

Event 1: A Merchandise Import
Event 2: A Merchandise Export
Event 3: A Foreign Citizen Traveling on a U.S. Carrier
Event 4: A U.S. Citizen Traveling on a Foreign Carrier
Event 5: The Purchase of an Apartment in Paris by a U.S. Citizen
Event 6: The Purchase of an Apartment in Miami by a French Citizen

What effect would each of the events in the illustration have on the balance of payments?

contained in the balance of payments shows net differences between U.S. government transfers to foreign lands and foreign government transfers to the United States and private transfers of a similar nature. As we can see in Table 23.3, unilateral transfers in 2001 amounted to

- an outflow of $17.3 billion resulting from transfers by government
- an outflow of $32.1 billion from transfers by private individuals and institutions.

⚡ The Capital Account

So far, we have been discussing the current account in the balance of payment statement. Now we will turn to the capital account. Since imports and exports of goods and services are never equal, additional funds need to be moved to bring the payments into balance. This occurs with the movement of capital.

The *capital account* describes how the inflows and outflows of payments were brought into balance. You will find these descriptions in the accounts headed "U.S. ASSETS ABROAD" and "FOREIGN ASSETS IN THE UNITED STATES."

Loans or investments made abroad by individuals, corporations, and governments are recorded as either outflows or inflows in the capital account of the balance of payments. Saudi Arabian investment in Iowa farmland creates an inflow of funds, just as the purchase by a U.S. corporation of an oil refinery in West Africa creates an outflow of funds. Over the years, the income, if any, generated by these investments will be noted under investment income in the current account.

In the course of a year, some Americans sell off their overseas assets while others purchase new ones. Similarly, some foreigners sell their holdings while others add to theirs. The net result of these transactions for one year is summarized in Table 23.3.

U.S. ASSETS ABROAD.   The value of the dollar in terms of foreign currencies is determined in the foreign exchange markets. One of the more important things that the U.S. government does to promote foreign trade is to enter the foreign exchange market as a buyer or seller. It does so to maintain the value of the dollar.

Since foreign exchange is used to purchase foreign goods and services, a decrease in the U.S. government's supply of foreign exchange is recorded as an outflow of funds in the balance of payments. Similarly, an increase in the government's supplies of foreign exchange is shown as an inflow.

In 2001, the purchase by private individuals and institutions of foreign assets (securities, corporations, etc.) is an outflow in the Capital Account of $371 billion.

Robert A. Mundell

In 1999, 11 European nations voted to adopt (to begin in 2002) the euro as a replacement for the francs, marks, liras, etc., that had long been their national currencies. Also in 1999, Canadian-born Professor **Robert Mundell** of Columbia University won the Nobel Prize in Economics. The two events were more than a coincidence.

In a series of studies in the 1960s, Mundell originated the idea that a single nation was not necessarily the best area for a currency. How much better it would be, he continued, if closely aligned nations with common trading interests shared a single currency. The EU nations are closely aligned and have common trading interests.

In the 1960s, it was generally believed that international trade had little, if any, effect on the overall economy. Mundell believed otherwise. He was among the first to describe the interrelationship of floating and fixed exchange rates with monetary and fiscal policies. In 1973, the United States abandoned fixed exchange rates and allowed the dollar to "float" against foreign currencies. Monetary policy, more so than fiscal policy, then became the major tool used to stabilize the U.S. economy. Here is why.

As Mundell argued, fiscal policy could not affect overall demand with a floating currency and free capital flows (which is what we have today). Why? Because (as discussed in Chapter 19) increased government expenditures give rise to a greater demand for money and tendencies toward higher interest rates. Foreign investors will take advantage of higher interest rates in the United States, and this inflow of foreign capital will cause the value of the dollar to increase relative to other currencies. A more expensive dollar, as discussed earlier in this chapter, results in lower net exports. A decline in U.S. exports contributes to a decline in business activity and, therefore, negates the entire expansive effect of higher government expenditures.

Under floating exchange rates, however, monetary policy becomes a powerful tool for influencing economic activity. Expansion of the money supply tends to promote lower interest rates, resulting in capital outflows and a weaker exchange rate, which in turn expand the economy through increased net exports.

Many of the leading economic decision makers in the United States today are adherents of Mundell's monetarist theories. Alan Greenspan, Chairman of the Federal Reserve Board, has made monetary rather than fiscal policy the major tool to stabilize the U.S. economy.

FOREIGN ASSETS IN THE UNITED STATES. Investments by foreign governments and private individuals and institutions in U.S. securities, real estate, business firms, and other assets appear as an inflow of funds on the balance of payments statement. Foreign assets in the United States in 2001 totaled over $752 billion.

STATISTICAL DISCREPANCY. Because the balance of payments accounts for literally millions of transactions in international trade, it is bound to have a number of errors. These are summarized under the heading "STATISTICAL DISCREPANCY." The *statistical discrepancy* is whatever it takes to bring the balance of payments into balance. In 2001, this amounted to $11.5 billion.

S U M M A R Y

The rate of exchange is the price of one country's currency in terms of another's. The value of a nation's currency depends on the supply and demand for that currency in the international market, which in turn depends on the demand for the goods and services of that nation.

Foreign exchange rates were fixed when most industrial nations adhered to the gold standard. In 1944, many countries adopted a standard of fixed exchange rates based on the U.S. dollar. In 1971, the United States devalued the U.S. dollar and would no longer exchange U.S. dollars at a fixed rate. Thus, the exchange rate began to "float" in value in accord with the supply and demand for the currency on the international market. Today, exchange rates fluctuate daily. Political and psychological as well as economic factors often influence these short-term changes in the value of currencies.

The U.S. Balance of Payments is a financial statement that summarizes the country's international transactions. Exports of goods and services cause funds to flow into the country. Imports of goods and services result in an outflow of payments. When imports exceed exports, a nation has an unfavorable balance of trade. When exports exceed imports, a nation has a favorable balance of trade. When the balance is not exactly equal, a balance is achieved by either an inflow or outflow of funds.

REVIEWING THE CHAPTER

BUILDING VOCABULARY

Match each item in Column A with its definition in Column B.

Column A

1. Special Drawing Rights
2. fixed exchange rate
3. Bretton Woods system
4. gold standard
5. floating exchange rate
6. statistical discrepancy
7. royalties
8. devaluation
9. balance of payments
10. balance of trade

Column B

a. a summary of financial transactions between one country and the rest of the world
b. the value of a currency that is determined by the laws of supply and demand on the open market
c. the reduction in the value of a nation's currency in terms of foreign currencies
d. the relationship between a country's merchandise imports and exports
e. credits to the account of member nations in the IMF that can be used to purchase foreign currencies
f. a system whereby currencies of most countries were exchangeable for a fixed amount of gold
g. the value of a currency that is set by a government
h. a summary of errors in recording transactions
i. a system whereby foreign currencies were exchanged for dollars at a fixed rate of $35 per ounce of gold
j. payments to authors of creative works, usually as a percentage of the sales price

UNDERSTANDING WHAT YOU HAVE READ

1. Which *one* of the following is the best explanation of why the Mexican peso has value outside Mexico? (*a*) Anyone can walk into a bank and exchange the peso for gold. (*b*) Merchants throughout the world will accept the peso in exchange for their goods. (*c*) The peso can be used to buy Mexican goods and services. (*d*) There is an ample supply of pesos.

2. Assume that the exchange rate for the Chilean peso is $1 = 135 pesos. How much would a U.S. importer pay in dollars for wool worth 202,500 pesos? (*a*) $15,000 (*b*) $1,500 (*c*) $150 (*d*) $15.

3. Suppose that a few days before the U.S. importer made payment on the wool purchased in question 2, the Chilean peso was devalued. What effect would this have on the importer? (*a*) It would have no effect. (*b*) It would make the wool more expensive. (*c*) It would make the wool less expensive. (*d*) It would make it impossible for the importer to make payment.

4. Assume that exchange rates are allowed to float and that the demand for Swedish kronor has been increasing. Under these circumstances, which of the following is most likely to occur? (*a*) It will take fewer dollars to buy Swedish kronor. (*b*) The price of Swedish goods in terms of dollars will fall. (*c*) Swedes will find that imported goods are getting more expensive. (*d*) Americans will have to pay more for goods made in Sweden.

5. If a nation's reserves of dollars or other foreign currencies were running low, it might look to the International Monetary Fund for (*a*) a loan of foreign exchange (*b*) the printing of any foreign currency it needed (*c*) an investment loan to build up-to-date production facilities (*d*) a market for its surplus production so as to restore a "favorable balance of trade."

6. Special Drawing Rights (SDRs) were created to provide all of the following, *except* (*a*) an international monetary reserve currency (*b*) an alternative to gold (*c*) currency that can be used by tourists as they travel from one country to another (*d*) a substitute for U.S. dollars as a "reserve currency."

7. Which *one* of the following was a serious weakness of the gold standard? (*a*) Having the gold standard made it difficult to determine rates of exchange. (*b*) People did not want to accept gold in exchange for a currency. (*c*) As the supply of gold in a country on the gold standard increased, imports became more costly. (*d*) Having the gold standard made it difficult for a nation to increase or decrease its money supply.

8. The euro is (*a*) a unit of currency (*b*) an organization of many European countries (*c*) a measure of the value of one ounce of gold (*d*) the European measure of weight.

9. A nation's balance of trade describes (*a*) the total flow of money into and out of the country (*b*) its exports and imports of merchandise (*c*) its overall economic health (*d*) how well it is doing in international trade.

10. A nation's balance of payments summarizes the nation's business transactions with (*a*) multinational corporations based in that country (*b*) the European Union (*c*) the International Monetary Fund (*d*) the rest of the world.

THINKING CRITICALLY

1. Sweater Trends, Inc., distributes sweaters manufactured to its specifications to department stores and boutiques around the country. In seeking a manufacturer for its latest design, Sweater Trends narrowed down its choices to three firms. One, a U.S. company, offered to deliver the sweaters for $10 each. The second, a Taiwanese firm, can do the same, including delivery to the United States, for 300 NT$ each. The third, a Mexican manufacturer, offered to deliver the sweaters for 100 pesos each.

    Exchange rates at the time stood at:

    $1 = 34.75 NT$
    $1 = 10.98 pesos

    Since the initial order was to be for 10,000 sweaters, Sweater Trends selected the manufacturer that made the lowest bid. (*a*) Which manufacturer did the distributor select? (*b*) Suppose that by the time Sweater Trends was ready to place its order, exchange rates had shifted so that $1 was now equal to 25 NT$ and 8.75 pesos. (*1*) Which manufacturer would Sweater Trends have then engaged? (*2*) What happened to the value of the U.S. dollar as a result of the shift in exchange rates? (*3*) How did the shift in exchange rates affect the standard of living in the United States? (*4*) What might have caused such a shift in exchange rates?

2. "A nation's exports pay for its imports." Explain this statement.

3. Even today, some economists argue that the world's trading nations ought to return to the gold standard. (*a*) What was the gold standard? (*b*) Identify and explain *one* advantage that the gold standard offered in international trade. (*c*) Identify and explain *one* principal weakness of the gold standard.

4. In the early 1990s, the dollar depreciated in value when compared with the currencies of Germany, Switzerland, France, and Japan. More funds were flowing out of the U.S. economy than were flowing in.

    a. Explain why the U.S. dollar depreciated with respect to the currencies of Germany, Switzerland, France, and Japan when more funds flowed out of the U.S. economy than flowed in.

    b. Discuss how a fall in the value of the U.S. dollar affected (*1*) U.S. demand for German, Swiss, French, and Japanese products, and (*2*) the demand for U.S. products by those countries whose currencies had appreciated in value relative to the dollar.

    c. How did a decrease in the supply of foreign funds affect the U.S. balance of payments?

    d. Why were U.S. workers involved in the import trade concerned when they heard that the value of the U.S. dollar was falling? How were U.S. workers involved in the export trade affected by a falling dollar?

SKILLS: Using a Foreign Exchange Rate Table

Imagine that you are on a long trip through Latin America, Europe, and Asia. To pay for purchases in each country you visit, you will exchange U.S. currency for the currency of the country you are in. Complete the following table. Use the information in Table 23.1 on page 520 to determine the cost in U.S. dollars and in a foreign currency for each of your purchases.

Country	Purchase	Cost in Local Currency	Cost in U.S. Dollars
Argentina	dinner for two	22 pesos	$?
France	perfume	100 euros	$?
China	ceramic vase	? yuan	$100
Mexico	shawl	100 pesos	$?
Sweden	hotel room	1,700 kronor	$?
Venezuela	rug	15,980 bolivars	$?
Russia	1 oz. caviar	? rubles	$150
Switzerland	1 lb. cheese	6 francs	$?
Taiwan	television set	5,272 NT$	$?

Note: To convert from a foreign currency to U.S. currency, divide the foreign currency by "How Much $1 U.S. Equals in Foreign Currency," or multiply the foreign currency by "How Much One Unit of Foreign Currency Equals in U.S. Dollars."

To convert from U.S. currency to foreign currency, multiply the amount in U.S. currency by "How Much $1 U.S. Equals in Foreign Currency," or divide the amount in U.S. currency by "How Much One Unit of Foreign Currency Equals in U.S. Dollars."

If you use two methods to compute a conversion, you may find a slight discrepancy. This happens because the numbers quoted in Table 23.1 are rounded off.

USING THE INTERNET

- The exchange rates change daily. To find the current exchange rate for any currency, you can log on to <<www.exchangerate.com>> or <<www.xe.com/ict/>>.

- A historical view of exchange rates can be obtained at <<www.oanda.com/convert/fxhistory>>. You might want to develop a table or graph of exchange rates for one or two countries as they fluctuate over a period of time when compared to the U.S. dollar. "FXHistory" is an easy tool to obtain the historical exchange rates for any currency pair. Select the language, the range of dates, and the currencies for which you would like to obtain exchange rates. Click on "Get Table" to obtain the historical currency exchange rates.

CHAPTER 24
Other Economic Systems

O V E R V I E W

A specter is haunting Europe—the specter of Communism. All the powers of old Europe have entered into a holy alliance to exorcise this specter. . . . The Communists disdain to conceal their aims. . . . They openly declare that their ends can be attained only by the forcible overthrow of all existing social relations. Let the ruling classes tremble at a Communist revolution. The proletarians have nothing to lose but their chains. They have a world to win.

—*Karl Marx and Frederick Engels,* Communist Manifesto, *1848*

In 1848, at a time of social unrest in Germany and elsewhere in Western Europe, **Karl Marx** and fellow socialist **Friedrich Engels** wrote the *Communist Manifesto.* It was not only a call for revolution but also a severe critique of capitalism. Many people in the 19th century blamed the capitalist economic system for the terrible working and living conditions in Europe. Western Europeans were going through the Industrial Revolution then. Unlike today, in the mid-19th century there were few labor unions to organize workers and help them demand better wages and working conditions. Governments were not yet involved in protecting workers from their employers. Socialism was in its infancy, and communism had not yet been born in 1848. Not until the 20th century would socialism and communism become strong competitors with capitalism as ways to organize economic society.

In this chapter, we will compare different economic systems. After briefly reviewing the market economy, we will discuss the theories of Karl Marx and the Communist economy of the former Soviet Union. Then we will look at democratic socialism as practiced in Sweden and elsewhere. Finally, we will discuss "managed capitalism."

COMPARING ECONOMIC SYSTEMS

The message of economics is as clear as it is universal: you can't have everything, we can't have everything, and they can't have everything.

—Anonymous

As discussed in Chapter 1, scarcity forces all societies to make choices and decide WHAT will be produced, HOW it will be produced, and WHO will receive it. You may recall from your reading of Chapter 1 that the way a group or nation organizes itself for production in order to answer these fundamental questions is known as its "economic system."

Thus far we have mainly described one economic system—capitalism. Although capitalism is the economic system of choice in the United States and in many other countries, other systems also exist. Indeed, prior to the 1990s, more of the world's population lived in socialist or Communist economies than in market economies. Since the collapse of the Soviet Union in 1991, however, most of the Communist and socialist countries have been converting their economic systems to include at least some capitalist principles.

The economic systems of nations today are mixtures of command, traditional, and free market. In a traditional economic system, people grow crops, raise herds, or fish, using the same tools and techniques that have been used for many generations past. The family is the main organizational unit of traditional economic life. WHAT is produced and HOW it is produced are not the result of conscious planning but rather a matter of custom and tradition.

In a command economy, the fundamental questions of WHAT, HOW, and WHO are pretty much decided by a central authority, usually the government. The degree of power exercised by the central authority may vary from one country to another, but the principal means of production remain in government hands. Since government owns most of the industry in command economies, government central-planning agencies determine WHAT to produce and HOW it will be produced.

We give the economic systems labels in an attempt to describe their main characteristics—labels such as "capitalism," "socialism," "communism," or "managed capitalism." As you read this chapter, though, remember that whatever we call the economy of a particular country, it is only a label. One has to search deeper in order to understand how the economy of that nation really works.

Economic systems are most frequently compared in terms of the ownership of the means of production and how these means of production are coordinated.

Ownership

Ownership as a trait of an economic system refers to the extent to which the means of production are either privately or publicly owned. In the United

Lukoil refinery and pipelines at Perm, Russia. The Russian economy is being transformed so that major industries such as this one, previously owned by the government, are now privately owned.

States, private individuals and corporations own most farms, factories, offices, shops, and other businesses. In some other countries, the government owns (and operates) a large share of the means of production.

Coordination

Coordination is a term economists use to describe the way an economic system answers the fundamental WHAT, HOW, and WHO questions. Nations organize their economic systems in one of three ways: (1) around the market, as in a capitalist system; (2) through government planning, as in a socialist system; or (3) a combination of the first two ways, in what is described as a "mixed economic system." Tradition may still play a role in economic activities, but the role of tradition diminishes as an economy industrializes. We begin our comparison of economic systems with a review of our own system of capitalism.

CAPITALISM

In Chapter 2, we described the U.S. economic system—capitalism. Here are the main points. In a capitalist or market economy, the means of production are, for the most part, privately owned. Prices, as determined by the forces of supply and demand, drive the system. Consumers cast their votes for WHAT is produced in the form of the prices they are willing to pay for particular goods and services. Producers try to satisfy those demands as best they can. When not enough of a product is offered for sale, prices rise until supply and demand are equal. When too much is produced, prices fall. As a result, output is reduced until supply and demand are once again equal.

Prices also determine HOW goods are produced. In their efforts to maximize profits, producers strive to combine productive factors in such a way as to achieve the highest level of output for the least amount of input. For example, manufacturers of loose-leaf paper use their machines, labor, and raw materials in such a way that they produce the greatest amount of paper (of a given type and quality) at the lowest possible cost. For their part, suppliers of raw materials used by paper producers will also do their best to offer their products and services at the prices that allow them to beat out their competition but still earn a profit.

It is important to note that the system of capitalism just described is an ideal. It does not exist as such in the real world. In the United States, for example, government ownership of productive facilities exists at the federal, state, and local levels. In addition, the Federal Reserve System manages the supply of money and credit in the economy. Monopolistic and oligopolistic firms (both discussed in Chapter 7) may interfere with the free forces of the market. Moreover, many government laws protect U.S. consumers. At the same time, some other laws help individual firms or industries. In short, the United States is really a mixed economy rather than a completely *laissez-faire* capitalist economy.

THE THEORIES OF KARL MARX

In the mid-19th century, Karl Marx wrote several powerful critiques of capitalism as it was developing during the Industrial Revolution. Marx's ideas became the basis for both modern socialism and communism. In studying his ideas, we can learn about both of these economic systems. The following are some of Marx's major theories.

The History of Society Is a History of Class Struggle

Marx argued that throughout history one class has dominated the others. He claimed that during the Middle Ages in Western Europe, church officials and nobility were triumphant. Later, these classes were replaced as the dominant ones by the *bourgeoisie* (people of the middle class, including capitalists). Marx claimed that capitalists grew fat through the exploitation of the *proletariat*—Marx's term for people who work for wages. He predicted that the proletariat would eventually overthrow the capitalists and create a classless society.

Workers Are Paid Less Than the Value of the Goods They Produce

Marx called the difference between the value of workers' wages and the value of the goods that workers produce *surplus value.* Many Marxists equate surplus value with profits and suggest that this surplus value rightfully belongs to the workers.

Capitalism Will Inevitably Lead to an Endless Round of Economic Depressions

Marx argued that because of competition among firms, capitalists are under constant pressure to reduce their costs. Capitalists reduce costs by investing in labor-saving machinery, reducing wages, or both. Since labor-saving machinery requires fewer workers to produce a given output, unemployment increases. Meanwhile, those firms unable to compete successfully are forced out of business, and their workers are added to the rolls of the unemployed. As unemployment mounts and wages decline, depression is the inevitable result.

The trend is reversed as wealthier businesses buy up those that have failed. As time goes by and surplus stocks are consumed, the remaining businesses hire increasing numbers of workers, and prosperity returns. Eventually, however, the cycle is repeated, more economic power is concentrated in fewer hands, and the proletariat endures greater suffering.

Marx predicted that under capitalism the rich would get richer, the poor poorer, and (with business firms' increasing reliance on machinery) the army of unemployed would grow and grow.

Revolution Is Inevitable

Marx believed that the mounting discontent among workers would unite them. Furthermore, Marx said, the proletariat would rise up, overthrow the capitalists, and establish a socialist state.

Communism Is the Ultimate Goal

Marx wrote that the ultimate goal for workers is communism. But to achieve this goal, he said, a society would have to advance through the stage of the dictatorship of the proletariat.

DICTATORSHIP OF THE PROLETARIAT.   If the proletariat are victorious, Marx argued, the country that they control would be immediately surrounded by hostile capitalist states. It would be necessary, therefore (claimed Marx), to establish a dictatorship in order to organize the state along socialist lines and to fight its capitalist neighbors. This dictatorship of the proletariat would permit the victorious revolutionaries to develop a socialist economy, one in which the workers or the government would own all the means of production.

COMMUNISM. Ultimately, Marx said, the socialist economic system would advance far enough technologically so that communism would be possible. Under *communism,* the economy would supply sufficient quantities of goods and services to satisfy everyone. All workers would work to the best of their abilities and would be paid in accordance with the principle "to each according to one's needs." There would be no classes under communism. Thus, the absence of want and of any struggle between classes would make government unnecessary. The state, declared Marx, would "wither away."

🗲 Theory and Reality

Although most Americans reject the theories and conclusions of Karl Marx, his ideas can hardly be ignored since they influenced the economic thinking of such a large portion of the world. Some things that Marx predicted about capitalism proved to be true. He was right when he predicted that there would be recurring depressions and that giant firms would come to dominate the industrial scene. Nevertheless, Marx's most important conclusion—that capitalism would inevitably collapse—has not been borne out. To the contrary, in the early 1990s capitalism replaced communism in many countries.

Why was Marx wrong? Why has capitalism survived? One answer is that governments with capitalist economies have protected consumers and workers. Marx pictured capitalism as a system that was completely dominated by the greed of the capitalists. As Marx saw it, a society so dominated would be incapable of reforming its economic system to give workers a greater share of the goods and services they produce. As a result, this exploited group would rise up and overthrow its masters. Beginning in the late 19th century and continuing into the 20th, however, the governments of many capitalist countries did many things to help workers. In the United States, for example, Congress passed laws that protect consumers and workers (as well as business firms) and promote the more equitable distribution of income. Moreover, contrary to Marx's predictions of class struggle, labor and management have learned to work together within the framework of the capitalist system.

Some of the most powerful countries in the world regarded Marxism as the theoretical basis of their economies. In the pages that follow, we will take a closer look at how the Soviet Union applied Marxist philosophy. To some extent, the Soviet system became a model for Communist systems in China, North Korea, Vietnam, Cuba, Hungary, Czechoslovakia, Yugoslavia, Bulgaria, Poland, Albania, Laos, Ethiopia, and elsewhere.

Karl Marx

To the world's Communists, the book *Das Kapital* (1867) is a kind of bible and Karl Marx is its prophet. Even socialists who are not Communists revere Karl Marx. Who was this dark-eyed, bearded man whose portrait peered down from walls in homes and offices wherever communism was the official state doctrine?

Karl Marx was born in the German city of Trier in 1818. Educated at the universities of Bonn and Berlin, he became a journalist. Forced to leave Germany because of his radical views, he settled in Paris, France. There Marx met Friedrich Engels (1820–1895), the son of a wealthy Prussian textile manufacturer. The two men became lifelong friends, a fact that is significant for several reasons. First, Marx and Engels collaborated on writing the *Communist Manifesto* (1848), which set forth a declaration of principles for a newly created Communist group known first as the "League of the Just" and later as the "Communist League." Second, had it not been for Engels's financial aid, it is unlikely that Marx would have finished writing his greatest work, *Das Kapital.*

Because of Marx's support for the 1848 revolution in Austria, he was banished from continental Europe. In 1849, Marx moved his family to London. There he spent nearly every day doing research and writing in the Reading Room of the British Museum. Marx and his family lived in wretched poverty for many years. Much of his meager income came from articles he wrote for a U.S. newspaper, the *New York Tribune,* and from money that Engels gave him.

In 1864, Marx helped to organize The International Workingmen's Association. The **First International**, as the association was commonly known, was a forerunner of modern Communist parties. Later, in 1867, the first volume of *Das Kapital* was published. After Marx's death in 1883, two more volumes of the work were edited by Engels and published, in 1885 and 1894.

THE SOVIET EXPERIENCE, 1917–1991

Prior to 1917, communism had not been tried by any country. In 1917, however, two revolutions took place in Russia. In the second one, the Russian Communist party under **V.I. Lenin** seized control. Thus began the first Communist state—Soviet Russia—whose name was changed to the Soviet Union in 1922. Although many observers predicted the imminent downfall of the Soviet experiment, its economy developed to a great extent. The Soviet government spent a large part of its resources building up heavy industry and a strong military. Within three decades of the revolution, the Soviet Union had become one of the two most powerful nations in the world (the other was the United States). Although Soviet leaders called their government and society "Communist," they did not claim that their economic system had achieved communism. Instead, communism was always a goal toward which the Communist party and its supporters were working.

Special Role of the Government in the Soviet Economy

The Soviet Union had a command economy. Because the Soviet State owned almost all the means of production and distribution (including factories, mines, farms, and stores), it determined how the basic questions of WHAT, HOW, and WHO would be answered. Moreover, because the Communist party was the only legal political party, it exercised ultimate power over the government. Thus, the Communists decided what the general economic goals for the coming

May Day (May 1) was a major holiday in the Soviet Union. This parade on May 1, 1960, in Moscow emphasized the country's military strength. The banner pictures Marx and Lenin and reads, "Forward, Toward the Victory of Communism!"

years would be. These goals were written down in formal plans for the coming years.

FIVE-YEAR PLANS.   When **Joseph Stalin** rose to power in the USSR in the mid-1920s, he found himself at the head of an industrially backward nation. In an attempt to modernize the Soviet economy as rapidly as possible, Stalin instituted a series of *five-year plans*. Each plan was a detailed statement of the nation's production goals for the next five years. The plans applied to all aspects of the economy, including industry, agriculture, trades, and the professions. For example, the government expected lawyers to handle their quota of cases, taxi drivers to log so many miles, and barbers to perform a minimum number of haircuts.

The five-year plans not only set forth production goals but also tried to *allocate* (assign) the resources necessary to achieve them. If, for example, Soviet leaders determined that steel production should be increased, the plan provided for the construction of additional steel production facilities and allocated the raw materials and labor needed to meet that goal. With the exception of the war years (1939–1945), five-year plans or their equivalent (there was one seven-year plan) were in force from 1928 to the end of the Soviet era in 1991.

DECIDING WHAT TO PRODUCE.   The Soviet agency responsible for preparing and administering the central economic plan was the State Planning Committee, or **Gosplan**. After consulting with the various economic ministries and industries, Gosplan prepared production quotas, or targets, for each of the 350,000 business enterprises within the Soviet economy and sent them on to the individual managers.

The managers then estimated the quantities of raw materials and the amount of labor they would need to meet their quotas. The managers' estimates were sent back to Gosplan. Since the managers' requests for inputs rarely matched the available resources, Gosplan had to modify many of its quotas and reassign tasks among the enterprises until a final plan was achieved. The plan, which was binding on all Soviet enterprises, set forth target quotas for sales, costs, profits, and productivity increases for the coming year.

DECIDING HOW GOODS WERE TO BE PRODUCED.   The responsibility for carrying out the annual plan rested with the managers of the local factories, farms, stores, and offices. They hired and fired workers, purchased machinery and equipment, and made the everyday decisions necessary to running a business. But unlike capitalist entrepreneurs (whose primary motivation is to earn profits), the Soviet managers' goal was to conduct their "businesses" in ways that would meet their quotas.

DECIDING WHO WAS TO RECEIVE THE GOODS AND SERVICES.   Since the government controlled nearly all of the nation's output, it could reward some people by allowing them to purchase goods and services that were unavailable

to most others. For ex
almost everyone could an
ments to go around. Neverthe

categories of workers who were
as Olympic athletes, scientists, and ment controlled rents so that
these officials and other privileged peoly were not enough apart-
stores set up for their exclusive use.   made available for certain
                                      the government, such
                                      officials. Similarly,

✷ The Failure of the Soviet Eco in scarce items in

The Communist party governed the Soviet Union until
with the economic system in chaos, Soviet leaders dissol
The collapse of both the Soviet economy and the Soviet
shock to most Americans. As recently as 1987, the U.S. Cen
Agency had listed Soviet production as greater than that of Japa
only to that of the United States. As events were to prove, the Soviet
in reality an impoverished nation whose collapse was largely the resu
failed economic system.

WHY DID THE SOVIET ECONOMY FAIL?   Although opinions differ, most experts agree that the system's inability to allocate scarce resources was a major reason for the failure of the Soviet economy. By allowing planners (rather than supply and demand) to determine what goods and services were to be produced, the Soviet economy was overwhelmed with products for which there were no buyers. At the same time, the Soviet economy was burdened with enormous shortages of products that were in demand.

Another major reason for the failure of the Soviet economy was the government's overemphasis on military expenditures. During the years 1945–1991, the Soviet Union devoted approximately 14 percent of its budget each year to defense. At the same time, however, Japan allocated only 1 percent of the yearly national budget for military expenditures. As a result of Soviet planners' decisions to emphasize military production, not enough resources were available for the production of consumer goods and services.

In the absence of a capitalist-type price system in the Soviet Union, the central planners often undervalued resources. This undervaluation, in turn, encouraged inefficient and wasteful manufacturing processes. Many plant managers, for example, looked on Soviet petroleum, natural gas, and other raw material as cheap and limitless. They had no need to conserve these resources and no incentive to change production methods to save money.

Under the Soviet system of low, fixed prices for consumer goods, people could afford to buy the food and appliances they wanted. The problem was that there often was not enough of these items to go around. So although the price of a commodity like eggs was low enough, at times there were not enough eggs produced to meet consumer demand. The same type of shortage existed for

A woman stands before empty shelves in a Soviet bakery. What does the photograph tell us about the Soviet economy?

automobiles, appliances, and other goods. In a free enterprise economy, you may recall, when demand outruns supply, the market is brought back into balance with price increases. But the Soviet Union had made a political decision to maintain fixed prices at levels that everyone could afford. Therefore, ways other than the price system had to be developed in order to allocate consumer goods and other resources. One way was waiting in long lines for scarce goods. Another was political favoritism. And a third was the illegal market.

LONG LINES.   When members of the general public wanted to buy food or clothing, they had to wait their turn in long lines outside shops that had something to sell. When one store ran out of merchandise, shoppers might then go to other stores and wait in lines there. Some people even sneaked away from work to get a good place in a line. This practice interfered with the efficiency of workplaces. Long lines in the Soviet Union served the same purpose as prices do in the United States. Both are ways of allocating resources.

POLITICAL FAVORITISM.   A second means of distributing scarce resources in the Soviet Union was political favoritism. Important government and party officials and other influential citizens could avoid the indignities of waiting in line by shopping at stores run exclusively for their benefit. There the shelves were always well stocked with goods unavailable to ordinary folk. Similarly, factory managers with the right connections could always obtain the materials needed to keep their operations running smoothly. Those without connections could buy their raw materials only when they became available from government sources.

ILLEGAL MARKET.   The illegal market provided a third means of distributing scarce resources. Soviet citizens commonly bought fruits, vegetables, meats, shoes, gasoline—in fact, almost anything they wanted—at illegal stands and stores. Products unavailable in the official government stores were often available, for a price, on the unofficial illegal market. The prices for goods in the illegal market were higher than the official prices for goods sold at government stores. But remember that the government stores often had shelves empty of certain desired items. So if a Soviet citizen wanted a certain product that was in demand, that person sometimes had to get it on the illegal market and pay the going price, or go without.

THE GORBACHEV YEARS.   For many years, the Soviet Union was able to make up for the scarcity of consumer goods by paying for imports with exports of its natural resources. By the 1980s, though, it was no longer possible to export enough raw materials to offset the shortages. In 1985, leadership of the Soviet Union and its Communist party passed to **Mikhail Gorbachev**. With the Soviet economy in a shambles, Gorbachev made economic reform a top priority. Toward that end, he introduced the policies of glasnost and perestroika.

Glasnost (the Russian word for "openness") encouraged discussion and some criticism of government programs by the press and the public.

Perestroika, or "restructuring," referred to the fundamental changes that Gorbachev began making to the structure of the economy and the political system. Economic changes included the introduction of limited private enterprise; the reform of the price system so that the costs of raw materials supplied to factories would be negotiated by buyers and sellers; and self-sufficiency for government-owned enterprises, which were told to earn a profit or be put out of business.

By 1991, *perestroika* still had not rescued the Soviet economy. Budget deficits had reached the highest levels since the end of World War II. The economic growth rate was declining, and food had to be imported in record quantities from the United States and elsewhere. Worse still, Soviet living standards, as measured by per capita gross domestic product, were far behind those in the West.

 # POST-SOVIET RUSSIA

Mortally weakened by its failed economy, the Soviet Union collapsed in December 1991. It was replaced by the **Commonwealth of Independent States (CIS)**, a loose association of 12 independent republics that had once been part of the Soviet Union. In Russia, the largest of the republics, the Communists gave up power to non-Communists. One former Communist, **Boris Yeltsin**, became the head of Russia.

⚡ Economic Reform in Russia

After his election as president in 1991, Boris Yeltsin continued Gorbachev's economic reforms and added some more radical ones. His goal was to revitalize the Russian economy and raise the standard of living. Some of the changes that Yeltsin and his advisers proposed were so drastic that they were characterized as "shock therapy." He called for

- lifting price controls
- ending central planning
- privatizing state enterprises
- balancing the national budget
- permitting the free movement of goods and capital in and out of the country.

Proponents of shock therapy said that free pricing and privatization would give profit-seeking enterprises the incentives they needed to produce the goods that consumers want. Meanwhile, opening the country to international trade and investment would provide much needed foreign technology and financing.

Yeltsin's economic reforms went into effect in January 1992. With abolition of price controls, store shelves began to fill and waiting lines outside shops disappeared. But the Russian economy was still in deep trouble. At the heart of the problem was the inability of business and industry to increase output. Morover, as the now privately owned firms struggled to earn profits, many workers were laid off.

Not all Russians suffered as a result of privatization. Those able to acquire the capital necessary to purchase government assets and start a business often succeeded. Unfortunately, a sizable proportion of those early entrepreneurs became members of organized crime. According to one report published by the Russian government, organized crime controlled between 70 and 80 percent of all banking activities. Another survey found that over 25 percent of Russia's entrepreneurs said that they had been pressured to make extortion payments.

Another consequence of the early failures of Russia's conversion to a market economy was that it added to the unequal distribution of income. According to a 1995 study, the richest 20 percent of the population earned 50 percent of the country's revenue, while the poorest 20 percent received only 3.5 percent. Worse yet, one-third of all Russians lived below the poverty line.

⚡ Putin

Yeltsin resigned the presidency in 1999, and **Vladimir Putin** became the acting president. In March 2000, Putin became the second democratically elected president of Russia. Putin continued to liberalize the Russian economy. He instituted banking and labor reforms, encouraged private property, and improved

"Now you'll learn the pleasures of capitalistic competition."

Why is the cartoonist portraying an unfair race?

a legal system so that business contracts became more in line with those of Western democracies. Economic conditions improved so that workers began receiving their wages on time and retired people, their pensions. How much of these changes were due to measures taken by Putin and how much to the rise in the price of oil, Russia's major export, is not clear.

Putin's critics say that every democratic institution in Russia became weaker after Putin came to power. They claim that he ran the privately owned television networks out of business, weakened the Russian Parliament, and used the worldwide war on terror to wage a brutal war against Chechnya (a breakaway province of Russia). It must be kept in mind that Putin was trained as a spy for the KGB (Soviet Secret Police) and had served as head of the Federal Security Service, the successor to the KGB. Moreover, President Putin placed many of his former KGB colleagues into executive posts.

COMMUNISM TODAY

Few countries today call themselves Communist. Examples include Mainland China, North Korea, Vietnam, and Cuba. While North Korea and Cuba have resisted introducing many elements of capitalism into their economies, China and, more recently, Vietnam are creating real mixed economies. Let us look at the example of China to see how well the label "Communist" can still be applied.

China

Mao Zedong and the Chinese Communist party came to power in Mainland China in 1949. They established a Soviet-style economic system there that included a planned economy and government ownership of most means of production. In 1978, Mao died. Leadership of the Communist party fell to **Deng Xiaoping**, who turned China toward a semicapitalist dictatorship. As one Chinese official jokingly commented on the changes, "Under the leadership of the Communist party, we're advancing from socialism to capitalism." At the 15th National Party Congress in September 1997, **Jiang Zemin** (who had just replaced Deng as Communist party leader and President of China) delivered a report extolling the Deng Xiaoping's theories that had implemented market features with Chinese characteristics. Jiang opened up party membership to China's private entrepreneurs but still favored state control over the economy. In March 2003, **Hu Jintao** replaced Jiang Zemin as President of China. Hu favored getting the Chinese government out of owning all but the most strategic industries, such as arms manufacturing and telecommunications.

THE RURAL SCENE. From the 1950s to 1979, farming in China was done on *communes* of 2,000 to 4,000 people each. Residents of the communes were organized military style in shared living quarters and mess halls. Everyone worked at assigned tasks and received wages. Private farms had been abolished. Nevertheless, the first to break with Communist tradition was the agricultural sector.

In 1979, the agricultural system was reformed to allow individual households and groups of households to lease land from the state for a specified number of years. During that time, the renters would have to pay taxes and fulfill planned production quotas. The goods produced to meet these quotas had to be sold to the state at set prices. After meeting these obligations, though, rural households would be free to produce what they could and sell surplus products on the free market at whatever price they could get. The rural reforms were very successful. Chinese farm output and the peasants' standard of living increased dramatically. China, however, has shifted its production efforts from agriculture to industry and services. Agriculture in 2001 amounted to only 17.7 percent of China's GDP, whereas industry was 49.3 percent and services comprised 33 percent.

INDUSTRIES AND OTHER BUSINESSES. Under Mao, the Chinese government controlled all factories, stores, and means of transportation. Copying the Soviet example, the government instituted five-year plans for all economic units. Then under Deng, the government encouraged private ownership of light and medium industries (such as the manufacturing of toys, textiles, clothing, shoes, and consumer electronics). Many state factories were privatized and sold stock to the public. China still has five-year plans that govern the state-run industries. Since Deng's economic restructuring began, though, the role of the state sector in the economy has been greatly reduced. The total number of private enterprises reached 2 million in 2001 (compared to only 90,000 in 1998). According to the Asian Development Bank, private businesses in 2002 accounted for 60 percent of China's GDP. Today, eight out of every ten new jobs in China are created by private, small and medium-sized enterprises. State-owned enterprises, though, still employ more than half of the workforce.

In addition to the private and the state-run factories, today many factories are owned collectively by local governments or by the people who work in the factories. Collectives account for one-third of industrial output.

State-owned trading corporations control foreign trade. China has given priority to increasing overseas trade and attracting foreign investments in Chinese factories and other businesses. As a result, many thousands of foreign business ventures have been set up in China. There are some 424,196 foreign companies doing business there, and by 2002, almost 100 million Chinese worked in foreign-related businesses or directly for enterprises backed by foreign investors. In fact, China surpassed the United States as the world's number one destination for foreign dollars in 2002.

China's combination of political dictatorship and limited capitalism has had considerable economic success. China's GDP, which amounted to $298 billion in 1980, increased to $5.9 trillion in 2002. Today, China ranks seventh in GDP among the nations of the world. As a result, consumption levels more than doubled, although its annual GDP per capita of $4,700 in 2002 was still relatively low compared with that of U.S. GDP (at $36,300) or Japan's (at $27,000). Keep in mind, though, that GDP per capita remains low because of China's huge population.

🌀 Problems Remain

The environment has paid a price for China's rapid industrialization. Pollution of the air, land, and water are major problems. With the increase in vehicular traffic and factories, there has been an increase in smoke laden with carbon dioxide spewing into the atmosphere. Many factories dump their industrial wastes into landfills and streams. Arable land has been lost in order to make space available for industrial projects and other aspects of urbanization. Adding to China's environmental problems are the intensified use of chemical fertilizers, soil erosion, and a fall in the water table level.

Corruption is widespread in China, especially among government officials. To conduct business, Chinese entrepreneurs must often bribe officials.

Economic growth in China has been achieved at a price. Inflation ran at around 20 percent through much of the 1990s. While many in the new middle

Shipyard and skyline of Shanghai, China, reflect advances in the Chinese economy.

class live well, inflation has been particularly hard on those living on pensions and other fixed incomes. Poverty is widespread in the countryside.

Nowhere has the income gap widened more rapidly than between the urban and rural areas. Although rural regions were among the first to benefit from privatization, many of the less efficient farmers found themselves unable to earn a good living. Some 100 million Chinese people are estimated to have moved from the countryside to the cities in search of work. These people form a vast, sometimes-migrating labor pool that entrepreneurs tap to keep their new businesses going. Unemployment and overcrowding in the cities have pushed up urban crime rates. Homelessness and begging are now common in Chinese cities. The income gap between rich and poor in this Communist country is wide. Whereas the lowest 10 percent of the population receives 2.4 percent of the nation's earnings, the top 10 percent receives 30.4 percent—hardly representative of an egalitarian society.

Although China is moving in the direction of free-market capitalism, it is not becoming democratic. It still has a one-party government. Communist party leaders are willing to free prices, but they are not willing to free the press. Nor does the party tolerate dissenters. In April 1999, more than 10,000 Falun Gong members gathered in Beijing. Falun Gong combines traditional exercise and breathing therapy with religious ideas borrowed from Taoism and Buddhism, the two major religions in China. The government outlawed the movement and has arrested and prosecuted many Falun Gong members. The party leadership believes that demonstrations, if left unchecked, could lead to the violent overthrow of party rule and social chaos. Despite international protests in support of the Falun Gong, the Chinese government insists that the movement is political and, as such, is a threat to the single-party state.

SOCIALISM

Socialism is not easy to describe because so many different nations have called themselves socialist. The Communist countries just described are (or, in some cases, were) socialist. In contrast to these examples is *democratic socialism*—the type of socialism that was or has been practiced in certain Western European countries and in India, New Zealand, Australia, and elsewhere.

A number of features help distinguish democratic socialism from communism. Although socialism is a form of a command economy, the degree of power exercised by the central government varies from one socialist country to another. For example, the government of Great Britain when socialists were the majority party had much less power than the Communist governments of China and Cuba. Government ownership of productive resources and government planning are limited in democratic socialist countries but are quite extensive in Communist countries. Although socialist and Communist economic systems are both forms of a command economy, communism is the more extreme model.

Democratic Socialism

In addition to having elements of command economies, democratic socialist countries have other traits in common. They have democratically elected governments with freedom for their population and press. They have all *nationalized* (taken control of by the government) major industries, such as coal, railroads, airlines, and banks. After World War II, democratic socialist countries, with their high taxes on wealth, established "cradle-to-grave" welfare services, including free medical care and generous pension benefits.

Democratic socialism still exists in some countries, but only periodically, after socialists are elected to power. After winning an election, socialist leaders typically introduce elaborate welfare programs and nationalize major industries. Also typically, though, socialist programs are cut back in these countries after the socialists lose elections or when economic conditions in the country deteriorate. In a sense, every country in Western Europe, and to a degree in the breakaway Eastern European democracies, has practiced socialism or, as it is more commonly called, welfare-state policies. Sweden is one nation that experimented with democratic socialism.

Sweden: The Middle Way

At one time, economists referred to the Swedish economy as the "middle way," meaning that the nation had adopted many socialist programs while maintaining the kind of private ownership normally associated with capitalism. Between 1950 and 1980, the public sector grew from 12.5 percent to 30 percent of GDP and employed one out of every four workers. The Swedish social welfare programs sought to achieve a more even distribution of incomes and wealth through transfer payments to households. Social insurance was universal and compulsory. One social program paid for all maternity expenses as well as paid leaves of absence for new parents. Even today, regardless of need, every family in Sweden receives a child-care allowance for each child. The government subsidizes child-care centers to keep costs low for working families. Another government program pays the entire cost of medical and dental care and guarantees close to a full income for people who become sick or unemployed. All Swedish children are entitled to a free education from kindergarten through college. Students' meals, books, and school supplies are provided without charge until they are 16. Thereafter, they receive a monthly allowance from the government for as long as they remain in school.

On entering the world of work, young adults become eligible for different kinds of government-sponsored benefits. Unemployment insurance reimburses them if they lose their jobs, and government programs train them for new ones. Free transportation is available if a new job involves commuting to another town. On retirement years later, Swedish workers receive pensions and other forms of government assistance, such as housing and health care.

The Swedish social welfare system was highly successful from the 1930s through the 1980s. Then Sweden (like much of Western Europe) went through a recession. Unemployment rates went from almost nothing in 1991 to 13 percent in 1994. Unemployment compensation and other government benefits surged, and so did the nation's deficit. Worse still, between 1991 and 1993, the country's economy shrank by 5 percent.

In an effort to pull itself out of its recession, Sweden cut many of its welfare programs. For example, the waiting period before one could receive unemployment benefits was extended, and the benefits themselves were reduced from 90 percent of one's former salary to 75 percent. These measures were also designed as a greater incentive to work.

Tax rates in Sweden were among the highest in the developed countries (to pay for their extensive welfare programs). Corporate tax rates were reduced to enable Swedish manufacturers to compete with companies operating under a more favorable tax system.

Sweden also deregulated many industries, dissolved some government monopolies, and introduced laws to encourage competition rather than collusion among competing firms.

Today, Sweden's economic system is very much like that of other European Union members. Sweden is a leading nation in technology, telecommunications, engineering, and pharmaceuticals. International trade, mostly with other countries of Western Europe, accounts for 47 percent of the nation's GDP. So far, however, Sweden has declined to give up its currency—the krona—to adopt the euro.

What benefits does the Swedish economy provide its people?

MANAGED CAPITALISM

For more than a hundred years, the world's wealthiest economies were to be found among the industrialized countries of Western Europe and North America. More recently, however, new names appeared on the rankings of middle- to high-income categories of national economies. Of these, the Asian nations of South Korea, Singapore, Thailand, and Malaysia have much in common.

Most striking, perhaps, were the rapid strides toward industrialization and economic growth experienced by all four. Starting in the 1960s, South Korea developed its textile and light manufacturing industries. During the 1970s and 1980s, the focus of development shifted to heavier industries such as steel and chemicals (followed by automobiles and electronics). With a colonial past stretching back over many centuries, Singapore finally achieved independence in 1965. Then Singapore became one of the world's fastest growing economies. With a per capita GDP of $24,700 in 2001, it ranked high among the world's most productive nations.

Economic development in Malaysia and Thailand followed similar paths. As in Singapore and South Korea, industrialization did not begin until the 1970s. But when it did, changes came rapidly.

Shared experiences were less than wonderful in 1997 and 1998 when an economic crisis raced through much of Asia. At its worst, the recession (or "Asian flu" as some described it) triggered a period of negative growth and a devaluation of the currencies in all four countries. The economic recession soon spread to Indonesia, Russia, and many other countries, even to Japan.

The economic system in South Korea, Singapore, Malaysia, and Thailand is often cited as the principal reason for the success of those economies in the 1980s and 1990s. Patterned after the economic system in Japan, *managed capitalism* relies on government intervention and cooperation among corporations to achieve its goals.

⚡ Japan's Managed Capitalism

One way of comparing the U.S. model and the Japanese version of capitalism is in terms of competition vs. collaboration. In the United States, competition among producers is the key to increased output, reduced costs, and improved living standards. Indeed, the principal goal of U.S. antitrust legislation is to encourage competition. In order to promote competition, the government prohibits efforts by firms in the same industry to collaborate in the production or distribution of their products. (This topic is discussed in Chapter 7, pages 151–156.)

In contrast to the emphasis the United States gives to competition among producers, the stress in the Japanese economy is placed on *collaboration* (active cooperation). This includes collaboration (1) between industry and government, (2) among groups of firms within and across industries, and (3) between limited numbers of shareholders and management.

COLLABORATION BETWEEN INDUSTRY AND GOVERNMENT.   As discussed in other chapters, government has an important role to play in the U.S. economy. In Japan, the relationship between government and industry is significantly closer. For example:

- By erecting tariff and nontariff barriers to trade, the Japanese government protects large sectors of its economy from foreign competition.
- Government policies encourage the formation of vertical, horizontal, and conglomerate combinations of firms.
- By limiting or prohibiting foreign investment, the government prevents takeovers of Japanese firms by overseas corporations.

COLLABORATION AMONG FIRMS AND GROUPS OF FIRMS.   The U.S. market system is based on head-to-head competition among rival firms. U.S. antitrust laws were specifically written to prevent one or more firms from gaining an unfair advantage over the competition. Quite the opposite is true in Japan where industry is dominated by the *keiretsu*. A *keiretsu* is a family of tens or hundreds of companies banded together for the mutual benefit of the "family" members. *Keiretsu* members are free to invest in one another's firms, share directors, and maintain close social links. The principal firms associated with the Sumitomo Group comprise one of Japan's largest *keiretsu*.

COLLABORATION BETWEEN SHAREHOLDERS AND MANAGEMENT.   Unlike in the United States, where private individuals primarily own corporations, controlling shares of large Japanese firms are primarily owned by other corporations. This is especially true among the *keiretsu,* where other member corporations may own as much as 60 to 80 percent of a corporation's stock. Since these shares are rarely (if ever) traded, member companies do not have to worry about falling stock prices, takeover attempts, and shareholder demands for dividend payments.

One of the benefits of collaboration between shareholders and management is that Japanese managers (unlike their U.S. counterparts) can focus on long-term rather than short-term results. For example, if forced to choose between skipping a dividend payment or laying off experienced workers, U.S. managers often keep their stockholders happy by paying the dividend and laying off these workers. The decision to lay off experienced workers is a short-term decision often connected with concern for end-of-year profits. Since an experienced staff is a valuable resource, laying people off can be damaging to a business in the long term.

COMPETITION AT HOME.   Much of Japan's success, prior to falling into a recession in the mid-1990s, was due to competition among its producers. Although collaboration between industry and government does restrict competition from foreign companies, competition is extensive within Japan. Japan has about 580 companies in the electronics business, 7,000 textile manufacturers, and 114 firms manufacturing machine tools. Price cutting in Japan is as ruthless as anywhere else.

IMITATING JAPANESE PRACTICES.   Japan rose like "a phoenix from the ashes" of World War II. Until it suffered through a recession in the 1990s, U.S. firms looked to Japan for answers to improved industrial production. There are a number of Japanese production techniques that have been copied by U.S. firms.

In the last decade, Japan has gone through several recessions with high unemployment levels. These unemployed workers are searching for jobs by using computers.

1. Quality Circles. One technique, *quality circles,* organizes employees into teams that work together to solve any production problems that arise. In the Japanese factory or office, a team of workers forms a quality circle. New ideas and production techniques are evaluated openly by the quality circle, and the whole team reaches a decision. All members of the quality circle receive credit, or take blame, for the team's results. Success is very important to Japanese workers. But success is measured in terms of group success, not individual success.

2. Inventory on Demand. A second Japanese practice that has gained favor among U.S. firms is *inventory on demand* (also known as "just-in-time manufacturing"). Traditionally, most U.S. firms have maintained large stocks of inventory at the factory. This practice, however, is expensive. With inventory on demand, supplies are kept by a wholesaler and delivered immediately when requested. When a production unit needs left front fenders, for example, an order is placed for left front fenders and the supplies are delivered from a warehouse that holds thousands of fender parts. Thus, Japanese firms do not need to carry large inventories at their production facilities. By keeping supplies to a minimum, Japanese firms save the costs of storage.

U.S. PRODUCTIVITY EXCEEDS THAT OF JAPAN.   A yardstick of international competitiveness is productivity, and the United States is the world leader in productivity per worker. Japanese factory workers, for example, produce 80 percent as much as U.S. workers on an hourly basis. Some U.S economists argue that the reason for the high productivity in the United States is that the government rejects managed capitalism and is reluctant to protect U.S. firms from the rigors of competition—domestic or foreign.

U.S. firms freely lay off unnecessary workers and close down outmoded plants. Japanese firms are reluctant to do so. When a new Japanese employee enters a company, the company becomes the worker's family. Therefore, while the jobs of some Japanese workers are protected, their production costs are higher than they need be.

CHANGES IN JAPANESE PRACTICES FOR THE 21ST CENTURY.   Facing a continued recession in the mid-1990s, some Japanese business leaders instituted reforms in the ways their firms operate in order to increase productivity and lower cost. For example, at management levels in many large Japanese firms, *merit pay* (pay in which those who perform better are paid more) is replacing seniority in determining salary. The Japanese institution of "lifetime employment" is also under attack as some workers are fired and others are being asked to retire early. These reforms are bringing practices to Japan that are similar to those common in the United States.

Some Japanese business leaders think that Japan should open up its economy more to foreign competition. They also think that there should be less collaboration between the Japanese government and Japanese firms. These measures, they claim, will make Japanese businesses more efficient and better able to compete on the world market.

======== S U M M A R Y ========

In capitalist countries, private ownership predominates and coordination is carried out through the marketplace. In socialist and the Communist countries, the means of production are principally owned by the state and coordination of economic activities is largely carried out through government planning. By contrast, the Japanese model of managed capitalism emphasizes cooperation and collaboration among firms and between the government and businesses.

In comparing the economic systems of two or more nations, labels can be confusing. All countries that call themselves capitalist (including the United States) have some degree of government ownership and planning. China, a Communist country, allows some private ownership of the means of production and has stock exchanges. Some democratic countries, such as Sweden, Australia, New Zealand, Britain, and France, have at times been labeled "socialist" even though in each country most of the means of production have been in private hands.

REVIEWING THE CHAPTER

BUILDING VOCABULARY

Match each term in Column A with its definition in Column B.

Column A

1. bourgeoisie
2. democratic socialism
3. *perestroika*
4. managed capitalism
5. commune
6. coordination
7. proletariat
8. surplus value
9. five-year plan
10. *glasnost*

Column B

a. people who work for hourly wages
b. the way an economic system answers the WHAT, HOW, and WHO questions
c. the difference between workers' wages and the value of the goods and service they produce
d. a market economy with strong government intervention and cooperation among firms
e. members of the middle class
f. an economic and political system characterized by free elections and by government ownership and management of economic institutions
g. a community of farmers who work collectively
h. a Soviet policy that encouraged public discussion and criticism
i. a detailed statement of a country's production goals and allocation of resources
j. the restructuring of the Soviet economy

UNDERSTANDING WHAT YOU HAVE READ

1. The first major nation to become Communist was (*a*) Russia (*b*) Germany (*c*) France (*d*) China.

2. In which type of economic system do the forces of supply and demand play the most important role? (*a*) capitalism (*b*) socialism (*c*) a command system (*d*) a traditional system.

3. In which respect did the economy of the Soviet Union differ from that of the United States? (*a*) the emphasis on technological progress (*b*) the use of money as a medium of exchange (*c*) the emphasis on continued economic growth (*d*) the manner of deciding what goods and services would be produced.

4. Which *one* of the following statements about socialism is *false*? (*a*) The concept of socialism has changed since the time of Karl Marx. (*b*) All socialist systems are the same. (*c*) Some socialist states nationalize privately owned businesses. (*d*) Socialism can exist in a democratic society.

5. Which *one* of the following was the most important factor in determining what goods and services would be produced by the Soviet Union's Communist economy? (*a*) supply and demand (*b*) government planning (*c*) labor unions (*d*) consumers.

6. All of the following reforms were introduced into the Soviet Union under the policy of *perestroika, except* (*a*) self-sufficiency of government enterprise (*b*) price reform (*c*) the profit motive (*d*) five-year plans.

7. Sweden was said to follow a "middle way" because it (*a*) maintained elements of both socialism and capitalism (*b*) combined a blend of totalitarian dictatorship with democracy (*c*) followed an economic path somewhere between communism and socialism (*d*) is geographically located between Eastern and Western Europe.

8. China in the 21st century (*a*) refuses to introduce any elements of a free market (*b*) discourages overseas trade and investment (*c*) prohibits private ownership of all factories (*d*) allows foreign companies to do business and own factories in China.

9. The Japanese version of capitalism differs from the U.S. model in that the Japanese government (*a*) encourages collaboration rather than competition among industries (*b*) discourages the formation of business combinations (*c*) allows foreign countries easy entry into the Japanese market (*d*) prohibits large corporations from owning controlling shares of other firms.

10. Lifetime employment, quality circles, and inventory on demand were characteristics of the economy of (*a*) the United States (*b*) Russia (*c*) China (*d*) Japan.

THINKING CRITICALLY

1. Economists usually look at the *ownership of means of production* and the *coordination of economic activity* when they compare economic systems. With reference to the italicized phrases, compare the economic system of a past or present socialist or Communist country with the economic system of the United States today.

2. Communism had its origins in the writings of Karl Marx. With respect to *two* of Marx's theories, (*a*) describe each theory, and (*b*) explain the extent to which you agree or disagree with it.

3. What were the inefficiencies in the Soviet economic system that may have contributed to the system's collapse?

4. Explain the role played by Mikhail Gorbachev in changing the Soviet economy.

5. Japan today is one of the leading industrial nations of the world. Its currency is usually strong. Japanese workers enjoy high wages and a high standard of living. Some economists and business leaders attribute the success of Japanese industries to the country's reliance on managed capitalism and Japanese production and employment techniques.

    a. Compare practices in the United States with those in Japan in terms of managed capitalism, production techniques, and employment techniques.

    b. Present arguments why the United States should or should not adopt the Japanese economic model.

SKILLS: Analyzing an Editorial Cartoon

Study the cartoon below and answer the questions that follow:

1. Who does the figure labeled "China" represent?

2. Identify the symbols at the ends of the balancing rod and explain what China is doing in this cartoon.

3. Why is the figure drawn standing on a razor blade?

4. What can you say about the cartoonist's point of view toward China?

5. What title would you give this cartoon? Why?

6. How does the cartoon relate to the discussion of economic systems in this chapter?

ARCADIO
LA NACION
San Jose
COSTA RICA

Arcadio, Cartoonists and Writers Syndicate/cartoonweb.com.

USING THE INTERNET

- For a discussion on how Russia has adapted to capitalism, read the article by the British economist David Lane at <<www.sps.cam.ac.uk/stafflist/Lane_D/russbanks.htm>>.

- *The World Factbook,* an annual book put together by the CIA, has information on almost every nation in the world. It is also available online at <<www.cia.gov/cia/publications/factbook/index.html>>.

CHAPTER 25

Economics of Development

OVERVIEW

More than half the people of the world are living in conditions approaching misery. . . . Their poverty is a handicap, and a threat, both to them and to more prosperous areas.

—*Harry S. Truman*

Little has changed since President Harry S. Truman spoke these words in 1949. The world is still divided between the wealthy countries and the poorer ones. Of course, poverty exists in all nations, including our own. In some countries, however, poverty is much worse.

Why should we, living in one of the most economically advanced countries, be concerned about the poorer countries? One answer, of course, is that we should be concerned with the plight of humanity everywhere. In addition, we are aware that it is in our self-interest to promote the well-being of nations everywhere. Why? Because of increasing international economic interdependence, economic conditions and policies in one nation affect economic conditions in many other nations, including our own. According to a World Bank report, misguided policies of the past have contributed to environmental disasters, income inequality, and social upheaval in some countries. The results have been extreme poverty, famine, and civil wars.

In this chapter, we will discuss how we measure and compare economic development in different nations, the factors that hinder development, and programs to promote economic growth in developing nations.

HOW CAN WE MEASURE DEVELOPMENT?

In measuring economic development, economists distinguish between developed and developing countries. The *developed countries* are industrialized nations with relatively high GDP and income per capita. *Developing countries*, by contrast, have basically agricultural economies, with relatively low income and GDP per capita. The United Nations uses slightly different terminology in discussing development. It differentiates between *more developed countries (MDCs)* and *less developed countries (LDCs)*. According to the UN, there are approximately 45 MDCs, mostly in Europe and North America. The UN lists more than 120 LDCs.

How do the less developed countries compare to the more developed ones? One basis of comparison is *quality of life,* that is, how well the average person in each country lives. The quality of life is relatively high in the United States and in the other more developed countries. People eat better, live longer, and are better educated and cared for. They have more material things. People living in the more developed countries are the major beneficiaries of humankind's scientific, technological, and cultural achievements. A child born in a more developed country is likely to grow to adulthood enjoying a higher quality of life than one born in a less developed country. A few statistics, summarized in Table 25.1, illustrate these differences.

1. Per Capita GDP

Poverty is the common denominator shared by the less developed countries, while the more developed countries are considered wealthier. One of the most frequently cited measures of a nation's wealth is per capita gross domestic product (discussed in Chapter 21). This statistic is determined by dividing a nation's total GDP by its population. Economists measure living standards by the amount of goods and services available to an individual or society. GDP per capita enables them to compare the living standard of one nation to that of another. Among the more developed countries in a recent year, per capita GDP averaged $26,283. Compare this figure with $440 for the less developed countries. The average income in the richest 20 countries is 37 times that in the poorest 20 countries. It is estimated that in order for the LDCs to reduce the percentage of those in poverty by just one-half, they will need to grow their economies at a rate of at least 3.6 percent.

TABLE 25.1 MORE DEVELOPED AND LESS DEVELOPED COUNTRIES: *MEASURING THE DIFFERENCES*

Regions or Country	Per Capita GDP (U.S. Dollars)	Infant Mortality (per 1,000)	Life Expectancy (years)	Literacy Rate (percent)	Energy Consumption Per Capita (kilowatt-hrs.)	2001 Population (millions)	Annual Population Growth Rate (percent)	Projected Population 2050 (millions)	Percent of GDP Devoted to Agriculture
More Developed Countries	$26,283	5.8	74.9	n.a.	8,038	995	0.2	1,014	2.3
Less Developed Countries	440	93.3	50.5	45	68.5.	4,865	1.1	8,141	30.8
Bangladesh	$ 1,546	67	57	53	198	131.3	1.6	254.6	30
Brazil	6,477	38	63	83	1,051	174.5	1.1	233.2	8
China	3,535	37	72	86	883	1,273.1	0.6	1,395.2	15
Egypt	3,552	40	64	51	688	69.5	1.5	127.4	18
Ethiopia	595	106	45	36	294	64.5	2.1	170.9	60
Germany	23,317	5	78	99	4,232	83.0	-0.2	79.1	1
India	2,136	65	63	52	447	1,205.1	1.2	1,531.4	31
Indonesia	2,863	40	68	84	682	214.8	1.4	280	19
Japan	24,848	3	81	99	4,085	126.7	-0.2	109.7	2
Kenya	1,482	59	54	52	497	5.2	1.4	6.5	21
Malaysia	10,063	10	72	90	2,310	22.2	1.5	33.3	24
Mexico	8,981	28	72	75	1,501	101.9	1.4	130	4
South Korea	15,961	7	75	98	3,856	47.9	0.6	50.7	7
Russia	7,699	17	67	95	4,009	145.5	-0.5	144.4	9
Switzerland	28,421	5	80	99	3,616	7.3	-0.1	6.3	1
United States	35,831	6.8	77	97	12,900	278.0	0.1	331.0	2

Sources: *CIA World Fact Book, 2002*, World Development Report, 2003, UNFPA, 2003.

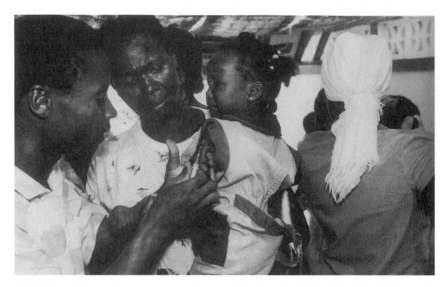

A Haitian child receives a vaccination provided by the United Nations Children's Fund (UNICEF). A country's medical services is one of the indicators of its economic development.

2. Medical Services

The next two columns tell something about the state of medical and public health services in various countries. *Infant mortality rate* is the number of babies (out of every 1,000 live births) who die before their first birthday. *Life expectancy* is the number of years the average newly born infant in the designated nation may expect to live. Once again, there is a difference between the more developed and the less developed countries. Infant mortality is only 5.8 per 1,000 in more developed countries as compared to 93.3 per 1,000 in the less developed countries. Life expectancy averages 74.9 years in the more developed countries, compared to 50.5 years in the less developed countries.

3. Literacy Rate

The ability to read and write is one of the essential ingredients in economic development. The percentage of an adult population who can read and write is its *literacy rate.* In the more developed countries (where compulsory education is a fact of life), most people are literate. In the less developed countries, low literacy rates are common. For that reason, governments all over the globe have declared universal literacy to be a principal goal.

The opportunity costs of universal education can be high, especially in the short run. In the desperately poor countries of Africa and Asia, parents often look to their children to help them scratch out a living. Thus, some are reluctant to have their children spend time in school. Similarly, governments intent on retaining or expanding political power are likely to give a higher priority to spending on their armed forces than on education. Education, however, is an essential ingredient in economic growth and development. According to a study of less developed nations:

> . . . economies—such as Japan and the Republic of Korea—which committed themselves to education and training made great strides in human development and economic growth. . . . A one-year increase in schooling augmented wages by more than 10 percent; raised farm output by anywhere from 2 to 5 percent; and resulted in an increase in earnings in family-owned business.
>
> —*International Bank for Development,* The Challenge of Development

4. Energy Consumption Per Capita

Energy is needed for heat, light, power, and transportation. Energy is created most commonly with the help of a variety of fuels, including petroleum, natural gas, coal, and nuclear varieties. A country's progress in making these vital fuels available is measured by the statistic *energy consumption per capita*—a nation's total energy consumption divided by its population. The statistics in this column are stated in terms of kilowatt-hours (kWh) per person.

5. Population Data

The next three columns compare the populations of more developed nations with that of less developed countries and show how they are changing. The first column lists the total population in a recent year. The second shows its present rate of population growth per year, and the third estimates the total population, based on the given rate of growth, for the year 2050. If the rates of growth continue as shown, the total population in the less developed countries will exceed that of the more developed countries.

6. Percent of GDP Devoted to Agriculture

The relative importance of agriculture in the more developed and less developed countries is illustrated in the last column. Nations obtain the food they need to feed their populations by either producing it themselves or importing it from abroad. The more industrialized a nation becomes, the fewer resources it needs to devote to growing its own food. This is true because (1) industrialized nations can use the proceeds from the export of manufactured goods to purchase food and (2) agricultural productivity in industrialized nations is generally higher than that in the less developed countries. In contrast to the situation in industrialized countries, agriculture generally plays a much larger role in the economies of less developed countries.

In Bangladesh, many farmers rely on animals to power plows. What percent of Bangladesh's GDP is devoted to agriculture?

 # THE STAGES OF DEVELOPMENT

Why are some countries more developed than others? Economist **W.W. Rostow** of M.I.T. made one of the most accepted explanations of economic growth. In his *The Stages of Economic Growth: A Non-Communist Manifesto,* Rostow argued that, at one time or another, all industrialized nations could have been classified as "less developed." At some later time, however, each began a process of development that transformed its economy. The process, as described by Rostow, involved five stages of economic growth: (1) traditional society, (2) pre-conditions for takeoff, (3) takeoff, (4) drive to maturity, and (5) age of high mass consumption.

Rostow's work provides a simple framework for understanding how nations increase real per capita income through the process of economic development. Let us take a closer look at each of the stages of economic growth.

Stage 1: Traditional Society

At the traditional stage, society has not yet come to use advanced technology to increase its production of goods and services. Because its methods of production are primitive, virtually all of society's productive energies must be directed toward feeding its people. The class structure of such a society is often rigid, and whatever surplus people produce inevitably finds its way into the hands of a small wealthy class. Since this surplus is not used to increase the level of production, economic life continues more or less the same from one year to the next.

Stage 2: Preconditions for Takeoff

Before a society can undertake a dramatic move toward development, it has to prepare itself by making certain breaks with the past. These preconditions, according to Rostow, are:

BREAKDOWN OF OLD TRADITIONS. The attitudes and traditions that dominated society in the past must be broken down so that new social, political, and economic methods may be introduced.

EMERGENCE OF NATIONALISM. It is easier to develop an economy along modern lines if a population accepts the rule of a central government. This was not the case in Europe during the Middle Ages. Under feudalism, a person's main allegiance was to the local lord rather than to a monarch. Similarly, some of today's less developed countries were established based on arbitrary lines drawn by the former colonial powers without taking into consideration ethnic groups within those areas. Consequently, individual loyalties in these states often lie with a tribe rather than a national government. This tendency serves as an obstacle to modernization because a central government is needed, among other reasons, to make laws governing commerce that apply to the whole nation.

DEVELOPMENT OF AN ENTREPRENEURIAL CLASS. Economic development requires a group willing to form businesses and take risks in pursuit of profit. Such a group is described as entrepreneurs.

ACCUMULATION OF SAVINGS. Before increasing output, a portion of the profits from current output needs to be saved for later purchases of capital goods. Closely allied with the accumulation of savings is the development of financial institutions and markets that can pool funds and make them available to businesses in need of capital.

Stage 3: Takeoff

Rostow defines *takeoff* as a dramatic movement toward development that includes increased productivity. Just as a plane becomes airborne at one point along the runway, so too will a developing economy "take off" with a sharp increase in output. As this occurs, production will increase at a faster rate than its population. Then, as the surplus is invested in capital goods, output will increase still further. The Industrial Revolution in the textile industry in 18th-century Britain is a classic example of what Rostow meant by "takeoff."

⚜ Stage 4: The Drive to Maturity

With production increasing faster than the population, living standards will rise. Simultaneously, the manufacturing and service sectors of the economy will increase in importance, while the agricultural sector will become less important.

⚜ Stage 5: Age of High Mass Consumption

Roughly 60 years after the breakdown of traditional society, said Rostow, the nation will mature to the point where it can produce or acquire anything that consumers want. With high mass consumption, consumers will have achieved a high standard of living. Meanwhile, society will be able to devote an increasing share of its resources to social welfare programs.

WHAT FACTORS HELP OR HINDER DEVELOPMENT?

Since the less developed countries are not all alike, any summary of the reasons for their poverty must be generalized. Each differs from the others in many ways. Each has its own strength and weaknesses.

Some 24 less developed countries (such as China, India, South Korea, and Mexico) are well on their way toward development. They seem to fall outside most of the generalizations that follow. Then, too, there are those less developed nations whose holdings of a natural resource are extensive. It is reasonable to assume that they will more easily be able to raise capital for development than the less endowed nations. One such group includes the nations of the Organization of Petroleum Exporting Countries (OPEC). Their wealth from the sale of oil gives them an enormous advantage over other developing nations and helps explain why two OPEC members—Kuwait and the United Arab Emirates—have already reached the fifth stage of economic growth. (The other members of OPEC are Algeria, Indonesia, Iran, Iraq, Libya, Nigeria, Qatar, Saudi Arabia, and Venezuela.) However, the reliance on revenue from a single natural resource, such as oil, is not always an aid toward development. These nations have less of an incentive to invest in other industries—ones that might not return such enormous revenues. Then, too, a fall in demand and, there-fore, in the price for that single resource could wreak havoc on an economy that is solely or largely dependent on one product such as oil, cacao beans, or coffee.

As we will read, money flowing into a country is not the only factor needed for growth. Many members of OPEC, despite their oil wealth, share some of the same obstacles to growth that the less fortunate developing countries experience.

In their fight against poverty, the less developed countries tend to suffer from some or all of the following handicaps.

1. Traditions That Are Obstacles to Economic Growth

Traditional societies need to overcome any number of obstacles in their efforts to meet the preconditions for takeoff. Deeply ingrained religious and social customs and traditions may limit their ability to increase production. In some Muslim countries, for example, women are excluded from the labor force because of custom. For a long time in India, the caste system locked many people in the social class into which they were born. Those in the lowest castes were not free to work where they chose.

People in traditional economic societies are often reluctant to adopt new methods of production. Farmers who barely grow enough to feed their families, for example, may be reluctant to try a new plowing technique because they fear failure, which could result in starvation.

2. Unfavorable Social and Political Conditions

History has shown that government can be a major factor in a society's economic growth and development. In many of the less developed countries, political instability and repression have added to the nations' woes. Many of Ethiopia's problems had their origin in the harsh policies of the Marxist government that ruled from 1974 to 1991. It forced 1.5 million farmers off their land, triggered a nationwide famine, and plunged the country into a civil war. In contrast, Vietnam moved from a strict, totalitarian Marxist economy to one having some elements of capitalism. Tourism and some foreign investment are being encouraged.

Some governments spend more on human development (health, education, and social services) than others, with predictable results. For example, in 1989, both Sri Lanka and Guinea had about the same per capita GDP. But the Sri Lankan government then committed more of the nation's resources to human development than did the government of Guinea. By 2003, Sri Lanka's GDP per capita was almost double that of Guinea. Moreover, life expectancy in Sri Lanka grew and is now 72 years (compared to 54 years in Guinea).

Military spending, particularly in developing countries, is another ingredient likely to affect economic growth and development. For a number of years, Angola, Cuba, Chad, North Korea, and Uganda—all poor countries—each spent more on its armed forces than it could afford. This money could have been better used to help develop industries or infrastructure. North Korea, for example, is a nuclear power with massive armed forces, yet it has difficulty feeding its own population.

Corruption is still another factor that can impede a less developed nation's efforts to grow its economy. Corrupt individuals steal much money from governments—money that could be used for development. Moreover, businesspeople often have to pay bribes to get matters approved by government officials. Corruption was a major justification for the military overthrow of the government of Nigeria in 1993. Yet corruption has continued in Nigeria.

3. Rapid Population Growth

As we can see in Table 25.1, the population in the less developed countries is growing at a much faster rate than it is in the more developed world (1.1 percent vs. 0.2 percent). At these rates, the average population in the less developed nations will increase by two-thirds by 2050, while population in the more developed nations will grow less than 2 percent. Imagine the kinds of problems the population explosion in the less developed nations might create. To maintain living standards at present levels, production in less developed countries would have to grow at the same rate as the population growth. But this increase in production is unlikely to happen. Less developed countries rarely achieve economic growth rates that exceed their population growth.

Remember, too, that life expectancy in less developed countries is 24 years less than that in the developed ones. Combined with high birthrates, lower life expectancy means that the less developed countries have a predominantly young population. As a result, an estimated half of the population of many of the less developed nations is too young to work. After adding the number of those needed to rear children and those who could be considered too old to work, we see that a substantial portion of the population is simply unavailable to join the labor force.

4. Shortage of Capital

The more developed nations possess the kinds of factories, equipment, and tools necessary to the tasks of modern production. Therefore, the more developed nations can turn out more goods and services than they need. Excess production can then be exchanged for the goods and services necessary to maintain and improve the nation's living standards. The less developed countries, by contrast, are woefully short of capital. They do not have the kinds of

Amartya Sen

Professor **Amartya Sen** of Cambridge University in England specializes in the areas of welfare economics and economic growth and development. A citizen of India, Sen was educated at Calcutta University in India and Cambridge University in Britain. He has taught at the University of Delhi, the London School of Economics, Oxford University, and Harvard University.

In his landmark study *Poverty and Famine* (1981), Amartya Sen argued that more lives could be saved by giving money instead of food to victims of famine. (*Famine* is defined as large-scale starvation.) In arriving at this conclusion, Sen used the following arguments:

One of the most desperate problems faced by certain underdeveloped nations has been that of famine. In their efforts to fight the malnutrition, hunger, and death that often follow in famine's wake, governments and international agencies strive to deliver and distribute food to those in need. In doing so, they undoubtedly save millions of lives. But as the death tolls show, food aid usually arrives too late to save everyone. Then, when help finally arrives, it often harms farmers who have crops or livestock to sell because people will not pay for food that they can obtain for free. As local farmers abandon the soil, the impoverished country finds itself even more dependent on outside aid when drought and famine return.

By way of illustration, Sen cited the famine in Ethiopia in 1973. Although the country as a whole in 1973 produced roughly as much food as in previous years, there was a famine in the province of Wollo, where food production suffered a big decline. Most of the famine victims were subsistence farmers whose crops had failed. They lacked enough money to buy food from elsewhere in Ethiopia, which had enough food. Trade was possible because the roads into Wollo were open. Indeed, some of Wollo's farmers had surplus food and sold it outside the province.

This scenario led Sen to suggest that cash, rather than food, would save more famine victims. Unlike food aid, cash can be dispatched quickly to the famine areas and is less disruptive to the local economy. With money in hand, those facing starvation can buy food from those who have enough. Moreover, cash aid pushes up food prices, thereby encouraging food imports and, even more important, greater production of food at home.

In 1998, Amartya Sen won the Nobel Prize in Economics for his study of the economic conditions that lead to poverty and famine.

Of course, cash aid works only if there is already enough food in a famine-stricken country to feed everyone, and only if food can be bought and sold relatively freely. As Sen's research has shown, these conditions exist more often than is usually supposed.

factories, equipment, and tools necessary to the tasks of modern production. Thus, they have much fewer surplus goods and services. But in order to acquire capital goods, less developed countries need to set aside enough savings to finance necessary investments. In the more developed countries, individual savings in banks and other financial institutions provide a pool of funds that can be borrowed and invested in capital projects. However, in places where most of the population lives at the subsistence level, little is available for savings and investment. Investment and an infusion of capital, therefore, must come from outside sources, that is, the rich nations of the world.

5. Poorly Educated Labor Force

Most economists would agree that education is essential for raising individual productivity. General education gives children skills that in later years they can transfer from one job to another. All too often, though, the labor force in less developed nations suffers from inadequate education and training. There is a direct relationship between education and productivity. A study found that farmers in China's Hunan Province, where education is a priority, outproduced less educated farmers in other Chinese provinces. Similarly, areas of India in which few farmers had primary schooling experienced less economic growth than other areas of India in which farmers were better educated. Evidence since then continues to suggest that educated farmers are more productive than those with little or no education.

A PROGRAM FOR THE DEVELOPING COUNTRIES

Economists have suggested that less developed countries follow a number of measures in their efforts to achieve economic growth.

1. Increase Farm Productivity

More than half the total labor force in the less developed countries works in agriculture. In the poorest nations, the average is closer to 60 percent. Contrast these percentages with 2.3 percent for the industrialized world's agricultural labor force. Agricultural productivity accounts for the difference. Modern technology enables farmers in the more developed countries to produce (with fewer workers) far more than their counterparts in the less developed countries. Whereas farms in the more developed nations typically produce a surplus, much of the agriculture in the less developed countries consists of *subsistence farming*. Farms operating at subsistence levels produce just enough to feed the farmers and their families.

A successful agricultural economy is one of the basic steps toward development. This Hmong woman works a field in Thailand.

If poor nations modernized their farming methods, fewer farm workers would be needed. Thus, additional workers would be available for service in other forms of production, thereby increasing total output. The increase in total output could lead to an overall improvement in living standards.

In addition to improved technology, some experts suggest land reform as a means to improve agricultural productivity in the less developed world. *Land reform* refers to the breakup by government of large estates into smaller plots that can be owned and farmed individually. The process of land reform gives those who work as tenant farmers an opportunity to own the land on which they labor. Those who favor land reform argue that farmers who own their land are likely to be more productive than those who work for others.

In Latin America, most farmland is still in the hands of giant landowners. Peasants work the land for a minimal wage and/or a share of an estate's resources. One of the earliest efforts at land reform in Latin America occurred in Mexico in the 1930s. During that decade, some 45 million acres of land acquired in the aftermath of that country's revolution was distributed to 800,000 peasant families. More recently, Guatemala, Bolivia, Venezuela, Cuba, Ecuador, Nicaragua, Chile, and Peru have broken up some estates and redistributed the farmland. Brazil has made it possible for poor people in some locales to gain title to their homes and land. Secure that they will not be evicted, these poor people have the motivation to invest to improve their holdings.

Land reform is not unique to Latin America. In Thailand, where 60 percent of the population still makes its living from the land, land ownership and reform is that nation's most sensitive political issue. The government of Indonesia also regards land reform as an essential part of that country's development plans. Similarly, land reform is at the top of the political agenda of the governments of South Africa and Zimbabwe.

Not all economists agree, however, that land reform leads to greater agricultural productivity. Some claim that dividing large estates into tiny, privately owned plots can be inefficient. A farmer with a small plot might not earn enough from the land to invest in agricultural machinery and make other improvements. Defenders of land reform counter with the argument that the new landowners who benefit from land reform could form cooperatives to purchase tractors and other expensive machinery. Members of the cooperatives would share the costs and the uses of such technology. However, increasing agricultural productivity in the developing nations is only part of the solution.

There also needs to be a market for this increased production. World markets, particularly in the industrialized countries, must be opened up to the less developed countries dependent on agriculture. To the contrary, the policies of the more developed nations hinder agricultural progress in the poorer nations. According to *The World Development Report, 2003* issued by the World Bank, the more developed countries spend $1 billion a day on agricultural subsidies to their farmers. These subsidies enable farmers in the more developed nations to sell their produce at prices below those of farmers in the less developed nations who are not similarly subsidized. Moreover, import restrictions imposed by the more developed nations on the agricultural products of less developed countries reduces still further the market for the agricultural products of the developing nations. (Chapter 22 discussed the effect of subsidies and tariffs on foreign trade.)

🧭 2. Reduce Population Growth

For a nation's per capita gross domestic product to grow, total GDP must increase faster than the increase in population. With this in mind, a number of less developed nations introduced family-planning programs. *Family planning* refers to efforts to limit the size of families. Family-planning programs vary from privately sponsored organizations that give out brochures and contraceptives, to clinics that perform abortions, to government-imposed limits on family size. China, for example, limits families to one child (there are exceptions to this rule) and imposes penalties on parents who have more than their limit.

While most people agree that population growth affects living standards, some efforts to limit family size are highly controversial. In some poor, agricultural countries, for example, family planning flies in the face of tradition. In those societies, people often look to their children as a kind of social security. By the time they are 10 or 11 years old, the children are expected to help the family work the land. In later years, when the parents are too old to care for themselves, the children are expected to attend to their parents' needs. Without children to care for them, many elderly people might die of hunger or neglect.

Family-planning programs often conflict with people's religious beliefs and practices. In India, where the population has been increasing by more than 10 million a year, opposition by followers of traditional Hinduism has been an obstacle to the success of that country's birth control programs. Similarly, the Roman Catholic Church has been a leader in opposing most birth control methods in countries around the world.

🎴 3. Accumulate Capital Goods

Modern production requires the application of machinery and tools and up-to-date manufacturing plants. Since the less developed countries are unable to manufacture most of their own equipment, they have to purchase it abroad. When they do set up modern manufacturing plants, they often need foreign assistance. Nevertheless, less developed countries do accumulate capital goods, in the following ways.

BUY EQUIPMENT WITH OWN FUNDS.   About 80 percent of the capital needed for development in the less developed countries comes from internal sources (that is, from within the countries).

ENCOURAGE FOREIGN INVESTMENTS.   Less developed countries often encourage foreign companies to establish businesses on their soil. These investments (along with domestic investments) stimulate economic growth. In keeping with this philosophy, in 1986 Vietnam launched its *doi moi* (economic renovation) policy, which, among other things, encourages foreign investment. As a result of the *doi moi* program, some 800 foreign firms have pledged more than $17 billion of investment in 1,400 different projects.

About one-third of cross-border private investments have been made to less developed countries. Of that, about one-third has been invested in China and another third in the Asian countries of South Korea, Malaysia, Indonesia, and Thailand. Other countries getting private investments include Mexico, Argentina, and Brazil.

Not everyone is in favor of extensive foreign investment in the less developed countries. Antiglobalization forces see a danger that it can lead to exploitation of labor and harm the environment (as discussed in Chapter 22, page 513). Multinational corporations in the less developed countries have been accused of paying slave labor wages and providing poor working conditions for their employees.

JOIN INTERNATIONAL FINANCIAL AGENCIES.   International organizations provide grants, loans, and technical advice to less developed nations. A major source of this aid is the United Nations and its affiliated organizations. The most important of these are the **International Monetary Fund (IMF)** and the International Bank for Reconstruction and Development (or as it is more commonly called, the **World Bank**). The IMF and the World Bank complement one another. They do this by specializing in different aspects of the financial problems most frequently faced by developing nations.

International Monetary Fund.   The IMF's job is to help ensure that in periods of economic downturn, the value of a nation's currency remains stable. This task is important because a fluctuating currency can interfere with a nation's foreign trade. For example, the IMF in 2003 gave Turkey $701 million as part of an $18 billion loan package. Turkey then was in the throes of a severe inflation, and its government was sinking in debt. As part of the deal, the IMF insisted that Turkey cut its government expenditures, balance its budget, and agree to new loan terms if it was to receive the remainder of the $18 billion.

World Bank. The fundamental role of the World Bank is to make loans to the governments of less developed nations that want to build expensive infrastructure projects, such as dams, power plants, and highways. Private investors are often unwilling or unable to fund such projects. Yet an infrastructure is necessary to attract private investment in other sectors of the economy, such as manufacturing and natural resource exploitation. For example, guarantees by the World Bank enabled Pakistan to raise additional funding from private sources toward the building of its Hub hydroelectric plant. The Bank also provided loans for road-building projects in Poland and India, and a railroad-improvement program in Bulgaria. Venezuela received a loan of $30.3 million from the World Bank to expand health coverage for the poor in its Caracas Metropolitan District.

With the assistance given to developing countries by organizations such as the IMF and the World Bank, one wonders why protest demonstrations have been directed against them. It is because these organizations are seen as setting standards and rendering judgments based on the interests of corporate powers. IMF and World Bank loans and investments require that each receiving nation adopt a set of financial and budgetary policies that stress fiscal responsibility, often at the expense of social and humanitarian needs. Thus, in a country with high unemployment and severe inflation, the international monetary organizations may insist on a reduction in government spending to achieve a balanced budget. Opponents of the IMF and the World Bank may demand an increase in government spending for health and welfare programs.

Regional Organizations. In addition to international agencies like the World Bank and the IMF, regional agencies (such as the Asian Development Bank, the Inter-American Development Bank, and the African Development Bank) make loans, but only to countries within their particular region. For example, in one recent year, the African Development Bank disbursed about $14 billion in loans for projects in Egypt, Nigeria, Morocco, Congo, Tunisia, Algeria, and Côte d'Ivoire.

ACCEPT GRANTS AND LOANS FROM PRIVATE BANKS AND CORPORATIONS. Private banks and corporations, if they feel that they have a reasonable chance to earn a profit, also invest in the less developed countries. Since making a profit is a primary focus of private funds, however, private sources generally prefer to do business in the stronger economies.

ACCEPT GRANTS AND LOANS FROM FOREIGN GOVERNMENTS. Since the end of the Second World War, economic and technical assistance from foreign governments has been an essential ingredient in the industrialization of less developed nations. However, the amount of assistance available for distribution to the less developed countries has been decreasing. In the late 1940s, for example, the U.S. government spent 2 percent of the country's GDP on foreign aid programs. The U.S. budget for 2004 provided only $8.7 billion for development and humanitarian aid programs. This was less than 0.1 percent of the country's GDP. (The United States provides additional billions in military aid.)

The industrialized nations of Europe have also been losing their enthusiasm for helping less developed nations. In 2002, the member nations of the EU agreed to continue to lend economic and technical assistance to 71 countries, mostly those that had been their colonies. This new agreement, the **Cotonou Partnership**, covers the period 2000–2020. Although direct aid predominates in the cooperative agreements between these countries and the EU, agreements are also reached on matters involving trade and developing infrastructure.

OTHER HELP.   Finally, U.S. government agencies such as the **Peace Corps** and a variety of religious and other nonprofit groups also contribute to the development process. By teaching, assisting in health projects, working on construction sites, and consulting with local leaders, they bring the benefits of modern technology to the developing nations.

🌀 4. Introduce or Improve the Market System

To promote efficiency in their domestic economies, less developed nations need to introduce or strengthen capitalism there. To do that, they need to strengthen the institutions that make a market system work and improve the infrastructure.

STRENGTHENING INSTITUTIONS.   To promote efficiency in their domestic economies, developing nations need to strengthen the institutions that make a market system work. In most instances, this means that government needs to create and protect financial institutions, such as banks, securities markets, and currency exchanges. The World Bank, for example, has a program to help the less developed nations set up their own stock exchanges. A market system works effectively only when it operates within the framework of a government of laws, not individuals. Individuals and businesses must be able to sign contracts with the expectation that the legal system will back up those contracts. Along these lines, bribery must be discouraged.

Private enterprise may be promoted by making it easier for entrepreneurs to obtain *microcredit* (small loans at very low interest) and obtain foreign currencies. Ghana has taken steps in this direction.

> Irene Dufu owns Cactus Enterprises, Ltd., a fishing company headquartered in Tema, Ghana. She started with only a single wooden vessel and a crew of 12. Mrs. Dufu credits her success to a government program that made it possible for her (and other small business owners) to obtain small, low-cost bank loans and foreign exchange. Microcredit enabled Mrs. Dufu to purchase and maintain three modern boats. She now employs 65 people on these boats.

Most U.S. economists agree that the less developed nations can benefit from open markets, fewer government regulations (deregulation), privatization of government enterprises, and fiscal discipline. But this path toward economic growth has its problems.

Latin America stretches south from the U.S.-Mexican border to the southernmost tip of Argentina and includes the Caribbean Islands. Throughout the region, nations have developed and modernized their industries. At the same time, they have opened up their markets to foreign investment, pulled down many of their protective barriers to trade, and created new jobs.

Shacks coexist with high-rise apartment buildings in Rio de Janeiro, Brazil.

Nevertheless, all is not well in Latin America. Violent crime is a problem in many countries. Armed criminal gangs engage in armed robberies, kidnappings, and drug dealing. Typical of the kidnappings will be the seizure of a businessperson and the setting of a ransom, to be paid before the kidnap victim would be released. Such an atmosphere is not good for attracting foreign investments. Moreover, some wealthy Latin Americans keep their money and their families in North America or Europe.

The economy of Venezuela is hurting because of conflict between two major forces—President **Hugo Chávez** (and his political party, which has the broad support of the poor) and the middle class (including most businesspeople). Chávez admires the Cuban example and has worked to nationalize major industries. In 2002, elements of the Venezuelan military, with support of businesspeople and some labor leaders, carried out a coup. Chávez was forced out of office, but a few days later other elements of the army brought him back to power. Then in 2003, striking oil workers in Venezuela called for an immediate referendum on whether Chávez should remain President. The strike lasted two months and nearly crippled the Venezuelan economy. This political uncertainty has hurt foreign investment and cut oil production—Venezuela's major industry.

Colombia and Peru have long had problems with Marxist revolutionary groups. The situation is most severe in Colombia, where the government has been in armed conflict with several guerrilla groups. The largest, the Revolutionary Armed Forces of Colombia (FARC), controls a large section of the country, taxing businesses and people living there and murdering local government officials and others who cooperate with the national government. From time to time, the Colombian government has sent troops into FARC territory to try to dislodge them. The U.S. government has provided funds and has helped train these Colombian troops.

The production and distribution of illegal drugs

is part of the problem in Latin America. Much of the world's cocaine is produced in Peru, Bolivia, and Colombia. Peasants in these countries find the production of coca leaves to be much more profitable than legal crops, but the governments (with U.S. help) have been eradicating coca fields. In Columbia, FARC has protected coca farmers and has taxed drug dealers. FARC demanded $15,000 per flight for every drug-carrying plane that departed from one of the airports or airstrips under its control.

The discontent in these countries, and elsewhere in Latin America, can be attributed to the fact that economic growth has proved very uneven. The rich are getting richer, while the poor are getting poorer. The few new jobs that have been created for the illiterate poor are largely low-paying and short-term ones. Some 38 percent of Latin America's population lacks basic minimums of income, food, shelter, health care, and education. UN economists estimate that 46 million people in Latin America are homeless, 85 million live in homes that deserve to be demolished, and some 100 million people lack water and electricity in their homes. Thus, a high portion of the area's population lives in poverty despite the economic growth brought about by the introduction of the market economy.

It is clear that more spending on social programs to develop the area's human resources is essential. But where will the money for these programs come from—private sources or government? Will wealthy Latin Americans accept paying a much larger share of taxes—something that they have not so far been accustomed to doing? Will high taxes discourage private investments?

Few economists will argue that introducing the market economy to Latin America has been a mistake or a failure. Opening the doors to more investment and to privatization is working. But in Latin America, old ways are not easily changed. Bureaucracies need to be streamlined, corruption and crime reduced, and more land reforms implemented. It may take some time before the benefits of these reforms trickle down to the mass of poverty-stricken people in Latin America.

According to Argentine economist **Miguel Angel Broda**, Latin American countries may either (1) turn to the economic model of the Western European social welfare state (where many people work in the public sector) or (2) follow the direction of the more market-oriented U.S. economic model. Broda argues that the U.S. model is more desirable in the long run. But the "long run" is little comfort to people who must buy food, pay rent, and support their families today. These hardships, coupled with the widening gap between rich and poor in Latin America, contribute to social unrest and political instability. Under such conditions, Latin Americans who have not benefited from the market economy might very well look to other economic models.

If you were an economist living in Latin America today, which path to economic development would you choose—the U.S. economic model or the Western European social welfare state?

IMPROVING INFRASTRUCTURE. Sanitation systems, transportation facilities, communications networks, and public utilities are examples of *infrastructure.* Many of these vital ingredients are lacking in the less developed countries. This situation discourages foreign investors and makes it difficult for poor countries to develop.

In Nigeria, for example, there was only one telephone line for every 500 inhabitants in 1993. Business firms had to depend on radios and messengers for basic communication. To expand and improve the nation's telecommunications networks, Nigerian leaders privatized them. As a result, the new telephone companies had more money to invest in expanding telephone service. Nigeria has had some success. By 2002, including mobile phones, there were about four telephones for every 500 persons. Nigeria still has a way to go to catch up to the more developed countries, which have one or more telephone or mobile phone per person. Other infrastructure programs in Nigeria are improving roads, water supply systems, solid waste disposal systems, and sanitation services.

RE-ESTABLISHING CREDIT.   Borrowing from abroad is a major means for less developed nations to finance capital investment. But many of the world's poorest countries can no longer borrow. They are so heavily in debt that they cannot meet interest payments on the loans that they already have. One of those is the African country of Guinea-Bissau. It is so heavily in debt that it would have to pay out two and a half times more than it earns in exports just to meet its import payments. In an effort to save Guinea-Bissau and other nations with similar problems from bankruptcy, the International Monetary Fund and the World Bank have provided them with additional loans.

In 1999, the Poverty Reduction Growth Facility was established as an initiative for some 75 heavily indebted poor countries. Experts from the World Bank and IMF work closely with an indebted country to develop an economic recovery plan. The World Bank and IMF then decide on new loans or debt reduction as determined by need. Borrowers pay 0.5 percent interest on the new loans and receive a grace period of 5½ years before beginning repayment. In order to receive these new loans, a nation must have a per capita income of $875 or less.

5. Invest in People

Few policies promote development as effectively as investments in human resources. These investments include expanding primary, secondary, and post-secondary education and improving health care. Increasingly important is the need to reverse the spread of HIV and AIDS, which are decimating populations in Africa and have the potential to do so in Asia. This will necessitate the immediate supply of medicines to combat the dread disease and a long-term educational program relating to health and sexual practices.

With two-thirds of its population illiterate, Bangladesh has undertaken to expand its primary schools. In order to accomplish its goals, the nation will look abroad for financial assistance.

S U M M A R Y

The more developed nations are industrialized countries with relatively high GDP and income per capita. The less developed countries, by contrast, have basically agricultural economies, with relatively low income and GDP per capita. The common factors hindering economic growth in the less developed countries include: (1) economic systems based on tradition that do not adapt easily to change; (2) unstable political and social conditions with a small, wealthy elite and a very large number of poor citizens; (3) a population growth at a rate greater than economic growth; (4) a shortage of capital needed for development; and (5) a need for education and training of a population that is largely illiterate.

Programs to help the less developed nations attempt to deal with the factors hindering economic growth include: (1) introducing modern technology to improve farm productivity, (2) land reform, (3) slowing down population growth, (4) encouraging foreign investment, (5) improving the market system, (6) introducing basic improvements in the infrastructure, and (7) improving the educational and health systems.

The less developed nations might choose a market system or a more socialized, welfare state path to economic development. Actions that strengthen the market system in the less developed nations have brought about economic growth, but the benefits of this growth have not been evenly distributed among the populations of these countries.

REVIEWING THE CHAPTER

BUILDING VOCABULARY

Match each item in Column A with its definition in Column B.

Column A	Column B
1. more developed country	*a.* an agricultural system in which each family produces just enough to feed itself
2. less developed country	*b.* the number of years a newly born infant is expected to live
3. family planning	*c.* large-scale starvation due to lack of food
4. life expectancy	*d.* a largely agricultural nation with low per capita GDP
5. infant mortality rate	*e.* efforts to limit the number of children that couples have
6. subsistence farming	*f.* the percentage of the adult population who can read and write
7. land reform	*g.* a stage in the economic growth of a country
8. takeoff	*h.* an industrialized nation with high per capita GDP
9. famine	*i.* government efforts to break up large landholdings
10. literacy rate	*j.* the number of infants per 1,000 born who die before their first birthday

UNDERSTANDING WHAT YOU HAVE READ

1. Which *one* of the following describes an aspect of life that is more characteristic of more developed than less developed countries? (*a*) a high birthrate (*b*) a shortage of capital goods (*c*) widespread poverty (*d*) a large, industrial labor force.

2. Roads, water supply, and communications networks are part of a nation's (*a*) infrastructure (*b*) subsistence farming (*c*) foreign aid (*d*) social order.

3. Land reform is frequently suggested as a key to solving some of the economic problems of less developed countries. Land reform is (*a*) the application of scientific farming methods (*b*) the use by farmers of only their most fertile land (*c*) programs that enable farmers to own land (*d*) a soil conservation program.

4. As compared to the more developed countries, less developed countries usually have (*a*) greater political stability (*b*) a greater willingness to accept change (*c*) a higher percentage of their GDP devoted to agriculture (*d*) larger accumulations of capital.

5. Which *one* of the following is an international organization known best for lending capital to needy nations for development projects? (*a*) World Bank (*b*) United Arab Emirates (*c*) European Union (*d*) OPEC.

6. According to W.W. Rostow, which of the following is *not* one of the five stages of economic growth? (*a*) traditional society (*b*) increased tribal loyalties (*c*) takeoff (*d*) high mass consumption.

7. A major problem facing less developed nations is (*a*) slow population growth (*b*) rapid industrialization (*c*) high living standards (*d*) low output per farmer.

8. The reason that the less developed nations are poor is that they (*a*) are located in Africa, Asia, and Latin America (*b*) are not yet industrialized (*c*) have a relatively small percentage of their population working on farms (*d*) have high rates of savings.

9. Less developed countries are (*a*) all exactly alike (*b*) likely to enjoy high life expectancy, high literary rates, and low birthrates (*c*) greater in number than more developed countries (*d*) incapable of change.

10. Japan is one of the world's leading industrial nations. This fact proves that (*a*) development is not limited to Europe and North America (*b*) only nations in Western Europe and North America are developed (*c*) it is relatively easy for a nation to industrialize (*d*) the Japanese people are naturally smarter than most other people.

THINKING CRITICALLY

1. The less developed nations need to accumulate capital goods in order to increase their productive output. Capital formation may be financed through *personal savings, taxation, borrowing,* or *aid from sources outside their own country.*
   a. With reference to *three* of the italicized items above, explain how each serves to finance capital formation.
   b. For *each* item you have selected, explain the problems that a developing nation might face in applying that method to finance capital formation.

2. Imagine that you are an economic adviser to the president of the United States. The leader of a less developed country in Asia visits you and asks your government for a loan of $40 billion to improve her nation's infrastructure, including hospitals, roads, schools, and communication networks. Your analysis shows that in the past much of the foreign grants and loans to this nation have been wasted or have gone into the hands of corrupt officials. Without U.S. help, however, the economy might collapse and a revolution or political coup might take place.
   a. Describe the economic, political, and strategic issues involved in this request.
   b. Based on your analysis, what would you advise the president to do?

3. A major problem facing the less developed nations is poverty. Economists have advised achieving economic development by opening up a country's markets, deregulating industries, privatizing state-owned industries, and promoting fiscal responsibility. Where such measures have been applied, however, economic growth has not reduced poverty. In fact, the gap between the rich and poor has widened. Because of this widening gap, some Latin American nations might imitate the economic policies of socialist countries rather than those of the United States.

a. What are the advantages and disadvantages of industrialization to a less developed nation?

b. Would you recommend that any areas of the economy of a less developed nation be in government hands? Explain your answer.

c. Is it in the interest of the U.S. government and people to be concerned with the problems of people in less developed countries? Explain your answer.

SKILLS: Constructing and Analyzing a Map of Economic Development

Use Table 25.1 on page 569 to help you construct a map of economic development in the world today. Do your work on an outline map of the world.

1. To get a better picture of where the more developed and less developed nations of the world are located, color yellow those nations that fit the description of less developed. Color green those nations that seem to be on the road to development, and color blue the developed nations.

   Use the following as guidelines to decide what stage of development a country has reached.

Stages of Development	Per Capita GDP	Energy Consumption Per Capita (kWh)	Percent of GDP Devoted to Agriculture
More Developed	$10,000+	5,000+	less than 6%
On Road to Development	$1,000–9,999	1,000–4,999	6–20%
Less Developed	under $1,000	below 1,000	more than 20 percent

2. (a) Using the same map, label all of the following regions: North America, Central America, South America, Western Europe, Eastern Europe and Russia, Middle East, Africa, South Asia, Southeast Asia, and East Asia. (b) Although you are working with a limited number of the nations of the world, what generalizations can you suggest concerning where (1) most of the more developed nations are located? (2) those that are on the road to development are located? (3) most of the less developed nations are located?

3. Mark with diagonal lines going like this (\\\\) those nations from the table whose literacy rate is 91 percent or greater; and use diagonal lines going like this (///) for nations whose literacy rate is 50–90 percent. What generalizations can you make with regard to the relationship between a nation's literacy rate and its level of economic development?

4. For extra credit, improve your map by gathering information about other nations of the world and adding the correct coloring and shadings of these nations to your map. You can find comparative international statistics in the *Statistical Abstract of the United States, The World Almanac, World Bank Atlas,* and *Information Please Almanac.*

USING THE INTERNET

- The World Bank prepares numerous studies and statistical data on the less developed countries. A branch of the World Bank, the International Development Association, provides long-term, no-interest loans to the poorest of these. Start at <<www.worldbank.org>>. From this point, you can enter many of their various locations centering on different areas of interest.

- The International Monetary Fund, like the World Bank, prepares studies, data, and research on economic and social conditions in the developing world. You might begin at their Web site at <<www.imf.org>>.

- The impact of microcredit in developing countries is emphasized at the Grameen Web site at <<www.grameen-info.org/mcredit/unreport.html>>.

- The Volunteer Services Overseas is a British organization that seeks experienced professionals for volunteer work to help fight poverty around the world. Their Web site is <<www.vso.org.uk/index.htm>>.

- Poverty Fighters is a group that helps coordinate efforts of institutions that raise and provide microcredit to individuals in developing countries. Their work and success stories may be found at <<www.povertyfighters.com>>.

GLOSSARY

ability-to-pay principle the idea that people who are best able to afford to pay taxes should pay more than others

absolute advantage a situation whereby one nation can produce a good or service at a lower cost than another nation

acceleration principle (or **accelerator)** the idea that small changes in consumption lead to proportionately greater changes in investment

administrative red tape bureaucrats' efforts to slow down the government's approval process

ad valorem **tariff** a tax on imports calculated as a percentage of their value

advertising paid announcements (**ads**) that call attention to one's products or services in hopes of attracting customers

affirmative action the active hiring and promotion of members of certain groups because of past patterns of discrimination

after-tax income the income that remains after paying taxes

agency shop a workplace where nonunion workers are required to pay dues to the union that represents them

aggregate demand the total of all spending by all sectors of the nation's economy: consumers, businesses, and government

allocate to assign parts of a whole

annual percentage rate (APR) the percentage cost of credit on a purchase, figured on a yearly basis

annual report a report by a company on its financial operations over the past year

annuity a fund purchased for a fixed sum in order to provide periodic income at a later time

antitrust law legislation that limits monopolistic practices

arbitration the process of settling a labor-management dispute by which an impartial third party renders a binding decision

arbitrator the third party in arbitration

arithmetic progression a sequence of numbers in which each number is increased by the same amount (e.g., 1, 2, 3, 4, etc.)

assessment the official determination of the value of a property

asset anything of value that is owned by an individual or a business

automated teller machine (ATM) a bank device that allows a customer to make deposits and withdrawals

automatic stabilizer a feature built into an economic system that automatically compensates for changes in the business cycle

automation the substitution of modern machinery for human labor in the production process

average unit costs total production costs divided by the total output

balanced budget one in which planned income and expenses are equal

balanced fund a mutual fund that invests in both stocks and bonds

balance of payments a financial statement that summarizes a nation's economic transactions with the rest of the world

balance of trade the difference between the cost of a nation's merchandise imports and the value of its merchandise exports

balance sheet a financial report that summarizes the assets, liabilities, and net worth of an individual or organization

bank card a plastic card used to facilitate electronic funds transfers (includes credit cards, debit cards, and ATM cards)

bank reserves the funds a bank sets aside to meet withdrawal demands

bankruptcy a legal declaration that a firm is unable to pay its debts

barter the exchange of a good or service for another good or service

bear an investor who acts in expectation that the price of a stock will decline

beneficial externality a side effect of an economic activity that provides a source of enjoyment for the public

beneficiary an individual named in an insurance policy who is to receive benefits

benefits-received principle the idea that taxes should be paid by those who will benefit from the money collected

bilateral having to do with two nations

bimetallic monetary standard a money system based on the ability to exchange currency for two metals, usually gold and silver

blank endorsement a check endorsement that transfers title to anyone holding the check

block grant federal aid to a state or local government to achieve broad policy goals

blue-collar worker one employed in craft, operative, or manual labor

board of directors the elected representatives of the stockholders of a corporation

bond a certificate issued by a unit of government or a corporation in exchange for a long-term loan

bond fund a mutual fund that invests only in bonds

bourgeoisie people of the middle class

boycott an organized refusal to buy goods or services from a company

brand name an adopted name given by a producer or seller to a good or service to distinguish it as produced or sold by that producer or seller

Bretton Woods system a worldwide money system based on the U.S. government promise to exchange dollars presented by foreign countries for gold at the rate of $35 an ounce

broker one who carries out customers' orders to buy and sell securities

budget a plan for dealing with future income and expenses

bull an investor who believes that the price of a stock will rise

bull market a general rise in prices of stocks

business cycle the fluctuations in a nation's economic activity

buying long purchasing securities in the expectation of selling them later at a higher price

by-product a secondary good produced along with a major item of production

capacity maximum output in the short run

capital machines, tools, buildings, and other things used to produce goods and services; money

capital account the summary of capital movements in a balance of payments statement

capital consumption the sums that all businesses set aside in a year to replace worn-out plant and equipment; also called **depreciation**

capital formation the production of capital goods

capital gain the profit realized from the sale of an asset

capital goods goods used to produce other goods

capital growth the increase in value of a stock over time

capitalism an economic system in which most of the resources of production are privately owned, and most economic decisions are made by individuals and business firms

capital movement an investment, loan, or gift from one country to another to settle differences between a country's imports and its exports

capital resource *see* **capital**

career an individual's lifelong work

cartel a group of sellers who formally agree among themselves to restrict output so as to control prices of their products

cash flow the movement of cash into and out of a business. If cash inflow exceeds the outflow, it is a **positive cash flow**; if the reverse, it is a **negative cash flow**.

cash in vault money that a bank has on hand to use

cash value the amount of money an individual will receive if an insurance policy is redeemed before its due date

caveat emptor "let the buyer beware"

ceiling price a maximum, government-set price for something

central bank a national institution that supervises other banks in a country; sometimes called a **national bank**

certificate of deposit (CD) a savings instrument in which a buyer agrees not to withdraw his or her deposit for a set period of time

certify to approve something officially

ceteris paribus the assumption that all things other than what is being considered will stay the same

charge account an arrangement that allows account holders to purchase goods on credit

charter a government license for people to form a corporation

check a written order directing a depository institution to pay a sum of money

checkable deposits balances in bank accounts that offer check-writing privileges

checkbook money that portion of the money supply represented by checkable deposits

checkoff a clause in some union contracts that requires the employer to withhold union dues from workers' paychecks

circular flow the movement of money, goods, and services through the economy

clearing a check the process whereby a bank deducts the amount of a check from the account of the person who wrote it

climate the pattern of the weather in a place over a long time

closed shop a business in which only workers belonging to a specified union may be hired

coincident indicator a set of data whose up and down movements parallel the business cycle

collaboration active cooperation

collateral any item of value that a lender may seize should a borrower default on a loan

collective bargaining a series of discussions between representatives of a union and representatives of management to arrive at a contract that will spell out the terms of employment

collision insurance financial protection from damage in an accident caused to a motor vehicle of an insured person

collusion a secret agreement or agreements among competing firms, usually to limit competition

command economy one in which decisions to allocate resources are made by the government

commercial bank a privately owned institution that provides a wide array of financial services, especially to business customers

commodity inflation general price increases caused by run-ups in the prices of key goods

common stock a stock that entitles its owners to vote for candidates to the board of directors

commune an community of farmers who work collectively

communism an economic and political system in which all property is publicly owned and the government makes all WHAT, WHO, and HOW decisions

comparative advantage the principle that a nation should specialize in the production of those goods and services in which it is most efficient, and trade its surplus goods and services for the things it needs

competition the rivalry for goods and services among buyers and among sellers

compound interest the interest earned on the principal and on the interest already earned

concentration ratio the percentage of an industry's output that is produced by its four largest firms

conditional sales contract an installment plan contract in which title to goods sold remains with the seller until the final payment is made

conglomerate merger one that combines firms that produce unrelated products

constant dollar a value of the dollar that has been adjusted to eliminate the effects of inflation or deflation

consumer one who buys goods and services for personal use

consumer cooperative a retail business owned by some or all of its customers

Consumer Price Index (CPI) a series of index numbers measuring changes in the level of prices over a period of time

consumer sovereignty the freedom consumers have to choose which goods and services to buy

consumption the act of buying final goods or services

contraction the phase of a business cycle during which economic activity is in decline

cooperative an association of individuals who wish to buy, market, or produce products as a group

coordination the way in which an economic system answers the WHAT, HOW, and WHO questions

copyright a government grant of legal control over literary, musical, and artistic works

corporate income tax one on net profits of incorporated businesses

corporate officer one of the top managers of a corporation, usually appointed by its board of directors

corporation a business chartered under state or federal law and owned by its stockholders

cost-benefit analysis a weighing of the costs and benefits of something to reach a numerical answer

cost-push inflation a rise in the level of prices caused by an increase in the cost of doing business

countercyclical fiscal policy one calculated to check excessive developments in a business cycle

counterfeit to produce something illegally

craft a skilled occupation

craft union an organization of members of the same skilled trade

creative destruction the economic theory that says that in order for a firm to remain competitive, it must be prepared to modify, revise, and/or abandon existing processes and products in favor of new ones

credit card a piece of plastic that allows holders to purchase goods and services on credit at participating businesses

credit history a record of how one has paid bills and repaid loans

credit union a depository institution whose members are its depositors and borrowers

currency that part of the money supply consisting of paper money and coins

current account the summary of all imports and exports of goods, services, income, and unilateral transfers in a balance of payments

current dollars dollar values or prices that have not been adjusted for inflation or deflation

cyclical unemployment the status of workers who have lost their job because of insufficient demand for goods and services during the downswing of a business cycle

debit card a plastic card that may be used in the same way as a check to purchase goods and services, which are immediately charged to the purchaser's checking or savings account

debtor one who owes money

deductible the initial portion of a year's worth of medical bills, not paid by the insurance company

deficit the status of a budget in which revenue is less than expenditures

deficit financing the policy of balancing a government budget with loans

deflation a general decline in prices

demand the quantity of a product or service that would be purchased at a particular price

demand curve a line on a graph that shows the amount of a product or service that will be purchased at each price

demand deposit an account in a bank that promises to pay on demand a specified amount of money

demand-pull inflation a rise in the level of prices caused by an increase in demand

democratic socialism an economic system with a command economy, elected government, and freedoms for the population and the press

deposit insurance federal guarantees of deposits of up to $100,000 in banks and thrift institutions

deposit multiplier the number of times deposits could be increased by the banking system for every dollar in reserves

depository institution a bank or thrift institution that holds funds or securities deposited by others

depreciation a decline in the value of capital assets caused by use, the passage of time, or both

depression a serious, long-lasting decline in a nation's business activity

deregulate to remove regulations

derived demand the demand for something that is caused by the demand for something else

devaluation a reduction in the price of one currency in terms of the currencies of other nations

developed country an industrialized country with relatively high GDP and income per capita

developing country one with a largely agricultural economy and relatively low income and GDP per capita

diminishing returns the point at which the extra output, resulting from the addition of more units of a productive factor, will begin to decline

direct deposit the transfer of funds, such as wages and tax refunds, by others directly into an individual's checking or savings account

direct payment the payment of bills electronically after customers authorize firms to deduct money from the customers' checking or savings accounts

direct tax a tax paid to a government by the person or business that is taxed; a tax that cannot be shifted

disability insurance financial protection from loss of income because of an extended illness or disability

discount rate the interest on loans that the Federal Reserve charges its member banks

discretionary fiscal policy a fiscal policy that the government may or may not use to regulate the economy

diseconomy of scale an increase in the cost of doing business that results when a business has grown too large

disposable income the income a person or family has left after paying personal taxes

dividends profits that are distributed by corporations to shareholders

division of labor the dividing of a production process into a series of jobs, thereby enabling workers to increase output through specialization

draft a written order, such as a check, on which one party directs a second party to pay a third party a sum of money

drawee the bank upon which a check is drawn

drawer the person writing a check

durable good a product that is expected to last several years

earned income tax credit a reduction in federal taxes for individuals and families who meet certain income and other guidelines

easy-money policy a Fed policy to expand the money supply

econometrics a branch of economics that uses mathematics and statistics in solving economic problems

economic efficiency a measure of how well a society uses its available resources to produce goods and services

economic growth the increase in output of goods and services over time; an increase over time in either real GDP or real GDP per capita

economic indicator a set of statistics about the performance of a sector of the nation's economy; often classified as either **coincident, leading,** or **lagging**

economic model a simplified representation (verbal, graphic, or mathematical) of an economic problem

economics the study of how people and societies use limited resources to satisfy unlimited wants

economic stability a period of modest changes in the level of prices, employment, and business activity

economic system the way in which a society answers the WHAT, HOW, and WHO questions

economy of scale a reduction in the cost of doing business that results from increases in the size of operations

educational attainment the number of years of school completed or degrees obtained

elastic currency one that expands and contracts with the needs of businesses

elasticity of demand the extent to which total spending for an item will fluctuate with changes in prices

elasticity of supply the extent to which the total spending for an item will fluctuate with changes in supply

electronic funds transfer (EFT) the transfer of funds electronically

embargo a ban on importing goods

embezzlement the stealing of funds from a firm, union, or other organization by an insider

eminent domain the right of government to acquire private property for public use by paying a reasonable price to the owner

endorsement the act of passing title to a check to another party

energy consumption per capita a nation's total energy consumption divided by its population

energy efficiency the relative amount of energy used to run an appliance or vehicle

EnergyGuide label one that provides an estimate of the yearly cost of operating an appliance and how that appliance compares in energy usage with competing products

energy tax a tax on the consumption of energy

Engel's Law the rule that as a family's income increases, the percentage spent on food decreases, while the percentage spent on luxuries, medical care, personal care, and savings increases

entitlements programs that automatically provide benefits to specified classes of individuals

entrepreneur a person who gathers together the factors of production to create and operate a business enterprise in the hope of earning profits

entrepreneurship the process of bringing together the factors of production

equation of exchange $MV = PQ$, where M equals the money supply, V equals velocity, P equals the average price paid, and Q equals the quantity of goods and services produced

equilibrium price the price at which the quantity of a good or service supplied equals the amount demanded

equity financing a corporation's method of obtaining capital by selling its stock

equity fund a mutual fund that invests only in corporate stocks

escalator clause a section of a union contract that ties wage increases to a cost-of-living index

estate planning the sum of all actions one takes to accumulate wealth to leave to one's heirs and to determine how to divide the estate among the heirs

estate tax a tax levied on a person's money or property at the time of death

euro the common currency of a number of European Union countries

excess reserves the funds held by a bank that are above the reserve requirement

exchange rate the amount of one currency that can be purchased for a certain amount of another currency

excise tax a tax on the manufacture, sale, or use of a good or service

exemption a deduction from earnings that are subject to income tax (given to individuals and their dependents)

expansion the phase of a business cycle during which the economy advances out of a trough

expenditures approach a way of calculating GDP by measuring purchases by consumers, businesses, and government, and by international buyers of U.S. goods and services

exports a nation's goods and services that are sold abroad

external causes events outside the economy that cause changes in the business cycle

external cost a business expense paid for by society as a whole

external debt money that the federal government owes to foreign institutions and individuals

externality an economic activity that is paid for or enjoyed by those who had neither produced nor consumed it

face value the dollar value of a security or insurance policy as printed on its face

fact-finding board one that investigates issues in a labor dispute and makes a report

factor of production a resource (such as labor, land, or capital) that is used to produce a good or service

family planning efforts to limit the size of families

famine a desperate shortage of food affecting large numbers of people

favorable balance of trade an excess in the value of merchandise exports over imports

federal funds rate the interest that banks charge one another for overnight loans of funds necessary to maintain their reserve balances in Federal Reserve banks

Federal Reserve note paper currency issued by the Federal Reserve System

fiat currency standard a money system that is not based on metals

final goods products sold at retail

finance charge the total amount one pays to use credit in a purchase

financial assistance cash payments by a government to individuals in need

financial plan a statement of one's goals that will cost money and the means of achieving those goals

financial resources money or assets that can be converted into money

fire insurance financial protection for the insured for damages caused by a fire to a home or other buildings and to furnishings

fiscal policy the use by the government of its powers to tax and spend in order to regulate the economy

fiscal year an accounting period of 12 months

five-year plan a detailed statement of a nation's production goals (and means of attaining them) for a five-year period

fixed costs those that remain unchanged regardless of the number of units a business produces

flat tax a tax with a single rate that is applied to all income above a certain level

floating exchange rate the value of a nation's currency that moves up and down to reflect roughly the laws of supply and demand

fluctuate to move up and down in value

401(k) plan a fund run by an employer into which a worker (and sometimes the employer) contributes to provide income upon retirement

fractional currency U.S. coins that are worth less than $1

fractional reserve banking a system in which only a fraction of the total deposits managed by each bank must be kept in reserve

frictional unemployment the status of workers who have left one job and are likely soon to find another

fringe benefit the compensation received by employees in addition to wages

full employment the condition in which all of an economy's resources are being utilized

full endorsement a check endorsement that transfers title of the check to a specific party

GDP per capita total value of all goods and services produced by a national economy in a year divided by the population

geometric progression a sequence of numbers in which the ratio of one number to its predecessor is always the same (e.g., 2, 4, 16, etc.)

gift tax a federal tax on gifts in excess of specified limits

glasnost a Soviet policy introduced by Mikhail Gorbachev that encouraged public discussion and criticism

global economy the combined economies of all nations

globalization the reduction of barriers to the movement of goods and services, workers, and capital among nations

global warming the idea that the Earth's surface temperatures are increasing over time

goldsmith a person who makes and sells articles of gold for a living

gold standard the tying of the value of a nation's currency to a fixed amount of gold

good a tangible item of value

goods-producing industry one that primarily makes goods

goodwill the value of a firm's intangible assets, such as its reputation or location

grant-in-aid a payment by one level of government to a lower one, usually designated to be spent for a specific purpose

Great Depression the severe economic downturn in the United States and elsewhere, 1929–1939

greenhouse effect the trapping of the sun's heat by atmospheric gases

Gresham's Law the idea that cheap money drives out expensive money

grievance a formal complaint by a union member against his or her employer

grievance machinery established methods of resolving complaints filed by union members against their employer

gross domestic product (GDP) the total value of all goods and services produced by a national economy in a year

gross expenses total of all expenses other than selling costs

gross income total sales minus selling costs

gross pay one's paycheck before any payroll deductions are made

gross private domestic investment the sum of business spending for new equipment, construction, and changes in business inventories

gross receipts tax one levied on a business firm's retail and wholesale sales

harmful externality a side effect of an economic activity, one that imposes costs on the public

hidden tax one included in the selling price of a good or service without the buyer knowing about it

holding company a corporation that has a controlling interest in the shares of one or more other corporations

home equity loan a consumer loan in which one's home is used as collateral

home mortgage a pledge of one's home as security for a loan to buy the home

homeowner's insurance protection to cover costs of various types of potential risks to the owner of a home

horizontal merger a merger of two or more firms that produce competing products

hospital insurance that part of health insurance that will pay all or part of the costs incurred in a hospital stay (other than surgical and doctors' fees)

human resources the people whose efforts and skills go into the production of goods and services

identity theft the assumption by criminals of the identity of a person for the purpose of gaining access to that person's financial accounts or obtaining credit in the name of that person

imperfect competition market classification falling between monopoly and perfect competition and consisting of **monopolistic competition** and **oligopoly**

import a good and service that is purchased from abroad

import restriction the imposition of a tariff, quota, or outright ban on foreign products as a means of protecting the domestic producers of those products

income approach a way of calculating GDP by measuring the total income of all employees and businesses

income security government welfare

incomes policy government efforts to control inflation by limiting increases in wages and prices

income statement a summary of the financial activities of a firm over a period of time

income tax a tax on a person's or company's income after certain items have been deducted

index number one showing percentage change of a variable from a base year

indirect tax a tax that can be shifted from the person or business taxed to someone else, who is frequently unaware of that fact

individual income tax one on the earnings of individuals and unincorporated businesses

individual retirement account (IRA) a fund into which an individual may pay a limited amount each year to provide income upon retirement

industrial production index a measure of changes in output in the nation's factories, mines, and utilities

Industrial Revolution a period of rapid mechanization of a nation's industry

inelastic demand a market situation in which a decrease in price results in a less than proportionate increase in the quantity demanded, and *vice versa*

infant industry an industry that is newly developed

infant mortality rate the number of babies (out of every 1,000 live births) who die before their first birthday

inflation a general rise in prices

inflationary gap the excess of aggregate demand over total output at full employment

infrastructure the physical capital that supports a society's activities (roads, power lines, water facilities, schools, etc.)

inheritance tax a tax levied on the property of a person who has died

injunction a court order to cease a certain activity

innovation a new way of doing something

installment plan a method of purchasing something on credit with payments scheduled over time

insurance a way of protecting oneself and others against money losses by sharing the risks with others

interest rate the price paid to borrow money

interlocking directorate a situation in which the same people sit on the boards of directors of competing firms

internal causes events within the economy that trigger changes in the business cycle

internal cost a business expense paid for by the firm incurring it

internal debt money that the federal government owes to U.S. institutions and individuals

Internet banking a system that allows individuals and firms to use the Internet to perform banking activities

inventory the goods that a business has on hand to sell and the materials used in their manufacture

inventory on demand a method of obtaining supplies needed for manufacturing only just before they are needed

inverse the reverse of

investing the use of savings to buy something that is expected to increase in value

investment that which people or institutions purchase while investing

investment bank an institution that underwrites corporations' issuing of stocks and bonds

investment-grade bond a bond ranked Baa or BBB and above

investor one who buys something of value for income and/or long-term growth

job outlook the chances of finding work in a particular occupation, region, or season

job security union-management agreements that make it difficult to dismiss workers without good cause

junk bond a highly risky bond ranked below investment grade

jurisdictional strike one caused by a dispute between two unions over which one can represent certain workers

keiretsu a closely knit network of business firms in Japan

labor the factor of production involving human effort

labor contract a written agreement between an employer and a union

labor force the number of people 16 years of age, or older, who are working or looking for work

labor productivity output per worker per time period

Laffer Curve a graphic representation of the relationship between tax rates and resulting tax revenues

lagging indicator a set of data that experiences the ups and downs of business activity some time after it occurs in the business cycle

laissez-faire a government's policy of not interfering with its nation's economy

land reform the breakup by a government of large estates into smaller, farmer-owned plots

Law of Demand the principle that the demand for a good or service varies inversely with its price

Law of Diminishing Returns the principle that in adding factors of production, a firm eventually reaches a point where productivity begins to decline

Law of Supply the principle that the quantity of a good or service supplied varies directly with its price

lawsuit a legal action in court taken against one individual or group against another

leading indicator a set of data that experiences the ups and downs of business activity some time before it occurs in the business cycle

legal tender a currency that by law must be accepted in payment of debt

less developed country (LDC). *See* **developing country**

leverage the use of borrowed funds to finance business operations

liability an obligation or debt

liability insurance financial protection for the insured against lawsuits for injuries to other persons or damages to their property

life expectancy the number of years the average newly born infant is expected to live

life insurance a policy that provides for a specified payment to one or more beneficiaries upon the insured's death

limited liability the legal exemption of stockholders from the debts of the corporation in which they own stock

limited liability company (LLC) one that combines the advantages of a corporation (limited liability) with those of a partnership (no double taxation)

line of credit a bank's arrangement with a firm that allows the firm to borrow whenever it needs money, up to a stated limit

liquidate to sell off the assets of a firm and go out of business

liquidity the ease with which an investment vehicle can be turned into cash

literacy rate the percentage of the adult population who can read and write

lockout the shutting down of a plant by management in hopes of getting its union workers to agree to certain contract proposals

long run a period of time during which any or all of the factors of production could vary

long-term financing loans that need to be repaid after a year or more

long-term goal one that you would expect to take more than a year to achieve

luxury a nonessential good or service that adds comfort and pleasure to life

M1 the nation's money supply as measured by the total currency, checkbook money, and traveler's checks in circulation on any given day

M2 the nation's money supply as measured by M1 plus individual savings accounts, money market funds, and certain foreign assets

M3 the nation's money supply as measured by M2 plus business and other large savings accounts

macroeconomics the study of the forces affecting the economy as a whole

managed capitalism a market economy with strong government intervention and cooperation among corporations

margin a down payment required when purchasing securities on credit

marginal analysis *see* **marginalism**

marginal cost the addition to costs resulting from the production of one extra unit

marginalism the evaluation of the usefulness of adding one more of an item to the production of a good or service

marginal productivity the value of the output of the last worker hired by a company

marginal propensity to consume (MPC) the rate at which the public spends as national income goes up

marginal propensity to save (MPS) the rate at which the public saves as national income goes up

marginal revenue the income from the production of one more unit

marginal utility the additional usefulness received from each added unit of a product or service

market a place where goods and services are bought and sold

market economy one in which the allocation of resources is determined by the free operation of the forces of supply and demand and market prices

market failure the inability of a market to allocate resources efficiently

market power the ability of buyers and sellers to influence prices

market price *see* **equilibrium price**

market risk the possibility that the value of an investment will be low when one wants to sell

mass production the making of a product in quantity, usually with machinery

maturity the date at which a bond is set to be redeemed at face value

maximize to make the most of

maximum employment a goal whereby everyone who wants to work has a job

maximum production the level at which entrepreneurs believe it no longer profitable to add more workers, land, or capital to the production process

maximum purchasing power consumers' ability to buy the greatest amount possible with limited numbers of dollars

median retirement age the age of retirement at which half of all new retirees are older and half are younger

mediation a nonbinding process in which an impartial party, or **mediator**, tries to bring both sides in a labor dispute into agreement

medical insurance protection from the costs of hospitalization, surgery, medicines, and general medical care

medium of exchange something readily accepted in payment for goods or services

mercantilism a set of economic practices of the 16th to 18th centuries based on the premise that a nation's wealth could be measured by its holdings of gold and silver

merger the absorption of one or more firms by another

merit pay a system of compensation based on the idea that those who perform better are paid more

microeconomics the study of the effects of economic forces on individual parts of the economy

mint to manufacture coins; a place where coins are made

monetary policies the actions taken by the Federal Reserve System to regulate the nation's supply of money and credit

monetary standard the commodity or benchmark that a society chooses to use for its money

money market fund a mutual fund that invests in short-term credit instruments such as Treasury bills

monopolistic competition a market situation in which there are many firms selling similar items on the basis of product differentiation

monopoly a market situation in which there is only one seller of a particular good or service

monopoly power the ability of a group of firms to act as if it were a monopoly

monopsony a market that has only one buyer

more developed country (MDC). *See* **developed country**

mortgage a pledge of property as security for a loan

most-favored-nation clause a treaty provision requiring a signatory to extend the same preferential trade terms to other signatories that it extends to a nonsignatory

motor vehicle insurance financial protection to help pay the costs of damages and injuries incurred as a result of a motor vehicle accident

multilateral having to do with many nations

multinational corporation a firm that has operations in two or more countries

multiplier (or multiplier effect) a numerical factor by which an increase in investment or spending is multiplied to find the effect on national income

mutual fund a corporation that uses the proceeds from the sale of its stocks to purchase the securities of other corporations

mutual savings bank a bank that is owned by its depositors

national debt the total of all money owed by the federal government

national income the total of incomes earned by individuals and business firms in the production of the GDP

nationalize to take control by the government of private industries

national union a labor group organized on a national level

natural resource a factor of production obtained from the land, sea, or air

necessity a product or service needed to sustain daily life

net exports the difference between a country's imports and exports of goods and services in a year

net income gross income minus expenses (also known as **net profit**)

net interest the difference between the total interest received and that paid out by all businesses in a year

net worth the value of a business as measured by its assets minus its liabilities

no-fault insurance financial protection whereby the injured party in a motor vehicle accident is paid by her or his insurance company, regardless of who was responsible for the accident

nominal interest rate the rate of return on a loan expressed in today's dollars

nondurable good a product that is quickly consumed or worn out

nonrenewable resource one incapable of being replaced or renewed

not-for-profit-corporation one organized to provide a social, educational, or other nonbusiness service, rather than to earn a profit

NOW (negotiable order of withdrawal) account a checking account that pays interest on deposited money

offshore tax shelter a strategy for avoiding certain U.S. taxes by opening an office in foreign countries where the taxes are lower

oligopoly a market dominated by only a few sellers

on-the-job training a program whereby workers earn money while they are learning a skill

open market operations the buying and selling of government bonds by the Federal Open Market Committee

open shop a workplace in which the employer is free to hire either union or nonunion workers

opportunity cost the amount of goods and services that must be done without in order to obtain another good or service

outlay an expenditure

output the total value of goods or services produced by a firm

outsource to have certain tasks done by employees of another firm, sometimes in another country

over-the-counter market places where stocks are bought and sold other than the stock exchanges

paradox of thrift the assertion that if individuals increase the level of their savings, society as a whole will have less to save

parity a price that gives farmers the same purchasing power from the sale of their goods that they enjoyed during certain base years

partnership an unincorporated business owned by two or more people

patent a government grant giving ownership rights to an invention

payee the person to whom a check is payable

payroll tax one levied on a business firm's payroll

peak the upper turning point of a business cycle

perestroika attempts at restructuring the Soviet economy under Mikhail Gorbachev to allow elements of free enterprise

perfect competition a market in which there are many buyers and sellers, none of whom alone can affect prices

personal consumption expenditures spending by consumers

personal income the total income received by all individuals before they pay income taxes

personal property tax a tax on one's property other than real estate

Phillips Curve a graph illustrating the trade-off between inflation and unemployment

picketing the marching of workers with signs outside a place of business, usually to proclaim a strike

pollution haven effect the result of having industrial firms in countries with strong environmental laws relocate to countries with lax environmental rules or lax enforcement

pool an agreement among two or more firms to share the market for their products and to fix prices

pork (or **pork-barrel legislation)** laws passed mainly to benefit people and businesses in an electoral district so that voters will reelect the legislators who supported the laws

preferred stock the shares of stock that are entitled to a fixed dividend before profits are distributed to holders of common stock

price-earnings ratio the current market price of a security divided by its earnings per share

price floor the minimum, government-set price for a commodity

price leadership a characteristic of an oligopoly by which firms match each other's price increases and decreases

price makers firms that can affect the price of the goods they sell by increasing or decreasing output

price rigidity a situation of having prices that are slow to adjust to changes in supply and/or demand

price supports a government program that sets a floor on the selling price of some farm products by offering to buy the products at that floor

price takers firms whose level of production will not affect the price of the goods they sell

principal the face value of a loan

private good or service one consumed by the person or family that pays for it

privatization the transformation of a publicly owned business into a privately owned one

producer cooperative an organization of producers who share in the costs of buying equipment and supplies and in marketing

product differentiation the creation by sellers of the appearance that their products are different from those of their competitors, while, in fact, they are similar

production possibilities curve a graph showing the various combinations of goods and services that an economy might produce if all its resources were fully and effectively employed

productive capacity the amount of goods and services that the economy is able to produce at a given time

productivity a measure of the efficiency of a factor of production as measured by *output per unit of input*

profit the income that remains after the costs of doing business have been deducted from the receipts of the sale of goods and services

profit maximization efforts to earn the greatest profits

profit motive the desire of business owners to earn the greatest profits

progressive tax one that increases in the percentage paid as the taxpayer's income increases

proletariat people of the working class

promissory note a written promise to repay a loan, plus interest, by a specific date

propensity to consume the tendency to spend a portion of one's income

propensity to save the tendency to save a portion of one's income

property insurance financial protection against loss or damage to an insured person's property

proportional tax one that applies the same rate to all persons regardless of their income

proprietors' income the profits earned by the owners of the nation's unincorporated businesses

prospectus a document for investors that describes the operations of a company that is issuing new securities

protective tariff a tax whose primary purpose is to protect domestic production from foreign competition

public franchise a government license to a business for an exclusive market

public good or service one that can be consumed by any or all members of society regardless of who pays for it

public utility an industry that produces a good or service in the public interest

purchasing power a measure of how much goods and services a dollar can buy at a given time

quality circle a team of employees who work together to solve production problems

quality of life how well the average person lives

quota a limit on the importation of a good; a limit on how much a producer can produce

rate of population growth the percentage that a population increases over a set period of time

real estate (or **real property**) land and buildings

real GDP (or **real gross domestic product**) the measurement of gross domestic product in constant dollars (dollars of a base year)

real GDP per capita the GDP of a country as expressed in constant dollars divided by the population

real interest rate the nominal interest rate minus the inflation rate

real property tax one on the value of land or anything permanently attached to it

recession a contraction in economic activity that lasts for six months or more

recessionary gap the amount by which aggregate demand falls short of the total needed to sustain full employment

reciprocal the reverse of something

recovery the expansion phase of a business cycle

redeem to convert a note, bond, or insurance policy to the issuer for cash

regional trade bloc a group of countries of the same region that have made a trade agreement

regressive tax one that takes a larger proportion of the earnings of people with low incomes than of those with higher incomes

renewable resource one capable of being replaced or renewed

reserve ratio (or **reserve requirement**) the percentage of its total deposits that a bank is required to keep in its Federal Reserve district bank or as cash in its vaults

resource a factor of production

restrictive endorsement a check endorsement that restricts how funds are to be used

retained earnings profits of a business that are not distributed to its owners

revenue income from sales of goods and services

revenue tariff a tax on imports whose primary purpose is to generate income for the government

revolving charge account one that entitles a buyer of different items at different times to repay on a monthly basis a portion of the outstanding balance

right to private property a principle that allows individuals to own property, use it, and depose of it in any lawful manner that they choose

right-to-work law a state regulation that makes it illegal to require workers to join labor unions

risk the possibility of financial loss or physical injury

risk management identifying the risks that one is exposed to and taking steps to reduce the monetary costs that may occur

royalty payments to creative individuals (such as inventors, songwriters, and authors) by those who use their works

run on a bank large withdrawals from a bank by many depositors at the same time

sales tax one on the value of the retail sales of certain goods and services

savings any income that is not spent

savings and loan association (S&L) a financial institution whose funds are used primarily to finance home mortgages

scarcity the condition resulting from the fact that there is not enough of everything to go around

S-corporation a type of small corporation that has the tax benefits of a partnership

seasonal unemployment that brought on by the status of work in certain industries at particular times of the year

secured bond one backed by collateral

securities stocks and bonds

selling short selling stock that you do not own (that you borrow from a broker) in the hope of buying it back later at a lower price

seniority the number of years a worker is employed in a workplace

service an intangible item of value, such as medical care

service-producing industry one that sells mainly services

service worker one employed in a service industry (transportation, trade, finance, government, etc.)

shareholder (or stockholder) one who owns shares (stock) of a corporation

shifting the process of transferring the burden of a tax to another party

short run the operation of a plant using existing equipment

short-term financing loans that need to be repaid within a year

short-term goal one that you would expect to achieve within a year

silver certificate former U.S. paper currency that could be exchanged for silver

simple interest the interest earned on the principal alone

sin tax one on products or services that a legislature says are undesirable

slowdown a deliberate reduction of output by workers

socialism an economic system in which the means of production are owned by the state and resources are allocated through central planning

sole proprietorship an unincorporated business owned by one person

Special Drawing Rights (SDRs) credits to the accounts of member nations in the International Monetary Fund that can be used to purchase foreign currencies

specialization a situation in which each nation, region, or firm produces a narrow range of products or services

specific tariff a tax on imports calculated by a set amount per unit

speculator one who buys things of value to turn a quick profit

stagflation a period of both a recession and inflation

standard deduction a set dollar amount that reduces the amount of earnings on which an individual or family may be taxed (available to those who choose not to itemize deductions)

standard of living the quantity and quality of goods and services available to an individual or society

statement of cash flows a summary of a firm's sources and uses of cash over time

statistical discrepancy a line in a financial statement that summarizes errors in recording transactions

stock a certificate that represents ownership in a corporation

stock exchange a place where shares in major corporations are bought and sold

stock market a collective term for places where stocks are bought and sold

straight-life insurance life insurance that also provides for forced savings and cash value

strike a work stoppage by a firm's employees

strikebreaker (or scab) one hired to replace a striking union member

structural unemployment the status of workers who have lost their job because of changes in technology, consumer preferences, or the movement of job opportunities from one region to another

subsidy a government payment to a producer of a good or service

subsistence farming the operation of a farm that produces enough to feed the farm family, but not more

supply the amount of a product or service offered for sale at a particular price

supply curve a line on a graph that shows the amount of a product or service that would be offered for sale at each price

supply restrictions a federal government strategy to increase the price of domestic goods (usually farm goods) by limiting the amount that producers can produce

supply-side economics an economic theory that calls for a shift in the focus of government from the demand (consumption) side of the economy to the supply (production) side

surplus the status of a budget in which revenue is greater than expenditures

surplus value the difference between workers' wages and the value of the goods and services they produce

sustainable economic growth the idea that every generation should pass on a stock of net resources to future generations

take-home pay gross pay minus payroll deductions

takeoff a dramatic movement toward economic development that includes increased productivity

tariff a tax on imports

taxable income that portion of an individual's or firm's earnings that is subject to an income tax

tax avoidance efforts to lawfully minimize one's tax liability

tax credit the amount one can reduce one's tax liability because of one's poverty status or participation in certain activities

tax deduction an amount that individuals and families can deduct from their taxable income

tax exemption a set amount of one's income that can be exempted by law from income taxes for each member of a family

tax incidence the person on whom the burden of a tax ultimately falls

technological revolution rapid changes in the ways of producing goods and services

technology a culture's methods and tools for making things

term-life insurance life insurance, usually for a one-to-five-year period, that may be renewed, but at a higher premium each term

thrift institutions a term used for mutual savings banks, S&Ls, and credit unions

tight money a Fed policy that attempts to slow the growth of the money supply

time deposit a bank account for which the bank might require of the depositor an advance notice of a withdrawal

token money coins whose metallic value is less than their face value

trade credit a payment delay granted by one firm to another

trade-off the giving up of one thing to obtain something else

traditional economy one in which resources are allocated according to tradition and custom, and people make a living in the same way as they have done for a long time

transfer payment a government money payment to an individual for which nothing is received in return

traveler's check a check that one can purchase at most banks and can easily cash at most places of business

trickle-down economics the belief that tax benefits given to the rich help everyone in an economy because the rich will save and invest more of their income, which will grow the economy

trough the lowest point in a business cycle

trust a large business monopoly of the 19th century whose shareholders placed control of the firm in the hands of trustees

trustee an individual appointed to administer the affairs of a company

underconsumption a time when consumer expenditures lag behind output

underground economy the part of the economy whose activities are not included in official government statistics

underwrite to assume financial risk. **Securities underwriters** assume the risk of marketing newly issued securities; **insurance underwriters** assume the risks of the perils listed in the policies that they sell.

unemployment compensation state-operated periodic cash payments for a limited period to workers who have lost their job

unemployment rate the percentage of the labor force that is jobless, looking for work, and available to work if offered a job

unfavorable balance of trade an excess of merchandise imports over exports

unfunded mandate a requirement imposed by one level of government on a subordinate level to enact some program for which no financing is provided

unilateral transfer a gift from individuals or institutions of one country to those of another

unincorporated income tax a tax on net income of businesses that are not incorporated

uninsured motorists policy insurance coverage for damages to the vehicle and for injuries to the insured and his/her family in cases where an uninsured motorist or hit-and-run driver is legally responsible for the losses

union shop a firm that has a union contract that states nonunion members may be hired on condition that they join the union

United States notes paper currency issued by the U.S. Treasury Department

United States savings bond a security representing a small loan to the federal government. It promises to pay both principal and interest to the buyer of the bond many years later.

unit production costs the average costs of producing an item

unlimited liability a situation in a sole proprietorship or partnership whereby the personal property of any of the owners may be taken to pay the debts of the business

unsecured loan one with no backing other than the creditworthiness of the borrower

user tax one imposed only on those who use certain products or services

variable cost one that increases or decreases with the level of production

variable-rate mortgage one whose interest rate goes up or down as general interest rates rise or fall

vault a protected storage area of a bank

velocity the number of times a given dollar is spent over a specific time period

vertical merger a consolidation of two or more businesses that are each other's suppliers or customers

wage-price spiral an inflation marked by rising wages causing prices to rise *and* by rising prices causing wages to rise

wealth anything that has money value or exchangeable value

weapons of mass destruction (WMD) nuclear, biological, and chemical ones

white-collar worker one employed in a clerical, professional, or managerial occupation

will a legal document that specifies how one's assets are to be distributed upon one's death

worker mobility the willingness of workers to move to where jobs are

yield the rate of return on an investment based on the purchase price

zero economic growth the idea that the GDP should increase only enough to accommodate population growth

INDEX

Chief executive officer (CEO), 88
Chile, 579
China, 470, 491, 545, 553; Communism in, 554–556; family planning in, 580; GDP of, 555; inflation in, 555–556; labor force in, 578; U.S. trade with, 495, 555
Circular flow of economic activity, 29–33, 218, 219; government and, 30–32
Civilian Conservation Corps (CCC), 451
Civil rights laws, 177
Civil War (1861–1865), 185, 339, 501
Clayton Antitrust Act (1914), 147, 152, 187
Clean Air Act, 283, 307, 481
Clinton, Bill, 451, 461, 479, 495
Closed shop, 189
Coast Guard, U.S., 293, 295
Coins, 18, 336, 337; role of Federal Reserve in supplying, 386–387
Collaboration: among firms, 499, 560; between industry and government, 560
Collateral, 97, 251
Collective bargaining, 185, 195–197; failures of, 197–203
Collision insurance, 262
Collusion, 139
Command economy, 11–12, 74, 541. *See also* China; Soviet Union
Commerce, U.S. Department of, 529
Commercial banks, 226, 361, 385
Commodity inflation, 352
Common Market, 504, 510
Common stocks, 98–99, 228–229
Commonwealth of Independent States (CIS), 551
Communism, 540, 544–545; today, 553–556
Comparative advantage, 492–495; Law of, 493, 494, 497
Competition, 27; brand names and, 241; global, 192; imperfect, 135; international, 156; monopolistic, 136–137; perfect, 61, 66, 134, 135–136; safeguarding, 279; in selected industries, 142
Compound interest, 215
Concentration ratio, 141–143
Congo, 582
Congress of Industrial Organizations (CIO), 188–189
Constant dollars, 412
Consumer action professionals, 243, 251

Consumer cooperatives, 85–86
Consumer demand: market system and, 40; monopolies and, 153
Consumer Price Index (CPI), 345, 348
Consumer Product Safety Commission, 242, 257, 283
Consumer reporting agencies, 251
Consumer(s), 3, 156; advertising and, 236–242; assisting and informing, 242–245; borrowing by, 245–251, 253; credit, 245–246; purchasing power of, 431; sovereignty, 26; in writing letters of complaint, 252
Consumer spending: economy and, 218–223; fiscal policies and, 445–446; as part of gross domestic product, 32, 218; psychological factors in, 404–405; underconsumption and, 405
Consumers' Research, 243
Consumers Union, 243
Cooperatives, 85–86
Copyrights, 140, 410
Corn Laws, 496, 497
Corporate bonds, 97–98, 226, 227; investing in, 106; sale of, to public, 100–107
Corporate income taxes, 83, 316–317, 323
Corporate stocks, 226; sale of, to public, 100–107
Corporations, 81–84; advantages of, 82; board of directors in, 86–87; defined, 81–82; disadvantages of, 83; government-owned, 85; liability for, 82; multinational, 488, 509–510; not-for-profit, 85; officers in, 86; organization of, 86–87; S-, 83; separation of ownership and control of, 87, 89
Cost(s): external, 41; fixed, 127; internal, 41; marginal, 130; opportunity, 8, 493–494, 495, 570; pollution-control, 480; unit production, 125; variable, 127
Cost-benefit analysis, 283
Cost of living, 193
Cost-push inflation, 350–352; curing, 432–433
Côte d'Ivoire, 582
Cotonou Partnership, 583
Council of Economic Advisers, 426, 479
Countercyclical fiscal policies, 445
Counterfeiting, 337
Craft unions, 184, 185
Creative destruction, 126

PHOTO ACKNOWLEDGMENTS

Unit VI

335, Federal Reserve System; 337, 338, U.S. Treasury Department, Bureau of Engraving and Printing; 347, UPI/Bettmann/Corbis; 351, Reuters NewMedia Inc./Corbis; 360, Bettmann/Corbis; 363, Gary Walts, Syracuse Newspapers/The Image Works; 368, Steve Ruark/Syracuse Newspapers/The Image Works; 382, Bettmann/Corbis; 388, Federal Reserve System.

Unit VII

397, Reuters NewMedia Inc./Corbis; 403, AFP/Corbis; 407, Bettmann/Corbis; 411, Bob Daemmrich/The Image Works; 427, Tim Boyle/Getty Images; 449, Fritz Hoffmann/The Image Works; 472, Bettmann/Corbis; 474, Steven Rubin/The Image Works; 477, Joe Sohm/The Image Works.

Unit VIII

487, Peter Blakely/Corbis SABA; 490, 493, UN/DPI Photos; 496, Culver Pictures; 498, Najiah Feanny/Corbis SABA; 500, Bettmann/Corbis; 503, Luis Galdamez/Reuters NewMedia Inc./Corbis; 505, AFP/Corbis; 511, Asea Brown Boveri (ABB); 521, AFP/Corbis; 527, UPI/Bettmann/Corbis; 542, Peter Blakely/Corbis SABA; 546, Bettmann/Corbis; 547, Library of Congress; 550, Reuters/Bettmann/Corbis; 556, Liu Liqun/Corbis; 559, Judy Gelles/Stock Boston; 561, Koichi Kamoshida/Getty Images; 570, Steve Winter/UN/DPI Photos; 572, K. Bubriski/UN/DPI Photos; 577, Harvard University News Office; 579, 584, UN/DPI Photos.